Ruairí Ó Brádaigh

Ruairí Ó Brádaigh

THE LIFE AND POLITICS OF AN IRISH REVOLUTIONARY

ROBERT W. WHITE

Indiana
University
Press

BLOOMINGTON AND INDIANAPOLIS

Indiana University Press
601 North Morton Street
Bloomington, IN 47404-3797 USA

http://iupress.indiana.edu

Telephone orders 800-842-6796
Fax orders 812-855-7931
Orders by e-mail iuporder@indiana.edu

The paper used in this publication meets the minimum requirements of American National Standard for Information Sciences—Permanence of Paper for Printed Library Materials, ANSI Z39.48-1984.

Manufactured in the United States of America

Library of Congress Cataloging-in-Publication Data

White, Robert W. (Robert William) date
Ruairí Ó Brádaigh : the life and politics of an Irish revolutionary / Robert W. White.
p. cm.
Includes bibliographical references and index.
ISBN 0-253-34708-4 (alk. paper)
1. Ó Brádaigh, Ruairí. 2. Revolutionaries—Northern Ireland—Biography. 3. Northern Ireland—Politics and government. 4. Northern Ireland—Biography. I. Title.
DA990.U452O27 2006
941.6082′092—dc22
2005014172

3 4 5 11 10 09 08 07 06

In memory of my mother,
Margaret Mary Hanrahan White,
and my father,
Howard Christy White

CONTENTS

A CHRONOLOGY OF KEY EVENTS IN THE LIFE OF RUAIRÍ Ó BRÁDAIGH (RÓB)

1890	Birth of his father, Matt Brady, North County Longford.
1899	Birth of his mother, May Caffrey, Belfast.
1914–1918	World War I.
1916	Easter Rebellion.
1919	Anglo-Irish War; Dáil Éireann formed. Matt Brady, Irish Republican Volunteer, shot; recuperates in Dublin.
1920	Government of Ireland Act partitions Ireland.
1922	Anglo-Irish Treaty ratified; Irish Civil War starts. Matt Brady returns to Longford and meets May Caffrey, who becomes secretary of the Longford County Board of Health.
1923	Irish Civil War ends, cementing partition of Ireland into Northern Ireland and the Irish Free State. The IRA and Sinn Féin refuse to recognize the authority of each.
1926	Sinn Féin splits; Éamon de Valera forms Fianna Fáil. Marriage of Matt Brady and May Caffrey.
1927	Éamon de Valera and Fianna Fáil recognize Leinster House, site of the Free State government.
1929	Birth of his sister, Mary (May Óg) Brady.
1932	Éamon de Valera and Fianna Fáil form coalition government of Irish Free State. Birth of Rory Brady, Longford, Ireland.
1934	Matt Brady and Seán F. Lynch elected to Longford County Council.
1937	Birth of his brother, Seán Brady.
1938	Delegation of powers of government from the Second Dáil Éireann to the Army Council of the Irish Republican Army.
1939–1945	IRA campaign in England and Northern Ireland. Fianna Fáil represses Irish Republicans.
1942	Death of Matt Brady.
1944	May Brady marries Patrick Twohig.

1946–1950   RÓB attends St. Mel's of Longford.

1946   Seán Mac Bride, former IRA chief of staff, forms Clann na Poblachta, which recognizes Leinster House. Mac Bride had resigned from the Republican Movement in 1938.

1950   RÓB enrolls at University College Dublin. Joins Sinn Féin. Changes name to Ruairí Ó Brádaigh.

1951   Joins Irish Republican Army in Dublin.

1955   Leads IRA Arborfield raid. Elected to IRA Executive Council.

1956   Joins Ard Chomhairle of Sinn Féin. Elected to the IRA Army Council.

1956–1962   Elected to Leinster House, interned in the Curragh, escapes, and becomes IRA chief of staff. Marries Patsy O'Connor and is chief of staff when the campaign ends.

1962–1969   Member IRA Army Council.

1969–1970   Sinn Féin and IRA split into "Officials" and "Provisionals" over recognition of Leinster House, Stormont, and Westminster. RÓB becomes president of Provisional Sinn Féin. Reported a founding member of the Provisional IRA.

1972   RÓB and Dáithí O'Connell develop Sinn Féin's federalism policy, often referred to as Éire Nua. RÓB is arrested (in May) and is on hunger strike until his release fifteen days later. First British-IRA truce. Arrested again (in December).

1973   RÓB is sentenced to six months' imprisonment on the opinion of a senior police officer that he is a member of the IRA.

1974   RÓB is excluded from the United States. Birmingham bombs lead to Feakle talks.

1975   Second British-IRA truce. RÓB is one of three Irish Republicans who meet with British representatives.

1976   RÓB is excluded from Great Britain and Northern Ireland. IRA prisoners go "on the blanket."

1979   RÓB supports Sinn Féin contesting first election to European Parliament but is outvoted on the Ard Chomhairle. Margaret Thatcher becomes prime minister.

1980–1981   IRA prisoner hunger strikes. Bobby Sands elected MP for Fermanagh–South Tyrone. Owen Carron elected in by-election occasioned by death of Bobby Sands.

1983   RÓB resigns as president of Provisional Sinn Féin. Succeeded by Gerry Adams.

1986   Sinn Féin recognizes Leinster House and splits. Formation of Republican Sinn Féin and the Continuity IRA. RÓB becomes first president of Republican Sinn Féin. Martin McGuinness and other leading Provisionals pledge to never enter Stormont.

1990   Provisional IRA enters into secret talks with British representatives.

1994   Provisional IRA cease-fire. RÓB is a leading critic.

1996   Canary Wharf bomb ends Provisional IRA cease-fire. Continuity IRA emerges.

1997   RÓB criticizes second Provisional IRA cease-fire, is excluded from Canada.

1998   Good Friday Agreement. Provisional Sinn Féin agrees to enter Stormont.

2005   Provisional IRA formally ends its campaign.

FOREWORD

BACK IN THE summer of 1980, I was commissioned by *Magill* magazine in Dublin to write a lengthy article about the Provisional IRA and Sinn Féin. *Magill's* editor was particularly interested in the internal politics of the Provos and whether rumours of a northern takeover and resulting divisions and tensions held any truth at all.

For me it was the start of a long career spent reporting on the Provisional movement, its leaders, and its politics, an experience that most of the time was fascinating, often frustrating, and occasionally disturbing. Throughout all those years I was painfully aware that the IRA and Sinn Féin were organisations defined by their secrecy and that as an outsider I would be lucky ever to learn more than a fraction of the truth of any story.

The IRA had a rule enforcing internal silence similar to the Sicilian Mafia's *omerta* and added to that was a long legacy of distrust of the media in all its forms and whatever the national origin. But there was another unwritten rule that governed the business of reporting the IRA, and that was the knowledge that though it might take years, the IRA could never keep a lid on all its activities and eventually stories its leadership would rather have kept suppressed would seep to the surface. Human nature eventually prevailed over autocracy, and the patient observer could enjoy a rich harvest.

My *Magill* commission became a metaphor, in its way, for all this. The IRA leadership agreed to cooperate with me, and the organisation's director of publicity, Danny Morrison, introduced me to various figures that I had asked to talk to. We spent many hours together that summer, often on the road, discussing the Provisional movement. The article was written, and looking back at the episode it is difficult not to conclude, unhappily, that much of it reflected the direction I was steered towards.

I was able quite easily to confirm that the Provisionals were indeed riven at that time with division and tension and two camps now existed, one represented by Gerry Adams and his young, militantly left-wing northern supporters and the other led by Ruairí Ó Brádaigh and Dáithí

Ó Conaill, the older, southern-based veterans who had been at the forefront of the first leadership of the Provisionals.

Bob White has, in this book, done an excellent and exhaustive job of examining the causes, course, and outcome of that division, and I need not dwell upon all that here. Suffice it to say that my article oversimplified the dispute to the advantage of the northerners, portraying it as being about left versus right, young and angry versus old and jaded, revolutionaries versus conservatives, the clever and imaginative versus the dull and gullible. I would not write the same article today but there is no doubt that at the time, Gerry Adams's camp was pleased to see it in print.

It would be twenty years before I would learn, courtesy of Ó Brádaigh, what happened after the article was published. The northerners may well have been happy with it, but they knew the Ó Brádaigh wing would be furious and suspicious that the northerners had connived to shape it. And so at the first meeting of the Ard Chomhairle, the committee that runs Sinn Féin, held after the article appeared, Danny Morrison proposed a motion expressing outrage at what I had written and instructing Ard Chomhairle members not to have any contact with me in the future.

From that point on, and for some years afterwards, none of the Ó Brádaigh-Ó Conaill camp would have any dealings with me, even going so far as to turn on their heels if they saw me approaching them during breaks at Sinn Féin's annual conference. The northerners had no such qualms and we carried on speaking to each other as if nothing had happened—and, as far as I was concerned, nothing had happened.

It was a classic Adams stratagem, one characterised by its multiple goals and a level of deceit in its implementation. At one stroke he insulated himself from criticism from the Ó Brádaigh camp and ensured that they and myself would be incommunicado, meaning that I would be deprived of their view of the world and they of my access to the print media, while Adams himself, either directly or via allies, was still able to influence how I regarded, interpreted, and reported Provisional politics.

Not long after Ó Brádaigh told me this story I confronted Danny Morrison. He denied it, but I did not believe him. It wasn't just because by that stage I had caught Danny telling so many lies that I could believe him about nothing, but I had heard exactly the same story told about another journalist—in his case the Army Council was warned off him—from an entirely different source in the movement. There was a detectable pattern of behavior, in other words.

The real importance of this story is that it is both a metaphor for the difference between Ruairí Ó Brádaigh and Gerry Adams and their brands of Irish republicanism and also a partial explanation of why Adams now leads a party that has elected representatives in four parliaments and is on the cusp of being in two governments while Ó Brádaigh heads a small group that seems destined to live out its life on the margins of Irish politics.

Adams had no compunction about deceiving his rivals, first by pretending he had been upset by and had no hand in shaping my article and second by ignoring the Ard Chomhairle decree to have no dealings with me. Ó Brádaigh and his supporters, on the other hand, felt obliged to obey the Ard Chomhairle edict. Or put another way, while Adams and his people were prepared to break the rules to advance their agenda, Ó Brádaigh believed in playing by the rules, even though they might damage his interests.

Another issue that graphically illustrates the difference between them was the question of their membership of the IRA. For many years now, long before the peace process, when asked by the media, Adams has routinely and occasionally angrily denied that he is, was, or ever had been a member of the IRA. When asked the same question Ó Brádaigh has simply refused to answer. Adams has lied about this matter—lied grotesquely, given all that is known about his IRA career—but Ó Brádaigh would not lie, although he would not admit the truth either. While Ó Brádaigh would often not tell the full story of an incident or issue or would dodge the matter altogether if it suited him, I never in all my dealings with him ever caught him out telling a lie. Adams, on the other hand, lied routinely, just as one inhales and exhales air, and so did his loyal lieutenants. In this respect, as in many others, Ó Brádaigh and Adams were the yin and yang of the Provisional movement.

Given this ethical difference, the outcome of the struggle for hegemony in the IRA and Sinn Féin was predetermined. Ó Brádaigh never really had a chance. While he and his allies lived by a set of rules and principles which they would not bend, the Adams group cared only about tactics, and they deployed these with ruthless zeal and efficiency. All that mattered for them was that they prevailed.

There are many possible explanations for the gulf between the two camps, but one stands out. In a very direct and meaningful way Ó Brádaigh and his supporters could trace their ideological and ethical roots all the way back to the 1916 Rising, the Anglo-Irish War, and, most important, the terrible civil war that followed the 1921 Treaty. While others, Collins and de Valera prominent amongst them, were happy to exchange principle for power, Ó Brádaigh and his colleagues came from the uncompromising wing of Republicanism for whom principles were sacred because Republicans had died and suffered for them, in Ó Brádaigh's case, his father.

Gerry Adams had family ties to all this, but his roots were in the northern IRA, and the northern IRA was always different from the IRA in the rest of Ireland. For instance, even though the Anglo-Irish Treaty threatened to separate them from the rest of Ireland, the sympathies of the northern IRA lay with the Treaty's co-architect, Michael Collins, because he waved a big stick at the Unionist and Protestant establishment in the north and stood up for Catholic rights.

And when the Troubles erupted fifty years later, northern activists sided with the Provisionals, not just because the left-wing constitutionalism of Goulding's Officials offended them but because the Provisionals offered a way to defend their areas from Protestant attack and gave the opportunity to strike back violently at the state and people that had for so long discriminated and oppressed their fellow Catholics.

The northern Provisionals came in large measure from the Defenderist and, it must be said, sectarian tradition of Irish Republicanism, while Ó Brádaigh and his supporters took their politics from Pearse, Mellows, O'Malley, and Liam Lynch. It was fear and loathing of Unionism less than the wish to break the link with Britain that inspired hundreds and thousands of northern Catholics to join the Provisional IRA and to follow Gerry Adams.

When defence was the priority, principle took a back seat, and this defining characteristic of Provisional republicanism, along with the ruthless pragmatism of the Adams camp, made the peace process possible. As long as he was able to assure his followers in the north that the IRA would continue to perform its defensive role, Gerry Adams was able to persuade the IRA and Sinn Féin grassroots to abandon acres of ideological high ground, thereby advancing the peace process agenda.

So it was that the main obstacle in Adams's path turned out not to be accepting the principle of consent—the idea that Northern Ireland would remain British as long as a majority of its population, in practice the Unionists, wished it to be so, a principle that ran like a golden thread through the Good Friday Agreement. Overthrowing the consent principle and reestablishing the right of all the people of Ireland, north and south, to determine their own future was the defining feature of the post–civil war IRA. It wasn't accepting this that caused Adams problems but the decommissioning of IRA weapons, the instruments of defence. Accepting the consent principle happened with scarcely a murmur of protest from the ranks in the north, but it took Adams years of careful maneuvering to persuade them to accept decommissioning.

There are other examples. When Adams moved against Ó Brádaigh, he used the latter's espousal of Éire Nua against him, knowing that the plan to create a federal Ireland in which the northern Protestants could still be a majority in the province of Ulster was unpopular with his northern supporters.

The two big splits in the Provisionals since 1969 have both been largely on north-south lines, first the exit of Ó Brádaigh and Ó Conaill and then the departure of the Real IRA, whose members came mostly from the southern-based quartermaster's and engineering departments of the IRA. Both were on grounds of principle, the first because abstentionism had been breached and the second because Adams wished to accept the Mitchell principles, which implicitly endorsed the consent precept. In both instances, Adams's pragmatism won out among his northern following. And so on, and so on.

In a very real sense, Ruairí Ó Brádaigh can thus be said to be the last, or one of the last, Irish Republicans. Studies of the Provisional movement to date have invariably focused more on the northerners and the role of people like Gerry Adams and Martin McGuinness. But an understanding of them is not possible without appreciating where they came from and from what tradition they have broken. Ruairí Ó Brádaigh is that tradition, and that is why this account of his life and politics is so important.

Ed Moloney
New York
April 2005

ACKNOWLEDGMENTS

THERE ARE SO many people who must be thanked for supporting this project that I fear missing someone. I especially want to thank the respondents, who gave generously of their time and their memories. Most important, Ruairí Ó Brádaigh patiently sat for interviews, responded to letters, and spoke with me on the phone. He generously shared his time, his papers, his opinions, and access to his colleagues, comrades, and family. I also want to thank Patsy Ó Brádaigh and Seán Ó Brádaigh and their families for all of their help. It was especially helpful that Ruairí Ó Brádaigh and his family let me form my own conclusions. Others would have been tempted to form them for me.

Two top scholars, David Rapoport and the late J. Bowyer Bell, have been ardent supporters. David is the masterful co-editor of *Terrorism and Political Violence.* He is open-minded, reasoned, and always charming. Bow Bell, from 1983, was always supportive, willing to answer questions and offer suggestions, and a fun person to meet on an Irish street. He set the standard for research on Irish Republicans and he is missed. The staff of the Linen Hall Library, especially Yvonne Murphy and the staff of the Northern Ireland Political Collection, are the best. Father Ignatius Fennessey of the Franciscan Library at Dún Mhuire, former repository of Seán Mac Eoin's papers, was especially helpful. The papers are now held by University College Dublin. A grant from The Harry Frank Guggenheim Foundation supported travel and research assistance and allowed a very fruitful sabbatical in Ireland in the fall of 1996. Grants from the Indiana University Office of International Affairs and the Indiana University Bloomington West European Studies Program paid for travel and/or research assistants. An Indiana University Arts and Humanities grant also supported travel and research assistance.

A lengthy list of research assistants has been a great help. They include Shannon Baldwin, Bruce Beal, Erin Bethuram, Karen Budnick, Evelyn Hovee, Amber Houston, Lori Langdoc, Libby Laux, Karen Patterson, Patricia Richards, Jasper Sumner, and Bridget Tucker. Others who offered help, insights, suggestions, and sometimes just listened to me include

Herman Blake, David Bodenhamer, Egan Dargatz, Scott Evenbeck, Charlie Feeney, Dave Ford, Toni Giffin, Velma Graves, Rick Hanson, Wayne Husted, Mel Johnson, Joy Kramer, John Leamnson, Gianni Lipkins, Mike Maitzen, Kevin Marsh, John McCormick, Fr. William Munshower, Fred Burns O'Brien, Gail Plater, Jane Quintet, Becky Renollet, Patrick Rooney, Mike Scott, Gen Shaker, Michelle Simmons, Catherine Souch, Margie Tarpey, Michael Tarpey, Rick Ward, and Tom White. Thanks go to Kevin Mickey and James Colbert for the maps. Over the course of writing this project I have served as Associate Dean for Academic Affairs and as Dean of the School of Liberal Arts. The dean's staff, many of whom are listed above, is extraordinary, and their support and friendship has been a great help. Special thanks go to Sue Herrell, my administrative assistant, and Carol Clarke, Merle Illg, and Mark Shemanski, the office receptionist/secretaries, for their help. Stephanie Osborne, formerly of the dean's staff, has great ideas and listens very well. Miriam Langsam, my teacher, colleague, friend, and fellow Acting Co-Director of the Women's Studies Program, read several chapters, offering her insight. Richard Turner, Mary Trotter, and the students of I300, Irish Tradition and Culture, offered their insights and gave me the opportunity to talk about my project. The students of R476, Social Movements, offered comments and perspective and were a pleasure to teach. Christian Kloesel and the late Tony Sherrill are and were sources of mirth and inspiration. Special thanks go to Val and Dolores Lynch and their family for their friendship. I especially want to thank Ed Moloney for his foreword and comments.

As "I poked about a village church and found his family tomb," my family has been a source of support and encouragement. My wife, Terry, patiently read every chapter at least twice and offered several suggestions that smoothed out the presentation. She and our children, Kerry and Claire, have participated in many an Irish adventure, have tolerated my constant telling of stories about this and that, and have patiently listened to my infrequent and mild complaints associated with academic administration.

Two people with me when I started this project, my mother, Margaret White, and my sister, Barbara White Thoreson, have left us physically but remain with me. *I measc Naomh is Laochra na hÉireann go raibh a n-anam uasal.*

RWW
Indianapolis
July 2005

INTRODUCTION

FRIDAY, SEPTEMBER 3, 1971, was an ugly day in Northern Ireland. In the four weeks since the introduction of internment without trial, gun battles on Belfast streets between the British Army and the IRA had been a daily occurrence. Similar violence was widespread throughout the province. On that Friday morning, three Provisional IRA gunmen shot dead 23-year-old Frank Veitch, a private in the Ulster Defence Regiment, who was on guard duty outside a joint British Army/Royal Ulster Constabulary base in Kinawley, County Fermanagh. He lived with his widowed mother and sister. The shooting was condemned by his neighbor and MP, Mr. Frank McManus, as "shocking and dastardly." That afternoon, in Belfast, 7-year-old Paula Gallagher was out for a walk with her 17-month-old sister, Angela. They were visiting their grandparents. As Angela pushed a doll's pram along the pavement, a sniper took a shot at British troops. The bullet ricocheted off a wall, passed through Paula's skirt, and struck Angela in the head. She died in Paula's arms.

That night, the Taoiseach (prime minister) of the Republic of Ireland, Jack Lynch, stated that "Nothing—no motive, no ideal—can excuse the killing of this innocent of the innocents. Cannot even this shameful act bring home to these men of violence the evil of the course they have taken? The sacrifice of this innocent life must surely convince them of the futility of their actions. The sympathy of the whole country goes out to the parents and family of this child." The minister for community relations for the Northern Ireland government at Stormont, David Bleakley, stated that those responsible for Angela Gallagher's death should be treated "like the lepers they are. They deserve neither comfort nor shelter—only cold contempt and utter rejection." The *Daily Mail* reported that Pope Paul VI condemned the shooting and quoted from his address to pilgrims and tourists, "We hope that this innocent blood may be worthy to beseech from God a true and just reconciliation among the people." Although the IRA's Belfast Brigade denied it, the evidence and the historians record that the sniper was a member of the Provisional Irish Republican Army.

The next morning, John Shaw of the Press Association telephoned

Ruairí Ó Brádaigh at his home in Roscommon. Ó Brádaigh was president of Provisional Sinn Féin, the political wing of the Provisional IRA. Questioned about Angela Gallagher, he stated that what "happened was one of the hazards of urban guerilla warfare . . . it was one of those unfortunate accidents."

The sound bite was picked up and condemned in the tabloids and by Ó Brádaigh's political opponents. Even the Provisional IRA chief of staff (C/S), Seán Mac Stiofáin, phoned and berated him for the comment. The rival Official IRA, which would later kill a number of civilians with its own activities, released a statement that included, "We have consistently attacked in the strongest possible terms all activity which would jeopardise the lives of innocent people and we do not subscribe to the policy of those who attempt to excuse death and injury to innocent civilians as the fortunes of war." Tomás Mac Giolla, former president of Official Sinn Féin, draws on incidents like this, describing Ó Brádaigh as "a very cold kind of person in many ways like that. Lacking any sort of human compassion." From an outsider's perspective, Ruairí Ó Brádaigh is the quintessential Irish nationalist who lives in the cloistered confines of the West of Ireland and clings to the myth that physical force can lead to a united, Gaelic, Catholic Ireland.

Yet there is more to Ruairí Ó Brádaigh. He did regret Angela Gallagher's death. He had spent about half of an hour on the phone with Shaw and the conversation had ranged from Dublin in 1920–1921 (when a number of civilians were killed) to Nicosia and activities in Cyprus to Saigon in Vietnam; the sound bite was the only part to be published. On the day Angela Gallagher died, Ó Brádaigh was 39 years old, married, and the father of six children—the oldest was 11 and the youngest was 18 months. He also told Shaw that what had happened was extremely regrettable, that nothing "would relieve the grief of the parents about the death of their child" and that "I would know how I would feel, and I have six children myself."

Ruairí Ó Brádaigh is a complex man. While raising a family and pursuing a career, he also lived the public life of a revolutionary political figure and the very private life of a guerrilla soldier. He is a second-generation Irish Republican and a second-generation college graduate. He joined the IRA and Sinn Féin in the 1950s and became a major figure in each; his tenure on the IRA's Army Council spans decades, he was the first president of Provisional Sinn Féin and is currently president of Republican Sinn Féin. He has lived most of his life in a small town in the West of Ireland, but he has also traveled the world—in support of the Republican cause and to examine other political systems for insight on how to achieve a lasting peace in Ireland. He is a conscientious Catholic, but his family background includes Swiss Protestants, and he publicly challenges the authority and the ethics of the Catholic hierarchy. Interpersonally, he is routinely described as polite and courteous, and countless articles have noted that he is a nonsmoking teetotaler. Even his political enemies comment on his humorous side. Tomás Mac Giolla also remembers Ó Brádaigh as "an individual you could get on with, have good fun with, and that." He is known to refer to himself and fellow Irish Republicans as "madmen like us," and in speaking about his children he is quick to laugh at how awkward it must be for future in-laws to meet for the first time a man vilified as one of the world's chief terrorists.

This biography is an attempt to understand the complexity of Ruairí Ó Brádaigh *and* modern Irish Republicanism. Aside from his own importance, Ó Brádaigh is the public face of a generation of Irish Republicans which, having fought in the IRA's Border Campaign in the 1950s, founded the Provisional IRA and Provisional Sinn Féin in 1969/70 and the Continuity IRA and Republican Sinn Féin in 1986. Ó Brádaigh's life is a window for understanding his generation of Irish Republicans and how they received the values of a previous generation and are transmitting those values to the next generation. He represents IRA and Sinn Féin members who, no matter what, will not "give up the gun" short of a declaration of an intention to withdraw from Northern Ireland by the British government. Because of people like him there will never be peace in Ireland without such a declaration—no matter the outcome of the current peace process.

Paula Backscheider, in *Reflections on Biography,* states that "getting to the person beneath, the core of the human being, is the biographer's job." Understanding the complexity of Ruairí Ó Brádaigh and those like him requires an in-depth examination of the personal and political events that shaped his life. In presenting this life, I have tried to describe his actions and choices as he experienced them, to understand his decisions based on the context and information that he had at the time rather than with the benefit of hindsight. In this process, I have relied as much as possible on contemporary accounts of events, including direct quotations from him at the time of a particular event. These accounts are complemented by hours of interviews with Mr. Ó Brádaigh, as described under "Sources." The reader will determine if the core of Mr. Ó Brádaigh has been revealed.

Ruairí Ó Brádaigh

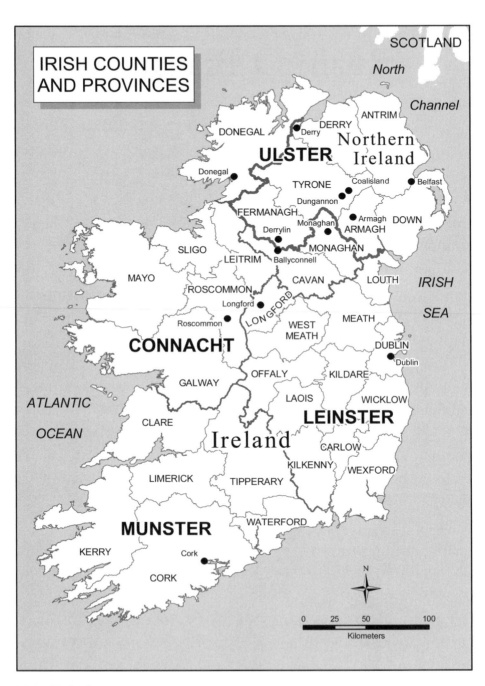

Map of Ireland

1

Matt Brady and May Caffrey

ANGLO-IRISH WARS in the seventeenth century consolidated English power over Irish affairs and placed a minority but loyal Irish Protestant elite in control of the majority Irish Catholic population. The Protestant Ascendancy ruled Ireland from their base in Dublin, but their greatest numbers were in the northeast portion of the province of Ulster. It was here that the Plantation of English and Scottish settlers into Ireland in the seventeenth century was most successful. In the 1790s, anti-English agitation in Ireland, as organized by the United Irishmen, adopted a Republican political philosophy. They tried to unite Catholic, Protestant, and Dissenter to establish an Irish Republic. They rebelled in 1798 and failed. Rebellions against English and British power in Ireland continued into the nineteenth century: by remnants of the United Irishmen in 1803, by the Young Irelanders in 1848, and by the Fenians at various points in the 1860s, 1870s, and 1880s. These rebellions were complemented by large-scale social protest movements that also challenged the status quo. In 1829, agitation led by Daniel O'Connell resulted in Catholics being granted the right to hold seats in Parliament. In the 1870s and 1880s, Charles Stewart Parnell and others involved in the Land League forced landlords, if only slowly, to return lands confiscated from the Irish people in the seventeenth century. Parnell, leader of the Irish Parliamentary Party at Westminster, was also a key proponent of a Home Rule for Ireland Bill. If enacted, the bill would not create an Irish Republic, but it would limit the power of the Protestant Ascendancy and give Irish people significantly more control over Irish affairs.

It was into this context that Matt Brady was born in 1890 in North County Longford in the townland of Gelsha, near Ballinalee. He was the youngest of eight children, and in a time of high infant mortality, only he and his siblings Hugh and Mary Kate lived to adulthood. Then, as now, the area was filled with trees, bushes, small farms, and little villages. Matt's father, Peter Brady, was married to Kate Clarke and worked a twenty-acre farm. Folklore has it that the Bradys were driven from Ulster by Orangemen. They were in North Longford by at least the 1840s, when Peter's uncle died of typhus during the famine. Peter Brady was active in local politics and is remembered for buying newspapers and reading them to his neighbors, giving them the news on Parnell, the Fenians, and other events. He was active in the Land League, and at one point he chose to go to jail rather than pay a fine for agitation.

County Longford is strategically located in the Irish midlands where the provinces of Leinster, Ulster, and Connacht come together, and it has a long military history. In the 1640s, General Owen Roe O'Neill, who was home from the Spanish Army, trained his Army of Ulster at the juncture of the three provinces. In 1798, a French expedition, under the command of Jean-Joseph Amable Humbert, invaded Ireland in support of the United Irishmen. Humbert landed at Killala in County Mayo and marched his troops through Mayo, Sligo, and Leitrim and into Longford, where he confronted British General Lake in what became known as the Battle of Ballinamuck. It is estimated that 500 insurgents fell in the battle. As Humbert described it, he was "at length obliged to submit to a superior force of 30,000 troops." The French were taken prisoner; the Irish were slaughtered. Among those captured and hanged were the United Irishmen Bartholomew Teeling and Matthew Tone, the brother of Wolfe Tone, who is considered the founding father of Irish Republicanism.

The effects of Ballinamuck weighed on the local peasantry and small farmers, who had risen against the Crown and paid a high price for it, and on the local elites, who feared it might happen again. Seán Ó Donnabháin, an Irish scholar who worked on an ordnance survey in North Longford, described the people of the area in an 1837 letter from Granard as "poor, and what is worse, kept down by the police." One of the few Irish soldiers to survive the battle was Brian O'Neill. People like him kept the memory of the battle alive, and it became a symbol of local resistance to British injustice. O'Neill's grandnephew, James O'Neill, was born on March 1, 1855, and over the course of his long life he was a keeper of the flame of Ballinamuck, a direct link between 1798 and decades of political activity in Longford, until his death in 1946. A contemporary of Peter Brady, he was involved in the Land League, was president of the Drumlish and Ballinamuck United Irish League, and was later active in Sinn Féin with Matt Brady.

In 1913, Matt Brady moved from Gelsha to Longford town and became a rate collector for the County Council. The town developed on the

Camlin River; in 1913 a main feature was two military barracks, one for cavalry and the other for artillery. The barracks indicated Longford's strategic location and a tradition of resisting the Crown's authority. It was a prosperous town, and architecturally it was and is dominated by the facade and tower of St. Mel's Cathedral. The foundation stone for St. Mel's was laid in May 1840, but the building was not completed until the 1890s. In 1914, after Matt's brother Hugh left for the United States, Matt continued his work for the county and maintained the small farm at Gelsha. World politics would soon set in motion events that would directly affect both Matt Brady and Longford.

When it became apparent that Home Rule would pass in Westminster, anti–Home Rule Unionists in Ulster organized the Ulster Volunteer Force and began drilling. The Irish Republican Brotherhood, heirs of the Fenians, countered this by forming the Irish Volunteers. When World War I began, Unionists supported the war effort and the Ulster Volunteer Force joined the British Army en masse. John Redmond, Parnell's successor as leader of the Irish Parliamentary Party, encouraged the Irish Volunteers to do the same, splitting the Volunteers.

In August 1914, the Irish Republican Brotherhood's Supreme Council met and determined that Ireland's honor would be tarnished if no fight was made for an Irish Republic during the world war. The Irish Republican Brotherhood planned a rebellion to coincide with the importation of arms from Germany at Easter 1916. The arms were to arrive in County Kerry, then be distributed throughout the south and west of Ireland. Instead, Irish Volunteers missed their rendezvous with a German Steamer, the *Aud,* which was eventually spotted by the Royal Navy. The crew scuttled the *Aud,* and her cargo, at the entrance to Cork Harbor. When word of the lost arms reached the rebel organizers, confusion set in and the Rising was postponed from Easter Sunday until Easter Monday. Rebels seized the General Post Office and other strategic buildings in Dublin, and Patrick Pearse, "Commander-in-Chief of the Army of the Republic and President of the Provisional Government," stepped forward and proclaimed the Irish Republic. The Irish Republican Army (IRA) took up positions throughout Dublin. So did the Irish Citizen Army, led by James Connolly, a socialist critic and labor organizer, who had formed the small (approximately 200-member) Citizen Army in 1913 as a defense force for workers during a bitter lockout.

British reinforcements quickly suppressed the rebellion; within a week, several parts of the city were reduced to rubble and 450 people were dead. The rebels' surrender was followed by large-scale arrests in Dublin and in the provinces, and general courts-martial were set up. One hundred and sixty-nine men and one woman, the Countess Markievicz of Connolly's Citizen Army, were tried and convicted by courts-martial. The Easter Rising's leaders—including the signatories of the Proclamation of the Irish Republic, Tom Clarke, Patrick Pearse, James Connolly, Seán Mac Diarmada, Eamonn Ceannt, Thomas McDonagh, and Joseph Plunkett—were executed. Over 1,800 men and five women were sent to Frongoch internment camp in Wales. Eight of them were from County Longford; three were from Granard.

Internees were quickly released; 650 after a few weeks, more in July, and the rest by Christmas 1916. They were welcomed home by crowds and bonfires. The prisoners had not wasted their time in the camp. Placed together in one location, they formed friendships, organized themselves, and plotted. When they were turned loose, they joined the political party Sinn Féin, the Irish Volunteers, or both. When it was announced that there would be a by-election for the North Roscommon seat at Westminster in February 1917, the Republicans had a chance to find out how much support they had. Count Plunkett was put forward as the representative of the new Irish nationalist direction in opposition to the Irish Parliamentary Party candidate. A prominent and respected member of the community, he was director of the National Museum, a papal count, and the father of the executed 1916 leader Joseph Plunkett. He ran as an independent, heavily supported by Sinn Féin, and won handily. After some pressure from Sinn Féiners, he declared he would follow Sinn Féin's policy of not taking his seat at Westminster. This decision continues to influence Irish politics.

In May 1917, there was another by-election, this time in South Longford. Mick Collins, who had been interned in Frongoch, was a conspiratorial genius. He arranged to have Joe McGuinness, who was imprisoned in England, nominated as the Sinn Féin candidate. McGuinness, a Dublin draper, was a native of nearby Tarmonbarry, and his brother, Frank, owned a small shop in Longford town. The campaign slogan was "Put him in to get him out." Republican Ireland descended on Longford; among those speaking on behalf of McGuinness were Margaret Pearse, widowed mother of the executed brothers Patrick and Willie Pearse, Count Plunkett, and Mrs. Desmond Fitzgerald, whose husband, a 1916 veteran, was in an English jail. Count Plunkett told one crowd, "Every vote for McGuinness [is] a bullet for the heart of England." The public was presented with two distinct choices, the moderate work-with-the-system approach of the Irish

Parliamentary Party versus the radical challenge-the-system approach of Sinn Féin. McGuinness won by thirty-seven votes. Around this time, Matt Brady joined the Irish Volunteers.

When McGuinness was released from prison, a rally in Longford brought together a who's who of Irish Republicans, including McGuinness, Count Plunkett, Arthur Griffith, Éamon de Valera, and Thomas Ashe. Griffith was the founder of Sinn Féin and the prime source of its abstentionist tactics; that is, the refusal of Republican elected officials to take their seats at Westminster. De Valera was the most senior 1916 rebel who had not been executed. In 1916, Ashe had led attacks on Royal Irish Constabulary (RIC) barracks in North County Dublin and directed a pitched battle with the RIC outside Ashbourne in County Meath. Collectively, they were key actors in a series of dramatic political events. Matt Brady was a witness to and participant in these events and probably heard Ashe introduced as "Commandant Thomas Ashe of the Irish Republican Army." Soon after the rally for McGuinness, under the Defence of the Realm Act, Ashe was charged with attempting to cause "disaffection" among the people while making a speech at Ballinalee, County Longford. He was sentenced to one year's imprisonment at hard labor and joined about forty other prisoners in Mountjoy Prison in Dublin. The prisoners attempted to distinguish themselves from the criminal population by requesting a number of special privileges, including unrestricted conversation, optional work, classes for study, and no association with ordinary criminals. When the privileges were refused, they embarked on a hunger strike. The prison authorities countered by force-feeding them, but liquid was pumped into Ashe's lungs instead of his stomach, causing his death in September 1917.

Republicans from throughout Ireland attended the funeral; years later, Ruairí Ó Brádaigh recalls his parents' account of the event. The First Battalion (Ballinalee) of the Longford Volunteers, including Matt Brady of the Colmcille Company, marched eight miles to Longford town to catch a special train to Dublin. There were so many passengers that extra carriages were attached as the train progressed. The funeral, an open display of contempt for the power of the authorities, brought the city to a standstill. After a volley of shots was fired over the coffin, the oration was given by Mick Collins. He was brief, but powerful: "Nothing additional remains to be said. The volley which we have just heard is the only speech which is proper to make above the grave of a dead Fenian." On detail was Matt Brady and his comrades in the Colmcille Company of the Longford

Battalion, Athlone Brigade, of the Irish Volunteers. As did many others, Brady took his turn "on guard over [the] corpse in the city hall . . . and then on duty at [the] funeral."

About this time, May Caffrey was an 18-year-old living in County Donegal. She was the daughter of John Caffrey, a municipal inspector for Belfast Corporation, and Jeanne Ducommun. Caffrey met Ducommun in London, where he was attending classes while she was working as a governess. He was an Irish Catholic interested in learning French. She was a Swiss Calvinist who was fluent in French, English, and German. In spite of, or perhaps because of, their different backgrounds, a relationship blossomed. They married and moved into a house on Clonard Gardens in Belfast. One of her first experiences there was watching the aftermath of a July 12th march commemorating the victory of the Protestant army of William of Orange over the Catholic army of James II at the Battle of the Boyne in 1690. She was amazed at the rioting. Their daughter, May Caffrey, was born in Belfast in 1899. In 1906, the family moved to Armagh City, where John Caffrey took a job as headmaster of the Technical Institute. May would later tell her children about how she always had to walk to primary school with a group of other children, for she had to pass through a Unionist area and her parents feared she would be attacked. In 1908, the family moved to Donegal Town, where John Caffrey became county engineer. He also became active in Sinn Féin. He attended the Dublin funeral of the Irish-American Fenian O'Donovan Rossa in 1915 and heard Pearse's famous oration there. In the 1918 national election, he seconded P. J. Ward, Sinn Féin's candidate for South Donegal, on Ward's nomination papers. (Ward was elected). Caffrey's children followed his politics.

Like Matt Brady, May Caffrey was a participant in the dramatic political events in Ireland. She was a member of the Gaelic League and was the captain of the first branch of Cumann na mBan, the women's wing of the Republican Movement, in Donegal town. She also organized the hinterland, cycling to Mountcharles and Frosses and other places. At one point, a local priest complained to her father that she was drilling the servant girls. The priest indicated that not only were her politics wrong but she was consorting with people beneath her. Her father ignored him and supported her.

As Sinn Féin, the Irish Volunteers, and Cumann na mBan grew and de Valera, Arthur Griffith, Mick Collins, and others toured the country, the authorities became concerned. Collins was arrested in Dublin in March 1918, transported to Longford, and charged with having "incited certain persons to raid for arms and carry off and hold same by force" in North Longford. He was found guilty and sent by train to Sligo Jail. In the same month, John Joe O'Neill (son of James O'Neill), was charged with drilling a squad of young men at Ballinamuck. Crowds of Sinn Féiners regularly attended the court proceedings, protested the results, and welcomed the prisoners home when they were released. According to the *Longford Leader,* among those who met Collins when he was released from Sligo Jail was Hubert Wilson, a former Frongoch internee and Matt Brady's battalion commander. Matt Brady was likely there, too.

In April 1918, the political situation became especially serious. The House of Commons voted to extend conscription to Ireland. Nationalist Ireland, Republican or not, was opposed. Most of the Catholic clergy were opposed. In Donegal, May Caffrey watched the local Hibernian priest share a platform with members of the Irish Parliamentary Party and Sinn Féin, united in opposition to conscription. In Longford Town, Sinn Féiners and Irish Parliamentary Party members shared the platform in a public protest. Energized by the crisis, Matt Brady and his comrades "organised resistance to conscription" in their area. In Ballinalee, Seán Mac Eoin, who had been appointed commander of the local unit of the Irish Volunteers by Mick Collins, was able to recruit a hundred people in one day. Mac Eoin later became a central figure in Matt Brady's life as a guerrilla leader transformed into a leading politician.

World War I ended in November 1918, and the British government called a national election in December. Sinn Féin seized the opportunity and in a stunning victory won seventy three of the Irish seats at Westminster. The Irish Party, representing constitutional Irish nationalists, took six seats, and the Unionist Party, representing Protestant and Northeast Ireland, took twenty-six seats. In Longford, Sinn Féin polled extremely well and Joe McGuinness was easily re-elected. Among the others elected was Countess Markievicz, in Dublin. She was the first woman to be elected in a British parliamentary election.

In January 1919, the elected Sinn Féin representatives put their abstentionist principles into action. Instead of going to London as Irish representatives to a British government, they formed a revolutionary government in Dublin, called Dáil Éireann (Parliament of Ireland). Éamon de Valera, president of Sinn Féin and the Irish Volunteers could not attend; he was imprisoned in England. In his place, Cathal Brugha, a 1916 veteran noted for his devotion to the Republican cause—he had suffered many bullet wounds—was elected president of Dáil Éireann. Members of the Dáil viewed themselves as the Parliament of the Irish Republic, "proclaimed in Dublin on Easter Monday, 1916, by the Irish Republican Army acting on behalf of the Irish people." Ireland was sliding into a revolutionary situation. Sinn Féin courts and arbitration boards were established and their decisions were accepted by the people. On the day Dáil Éireann was formed, Irish Republican Army volunteers in Tipperary killed two members of the Royal Irish Constabulary and seized a cartload of explosives.

Under the authority of Dáil Éireann, the Irish Volunteers formally became the Irish Republican Army. The IRA in North Longford reorganized under the command of the Longford Brigade. Seán Mac Eoin became Ballinalee battalion commander. John Murphy was his vice-commandant and Seán Duffy his adjutant. Battalion companies were located at Edgeworthstown (Mostrim), Killoe, Mullinalaughta, Drumlish, Ballinamuck, Colmcille, Granard, Dromard, and Ballinalee; Matt Brady was a lieutenant with the Colmcille Company. Similar reorganizations occurred across the country, and the IRA began to flex its muscles. Seán Mac Eoin led a raid into County Cavan that recovered shotguns impounded by the RIC. In Limerick, the IRA tried to free a hunger-striking Republican prisoner from the hospital. The prisoner, a police officer, and a prison guard were shot dead and another guard was wounded. The authorities proclaimed Limerick a military area, and tanks and armored cars paraded the streets. By the end of April, Counties Limerick, Roscommon, and Tipperary were under British military control.

On Sunday, April 27, 1919, one week after Easter, there was an *aeraíocht* in Aughnacliffe, a sort of outdoor contest and sports festival with bands and dancing. Such events build community spirit and allow people to enjoy the day. Several Sinn Féin members spoke there, including Joe McGuinness. In the evening, there was a concert. Given the political climate, extra police were brought into the area. Unknown to them, Seán Mac Eoin was using the event for an IRA Brigade Council meeting.

As the concert was starting, Matt Brady and Willie McNally, who were both in the IRA, went for an evening walk with Phil Brady, a Sinn Féin candidate in the upcoming local election. At about 9 PM, they left Phil Brady "on his way home" and were returning to the concert when they saw two RIC constables, Fleming and Clarke, cresting a hill on bicycles. The off-duty constables were returning to their barracks at Drumlish. Brady and McNally decided to seize their weapons. Each jumped a constable; the men starting wrestling, but McNally had trouble with his man. A shot rang out and McNally, hit in the head, collapsed. The RIC men then turned on Matt Brady, shooting him five times. Frightened and angry, they smashed the butts of their rifles into Brady's and McNally's faces. Phil Brady heard the shots and turned back to investigate, passing Fleming and Clarke running with their bicycles in the other direction. He found Matt Brady riddled with bullets. He had been hit at least twice in the chest and his left thigh was a mess. Bullets had gone through both hands. McNally was bleeding from a nasty but not dangerous wound over his left eye. Phil Brady ran to get help, shouting that there had been a murder. As more people arrived, they discovered that both men were still alive.

Seán Mac Eoin arrived quickly and took charge. He sent Seán F. Lynch, a Sinn Féiner involved in the court system, in search of a doctor and oversaw the removal of Brady from the edge of the road to the kitchen of a local house. Two local physicians arrived and began treating the wounded men, and the RIC returned. A district inspector announced that "under the authority of the Crown" he was going to arrest the two men. Mac Eoin responded, "under the authority of the Irish Republic," that they would not be arrested. He revealed that he was armed and the RIC withdrew. The incident was indicative of the growing conflict in Ireland.

The next day, as IRA volunteers watched over him, Matt Brady was moved by British military ambulance to the Longford Infirmary, where he recovered slowly, under the watchful eyes of both the IRA and the RIC. In October, Mac Eoin was alerted by Crown Solicitor T. W. Delaney that a warrant was to be issued for Brady's arrest. The IRA got there first and moved him to the Richmond Hospital in Dublin, under the care of friendly physicians. Mac Eoin was probably also the source of a *Longford Leader* article that gave Matt Brady a cover story that explained his injuries:

> On Thursday forenoon as Mr. Matthew Brady, a well-known Longford horseman, was riding a thoroughbred into town the horse slipped opposite the pump in the Market Square and threw him violently to the ground. Blood gushed from his mouth and nose and he was rendered insensible. A large crowd quickly collected and the priest and doctor were sent for. Rev. Father Newman, Adm., on arrival considered the case so bad that he anointed the injured man on the spot. Subsequently a motor car was procured and the priest and Mr. P. H. Fitzgerald, U.D.C., took him to the Co. Infirmary, where he lies in a very precarious state.

From the spring of 1919 the IRA grew quickly and its capabilities expanded rapidly. In Dublin, it was led by Mick Collins, who was ruthless. On Sunday morning, November 21st, 1920, IRA men under his direction broke into homes and hotel rooms and executed fourteen suspected British spies. Some were shot in front of their wives. That afternoon, also in Dublin, British forces took their revenge by firing indiscriminately into a crowd at a football match in Croke Park, killing twelve and wounding sixty. In the countryside, the IRA was especially active in Cork, Tipperary, Clare, Kerry, Limerick, Roscommon, and Longford. Noteworthy IRA leaders were Tom Barry in Cork and Seán Mac Eoin in Longford. Barry directed the IRA in battles at Kilmichael and Crossbarry. His policy was to burn out two pro-British homes for every pro-Republican home burned out. Seán Mac Eoin directed the IRA in what became known as the Battle of Ballinalee. In October 1920, the IRA executed an RIC inspector in Kiernan's Hotel in Granard. In response, British auxiliary troops, in spite of fire from Mac Eoin's men, torched buildings in the town. A few days later, the auxiliaries set out on a reprisal raid on Ballinalee. Alerted to what was coming, Mac Eoin arranged an ambush, killing several auxiliaries.

Mac Eoin's exploits became the stuff of legend. In January 1921, he was staying with sympathizers when the home was raided. He escaped, but an RIC district inspector was killed. Mac Eoin then led another guerrilla ambush at Clonfin, during which several British forces were killed. In March 1921, after visiting IRA general headquarters in Dublin, where he met with Collins and Cathal Brugha, Mac Eoin was arrested on the train at Mullingar. He tried to escape and was wounded for his efforts. In prison, he was elected as a Sinn Féin TD (Teachta Dála, member of the Dáil) to the Second Dáil Éireann. In court, he was charged with murder. He fought the charge but was found guilty and sentenced to death. Twice Mick Collins tried to break him out of prison. Mac Eoin's reprieve came when the IRA and British authorities entered into a dialogue that led to a truce and Collins and Éamon de Valera insisted that he be released. At the first session of the Second Dáil Éireann in August 1921, IRA commander and rebel politician Seán Mac Eoin was granted the honor of proposing de Valera not as president of the Dáil but as president of the Irish Republic.

Matt Brady missed direct involvement in Mac Eoin's rise to fame. He rode out the Anglo-Irish War (also known as the Black and Tan War) in hospitals in Dublin under the nom de guerre Tom Browne. It was not an easy existence. RIC and British troops were in and out of the hospitals as patients; when he played cards he would hold his hand so that the obvious bullet wound there was not recognized. The hospitals were also raided regularly. He was moved at various points to the Mater Hospital, to Linden Convalescent Home, and to private homes. There were some problems with hospital staff. A nurse at Richmond Hospital reported to the secretary that Brady suffered from a gunshot wound, not the kick of a horse. Dublin Castle, the seat of British power, got the report, but Mick Collins had agents there. When the British arrived, Brady's hospital bed was empty. The IRA ordered the hospital secretary to leave Ireland within twenty-four hours and the nurse had her hair cropped.

Matt Brady's presence in Dublin was an open secret among Longford Republicans. He was "available" for his officers, and engaged in "I.O. [Intelligence Officer] work in [the] Mater and Richmond Hosp." Certainly wounded RIC and British troops were a source of information that he passed along. Longford people visited him, including Joe McGuinness's wife. While "in his own keeping," he followed the revolutionary situation in Dublin. From the Mater he watched cabs and lorries arrive with prisoners at nearby Mountjoy Prison. He later recalled for his children a demonstration outside the prison as six IRA members were hanged there, in pairs, on March 14, 1921, two at seven, two at eight, and two at nine in the morning.

Also in Dublin at this time was May Caffrey. A graduate of the St. Louis Convent in Monaghan, she spent a year back in Donegal studying Irish and then qualified for the National University in Dublin. On campus, she majored in commerce and played camogie, which is similar to hurling. She was on the 1921 team which won the prestigious Ashbourne Cup; the team photo is proudly displayed in Ruairí Ó Brádaigh's home. Her teammates included fellow Republicans, including the sister of IRA member and future Taoiseach (prime minister) Seán Lemass. Off campus, she transferred to Dublin Cumann na mBan. Her brother Jack was also at the university and in the IRA; during holidays, she continued to organize Cumann na mBan in Donegal. As a Cumann na mBan volunteer in Dublin, she helped provide packed lunches for Sinn Féiners on polling day in the local council elections in 1920, helped hide "wanted" men, and marched in formation to protest meetings and demonstrations outside prisons during hunger strikes and executions. It was standard practice for RIC men based in the countryside to visit Dublin and help the police identify people from their areas who might be on the run or visiting on business; Seán Mac Eoin was captured returning to Longford from an IRA meeting in Dublin. As a counter, the IRA asked people from the country living in Dublin to identify these RIC officers. May Caffrey was asked to identify an inspector from Donegal who was expected to arrive in Dublin on a particular train, presumably so the IRA could assassinate him. She was at the station with the IRA when the train arrived, without the RIC officer.

In July 1921, the British entered into a truce with the IRA, presenting an opportunity that brought Matt Brady and May Caffrey together. Matt, under relaxed conditions, transferred to Longford County Home and took a job as a steward. May, who had finished her degree in commerce, was teaching in Bray, County Wicklow. The job of secretary to the County Longford Board of Health became available, and they met when both took the civil service examination. With her degree, May Caffrey was better qualified and she got the job, commencing December 5, 1921. Her letter of appointment was signed by Liam T. Cosgrave, Aire Rialtais Áitiúil (minister for local government) of the Second Dáil Éireann. She took up residence in the County Home. Among her duties were the registration of births, deaths, and marriages in County Longford and sending board meeting minutes to the department of local government of the still-revolutionary Dáil Éireann via a "cover address" in Dublin.

In 1920, Westminster passed the Government of Ireland Act, which created two Home Rule Parliaments in Ireland, one in Belfast for the six northeastern counties and one in Dublin for the rest of the country. Republicans rejected the bill, but Unionists immediately formed a government for Northern Ireland, with Sir James Craig as prime minister. In 1921, with a truce and negotiations under way, Republicans believed they could reunite the country and achieve international recognition of the Republic. Instead, in London, representatives of Dáil Éireann—including Arthur Griffith and Mick Collins but not Éamon de Valera—signed the Anglo-Irish Treaty on December 6, 1921. The Treaty confirmed partition, contained an oath of allegiance to the British monarch, and placed the 26-county Irish Free State firmly in the British Commonwealth.

Republicans split over the treaty, which was ratified by the Dáil. Pro-treaty Republicans included Mick Collins, Arthur Griffith, and Seán Mac Eoin. Mac Eoin, in the Dáil, seconded Arthur Griffith's motion "that Dáil Éireann approves of the Treaty between Great Britain and Ireland, signed in London on December 6th 1921." Éamon de Valera led the opposition. When it was ratified, he resigned as president of the Republic, moving Ireland from rebellion against the British government and closer to civil war. Arthur Griffith formed a pro-treaty ministry, and Mick Collins became president of the Provisional Government of the Irish Free State. The anti-treatyites refused to recognize the authority of the new government. Matt Brady and May Caffrey sided with de Valera and the anti-treatyites. Brady was a determined man. His injured leg was rigid and

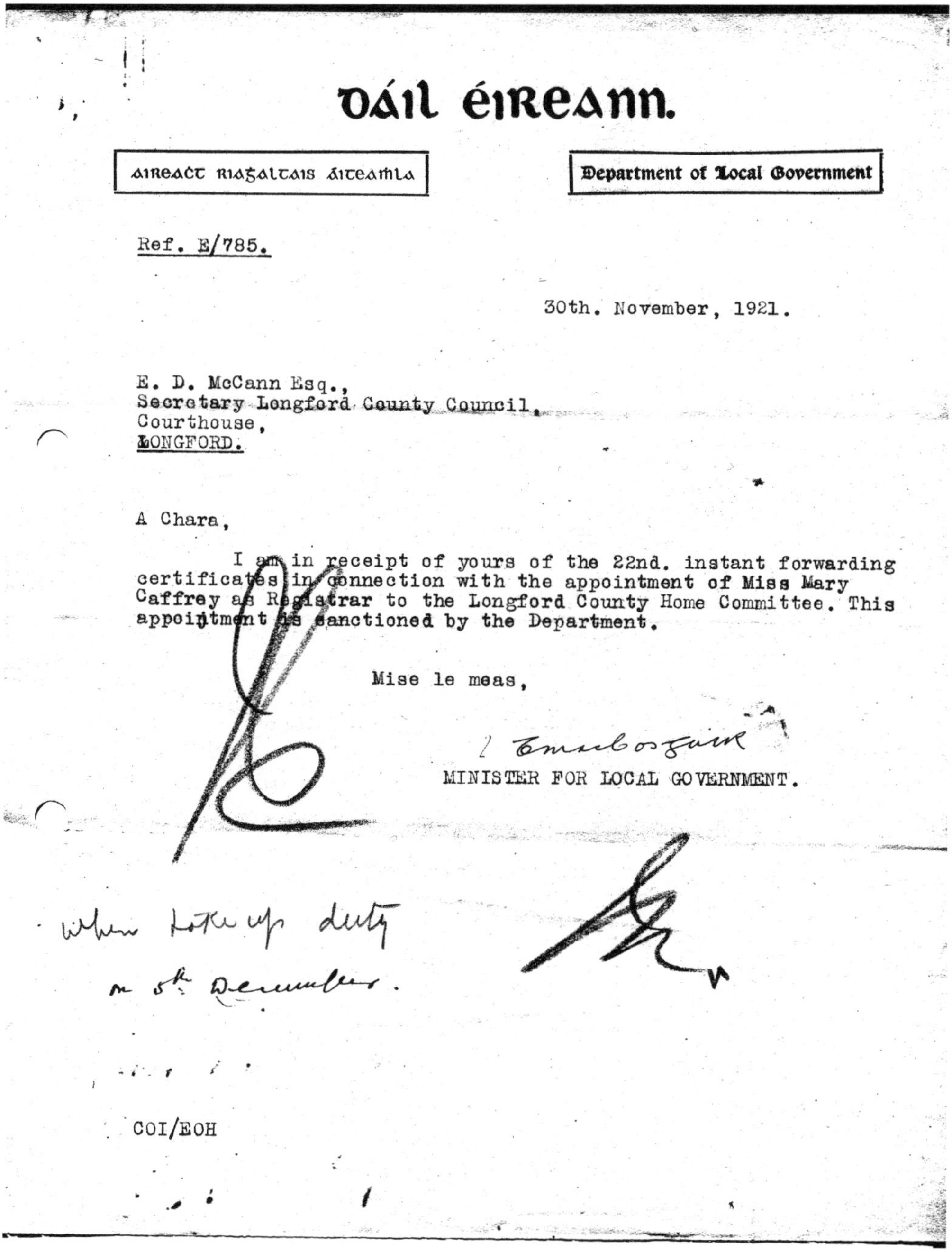

DÁIL ÉIREANN.

AIREACHT RIAGHALTAIS ÁITEAMHLA

Department of Local Government

Ref. E/785.

30th. November, 1921.

E. D. McCann Esq.,
Secretary Longford County Council,
Courthouse,
LONGFORD.

A Chara,

I am in receipt of yours of the 22nd. instant forwarding certificates in connection with the appointment of Miss Mary Caffrey as Registrar to the Longford County Home Committee. This appointment is sanctioned by the Department.

Mise le meas,

L Mac Cosgair

MINISTER FOR LOCAL GOVERNMENT.

When take up duty on 5th December.

COI/EOH

1921 letter from Liam Cosgrave appointing May Caffrey secretary/registrar of the County Longford Board of Health. Ó Brádaigh family collection.

shortened by several inches and he was forced to wear a surgical boot and walk with a cane, but he was still a "Brigade Staff" officer in the IRA. Prior to the treaty he was "preparing forms for intelligence reports from units and indexing correspondence [of] GHQ Brigade and Gen Staff." After the treaty, he "left Brigade Head Q's . . . and started organizing against [the] Treaty."

In Dublin, IRA (anti-treaty) forces established their headquarters in the Four Courts, the country's legal center. The Free State government demanded that they surrender. They refused, and civil war broke out. The IRA was disorganized from the start, and the Free State forces, backed by the British, drove them from Dublin and pursued them into the country-side. In August, Arthur Griffith died of a heart attack and Mick Collins was killed in an ambush in Cork. Liam Cosgrave, 1916 veteran and the person who appointed May Caffrey as secretary in Longford, took over as president of the Irish Free State. Attitudes on both sides hardened. The 26-county Third Dáil of the pro-treatyites, referred to as Leinster House (where it met, in Dublin) by the anti-treatyites, granted the Free State government the power to impose the death penalty. Executions led to reprisals, which led to more executions. On December 8, 1922, the Feast of the Immaculate Conception, four prominent anti-treaty Republicans who had been imprisoned without charge or trial for five months—Liam Mellows, Rory O'Connor, Joe McKelvey, and Richard Barrett—were taken out and shot. Between November and May 1922–1923, more than eighty Republican prisoners were executed. Seán Mac Eoin, a general in the Free State Army, had under his command Athlone Barracks. Five anti-treaty Republicans were executed there in January 1923.

In Longford, most of the IRA activists supported Mac Eoin, but there was enough opposition that Mac Eoin singled out Seán F. Lynch in a letter, complaining of Lynch's anti-treaty activities and noting that "it is time to relegate this man to his proper sphere of duties." Lynch's brother-in-law, Tom Brady, also rejected the treaty and tried to reorganize the IRA. The IRA was beaten down in Longford and elsewhere, however. Liam Lynch, its chief of staff, was killed in action in April 1923. Soon after this, de Valera met with Lynch's successor, Frank Aiken, and they ended the fight. De Valera issued a famous statement to the "Soldiers of the Republic, Legion of the Rearguard" and declared that "[the] Republic can no longer be defended successfully by your arms." Aiken issued a cease-fire order to soldiers still in the field. Thousands of anti-treaty Republicans were in prison, and still more faced prison if they surfaced. Tom

Brady remained on the run until 1925. Militarily, the cost of the Civil War was relatively small, with probably less than 4,000 casualties. Politically, the Civil War created bitter political divisions. Sinn Féin remained the primary opposition party, but they refused to participate in the Free State Parliament. For them, the Second Dáil Éireann remained the true government of the Republic and Free Staters were traitors who had sold out the Republic for political power in a truncated, unfree Irish state. Abstention from Westminster had led to the creation of Dáil Éireann. Abstention from Leinster House, site of the Dublin government, left Liam Cosgrave and the pro-treatyites in unchallenged control of the Irish Free State.

As for Matt Brady and May Caffrey, they found each other in the midst of the truce. They were a perfect match—almost. She was a Cumann na mBan veteran, he was an IRA veteran. Each of them rejected the treaty. They were both ardent proponents of the Irish language. Yet May's parents worried about the future of their young healthy daughter who was involved with a man nine years her senior who had not, and probably never would, recover from devastating war wounds. Her sister Bertha told her in fun, "You are running around with a broken soldier." May was unhappy with the comment. Complicating their situation, each was employed at the Longford County Home. An employee there was not allowed to supervise the work of one's spouse. If they married, one of them would be out of a job.

For four years they wrestled with these issues. In considering their options, they enlisted the support of the most powerful person they knew, Major General Seán Mac Eoin. Mac Eoin had saved Matt Brady's life and kept him out of harm's way as he recovered. While they differed totally in politics, they respected each other, and with May Caffrey the three of them had a personal relationship that transcended their political differences. This is clearly evident in letters found in Mac Eoin's papers. Unfortunately, the best that Mac Eoin could do was to give an assurance that if May Caffrey resigned her job, Matt Brady would receive "the fullest possible consideration" for the position of superintendent assistance officer at the County Home. Making the best of a difficult situation, Matt Brady resigned his job. May Brady would be the breadwinner in the family.

They were married on August 26, 1926, at Castlefinn, County Donegal, where her parents lived. They passed through London on their honeymoon. May later recalled the trip for her children, finding humor in Matt's reaction. She enjoyed the sights, but he instinctively wanted to get

Wedding photograph of May Caffrey and Matt Brady, August 1926. Ó Brádaigh family collection.

out of the place as fast as possible; as far as he was concerned, England was the fountainhead of all that was bad in the Irish world. They moved on and visited her relations in Switzerland. When they finally arrived back in Longford, May went to work as the secretary of County Longford Board of Health. Matt was unemployed but helped out as she went about her business, and they looked forward to raising a family.

2

The Brady Family

IRISH REPUBLICANS IN THE 1930S AND 1940S

POLITICAL EVENTS IN THE 1920s split people into two camps: pro- and anti-Treaty, which became defined as anti- and pro-Republican. In the 1930s and early 1940s, the anti-Treaty Republicans split again, for or against involvement in constitutional politics. These divisions directly affected the lives of Matt and May Brady and their children.

In 1925, the IRA formally withdrew itself from the authority of the Second Dáil. The two organizations still sought an Irish Republic, but they drifted apart. The anti-Treaty Second Dáil Teachtaí Dála considered themselves to be the de jure government of *all* of Ireland. Their abstentionism, however, locked them out of participation in the Free State government. In 1926, at the Sinn Féin Ard Fheis (convention), Éamon de Valera asked the delegates to drop the abstentionist policy with respect to both Leinster House and Stormont (the Parliament of Northern Ireland). When his request was denied, de Valera resigned as president of Sinn Féin and formed a new political party, Fianna Fáil. Fianna Fáil and Sinn Féin contested seats in the June 1927 Free State general election to "Leinster House"—Republicans refused to label the government "Dáil Éireann." Under the direction of the charismatic de Valera, Fianna Fáil virtually wiped out Sinn Féin as the Republican alternative in the election, but it did not win enough seats to form a government. Instead, William Cosgrave and his pro-Treaty Cumann na nGaedheal Party remained in power. This power was unchecked because entering Leinster House required an oath of allegiance to the Crown, which de Valera and the other Fianna Fáil TDs refused to take. But political events would lead them to compromise.

Many Republicans held Kevin O'Higgins, Free State minister for justice during the Irish Civil War and subsequently the state's vice-president, responsible for the executions of 1922–1923. In July, 1927, freelance IRA volunteers shot him dead. Cosgrave responded by introducing severe anti-Republican legislation, and there was no opposition party to stop it. In a dramatic move, de Valera led his followers to Leinster House, signed the oath of allegiance, and entered Parliament. The decision haunts his place in history. Taking his seat did not prevent more repressive legislation, and purists believed he had compromised his principles. Because it was only the opposition party, Fianna Fáil continued its Republican rhetoric and kept an uneasy peace with those suspicious of de Valera's motives. As the 1932 Free State general election approached, de Valera was an untested alternative to the anti-Republicanism of Cosgrave. The IRA actively supported Fianna Fáil, and the party won enough seats to form a coalition government with Labour. For the next sixteen years, Fianna Fáil was in power either in coalition or on its own.

Fianna Fáil acted like a Republican government. IRA prisoners were quickly released, the IRA was deproscribed, legislation removing the oath of allegiance was introduced, and the governor general was replaced with a de Valera loyalist. Fianna Fáil also refused to pay land annuities to the British created by the Government of Ireland Act (1920) and the Treaty. The first strain in the Fianna Fáil–IRA relationship appeared as fascism swept across Europe and landed in Ireland as the Blueshirts, a right-wing group that clashed with the IRA. The Fianna Fáil government could not tolerate this; it seized propaganda material and arrested Blueshirts and IRA members. The Blueshirts were short lived; they were harassed by the IRA, arrested by the government, and abandoned by mainstream politicians.

The IRA, still a large organization with generations of experience with conspiracy behind it, presented a more difficult problem. De Valera used his power to wean support from the IRA. In 1933, the Fianna Fáil government established an army volunteer reserve; the goal was to attract potential IRA recruits to the forces of the state. In 1934, a military service pension was introduced for old IRA men. Caught up in the Depression, some anti-Treaty Republicans were faced with living in poverty, emigrating, or recognizing the government and taking a pension. The IRA saw the pensions as an attempt to "seduce Volunteers from their allegiance" and rejected them. Able-bodied IRA veterans who accepted pensions were viewed as sellouts, but disabled veterans were allowed to accept. Matt Brady qualified for and received a pension.

National politics were played out on the local level throughout the Free State. Seán Mac Eoin retired as chief of staff of the Irish Free State

Army and became a full-time politician. In June 1934, the Blueshirts came to North Longford and Mac Eoin, a United Ireland Party TD (which was reorganized from Cumann na nGaedheal and later referred to as Fine Gael, the party's Irish name), supported them. Seán F. Lynch organized against the rally, asking people to stay away "from the Blueshirt parade" because they were there "to create trouble and disturb the peace."

That same June, the IRA staged a rally in Longford "in support of a demand for the release of Republican prisoners and the abolition of the Public Safety Act," which was enacted by Cosgrave's government and then used by de Valera's government against the Blueshirts *and* the IRA. Forming up on Battery Road, 300 members of the IRA and its youth group, Na Fianna Éireann, carried banners with slogans such as "Join the IRA" and "Smash Partition" and marched to the courthouse. Mick Ferguson, the Longford Battalion commanding officer, presided, and the crowd was addressed by leading IRA figures who had come down from Dublin. As he addressed the crowd, Michael Fitzpatrick commented on the upcoming local elections: "We of the Republican Army have no interest—no definite interest—in the Local Government elections." As far as the IRA was concerned, when the local governments functioned, they supported the governments in Dublin and Belfast, which were "functioning in the interests of the British Government." He also attacked Fianna Fáil:

> A number of you may think that we don't give Fianna Fáil a chance and that they are doing their best. But if they are doing their best we came here to tell you that their best is not enough. The attitude they are adopting is the same as that adopted by their predecessors. They have more republicans in prison than were in it at any time during Cosgrave's term in office.

Three local Republicans who agreed with most, but not all, of the IRA's message were probably in the crowd that day. Seán F. Lynch, his brother-in-law Tom Brady, and Matt Brady were Independent Republican candidates in the local government elections.

Irish politics were in a state of flux. Fianna Fáil began the 1930s as the leading Republican challenger, but its success was in part the result of the compromises it made. In order to present his message to the people, de Valera had launched the *Irish Press* in 1931. The daily paper was financed by subscription shares. Among those who purchased shares were Matt and May Brady. They probably supported Fianna Fáil in 1932. But by 1934, distrust of Fianna Fáil kept Matt out of that party, and Sinn Féin was not fielding candidates. Running as Independent Republicans gave Matt Brady, Seán F. Lynch, and Tom Brady the opportunity to express their Republican aspirations.

At this point, Matt and May Brady were the parents of two children—Mary, born in August 1929, and Rory, born October 2, 1932. Mary was referred to as May Óg by the family, Óg being the Irish word for young or "junior." Rory's full name was Peter Roger Casement Brady. He was named Peter after his grandfather and Roger Casement after the 1916 leader who was hanged in Pentonville Prison in London. Sir Roger was knighted for his work exposing the abuses of natives in the Belgian Congo and in the Putumayo area of South America. Born into an Anglo-Irish family, he arranged the arms shipment from Germany for the 1916 Irish rebels. He was arrested and tried in England, where his name was smeared with the selective and controversial release of alleged diaries indicating he was a homosexual. In naming their child after him, the Bradys indicated their allegiance to Republicanism. The child was called Rory, the Hiberno-English translation of Roger; in the Irish language, it is Ruairí.

The Bradys had moved from a two-room flat over a mechanic's garage to Silchester, on Battery Road. The IRA march in June 1934 probably formed up in front of Silchester or marched by it. Silchester was actually two sets of two semi-detached two-story homes connected to the main road by a long—perhaps one hundred yards long—avenue. The grounds were spacious, with tall hedges and apple trees and plenty of room for Matt to plant a garden for vegetables, which supplemented the family's income, making them relatively self-sufficient.

On June 16, 1934, Matt Brady's "election address" was published in the *Longford Leader*; it was titled "To the Electors of Ballinalee County Electoral Area." He pledged "to support the present Government as long as they endeavor to obtain the complete independence of our country" and to "do all that is in my power to foster the revival of our mother tongue, the Irish language, for it is my firm belief that we can never become truly Irish and free until our own tongue is a living language in our midst." He saw no reason why Ireland could not become bilingual, as was the case in Belgium. He also pledged to "do my best in the interests of the ratepayers" while at the same time trying to maintain an efficient local administration. He had "plenty of time at my disposal to devote to this work, and my services will always be available." He was interested in the welfare of the "bona fide labourer" and in the state of roads and passes in the area, which were "badly in need of repair." Not mentioned was a practical benefit to the Brady family if Matt was elected. As secretary of the

Board of Health, May Brady was an employee of the County Council. Although council seats were unpaid positions, Matt's presence on the council would guarantee her a fair hearing if there were ever difficulties.

In the election, Fianna Fáil repeated its success of 1932 and won control of a majority of the County Councils. In Longford, Fianna Fáil won thirteen of twenty-six seats. The other thirteen seats were split between the United Ireland Party (ten seats), the Independent Republicans (two seats), and the Independent Labour Party (one seat). Because ballots call on voters to rank candidates, a complex series of counts is taken to determine the winners. In Drumlish, Seán F. Lynch topped the poll (received the most votes) and was elected on the first count. In Ballinalee, on the sixth and final count, Matt Brady was elected. When the council met for the first time after the election, a Fianna Fáiler was elected the chair and Seán F. Lynch was elected vice chair. More relevant to the Brady family, Seán F. Lynch was appointed to the Board of Health and became its chairman and as such nominally oversaw the work of May Brady. Together, Lynch and Matt Brady used their positions on the County Council to support the Republican cause. Because they were there together, each could second the other and force the discussion of issues. Their importance was enhanced because no party had an overall majority. A high point of their collaboration was in 1937, when Lynch was an unsuccessful candidate for Leinster House and Matt Brady was his election agent. They publicly supported the IRA and the oppressed.

The Depression was especially hard on tenants, whose rents were fixed but whose incomes were declining. At the Sanderson Estate, near Edgeworthstown, Gerald More O'Ferrall was unable to collect from tenants, who demanded a 50 percent reduction in their rents. When he threatened eviction, he received threats. When he initiated eviction proceedings, the Edgeworthstown Town Tenants' Association turned to the IRA. At a public meeting, IRA representatives, in the tradition of the Land League and the Fenians, pledged "the support of the I.R.A. to the tenants in their fight against landlordism." One speaker bluntly stated that "if the forces of the state are called in to protect the bailiffs, then force must be met by force." Opposition to landlords, bailiffs, and sheriffs has a lengthy and violent history in Longford. In the 1830s, tenants who supported landlords were killed, as was a bailiff. In the 1930s, landlords who insisted on their rents were courting trouble. The IRA waited through the Christmas season, then set out in February 1935 to humiliate O'Ferrall by dousing him with tar. It ended in tragedy. Dressed as police officers, IRA men barged into his house. In the scuffle that followed, Gerald More O'Ferrall was beaten and his son, Richard, was shot in the back. He lingered for eleven days and then died.

The attack was denounced all over Ireland, especially by the Catholic clergy. The Dublin County Council passed a resolution condemning the "foul murder of the late Mr. More O'Ferrall in his house," called on the "Government to make every effort to bring the perpetrators of this foul crime to justice," and asked that other councils endorse the resolution. At the next meeting of the Longford County Council, Mr. Dunne of the United Ireland Party brought up the resolution. Matt Brady immediately protested with, "I would like to propose that we go on with the next business as that resolution is political. If it was a poor man's son there would be very little about it."

Dunne replied, "No matter about that, I have a resolution to propose. It is that we condemn the shooting of any man whether he is rich or poor. There ought to be a way out of these things without going to the extreme of murder. It is a terrible thing that a man can be murdered in his own house."

Brady persisted, "I protest against that resolution."

The chairman, Mr. Belton of Fianna Fáil, stated, "Resolutions will not do any good anyway."

Dunne argued that "if we are not in agreement with [the shooting] we should condemn it. I don't know why Mr. Brady objects to it."

Brady held his ground: "The resolution of Dublin County Council is political." Eventually the chair ruled "the whole thing out as it has been turned into politics." Dunne walked out of the meeting.

Police in Longford and Leitrim arrested seven people, four of whom were charged with the More O'Ferrall murder. But there was more trouble in Longford when three families were evicted from the Sanderson Estate. At a public protest, a crowd of about 200 was monitored by "a large force of Gardaí [Irish police] and detectives." The first speaker, a Fianna Fáil member of the County Council, was applauded for proposing a "resolution to stand by the men in jail who [are] fighting our fight for us." He was followed by Seán F. Lynch, who stated that "the place for any public man is where the people are in trouble." He encouraged the people to stand by their tenants' association. Matt Brady followed Lynch, and his comments offer insight into his attitude on the shooting and his general approach to politics. He began by commenting on himself; he had not been on a public platform since the general election in 1918. He was there as a "representative of the people" of the area (Edgeworthstown was in the Ballinalee electoral area) and was not a "speech-maker." But he would "always stand behind the underdog." He encouraged the tenants to stick together and he seconded the proposition that the assembled crowd stand by the arrested men. He also voiced his concern that the accused would not get a fair trial: "It is a terrible thing that resolutions are being passed describing it as wilful murder. It is for a judge and jury to decide that; and how can a jury come to a fair decision when all this sort of thing is going on." Matt Brady believed that the IRA had not set out to kill Richard More O'Ferrall. In their actions on behalf of the working poor of the area, an accidental tragedy had resulted. He supported the IRA's action on behalf of the underdog.

The four men accused of the murder recognized the court in Dublin and fought the charges. The result was a hung jury. In a retrial, they were found not guilty on the direction of the judge and set free. Officially, the case was never solved. It was a victory for the IRA, and the accused were welcomed at several public meetings. They were sent off from Dublin by the cream of the IRA, including Moss Twomey, the chief of staff. At Edgeworthstown, they were met by the Tenants Association and the local IRA. Irish flags (tricolors) were flying, as was a banner inscribed with "Welcome I.R.A. Prisoners." Several of them addressed the crowd, as did Moss Twomey and Matt Brady. This meeting concluded with the singing of the Irish national anthem, and the ex-prisoners moved on to Longford town, where Matt Brady presided over another welcoming reception.

Fianna Fáil and the IRA both wanted a 32-county Republic. Those in Fianna Fáil thought they could bring it about through constitutional means. Those in the IRA appreciated constitutional changes consistent with a Republic, but they also wanted direct action to end partition and reunite the country. The More O'Ferrall shooting was one of a number of incidents in which the IRA flouted the authority of the Free State. No government can long tolerate a paramilitary army undermining its authority. On June 18, 1936, Fianna Fáil proscribed the IRA once again. The annual Republican parade to Wolfe Tone's grave at Bodenstown, scheduled for the next day, was banned. A thousand troops and 500 police officers kept Republicans out of the cemetery. In its lengthy history, dating from the 1790s, the military wing of Irish Republicanism had been legal for only four years. Proscribing the IRA and banning Republican activities made life difficult for the Republican Movement, but it was the usual situation for a group of people who had a history of adapting to such conditions.

In Longford, Matt Brady took on Fianna Fáil. At a County Council meeting he proposed a resolution protesting the use of solitary confinement and the denial of political status in Irish prisons, demanding the immediate release of all political prisoners, and protesting the ban on Bodenstown. He was seconded by Seán F. Lynch. The chairman, who was from Fianna Fáil, ruled the motion out of order because he had not been notified in advance. He also noted that the year before, he had ruled another motion out of order on the grounds that it was political, as was this motion. Brady replied that it was not "political" but "national." There were heated exchanges and he attacked Fianna Fáil and de Valera: "The Government should be ashamed of themselves, and particularly the President." A Fianna Fáil councilor defended de Valera, "as our leader, Mr. de Valera[,] says, we want to live in peace and harmony with our neighbour, England, too." Brady responded with, "Oh, I see. Do you stand for coercion, Mr. Walsh?"

Opposition or not, Éamon de Valera continued on his quest to minimize the 1921 Anglo-Irish Treaty. He directed the development of a new Constitution that was ratified by the Free State electorate in 1937. Article 2 stated that "the national territory consists of the whole island of Ireland, its islands and the territorial seas," and Article 3 claimed for the Dublin Parliament the right to exercise jurisdiction over the entire island, "pending the reintegration of the national territory." In 1938, as Taoiseach under the Constitution, he engineered the British return of control of Irish ports that had not been released with the 1921 Treaty. This helped Ireland stay neutral in World War II, perhaps his greatest achievement.

In the summer of 1938, Matt Brady experienced what was probably his finest moment as a public person. On September 8, Longford celebrated the 140th anniversary of the Battle of Ballinamuck. Matt Brady chaired the commemoration committee. On a sun-filled day, thousands of people, including May, Mary, Rory, and presumably the youngest member of the family, infant Seán, assembled on the battlefield. The village and battlefield were decorated with side-by-side French and Irish tricolors. A collection of relics from the battle was on display in the village courthouse. It was an all-day event; the committee and bands traveled throughout North Longford, laying wreaths, reciting a decade of the rosary in Irish, and playing the national anthem and similar tunes at numerous sites marking Republican events from 1798 through the 1920s. When it arrived in Ballinamuck, the commemoration committee made its way to the platform and watched as speakers and marchers, including a procession of the IRA dressed as 1798 pikemen, arrived. Finally, Reveille was sounded and Matt Brady hoisted the Irish tricolor from half to full mast.

On the platform was a who's who of past and present Longford Republicans. Matt Brady, Seán F. Lynch, Hubert Wilson, and Tom Brady, who had all rejected the Treaty, were joined by Seán Mac Eoin, a Fine Gael TD, and James Victory and Erskine Childers, Fianna Fáil TDs. Political differences aside, they all recognized and appreciated the significance of 1798. Each wanted a united Ireland; they differed in how they believed it was best to bring this about. Matt Brady began the formal commemoration with a quotation from John Kells Ingram's famous poem, "The Memory of the Dead":

> All, all are gone, but still lives on
> _the fame of those who died,
> And true men, like you men,
> _remember them with pride.

The husband of a Cumann na mBan veteran and career woman, he welcomed the "exceedingly great number of 'true men' and women, 'like you men' and women here to-day." He noted that "since the Norman Invasion the chequered history of our country consists of a series of attempts on the part of its people to regain their independence. These attempts were made, both with the sword and the pen, in nearly every generation." For Brady, the struggle against England and the United Kingdom was continuous and consistent over time. These same motives and actions were present in 1938 Ireland: "We have all seen them in our own day, and they will continue till the end is achieved. The soil of our country has been wet with the blood of martyrs in this cause, its sod is dotted over with their graves." A previous struggle was being commemorated; it was not to be forgotten, it was to be emulated:

> It is to celebrate such an attempt that we are here now. So long as we continue to do so all will be well, but woe betide the day when we begin to forget, the day when we cease to remember the dead who died for Ireland.

With this he concluded his remarks and introduced the other speakers, including Seán Mac Eoin and, at age 82, James O'Neill, the grandnephew of Brian O'Neill, the survivor of the Battle of Ballinamuck. The proceedings concluded with bands playing the French and Irish national anthems; the crowd sang the Irish anthem.

The nonpartisan nature of the commemoration was an aberration. In spite of his successes, de Valera had not ended partition. Irish Republicanism was a mass movement in the years 1918–1922. Splits, defections, the pension issue, arrests, and time had reduced it to a small, isolated, clandestine group—its condition before 1916. Nevertheless, the IRA was preparing for war. During the Anglo-Irish War, the First Dáil had passed a resolution such that a provisional government could be formed if repressive conditions significantly reduced its number and threatened its operation. After the Treaty, the Second Dáil TDs, with the support of the IRA, formed an emergency government. In their view, this was the de jure government of the Republic, led by an Executive Council. Over the years, the Executive Council met as a shadow government of the Republic. By 1938, a hard core of absolutist Republicans were on an Executive Council that included Count Plunkett; Mary MacSwiney, whose brother died on hunger strike in 1920; and Tom Maguire, whose brother was executed by the Free State. The IRA leadership asked the council to transfer its executive power to the IRA. They agreed, and in purist Republican terms, the IRA's Army Council became the de jure government of the Republic. This was, and is, important; it gave the IRA the legal and moral authority to wage war in the name of the Republic. In making the transfer, the surviving Second Dáil deputies empowered men much like themselves, purists left over from the 1910s and 1920s who refused to accept the Free State and Northern Ireland. The IRA chief of staff was Seán Russell; he had been IRA director of munitions in 1921. Also on the Army Council was George Plunkett, one of the Count's remaining sons, and Larry Grogan, who had been imprisoned in Mountjoy in 1922 when the Free State began executing prisoners. In January 1939, the IRA demanded that the British withdraw from Ireland and asked for a response. When none was forthcoming, explosions rocked London, Manchester, and Birmingham. After nearly twenty years, the IRA was back at war.

The Dublin government quickly introduced repressive legislation, including a Treason Bill and the Offenses Against the State Act. The prescribed penalty for treason was death; the Offenses Against the State Act allowed the reintroduction of military tribunals and internment without trial. Opponents of the legislation mobilized, but with Fianna Fáil firmly in the majority, repressive legislation was destined to be enacted. At a meeting of the Longford County Council, Matt Brady proposed a resolution protesting the legislation "on the grounds that there is not occasion for it." As far as he was concerned, it was peaceful in Longford and "anything that happened has happened at the Border or in England, and thank God we have young men sufficiently alive to the national inspirations that it is into the enemy camp they are carrying the work and are hitting at the hub of the Empire, which is the proper place to hit, and the best of luck to them." He was supported by members of Fine Gael, who tended to oppose anything put forward by Fianna Fáil. The council passed the resolution, which was forwarded to the TDs of the area, including Seán

Mac Eoin. In the Dáil debates on the Offenses Against the State Act, Mac Eoin said it was "astonishing" that Fianna Fáil was criminalizing activities that its ministers had once pursued. Fianna Fáil's position was that they had a "duty to protect the State and its people" and the new Constitution negated any "moral justification" of the IRA. Irish Free State jails began to fill with suspected and active IRA members.

In August 1939, disaster struck in Coventry, England. Five people were killed and sixty were wounded when a bomb exploded in a crowded street. The action was contrary to IRA policy, but that did not help the victims or concern the police. Five Irish people living in Coventry were arrested, including Peter Barnes, who was originally from County Offaly, and James McCormick, who was from Mullingar in County Westmeath. Barnes was in the IRA and McCormick was present when the bomb was made, but neither was directly responsible for the premature detonation. Each pleaded innocent, was found guilty, and was sentenced to death. In spite of widespread appeals for clemency, they were hanged in a Birmingham jail on February 7, 1940.

That morning, as his 11-year-old daughter Mary and his 8-year-old son Rory were getting ready to leave for school, Matt Brady pulled out his pocket watch. When the watch hit nine o'clock, he turned to them and said, "Kneel down and say your prayers. Two Irishmen now lie into quicklime graves in Birmingham." It was Ash Wednesday, making it that much easier for Rory to remember the event. Ireland went into mourning for Barnes and McCormick. In Longford, both cinemas closed the night of the hanging and the next day all shops drew their blinds. The courthouse flag was flown at half mast. The next Saturday there was a large protest meeting at the Longford Courthouse, where Republicans Hubert Wilson and Seán F. Lynch spoke. At the next County Council meeting, Matt Brady proposed a resolution "of protest against the English executions and sympathy with the relatives of the executed men." After passing the resolution, the council adjourned for half an hour out of respect. McCormick had been from Mullingar, and Brady was a member of the Mullingar Mental Hospital Committee. At their next meeting he aired his feelings on the executions. In seconding a vote of sympathy, he stated that the men were "murdered." As reported in the *Westmeath Independent,* he said that Barnes and McCormick would

> go down in history as martyrs like Kevin Barry and Pádraig Pearse. They had gone now to their reward as he was sure they were in heaven. They had stood out for the complete freedom of their country. They were not Com-

munists or Socialists or anything of that kind as some people would put them down to be. They were good Irish men, and went to their death with a smile. Their blood would not be shed in vain.

1940 was a particularly bad year for the IRA. There were mass arrests in Britain, in Northern Ireland, and in the Free State. Prison conditions were bleak. Arbour Hill Military Detention Barracks in Dublin was reported to be the coldest prison in Europe. People who had been arrested but not charged with a crime, "internees," were sent to the Curragh Military Camp in County Kildare. The camp consisted of wooden stables left over from the British Army, surrounded by barbed wire. As they had during the Anglo-Irish War, IRA prisoners fought the conditions and eventually turned to the hunger strike as their most potent weapon. Among the strikers was John Plunkett, yet another of the Count's sons. Two IRA men, Tony D'Arcy and Seán MacNeela, died before the IRA called off the strike. At D'Arcy's funeral a confrontation between the police and the Republican crowd caused the coffin to be knocked to the ground.

These events were closely followed in the Brady household. One of the funerals traveled through Longford, and the Brady family paid their respects as the cortege passed by. Rory Brady remembers that he "couldn't understand this at all." He knew that the British had left Longford in the early 1920s, "but why were men dying on hunger strike in Dublin?" He asked questions and discussed politics with his schoolmates, some of whom said it was suicide. He remembers, "I was politically aware enough to say, 'Well, what about Terence MacSwiney?' They'd say, 'Ah, well, that's different.' Well, how different? It's the principle of it." MacSwiney had died after a 74-day hunger-strike. He is perhaps best known as the author of *Principles of Freedom* and for the quotation "It is not those who can inflict the most, but those that can suffer the most who will conquer." In the Brady household, there was no difference between Terence MacSwiney in 1920 and Tony D'Arcy and Seán MacNeela in 1940.

As the IRA campaign continued, Fianna Fáil set out to destroy the organization. The Longford IRA was especially hard hit. Barney Casey, the Longford commanding officer, was arrested and sent to the Curragh, where the situation was tense. In December 1940, the prisoners burned down several of the huts. Fighting broke out between prisoners and warders, and several prisoners were wounded. A few days later, Barney Casey was shot in the back and killed. For Casey's funeral, the IRA provided a coffin and hearse. Republicans, wearing tricolor armbands, marched alongside the hearse. The mourners included Kathleen Clarke and Maud Gonne Mac Bride, widows of executed 1916 leader Tom Clarke and John Mac Bride. Busloads of people arrived from throughout the country, including one organized by Seán F. Lynch. Matt Brady and Hubert Wilson were there together, and after the funeral they were harassed by Free State troops. Richard Goss, the IRA's North Leinster–South Ulster Divisional commanding officer, was arrested in County Longford after a shootout in which two soldiers were wounded. Under the Emergency Powers Act of 1939, anyone found guilty by the military tribunal faced a mandatory death sentence. Goss was executed by firing squad in Port Laoise Prison on August 9, 1941. With him, for all practical purposes, died the Longford IRA.

Matt Brady had never recovered from his wounds of 1919. As a youngster, Rory would climb into bed with his father and spot a red stain about the size of a sixpence on the man's pajamas; he was still bleeding after twenty years. Not long after the Casey funeral and the Goss execution, Matt Brady's health declined further. He was in Dublin's Mater Hospital twice in 1942, to no avail. On Sunday morning, June 7, 1942, he died at the family residence; he was 51 years old. In passing a resolution of sympathy for the family, a member of the Board of Health stated, "A fairer or straighter or more honourable man I never met in my life." An obituary described him as "a man of sterling national principles and unrelenting patriotism throughout the whole period of his career, fair in criticism and unfailing in the cause of justice." He was described in tributes as the first man in Longford "to shed his blood for the Cause" in the Anglo-Irish War and as a "die-hard Republican." He was given a soldier's funeral.

The funeral Mass was held at St. Mel's Cathedral in Longford. Burial was in Ballymacormack Cemetery, near the town. Behind the ruined walls of a twelfth-century church, Matt Brady's old comrades formed a guard of honor under the command of Seán Duffy of Ballinalee. The surviving family watched as the guard exited an ancient door, marched to the gravesite, and fired three volleys over the tricolor-draped coffin. Seán Mac Eoin had asked May Brady if she would like a bugler to sound The Last Post. She agreed, but only if the bugler was not in uniform. Mac Eoin offered a graveside oration for the man he had saved so many years before. In 1921, they had made different choices on the Treaty. Over time, each remained true to his convictions. They respected each other and the choice each had made, and they remained on good personal terms throughout the tumultuous 1930s and 1940s. For Matt Brady, Seán Mac Eoin was a political opponent and personal friend, but de Valera and Fianna Fáil were

Firing party at the funeral of Matt Brady, June 1942. Ó Brádaigh family collection.

bitter enemies who had betrayed the Republic. A tombstone, designed by May's younger brother, Eugene, an architect, was later added to Matt Brady's grave. Engraved on the front is an Easter lily, the symbol of 1916 and the continuing struggle; on the back is a reversed rifle, symbol of a fallen soldier.

Matt Brady's Republicanism had several dimensions that combined an interest in history and culture and direct methods of physical force to bring about the Republic. His family and the people of Longford watched him act on each. At home, he spoke the few words of Irish that he knew. On the County Council, he supported changing the name Edgeworth-stown to Mostrim, the area's name prior to the arrival of the famous Edge-worth family. His support for the IRA was unwavering. In 1938 an IRA volunteer from Longford was killed in a premature explosion at the border. When a member of the County Council did not stand in silence for the deceased, Brady told him, "You should be ashamed." He regularly served as chair of Longford's 1916 commemorations. The first Easter Commemoration Rory Brady attended was in 1941, at Clonbroney, Balli-nalee; he was there with his father, his sister Mary, and Hubert Wilson.

Matt Brady had also married a woman ahead of her time. Thirteen-year-old Mary, 10 year-old Rory, and 5-year-old Seán were in good hands. She was the family's source of income and she was not afraid to stand up for herself. In the early 1930s, she was dissatisfied with the organization of the Board of Health. At one County Council meeting, which took place after Matt Brady and Seán F. Lynch had joined the council, she expressed her dissatisfaction and asked for change. When two councilors indicated that they were content with the organization, she challenged them, "I am not content at all. I have to sign things I know nothing about." She explained that she could be held liable if illegal payments were made by the board. A councilor stated, "Nothing will satisfy Mrs. Brady until this Board gives her full control. Is that so, Mrs. Brady?" She replied, "Yes, I have stated that several times." In her early 40s, she was still young and fit. She played for St. Ita's Camogie Club of Longford; they were county champions from 1935 until Seán was born in 1937. After Seán's birth, she switched to referee. She was chair of the County Longford Camogie Board and an active member of the Irish Language Gaelic League. There was also a scholarly side to her. Matt Brady had introduced her to the poetry of his cousin, Pádraic Colum. In 1954, she offered a public lecture on this topic. She had her own Republican credentials and a keen interest in the North of Ireland. She was born in Belfast, where an aunt and her family were burned out and traumatized during the sectarian rioting of the early 1920s. She still had family in Donegal and they were Republican, too. In August 1942, Mary and Rory, in Dublin on holidays with their maternal grandmother, attended the large funeral of Father Michael O'Flanagan. O'Flanagan, vice president of Sinn Féin from 1917 and president of the organization in 1933–1935, had twice been "silenced" by the Catholic hierarchy, in 1917 and in 1925.

After Matt Brady's funeral, May went back to work for the Board of Health and the children went back to school. They attended Melview, about two miles outside Longford. From the front of the school, the spire of St. Mel's Cathedral is visible on a clear day; hence the name. Mary took Seán to school on his first day. The two older children watched out for Seán; he remembers them being very protective of him. Then, in August 1944, May Caffrey Brady married Patrick Twohig, a native of West Cork, Melview's principal and one of its three teachers. Twohig had his own political history. He was a member of both Sinn Féin and the Irish Volunteers and on Easter Monday, 1916, he was arrested by the RIC when he arrived in Longford by train from Dublin. In the period 1919–1921, he was a married man with young children and he was not on active service with the IRA, but he did help out. He was battalion engineer for the Drumlish IRA and worked with the brigade engineer on various projects; in fact, in 1919, he had attended the *aeraíocht* in Aughnacliffe and had traveled the same road home on which Matt Brady and Willie McNally encountered the RIC. After the Anglo-Irish Treaty was signed in 1921 he withdrew from politics. He initially supported the Treaty but over time he became disillusioned; in the late 1940s, he supported a Republican alternative to Fianna Fáil, Clann na Poblachta.

Twohig, a 57-year old widower with grown children, was for two years the teacher and stepfather of Rory Brady. Mary, three years older than Rory, and Seán, five years younger, liked Twohig immediately. Rory, who was becoming a teenager, took a little longer, but he remembers Twohig now with affection, noting, "It was a difficult situation for both of us; the teacher getting married to your mother." Patrick Twohig's greatest influence on the Brady family involved the Irish language. Twohig, an award-winning teacher of the language, spoke Irish around the house, encouraged the children to do the same, and supported their interest in the language. Starting in 1945, Rory spent a month each summer in the Irish-speaking Gaeltacht in Spiddal, County Galway. Rory today believes that he owes his love of the Irish language to his stepfather.

At age 13, as he approached graduation from Melview, Rory sought a scholarship to attend St. Mel's College in Longford. The school, which was founded in 1865, was open to all students, but its main objective was providing priests for the local Diocese of Ardagh and Clonmacnoise. There were about 170 students—120 boarders and forty to fifty day students, scattered over five grades. The curriculum was demanding and the schedule firm; September to Christmas, after Christmas to Easter, and after Easter to summer, with no other breaks. Family members could visit boarding students for half an hour on Saturdays. Among the notable graduates of the school are John Wilson, class of 1942 and Tánaiste (deputy prime minister) in Albert Reynolds's government; Bishop Colm O'Reilly, class of 1953; and Ruairí Ó Brádaigh.

Rory Brady was admitted to St. Mel's in 1945 without a scholarship. He stayed at Melview another year, studied Latin with a tutor, and then earned the scholarship that paid half of his expenses. When he enrolled in 1946, he was immediately moved into the second-year curriculum. Eugene McGee's *St. Mel's of Longford* has a photograph of the entering class of 1946. In the photo, we see Rory Brady as a 14-year-old with jet black hair and arms crossed casually. He has grown to his adult height, five foot seven and a half, making him taller than most of the other children. Already shaving and stoutly built, there is a certain self-assuredness evident in the picture.

Rory Brady on entering St. Mel's, back row, third from the right, 1946–1947.
Ó Brádaigh family collection.

In her exposé *To Take Arms: My Year with the IRA Provisionals,* Maria McGuire comments that Rory's "mother took a second husband, a school-teacher whom [he] disliked and so was not displeased at being sent away to boarding school." But according to Rory, he had the option of attending as a boarder or as a day student; he was not sent out of the house. His decision to board was probably met with relief in the household, for at age 14 he had already developed a strong independent spirit. It was a St. Mel's tradition and rite of passage, for instance, for second-year students to attend a formal ceremony in which they took a pledge not to drink liquor. In return, they received the Badge of the Pioneer Total Abstinence Association, to be worn on the lapel. Brady objected, not to the badge, but to the unfairness of not being given a choice in the matter. It was assumed that students would attend the ceremony and take the pledge. He refused to do either and was supported by his mother. He subsequently determined that he did want the badge and as a senior student went with the second-year boys and took the pledge. He obtained his Pioneer Badge on his terms, and he wore it proudly for almost forty years.

St. Mel's was a hotbed of Irish football; the school won the All-Ireland Championship in 1948. Rory played football with his friends, but he was not on the school's team. His heart was elsewhere. It was against the rules, but Mary Brady, who by then was a student at University College Dublin, sent him clippings of political events. He read them in the toilet, including accounts of the funerals of people such as Richard Goss, Patrick McGrath, and Charlie Kerins. McGrath was arrested after a shootout in which two police officers were shot dead. In 1940, he was executed by firing squad at Mountjoy. Charlie Kerins, the IRA's chief of staff, was implicated in the killing of a Special Branch police sergeant. In 1944, he was hanged at Mountjoy. Their bodies were buried in prison yards until September 1948, when they were released and reinterred with proper Republican funerals.

In the library at St. Mel's, he read the available Republican literature, including John Devoy's *Recollections of an Irish Rebel*. He was particularly interested in Devoy's chapter on the Catholic Church and Fenianism. The chapter begins, "The hardest test the Fenians had to face was the hostility of the authorities of the Catholic Church." Devoy summarizes his perspective on the Church and the Fenians with, "We'd have beaten the Bishops only for the English Government, and we'd have beaten the English Government but for the Bishops, but a combination of the two was too much for us." Rory had purchased issues of Brian O'Higgins's *Wolfe Tone Annual* and on a visit his mother brought them to him. One of O'Higgins's *Annuals* carried a reference to Seán McCaughey, who died in Port Laoise Prison in 1946 after a horrific hunger and thirst strike. Brady wrote under the reference, "Died for Ireland on hunger strike." Another student saw this. In study hall, where talking was forbidden, he sent a note reading, "He didn't die for Ireland, he died to raise trouble." Brady replied to the contrary. He pursued his interest in Republican politics when he was not at St. Mel's. In the offices of the *Longford Leader*, he went through newspaper accounts of his father's career. He also spoke with his mother about his father and about the Republican Movement. She encouraged his interest. For Christmas 1949, she gave him a copy of Tom Barry's *Guerrilla Days in Ireland*, a classic account of guerrilla warfare and the Cork IRA in the 1920s. Her comment was, "This is what good Irishmen should be reading." She also encouraged him to read Peadar O'Donnell's work, including *The Gates Flew Open*. It had been banned by the state but she brought in a copy from Scotland. O'Donnell, who was from Donegal, was a key figure among a group of leftist Republicans of the 1930s.

Of the twenty-eight students in St. Mel's class of 1950, eighteen went off to become priests. Rory had other plans. While at St. Mel's, he had followed another split in the Republican Movement. Seán Mac Bride, the son of executed 1916 leader John MacBride and a former IRA chief of staff, had resigned from the IRA, although he remained sympathetic and continued to defend Republicans in court. In 1946, he formed the political party Clann na Poblachta. After what they had been through with de Valera, the faithful few who remained in the IRA expelled supporters of the new party. In the 1948 Free State election, Clann na Poblachta won ten seats and entered government as the junior partner to Fine Gael, with Mac Bride as minister for external affairs. It was the first non–Fianna Fáil Irish government since 1932. In 1949, the new government declared the 26-county state the Republic of Ireland. The IRA and Sinn Féin rejected this label and continued to call it the "Free State"; they reserved the term "Irish Republic" for the 32-County state they sought. Rory Brady agreed with them. For him, it was a Republic in name only, and the constitutional politics of Clann na Poblachta, like the constitutional politics of Fianna Fáil and Fine Gael, would not end partition and create a united and free Ireland. From his parents, and from his own studies, he knew his Irish history.

In the spring of 1950, he attended his first Easter Commemoration as an adult, at Cloonmorris Cemetery in County Leitrim, at the gravesite of James Joseph Reynolds. The event is noteworthy for a number of reasons. The movement's paper, *The United Irishman,* was on sale. He signed up for a subscription; ten years later, he would edit the paper. The event was a joint Leitrim-Longford effort because the cemetery straddles the border of the two counties. Reynolds, who was killed in a premature explosion in 1938, had been one of the accused in the More O'Ferrall killing. His death had prompted the moment's silence by the Longford County Council and Matt Brady's statement that one of the councilors should be ashamed for not standing for the moment's silence. Hubert Wilson was the chairperson, and a keynote speaker was John Joe McGirl, a 29-year-old publican from Ballinamore in Leitrim who was fast becoming prominent in the movement. A veteran of the IRA's 1940s campaign and a key figure in the reorganization of the IRA in the late 1940s and early 1950s, he was to become a close comrade of Brady for thirty-five years.

That summer, Brady attended summer school in the Gaeltacht for the last time. He met young men from Dublin who were active Republicans. As they spoke, the conversation drifted to politics and he found them like-minded, which was encouraging. That fall, he left for University College Dublin and the Republican Movement.

3

Off to College and into Sinn Féin and the IRA

1950–1954

IN THE FALL OF 1950 Rory Brady left Longford for Dublin, where he went into digs with a friend of his Aunt Bertha, who set up the arrangement. University College Dublin's campus was located a bicycle ride away, just up from St. Stephen's Green. It was a time for several key events in his life. He adopted the Irish form of his name, changing from Rory Brady to Ruairí Ó Brádaigh (his younger brother had already changed his name and was known at St. Mel's, class of 1955, as Seán Ó Brádaigh). Dublin, Ireland's capital, was the site of the headquarters of Sinn Féin, which he joined. The first Republican event in Dublin he attended was a *céilí* (an evening of Irish dancing) that was held in a hall in Parnell Square in honor of Hugh McAteer, Liam Burke, and Jimmy Steele, three prominent IRA men who had recently been released from prison in Belfast and were among the last of thousands of prisoners in the 1940s.

Sinn Féin has a hierarchical structure that begins at the lowest level with a *cumann* (club), which is usually named after a deceased activist. Ó Brádaigh joined the Paddy McGrath Cumann, named for the man whose reburial he read about in 1948. Each *cumann* has five to ten members and meets weekly. *Cumainn* send two delegates to the Sinn Féin Ard Fheis (annual conference), which is usually held in Dublin. At the Ard Fheis, the delegates elect the Sinn Féin Officer Board and the party's Ard Chomhairle (Executive). Even though he was one of its newest members, Ó Brádaigh attended the Ard Fheis, which was held at the Sinn Féin head office at 9 Parnell Square, as a delegate. On November 19, 1950, about seventy delegates took their seats in a large front room on the first floor of the building.

He saw several prominent activists firsthand at what was an historic Ard Fheis. Margaret Buckley, the party's president since 1937, stepped down, although she remained on the Ard Chomhairle. She had been a member of the Irish Women Workers' Union and a judge in the revolutionary Sinn Féin courts and was imprisoned in Mountjoy and Kilmainham jails for her Republican efforts. In 1938, she published her jail journal, *The Jangle of the Keys*. Because of his mother's background, Ó Brádaigh found Buckley especially interesting. Paddy McLogan succeeded her as president. McLogan, Tony Magan, and Tomás Mac Curtáin were the "three Macs" who dominated the IRA and Sinn Féin in the early 1950s. McLogan's assumption of the Sinn Féin presidency was in fact the result of a friendly coup organized by the IRA. As they picked up the pieces in the late 1940s, the IRA's leadership realized that they needed a public political vehicle to complement their clandestine activities. After twenty years of estrangement, they adopted Sinn Féin as that vehicle. McLogan, Magan, and Mac Curtáin, and the IRA in general, were not interested in recognizing Leinster House or Stormont, and Sinn Féin's policy of abstentionism from those bodies and Westminster was consistent with IRA policy. IRA volunteers were "infiltrated" into Sinn Féin; Sinn Féin welcomed them and became the political wing of the Irish Republican Movement.

Magan, McLogan, and Mac Curtáin were hard men who were dedicated to the cause. Each had impeccable credentials. McLogan was born in 1899 in South Armagh, in what became the Six Counties of Northern Ireland. He was on hunger strike at Mountjoy Prison with Thomas Ashe in 1917 and was later held under an assumed name in Belfast Jail while the police searched for him outside on a charge of murder. In the 1940s, he was interned in the Curragh Military Camp. He made his living as a publican in Port Laoise. McLogan is described as "placid in temperament and ice cold in contention, but easy to trust" and "the Father of Republicanism, the austere plotter from a previous generation." Deeply religious, he had met his wife on a pilgrimage to Lourdes. Tony Magan, the IRA's chief of staff, was in his late 30s. He was from County Meath and had joined the IRA in the 1930s; he was also interned in the Curragh. A bachelor and devout Catholic, he is described by J. Bowyer Bell as "a hard man, tightly disciplined, and utterly painstaking." Tomás Mac Curtáin, the youngest of the three, was in his mid-30s. He was the son of Tomás Mac Curtáin, the Sinn Féin mayor of Cork who was murdered in 1920, allegedly by members of the Royal Irish Constabulary. The younger Mac Curtáin was a member of the IRA's Army Council and, in the late

1950s, of Sinn Féin's Ard Chomhairle. He was on the 1940 hunger strike at Mountjoy. After the strike was called off, he was sentenced to be hanged for shooting dead a Special Branch detective. Because he was the son of a Republican martyr, he was given a last-minute reprieve and was transferred to Port Laoise Prison, in County Laois. In Port Laoise, he and his fellow prisoners refused to wear prison uniforms or follow the routine. They spent years in solitary confinement, naked, wearing only blankets. Their resistance culminated in the death, by a hunger and thirst strike, of Seán McCaughey in 1946.

Two of the three Macs and other hard-liners who helped reorganize the IRA were not universally loved, at least not by their comrades in the Curragh. Uinseann Mac Eoin's *The IRA in the Twilight Years: 1923–1948* offers interviews with people interned with Magan and McLogan. Life in the camp was rough, and because they were internees—they were never charged with a crime—there was no release date in sight. Fianna Fáil exacerbated the situation by offering parole to prisoners who recognized the state and pledged to forgo future participation in the Republican Movement. Some prisoners accepted the offer. The camp split over the best approach: take a hard line and refuse compromise with the authorities versus go softly and get through it. Magan and McLogan were with the hard-liners. Depending upon one's perspective, they were part of a group of disciplined orthodox soldiers or they were autocratic martinets. When the division came, the hard-liners made their choice and stuck with it. An ex-internee who was on the other side of the divide recalls saying hello to Magan. "F off" was the reply. Another ex-internee describes Paddy McLogan as "a grand man, but if Paddy ever went to heaven he would cause trouble there; it was in his nature to cause trouble." Yet because of their steadfast position, people such as Magan and McLogan kept the movement alive after the 1940s campaign. Their convictions got them through the Curragh; their convictions helped them reorganize the IRA and Sinn Féin. To young recruits such as Ó Brádaigh, the three Macs provided an example of how to sustain and lead the Republican Movement.

The IRA's headquarters were also in Dublin. As he continued his studies and attended Sinn Féin meetings, Ó Brádaigh sought membership in that organization. He figured out who in Sinn Féin was also in the IRA and mentioned that he wanted to join. The next time he met the person, he asked "Did you do anything about that?" To an eager recruit, the process was slow. About six months after joining Sinn Féin, he was admitted to a recruits class that had five or six other potential IRA members. The class was directed by Mícheál "Pasha" Ó Donnabháin (Michael O'Donovan), a staff member of the Dublin unit. His lectures covered things such as the Constitution of the IRA, the Army's general orders, and Irish and Irish Republican history. His job was to separate the reliable from the unreliable. He reported on who was ready to move from recruit to volunteer and who was not. Some never moved out of recruits classes. Ó Brádaigh, who was courteous, well-educated, and obviously motivated, quickly moved from recruit to IRA volunteer. He formally pledged the declaration (word of honor) to the Irish Republican Army in a ceremony held at 44 Parnell Square in Dublin; the building has been in Republican hands for decades.

Ó Brádaigh was fairly typical of IRA recruits at this time. He was in his late teens and he was the child of activists from the 1916–1923 period. The fact that he was a second-generation Republican in and of itself probably did not influence his admittance to the IRA. A recruiting officer might find a parent's activities interesting, but recruiting officers are most interested in the merits of the recruit. Yet the Republican background of someone like him would have been so self-evident that his recruitment into the IRA was natural. According to senior Republicans at the time, Ó Brádaigh's background "was written all over him." He describes himself as "ready made"; it was evident to senior Republicans. If necessary, informal background checks were readily available. After joining the IRA, Ó Brádaigh for a time reported directly to Tony Magan as he sought to organize a unit in Longford. He was amazed at how much Magan knew about Longford. In the early 1950s, the Republican Movement was not very large, but its networks connected people throughout the country. Ó Brádaigh later discovered that Magan's sisters lived in Longford. Through them, Magan knew what was happening there. He also knew of Matt Brady and May Brady Twohig; one of his sisters had been captain of St. Ita's camogie team. These connections probably did not significantly influence Ó Brádaigh's recruitment into the IRA. If he had been found unreliable, he would not have been accepted. Being from good stock was a bonus, but it was not essential.

In joining the IRA, the young recruits were not joining a country club or fraternal organization. They were joining a guerrilla army that was planning for war. In this they were not unique to Ireland. From the late 1940s through the 1950s, there were a number of active guerrilla campaigns throughout the world in places such as Aden, Algeria, Cuba, Cyprus, Kenya, Malaya, Palestine, and Vietnam. On July 26, 1953, Castro began the military campaign that resulted in his seizing control of Cuba on January 1, 1959. In Vietnam, Dien Bien Phu fell in May 1954, marking the end of French control in Vietnam. The guerrillas involved in these events were inspired by nationalism and were given the opportunity for campaigns by the decline of the colonial powers after World War II. The 1960s would be the decade of student protest, but the 1950s was the decade of the guerrilla. Irish Republicans were aware of other guerrilla wars, in part because many of them, including those in Cyprus and Kenya, were directed against British forces. Many of the volunteers viewed 1916 as the first of the assaults against the British empire in the twentieth century. Colonialism appeared to be dying, and it appeared that other nations had passed by the Irish. The young volunteers believed it was their job to finish the Irish struggle for independence.

Combining his studies with his Republican activities, Ó Brádaigh soon became a recruiting officer for the IRA in Dublin and in Longford. On weekends and holidays he took the train, hopped a bus, or hitched a ride home and began reorganizing the Longford IRA; one ride was given by Seán Mac Eoin, who described Matt Brady's activities to him. Organizing Longford required effort. The Free State had killed key people such as Barney Casey and Richard Goss, constitutional politics had attracted others, and the rest were too old and too tired. Ó Brádaigh began by taking part in Longford's Easter Commemorations. At Easter 1951, the commemoration was at Killoe Cemetery, the burial site of Barney Casey. A parade, headed by the Drumlish Brass Band, marched to the cemetery. Casey's family was there; Matt Casey was to become a fixture at Longford Easter commemorations, leading the way, bearing the Irish flag. Among those in attendance at this and subsequent commemorations were people from the previous generation, including May Brady Twohig, Hubert Wilson, Pat and Maggie Healy, and Seán F. Lynch, who was still on the County Council as an Independent Republican, and younger people, including Seán and Mary Ó Brádaigh and Seán F. Lynch's son, also named Seán.

There is a routine to Easter commemorations: the 1916 Proclamation and the IRA's Easter message are read to the crowd, as is the County Roll of Honour, a list of names of Longford's soldiers who have died in the fight for Irish independence. A decade of the rosary is recited in Irish; The Last Post, Taps, and Reveille are sounded by a bugler; and wreaths are laid on behalf of relatives and various organizations, such as Sinn Féin or Óglaigh na Éireann (the IRA's Irish name). One person usually presides over the ceremonies and introduces the keynote speaker, who is usually the most prominent Republican available. At Easter 1951 in Longford, the main oration was given by Michael Traynor of Belfast and later of Dublin Sinn Féin. Traynor appealed to the local crowd by outlining the circumstances of Barney Casey's death and linking his death with the larger Irish Republican cause: "It was because Barney Casey was a Republican and a Separatist that he was arrested and interned in the Curragh in 1940, and because he was in the Curragh on that morning of December 16th, 1940, he was brutally shot for being faithful to the people of Ireland. Long may his memory and his ideals live in the hearts of his countrymen." The 1952 commemoration attracted a larger crowd. Hubert Wilson presided and Hugh McCormack of Dublin delivered the oration. He linked the honored Republican dead to the current Republican goals: "We should remember that it was not for a sham republic in a partitioned and anglicised Ireland that Seán Connolly, Tommy Kelleher and Barney Casey died; and unless we are blind to the lessons of history we will find that the method which they adopted—physical force—is the only way to make England withdraw her occupation forces from our country." He also looked to the future: "We must endeavour to build anew the national movement, which led the people to the verge of freedom in the years 1916–21 until it was betrayed by weakness and treachery at the top."

Ó Brádaigh helped organize the 1953 commemoration in Ballymacormack and in 1954 he presided at the event at the memorial cross in Drumlish for Thomas Kelleher. The oration was delivered by Tom Doyle, who was serving as president of Sinn Féin for a brief period—McLogan returned to the post soon after this. In his remarks, Doyle reminded the audience that the "objective of those we commemorate has not yet been achieved." He continued: "One fact we must keep constantly before us—the fact that British forces of occupation still hold six of our Irish counties against the will of the Irish people and by holding those six counties they dominate and control the life of the whole thirty-two." He finished with an appeal to action: "Let us get rid of the invader out of every last inch of our territory—then and only then can we celebrate with a full heart—then and only then can we say that we have truly honoured our glorious dead." Easter commemorations gave Ó Brádaigh an opportunity to recruit for the Longford IRA. He read the IRA's Easter statement every year. Potential recruits could approach him and indicate that they were interested in more than Sinn Féin. Ó Brádaigh would then check the person's background, a relatively easy task in a small county such as Longford. A prime resource was senior people, including Hubert Wilson and Seán F. Lynch. Like Pasha Ó Donnabháin, Ó Brádaigh's job was to separate the reliable from the unreliable.

Ó Brádaigh was first a section leader of the Longford unit of the IRA. The section was attached to the Leitrim IRA, which was under the com-

mand of John Joe McGirl. Although it was only a nominal attachment—
they only met once or twice a year—it was significant. McGirl, who was
about ten years older than Ó Brádaigh, was rebuilding the IRA in the
area. He was reasonable and, more important, very enthusiastic. After two
years, this arrangement was dropped and the small five-member Longford
unit of the IRA became independent, with Ó Brádaigh as commanding
officer reporting directly to Tony Magan. A perquisite of an independent
unit is that it may send a delegate to the IRA's annual convention. As an
elected delegate, Ó Brádaigh attended the IRA's 1953 convention. Aside
from providing opportunities to participate in decision making and learn
policy firsthand, conventions also bring together Republicans from throughout Ireland. One of the other delegates was Joe Cahill from Belfast. Cahill,
in his early 30s, was one of six people arrested in 1942 and charged with
the death of a Royal Ulster Constabulary (RUC; reformed for Northern
Ireland from the Royal Irish Constabulary). Five of the sentences were
commuted. Nineteen-year-old Tom Williams, the commanding officer of
the unit that killed the constable, accepted responsibility for the action,
and even though he did not fire the fatal shot, he was hanged in prison in
Belfast. Cahill was among the last of the 1940s IRA people to be released.
He was to become a key figure in the Republican Movement in the 1970s.

Attending the convention gave Ó Brádaigh the opportunity to see at
first hand how the IRA worked. Although it is a clandestine organization,
the IRA has a structure to govern its members. The twelve-member IRA
Executive calls the conventions, and this is an important source of its
power. In calling a convention, the Executive sets in motion the process
of creating a new IRA leadership. The convention is the IRA's supreme
authority, and it is here that delegates debate policies, tactics, strategies,
motions, and so forth. The convention delegates directly elect the IRA
Executive, which remains in place until the next convention. If someone
is arrested or leaves for another reason, a new member is asked to join, or
"co-opted," onto the Executive until the next convention. The chair of the
IRA convention convenes the Executive's first meeting; if that person has
not been voted onto the Executive, he or she retires. The Executive elects
its own chair and secretary.

The IRA Executive then elects the seven-member Army Council, the
size of which is derived from the number of people who signed the Proclamation of the Irish Republic in 1916. The Army Council appoints a
chief of staff, who subsequently appoints a staff: adjutant general, quartermaster general, director of intelligence, and so forth. These staff appoint-
ments are ratified by the Army Council. Because the Army Council can-

not be in continuous session, it lays down lines of policy for the chief of staff to carry out. In that way the chief of staff is answerable to the Army Council, which in turn is derived from the Executive. The Army Council generally meets on a monthly basis. Unless there are leaks or they participate in the process, volunteers do not know who is on the Executive, the Army Council, or the chief of staff. In his dealings with Magan, Ó Brádaigh knew that Magan was a member of general headquarters staff, but he did not know he was chief of staff until later.

As commanding officer of the Longford unit, Ó Brádaigh's primary activity was training people in weapons and explosives. The unit possessed a number of weapons, including a revolver, a pistol, a rifle, and a Thompson submachine gun. Gelignite detonators and fuses were also available. If they lacked particular equipment, loans were arranged from other units. The training goal was to make people familiar with all aspects of the arsenal. They met weekly. On occasion, more-intensive training camps, involving weekend overnights, were organized. For each situation, Ó Brádaigh began by arranging a secure area and the transportation of weaponry. Firing practice was often undertaken in County Leitrim, one of Ireland's most underdeveloped areas. The unit also practiced advanced fieldcraft: battle techniques, ambushes, and attacking barracks. At some of the camps, the director of training, Gerry McCarthy, and a training officer, perhaps Charlie Murphy, Magan's adjutant general, came down from Dublin and offered expertise. Ó Brádaigh was aided in this activity by his mother (who probably knew what he was doing) and the design of Silchester. May, who was widowed again—Patrick Twohig had passed away in March 1951 and was buried next to Matt Brady—loaned him her Model Y automobile. The hedges surrounding her home presented a cover such that he could walk out the back door with a rifle and head off down the lane.

Although Ó Brádaigh was devoted to the IRA—he traveled home on weekends so he could run training exercises—he found time for other activities. He was an avid attendee at *céilís* organized by Republicans and non-Republicans. He was also active in extracurricular activities at University College Dublin. He has fond memories of the college boxing club, which met during the week. The gym was in a part of the university's buildings that backed up to Irish government buildings. The students used to joke about tunneling through and setting off explosives. There were no showers, and they would clean off by dipping towels in a water bucket. One particular boxer, a flyweight from Belfast, would stand in the bucket, splash himself clean, and then announce that the bucket was available for the next person to wash his face. Ó Brádaigh and the others learned quickly to get to the bucket before the flyweight.

Irish literature and economic and industrial history were his favorite courses. His mother encouraged his studies in the field of commerce, which included accounting, organization, and business statistics. He also continued his study of the Irish language. Ó Brádaigh was starting to consider teaching as a profession when he attended an intensive course in the summer of 1952 at the Galway Gaeltacht, which was designed for people with college degrees who wanted a qualification in teaching Irish. As a training officer for the IRA, he had experience with addressing a group of people, commanding their attention, and running them through drills. The Irish instructors, who were unaware of his clandestine activities, thought he was a natural teacher and told him so. It was a key point in his academic career, and when he returned home he told his mother that he would seek a career as a teacher. His sister Mary, who had graduated from University College Dublin in 1951, had already made the same choice. Thus, in the spring of 1954, Ruairí Ó Brádaigh graduated from University College Dublin and received a degree in commerce and certification to teach that subject and the Irish language.

Like most college graduates, he applied for jobs "all around the place." He received two offers, one from a school in Athlone and the other from Roscommon Vocational School. He chose the job in Roscommon because it was closer to Longford than Athlone and the bus service suited his needs. He wanted to be close to his twice-widowed mother and to stay involved with the Longford IRA. He moved home and, starting in the fall of 1954, took a bus to Roscommon, spending the week there. By this time, Seán was attending St. Mel's as a day pupil. Because jobs were scarce, Mary was teaching in a primary school in Birmingham, England. Longford, which is in the province of Leinster, is lush with trees and vegetation, like much of the Irish midlands. Roscommon, only twenty miles away, is in the province of Connacht and is on the edge of the west of Ireland. From Roscommon to the Atlantic, trees and vegetation give way to hills and rocks, small sheep farms and stone walls, and fewer and fewer people.

The IRA leadership, which was apprised of Ó Brádaigh's career plans, put him in touch with Tommy McDermott, who had been in the IRA in London when Terence MacSwiney died on a hunger strike in Brixton Prison in 1920. At the age of 18, McDermott had marched in Mac-Swiney's funeral in London. He initially took the Treaty side in the Civil

Ruairí Ó Brádaigh on graduating from University College Dublin, 1954. This photo accompanied several articles that appeared in the *United Irishman* of the 1950s. Ó Brádaigh family collection.

War, but when the executions started, MacDermott took his rifle and deserted to the anti-Treaty side. Never married, he was interned in the Curragh in the 1940s. Ó Brádaigh viewed McDermott as a lodestone, a role model who attracted the next generation of Republicans. According to Ó Brádaigh, he was a person who "went through it all, took all the hard knocks, and in good times and in bad he didn't change his views or his principles to suit the tide of the time." People such as McDermott stood out and "immediately attracted all the disenchanted." They were very important for the maintenance of the IRA in lean times.

McDermott, who by this time was in his early 50s, was the South Roscommon commanding officer; Ó Brádaigh, who was in his early 20s, complemented him as the South Roscommon training officer. Together, they built up the IRA in the area. One of their recruits was Seán Scott, who joined the IRA in 1955. Scott approached McDermott and through him met Ó Brádaigh. According to Scott, McDermott was "a very, very sincere man. . . . He was very dedicated, and he wasn't prepared to deviate . . . one iota from what he believed." McDermott saw that "the

British were in the country [and] there was only one way that they were going to leave, through force. He was an absolutely committed soldier." Scott found Ó Brádaigh "a lovely fella. Very energetic, full of action, very approachable. Ó Brádaigh had sincerity written all over his face. Anything that he said you knew that he meant it." As a training officer, Scott found him "very dedicated." He "was good at his job"; "he expected you to pay attention, as any good teacher would."

By the mid-1950s, Ó Brádaigh was involved in training camps outside Longford and Roscommon. These camps, like the IRA conventions, enabled volunteers from various parts of the country to meet each other. Scott's comments were echoed by an IRA veteran from Belfast, who first met Ó Brádaigh at a training camp in the Wicklow Mountains in the mid-1950s. This volunteer found him "very forceful."

4

Arms Raids, Elections, and the Border Campaign

1955–1956

As Tommy McDermott and Ruairí Ó Brádaigh were building up the IRA in Longford and Roscommon, similar progress was under way throughout the country. In order to get weapons and publicity, the IRA raided British Army barracks in the Six Counties of Northern Ireland (Antrim, Armagh, Derry, Down, Fermanagh, and Tyrone) and in England. The first raid was in June 1951 at Ebrington Barracks in Derry; it netted rifles, machine guns, and ammunition. A raid in England in July 1953 went less well. Three volunteers, Cathal Goulding, Manus Canning, and Seán Stephenson, sneaked into Felstead School Officers' Training Corps in Essex and loaded a van with rifles and machine guns, including a Browning machine gun and an anti-tank gun. The van, which was overloaded and traveling poorly, aroused the curiosity of police. The IRA team was stopped, arrested, and subsequently sentenced to eight years in prison. The loss of Goulding was especially important, as he was in the thick of the IRA's reorganization.

The failure at Felstead was followed by a successful raid on Gough Barracks in Armagh. An IRA training officer, Leo McCormack, noticed that there were no magazines or ammunition in the guns of the barracks guards. He passed this information on to general headquarters in Dublin, who investigated further. The raid was primarily planned by Charlie Murphy, Tony Magan's adjutant general. Among other things, Murphy had Seán Garland from the Dublin IRA enlist in the British Army at Gough Barracks, which enabled Garland to supply inside information. In June 1954, the IRA seized an armed sentry whose weapon was not loaded, replaced him with a uniformed and fully armed IRA man, and backed up

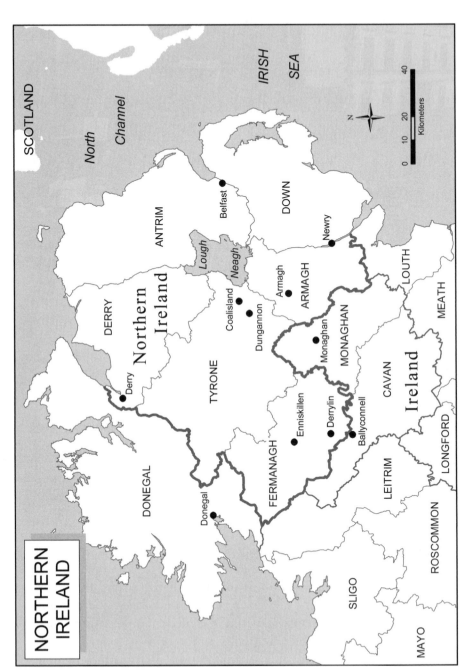

Map of Northern Ireland

a truck to the armory. The truck was filled with weapons and driven off through the gate, picking the IRA sentry up on the way out (Garland remained behind, "deserting" back to the IRA later). In October 1954, the IRA raided the Royal Inniskilling Fusiliers barracks in Omagh, scaling the walls at 3:30 A.M. A sentry, with a knife to his throat, screamed out and raised the alarm. Shots were exchanged and two IRA volunteers, Joe Christle and Joe Mac Liatháin, were shot. Five British soldiers were wounded. The camp's lights were turned on and the IRA, including Christle and Mac Liatháin, retreated. IRA men jumped into waiting cars that sped off, leaving a number of volunteers behind who were captured by the local police force, the Royal Ulster Constabulary, and the B Specials, Northern Ireland's armed militia. After the Omagh raid, the IRA leadership, aware that their activities in the north would raise concerns with the Dublin government, instituted General Order No. 8, which directed volunteers about to be caught with arms in the south to dump them or destroy them. It proscribes defensive action. It was a pragmatic decision, taken by people leading an organization that had almost been destroyed by Fianna Fáil in the 1940s. Throughout the 1950s, the leadership was at pains to not antagonize the Dublin government.

Concurrent with this military activity, the leadership also built up Sinn Féin. Paddy McLogan, Michael Traynor, and another Republican, Frank MacGlynn, drew up far-reaching amendments to its Constitution which were accepted at the 1950 Ard Fheis. Sinn Féin remained committed to the Irish Republic that had been proclaimed in 1916, but it also sought to establish "social justice, based on Christian principles, by a just distribution and effective control of the Nation's wealth and resources." As it was in the 1930s, when Matt Brady supported those accused of killing Richard More O'Ferrall, a fundamental element of Irish Republicanism is a commitment to social change in favor of people who have been underprivileged, oppressed, and victimized by the powers that be, whether they be landlords, employers, or Irish and British politicians. There is among Republicans a gut-level understanding that a commitment to social justice is embedded in their fight for national liberation. This commitment resonated with Ó Brádaigh. His father publicly supported the underdog, and Ruairí had chosen a career teaching teenaged students in a vocational school rather than the university-bound children of wealthy people. As part of Sinn Féin's political development, the party put forth an abstentionist candidate in a 1954 by-election in Louth for a vacancy in the Dáil/Leinster House. Ó Brádaigh, among others, worked for Sinn Féin in the election.

Because it is an all-Ireland political party, Sinn Féin was keenly interested in building a constituency in the North. Unionists—who are largely
Protestant and support the union between Northern Ireland and the
United Kingdom—constituted roughly two-thirds of the northern population. Nationalists—who are largely Catholic and support a united and
free Ireland—constituted roughly one-third of the population and suffered at the hands of Unionists, who viewed them as traitors. Sinn Féin
saw the May 1955 Westminster election as an opportunity to present itself
to its natural constituency, the second-class citizens of Northern Ireland—
Irish Nationalists. Sinn Féin nominated candidates in all twelve constituencies, half of whom were in jail following the Omagh raid. The moderate
Nationalist Party was caught by the move. If it put forward candidates, it
would split the Nationalist vote and guarantee Unionist Party success.
Such a move would also challenge IRA prisoners who were in jail in support of Northern Nationalists. The Nationalist Party skipped the election.

On weekends, southern Republicans, including Ruairí Ó Brádaigh,
went north in support of Sinn Féin's campaign. The Sinn Féin candidates,
who were abstentionists, pledged to take their seats only in an All-Ireland
Parliament and received more than 150,000 votes. Two IRA prisoners
from the Omagh raid, Phil Clarke for Fermanagh–South Tyrone and Tom
Mitchell for Mid-Ulster, were elected. This was a slap in the face to the
Stormont and British governments and set off maneuvering to overturn
the elections. As convicted felons, Clarke and Mitchell were not eligible
to hold their seats. Clarke's opponent filed a petition and was declared the
victor. The *Irish Times* commented that only Sinn Féin welcomed the petition, for it allowed the party to claim that the majority of voters in
Fermanagh–South Tyrone were disenfranchised. Mitchell's situation was
less clear cut. His opponent did not file a petition and the seat was declared vacant. In an August 1955 by-election, Mitchell won again and his
margin of victory increased. A petition was filed and Mitchell was disqualified, but further investigation led to the disqualification of the Unionist candidate. In a second by-election, a Nationalist Party candidate
entered the contest and split the Nationalist vote, and a Unionist was
elected.

Sinn Féin also stepped up its activity in the south. In June 1955, a
number of candidates contested the 26-county local elections, and not as
abstentionists. The party adopted the view that participation in a County
Council was not tantamount to recognizing the state. There would be
County Councils in the All-Ireland Republic and participating in them
offered Sinn Féin members an opportunity to serve constituents and build

the political side of the Republican Movement. Among those working for Paddy Ruane, a candidate for the Galway County Council, was a young Republican from Milltown, Frank Glynn, and Ruairí Ó Brádaigh. Glynn remembers Ó Brádaigh as someone who "never took no for an answer." When people complained that something was not getting done, Ó Brádaigh's view was that the person should "just get out and do it." Ó Brádaigh "led from the front." Sinn Féin's efforts in Galway were successful, and Ruane was one of seven Sinn Féiners elected to county or city councils.

North and south in the mid-1950s, Sinn Féin, the IRA, and Irish Nationalism in general were on the rise. Southern politicians were concerned but took no direct action against Republicans. In the north, the Stormont government saw trouble brewing and acted. In July 1955, Nationalists in Newtownbutler organized the County Fermanagh Feis, an annual festival celebrating Irishness. The *feis* was an affront to those who claimed Northern Ireland for Britain. That the prime organizer of the *feis,* Canon Tom Maguire, was joined on a platform in the *feis* field by Tomás Mac Curtáin of Sinn Féin and the IRA demonstrated that the *feis* was a cultural *and* political event. It was a day filled with clashes with the RUC. Stormont had banned any parades or processions associated with the event. Following Mass, a group of people wearing white shirts with green armbands and carrying a banner with a picture of Patrick Pearse, the 1916 leader, set off for the field. A group of about twenty police officers tried to stop them, and the two groups fought for 300 yards, until the marchers folded their banner and were allowed to proceed unhindered. About an hour later, police arrested a man at the railway station next to the field, and part of the crowd responded by stoning the police. The police countered with pressure hoses but were met with a hail of stones, which drove them back from the field. Outfitting themselves with steel helmets, the police drew their batons and charged. The melee ended when Canon Maguire left the platform and called for peace. He was sprayed by water cannons. The RUC later issued a statement that they were simply enforcing an order prohibiting processions.

Around this time, Ruairí Ó Brádaigh moved into the IRA leadership. In June 1955, the IRA convention met at a hall in Parnell Square, Dublin. The delegates were enthusiastic. Arms raids had raised the IRA's profile. The votes for Sinn Féin in Northern Ireland were amazing. The Clarke and Mitchell elections showed the hypocritical nature of democracy in Northern Ireland and demonstrated a large amount of support for the Republican cause. The local elections in the Twenty-Six Counties showed that Sinn Féin had a smaller but still significant constituency there. The movement was building itself into something formidable. At least it seemed that way to the delegates. The leadership had recognized Ó Brádaigh's commitment and his competence, and as a complement to his responsibilities as a training officer in Roscommon he had been attached to IRA general headquarters as a staff officer. At the convention, he was elected to the IRA's Executive. He was also placed in charge of an IRA raid in Britain.

In late 1954, Frank Skuse, who was from West Cork, was serving with the Royal Electrical and Mechanical Engineers of the British Army. He sent word to the IRA that he was willing to help arrange a raid. Tony Magan turned the case over to Charlie Murphy, who visited Skuse in Wales. They determined that a raid in Wales was not feasible, but when Skuse was transferred to Arborfield, which is not far from London, Murphy paid him another visit and began planning a raid. Because of problems with previous raids in Britain, Magan bypassed IRA members in London and created a special seven-man team. Murphy, who was a logical choice to lead the raid, was deemed too valuable to risk. Magan, recognizing his talents, selected Ó Brádaigh as the commanding officer for the special operation.

Ó Brádaigh was briefed by Magan and Murphy, and in July he traveled to London and met with Skuse. Skuse, who was serving at a British base at Blandford, arranged for Ó Brádaigh and himself to tour the Arborfield base, posing as off-duty members of the British Army. When he first met Ó Brádaigh, Skuse was disappointed. Murphy was outgoing, flamboyant. Ó Brádaigh was quiet, reserved. He was also a potential security problem; Ó Brádaigh laughed too much, thought Skuse. During the initial tour of Arborfield they came across Irish Army officers in uniform who were attending a training school. Ó Brádaigh joked that they would get credit for the raid, prompting Skuse to caution him. Yet over the next several weeks, he found Ó Brádaigh's sense of humor contagious and learned that he was a meticulous soldier and someone he could trust. Ó Brádaigh carefully checked every detail of the camp, every routine—the times of local pubs, the soldiers' drinking habits, the local bus schedules, the names and times of films at local theaters, and so forth.

Back in Dublin, Ó Brádaigh organized a special training course for those involved in the raid. Maps, drawings, and photographs were pored over. Nothing was taken for granted. As far as he was concerned, there was no such thing as a dumb question, from him or anyone else. Each volunteer was given detailed instructions on how to travel to England, how they would meet up, and what they would do on the raid. A group of them traveled to England in early August to make final arrangements. They rented a dilapidated shop in London; the arms were to be stored there and later shipped to Ireland. Ó Brádaigh and a few others familiarized themselves with the roads by driving from the shop to Arborfield and back several times. On one trip, they gave hitchhiking British soldiers a lift to the barracks. Discreetly, they asked the soldiers questions about their surroundings. On Thursday, August 11, 1955, the rest of the raiding party arrived and registered in a London hotel.

The raiders had detailed information on Arborfield, to the point that they knew the numbers of the keys for the armory and the magazine. In discussing the plans with Magan, Ó Brádaigh asked what he should do if the keys were not where they were supposed to be. Magan told him to get a "jemmy" and go straight into the lock. On the morning of the 12th, Ó Brádaigh visited a tool shop in North London. He picked up various instruments for the raid, including a hacksaw and spare blades, and asked the man behind the counter for a jemmy. Picking up on Ó Brádaigh's accent, the shopkeeper was amused. He laughed and turned to his apprentice, saying, "Paddy wants a jemmy." Ó Brádaigh replied that he needed it for "bursting bales or opening wooden containers, that type of thing." "Ah," the shopkeeper replied, "what you want is a case opener." "Yes," Ó Brádaigh agreed, he wanted a case opener. The shopkeeper produced two, one big, one small, and asked, "Which of them, now?" Ó Brádaigh pointed to the big one. "Ah," said the shopkeeper, "I thought so." He wrapped it up in paper, looked at Ó Brádaigh and, performing for his apprentice, said, "Now, you catch it like this and you bonk him over the head like that." Ó Brádaigh ignored the quip and gathered up his purchases. When he got to the case opener, he slid it up the sleeve of his sports coat. The shopkeeper commented, "Ah, see where Paddy hides his jemmy." At this Ó Brádaigh laughed along with him, bade him farewell, and left the shop. Outside, he said to himself, "That was bad." Undeterred, he went on and hired two vans and a car for the raid. Aware of what could happen, he also found time to go to confession.

Early in the morning of Saturday, August 13th, the IRA team, including Frank Skuse, traveled from London in two large vans and a car, arriving on the outskirts of Arborfield. The raid was scheduled to begin at 2:10 AM, just after the sentries were changed. The driver in each van had instructions to enter the barracks at a prearranged time. The car was parked nearby. Six members of the team walked to the barracks entrance. Ó Brádaigh and two others, one in uniform, led the way. The sentry, assuming they were soldiers returning from a night out, said "Right" as he left his box and lifted a barrier for them. "Right," they replied as they passed under. Inside the camp, the guardroom was on the left, the armory on the right. They went straight to the guardroom. As they entered, guns drawn, a second group of IRA men reached the barrier, grabbed the sentry, and dragged him into the guardroom. A Dublin volunteer in British uniform took the sentry's place. They had less than two hours to complete their work—a patrol check and a new sentry were due to arrive at the guardroom at 4 AM.

In the guardroom, the sergeant jumped up from his table to the words, "Get up your hands." He and the sentry were spread-eagled against a wall. IRA men moved into the sleeping quarters of the guardroom, awakened the soldiers, and hustled them into the largest room in the complex. Just to be sure, they searched toilets and the area behind the building. The sergeant, who was responsible for camp security, was bound and gagged and held in a separate room. Two volunteers sought out the duty clerk in charge of the telephone exchange. He awoke with the question, "Who sent you?" They put him in handcuffs. In all, the IRA captured nineteen soldiers. Each was bound at the hands and the ankles and then they were all bound together and gagged. As this was happening, the vans were driven past the IRA sentry and backed up to the armory.

As feared, the keys to the magazine and armory could not be found. They forced the doors with the case opener. At 2:50 AM, they began loading the first van with literally tons of guns and ammunition; its springs sagged from the weight. Ó Brádaigh was concerned, but about 3:15 AM he sent it off to London. A half an hour later, the second van was on its way. In the two vans were 55 Sten guns, 10 Bren guns, more than 75,000 rounds of ammunition, selected weapons and magazines, and one pistol. To provide more time for the vans, two IRA men in British Army uniform were left behind. When the patrol and new sentry arrived at 4 AM they were captured at gunpoint, bound, and gagged. This done, the two volunteers sped off for London in the rented car. Six hundred soldiers slept through the raid. The alarm was finally raised by the sergeant, who wiggled himself loose, hopped across the road, and banged his head on the door of the regimental sergeant-major.

Probably at about the time the sergeant-major sounded the alarm, the first van was being pulled over. They were traveling too fast, and they caught the attention of police officers who took up pursuit. When the police caught up with the van, they found its cargo and arrested two IRA men. This van was pulled off to the side of the road as Ó Brádaigh and the others drove by in the second van. They stopped, considered going back, but decided against it. Magan had told them to get home safely, even if it meant leaving their goods behind. Also, their own haul was significant and there was not a lot they could do to help the others. Ó Brádaigh drove on to London, dropping Skuse off on the way so he could return to Blandford. In London, they unloaded the van at the rented shop. The plan was to wait out what was likely to be a storm of publicity and high security and then quietly ship the guns and ammunition to Ireland.

According to newspaper accounts, Scotland Yard and MI5 organized a manhunt involving 50,000 people. Sea and air routes were watched and Irish neighborhoods in larger cities were combed. Building sites, where many Irish immigrants were employed, were watched. Two days later, soldiers at a base in Wales claimed they had foiled a raid there. It was a hoax, but it added to the tension as Ó Brádaigh and his colleagues made their way back to Ireland. The team split up to make themselves less conspicuous. Ó Brádaigh took with him another volunteer, who seemed more nervous than the others. On Sunday, while riding on a train, an elderly lady across from them was reading a paper, *The News of the World*, with the headline, "All Britain Man Hunt; Armed and Dangerous." She set it down and began checking out the two young Irishmen. As she became more and more curious, his compatriot became more and more nervous. Ó Brádaigh, a polite and well-spoken young man, struck up a conversation with her about the weather, thunder, lighting, and anything else available. He presented himself as a "nice boy," and it worked. They were in Dublin by the following Saturday. Ó Brádaigh tracked down the newspapers for Monday through Sunday and read the accounts. His own account of the event appeared in the November 1955 *United Irishman* as "The Arborfield Raid by One of the Volunteers Who Took Part in It."

Bad luck led to the capture of the first van and the arrest of Dónal Murphy (Charlie's brother) and Joe Doyle. Police searching the van found maps and receipts which led to the discovery of the arms in the rented shop and the arrest of James Murphy (no relation). Although the raid was not a success, it was not a complete failure either. The IRA had demonstrated daring and courage and had embarrassed the British Army in England. And Ruairí Ó Brádaigh had demonstrated his ability to organize the raid, carry it off, and return safely to base. He also became very aware of the risks he was taking. When the arrested volunteers went on trial in September, a soldier testified that "one man sounded very well spoken, like a university student." The IRA then, as it is now, was primarily comprised of people with working-class and small-farmer backgrounds.

Relatively few of them are university educated. This reference to Ó Brádaigh caught his attention. Fortunately for him, there were no repercussions.

That fall, Seán Cronin arrived back in Ireland. Originally from the Gaeltacht in County Kerry, Cronin was a veteran of the 1940s Irish Free State Army, not the IRA. He was married, in his early 30s, and he had been working in the United States as a journalist. He settled in Dublin, took a job with the *Evening Press,* and sought out the IRA. Cronin was special, a guerrilla leader in waiting. His recruiting officers found that he knew more about military affairs than they did. He was quickly moved on to the IRA's general headquarters staff and charged with developing a new training program. He also began working on what became Operation Harvest, a plan of attack on the Six Counties. Cronin was not interested in more arms raids; he wanted a campaign. Before long, he was IRA director of operations.

The IRA was becoming more professional and the Irish government was getting more nervous. John A. Costello, the Fine Gael Taoiseach, was caught in a dilemma. Like most people living in the south, he wanted a united Ireland. Yet as Taoiseach, he could not stand by and watch his authority be undermined by a guerrilla army that was launching arms raids on the territory of another government, even if the Irish Constitution claimed that territory. In November 1955, he addressed the Dáil, trying to forestall what seemed inevitable. He threatened the IRA: "We are bound to ensure that unlawful activities of a military character shall cease, and we are resolved to use, if necessary, all the powers and forces at our disposal to bring such activities effectively to an end." Yet he was not willing to cooperate with the northern authorities or the British and stated there would be "no question of our handing over, either to the British or Six-County authorities, persons whom they may accuse of armed political activities in Britain or the Six Counties." Costello, like most people in the south, believed that the only reason there was a Northern Ireland was because Britain was more powerful than Ireland, "This ancient nation, whose geographical extent is defined by nature as clearly and as unquestionably as that of any nation in the world, has, for many years, been divided in two by the act of a more powerful State, against the will, repeatedly expressed, of the overwhelming majority of the Irish people." He also argued that times had changed, that "now we have an Irish Government and Parliament, free and democratic, to speak and to act in the name of Ireland."

The Catholic Church supported Costello. In January, 1956, the Irish hierarchy issued a statement condemning the use of force that was read at all Masses in Ireland. The IRA leadership, through the pages of the *United Irishman,* replied that the people in Ireland who bore arms illegally were the British Army. Ó Brádaigh agreed with the leadership, but he was troubled enough that he discussed the condemnation with his mother. She placed the hierarchy's condemnation in perspective, commenting, "De Valera and the whole Republican movement in 1922 were excommunicated with bell, book, and candle. And they are now at high masses and all this kind of thing." She did not recall the excommunication being lifted. Her opinion was that the Irish people had clung to their religion "in spite of the bishops." The conversation cemented a personal view he still holds, that "you cling to your religion in spite of the politics, the passing politics." Most volunteers took the same perspective, and only one left the movement because of the statement; he was back within a year.

The Stormont government was not caught in a dilemma. Faced with opposition, they repressed it. In November 1955, the Northern Ireland minister for home affairs, G. B. Hanna, passed regulations allowing the arrest and detention, without warrant, of any person for up to twenty-four hours. In July 1956, his successor, Captain Terence O'Neill, banned processions associated with another County Fermanagh Feis in Newtown-butler. One hundred police officers, many in riot gear and steel helmets, invaded the village of perhaps 400 residents and enforced the ban. There were no processions, no baton charges, and no water hoses and the event passed peacefully. The only altercation of any kind was when the RUC ordered a band to stop playing. They were crossing a street and therefore engaging in a procession on a public road. The Stormont government forced the peace in Newtownbutler, but it was a short-lived peace.

The appeals of Costello and the Catholic Church and the repression from Stormont did not deter the IRA. The Westminster elections showed that it had support. Many in the leadership were influenced by Seán Cronin's enthusiasm and his abilities. Cronin had produced a manual called *Notes on Guerrilla Warfare* and a series of battle lectures, and was pushing for a campaign. The Army Council, a mix of senior and junior people, considered the possibility. Tony Magan, the chief of staff, was complemented by two veterans from the 1940s, Tomás Mac Curtáin and Paddy Doyle, and by Larry Grogan, a veteran from the 1920s. The younger people were Charlie Murphy, Robert Russell (a nephew of Seán Russell, chief of staff in the 1930s), and Ó Brádaigh, who was co-opted onto the council in July 1956. While the younger people tended to be enthusiastic, as was Ó Brádaigh, Mac Curtáin was not convinced that the

IRA was ready. He believed that the political situation in the north was not quite ripe and argued that a passive resistance campaign by northern Nationalists should precede an IRA military campaign. He suggested that Stormont elections, which were scheduled for 1958, offered an opportunity to organize civil disobedience and noncooperation. The council voted in favor of a campaign but did not set a specific start date. They did set up a summer "battle school" under Cronin's direction. Ó Brádaigh attended it.

The Army Council's plans were interrupted by a split in the IRA. Joe Christle, who had been shot during the Omagh raid, was a maverick with an ego who thought the leadership was too conservative. He grated on Tony Magan, who insisted on complete loyalty and dismissed him. Christle took with him several members of the IRA's Dublin unit. They organized themselves, linked up with other dissidents, and in November 1956 they began their own campaign by blowing up five unmanned customs huts along the Northern Ireland/Republic of Ireland border. They burned a sixth hut to the ground.

This adventure had no attraction for Ó Brádaigh. Many of Christle's followers were recent recruits who had been attracted by the arms raids. Ó Brádaigh, in contrast, had been in the IRA for five years; had been a delegate at conventions in 1953, 1954, 1955, and 1956; and was in the leadership. Christle was impatient. Ó Brádaigh is careful and meticulous. Some of those who went with Christle were "young turks," full of energy and, to a degree, themselves. Ó Brádaigh was the opposite. On the Army Council he was surrounded by men who had been in the leadership for decades. He was so full of trepidation that he did not even speak at his first two council meetings. Magan, Mac Curtáin, and Grogan, and McLogan in Sinn Féin were building for a military campaign. As veterans of previous campaigns, he knew, they wanted a *successful* military campaign. It was a question of when, not if. The Christle crowd, less cautious, seemed most interested in simply having a go at the British.

But Christle's activities put pressure on Magan and the Army Council. More defections were likely, and when the Dublin authorities went after Christle they would also go after Sinn Féin and the IRA. They decided to skip the passive resistance phase and begin a campaign in December 1956. It has been asserted that Belfast was excluded from the campaign because the leadership feared that including it would lead to sectarian conflict. In truth, Belfast was excluded because Paddy Doyle, an Army Council member and the Belfast commanding officer, had been arrested, which created disorganization there. Four flying columns, mobile groups of IRA volunteers modeled on the guerrilla columns of the 1920s IRA that operated in the countryside for extended periods, would be sent north. The columns, operating along Northern Ireland's 240-mile border with the Irish Republic, were named for Irish patriots: Patrick Pearse, Liam Lynch, Bartholomew Teeling, and Tom Clarke. Under Cronin's original Operation Harvest plan, each column would have twenty-five members. The columns were cut to fifteen members, armed with Bren light machine guns, rifles, Thompson machine guns, and pistols but no heavy gear such as bazookas or mortars. Gelignite was the primary source of explosives. The columns were supposed to link with local IRA units and attack high-priority targets, including police stations and British Army barracks. Local units were also to pursue their own—mainly sabotage—operations. It was hoped that a quick start would bring new recruits and the campaign would expand in quality and quantity. To fill the columns, the leadership drew on the best members of the various units available. Following the rules of the Geneva Convention, members of the flying columns dressed in uniform—a mix of British, U.S., and Irish fatigues—and wore black berets. On their shoulders they sewed tricolor patches (flashes) indicating they were soldiers in the Irish Republican Army.

On the night of December 11–12, 1956, the campaign began with a bang. Bridges were blown up and shots were exchanged with RUC patrols. In Magherafelt, a courthouse was bombed. In Derry, a BBC transmitter was blown up. In Armagh, Gough Military Barracks was attacked and there was a gun battle. On the 14th, police stations in Lisnaskea and Derrylin were attacked. A Sinn Féin manifesto was released: "Irishmen have again risen in revolt against British aggression in Ireland." Early estimates were that 150 IRA volunteers were involved in the various assaults.

The Stormont government immediately authorized internment, the arrest and detention without trial of persons suspected of involvement in the campaign. British Army troops were rushed to Enniskillen from Ballykinlar Camp in County Down and ordered to stand ready for action against the IRA. British Army engineers destroyed bridges crossing the border and rendered side roads impassable with spikes, barriers, and obstructions. The next day, police rounded up thirty Republicans from across the north, including Sinn Féin activists. In the last week of December 1956, the northern government banned Sinn Féin, making the party an illegal organization. Belfast Sinn Féin headquarters were raided, equipment was confiscated, and Sinn Féiners were interned. In the south, Costello's cabinet met and released a statement that the guerrilla activity might lead to civil war. Irish police and army personnel arrested and questioned suspected IRA activists along the border but released them for lack of evidence. Toward the end of the month, Costello urged Anthony Eden, the British prime minister, to allow Northern Ireland to unite with the Republic, which would end the guerrilla attacks.

Ruairí Ó Brádaigh, an Army Council member and a general headquarters staff officer charged with raising and training the Teeling Column in the West of Ireland, missed the opening of the campaign because he was teaching in Roscommon. Tony Magan instructed him to help organize supplies for the columns but to remain at his job until the Christmas holiday, which began on December 20th. After that, he was available full-time. As his students left for vacation, Ó Brádaigh "gathered up selected people from the West, and moved up" to South Fermanagh, just below the lakes. He joined the Teeling Column as second-in-command to Noel Kavanagh, the commanding officer.

5

Derrylin, Mountjoy, and Teachta Dála

DECEMBER 1956–MARCH 1957

IN LATE DECEMBER 1956, Noel Kavanagh brought together the Teeling Column, including Ó Brádaigh's section and Charlie Murphy, who was down from Dublin. Bases had been established, and the column spent the nights of December 28th and December 29th in the field, planning their next move. Kavanagh decided to attack the RUC barracks in Derrylin in South Fermanagh. It would be a return visit; the smaller column had attacked the barracks on December 14th. With the addition of Ó Brádaigh's section, Kavanagh hoped that the barracks could be destroyed.

On Sunday night, December 30th, Kavanagh arranged for a local IRA unit to block the roads into Derrylin, which would slow down RUC reinforcements. The column traveled on foot into the village and split into two groups, a cover party and an assault team. Ó Brádaigh, who was in charge of the cover party, had a Bren light machine gun. The volunteers with him were armed with Lee-Enfield rifles captured from the British Army in the raid on Armagh military barracks in June 1954. Kavanagh was in charge of the assault team. Seven RUC men were inside the barracks.

The barracks sat on ground about five feet higher than the road that fronted it. Along its sides and in back were trees and thick vegetation. The cover party set up on a grass margin of the road and took cover behind the trees growing through a boundary fence between the road and the barracks. The assault team crept up to the barracks. At about 10:20 in the evening, the RUC men were sitting around the fire listening to the Radio Éireann news bulletin when Ó Brádaigh's group opened fire, shooting through the windows and front door. Constable John Scally was hit in the back in the first burst of fire. He suddenly stood up and fell to the floor, groaning. Shots poured into the door and windows of the station as RUC men ran to help Scally or get up the stairs to see what was going on.

There was a brief lull, and the IRA called for those inside to surrender. The RUC men responded by returning fire through the second-floor windows. In front of the boundary fence was a shallow furrow filled with water. The return fire hit the water, which splashed Ó Brádaigh on the forehead. It was his first time under fire and his immediate thought was, "That bastard's shooting at me!" He and the rest of the cover party kept firing; the shooting waxed and waned as volunteers moved about, reloaded, and fired.

Kavanagh and Pat McGirl (no relation to John Joe McGirl) placed a homemade mine—a sack filled with gelignite—against the door of the barracks. While McGirl prepared the fuse, Kavanagh ran on and shot out the front light with his Thompson machine gun. He then heard the radio room above him. One of the constables, Cecil Ferguson, was calling for help. Kavanagh tossed a grenade through the second-story window and went back for another mine. The grenade went off, destroying the radio and blowing debris back out the window. The cover party continued firing. Kavanagh arrived with a second mine as McGirl lit the fuse of the first. He dumped the mine and ran as the first one went off, blowing in the door and demolishing the stairs. Ferguson, who was returning fire through a second-floor window, was knocked to the floor. Rubble from the ceiling fell in on him. As the RUC men recovered from the blast there was another lull, and again the IRA called for those inside to surrender.

Kavanagh was considering a frontal assault into the barracks when the RUC started firing again. Realizing that reinforcements were probably on the way, Charlie Murphy recommended that they withdraw. It had been twenty minutes of intense battle. Volunteers were tiring and it showed; their fire had slowed and was less organized. Kavanagh ordered the column back together and as two groups they took off along either side of the road. They had not gone far when an RUC Land Rover with its lights off appeared. They considered an ambush but instead allowed it to pass unmolested.

Behind them they left a wrecked police station. An RUC officer later overestimated that forty IRA volunteers were involved in the attack. Broken glass and debris were scattered inside and outside of the building. Walls were pitted with bullet holes. Broken planks and twisted iron were in front; piping and wiring hung from the roof. A first-floor ceiling "dangled to the floor." The second floor was a mess. A priest was called for Constable Scally, who was taken by ambulance to Fermanagh County

Hospital in Enniskillen. He died en route from shock and bleeding. An autopsy showed that bullet fragments had severed his spinal cord and lacerated his spleen. He had been engaged to be married.

After the RUC Land Rover had passed, the column moved south toward their County Fermanagh base near the border. As they made their way into the hills at the foot of Slieve Rushen Mountain, they saw warning flares going off in the sky. Because they had withdrawn quickly, they were safely beyond the British Army and RUC cordon. Several men were tired, and Murphy wanted to stop and rest. Kavanagh pressed on, and the column spread out. Snow began to fall and it got colder. The mountain's iron ore deposits rendered their compasses useless and they got lost and wandered about. They were cold and exhausted, and someone produced a bottle of Advocaat, a liqueur. Ó Brádaigh, true to his Pioneer Badge, had always been an abstainer, but he was persuaded to take a few drinks for medicinal purposes. They went straight to his head and he felt he was walking on air, to the amusement of his comrades. Finally getting their bearings, the group made their way up and over Slieve Rushen, missing their base and ending up in the Ballyconnell district of County Cavan. As they came down the mountain, they could see Gardaí behind them on the mountainside, searching for them. Kavanagh, exhausted, was left in a friendly house. The column split into groups and sought refuge in other houses in the general area. It was a hit-or-miss proposition, and several volunteers were lucky and escaped arrest. Kavanagh, who was not so lucky, was arrested. So were Ó Brádaigh and his group.

Rainsoaked and covered with dust, Ó Brádaigh and five others ducked into a house in the tiny village of Clinty, about a mile from Ballyconnell. Gardaí surrounded the house, saw the men inside, and entered through the back door. When a superintendent asked who was in charge, Ó Brádaigh said that he was and instructed the others to provide only their names and addresses. They had dumped their weapons and were unarmed, but Ó Brádaigh had a haversack that contained ammunition, a practice grenade, and a copy of Cronin's *Notes on Guerrilla Warfare*. They were put into police cars and taken to Ballyconnell police station. On the way, he quietly tossed the ammunition out of the car's window, but the police spotted this, retrieved the ammunition, and then went through the haversack.

It was in the house that they learned of Constable Scally's death. The civil and religious authorities, north and south, viewed the killing as murder. At the coroner's inquest on the death, an RUC Inspector stated that the attack had achieved nothing and that it personified, quoting Robert

Burns, "Man's inhumanity to man." Ó Brádaigh and his fellow volunteers had a different view. Scally was a victim in a war of national liberation. It was nothing personal against Scally; Ó Brádaigh, after thinking that a "bastard" (later identified as Constable Ferguson) was trying to shoot him, immediately recognized that the man had every right to shoot back. The IRA were soldiers fighting against British colonial interests in Ireland; Scally, as a uniformed and armed member of the state's militarized police, directly supported those interests. As soldiers, they knew that eventually they would kill someone, just as some of them might be killed. It was what they had been training for. It was never clear who fired the fatal shot (the Bren and the rifles used the same ammunition), and the raiders collectively shared responsibility. In 1991, Joe Jackson interviewed Ó Brádaigh for the magazine *Hot Press*. Jackson asked Ó Brádaigh if he knew who fired the shot that hit Scally. Ó Brádaigh replied, "I'd say everyone who took part in the attack shared responsibility, not just the man who shot the bullet. It can't be blamed on anyone in particular." Scally was the first fatality of the campaign.

At the police station, Ó Brádaigh requested that his initial interview, with Garda Superintendent Kelly, be in Irish. Instead, the relevant section of the Offenses Against the State Act was read to him in English. He put his fingers to his ears. Kelly then used Irish to ask him to account for his activities. Replying in Irish, he refused to answer. According to Ó Brádaigh, Kelly took him into a separate room and asked for the whereabouts of other members of the column. He offered to bring them in off the mountain and, in the rain and sleet, have them driven home. He also offered to drop charges related to the items in the haversack if Ó Brádaigh provided information on the IRA volunteers still at large. Ó Brádaigh refused. A Special Branch inspector, Philip McMahon, arrived and also spoke to him privately, asking him to reveal the whereabouts of the rest of the column. Again he refused. At about 8:30 in the evening the seven prisoners were taken from the police station, placed into two police cars, and transported to the Bridewell Detention Centre in Dublin.

While Ó Brádaigh and his group were being interrogated in Cavan, Seán Garland, commanding officer of the Patrick Pearse Column, received information on the Derrylin raid. His column, which included Seán Scott and a young volunteer from Cork, Dáithí O'Connell, had been unsuccessful in their attempts to ambush an RUC patrol. Garland decided to attack the RUC's Brookeborough Barracks, also in County Fermanagh. On New Year's Day they seized a truck and drove to the barracks. Like the IRA at Derrylin, they were armed with gelignite mines, machine guns, and rifles.

Unlike Derrylin, this raid did not go well. The mines did not go off and the RUC return fire found its mark. Several volunteers, including Garland, were shot. The IRA withdrew in the truck and crossed a mountain back over the border into County Monaghan. Two of the wounded, Seán South and Feargal O'Hanlon, were dying. They were left in a farm shed in County Fermanagh and local people were asked to call a priest and a doctor. The other volunteers abandoned the truck and dumped their arms but were arrested on the morning of January 2, 1957. The wounded were sent to hospitals; the healthy were sent to Mountjoy Prison in Dublin. South and O'Hanlon died in the barn and became legends.

In the popular imagination of Irish Nationalists, the tragedy of the raid at Brookeborough, where two IRA volunteers died, eclipsed the tragedy at Derrylin, where a member of the RUC died. South and O'Hanlon were immediately canonized as martyrs for the Republican cause. They were viewed as idealistic young men who died for something most Irish people wanted but were unwilling to sacrifice for. O'Hanlon, who was only 21 years old, was a prominent Irish-speaker and Gaelic footballer in Monaghan. South, who was eight years older, was from Limerick. He was known for his devotion to Catholicism and the Irish language. Each became the subject of a popular ballad: for South, "Seán South of Garryowen," and for O'Hanlon, "The Patriot Game." O'Hanlon was buried not far from where he died. South's funeral procession, which traveled from Monaghan to Limerick via Dublin, affected thousands of people in the Twenty-Six Counties. In Dublin, the IRA staged a large rally with volunteers standing at attention beside the hearse. In Limerick, 50,000 people attended the ceremony.

The Derrylin prisoners—Kavanagh, Ó Brádaigh, Pat McGirl, Paddy Duffy, Joe Daly, Dermot Blake, and Leo Collins—spent New Year's Day in solitary confinement in the Bridewell. The next day they appeared in Dublin District Court, dressed in a mix of military uniforms that included British Army battle dress, a British Army officer's tunic, weatherproof jackets, and British Army and black berets. Each had a tricolor flash on his left sleeve. Because they were in uniform and under the command of a superior officer, they were prisoners of war under the IRA's interpretation of the Geneva Convention. The Irish authorities treated them as criminals.

Late in the afternoon they appeared before Justice Michael Lennon and were charged under Section 52 of the Offenses Against the State Act with failing to account for their movements. It was the same Offenses Against the State Act that Matt Brady had protested in 1939 when it was first proposed. Detective Inspector John O'Flaherty of the Special Branch informed the justice of the charges. The justice, an old Sinn Féiner and Irish Republican Brotherhood man, raised a technical issue. Under Irish law, Section 52 came into force via a public proclamation from the government. Lennon asked for proof that this had happened. O'Flaherty did not have evidence of a proclamation, and the justice dismissed the charges against all seven. (Justice Lennon subsequently resigned at the government's request.) They were not immediately released but were returned to the Bridewell. Because he was unarmed and arrested by himself with no incriminating evidence, Kavanagh was later released. The others, who were implicated by the items found in Ó Brádaigh's haversack, spent the night in the Bridewell. That same day, eight of the captured Brookeborough raiders appeared in another court and were remanded to Mountjoy.

On January 3rd, Ó Brádaigh, Pat McGirl, Joe Daly, and Dermot Blake were back in court, this time facing District Justice Reddin. Paddy Duffy and Leo Collins were sick and unable to attend. The prosecution was ready and offered evidence that the government had publicly proclaimed that the IRA was an unlawful organization and that the Offenses Against the State Act was in force. The group was then formally charged with five offenses: membership in an illegal organization, refusing to account for their movements on the evening of December 30 and the morning of December 31, possession of fourteen rounds of .303 ammunition, possession of a practice grenade, and possession of an incriminating document—Cronin's *Notes on Guerrilla Warfare*. As they were IRA prisoners in a court that they did not recognize, the proceedings consisted of Detective Inspector O'Flaherty describing the respondents' refusal to answer questions. When O'Flaherty read the charges to them, Ó Brádaigh responded in Irish: "*Ní fheádfadh fios a bheith ag aon duine des na fearaibh eile faoi a raibh I mo mhála agus ní raibh aon bhaint acu len a raibh i mo mhálá*" [It would not be possible for any of the other men to know what was in my bag and they had no connection with anything that was in it]. When offered the chance to provide a statement, the others had responded with, "Nothing to say." In response to the charge of failing to account for their movements, Ó Brádaigh replied, "*Níl aon rud le rá agam*" [I have nothing to say]. In court, when the justice asked if they had any questions for the inspector, none of them replied. When he finished presenting the evidence, Walter Carroll, of the chief state solicitor's office, asked that the men be remanded in custody for another week.

Justice Reddin then asked the prisoners if they had anything to say. Ó Brádaigh spoke for them: "We have already been three days in solitary confinement, and on New Year's Day we were not permitted to go to Mass. On behalf of the men I wish to make a protest in the strongest possible form against their treatment." The prosecutor said he was surprised to learn this, but added, "I cannot make any comment." Ó Brádaigh could: "We made several objections and were told there were no facilities for hearing Mass in the Bridewell." He also complained that they were being held illegally. Under the Offenses Against the State Act they could only be held for forty-eight hours without being charged. "Our period of detention was up yesterday [January 2nd] at 4.30 p.m.," he said. "We were brought into Court and the charge was dismissed. We were not allowed to leave the Bridewell until 12.30 this morning when we were again charged. It would appear to us that our detention on the third day is illegal." O'Flaherty and Carroll countered that they had been charged within the 48-hour period. The justice accepted this and asked the prisoners if they objected to being held on remand for a week. Ó Brádaigh replied, "I have no objection to a remand, but we would prefer that it would not be in the Bridewell again in solitary confinement." Informed by the prosecutor that the remand would be to Mountjoy, he replied, "Very good." Justice Reddin then asked if any of them sought bail. Speaking for the group, he replied, "No sir."

Prisons north and south were filling with Republicans. On January 8th, Irish police officers spotted Seán Cronin, Robert Russell, Noel Kavanagh, and Paddy Duffy—who had escaped from a hospital near the Bridewell—in a car outside Belturbet in County Cavan. They were arrested and sent to Mountjoy. On January 12th, 100 people were arrested in Belfast. That same day, Tomás Mac Curtáin addressed a large crowd at College Green in Dublin. He argued that the IRA did not threaten the Dublin government and that volunteers would not return the fire of the Irish Army. It did not help. The next day most of the IRA's leadership, including Tony Magan, Larry Grogan, Charlie Murphy, and Tomás Mac Curtáin, were arrested; they too ended up in Mountjoy.

On Monday, January 14, 1957, the Derrylin raiders made their final court appearance, before Justice Fitzpatrick. They marched in and remained at attention. The justice informed them that they could be seated and Ó Brádaigh issued the order "*Suígí síos*" [Sit down]. Informed that they had the right to a trial by jury, each replied, "I am not interested." The prosecutor, Mr. Carroll, described their arrest, including Ó Brádaigh's attempt to toss items out the car window. When Superintendent Kelly, one of the arresting officers, took the stand, Justice Fitzpatrick offered Ó Brádaigh the chance to question him. Ó Brádaigh began by asking

Kelly if he wanted to speak in Irish or English. Kelly replied that it did not matter. The justice asked for an interpreter, stating, "I recognise your right to speak the Irish language, but I would like to have an interpreter as I do not know it." Superintendent Kelly then said that he would prefer to have the questions in English, as he did not know enough Irish.

Ó Brádaigh proceeded in English. When he came to Kelly's offer to drop the charges in exchange for information, Kelly denied that he had made such an offer:

Ó Brádaigh: "Do you remember having a private conversation with me in one of the rooms of the police barracks?"

Kelly: "Yes."

Ó Brádaigh: "Do you remember showing me a tin with a number of rounds of ammunition?"

Kelly: "Yes."

Ó Brádaigh: "Did you ask me to take responsibility for that ammunition?"

Kelly: "No."

Ó Brádaigh: "Did you promise me on that occasion there would be no charge in relation to those rounds contained in the tin?"

Kelly: "No, no, I did not give any promise at all of that."

Ó Brádaigh: "Did you at the same time ask the whereabouts of other members of our party?"

Kelly: "Yes."

Ó Brádaigh: "Did you press me hard as to where they were?"

Kelly: "I do not know whether you could say I pressed you hard."

Ó Brádaigh: "Did you ask me would I give my word of honour as to where they were?"

Kelly: "I did."

Ó Brádaigh: "Do you remember taking me aside and promising that the men now in Court would be driven home?"

Kelly: "I did not give a definite promise at all."

The judge, who was interested in the line of questioning, interjected with, "Did you give a promise of any sort?" Kelly replied, "No." As Ó Brádaigh remembers it, Kelly "had the grace to blush when the Judge pressed him." Ó Brádaigh, who was inexperienced at dealing with police officers, was shocked by the denial under oath.

Detective Inspector O'Flaherty also appeared as a witness. Ó Brádaigh used him to make political points. The Hungarian Revolution against the Soviet Union had begun in October 1956, and Imre Nagy had been appointed prime minister of Hungary. In November, Soviet troops attacked Budapest and Nagy fled. Janos Kadar formed a countergovernment with Soviet support. Ó Brádaigh asked O'Flaherty, "Would you agree that the Government of Northern Ireland has no more legitimacy than the Kadar regime in Hungary?" O'Flaherty replied: "I am afraid I could not express an opinion on that." Ó Brádaigh persisted: "If the freedom fighters of Hungary were forced to cross the Austrian Border would they not have received better treatment than we did?" The Justice intervened, "You need not answer that question. It is not relevant."

The state rested its case and the IRA prisoners were asked if they wanted to give evidence or call witnesses. They declined. Justice Fitzpatrick then found them guilty of the charges and imposed a sentence of six months in prison for each. Ó Brádaigh then asked for permission to address the court. The Justice stated, "The case is finished. I gave you an opportunity of giving evidence and calling witnesses and you said you did not wish to do so. I will listen to you but I will ask you not to make anything in the nature of a political speech." Ó Brádaigh pleaded ignorance of court procedures and tried to make a political speech.

He was frustrated that the Irish authorities would repress the IRA but offer sympathy to movements outside of Ireland that also used physical force. In the 1930s, there had been widespread support among politicians for an Irish Brigade that went to Spain in support of Franco and fascism. In the 1950s, Soviet repression of the Hungarian rebellion had generated sympathy throughout the Western democracies for the Hungarian people and for Hungarian activists who used physical force against the Soviets. In Cyprus, British repression of EOKA (Ethnica Organosis Kyprion Agoniston; National Organization of Cypriot Fighters) activities and the general Greek population had contributed to anti-British sentiment in Ireland and official concern from Irish politicians. Ó Brádaigh tried to point out this inconsistency: "I have little to say other than that, as members of the Irish Resistance Movement against British occupation in Ireland, we resent it very much indeed being arrested by fellow Irishmen while fighting against British occupation in Ireland. Had we banded ourselves together to go to fight for Hungary or Cyprus or formed an Irish Brigade to go to Spain—." Justice Fitzpatrick cut him off in mid-sentence, "I am sorry. This is a speech on matters which you might regard as national or international or, indeed, embracing the whole world. But that is outside my jurisdiction. I have already dealt with the case and I do not propose to listen further." This ended the case. In response to Ó Brádaigh's orders, which were given in Irish, the prisoners marched out of the dock. They were sent back to Mountjoy, where they were soon joined by those sentenced for their participation in the Brookeborough raid. They had also received a six months' sentence.

The campaign, at least from the IRA's perspective, had been going well. In Seán Cronin's Dublin flat, the Gardaí had found an IRA document that was probably written in early January and titled, "Outline of Operations to Date." It stated:

> From the Fermanagh experience we can prove that where guerrillas are active and aggressive the enemy becomes scared and confused. If we had Fermanagh activities all over we would be in a tremendously strong position in the Six Counties. We still hold the initiative in all areas and our limited supplies in most cases remain intact. We got more gelignite than we ever hoped for.

In early January, IRA columns had been reorganized into battle teams, which were effective, but there was room for still more improvement:

> Among the lessons we have learned are: The training of our men is still very spotty. The battle teams are only beginning to work in Fermanagh. Men are quite close to panic during the withdrawal phase. There is lack of battle discipline. Too many shout orders. Too many act without an order at all. This can cause loss of lives. The way to cure this is to make the column a well-moulded fighting team of battle teams, sections—all integrated in the column, every man given a job in the attack. No firing without an order.

By the end of January 1957, however, almost all of the IRA leadership was in Mountjoy, including Tony Magan, Tomás Mac Curtáin, Larry Grogan, Charlie Murphy, Seán Cronin, Robert Russell, and Ruairí Ó Brádaigh. Paddy Doyle was in Crumlin Road Prison, Belfast. This hurt the campaign, which was in the hands of a temporary IRA Army Council that included Tomás Ó Dubhghaill and Paddy McLogan as an observer.

Ó Brádaigh found Mountjoy to be "all right," although the food left a great deal to be desired. Conditions were not exceptionally harsh and prisoners were not abused by the warders. The negative aspects of being in prison are numerous: loss of freedom, loss of personal space, and so forth. Perhaps the only benefit is that it brings together Republicans from throughout Ireland and allows them the chance to build camaraderie. In 1916, the British had placed a large number of rebels in the same internment camp in Wales, Frongoch. Out of that camp the Republican Movement rebuilt itself in 1917. Forty years later, the benefits of bringing together people in Mountjoy were not as striking as in 1916, but significant relationships were formed there that continue to influence Ruairí Ó Brádaigh.

In prison, IRA members lose their rank and the prisoners elect their own commanding officer. An IRA chief of staff on the outside becomes a regular volunteer on the inside. This allows for continuity of leadership in the prison and for smoother relations. If an IRA officer were to enter a prison and attempt to take over and issue commands, it might breed confusion and factions. The IRA's leadership did not assume the leadership in Mountjoy; Dáithí O'Connell had been elected commanding officer by the first set of prisoners and he remained so.

Many of those in the leadership, including Mac Curtáin, Tony Magan, and Larry Grogan, were in prison in the 1940s; Grogan had been in Mountjoy in the 1920s. Ó Brádaigh remembers them taking to prison like "ducks to water." He gravitated toward the senior people. Pragmatically, he figured he could draw on their experiences to make the time pass more easily. The younger people in general tended to follow the lead of the senior people. He also saw an opportunity to add to the record of Irish history; he saw the senior people as actors in events that had often gone unrecorded, and he did not want this lost to posterity. Today, some of their stories appear in his "50 Years Ago" column in Republican Sinn Féin's paper, *SAOIRSE*. His interest in history was such that he even talked to some of the senior warders who had witnessed the executions and later exhumations of people such as Charlie Kerins and Paddy McGrath.

Tomás Mac Curtáin was particularly interesting. Mac Curtáin had been within hours of his execution in 1940. He saw what was to be his coffin brought into the prison and he knew that the hangman, who had been imported from England, was on site. His cell in 1940 was the prisoners' recreation room in 1957. The execution chamber was at the end of the wing. According to Ó Brádaigh, Mac Curtáin was convinced that upon his execution he would go "straight up to heaven." He had settled his affairs, was prepared to die, and did not expect to be reprieved. When the reprieve came the night before the scheduled execution, it caught him by surprise. The next morning, he told Ó Brádaigh, "I just simply didn't know what to be doing." Mac Curtáin was not confused for long. After he was moved from the cell for condemned prisoners, he began organizing the other prisoners. The authorities transferred him to Port Laoise Prison in County Laois. There he refused to wear a prison uniform or do prison work and was placed in solitary confinement (Ó Brádaigh refers to him today as the first "blanketman"). In solitary, Mac Curtáin searched for ways to break the monotony. When a mouse joined him in the cell, he tried to train it to run up one arm and down the other. On the third attempt, it bit him.

Among the younger prisoners that Ó Brádaigh became close to was David O'Connell. Formally, O'Connell went by the Irish version of his name, Dáithí. Informally, he was "Dave." Tall, thin, and with a Cork accent, he was only 18 years old. He looked to have a good future as a cabinetmaker; in 1955, he had been awarded first prize in Ireland and Britain in his apprenticeship examination and had received a gold medal. Like Ó Brádaigh and so many of their contemporaries, he was from a Republican background; an uncle was bayoneted to death by British soldiers in 1921. The 1955 local elections in the Twenty-Six Counties had caught O'Connell's attention and he had sought out the Republican Movement. He was interviewed for IRA membership by Mick McCarthy. McCarthy remembers that O'Connell was concerned that he would not be eligible for membership because he had briefly joined the Irish territorial army, the Fórsa Cosanta Áitiúil (FCÁ, "Local Defense Force"). He feared that this implicit recognition of the state would make him unacceptable. It was not a serious issue, and O'Connell was recruited into the IRA. O'Connell's concern is indicative of his intensity and of how careful Republicans were not to recognize the state. He was so intense that in prison he was referred to as "Mise Éire," or "I am Ireland." Ó Brádaigh first met O'Connell on St. Stephen's Day, 1956. Ó Brádaigh, as second in command of the Teeling Column, transferred some men to O'Connell, who was second in command of the Pearse Column. In Mountjoy, they developed a friendship that lasted until O'Connell's death in 1991.

While in prison Ó Brádaigh was visited regularly by his family. For many families, it would be a disaster to have a son and brother arrested for his involvement in the killing of a police officer. The Ó Brádaighs, who knew that Ruairí was involved in the campaign, were not surprised that he ended up being arrested. It was a likely outcome of being an activist. As far as they were concerned, Scally was a regrettable casualty of war. They did not rejoice at the death but neither were they repulsed by it. The family knew well the risks of involvement in the IRA; Matt Brady had been shot by the RIC, the RUC's predecessors. Seán Ó Brádaigh's reaction to Ruairí's arrest was to be annoyed with the Irish government—in trying to seal the border and in arresting IRA personnel, they were collaborating with the British government. For many people, Republican and Irish Nationalist, the killings of South and O'Hanlon put the killing of Scally into perspective; both "sides" were suffering in a military campaign. The huge funerals for South and O'Hanlon were a source of pride in the cause.

The family visited Ruairí whenever they could. His mother May traveled by train from Longford to Dublin. On occasion, she was joined by Ruairí's sister, Mary, who had returned to Ireland in 1955 to study for an MA in English (focusing on John Millington Synge) at University College Dublin. There she had met James Delaney, who was also pursuing an MA. They had married and temporarily moved in with her mother. Under the 1937 Irish Constitution, as a married woman, Mary was ineligible for employment by the state; they were planning a family. Visiting Mountjoy was easiest for Seán, who had followed Mary and Ruairí on to University College Dublin and, like his siblings, was studying to become a teacher. Another regular visitor was Patsy O'Connor, a teacher at Roscommon Vocational School. Patsy, a graduate of University College Galway, had joined the staff in 1953, a year before Ruairí. Her degree was also in commerce; she taught bookkeeping, business methods, shorthand, and typing. They had much in common, including a love of books. She had attended an all-Irish secondary school, and although she was not fluent, she shared his interest in the language. As Patsy describes it, "We could talk about anything. And we still do." Although they were not engaged, they had an understanding that they would be married. Patsy would take the bus from Roscommon to Longford and then ride to Dublin with May.

Assorted aunts, uncles, and cousins also visited, including his Uncle Eugene's family, which was living in Dublin. The families were close, and the Ó Brádaighs had often visited the Caffreys in Donegal. On one of these visits, when Ruairí was 10, he had worn a blazer with several pockets. The pockets fascinated his 2-year-old cousin Deirdre, who went through each one of them. Ruairí, a very serious youngster, told her mother that she should teach the child to not go through men's pockets or else when she grew up she would go to jail. On her first visit to Mountjoy, Deirdre, now 16, bounced into the visitor's box, looked at Ruairí, and asked, "Who went to jail?" It became a standing inside joke between the two of them.

Life and politics go on outside of prison. So do IRA campaigns. Republican prisoners follow external political events as closely as they can. Visits from family and friends are important sources of information. On occasion, IRA prisoners become central players in external political events; in late January 1957, Seán Mac Bride, TD, put forward a motion of no confidence in the government, primarily because of Costello's actions against the IRA. The government fell and Costello called an election for March 5th.

Republicans are always interested in elections, even when they do not participate in them. March 1957 was great timing for participation. The campaign had made Northern Ireland an important issue in 26-county politics. The deaths of O'Hanlon and South had generated enormous sympathy for the cause, and the movement had several promising candidates to offer the public, including Feargal O'Hanlon's brother, Éighneachán. Others included Paddy Mulcahy, a city councilor in Limerick; John Joe McGirl, the highly respected Leitrim publican and a prisoner in Mountjoy; and Ruairí Ó Brádaigh. At the encouragement of the Ó Brádaigh family, Ruairí was selected as Sinn Féin's candidate at a Longford-Westmeath constituency convention. In Mountjoy, and with some hints from Tony Magan, he wrote his first election address. It was later adopted as Sinn Féin's general manifesto for the election. He pledged to work for the unity and independence of Ireland and to take a seat only in a 32-county All-Ireland Parliament.

Ruairí Ó Brádaigh was an ideal candidate for a seat in Longford-Westmeath. Longford had a history of electing Republican prisoners; in 1917, Joe McGuinness won in South Longford. Ó Brádaigh's campaign adopted McGuinness's slogan: "Put him in to get him out." Ballads were composed, including one that began, "In Bridewell court one Monday morning, In this land the State calls Free." The Ó Brádaigh name was prominent throughout the constituency. Older people remembered Matt Brady, a county councilor from 1934 to 1942 and a member of the Mullingar Mental Hospital Committee. For thirty-six years, May Brady Twohig had been the secretary of the Longford Board of Health, certifying birth, death, and marriage records. Mary Delaney was Ruairí's election agent, and May and Seán actively worked on the campaign.

Republican Longford rose to the occasion. People who for years had rejected any form of constitutional participation were mobilized. Seán F. Lynch's mother-in-law, a staunch Republican, voted for Ó Brádaigh; it was the first time she had voted in a general election since the 1920s. The family's efforts were not without their humorous side. Calling at a house one day, Seán asked the occupant if he would be willing to work for

Ruairí's campaign. The man replied, "Yes, of course I will work for your brother. I voted for Joe McGuinness in 1918 [to re-elect McGuinness], I voted for de Valera in 1932, and I voted for Seán Mac Bride in 1948. And of course I will vote for your brother now." In each case, he had voted for the most "Republican" candidate available. Seán kept to himself the view that de Valera had gone on to arrest and execute Republicans and that Mac Bride had entered Leinster House.

Sinn Féin's intervention was an incredible success. With a total of nineteen candidates, the Party won 65,000 first-preference votes and elected four candidates: Éighneachán O'Hanlon in Monaghan; John Joe Rice, a Republican veteran of the 1920s, in South Kerry; John Joe McGirl in Sligo-Leitrim; and Ruairí Ó Brádaigh in Longford-Westmeath. McGirl topped the poll in Sligo-Leitrim. In Longford, Seán Mac Eoin topped the poll, as usual. But Ruairí Ó Brádaigh finished second with more than 5,500 first-preference votes and was elected. In the complicated system of vote transfers and multiple seats in one constituency, Ó Brádaigh replaced a Fianna Fail incumbent. It was an amazing result for a party that endorsed a paramilitary campaign and rejected participation in Parliament.

The day after the count over 1,000 people attended a rally in Longford in support of their jailed abstentionist Teachta Dála. A band played marches and the town courthouse was decorated with Irish flags and a Sinn Féin banner. Thomas Higgins of Longford Sinn Féin read a letter from Ó Brádaigh to the crowd. He thanked his supporters for their work and then drew a parallel to the 1917 election: "Longford and Westmeath have matched their achievement of 40 years ago, and have written yet another page in the history of our struggle for unity and independence." He also looked to the future, "If 1957 has been another 1917, then let us in God's name look forward to another 1918, to the day in the near future, when the All-Ireland Parliament, pledged to legislate for the whole 32 Counties will be re-assembled." Another speaker was Seán Ó Brádaigh, who stated, "We want to end the corruption, graft and hypocrisy that has been going on for the past 35 years." The rally ended with the singing of "A Nation Once Again" and the national anthem.

From a revolutionary Republican point of view, the election was a watershed, Sinn Féin's best showing in the Twenty-Six Counties since 1927. Combined with the Mid-Ulster and Fermanagh–South Tyrone results from 1955, Sinn Féin had elected six deputies to an All-Ireland Parliament. From the perspective of constitutional politics, Sinn Féin's success was less dramatic. The party had elected four of 147 members of Leinster House. And because they were abstentionists, those four people

Mary Ó Brádaigh Delaney at a
Sinn Féin rally in support of
her brother, Ruairí Ó Brádaigh,
TD, Longford, 1957.
Ó Brádaigh family collection.

would have no voice in the formation of the new government. Neither
would Seán Mac Bride, who lost his seat. The big winner was Fianna Fáil,
which elected seventy-eight Teachtaí Dála and formed yet another government with Éamon de Valera as Taoiseach. De Valera, the most successful
Irish politician of the twentieth century, was interviewed soon after the
election. The most important issue for him was the Irish economy, which
was forcing people to emigrate—"Unemployment is the one thing I am
thinking at the moment." He was also asked, "As an old I.R.A. fighter
yourself, what is your present view towards the revival of this extreme
national movement?" His reply brought no comfort to Sinn Féin and the
IRA, "As far as this part of the island is concerned, we have here a democratic system completely free and you cannot have two armed forces obviously."

6

TD, Internee, Escapee, and Chief of Staff

MARCH 1957–JUNE 1959

SINN FÉIN AND THE IRA were spurred on by the election. In March 1957, John Joe McGirl was released from Mountjoy and given a hero's welcome when he arrived home in Ballinamore, Leitrim. In Limerick, Seán South's home area, Sinn Féin established eight new *cumainn*. The election elevated Ó Brádaigh, McGirl, O'Hanlon, and Rice to the status of Teachtaí Dála, and their enhanced status was used to promote their cause. Soon after the election, Ó Brádaigh's election agent, Mary Delaney, sent a letter to the European Court of Human Rights at Strasbourg, concerning the imprisonment of a TD, her brother Ruairí. She called on the European Commission on Human Rights to investigate the provisions of Ireland's Offenses Against the State Act, which she believed to be "the very negation of democracy and of all human rights." It was the first attempt by Irish Republicans to seek redress from the commission.

Several prisoners in Mountjoy had received a three months' sentence in January. Soon after the election, there was a series of releases and by the end of April most of the IRA's leadership was back in place, with Tony Magan as chief of staff. The campaign had survived and was rejuvenated by their return. Early in the morning of Thursday, July 4th, the IRA ambushed an RUC patrol near Crossmaglen in South Armagh. An RUC commando was killed and another injured. That night, RUC posts in Fermanagh and Tyrone were wrecked by time bombs. To this point, the new Fianna Fáil government had not directly confronted the campaign. The attacks demonstrated that arresting people along the border and giving them light sentences was not enough. On Friday, July 5th, with Dáil Éireann/Leinster House closed for its summer recess, the Dublin government invoked Part Two of the Offenses Against the State Act, which allows for detention without trial—internment. On Saturday, the Special Branch raided the country, arresting sixty-three people. In Dublin, Sinn Féin's head office and the offices of *The United Irishman* were raided. An Ard Chomhairle meeting was in session, and Paddy McLogan, Tony Magan, Robert Russell, Michael Traynor, and Tomás Mac Giolla were arrested. In Cork, Tomás Mac Curtáin was arrested as he got off a train. The one person at Sinn Féin headquarters who was not arrested was Vice President Margaret Buckley; she left the building and tried to warn others that internment was under way.

On Sunday, the Curragh Camp, which was being used as a military prison for the Irish Army, was again an internment camp. Those arrested on Saturday were taken from the Bridewell in Dublin and shipped to the Curragh. The Government Information Bureau, on behalf of the minister for justice, released a statement claiming that people were arrested because they were believed to be involved in military activities. It said that "no one has been arrested because of membership of the Sinn Féin organisation." Because the Ard Chomhairle of Sinn Féin, a legal political party, had been picked up virtually en masse, the statement's sincerity was subject to question. An editorial in the *Irish Times* supported the government, stating that internment was a necessary evil: "It is a sickening thought that, once again, circumstances exist which force the Government to revive the special powers of arrest and detention available under a section of the Offenses Against the State Act. In a democratic country nobody relishes the invocation of authority to bypass the ordinary processes of law. At the same time, it is difficult to see how the Government could have acted otherwise." Within a matter of days there were fifty-six internees in the Curragh.

When internment was introduced, there were sixty-two convicted Republican prisoners in Mountjoy. Fifteen of them, including Ruairí Ó Brádaigh, were due for release on July 13th. The prisoners, their guards, and the newspapers speculated on whether or not they would be released or interned. The *Irish Times* reported that military guards had been added at the Curragh and that repairs were under way on wooden huts that had held German airmen and seamen during World War II. Because he was a TD, Ó Brádaigh's situation was especially interesting. Various warders told him that although the others would be interned, he would be released. Ó Brádaigh, who knew his Irish history, doubted it; to him, it appeared that de Valera was still living in 1940. Officially he was an elected member of the Dublin Parliament, but he expected the same treatment as the others. He had little faith in the 26-county political system and believed that the government would intern a majority of the TDs if necessary, let alone one.

The prisoners were due for release at 7:30 AM. The night before, the chief warder, who was friendly as a person, went to the prisoners' wing and told Ó Brádaigh that there had been a phone call from the Department of Justice. All of them would be interned. The prisoners expected to see their families, and protesters, as they were released and taken back into custody. Instead, they were awakened early, at 5:30 AM, given tea and a slice of bread, and sent to the gate, where lorries awaited them. Ó Brádaigh was the first to be released. As he stepped through the main prison gate, Inspector McMahon said, "Ruairí," tapped him on the shoulder, and pointed to a lorry. Very quickly the fifteen prisoners were transformed into internees and were on their way to the Curragh.

Their families arrived at Mountjoy's gate about 7:00 AM. The guard, presumably following orders, told them the prisoners had been released. When asked where they were, he said he did not know. The justice department, when phoned, offered no information on their whereabouts. The full story was not known until the evening papers came out. The title of an *Evening Press* article summed up the event, "15 Released—Then Interned *Rearrested Outside Jail* Sinn Féin T.D. Sent to Curragh." The London *Times* stated that "the sudden and drastic arrests are proof that Mr. de Valera in old age is still the most formidable leader in his country." A *United Irishman* article on internment entitled "British Whip" stated that de Valera had acted after being delivered a note from the British government.

By the end of August the 115 internees in the Curragh included most of the IRA and Sinn Féin leadership—Tony Magan, Paddy McLogan, Tomás Mac Curtáin, Larry Grogan (whose son joined him in January 1958), Robert Russell, Ó Brádaigh, and others. Several of the internees would become prominent in the movement in the late 1950s and 1960s, including Dáithí O'Connell, Éamonn MacThomáis, Seán Garland, Tomás Mac Giolla, and Proinsias de Rossa. Except for Vice-President Buckley and one other person, May Smith, one of the general secretaries, Sinn Féin had been beheaded and the Ard Chomhairle was in the Curragh. With McLogan as president, the internees began holding Ard Chomhairle meetings. Through visitors, the internees sent notes to May Smith and the organization continued on the outside. At the Sinn Féin Ard Fheis in October, McLogan was re-elected president and seven other internees were elected to the Ard Chomhairle, including Ó Brádaigh. Minus the internees, the reconstituted Ard Chomhairle began holding its own meetings in the Sinn Féin offices in Dublin. It was a signal to the state's authorities that, internment or not, Sinn Féin would not roll over.

Neither would the IRA. A camp council that included Magan and McLogan was elected, with Mac Curtáin as commanding officer. The 1940s campaign and their experiences in the Curragh had left an indelible mark on them. Confrontation with Dublin had been a disaster. Avoiding confrontation had allowed them to rebuild the movement. As a result, they adopted a narrow nonconfrontational approach, which eventually caused problems. Initially everyone supported the council, which organized leathercraft projects, Irish-language classes, and other activities—Mac Curtáin and Ó Brádaigh taught Irish. For a group of men engaged in a political and military campaign against a colonial power, there were any number of topics available for discussion: Castro and Cuba; Nasser and the Suez Crisis; the FLN, the Colons and the French in Algeria; the EOKA, the Cypriots, and the Turks; and Dien Bien Phu and its ramifications in Vietnam. They were especially interested in the role of physical force in social change.

India and Ireland experienced similar treatment from the British after World War I. The British had promised Home Rule for Ireland in 1914, only to defer implementation until after the war. Before the war ended, the Easter Rebellion had occurred, which led to the 1918 election and Dáil Éireann; instead of Home Rule, the Irish got repression. India had been promised political reform during World War I, but the British extended wartime emergency measures in 1919 with the Rowlett Acts and Indian leaders felt betrayed. When Mahatma Gandhi spearheaded a campaign to repeal the acts, the British responded with repression, including the Amritsar Massacre in April 1919, when British troops opened fire on a huge crowd of protesters in a small park surrounded by high walls, killing about 400 people.

The agitation in Ireland resulted in a partitioned country, not a Republic. Because of this, there was still an IRA. India had achieved independence, however, and the hunger strikes and nonviolent civil disobedience campaigns of Mahatma Gandhi were often presented as evidence that independence could be won without physical force. To the internees, it seemed evident that Gandhi must have known that people would suffer and die because of his actions. Most important, they believed that the options and resources available to the Indian leaders were not available to them. In India, a huge population was ruled by a small number of British personnel. The British Army could not control the population if a large percentage of it engaged in civil disobedience. In Ireland, the British and the Unionists had carved out an area where their sympathizers were by far in the majority. Politicians in Dublin claimed sovereignty over a 32-county Irish Republic, but they were no match for the British government, who ruled Northern Ireland. Civil disobedience was an effective option in India; it was less so in Ireland. This, for the internees, had been confirmed by events in Fermanagh.

Some of the internees had experienced the civil disobedience campaign of Canon Thomas Maguire in Fermanagh. In Northern Ireland, under the Flags and Emblems (Display) Act of 1954, a Union Jack was afforded special protection; it was an offense to interfere with the display of a British flag. In contrast, a police officer could require a person to remove any other "emblem," including an Irish flag. If a person refused to remove an offensive "emblem," the police were authorized to enter buildings or homes and remove it. To raise awareness of discrimination against Nationalists in Northern Ireland, Canon Maguire would lock his door and hang an Irish flag from a window. Rather than kick in the door, the police would get ladders. As they were climbing up to capture his Irish flag, Maguire would reach out of the window and take it in. Although events like this might lead to press coverage, given Unionist domination of the Northern Ireland Parliament, they would not change the basic social and political arrangements there. Similarly, in organizing marches such as those associated with the Fermanagh Feiseanna, Maguire instructed people to march up to the RUC, filter through the police line one at a time, and then regroup and continue marching. It was a great action in principle, but in practice marchers were attacked with police batons and water cannons. The attacks also led to press coverage, but no one put external pressure on the RUC as a result; the Northern Ireland government defended the RUC, the Irish government was powerless, and the British government did not care.

Ó Brádaigh was among those internees who concluded that there was a place for civil disobedience in the Republican Movement's repertoire, but in and of itself civil disobedience would not bring about a united and free Ireland. Based on his interpretation of Irish and more general colonial history, civil disobedience usually caused "action that would be taken by the Imperial power [that] would result in physical confrontation"—civil disobedience, in a colonial setting, generates state repression. In the face of state repression, the question was whether or not people would defend themselves or be driven into submission. Some people might submit. But "given our roots and our background and our experience and all that type of thing, we would be a people who would fight back." Civil disobedience could be used to raise people's awareness and to expose the illegitimacy of the colonial power, setting the stage for a military campaign. This was the goal of the planned "passive resistance campaign" that had not materialized before the Border Campaign. Gandhi's hunger strikes, Canon Maguire's violation of the Flags and Emblems Act, and the physical force the IRA used were all on a continuum—each was a weapon to be used against an unjust colonial oppressor.

Physically, conditions in the Curragh were crowded and cramped. The camp was old and had not been maintained. The exercise area was a muddy field that got worse and worse until the ground was no good for sports. The roofs leaked and sanitary conditions were poor. Toilets without doors were available outside the huts. The inside toilet facility was a large bucket in the corner of each hut. The internees wrote letters to the Irish Red Cross, which is funded by the Irish Department of Defense; their complaints were ignored. They also appealed to the International Red Cross. This effort received help from an unexpected source. Ó Brádaigh's grandmother was Swiss and his mother had Swiss first cousins. One of them, Charles Girardclos, had married a French woman and lived in Paris. In August 1957 he took his wife on a holiday to Ireland. Not surprising, he found it curious that his cousin's son, a member of the Irish Parliament, was interned. Girardclos was a dentist, and he informed the Ó Brádaighs and Caffreys that the secretary general of the International Red Cross was one of his patients. The families arranged for Girardclos to visit Ruairí, and he surreptitiously photographed the camp, with Ruairí standing by the fence wire. The photo was later published in the *United Irishman*. When Girardclos returned home he contacted the International Red Cross.

In October the Irish Department of Defense was notified that the International Red Cross wanted to inspect the facility. Whether or not this was prompted by Girardclos's letter, it helped the internees. By the time of the inspection in the spring, the roofs were repaired, new toilets were installed, new beds were distributed, a physician had visited each internee, and a section of the camp was set aside as a sports field. A barbed-wire tunnel was built and internees had access to the field mornings, afternoons, and, as spring passed into summer, late into the evening. Gaelic football matches were organized. Ó Brádaigh did not play football, so he stayed in shape by running the perimeter of the camp regularly with Dáithí O'Connell. But a football match was the setting for his escape from the camp.

As conditions in the Curragh improved, the situation outside deteriorated. By July 1958, there were 160 Republicans in the Curragh and the leadership needed help. The internees' leaders were upset to discover Chief of Staff Seán Cronin and Charlie Murphy, his adjutant general, were working with people who had drifted away from the IRA. Magan, Mac Curtáin, and McLogan, with reason, viewed them as ill-disciplined and unreliable. Cronin and Murphy, who were busy fighting a war, saw them as resources at their disposal. They were also upset that internees, who were removed from the situation, were trying to tell them what to do. They sent in a note to this effect which, predictably, made things worse. Because the two groups could not meet, the situation festered. Still, in the summer of 1958, an opportunity arose for the camp leadership and the Army Council to work together. The sports field's grass was cut regularly and turned into hay, which was tossed into piles that eventually covered the first lane of several safety fences. The internees noted this and a couple of them, including Dáithí O'Connell, suggested to Mac Curtáin that one or two internees could hide under the grass during the day and then, under cover of darkness, cut through the wire and escape. Mac Curtáin sent this information out to Seán Cronin and suggested that one of the interned IRA leaders be included in the escape. Word came back from the Army Council that they wanted younger volunteers with operational experience. At the top of their list was J. B. O'Hagan, an important IRA commander in the North who was interned in January 1958. The camp's escape committee made the final decision and chose Ó Brádaigh and Dáithí O'Connell. Ó Brádaigh was probably chosen because of the combination of the propaganda value of having an escaped TD and his experience in the field. O'Connell, everyone agreed, was one of the IRA's top soldiers. Seán Cronin describes the choice of O'Connell as putting the "hammer" in. All Ó Brádaigh remembers is Mac Curtáin telling him "You are escaping." A loyal soldier, he never bothered to ask why he was selected.

On September 24, 1958, a spirited football match, with lots of cheering and standing, diverted the eyes of the warders. Ó Brádaigh and O'Connell slipped behind cheering internees, and Noel Kavanagh, former commanding officer of the Teeling Column, used wire cutters on the bottom strand of wire at a pole. While the sentries watched the football match, Ó Brádaigh and O'Connell took the wire cutters and crawled under an overcoat that was disguised to look like a blanket and made their way under the wire; the overcoat had belonged to Ó Brádaigh's father. Kavanagh used spare wire to reattach the bottom strand. The match ended about 7:30 in the evening. As Ó Brádaigh and O'Connell kept quiet, the other internees returned to barracks and placed dummies in their beds. They waited until it was dark, cut through more wire, and climbed into a fifteen-foot deep dry moat and followed it, moving away from the search lights. After about 45 minutes they had covered about 500 yards and were on the Kildare-Brownstown Road. Awaiting them was a car and driver. Ó Brádaigh told him to head northwest, to Longford-Westmeath. He knew the area and the people and they knew him; after all, more than 5,500 of them had voted for him in the election.

The escape was not discovered until roll call the next morning. A general alert was declared, roadblocks were set up, and cars passing the camp were stopped and searched, but it was too late and Ó Brádaigh and O'Connell were safely hidden. Ó Brádaigh was the first Sinn Féin TD to be "on the run" since the 1920s. The two found themselves in a strange situation. They had escaped from an internment camp, not from a jail. There had been no charges against them, but now they could be arrested for escaping. For the next couple of weeks they hid in safe houses in the Longford-Westmeath area and went out only at night. During the day, they read, discussed the state of things with each other, and kept a low profile.

The escape was a morale booster for a cause that continued to suffer. Ó Brádaigh had escaped hoping to rejoin the campaign as a volunteer. But while he and O'Connell were lying low, Seán Cronin, Mick McCarthy (a member of the Army Council), and three members of IRA general head-quarters staff were arrested and interned. The arrests hurt the IRA, which was very much centered on Cronin. A temporary three-man Army Council remained in charge—Chief of Staff John Joe McGirl was joined by Myles Shevlin, a solicitor from Carlow who was Cronin's adjutant general, and Paddy Murphy, from Kilkenny. After waiting a couple of weeks, Ó Brádaigh made contact with the local IRA, who sent word to general headquarters, and a meeting was arranged. To his surprise, he was elected chief of staff. His initial reaction was that he should have stayed in the Curragh. In fact, he was a likely choice. At age 26, he was young, fit, and had operational experience. He was also the only member of the December 1956 Army Council who was at large. And because he was on the run, he could devote all of his time to the IRA. John Joe McGirl, Paddy Murphy, and Myles Shevlin remained on the council. Later, Paddy Mulcahy of Limerick was co-opted, as was another person, from County Down. The seventh member was Dáithí O'Connell.

There are three key jobs in the IRA, chief of staff, adjutant general, and quartermaster general. The Army Council is in charge of the IRA except when the army meets in convention. The chief of staff directs the IRA on behalf of the Army Council. Essentially, the chief of staff is the chief executive officer of a voluntary, not-for-profit, clandestine organization. In the mid- to late 1950s, there were probably 600–700 active members of the organization, of whom perhaps 400–500 were in prison or were interned. When Tony Magan was chief of staff, he had gone on operations in the early 1950s. But by 1958, the IRA had expanded and Cronin and then Ó Brádaigh functioned more as directors than operators, although both stayed as close as possible to what was happening. The adjutant general is an administrative officer in charge of communications and discipline; the position is like that of a general secretary or administrative assistant. The adjutant general might be involved in military operations, but the job is primarily that of a coordinator who is also in charge of IRA courts of inquiry and courts-martial. The quartermaster general is in charge of procuring, transporting, storing, and allocating material.

These three positions are complemented by general headquarters staff positions, including the director of finance, the director of intelligence, the director of publicity, and the director of operations. The duties of the positions are for the most part evident in their titles. At the October 24th meeting, Dáithí O'Connell became director of operations. Like Ó Brádaigh as chief of staff, he was a likely choice for the position. He was in good shape, had operational experience, and he was available full-time. As director of operations, he worked closely with Ó Brádaigh and the adjutant general in planning operations. Up through the mid-1960s the director of publicity oversaw publication of *An tÓglách* (*The Volunteer*), the IRA's small mimeographed internal newspaper that dated from 1914 and the Irish Volunteers. The IRA expands and contracts. When the army is small, one person will fill more than one position; the adjutant general, in charge of communications, will probably also serve as director of publicity. In an expanded period, as in the mid- to late 1950s, positions will be held separately. When things were especially active in the late 1950s, there was an assistant adjutant general.

Although the IRA's administrative structure is constant, with a chief of staff, an adjutant general, the Army Council, and so forth, the IRA had changed its operations a great deal since December 1956. The high level of operations of the first several months had declined, especially after internment was introduced in the Twenty-Six Counties. From January, 1957, the Army Council had been in a constant state of flux; people were arrested, their replacements were arrested, the original people were released and rejoined the council only to be rearrested, and so on. By October 1958, Tomás Mac Curtáin, Tony Magan, and Larry Grogan had been interned for more than a year. J. B. O'Hagan was arrested in January 1958 and Charlie Murphy was arrested in May 1958. Pat McManus, a member of the Army Council, was killed in a premature explosion in July 1958. Seán Cronin, Mick McCarthy, and other general headquarters people were arrested in October 1958. A substantial number of IRA leaders were unavailable.

After nearly two years out of action, Ó Brádaigh began by familiarizing himself with the situation on the ground and reestablishing contact with IRA units along the border and in the North. He also worked at getting used to operating on the run. Cronin had kept things so much to himself that when weapons were needed, a note had to be smuggled in to him asking for the location of gun magazines and clips. The reply was decoded and led to an individual who provided ample magazines. Finding out who was doing what, and where, took time, however. The structure of the IRA units had also changed. Before the campaign Paddy McLogan had argued that smaller five-person sections composed of two battle teams and a section leader would be more mobile and more effective than the larger columns. He was right, and the change was made in January 1957. The basic goal of the units had not changed. The IRA was trying to establish liberated areas in the countryside, where they could dominate and attack any RUC or British forces who entered. In this, Pat McManus had been a leader and his loss was keenly felt—he had established a series of dugouts across Fermanagh.

Morale in the IRA was "reasonable," but problems in the Curragh made things more difficult. Ó Brádaigh and O'Connell's escape encouraged internees who wanted confrontation and more escapes. Tomás Mac Curtáin demurred. In September, Charlie Murphy was transferred from Mountjoy to the Curragh, and he became a leading dissenter against Mac Curtáin. With little for internees to do but complain, the situation deteriorated. Speculation on what lay in the future contributed to the complaints. The campaign had faltered and there were rumors that the government would close the camp. Some internees who had become convinced that the Irish soldiers guarding them would not shoot escaping internees organized an unofficial escape. Early in December 1958, during another football match, Charlie Murphy and another internee ran to the fence and cut a large hole. As they held the fence open, groups of internees ran off over the fields. When the guards realized what was happening they fired shots over their heads. Sixteen men got away before the shots and tear gas brought the situation under control. Only two of them were rearrested. Although it was a success, the escape violated IRA policies and Mac Curtáin was furious. IRA general regulations state that members who engage in unofficial operations incur automatic dismissal. Mac Curtáin sent word to the Army Council that the escape was unofficial and that, by definition, the escapees were dismissed from the IRA. Into Ó Brádaigh's and the Army Council's collective lap fell fourteen motivated young men seeking active service. The leadership at the Curragh considered them former IRA members, but the Army Council needed soldiers. It was a sticky situation. The pragmatic needs of the IRA outweighed Mac Curtáin's condemnation. The Army Council arranged interviews with the escapees. Each stated that his excuse for violating policy and escaping from the camp was a desire to return to active service. Each applied for readmission to the IRA and each application was accepted. Mac Curtáin was not pleased, but he could do little except complain.

The rumors of the Curragh's imminent closing were true and the internees were released in March 1959. The end of internment reflected political changes that would have immediate and long-lasting effects in Ireland. The IRA's campaign had slowed significantly and there was less need for internment. And 77-year-old Éamon de Valera was stepping down as Taoiseach and was a candidate for the Irish presidency in an election scheduled for June. Internment, an affront to civil liberties, had become a liability. The Curragh Camp was officially closed on March 15, 1959. In the presidential election, de Valera defeated Seán Mac Eoin of Fine Gael handily. Seán Lemass, aged 60 and a 1916 veteran who had been linked with de Valera for decades, became Taoiseach. The change was part of a more general opening up of Irish society that began in the mid- to late 1950s and led to significant shifts in the Irish economy, freeing trade and encouraging foreign investment.

Closing the Curragh allowed Ó Brádaigh and O'Connell to move about more freely, but it also released Tomás Mac Curtáin and Tony Magan, who were still upset about the unofficial escape and the "conspiracy" of readmitting the escapees into the IRA. Their release also confused things; those who had led the IRA into the campaign were again available for leadership positions, while those who had filled in for them, including Ó Brádaigh, still held those positions. Just before Easter 1959, a meeting was arranged for the fifteen or so people who had been on either the Army Council or the Army Executive Council since December 1956. A long meeting produced two decisions. First, a statement would be circulated to all units explaining what had happened in the Curragh and, second, there would be a general Army convention.

Ó Brádaigh, an educator with obvious writing skills, was chosen to write the statement. He had also managed to remain on friendly terms with both the Curragh leadership and the dissidents. Partly this was due to his nature—even his political opponents note that he is polite and easy to get along with. It was also because of his age and position in the IRA at the time of the mass escape. He was much younger than Magan, Mac Curtáin, and McLogan and had only been in the leadership about a year when he was arrested. When he was in the Curragh, the IRA people on the outside identified more with him than they did with Magan and his peers. Yet it was Magan's group who brought Ó Brádaigh into the IRA's leadership. He respected them and got along with them in the Curragh. Ó Brádaigh tended to agree with the dissidents about the escape; he felt that the Curragh leadership had been too conservative. But this did not justify a blatant disregard for camp policy. Most important, he wanted to keep the IRA from splintering and he wanted to move ahead with the campaign. He discussed the situation with Cronin, who reduced the controversy to a question about the nature of the Republican Movement: Is the Republican Movement a self-perpetuating religious sect or is it the instrument of the freedom of Ireland? If it was a self-perpetuating religious sect, it was time for absolute discipline. If it was the instrument of the freedom of Ireland, then the situation had to be dealt with pragmatically. Cronin was not interested in the dispute; he wanted to get on with the campaign. Ó Brádaigh, and Dáithí O'Connell, agreed with him—time was being wasted and dismissing people would be a waste of talent.

Ó Brádaigh's document carefully laid out the facts, and both the Curragh leadership and the dissidents accepted this part of the presentation. The final paragraph stressed that IRA volunteers should guard against disunity. Mac Curtáin, who was interested in discipline, argued that the interim leadership had straddled the position: they recognized that a breach in discipline had taken place, but they allowed the violators to rejoin the IRA. He wanted vindication and had not received it. The dissidents criticized the statement from the other direction. They wanted explicit support for their actions. From their perspective, there should have been more escape attempts and the Curragh leadership had been too conservative. Neither side was satisfied, and Mac Curtáin and Magan continued to criticize Charlie Murphy, seeking his dismissal. Murphy, who was tired of the whole thing, asked for a court of inquiry. The court found against him and he resigned from the IRA. But the controversy still had not ended. Magan and Mac Curtáin believed that their reputations had been tarnished and looked to the upcoming IRA convention as an opportunity to clear their names.

The convention was held at the end of May 1959. Paddy McLogan, who had been released from the Curragh prior to the escape, was less involved in the dispute than Magan and Mac Curtáin and was elected the convention chairman. The agenda included resolutions condemning the escapees and resolutions congratulating them. When the first Curragh resolution came up for discussion, a counterresolution was offered from the floor: "That this Convention refuse to discuss the Curragh Camp and concern itself with the future of the Army and the Campaign of Resistance." Tony Magan argued against the motion and lost. He refused to let go. After losing the vote, Magan asked that he, on behalf of the 1956 Army Council, be allowed to make the report that each outgoing Army Council presents to the delegates. Magan was granted one hour. It was a security measure; the longer a large number of Republicans are gathered, for whatever reason, the greater the likelihood that they will be discovered by the police. Magan agreed and then ignored the limit. After about two hours, with some delegates getting very angry and the possibility of a split becoming real, Paddy McLogan, as chair of the convention, finally pushed Magan into concluding.

In its final act the convention elected a new twelve-member Army Executive. Magan, Mac Curtáin, and McLogan were nominated, but Magan and Mac Curtáin asked that their names be withdrawn. The request was rejected. Each stated that he would resign if he was elected. Each was elected. At the first meeting of the new Executive Council, each resigned. They were replaced, and then a new seven-member Army Council was elected that chose Seán Cronin as its chief of staff—a decision Ó Brádaigh endorsed wholeheartedly. Cronin was ten years older, had more experience, was exceptionally able, and Ó Brádaigh had great respect for him—he considers Cronin an incredibly just person and one of the people who has had the most influence on him. Ó Brádaigh was also elected to the Army Council and became Cronin's adjutant general. Cathal Goulding, who had returned to Ireland after six years in English prisons, was elected to the council and became quartermaster general. Others on the council included John Joe McGirl and J. B. O'Hagan.

With the clandestine activities of the IRA finally in order, Ó Brádaigh took a more public role. At a Sinn Féin rally in Mullingar, on Sunday, June 7th, he made his first public appearance in two years. He remembers the event because it was his first in-person address to his constituents and because it was the seventeenth anniversary of his father's untimely death. He was met on the outskirts of the town by the local brass and reed band and was escorted by a fleet of cars. As reported in the *Roscommon Champion,* he challenged Fianna Fáil on internment, "The men who came into power simply did this and they would continue to do it until the people said 'No.'" He spoke in Longford that evening. A week later, he made his first public appearance in Roscommon at another Sinn Féin rally. His remarks reflected his commitment to the campaign: "I undertook to sit only in an All-Ireland Republican Parliament, and I do not believe that the battle for the freedom of this country can be fought in Leinster House, Stormont, or any other assembly set up here by English Act of Parliament. I believe this battle must be fought and won elsewhere." The Curragh Camp was closed, but the threat of arrest remained. Predicting what was to come, he stated, "It is highly probable that I shall be sent back to jail."

These public appearances served as a buildup to the most significant event on the Republican calendar, the annual commemoration of Wolfe Tone's birth, on June 20th, 1763. The commemoration is held at Tone's tomb at the family's plot in the cemetery at Bodenstown in County Kildare, on or about the third Sunday in June. In 1959, it was held on Sunday, June 21st. Typically, the event draws people from all over Ireland and the diaspora in England, the United States, and sometimes Australia. The event serves as a direct link between the United Irishmen of the 1790s and contemporary Irish Republicans of many persuasions. In 1959, Fianna Fáil and Sinn Féin held commemorations at the tomb.

The commemoration generally begins with a parade from the nearby village of Sallins. In 1959, it was organized by Cathal Goulding, who served as chief marshal. Included in the parade were uniformed members of Cumann na mBan and the Republican youth groups Na Fianna Éireann and Cumann na gCailíní. Tomás Mac Giolla presided at the graveside. Broadly defined, the leadership of the Republican Movement is the Army Council of the IRA and the Ard Chomhairle of Sinn Féin. Each year, the leadership picks a prominent person to deliver the keynote address at Bodenstown. In 1959, it was Ruairí Ó Brádaigh.

The campaign had lost momentum and wrangling over the Curragh had taken its toll. The situation required a speech looking to the future. He delivered, beginning with, "We are assembled at this sacred place to do honour to the man whose remains rest here for over 160 years—Theobald Wolfe Tone." Tone, "the greatest Irishman who ever lived," had "defined

Irish Nationhood" and had "outlined the basis on which would be built a free and upright Irish Nation." Tone, who had pledged "'never to desist in his efforts' to secure the freedom of Ireland," had "laid the groundwork of the great National Uprising of 1798." Thus, "His last mortal remains are laid here, and to this spot succeeding generations have come to do him honour and to derive inspiration to complete his unfinished work." Since Tone's time, the Republican Movement had striven in every generation to follow his programme, and "the present generation, to their everlasting credit, has not been an exception. . . . They will fight on till the goal is achieved." He concluded with a quotation from Patrick Pearse, the 1916 rebel, "O my brothers, were it not an unspeakable privilege, if, to our generation, it should be granted to accomplish that which Tone's generation, so much worthier than ours, failed to accomplish?"

7

Marriage and Ending the Border Campaign

JUNE 1959–FEBRUARY 1962

AFTER THE COMMEMORATION at Bodenstown, the IRA went back to the campaign and Sinn Féin started working on the upcoming Westminster election, which was scheduled for October. The 1955 Westminster election had given the movement a tremendous lift, but by 1959 the situation had changed markedly. During an IRA military campaign, harassment increases and electioneering is especially difficult; the ban on Sinn Féin that the northern government imposed in December 1956 made campaigning all but impossible. Candidates could run only as generic "Republicans," for example. In the fall of 1959, according to *The United Irishman,* Republican organizers were "dragged into police stations and beaten up." When they tried to canvass an area they were stopped by the police, searched, let go, and then stopped and searched again and so on, every several hundred yards.

Sinn Féin's best chances were in Fermanagh–South Tyrone and Mid-Ulster, where Phil Clarke and Tom Mitchell won in 1955 and where there were still Nationalist majorities. Mitchell, who was still in Crumlin Road Prison, was again nominated for Mid-Ulster. Another prisoner, Henry Martin, was nominated for Fermanagh–South Tyrone. The highs of 1955 were not repeated; Sinn Féin's vote fell from 152,000 to 64,000 and Unionists were elected in each constituency. The Nationalist Party, which did not put forward candidates, blamed Sinn Féin's "disastrous intervention" for the Unionist victories. Sinn Féin blamed it on "intimidation and the operation of the North's Special Powers Act." Unionists described Sinn Féin's decreased vote "as a rejection of violence by the northern minority." The election was a harbinger of things to come for the Republican Movement.

In contrast to the disappointing election results, Ó Brádaigh's personal life was going well. While on the run, he had continued to call on Patsy O'Connor. After the Curragh was closed, he saw her more frequently, and they were wed on October 3, 1959, in the Church of the Sacred Heart in Roscommon. Ruairí's best man was his brother Seán. Patsy's first cousin, Mairéad O'Connor, was bridesmaid. The bride and groom's families attended, as did a number of people from the Republican Movement, including Dáithí O'Connell. While on the run earlier in the year, Ó Brádaigh and O'Connell had arrived unannounced at the home of Ruairí's Uncle Eugene and Aunt Margaret in Dublin, where O'Connell met Deirdre Caffrey; their first date was the Ó Brádaigh-O'Connor wedding.

Patsy knew what she was getting into. Even though he had tried to conceal his activities, by 1959 everyone in Ireland knew that Ruairí Ó Brádaigh was a prominent member of the IRA. In fact, Ruairí's involvement did make Patsy nervous. But she agreed with his politics, they had been informally engaged since 1956, and she wanted to marry him. Unemployed as a teacher, Ruairí was essentially working full-time, at no pay, for the Republican Movement. Because there was no end in sight to the campaign, they agreed that instead of getting their own place she would continue to live in a flat she shared with other women; their life together took a back seat to his politics. The biggest issue they faced involved not Ruairí's activism but the treatment of married women under Irish law. When Patsy married, she forfeited the right to work full-time as a teacher. She applied for a "temporary" full-time position and was allowed to continue teaching while the Roscommon Vocational Educational Committee and the minister for education considered her request. After a brief honeymoon in West Cork and Kerry, Patsy returned to her flat and work. Ruairí returned to the IRA and continued to move from place to place. He was not on the run, but the police knew who he was and the threat of arrest was real.

The IRA was strongest in the border areas, and most of its activities were there. To expand the campaign, they tried to reorganize other areas, including the area around Lough Neagh in County Tyrone. On the night of November 10th, Dáithí O'Connell, J. B. O'Hagan, and a local Republican, Mark Devlin, were walking along a road outside Ardboe when they passed a parked laundry van. Later, the van drove by and parked on a side road, and RUC men and B Specials set up an ambush. As O'Hagan, O'Connell, and Devlin walked by, the police shouted at them to stop. O'Hagan and Devlin did, putting up their hands. O'Connell took off running and in a hail of bullets was shot six times, twice in the lower chest and superficially in four other places. He kept running through the rough countryside and finally arrived at a farmhouse, knocked on the door, and identified himself as "the police." The lady of the house let him in and the RUC found him, exhausted, bloody, and seated by the fire. He lost his spleen, suffered damage to a kidney, and eventually joined O'Hagan and Devlin in Crumlin Road Prison. Among his regular visitors were his mother and Deirdre Caffrey. The loss of O'Hagan and O'Connell hurt the IRA. The shooting marks the end of the IRA's ability to operate effectively away from the border.

Ó Brádaigh met Patsy in Roscommon on the weekend of November 20–22. On the 22nd, they paid their respects to the headmaster of their school, who had passed away. After the service they were walking out of the church grounds and past the local Garda barracks when a group of police officers approached Ruairí. A detective sergeant told him that he suspected Ó Brádaigh was "in possession of information" and arrested him under Section 30 of the Offenses Against the State Act. As they entered the police station, Ruairí noticed that Patsy, who was pregnant, looked pale. He was asked twenty-four standard questions, including questions on his movements since the wedding. He remained silent and was held overnight. Patsy returned to her flat.

The next evening, with Ó Brádaigh in the Roscommon Garda station, the Roscommon Vocational Education Committee met and considered Patsy's request for a temporary full-time job. The chief executive officer, Mr. Ó Meiscill, informed the committee that the minister for education had rejected her request but had sanctioned her for a part-time position. The committee agreed to hire her. Ó Meiscill also informed the committee that Ruairí's salary was budgeted for the upcoming school year, indicating that his job was being held for him. Although he was being held in Roscommon Garda Station, the committee made public its support for Ó Brádaigh. Members of the committee represented a variety of political approaches, including Fianna Fáil, Fine Gael, and independents. The local Protestant minister was a member of the committee. Irrespective of their own politics, and the Ó Brádaighs' politics, committee members respected Ruairí and Patsy as people and as educators.

On Friday, November 27th, Ó Brádaigh was driven from Mountjoy to Ballymahon, Longford, where he again faced charges under the Offenses Against the State Act (for failing to answer questions). A large crowd, carrying signs that read, "Release Our T.D." and "Stop This Collaboration with England," stood outside the courthouse. Inside, Ó Brádaigh refused to recognize the court but reserved the right to cross-examine witnesses and make a statement. A detective sergeant testified that he had arrested Ó Brádaigh "under orders." Ó Brádaigh used this to charge that Fianna Fáil was using the Offenses Against the State Act to "to silence me as a public representative." He asked rhetorically if he had been stopped and questioned only because the authorities knew he would refuse to answer and therefore be subject to imprisonment. The response: he was found guilty and sentenced to six months in Mountjoy.

In Mountjoy, he experienced the low point of this period of his life. In early December, a letter arrived from his mother with the news that Patsy had suffered a miscarriage. The news hit him hard; in jail, he could not comfort his wife. He had been an idealistic newlywed filled with dreams about his future family. Distressed, he cried in his cell. In and of itself, prison was not a problem. Given the times, Ó Brádaigh had expected rearrest and knew how to cope with prison life. But being unable to help Patsy was hard. It was the only thing in the course of his early career as a Republican that truly upset him. A high point of his stay was Seán Mac Eoin's statement that while he disagreed with Ó Brádaigh's politics, his credentials as a TD representing a particular viewpoint could not be questioned. Mac Eoin added that while Ó Brádaigh had appeared publicly in several places, he had been arrested at a private funeral. Another positive was that when he was released, on May 26th, 1960, he was met by his Aunt Margaret rather than a tap on the shoulder and internment. On the way to Longford they were met by crowds in Ballinalack, Rathowen, and Mostrim and then escorted into Longford town by a band and fleet of cars for an enthusiastic public meeting.

The stay in Mountjoy had not deterred him. On Sunday, May 29th, following a Longford-Dublin football match, Ó Brádaigh addressed more than 2,000 people attending a Sinn Féin rally in Mullingar. When he was heckled by a plainclothes police officer, who kept shouting "Up Dev [de Valera]" and "Up Mac Eoin," the chairman of the rally informed the crowd of the heckler's occupation; the officer moved out of the crowd. Ó Brádaigh thanked those present for their support and thanked the Longford District Urban Council and the Granard Town commissioners, who had publicly protested against his arrest and imprisonment. Most important, he commented on a resolution that had been passed by Roscommon County Council while he was in Mountjoy. As an amendment to a motion "deploring the continued operation of the Offenses Against the State Act," the resolution called for the four Sinn Féin TDs to take their seats in Leinster House. It was rejected by Sinn Féin at the time. Now out of prison, Ó Brádaigh also rejected the resolution. In his comments, he explained why he opposed participation in Leinster House and

Sinn Féin rally in Longford, probably the May 1960 rally welcoming Ó Brádaigh home after his release from Mountjoy Prison. Ó Brádaigh family collection.

said that he would continue to uphold the policy that the electorate of Longford-Westmeath had endorsed: "I will sit only in an all-Ireland Parliament."

Ruairí Ó Brádaigh is a remarkably consistent person. The position he took that day on participation in Leinster House is the position he holds today. To him, participation in Leinster House was (and is) illogical at its most fundamental level. He told the crowd, "Sinn Féin aims at abolishing both the Leinster House and Stormont Parliaments, and substituting for them an All-Ireland Republican Parliament. How could Sinn Féin contribute towards the abolition of the 26-County Parliament by sitting in it and actually consolidating it?" In electing him, his constituents had endorsed his abstentionism. Even though he was a TD, he had been accosted on the street, arrested, and sent to jail simply because he refused to compromise his principles and recognize the authority of the 26-county state. The Roscommon resolution was asking the Sinn Féin TDs to "[a]bandon your principles and programme and do as we do; surrender, then you may be immune from arrest and imprisonment." Ó Brádaigh wanted no part of this kind of quid pro quo: "I refuse to become a party politician of the 26–County brand, and will continue to uphold the policy which the electorate of Longford-Westmeath have endorsed. I will sit only in an All-Ireland Parliament and will continue to strive to make such an institution a living reality." For Ó Brádaigh, participation in Leinster House would only delay the Republic of Wolfe Tone. His proof lay in the actions of Leinster House politicians, who seemed more interested in maintaining the status quo than in ending partition or helping the people of Ireland. "Your elected representative has gone to jail and he has returned. What good has his imprisonment done to this country or the people of this country?" he asked. "Has one person been placed in employment as a result; has one family been stopped from closing its house—if it had one—and emigrating to England or America? No good has been done to anyone, but the British Government has been appeased and the Border has been guaranteed. "

When he was arrested, Ó Brádaigh was replaced as adjutant general. An IRA convention had been organized for late spring, and he was released from Mountjoy in time to attend the general headquarters unit convention, which was held about ten days before the general convention. At the unit convention, he was selected as a delegate to the general convention. The general convention was held in June in County Meath and attracted more than 100 delegates. At the start, Ó Brádaigh was elected to chair the convention. As it had been for McLogan the year before, it was not an easy job. In 1959, the Curragh issue had dominated the convention. In 1960, the big issue was whether or not to continue the campaign. The Cork unit put forth a motion to end the campaign; Frank Skuse argued "that the campaign stood no chance of success, that its continuation would only further weaken the movement and prevent the early release of prisoners in English jails, that it was time to call a halt, hold on to any gains and conserve the remaining resources of the movement." Seán Cronin, who had spent the year reorganizing the IRA, strongly opposed the motion. Cronin believed the army was in a position to repeat the successes of December 1956 and early 1957. Ó Brádaigh also opposed the motion, but as he saw it, his job was to run the convention, not to publicly support one or another argument—to "put the facts on the table and let's make an assessment of it." Cronin responded to Skuse's argument by calling it "pure vituperation" and called for continuing support for the campaign. Tony Magan then criticized the campaign, sarcastically commenting that it was never meant to be a series of incidents along the border. Cronin, upset, jumped up to respond, only to have Ó Brádaigh allow Magan to finish his point. As far as Ó Brádaigh was concerned, everyone would receive a fair hearing or they could get a new convention chairman.

In the end, the motion received two votes—from Skuse and Derry City—and failed.

Near the end of the convention there were two resolutions that Ó Brádaigh strongly opposed. The first would allow the IRA to attack British warships when they came into 26-county ports. The second would allow the IRA to attack British forces when they were found in the Twenty-Six Counties. It was understood that if British soldiers pursued the IRA across the border, IRA members could defend themselves. The second resolution would allow the IRA to ambush British forces along concession roads, which run from the Twenty-Six Counties into the Six Counties and back out to the Twenty-Six Counties and so on. British forces were using them, and some people in the IRA wanted to stage ambushes in the 26-county sections of the roads. Ó Brádaigh was opposed because he feared this would draw the IRA into open conflict with the southern security forces and the Dublin government. Public opinion would support the government, which would come down hard on the movement. It is an unusual army that takes votes on its tactics, but the IRA is a voluntary organization. Both resolutions were passed.

Skuse was elected to the IRA Executive Council and Seán Cronin and Ruairí Ó Brádaigh were unanimously elected by the Executive to membership on the Army Council. The council then re-elected Cronin as chief of staff. Ó Brádaigh disagreed enough with the two resolutions that he declined membership on the council and did not take a headquarters staff position. He did remain in the army. However, two days after the convention, Cronin was spotted by police, refused to answer questions, and ended up back in Mountjoy. The Army Executive approached Ó Brádaigh and asked him to be chief of staff. He was interested, but he was concerned about the two resolutions. Ruairí Ó Brádaigh is a detail person; he does not play loose with facts and he does not ignore procedures. A majority of the convention delegates had voted for the two resolutions. If he was to be chief of staff, he wanted an extraordinary IRA convention that would reverse them. The Executive felt that his request was impractical and suggested that he pretend they had never been passed. He turned them down. There is a pragmatic side to his approach to detail. He knew that at some point his authority might be challenged on either resolution. If a unit proposed an ambush and cited the resolutions, he would be caught in the middle and it could result in a dispute like the one caused by the Curragh mass escape. Ultimately, a compromise was reached. Security issues precluded another general convention, but there would be four provincial conventions (Leinster, Munster, Connacht, and Ulster) for the general convention delegates. At the provincial conventions, Ó Brádaigh's position would be explained and delegates would be asked to agree to suspend the resolutions. The delegates accepted the suspension and Ó Brádaigh went ahead as chief of staff. Although he was not a member of the Army Council, the IRA Constitution allows the chief of staff (and the adjutant general and quartermaster) to participate in meetings but without the right to vote. He attended council meetings and had an important voice in their deliberations.

Cronin, a professional journalist, was editor of *The United Irishman* prior to his arrest in October 1958. The paper, a monthly, had a circulation of 120,000 copies. Seán Ó Brádaigh had replaced him as editor in 1958. In 1960, Ruairí Ó Brádaigh replaced him as editor. Like Cronin, he carefully organized his movements and his time. The Offenses Against the State Act precluded easy entry and exit from the paper's office in Dublin. Cronin had set up couriers who picked up information at the office and delivered it to a drop house or returned it from the drop house to the office. Ó Brádaigh adopted his system. *The United Irishman,* a monthly, was put together during two periods of intense activity that required Ó Brádaigh's presence in Dublin or nearby twice a month. Early in the month, he and his assistants would set a framework for the next edition; later in the month they would put it together. A group of regular contributors were assigned topics. In the office, the assistants went through the daily papers, such as the *Irish Press,* the *Irish Times,* and the *Belfast Telegraph,* and clipped relevant articles. Their other primary source of information was Irish radio; Irish television began broadcasting on New Year's Eve 1961.

Even before Ó Brádaigh resumed the role chief of staff and became editor of *The United Irishman,* the movement was facing the 26-county local elections that were scheduled for June 1960. This election, in retrospect, was especially important because it signaled the beginning of a broader politics for Sinn Féin. In 1955, seven Sinn Féiners were elected to county councils; unlike the party's Leinster House candidates, these candidates took their seats. The party's philosophy was that participation in local government made Republicans more aware of everyday political issues facing the Irish people. This action was complemented by discussions that addressed issues of social and economic justice in the Curragh and in Crumlin Road Prison, Belfast. The discussions were part of a more general awareness that there were serious problems with the Irish economy. Ó Brádaigh's comments at the rally in Roscommon in May, which mentioned problems with employment, emigration, and housing, were indicative of this development. On a personal level, he was very aware of economic hardship and poverty. In his early years, when his father was a councilor, people would call at the house, seeking help. He attended a rural primary school (Melview), where he mixed with the children of small farmers and agricultural laborers. In the movement and while canvassing for Sinn Féin, he met people from all walks of life. Sinn Féin's involvement in local politics, the discussions in the Curragh, and personal interest in the welfare of people raised his awareness of social and economic issues.

Over the centuries, Republicans have never viewed physical force as the only method of bringing about the Republic. The prominence of physical force has waxed and waned over time. The 1916 Easter Rising was almost exclusively a military affair. In 1919–1922, the movement combined physical force with more traditional political agitation, which led to a partial Republic. In the 1930s, socialists such as Peadar O'Donnell, George Gilmore, and Frank Ryan called for radical social and economic reform; Ryan went to Spain as part of the International Brigade. In this period of rabid anticommunism, linking socialism with Republicanism led to disagreements, splits, and factions. The people who rebuilt the movement after the 1940s—Magan, Mac Curtáin, McLogan, Larry Grogan, and others—were incredibly wary of involvement in political agitation and did not want to be smeared with any association with communism. By the late 1950s, their influence was on the wane and events had demonstrated that the movement needed a broader focus. Sinn Féin's success in 1955 and 1957 contributed to a push for a broader agenda. This broadening was reflected in Sinn Féin's manifesto for the southern local elections in 1960. It began:

> The objectives of Sinn Féin are: to break the connection with England; to end the entire British Imperial system in Ireland; to end poverty and insecurity; to abolish the existing partition institutions of Government in Ireland, and to replace them by a National Government having complete and effective jurisdiction over the entire territory of the Nation.

A central issue was social welfare: "The need for the 'dole,' home assistance, free milk schemes, children's allowances, health services administered through dispensaries, etc., is mostly due to unemployment and low wages." The party called for a comprehensive scheme of national health insurance. Sinn Féin did relatively well with this program in the southern local elections in 1960; sixteen people were elected to ten different county councils and fourteen people were elected to town councils. The results followed a pattern that still holds: Sinn Féin polled well along the border and in the west. Eight candidates were elected in five border counties: Cavan, Donegal, Leitrim, Monaghan, and Sligo. John Joe McGirl was elected to the Leitrim County Council, and Seamus McElwain was elected to the Monaghan County Council. In the west, Sinn Féin elected candidates in Clare, Cork, Galway, and Kerry. Paddy Ruane was returned to the Galway County Council.

In spite of, or perhaps because of, their modest but important electoral success, Irish police harassed Republicans on a continuous basis. Soon after Ó Brádaigh was released from Mountjoy, May Brady Twohig's home was raided. Ó Brádaigh had been a TD for more than four years and was not wanted for any crime, yet he had to watch his movements carefully. On the evening of December 8th, on a visit to prominent Republican Paddy Fitzgerald in Midleton in County Cork, he was traveling in a car with his adjutant general, Martin Shannon of Dublin. Shannon stopped at a gate, Ó Brádaigh got out to open it, and there was a shout of "Halt!" Police officers hiding in ditches on both sides of the road stood up and grabbed him and Shannon. He was pulled over to the grass margin of the road and searched from head to toe; his coat was torn in the process. Everything in his pockets—fountain pen, rosary, and comb—was removed. Personal letters fell into the mud on the roadside. His shoes were removed and searched. Shannon received the same treatment. As they searched, the police officers, who had not identified themselves, shouted questions. They were handcuffed together, frog-marched to their car, and informed that they were being detained for twenty-four hours. Although they were continually questioned, they refused to answer. At about 11:30 that night, they were placed in cold separate cells in the Bridewell in Cork City. The next afternoon, after refusing to answer more questions, they were informed that they could go free and that their car awaited them at Midleton. They got a ride to Midleton and then drove back to Dublin. When they reached Shannon's house, in the Finglas area of Dublin, they learned it had been raided by the Special Branch.

There was not much Ó Brádaigh or any other Republican in a similar situation could do about harassment like this. It was all legal. In fact, they were aware that they could have been charged and convicted for refusing to answer questions. One night in jail was getting off easy. Ó Brádaigh did take advantage of his position as a TD and released a statement that was picked up by the *Longford Leader* and the *Westmeath Examiner*. It ends with, "I am anxious that the people of Longford/Westmeath who elected me to an All-Ireland Parliament four years ago should know of the treatment meted out last week to their elected representative and his companion by the 26-County police. There was no explanation offered and no apology."

The campaign, as Tony Magan complained, had been reduced to a series of incidents against the RUC. In the south, the state harassed Republicans. In the north, where the IRA was attacking them, the RUC response was more harsh. In August 1958, the RUC crossed the border with County Cavan and ambushed a Sinn Féin organizer, James Crossan. It is believed that they were going to seize him and take him across the border for arrest. Crossan was found dead on the Cavan side of the border. No one was ever prosecuted for his death. In December 1960 or January 1961, an IRA unit in Monaghan reported to the Army Council that a member of the RUC was regularly crossing the border, either dressed in civilian clothes or with a civilian coat over his uniform, his cap left behind. Local informants reported that he was involved with a 15-year-old girl who lived in County Monaghan. The constable, Norman Anderson, was also known to drive around the area in an automobile. He had been crossing the border for six months and he was being watched by the IRA. He was either very foolish or he was spying; given that it was the hottest area along the border, the local IRA suspected that he was spying and asked the Army Council for permission to assassinate him. As chief of staff, Ó Brádaigh was one of those who ruled on the request. Anderson was not a "target of opportunity"—the Army Council had time to weigh the facts and make an informed decision. But from the perspective of members of the council, the evidence strongly supported the assertion that Anderson was engaged in espionage. They sanctioned his killing. On January 27th, 1961, after leaving his girlfriend's house, he was shot dead on the County Fermanagh side of the border. The *Belfast Newsletter* later referred to the attack as one of the "savage crimes" of the campaign, noting that Anderson's coat had fifteen bullet holes. The killing was condemned by political leaders on both sides of the border.

Subsequent events supported the interpretation of Ó Brádaigh and the IRA that Anderson had been engaged in espionage. Immediately after the assassination, RUC personnel vanished from the border areas. An RUC member who was visiting a shop in Clones at the time of the assassination was phoned from the RUC's Newtownbutler Barracks and told to stay there until they picked him up. Phones in the area were not on a dial system and the call was intercepted by an IRA sympathizer. The attack on Anderson was explained in a leaflet distributed the following week with the title "The Penalty Is Death." With reason, and to the IRA's benefit, RUC personnel were more careful after Anderson's death. Anderson's killing marked the beginning of a series of attacks that included mining bridges, cutting up roads, and blowing up customs houses. It was a short-lived resurgence in the campaign.

In August 1961, Seán Lemass, as Taoiseach, announced a general election to be held in early October. With four TDs up for re-election, it was a chance for the movement to complement the military campaign with electoral success. Lemass also announced that the state would apply for membership in the Common Market, the precursor of the European Union. In discussing the application, Irish leaders made it clear that they would follow through on the application only if the British followed through on their application; they were following the British lead. Most people in Ireland supported the application to join the Common Market. It was evident to virtually everyone that something had to be done to the Irish economy; as reported in *The United Irishman,* over 1,000 people a week were emigrating. Many people also believed that with Ireland and the United Kingdom in the Market the border with Northern Ireland would no longer be necessary, that membership in the Common Market would help cause the border to wither away. In the face of widespread support for joining the Market, Sinn Féin was strident in its opposition. The party position, which Ó Brádaigh supported, was that the application was driven by British politicians and the needs of the British economy rather than by Irish politicians who, they believed, should focus on creating an Irish economy that was less dependent on the British economy. Further, they believed that membership in the Common Market would not cause the border to wither away but in fact might further enmesh the border in a political bureaucracy that would make it more difficult to reunite the Republic of Ireland/Twenty-Six Counties with Northern Ireland. Finally, membership in the Common Market posed a potential threat to Irish culture. Ó Brádaigh addressed the issue in August 1961 at an *aeraíocht* at Loch Bán on the Meath-Westmeath border.

An *aeraíocht* is a cultural festival; Seán Mac Eoin had used one as a cover for an IRA Brigade Council meeting the day Matt Brady was shot in 1919. At Loch Bán, the program included a champion ballad singer, a pipe band, troupes of Irish dancers in traditional costume, and traditional Irish singers. There was also a children's choir—composed entirely of native Irish-speakers—from Athboy in the County Meath Gaeltacht. In his first public address in nearly twelve months, Ó Brádaigh commented on the "three car-loads of detectives" in the area and then focused on the importance of Irish culture. He praised the "fine turn-out to support our native language, music, dancing and singing." It was a tribute to the crowd's "sincerity and earnestness in the cause of Irish-Ireland." He urged the crowd to "to cling even more tenaciously to our cultural heritage. The forces of materialism and commercialism are stronger than ever today." And he addressed the potential impact if Ireland joined the Common Market: "Not alone is the political and economic objective our fathers fought for being lost sight of in the move to link a divided, dependent and underdeveloped Ireland with the European Common Market countries. Our Gaelic civilisation—that is, what remains of it—may be completely swamped."

The economic situation, the application to the Common Market, and the loss of support for the IRA's campaign all worked against Sinn Féin. In the spring of 1957, the campaign was fresh and the deaths of O'Hanlon and South had generated sympathy for the cause. By 1961, much of the support had faded away. None of Sinn Féin's candidates was elected and the first-preference vote fell from more than 65,640 in 1957 to 36,393. In contrast, Fianna Fáil received 512,000 first-preference votes; Fine Gael received 374,000, and Labour 136,000. Fianna Fáil formed another government with Seán Lemass as Taoiseach. Compared to the local elections the year before, the results were disappointing, and some people wondered if the problem was abstentionism—locally elected Sinn Féiners took their seats and represented the people, but Leinster House candidates did not. As for Ó Brádaigh, unlike 1957, he received only 2,598 first-preference votes. In his concession speech, he thanked "that gallant band of election workers in both counties who did not spare themselves in their efforts for the All-Ireland Republic." Taking advantage of the opportunity, he also made political points. He noted that "this is my first time to speak here at the conclusion of a count. On the last occasion I was in jail under a Coercion Act. When I was elected here in 1957 one of the Fianna Fáil T.D.s returned said that they could now form a government and they 'would rule with an iron hand.' We have felt that iron hand."

> I, the newly-elected Sinn Féin T.D., was taken from jail and thrown into the Curragh Concentration Camp. I was held there without charge or trial for well over a year until I escaped from it. Had we been successful on this occasion also, there is no guarantee that the same thing would not happen again.

He finished: "We have lost support but we have lost nothing else. We have not lost our self-respect, nor have we bartered our principles or compromised the full national demand. We have gone down fighting and, please God, we'll come back fighting."

Although the election had not gone well, it did offer a poignant moment for the Ó Brádaigh family. In the fall of 1960, Patsy had become pregnant again. She continued teaching at Roscommon Vocational Technical School until the Christmas break and then moved to her parents' house in Galway. Many parents would have been very concerned that their son-in-law, unemployed and harassed by the police, could not provide a home for their daughter and their future grandchild. Patsy's family took the situation in stride. Her father was a tailor and her mother ran a guesthouse. Patsy helped her mother, and her parents "never made me feel I was in the way." When their grandson was born on March 10th, 1961, they welcomed him into the family. He was named Maitiú, the Irish form of Matthew, after Ruairí's father. Ruairí was able to visit his wife and new son in the hospital only for a brief visit. He did manage to visit them occasionally in Galway, and they were able to visit his mother in Longford. In September 1961, in Longford during the election campaign, Ruairí, Patsy, Maitiú, and May Brady Twohig were in the town when they ran across Seán Mac Eoin, who also was a candidate. May called Mac Eoin over and introduced him to "Matt Brady." Indeed, Ó Brádaigh encountered Mac Eoin at several points during the campaign, typically at "church gate" meetings after masses in various villages and towns. Mac Eoin was always respectful and never condemned him or the movement.

The election losses affected morale in the IRA, which compounded other problems, and the army's operational capabilities fell. Money from U.S. supporters had dried up. Simple things like arranging transportation and training areas and paying bills had become difficult. The number of volunteers in the field had declined, perhaps to 50. In 1957, there had been 341 IRA incidents. In 1959, there were only 27. At the 1960 IRA convention, Seán Cronin had successfully argued that the campaign should continue, only to be arrested himself. Ó Brádaigh and the Army Council were unable to turn things around. Throughout the summer of 1961, the IRA tried to attack British soldiers in Northern Ireland, a "high yield" target. None of several planned operations came off. Instead, in November 1961, an IRA unit ambushed an armored RUC patrol, killing a constable and wounding three others. As J. Bowyer Bell notes, instead of acting as a catalyst for more action, the killing was widely perceived "as the most useless of all since the 'campaign' had obviously failed." The action only led to more repression. Charles Haughey, the son of an IRA veteran, an up-and-coming member of Fianna Fáil, and the son-in-law of

Seán Lemass, had been appointed minister for justice in the new Dublin government. The Irish government reintroduced military tribunals, in which accused IRA prisoners appeared before a three-person board of Irish Army officers instead of a judge. In the early part of the campaign, conviction for refusing to answer questions typically resulted in six months in Mountjoy. After the military tribunals were instituted, sentences were handed out in terms of years. In and of itself, repression would not stop the IRA, but it contributed to the difficulties of the time.

There were also personnel problems. Ó Brádaigh dismissed a Dublin volunteer who refused to go on active service; he remained in Sinn Féin. At the Army Council, Ó Brádaigh felt isolated. He was the only one left of those who had started the campaign in 1956. In 1961, internment was ended in the north and Paddy Doyle, who had been on the Army Council in 1956, was available. Ó Brádaigh wanted him back in the leadership. A meeting was arranged and a long conversation ensued, but Doyle was not interested. On January 18, 1962, the Army Council met and considered ending the campaign. They had to either pull off a major operation and generate some enthusiasm or quit; it made no sense to continue if all they could do was blow up bridges and customs huts. Ó Brádaigh believed that without a major operation the IRA would continue to decline, support would fragment into pockets, the organization would have no real military capacity, and it would take years to recover, assuming that recovery was possible.

Over the course of his tenure as chief of staff, the council had followed standard procedure and used a co-optation process to replace people who were arrested. In 1961, those most recently arrested were Cathal Goulding, Paddy Mulcahy, and Paddy Murphy; the addition of their replacements meant that perhaps fifteen people had served on the council while Ó Brádaigh was chief of staff. They were a mix of senior people and post-1956 recruits who, like Ó Brádaigh, were part of a new generation. Most of them were from the south and were from Republican families. The senior people at the January 18th meeting were Tom Mitchell, who had finally been released from Belfast Prison; Paddy Fox from Galway; and Redmond O'Sullivan from Kerry. The younger people were Seamus Costello from Wicklow; Denis McInerney from Clare; and one other person. Also attending the January 18th meeting were Ruairí Ó Brádaigh, chief of staff, and Martin Shannon, his adjutant general.

The situation reminded Ó Brádaigh of December 1956, when another difficult decision had been made. Tomás Mac Curtáin had been reluctant to go ahead with the campaign; his opinion had generated a careful examination of the options available. The Army Council and the Army Executive had been consulted and offered input. Ending a campaign also required a careful examination of the situation. The January 18th meeting did not end with a decision, but the council agreed to meet again two weeks later, on February 3rd. At that meeting they agreed, unanimously, to end the campaign. The Army Executive endorsed the decision and on February 5th an order was sent to IRA units telling them to put their arms in storage and to retire from the border. Ó Brádaigh was charged with drafting a formal statement for the media. It was a comprehensive statement that brought everything to a conclusion. When the draft was complete, he shared it with the other members of the council, who went through it with a "fine tooth comb." The final product was a collaborative effort and a declaration from the leadership, the Army Council, and the Executive.

The statement was released on the evening of February 26th, 1962, under the nom de guerre "J. McGarrity." It was addressed "To the People of Ireland" and stated that "Foremost among the factors motivating this course of action has been the attitude of the general public whose minds have been deliberately distracted from the supreme issue facing the Irish people—the unity and freedom of Ireland." People had been told that the border would fall if Ireland joined the Common Market. "This calculated emphasis on secondary issues by those whose political future is bound up in the status quo and who control all the mass media of propaganda is now leading towards possible commitment of the people of the 26 Counties in future wars." Included in the statement were comments on the "fantastic odds" the IRA had faced, including, "5,000 British regular troops, 5,000 territorials, 12,500 B-Specials, 3,000 R.U.C, 1,500 specially trained Commandos and sundry security guard forces totaling close on 30,000 armed men." These forces had at their disposal British armaments, "terroristic tactics," "draconian laws," the "collaborationist role of successive 26-County Governments," and a "muzzled press." Most important for the IRA and for its critics, the statement concluded with, "The Irish Resistance Movement renews its pledge of eternal hostility to the British Forces of Occupation in Ireland. It calls on the Irish people for increased support and looks forward with confidence—in co-operation with the other branches of the Republican Movement—to a period of consolidation, expansion and preparation for the final and victorious phase of the struggle for the full freedom of Ireland." An editorial in the *Belfast Newsletter* stated: "On the face of it, therefore, this is not an abandonment of the campaign, but a strategic retreat, with the intention of fighting another day."

Over a five-year period, the IRA had carried out a significant guerrilla campaign. The *New York Times* estimated that the campaign had incurred $14 million in damages to Northern Ireland's infrastructure. It was also estimated that the Belfast and Dublin governments had spent $28 million maintaining their security forces. Hundreds of Republicans had been arrested; many, like Ó Brádaigh, more than once. At the time of the ceasefire there were forty-three Republican prisoners in Crumlin Road in Belfast; forty-two prisoners in Mountjoy Jail in Dublin; and two more— Dónal Murphy and Joe Doyle, who had been held since the Arborfield raid—in England. The IRA had killed six members of the RUC and had injured thirty-two members of the British security forces. Ten Republicans had been killed: eight IRA members, one Sinn Féin member (James Crossan), and one IRA supporter, who was killed in a premature explosion.

Comments on the statement and summaries of the campaign may be found in numerous sources, including J. Bowyer Bell's *The Secret Army,* Tim Pat Coogan's *The IRA,* Seán Cronin's *Irish Nationalism: A History of Its Roots and Ideology,* and M. L. R. Smith's *Fighting for Ireland?* In general, these authors criticize the statement terminating the campaign, misinterpreting the comments about the "attitude of the general public" to mean that the IRA was blaming northern Nationalists for not supporting the campaign. In fact, the "distracted" public was a reference to Ireland's application to the Common Market and the belief of some that it would create a shortcut to ending British rule in Ireland. That is why the statement referred to the Twenty-Six Counties being committed in future wars.

The summaries point to a number of errors by the IRA that hindered the campaign. When they created the flying columns, the leadership brought together the best people, but the cohesion of people who had trained as a unit was lost. More important, the leadership did not anticipate and prepare for internment in the south. Over one weekend, in July 1957, most of the IRA's and Sinn Féin's leadership was picked up and put away for an indefinite period of time. The authors agree that the leadership's focus on physical force led to this lack of foresight. They were motivated by nationalism which, in Cronin's words, "may well be admired but is never going to attract mass support." Internment in the north and the declaration of Sinn Féin as an illegal organization restricted political development there; internment in the south added to these restrictions. The movement was left with no room to maneuver, despite the election results of 1957. M. L. R. Smith's assessment is the most critical: "The elitist attachment to violence, combined with doctrinal inflexibility, excluded all potential for either the consideration of alternative non-military options or the modification of political goals to accommodate actual military capabilities. As such, republican strategic thought was confined largely to a few simplistic precepts. The ideology defined the political object—a united independent republic. It defined the enemy—Britain. And it defined the means to challenge the enemy in order to attain the object—military action. Yet, as five and a half years of wasted effort testified, it also defined the most likely outcome—isolation and defeat."

The isolation of Republicans dated in part from the 1600s and the Plantation of Ulster. As IRA historian J. Bowyer Bell notes, "[T]wo-thirds of the population [in the North] were Unionists, dedicated and determined enemies of Irish republicanism." The 1956 leadership never adequately confronted this. They were steeped in the success of the IRA in the 1919–1922 era and wanted to recreate a mass nationalist movement. To them, the Unionist majority was a false one, created by a gerrymander that was opposed by the majority of the Irish people. The IRA made no sectarian attacks against the Protestant population in Northern Ireland during the Border Campaign, but it also made little attempt to attract Protestants to the Republican cause. A piece written by Seán Cronin that was published in *The United Irishman,* titled "Appeal to Unionists," was a notable exception.

Seán Stephenson, who was arrested with Cathal Goulding and Manus Canning at Felstead, England, in 1953, was released from prison in 1959. In prison, he had learned Irish and adopted the Irish form of his name, Seán Mac Stiofáin. His wife, Máire, was from north County Cork. They moved to Cork City, and in 1961 Mac Stiofáin became IRA commanding officer in Cork. Ó Brádaigh remembers discussing the state of the movement with Mac Stiofáin around the time the campaign ended. Mac Stiofáin commented that even though things did not look good, Sinn Féin had polled 64,000 votes in the 1959 Westminster election and more than 36,000 in the 1961 Leinster House election. From his perspective, the Republican Movement still had more than 100,000 supporters. Michael Farrell, in *Northern Ireland: The Orange State,* would later comment with respect to the North that "it was a sizable hard core of intransigents for any state to have. And the polices which had produced the IRA campaign hadn't changed." While M. L. R. Smith views the 1950s Border Campaign as "wasted effort," people like Ó Brádaigh and Mac Stiofáin believed that they had once again validated Ireland's claim to full independence. They looked forward to the next phase of the struggle. The IRA was going into hiatus, but it was not dead.

8

Political and Personal Developments in the 1960s

MARCH 1962–1965

AFTER THE CAMPAIGN ended, the main issue that threatened the movement was dissension in the ranks. Through 1961, the relationship between the Army Council and the Sinn Féin Ard Chomhairle had deteriorated; Tony Magan and Paddy McLogan refused to let the Curragh issue die. The Ard Chomhairle repeatedly asked that the IRA issue a public statement supporting the Curragh leadership. The Army Council consistently refused to do so.

The way the Army Council ended the campaign exacerbated the problem. It was not publicly known that the Sinn Féin leadership had not been consulted, and McLogan and Magan believed that they were being blamed for the failure of the campaign. In mid-March, the Army Council received a request that they state publicly that no member of the Sinn Féin Ard Chomhairle had any responsibility in the decision to end the campaign. The Army Council refused, and noted that such a statement would suggest that there was a split between the IRA and Sinn Féin. The Ard Chomhairle then requested that Sinn Féin be allowed to issue its own statement. The Army Council rejected that request, too, reminding the Ard Chomhairle that they had not been consulted on the decision to start the campaign, adding that the only statement Sinn Féin could issue was one supporting the decision to stop the campaign. Paddy McLogan then resigned as Sinn Féin's president and quit the Ard Chomhairle, but he remained a member of Sinn Féin. On April 30th, he resigned from the IRA.

In an attempt to reconcile their differences, representatives from the Ard Chomhairle and representatives from the Army Council, including Ruairí Ó Brádaigh as chief of staff, met on May 13th, 1962. The meeting lasted eight hours, from 1 to 9 PM. By any standard it must have been difficult, especially since nothing was resolved. The Army Council representatives made clear three points: the Army Council was the government of the Republic and the supreme authority in the Republican Movement; Sinn Féin is an autonomous and independent organization, but if it was to remain a part of the Republican Movement then Sinn Féin policy had to conform to IRA policy; and, if Sinn Féin issued a statement about the end of the campaign, the statement had to support the Army Council's decision. Presented with these points, Tony Magan asked what would happen if Sinn Féin went ahead and published its own statement. Given that Magan was chief of staff when the IRA went into partnership with Sinn Féin in the 1940s, he must have known the answer before asking the question. He was told that "it would be a major deviation from accepted procedure and a departure from Republican policy which would amount to a split in the movement, resulting in taking Sinn Féin outside the movement, as it would be directly opposed to Army policy." Magan ignored the warning.

At an Ard Chomhairle meeting on May 26th, a member proposed that Sinn Féin issue a statement disclaiming responsibility for ending the campaign. Tony Magan seconded it. The motion failed. Those who voted for the resolution resigned from the Ard Chomhairle but remained in Sinn Féin. Acting officers and Ard Chomhairle members were installed to replace those who had resigned. Seán Ó Brádaigh, who had left his teaching job and was working in human resources for Córas Iompair Éireann (the Irish Transport Network), became the acting secretary of Sinn Féin. The new Ard Chomhairle then discovered that someone from the old group had taken a copy of the names and addresses of the secretaries of Sinn Féin *cumainn* throughout Ireland and used the information to circulate a memo supporting those who had resigned from the Ard Chomhairle. A Sinn Féin court of inquiry was established, but those who issued the circular refused to appear. The group, which included Tony Magan and Paddy McLogan, was expelled from Sinn Féin.

Personally, Ruairí Ó Brádaigh regretted the losses, especially McLogan and Magan. He had worked closely with each; each had strongly influenced his Republican outlook. They had been model Republicans who had given outstanding service to the cause and had kept the IRA together through the difficult period of the late 1940s. Magan's devotion to the movement was beyond question. His politics guided his personal choices. His family had owned a farm in County Meath, the richest farming area in Ireland. He could have lived out a comfortable life on the farm. Instead, he sold the farm and donated the proceeds to the movement. Ó Brádaigh describes him as "utterly dedicated." He also acknowledges the importance of McLogan's influence. McLogan was a very resourceful person who believed he always had options; he faced difficult situations, examined his choices, and then acted. He was, Ó Brádaigh remembers, the kind of person who might recognize that his only option was something extreme, but for McLogan it was an option that might lead to something. This approach has helped Ó Brádaigh over the years.

Throughout much of the dispute, meetings were held in a semi-clandestine fashion. The campaign had ended, but in the short term, the authorities, north and south, continued to pursue Republicans. In response to the February statement, Brian Faulkner, the minister for home affairs at Stormont, stated that "there would be no amnesty" for the men in Crumlin Road Prison. The Dublin government announced it was keeping its security forces at the border. But by April, the campaign was clearly over and the governments began letting up. In the south, a final group of twenty-nine prisoners was released on April 20, including four who would be prominent in the movement in the 1960s: Tomás Mac Giolla, Cathal Goulding, John Joe McGirl, and Paddy Mulcahy. Mac Giolla replaced McLogan as acting president of Sinn Féin. In his late 30s, he was originally from Tipperary. Tall, thin, and balding, Mac Giolla—like Ruairí Ó Brádaigh—was a graduate of University College Dublin, had a degree in commerce, and had been interned in the Curragh in the 1950s. He was employed as an accountant by the Electricity Supply Board in Dublin prior to his first arrest and imprisonment in January 1957. The supply board, a semi-state body, was slow to reinstate him. It was not until 1963, after Sinn Féin had mounted a campaign in his support, that he was re-employed. In the north, releases were slower, but steady; in May, Seán Garland was one of two people released from Crumlin Road Prison. Dáithí O'Connell was one of the last to be released, in 1963. In the visitor's box of Crumlin Road Prison, Deirdre Caffrey's relationship with O'Connell had blossomed. They were married in September 1964.

By June of 1962 things had settled enough that suspected IRA people could surface and attend the annual Bodenstown Commemoration. The oration was given by Tomás Mac Giolla. Ruairí Ó Brádaigh and Martin Shannon, who were busy with army reorganization, did not attend; their absence generated renewed Special Branch activity. June was a busy month for the Ó Brádaighs. On the 24th, the Sunday after Bodenstown, Patsy gave birth to another son, Ruairí Óg. The family still had no home of their own and Ruairí still had no job. Soon after Ruairí Óg's birth, his father applied to the County Roscommon Vocational Education Committee for reinstatement as a teacher.

Ó Brádaigh's reinstatement was not guaranteed. The minister for education had circulated a notice that said that persons convicted under the Offenses Against the State Act should not be reappointed, that they had forfeited their jobs and their pensions and were disqualified for reappointment for seven years. This potentially applied to Ó Brádaigh, but he also had several interests in his favor. An attraction of working in a vocational school is that the employer is a subcommittee of the County Council and it meets in public. Based on his previous experience with the committee, he expected a fair hearing. Ó Brádaigh also had a personal resource in his mother. May Brady Twohig, the widow of a prominent teacher and respected in her own right, lived in Longford, twenty miles from Roscommon. She knew a number of people in Roscommon, including Mícheál Ó Meiscill, the chief executive officer of the Roscommon Vocational Education Committee. She approached Ó Meiscill and asked what Ruairí had to do to get his job back. Ó Meiscill suggested that Ó Brádaigh send him a note indicating his desire to teach again.

The Roscommon Vocational Education Committee met on June 29th and considered Ó Brádaigh's request. When a committee member brought up the minister's circular, Ó Meiscill stated that it did not apply to Ó Brádaigh. The committee accepted this. One of the members, a Fianna Fáil person, according to Ó Brádaigh, wondered if he should apply directly to the minister rather than to the committee. According to an account published in the *United Irishman,* another member replied that "there was no harm in their recommending to the Minister that he lift the suspension. The man [Ó Brádaigh] had sacrificed almost six years salary and now was being asked to go hat in hand to the Minister to re-employ him[?]" The committee voted unanimously to ask the minister for education to lift Ó Brádaigh's suspension. Because it would be very unlikely for the minister to reject a unanimous vote, Ó Brádaigh knew he had his job back. Before returning to teaching, however, he had one more piece of IRA business to complete.

The intense scrutiny of Republicans that was caused by the IRA's campaign had made it impossible for the organization to hold a convention in 1961. Once the problems with Sinn Féin were settled, a convention was scheduled for the beginning of September 1962. It was a difficult time. The absence of people such as McLogan and Magan, who had been mainstays since 1948, was palpable. There were still volunteers opposed to ending the campaign and their desire to renew the campaign had to be dealt with. Yet in spite of the problems since February, Ó Brádaigh was pleased with his own performance as chief of staff. His goal had been to bring the campaign to a close in such a way that the IRA did not split. Certainly the IRA was at a low point, and it has been described as a shattered army at this time. But Ó Brádaigh knew that things would have been much worse if the IRA had split. What was a difficult situation might have become a disaster.

The most important decision facing the IRA was the election of a new Army Council and chief of staff. Although some people expected that Ó Brádaigh would remain as chief of staff, he was not interested. He was exhausted, he wanted to pull his family together, and he wanted to teach. Like his peers, he had put much of his life on hold because of the campaign. Even if he wanted to be chief of staff, Ó Brádaigh was staying in Roscommon and the position required someone who could be reached easily, someone living in or around Dublin or perhaps Belfast. The problem was that as Ó Brádaigh was getting on with his life, so were his contemporaries. No one wanted to be chief of staff.

As usual, an IRA Executive and an Army Council were elected at the end of the convention. When the Army Council met, they discussed the situation and someone suggested Cathal Goulding as chief of staff. Goulding, who did not volunteer for the job, said he would consider the possibility and asked Ó Brádaigh to continue for another week. During the week, Goulding thought about the position, agreed to take it, and began making arrangements to succeed Ó Brádaigh. This fit with Ó Brádaigh's schedule. When Mícheál Ó Meiscill had informed him that the suspension was lifted, Ó Brádaigh asked when he would start. School was scheduled to begin on the first Monday of September, but the first week would be filled with a religious retreat. Ó Meiscill told Ó Brádaigh he could miss the retreat and start the following Monday. On the Friday of the first week of September 1962, Ruairí Ó Brádaigh formally turned over the chief of staff position to Cathal Goulding. The next Monday, for the first time since December 1956, he went to work as a teacher. Six weeks later, he and Patsy picked out a modest three-bedroom home in Roscommon and took out a bank loan.

At age 40 and at five feet five inches tall, Goulding was ten years older and several inches shorter than Ó Brádaigh. He also had impeccable credentials to be chief of staff. His record suggested that he was more of a militarist than the political figure he was to become; Goulding was not even involved in Sinn Féin until the mid-1960s. The family had a Republican history dating from the Fenians. His father and uncles are found among the list of prisoners deported and released in the *1916 Rebellion Handbook*. He was born into a working-class Dublin family, joined the IRA in the 1930s, and was interned in the Curragh in the 1940s. One of Goulding's closest friends was John Joe McGirl, and the two of them played a significant part in helping Tony Magan, Tomás Mac Curtáin, and Paddy McLogan rebuild the IRA in the late 1940s and early 1950s. Goulding was arrested at Felstead with Seán Mac Stiofáin and Manus Canning, and he returned to Ireland upon his release from prison in 1959. He was on the Army Council from 1959 until his arrest in 1961 and was in prison when the campaign ended. By April 1962, he was out of prison and working in the family business as a painting contractor.

Other than Goulding, it is not publicly known who was elected to the Army Council in 1962. Ruairí Ó Brádaigh confirms his own election to the council and the membership of three others on the council in the early 1960s: the late Seámus Costello, of Bray in County Wicklow; the late Paddy Mulcahy, of Limerick; and Denis McInerney, of Clare. Mulcahy, in his 50s, had been in the IRA since the mid-1930s. He was an insurance agent and former city councilor in Limerick. Costello and McInerney, who were in their mid-20s, were from the next generation, having joined the movement in the mid-1950s. They had progressed up the ranks and were on the Army Council when the campaign ended. McInerney had not been interned, but Costello had been; Costello carefully followed the military conflict in Vietnam while in the Curragh. In 1962, he was a car salesman in Dublin. McInerney was a printer with a local newspaper in County Clare. Ó Brádaigh, Costello, and McInerney provided continuity from the campaign's end to the reorganization of the 1960s. Another key person, and likely a member of the Army Council at this time, was Seán Garland of Dublin. He was on the Brookeborough raid that resulted in the deaths of Seán South and Feargal O'Hanlon. In *The IRA 1968–2000: Analysis of a Secret Army,* J. Bowyer Bell describes Garland and Dáithí O'Connell, who was also on the Brookeborough raid, as the most prominent volunteers at the end of the campaign.

Typically, Sinn Féin Ard Fheiseanna follow IRA conventions, which makes it easier for Sinn Féin policy to follow the IRA's lead. It also helps place IRA people in leadership positions in Sinn Féin; typically, some members of the Army Council or Army Executive are members of the Sinn Féin Ard Chomhairle. The 1962 Ard Fheis was held in Dublin on the weekend of October 27–28. The delegates endorsed the expulsion of McLogan, Magan, and the others and they formally elected a new Officer Board with Tomás Mac Giolla as president. Larry Grogan was elected one of two Sinn Féin vice presidents and Tom Mitchell was elected as a joint secretary. Others elected to the Ard Chomhairle included Seán Ó Brádaigh, Dáithí O'Connell (even though he was still in prison in Crumlin Road), Gerry McCarthy of Cork, and Paddy Mulcahy. Grogan, Mitchell, O'Connell, McCarthy, and Mulcahy were IRA veterans.

Ó Brádaigh remained on the Army Council, but most of his activity was at the local level. In the IRA, it is common for people to perform multiple roles, especially when the army has contracted. Tommy McDermott, who had been co-opted onto the Army Executive in 1960, was the South Roscommon commanding officer. Ó Brádaigh once again became McDermott's adjutant. In 1964, the IRA was reorganized, and he became commanding officer of Roscommon-Galway and worked with units in Longford and Westmeath. Most of his Sinn Féin activity was also at the local level. Ó Brádaigh attended the Ard Fheis as a delegate from Roscommon but did not stand for the Ard Chomhairle. However, in December he was elected pro tem Cathaoirleach (chairperson) of Roscommon Sinn Féin. He also became involved in other Republican-minded activities. Beginning in 1950, Roscommon Republicans had begun to erect a memorial to the county's patriot dead. The huge monument, which had an eighteen-foot base and three twelve-foot-high figures, was unveiled at Shankill Cross, Elphin, in September 1963.

The unveiling was performed by 71-year-old Tom Maguire, a well-known veteran Republican. Maguire had been the IRA's general commanding officer of the Second Western Division in the 1920s; the South Roscommon brigade had been under his command. As a member of the IRA's Executive and a TD in the Second Dáil, he had voted against the Treaty. He was arrested by Free State forces and was told he would be executed. His life was spared, probably because he was a member of the Second Dáil, but his younger brother, Seán Maguire, was executed by the Free State. Maguire rejected de Valera's attempt to take Sinn Féin into Leinster House, and in 1938 he was among those on the Executive Council of the Second Dáil who delegated to the IRA Army Council the "powers of government," which allows the Army Council to describe itself as the government of the Republic. By September 1963, Maguire was the only surviving TD from the Second (All-Ireland) Dáil who continued to reject the Treaty and participation in Leinster House and Stormont. His active involvement in the IRA had ended years earlier, but his continued participation in memorials, marches, and other activities provided a direct link between the Second Dáil faithful and the contemporary Republican Movement.

Ó Brádaigh first saw Tom Maguire speak in Galway in 1952. Then Ó Brádaigh was a young volunteer and had been too shy to introduce himself. By the time of the Elphin unveiling, he had joined Maguire as an abstentionist Sinn Féin TD, had served as chief of staff, and was very comfortable introducing himself. Out of the unveiling ceremony the two of them developed a lasting friendship. Ó Brádaigh found Maguire's personal history compelling and his devotion to the All-Ireland Republic inspiring. From this point until Maguire's death in 1993, at the age of 101, Tom Maguire played an important part in Ruairí Ó Brádaigh's life. In the 1990s, Ó Brádaigh would write Maguire's biography, *Dílseacht: The Story of Comdt. General Tom Maguire and the Second (All-Ireland) Dáil.*

For a group of people who had spent years, some of them decades, fighting for the Irish Republic in a variety of ways, the failure of the military campaign was a setback. But as Seán Conin states, "[F]ailure is a relative term as far as Ireland is concerned." Rather than quit, they would change tactics. The almost-exclusive focus on national liberation through military means had not worked. In response, they sought to expand the movement's appeal in two complementary directions, to the political left and in the direction of moderate Protestants in Northern Ireland. Because the movement had been formally anticommunist since the 1930s, and because the Cold War was well under way, the IRA's move to the left was cautious at first. It began with a rejection of Western materialism but did not go as far as embracing socialism or communism. In his first presidential address, at the 1962 Ard Fheis, Tomás Mac Giolla rejected materialism in all its forms: "In so far as the Communist menace is a battle for men's minds, we should undoubtedly be playing a leading part in the fight against it, as we should in the fight against materialism of every brand. . . . This life of the spirit in the Irish people is being slowly asphyxiated by American and British materialism and it is now to be finally extinguished in the new materialist Europe on the specious plea that we are aiding in the fight against Communism." Nineteen-sixty-three marked the 200th anniversary of the birth of Wolfe Tone. To mark the occasion and to help establish links with Protestant intellectuals, the Republican leadership founded the Wolfe Tone Society in Dublin. The plan was to sponsor discussions, seminars, and lectures that would lead to interaction between Republicans and non-Republicans. Wolfe Tone Clubs were formed in Dublin and Belfast and in other selected Irish cities such as Cork and Galway.

Cathal Goulding was the primary force behind the society, whose founders included Dublin-based Republicans such as Tomás Mac Giolla,

Seán Cronin, and Éamonn Mac Thomáis. Another founding member was Jack Bennett, who did not have an IRA or Sinn Féin past. Bennett was from a Belfast Protestant background and as a young man was politically involved as a communist. After emigrating to England, he joined the leftist Connolly Association, named for James Connolly, the executed 1916 leader. The Connolly Association campaigns for an independent Ireland and supports the rights of the Irish in Britain, but it rejects physical force. Bennett returned to Belfast in the early 1960s, took a job as a journalist with the *Belfast Telegraph,* and served as a link between the Wolfe Tone Society in Dublin and its target audience, Protestants in Belfast. He was one of three key people (the others were Roy Johnston and Tony Coughlan) who had been involved with the Connolly Association and then became influential in the Republican Movement via the Wolfe Tone Society.

Roy Johnston describes himself as a Marxist "in the spirit of Connolly, Gramsci, etc." He had lived in France in the 1950s, returned to Ireland, and then lived in England from 1960 to 1963. In England, he joined the Connolly Association. He returned to Ireland in 1963, took a position with the Dublin Institute for Advanced Studies, and became involved with the Wolfe Tone Society. Tony Coughlan had left Ireland for England in 1958 for postgraduate work. In England, he had been a fulltime organizer for the Connolly Association. Among his activities, he had organized a protest march from London to Birmingham against Unionist rule in Northern Ireland. In 1961, Coughlan accepted a position as a lecturer at Trinity College, Dublin, and he returned to Ireland. In 1964, he started attending Wolfe Tone Society meetings. The influx of people such as Bennett, Johnston, and Coughlan put the Republican leadership in a curious position, given that the movement had repeatedly rejected communism and connections with the Connolly Association.

In their involvement with the Wolfe Tone Society, people such as Bennett, Johnston, and Coughlan were not necessarily endorsing the physical force methods of the IRA or the politics of Sinn Féin. Rather, the Wolfe Tone Society promoted discussion and intellectual debate among a group of people who were interested in social and national issues in Ireland. Tony Coughlan never joined Sinn Féin. From his perspective, people such as Goulding, Mac Giolla, Garland, and their peers in the Wolfe Tone Society were looking for a way of "becoming politically relevant" in the aftermath of the Border Campaign; the Wolfe Tone Society was part of that process. Of the three, Johnston was probably the most important for the Republican Movement. He joined Sinn Féin, became prominent in the movement, and advocated an economic resistance campaign against imperialism and, later, the ending of abstentionism. As described by Pat Walsh in *Irish Republicanism and Socialism: The Politics of the Republican Movement, 1905 to 1994,* Johnston viewed abstentionism as a "rigid, legalistic tradition handed down by the rump of the Second Dáil" that hampered a new "principled political stand" which could be made in the Dáil to the advantage of Sinn Féin. From his perspective, some Republicans supported abstentionism "because they wouldn't know what to do if they were actually in office."

As the IRA campaign ended, there was speculation in the *Belfast Newsletter* that a radical party would emerge from the Republican Movement. And in 1962, the Sinn Féin Ard Chomhairle established a subcommittee to draft headings for a new social and economic program. The Wolfe Tone Society and the arrival of Bennett, Coughlan, and Johnston spurred the program's development. The headings (Sinn Féin's term for an outline) were put to the Sinn Féin Ard Fheis in December 1964 and were adopted. In 1965, at the direction of the Ard Chomhairle, they were developed by Roy Johnston and Sean Ó Brádaigh, but they were never published. Instead, the question of whether or not the Republican Movement should embrace constitutional politics came to dominate debate. Early in 1965, the movement organized a conference "to discuss political tactics, policy and internal organisation and make recommendations." Ten points emerged, and they reflected the influence of the Connolly Association. One point called on Sinn Féin to recognize Westminster, Stormont, and Leinster House. Another called for "co-operation with other radical groups," including the Communist Party of Northern Ireland, the Irish Workers' Party, and the Connolly Association. They were placed on the agenda of an extraordinary IRA convention.

Seán Mac Stiofáin, the IRA's organizer in Cork and Kerry, was a delegate at this convention. Mac Stiofáin was 36 years old and was employed as an organizer for Conradh na Gaeilge, the Irish-language organization. He was from London and spoke fluent Irish with a bit of an English accent. He was a big man, about six feet tall, broadly built, and he was more aggressive than many of his contemporaries. In his memoir, *Revolutionary in Ireland,* he records the reaction to the new program, "I and many others opposed the [ten] proposals head-on." Ruairí Ó Brádaigh was prominent among the "many others." The delegates rejected most of the proposals. With respect to abstentionism, Mac Stiofáin comments, "We defeated the key proposal on the abstentionist issue by a large majority." The proposals were next put to an extraordinary Sinn Féin Ard Fheis in May 1965. In an attempt to heal the damage of the extraordinary IRA convention, Cathal Goulding appointed Ó Brádaigh as chairman of the Ard Fheis. The proposals were again controversial and most were again turned down. As chair of the Ard Fheis, however, Ó Brádaigh did not participate in the spirited debate.

The IRA is like many volunteer organizations in that the people who lead it, especially during lean times, are those who are willing to speak out and take responsibility. Seán Mac Stiofáin was especially vocal in his opposition to the new direction. At the convention, he was elected to the Army Council. Immediately after joining the council, he went after Roy Johnston, whom he described as "a Marxist whom I knew to be Moscow-oriented, and who had been in the CPGB [Communist Party Great Britain] and the Connolly Association." Mac Stiofáin was not opposed to "social and economic agitation on a proper basis," and his opposition to Johnston was "nothing personal." His complaint was that Irish and British communists tend to condemn armed struggle in Ireland but support it elsewhere. At his first Army Council meeting, Mac Stiofáin argued that IRA General Order No. 4 prohibits membership in the Communist Party and that, therefore, Johnston's membership in the movement should be withdrawn. Goulding countered that Johnston was the best thing that had happened to the movement in some time and that if Johnston went, so would he. It was not an idle threat, and Mac Stiofáin was rebuffed.

According to Mac Stiofáin, in 1965 the Army Council became split; three people supported the new program, three people were opposed, and one person was studiously neutral. Ruairí Ó Brádaigh confirms this. The three opposed to the change of direction were Mac Stiofáin, Ó Brádaigh, and probably Paddy Mulcahy of Limerick. Those in favor of constitutional action were Goulding, Seámus Costello, and presumably Seán Garland. The studiously neutral person was Tomás Mac Giolla. Ó Brádaigh, like Mac Stiofáin, was highly suspicious of Johnston. But Ó Brádaigh also had reservations about Mac Stiofáin's approach. Mac Stiofáin had a tendency toward brash statements and head-on confrontation; his approach was not always successful and often created hard feelings. He failed to get rid of Johnston and he lost some goodwill in the process, especially with Goulding.

Ó Brádaigh was not opposed to political development and was self-assured enough not to be threatened by communists. He was a fan of Peadar O'Donnell, one of the leading leftist Republicans of the 1930s. In 1963, O'Donnell published *There Will Be Another Day*, his personal account of land-annuity agitation in the 1926–1932 time period. Ó Brádaigh read it enthusiastically and welcomed O'Donnell's reemergence as an in-fluential Republican in the 1960s. For Ó Brádaigh, the drift to the left was part of a trend, part of the zig and zag of Irish Republican politics. The movement had swung to the left in the 1930s, had swung back in the 1940s and 1950s, and was moving back to the left in the 1960s. The movement had survived the 1930s and it would survive the 1960s; as he states, "[I]n the early '30s the movement was accused of flirting with the Communist Movement. But the [Republican] Movement got over that." As far as he was concerned, the shift to the left in the 1960s "was a policy that could be corrected," if necessary.

Ó Brádaigh was committed to social change, but he wanted to know where it would lead and what form it would take. With others, he shared a practical concern that the movement would be smeared with a commu-nist label, as it had been in the 1930s. He was also concerned with the totalitarian tendencies of the governments of Eastern Europe. Most im-portant, he worried that the political developments would lead to involve-ment in constitutional politics, a violation of "fundamental principle." In a sense, Ó Brádaigh accepted Roy Johnston's assessment that some in Sinn Féin supported abstentionism because they would not know what to do if they were elected. Ó Brádaigh believed that if they were elected and took their seats in a Parliament—Leinster House, Stormont, or Westmin-ster—Sinn Féin representatives would be inexperienced and in the mi-nority, and they would be confronted by veteran parliamentarians. It was naive to believe that Sinn Féiners in a Parliament would not be out-maneuvered or co-opted or both. As had historically happened, they would fail their constituency and compromise their principles. Another concern was that the IRA was being run down, that volunteers were being diverted to political action rather than IRA activities. As a training officer and former chief of staff, he pushed for additional training but found that those pushing political development were not interested. He interpreted this as evidence that the reformers wanted to embrace constitutional poli-tics. At the extraordinary IRA convention in 1965 and in subsequent meetings, he made his concerns known. Those who agreed with him came to be seen as "militarists." Tomás Mac Giolla describes Ó Brádaigh as the "leader of the militarists."

Seán Mac Stiofáin pushed very hard against change. People in support of the new direction were also strident. In March 1965, the editor of *The United Irishman,* published an editorial with the title "Live Horse." The editorial attacked the "utopian" elements in Sinn Féin who saw the Re-public as the answer to all of Ireland's questions but who were unwilling to work for social change until the Republic had been achieved. He called on Republicans to put policy into practice, and advocated going into "all forums," including Westminster, Stormont, and Leinster House. It is reported that Seán Ó Brádaigh refused to sell the edition and that some *cumainn* in Dublin returned their copies to the head office in protest. In general, the paper began to place less emphasis on traditional Republican events, such as commemorations, and to provide more coverage of social issues, including agitating against very poor housing conditions in Dublin.

The early 1960s was a period of social and political ferment throughout the Western world. The end of the IRA's campaign in 1962 and a turn to politics by Irish Republicans seemed part of a general opening up that included Vatican II, the Beatles, civil rights protests in the United States, and protests against the Vietnam War. Tension developed between Irish Republicans who believed that social and economic agitation could form the basis of national liberation, a way to reunite the Six Counties of Northern Ireland with the Twenty-Six Counties of the Free State/Republic of Ireland, and Irish Republicans who suspected that social and economic agitation would lead to involvement in constitutional politics and co-optation of the movement. At the 1965 Sinn Féin Ard Fheis, abstentionism was hotly debated and a sort of compromise was reached—Sinn Féin candidates could take their seats in Leinster House only if the party should win a majority of the seats and invite six-county elected representatives to take part in an All-Ireland Parliament.

The compromise did not solve the basic tension in the movement, and those opposed to the new direction had two options: quit, or stay and fight. A few resigned from the movement, the most notable of them being Joe Cahill, who left the IRA in 1965. When he was interviewed for the book *Provisional Irish Republicans: An Oral and Interpretive History,* Cahill discussed his resignation. From his perspective, "there were moves afoot to run down the military wing, to run down the IRA, and to supersede the whole thing just into a purely political action. . . . I was probably more militant than ever, at that particular time." Cahill later realized he had made a mistake. His resignation isolated his dissent. In his words, "I should have stayed within it and fought and argued the point." Most IRA leaders stayed involved. They knew trouble was coming but they also believed the movement, and their interest in it, would be best served by waiting to see what happened. According to Ruairí Ó Brádaigh, "I was very clear that if the Leinster House thing was passed that very first time it was brought up in 1965 [at the IRA's extraordinary convention], I was very clear in my mind what I was going to do. And I would organize the minority which lost to elect a separate leadership, have a separate Movement." He knew that people such as Seán Mac Stiofáin agreed with him. Unlike Mac Stiofáin, he did not show his full hand: "I didn't tell Goulding of my intentions. Nor would I come out brash like Mac Stiofáin." Ó Brádaigh had been working with Goulding, Garland, Costello, and their supporters for more than a decade. He was willing to continue to work with them, to argue his case, and to keep his options open until "fundamental principle" was violated.

9

Dream-Filled Romantics, Revolutionaries, and the Northern Ireland Civil Rights Association

1965–AUGUST 1968

THE POLITICAL AND social awakening of the 1960s had a special impact on Northern Ireland, where there seemed to have been literally no social change since the foundation of the state in 1920. Change began at the top in 1963, when Viscount Brookeborough (Basil Brooke), prime minister at Stormont since 1943, retired. He was 75 years old; his successor, Captain Terence O'Neill, was 49. O'Neill and Seán Lemass, Éamon de Valera's successor as Taoiseach, could do things that their predecessors could not. Brookeborough was known for his anti-Catholic comments. O'Neill made significant gestures in support of the northern Catholic community, including highly publicized visits to Catholic elementary schools. In January 1965, he did the unthinkable and met with Lemass at Stormont; they discussed north-south economic arrangements. In April 1966, he visited Corrymeela in County Antrim, a community center designed to bring together people from different backgrounds. He spoke to an audience of leading Catholics and Protestants. In spite of protests by Protestant extremists—Rev. Ian Paisley began an "O'Neill Must Go" campaign—O'Neill seemed to indicate that real change was possible, that the traditional Protestant subjugation of northern Catholics might end.

Economic and social forces complemented the political change at Stormont. Traditionally, middle-class Catholics were employed as teachers or entered the clergy. In the late 1940s, free higher education was extended from Britain to Northern Ireland, and in the late 1950s and early 1960s, young better-educated Catholics were entering the labor force. At the same time, the northern economy was modernized and foreign capital was introduced. This created more opportunities for educated Catholics, whose expectations for themselves and their community exceeded those of previous generations. This was especially evident in Dungannon, County Tyrone. Dungannon was evenly split between Catholics and Protestants, but through gerrymandering, Unionists controlled the town and the allocation of council housing. To control voting strength, Unionists had not allocated permanent housing to any Catholic families for thirty-four years. A local physician, Dr. Conn McCluskey, and his wife, Patricia, formed the Homeless Citizens League. League members organized protest marches and squatted in unallocated empty homes. In January 1964, the McCluskeys helped form The Campaign for Social Justice in Northern Ireland, which raised awareness of discrimination against Nationalists/ Catholics.

An indicator that change was under way came in 1966 when Harold Wilson, the prime minister at Westminster, called an election. Sinn Féin's constitutional counterpart in Northern Ireland, the Nationalist Party, had a checkered history of participation in government and did not even put forward candidates for Westminster elections in 1955, 1959, and 1964. Tired of the Nationalist Party and not attracted to the abstentionist policies of Sinn Féin, a group of middle-class Catholics founded National Unity, which McCluskey describes as "unashamedly anti-partition and middle class but full of ideas." They accepted the Constitution of Northern Ireland, opposed IRA violence, and sought reform through participation in constitutional politics. They contested local and Stormont elections, and in 1966, they contested Fermanagh–South Tyrone in the Westminster election. The constituency had a slight Nationalist/Catholic majority and a history of non-Unionist victories, including Phil Clarke's in 1955. National Unity believed they could win the seat if the incumbent, the Marquis of Hamilton (James Hamilton) was opposed by only their candidate. A series of meetings were held throughout the constituency and then a National Unity convention selected J. J. Donnelly, owner of an antiques business and a councilor in Enniskillen, as their candidate. Unfortunately for National Unity, Sinn Féin had its own plan. Republicans, who had contested the seat since the mid-1950s, organized a constituency convention in Enniskillen and on February 7, 1966, selected Ruairí Ó Brádaigh as their candidate.

Peace brought stability to the lives of Republicans, and many of them responded by increasing the size of their families. The young IRA volunteers of the 1950s were becoming middle-aged family men. Ó Brádaigh,

Ruairí Ó Brádaigh, 1965. This photograph was used in publicity for the 1966 Fermanagh–South Tyrone election. Ó Brádaigh family collection.

who was still teaching in Roscommon, was now 34 years old and the father of four children. Fraternal twins, Conchúr and Deirdre, had been born in November of 1964. Although he did not live in Fermanagh–South Tyrone or even Northern Ireland, was a candidate for a banned political party (he ran as a "Republican"), and would not take his seat if elected, Ruairí Ó Brádaigh and his fellow Republicans took his candidacy seriously. It was a chance to determine how much support they had in the area and to present the movement's new policies. To properly campaign, he had to spend time in the constituency. The two largest towns are Enniskillen in Fermanagh and Dungannon in Tyrone, 66 miles and 106 miles, respectively, from Roscommon. With Patsy's support and the education committee's blessing, he took a month-long unpaid leave of absence from Roscommon Vocational School.

Ó Brádaigh knew the area and its people. He had campaigned for Phil Clarke in 1955, and during the Border Campaign he had traversed the area clandestinely as a guerrilla. Sinn Féin hired a caravan and parked it in Ann Street in Dungannon; it became the operations center for Ó Brádaigh's candidacy. Volunteers distributed 30,000 leaflets, but his primary activity involved a direct appeal to voters that he met at "Chapel-gate meetings" at churches throughout the constituency. On one tour of Fermanagh he visited Derrylin, the site of the 1956 raid that had led to his first arrest; he noticed that the RUC station there had been converted into a family dwelling. His election manifesto, which was released three weeks before the election, asked the people of the north "to root out petty sectarian bitterness and determine to work for the good of this nation, which is theirs to develop and expand." As reported in the *Irish Times,* the manifesto announced the Republican Movement's "comprehensive social and economic programme to ensure the development of Ireland's natural resources in the interests of the Irish people." The program was not socialist, but it advocated "many radical social reforms," including control over the import and export of capital and the nationalization of some industries in order to "protect the interests of the employees and the economy." The program wanted to "ensure a just distribution of the nation's wealth," it called for a free health service and free educational facilities, it allowed only Irish people to own Irish agricultural land, and it limited the size of farms. As always, the manifesto called for the establishment of an All-Ireland Parliament.

Godfrey Fitzsimons of the *Belfast Telegraph* interviewed the three Fermanagh–South Tyrone candidates, the Marquis of Hamilton of the Unionist Party, J. J. Donnelly of National Unity, and Ruairí Ó Brádaigh. The Ó Brádaigh interview offers an external observer's view of him. On the surface, he was "everybody's image of a Republican." Both of his parents had been Republican activists and his official name was Peter Roger Casement Brady. When Fitzsimons commented that the pen in Ó Brádaigh's breast pocket was red, white, and blue, the colors of the Union Jack, he "took it out and put it away." Ó Brádaigh remembers that Fitzsimons did not report his reply that ownership of "the economy of the country, not just symbols, was the real issue." Fitzsimons did report on Ó Brádaigh's Pioneer Badge—which he had worn since his days at St. Mel's, indicating that he was a teetotaler—and his gold *fáinne*—a circular pin indicating fluency in Irish. Ó Brádaigh's platform included support for the Irish language. He had a "ready laugh" and a "genuine friendly" manner. Politically, Fitzsimons found him "one of the more realistic of the Republicans," stating: "He sees the day when the border will disappear as far distant, and he has social plans in the meantime." The way to prosperity, he told Fitzsimons, was through a system of self-help. Ó Brádaigh referred to the cooperative activities of Father James McDyer of Glencolumbcille in Donegal and noted his support for credit unions and community projects.

Election day was March 31st. The loser, in a relative sense, was the Unionist Party. Unionists won eleven of twelve Northern Irish seats, but their majority declined in most constituencies. In a surprise result, Gerry Fitt of the Republican Labour Party won in West Belfast. As an MP in London, Fitt became a link between the Campaign for Social Justice and members of the British Labour Party. In Fermanagh–South Tyrone, the Nationalist vote was split and the Marquis of Hamilton was elected with 29,352 votes. J. J. Donnelly received 14,645 votes. Ruairí Ó Brádaigh finished third with 10,370 votes. Compared to the 1964 election, the Marquis increased the Unionist majority in the constituency. In the *Irish Times,* Wesley Boyd offered a detailed examination of the election returns. Boyd showed that while there was no dramatic change in voting patterns— Protestants still tended to vote for partitionist candidates and Catholics still tended to vote for anti-partitionist candidates—there were "signs that support is increasing for parties concentrating on social and economic issues." He noted that in the two constituencies where voters could choose between constitutional Nationalists and "extremist Republicans" (Fermanagh–South Tyrone and Derry), the Republican vote dropped sharply. The IRA and Sinn Féin leadership followed the 1966 election carefully, and they were aware of the interpretations of people such as Wesley Boyd. Those advocating a broadening of the movement—people such as Cathal Goulding and Séamus Costello—no doubt interpreted the results as support for their perspective.

Nineteen-sixty-six marked the fiftieth anniversary of the Easter Rising. Nationalist-minded people throughout Ireland celebrated the event. Official Ireland, represented by people such as Éamon de Valera, who was still president of Ireland, was prominent in commemoration activities. Veterans of the 1916–1923 era, both pro- and anti-Treaty, were involved in state-sponsored Easter commemorations, television programs, and commemorative publications. All of these people considered themselves Republicans. A small minority of Republicans avoided the official ceremonies and held their own events. On Easter Sunday, April 10th, there was a huge commemoration in the Gaelic football park in Coalisland, about four miles from Dungannon. More than 20,000 people and twenty bands attended the ceremonies. The *Irish Independent* reported that more than seventy members of the RUC watched as the "streets were thronged with visitors" and "those on parade included former local IRA members now living throughout the country." The 1916 proclamation was read by Paddy Crawford, a 1916 Volunteer, and a decade of the rosary was recited in Irish by the local priest, Rev. Charles McGarvey. The keynote speaker was Ruairí Ó Brádaigh. Despite his loss in the polls, Ó Brádaigh and the Republic still generated interest in the area. In his oration, he "spoke of Tom Clarke, the first signatory to the Proclamation, who had spent his early life in Dungannon." He also "saluted 'the five men languishing in prison at Crumlin Road, Belfast, for they are our true comrades'" (they had been arrested in Belfast). When he finished, a parade left the park and moved to the local parochial hall, where Joseph O'Neill, another 1916 veteran, unveiled a plaque commemorating the involvement of men from Antrim, South Derry, and Tyrone, in the Easter Rising.

A developing fragmentation of the Republican Movement underlay these events. Richard Behal, who later became a thorn in the side of both the Dublin government and the IRA leadership, was a principal figure in this fragmentation. Behal, from Kilmacow in Kilkenny, was in his late 20s and was an electrician and independent businessman, working with his father in a family-run electrical manufacturer. He was one of a growing number of IRA volunteers who was willing to act on his sense of frustration with the movement's new direction. A contemporary description states that he was a "rural republican" with a simple appeal and that his "speeches were more emotional, more militant and had less reference to social and economic thinking than those of his colleagues in the cities and big towns." He is described as having a "strong reputation for idealism," as being "impatient," and as having a "fondness for action, sometimes grandiose and often carried out with skill and daring."

Behal first met Ruairí Ó Brádaigh somewhere along the border in late 1958, although Ó Brádaigh knew of him before this. An IRA training camp in Kilkenny had been raided while Behal was on a bicycle tour with another IRA volunteer. When they returned, their homes were raided. Behal realized that if they did not account for their movements it would look suspicious and might compromise others. They answered questions honestly, their story checked out, and they were released. Afterward, Behal realized that he had violated IRA orders against recognizing or speaking with the police. He was so upset, and so idealistic, that he actually put himself on trial; he wrote out a report and gave it to his local commanding officer. His superior told him not to worry about it, but Behal persisted—he wanted his conscience clear. The report went up the line to the chief of staff, Ó Brádaigh. As Behal remembers it, "Ruairí came across it and he couldn't believe that anyone would be so upset." Ó Brádaigh sent word back to Behal that his status as a volunteer had not been compromised. When they met for the first time, Ó Brádaigh started the conversation with "So you're the guy with the conscience." They became friends and remain on good terms. Their relationship will always benefit from Ó Brádaigh's support for Behal when he was sentenced to death by an IRA court in 1966.

The Cold War was on and Ireland, an island in the North Atlantic, was strategically important. Ireland was non-aligned, but it welcomed U.S. and British navy ships at its ports. Behal and some others approached Cathal Goulding and argued that the IRA should confront such visits, especially by British naval forces. It was an opportunity to demonstrate the IRA's opposition to the military forces of Western imperialism. As part of their argument, they pointed out that an IRA convention had passed a resolution waiving restrictions on attacks on British forces in the Twenty-Six Counties. Goulding reluctantly supported their request and offered the use of a bazooka. Behal had reservations. No one involved had experience with the weapon and a bazooka increased the possibility of civilian casualties. IRA units would be firing on a target from the banks of Waterford Harbor. If they missed or if the round skipped off the target and continued across into the city it could be disastrous. Goulding allowed them to procure a Boyes anti-tank rifle, which fires a .55 inch round and has armor-piercing capabilities.

In September 1965, the British torpedo boat *Brave Borderer* was received in Waterford. The IRA was waiting, and a round from the Boyes rifle hit one of its engines. The other engine continued operating and the boat hopped all over the place. The sound of ripping metal then echoed across the harbor, the boat was engulfed in smoke, and the IRA team thought they had sunk the vessel. The high-profile attack was widely condemned in the press and by state authorities. It was also condemned by some people in the IRA leadership. According to Behal, general headquarters went "bloody bananas." It undercut the activities of those pushing for political development and involvement in social, not military, agitation. The attack also showed the state's authorities that even if the IRA's rhetoric was changing, it was still capable of causing trouble. With satisfaction, Behal notes that the attack had its desired effect; it "finished British naval visits for over thirty years."

Behal and two others were arrested and faced multiple charges, including possessing the anti-tank rifle and resisting arrest. He was sentenced to nine months in prison on the charge of resisting arrest and was scheduled to return to court to face charges the first jury disagreed on.

He took matters into his own hands and escaped from Limerick Prison. On the run, Behal and associates launched a minor campaign in Kilkenny. Cathal Goulding and Seán Garland had been arrested for possession of a revolver and ammunition. Their court appearance was postponed several times, and essentially they were interned without trial. In protest, Behal and associates blew up a telephone exchange in Kilmacow. On April 10th, the same day as the commemoration in Coalisland, Behal appeared as a surprise speaker at a *céilí* in Thomastown, County Kilkenny, where he addressed 300 dancers. Behal's activities fueled speculation that there had been a split in the IRA. Even though he denied it in the press, such speculation was not good. If some people were upset with the attack on the torpedo boat, his activities after his unauthorized escape went too far. He was too much of a maverick, and he was taken into IRA custody.

Complementing the problems created by Richard Behal, Seán Mac Stiofáin and Roy Johnston were involved in a high-profile disagreement in May 1966. Johnston believed that commemoration speeches should be used to push the movement's new direction. Instead, the speeches tended to follow the same script, focusing on Republican traditions and sacrifices. The commemoration at Coalisland and virtually every other commemoration that Easter followed this script. At Coalisland, two key participants were elderly veterans of 1916 who were remembering the past rather than looking to the future. Johnston wanted speakers to push for social agitation. Another staple of commemorations that bothered Johnston was the recitation of the rosary, as at Coalisland. The May issue of *The United Irishman* published a letter to the editor from Johnston in which he stated that Republican commemorations were sectarian because they were held in Catholic cemeteries and followed Catholic rituals.

The letter caught everyone's attention. It especially grated on Seán Mac Stiofáin, a conservative Catholic. Mac Stiofáin believed "the real target of this Marxist criticism was not sectarianism, but religion as such." He also found it offensive that someone would dictate how people should pray. He stopped distribution of the paper in his areas, Cork and Kerry, and he encouraged others to do the same. Denis McInerney supported Mac Stiofáin, not out of religious conviction but because he opposed Johnston's condemnation of how other people expressed their religion. Ruairí Ó Brádaigh also supported Mac Stiofáin. He was concerned that the movement would begin to dictate how people should express their religion. Most, though not all, of the IRA volunteers who had died in active service were Catholic, or at least they were raised as Catholics.

Commemorations were often held at cemeteries that hold the remains of fallen volunteers, and the commemorations often attracted the families of volunteers. These family members, like the fallen volunteers, were usually practicing Catholics. If the family wanted a decade of the rosary, Ó Brádaigh believed, it was not because they were sectarian but because they were practicing their religion in the way they knew how. In Ó Brádaigh's experience, when the fallen volunteer was not Catholic, the rosary was not recited. The rosary is not part of the Wolfe Tone Commemoration at Bodenstown, which is held in what was a Protestant cemetery. The death of James Monds, a Protestant from Castlerea who was killed in 1921 by British soldiers in County Roscommon, is remembered at the gravesite in a Church of Ireland cemetery, but the rosary is not recited. When Cathal Goulding was arrested, Séamus Costello replaced him as chief of staff. Costello supported Roy Johnston. When it was learned that Mac Stiofáin had stopped circulation of *The United Irishman,* he was ordered (presumably by Costello) to distribute the paper. Mac Stiofáin followed orders, but he was summoned to Dublin and suspended from the IRA for six months. This put him off the Army Council.

Compared to Richard Behal, Mac Stiofáin got off easy. Behal was tried by an IRA court-martial, he was found guilty of engaging in unauthorized actions, and he was sentenced to death. Ruairí Ó Brádaigh was not involved in Behal's court-martial, but when the death sentence was referred to the Army Council for confirmation, he became involved. The council discussed the situation at length; some people argued that an example should be made of an out-of-control volunteer. The council split on the issue; three (including Costello) were solidly in favor of execution. Ó Brádaigh was strongly opposed. Behal was certainly guilty of engaging in unauthorized actions, but his opponents included the attack on the *Brave Borderer* as one of his transgressions—Behal describes the attack as a "semi-unofficial action." Ó Brádaigh questioned the wisdom of executing Behal and was troubled by the *Brave Borderer* incident. He knew that Goulding, reluctantly or not, had approved use of the anti-tank rifle. It was unfair for general headquarters to approve an action and then condemn it. The final vote was 4–3 against executing Behal. His life was spared, but he was dismissed from the IRA. On informing the IRA he planned on going abroad, he was told not to return and not to speak to the media. In October 1966, the press reported that Behal had been driven to Belfast, where he "disappeared," presumably first to Britain, then to the continent, and finally to the United States. As it worked out, he was not gone long, from either Ireland or the Republican Movement.

At the IRA convention in the fall, the debate again centered on a motion to drop abstention from Leinster House—and Ó Brádaigh may have made an enemy. Tomás Mac Giolla, a member of the Army Council, again chaired the event. In 1965, following standard procedures for changing the IRA's Constitution, approval of the motion required the support of two-thirds of the delegates. The motion failed. In 1966, unexpectedly, the same chairman with the same motion stated that approval required only a simple majority. Ó Brádaigh immediately objected, asking why it required only a simple majority when the year before it had required a two-thirds majority. Mac Giolla replied that he could not remember the situation of the previous year. Ó Brádaigh would not allow the vote to rest on the improper application of procedures or a parliamentary sleight of hand. He stood up and proposed a vote of no confidence in the chair. He expected support, but no one seconded him. John Joe McGirl was sitting next to him. Ó Brádaigh knew that McGirl opposed the motion, so he kicked him. McGirl then seconded the challenge. In the discussion that followed, some wise guys proposed that a simple majority vote should decide whether or not a two-thirds majority was required for the vote on participating in Leinster House. The humor was lost on Ó Brádaigh, who again objected. Mac Giolla survived the vote of no confidence and insisted that the motion only required a majority vote. At that, the motion failed. But when the convention broke for tea, Ó Brádaigh caught Mac Giolla giving him a wounded look. He was unconcerned, because from his perspective he was "defending the Republic" and he would not put up with "creeping treachery." Most important, he "wanted to set down a marker that this was something enormous."

Seán Mac Stiofáin had served out his six-month suspension and attended the convention as a delegate. In *Revolutionary in Ireland,* Mac Stiofáin states that he was re-elected to the Army Council and that he was subsequently appointed IRA director of intelligence. Cathal Goulding and Seán Garland had served their time in prison and were also there. They were also elected to the Army Council, and Goulding replaced Costello as chief of staff. At the close of the convention, the Army Council was again split with three people pushing the new political direction—Goulding, Garland, and Costello—three people opposed—Ó Brádaigh, Mac Stiofáin, and Paddy Mulcahy—and Mac Giolla—a semineutral as far as Ó Brádaigh was concerned.

At the Sinn Féin Ard Fheis in November 1966, Tomás Mac Giolla noted that it had been an historic year—"The 50th Anniversary of Easter Week"—but other than mentioning "Pearse, Connolly and Clarke" and the hypocrisy of 26-county politicians celebrating "the Freedom we have won," the focus was on economic and social conditions in Ireland, especially in Northern Ireland. Special attention was paid to the western half of the Six Counties, the area west of the River Bann where there was a Nationalist/Catholic majority. Derry, the second-largest city in Northern Ireland, was "the most depressed city in Ireland," yet a "powerful economic pale [was] being created within a radius of approximately 35 miles from the city of Belfast . . . East of the Bann." Mac Giolla charged that there was an "elaborate plan to eliminate the small farmers of Derry, Tyrone, Fermanagh and other regions and to amalgamate their holdings into larger farms." Mac Giolla also addressed the forces pulling the movement apart. "The question of becoming another Free State political party was discussed openly and at length by our organisation last year and there was an overwhelming decision against it," he noted. "At the same time it was decided that the Sinn Féin organisation must become more active than ever in the social, economic and cultural life of the country. It is our aim and objective to endeavour to put into effect, in so far as possible, the ideas and policies laid down in our Social and Economic Programme."

The vast majority of those in Sinn Féin who disagreed with the new political direction stayed and argued their perspective. As a result, the Sinn Féin leadership was relatively stable through the 1960s. Mac Giolla was re-elected as president and Larry Grogan and Joe Clarke, a 1916 veteran, were each elected as vice presidents. Mac Giolla and Grogan had been officers since 1962. The other officers were Éamonn Mac Thomáis and Máirín de Búrca, joint secretaries; Tony Ruane and Niall Fagan, joint treasurers; and Seán Ó Brádaigh, director of publicity. The Ard Chomhairle included Cathal Goulding, Séamus Costello, Roy Johnston, Tom Mitchell, and Seán Mac Stiofáin. Goulding, Costello, Johnston, and de Búrca were relatively new Sinn Féin leaders who supported the new political direction, although Goulding had been in the IRA since the late 1930s. Seán Ó Brádaigh, Tony Ruane, and Seán Mac Stiofáin were all opposed to the new direction; Mac Stiofáin was a relatively recent addition to the Ard Chomhairle. Mac Thomáis and Mitchell were sort of caught in the middle. Both were for social agitation. Mac Thomáis was for abstention while Mitchell was against it with respect to Leinster House, but he was uneasy with the internal methods of Goulding, Costello, and Johnston.

When they could, those in Sinn Féin who supported the new direction pushed aside their opponents. In the 1966 Irish presidential election, Éamon de Valera was re-elected by a slim margin over Thomas O'Higgins of Fine Gael. Although they did not put forward a candidate, the Sinn Féin leadership tried to influence the election. Sinn Féin members were asked to clandestinely distribute an anti–de Valera leaflet. For many people, the tactic seemed naive at best. It might work in a large city like Dublin, but in rural areas where everyone knows everyone else, especially Republican activists, it was not feasible. Upset with the directive, and with the leadership in general, North Kerry Sinn Féin refused to circulate the leaflet. In February 1967, the entire North Kerry Comhairle Ceantair (regional council), which was composed of thirteen *cumainn* and 250 members, was expelled for the refusal.

Younger people started taking matters into their own hands. A group in Cork organized themselves as the Committee for Revolutionary Action and established a small Marxist group, Saor Éire (Free Ireland). Through a small booklet-sized publication, *An Phoblacht,* they severely criticized Goulding and company. The May/June 1967 edition argued that the movement was controlled by a left-wing Dublin-based group that was working in the interests of the "the British Communist Party, and its Irish sections, which are in turn directed from Moscow." Another group, a mix of 1950s veterans and younger people, formed a paramilitary organization, the Saor Éire Action Group. They were distinct from the group in Cork and robbed banks to raise funds; in one bank raid, a member of the Gardaí was killed. The group in Cork and the Saor Éire Action Group were not serious threats to Goulding's leadership or the IRA in general, but their emergence signaled that the movement was starting to splinter.

Cathal Goulding and his supporters were undeterred by dissension in Sinn Féin or the IRA. This was made especially clear at the annual Wolfe Tone Commemoration in June 1967. In his keynote address, Goulding confronted the opposition head on. He attacked those people who focused too much on the border: "While the IRA faced North, its sole aim being the ending of partition, the salesmen of imperialism aided by their native servants commenced a systematic take-over of Irish assets, a systematic speculation in Irish money, Irish manpower, Irish land. The army guarded a frontier while the imperialists quietly entered by another and laid claim to Ireland." Goulding blamed himself and his colleagues for the situation: "That this happened is our own fault and that of our history as a movement. Victory in any struggle is forged with many and various weapons. Historically we chose only one [physical force]." He described the contemporary attempt to broaden the movement and argued that this too had failed.

> We decided, you and I, in Convention and Ard-Fheis, at Comhairli Ceantair and staff meetings, to make an all-out attack on the takeover of Irish assets by foreign interests. We decided that the best method of preventing the deg-

radation of our people by these foreign interests was for us to develop the spirit and practice of co-operation in our local areas, to develop the credit-union idea so that our people would be rescued from the exorbitant rates charged by the almost exclusively foreign H.P. [Hire-Purchase] companies. We decided that we would organise resistance to the exploitation of Irish workers and farmers. We decided to do quite a lot in this line of country, you and I. I know it is almost unnecessary for me to state that, with a very few honourable exceptions, we have done almost nothing.

After asking, "Why not?" he answered by attacking "traditionalists" who were "tired."

It isn't easy to state that one hankers for a quick, glory-full military victory with none of the painful, slow, grueling work necessary to create the situation where we can grasp this victory. This is not any longer a movement for dream-filled romantics, who have been fed on [Tom] Barry's 'Guerrilla Days' and have never taken the trouble to read [Dorothy] McArdle's 'Irish Republic' or [James] Connolly's 'Workers Republic.' This movement has room only for revolutionaries, for radicals, for men with a sense of urgent purpose who are aware of realities, who are not afraid to meet hard work, men who will not be defeated and who will not be deceived.

He continued:

We cannot justify our existence as a movement by a simple faith in the morality or dejure-ness of our position. Faith, we are told in another context, is dead without good works. The same dogma holds good for Republicanism. We must work to justify our claim on the Irish people.

It was a hard-hitting, challenging speech.

Ruairí Ó Brádaigh, who was in the crowd at Bodenstown, agreed with much of what Goulding said. Goulding called for people to be involved in cooperatives. Ó Brádaigh supported cooperatives and credit unions and self-help community projects. In November 1966, he was one of a number of speakers to address a Sinn Féin Education Conference that focused on the cooperative movement and the restoration of fishing rights in lakes and rivers as they related to the west of Ireland. He practiced what he preached. Ruairí and Patsy were actively involved in the development of a credit union in Roscommon. Ó Brádaigh also agreed that a great deal of work had to be done before the border disappeared, by whatever means. That was one reason Godfrey Fitzsimons had described him as "one of the more realistic Republicans." Still, Goulding's hard language—"dream-filled romantics" and "a simple faith in the morality or dejure-ness of our position"—was worrisome. The "dejure-ness" of the Republican position was not simple or unimportant. The IRA had for years killed people in defense of the Republic. If it was the de jure government of the Republic, then it had the moral and legal right to defend it. If it was not the de jure government, then in whose name did it kill? And, at what point did that killing become murder? On a practical level, abstentionism, Easter commemorations, the annual trek to Tone's grave, and so forth helped keep the Republican Movement going during the lean years. Some of the "dream-filled romantics"—perhaps Paddy McLogan and Tony Magan in the 1950s and Tom Maguire, Joe Clarke, and Larry Grogan in the 1960s—were people Ó Brádaigh respected. They helped create traditions that had practical benefits. Abstentionism staved off absorption into a constitutional system that from his perspective corrupted everyone, from Mick Collins to Éamon de Valera to Seán Mac Bride. Ó Brádaigh also questioned the suggestion that those faithful to Republican traditions were somehow less revolutionary than those willing to jettison them. Everyone agreed that the Dublin Parliament was a neocolonial apologist for British imperialism. How was the person who was willing to cooperate with that Parliament more revolutionary than the person who refused such cooperation?

The reservations of people such as Ó Brádaigh aside, Goulding's call for more involvement in social agitation and the general shift to the left was unabated. At an IRA conference in August 1967 and at the Sinn Féin Ard Fheis in November, the movement openly declared that it sought a 32-county democratic socialist republic. In the south, the movement continued to push the cooperative movement, called for careful examination of who owned Ireland—the Irish people or absentee landlords, and agitated for better housing for poor people. Land had been returned to the Irish people through agitation in the late nineteenth century, but many landlords had retained fishing rights. "Fish-ins" were organized where groups of people fished without paying for a license and then gave away their catch or raffled it in aid of a good cause. The Dublin Housing Action Committee was created in May of 1967. The committee had no political affiliation, but Sinn Féiners were prominently involved, including Máirín de Búrca and Proinsias de Rossa. Among other activities, they chained themselves to condemned houses and interrupted meetings of the Dublin City Council. In January, 1968, twenty-six people were arrested in a "brawl" that erupted when bailiffs arrived to evict two families in Dublin. Among those arrested was Séamus Ó Tuathail. He was not a member of Sinn Féin, but he was the editor of *The United Irishman*.

In the north, in August 1966, the Wolfe Tone Societies of Dublin, Belfast, and Cork sponsored a conference on civil rights in Maghera, County Derry. A similar meeting was held in Belfast in November. On January 29, 1967, a public meeting on civil rights at the International Hotel in Belfast attracted eighty people. At this meeting, the Northern Ireland Civil Rights Association (NICRA) was created. By design the focus was British rights for British subjects. NICRA's concerns were discrimination in jobs, housing, and politics. A five-point outline of objectives was released:

> To defend the basic freedoms of all citizens;
> To protect the rights of the individual;
> To highlight all possible abuses of power;
> To demand guarantees for freedom of speech, assembly and association;
> To inform the public of their lawful rights.

For Republicans, NICRA was the culmination of years of hard work. The thirteen-person founding committee included two members of the Wolfe Tone Society, Jack Bennett and Fred Heatley, and Kevin Agnew, a prominent Republican attorney in County Derry. Other committee members included Conn McCluskey, Betty Sinclair, and Paddy Devlin of the Northern Ireland Labour Party and Robin Cole of the Young Unionists'. In February 1968, Betty Sinclair of the Communist Party was appointed the first chair of NICRA.

Through 1967 and into 1968, NICRA organized itself and arranged for the distribution of information on topics such as unfair housing procedures, unfair bans on Republican parades when Loyalist parades were allowed, and discrimination in jobs. NICRA also became involved in direct action. In Caledon in County Tyrone, Catholics without homes often squatted in unoccupied houses. When they were evicted and one of the homes was allocated to a single 19-year-old Protestant woman, Austin Currie, a Nationalist Party MP at Stormont, joined two other people and squatted in the house in protest. They were evicted and fined. Currie attended a meeting of the NICRA Executive, held in Kevin Agnew's home, and NICRA agreed to sponsor a civil rights march in support of the Caledon protests. The march, from Coalisland to Dungannon, was set for August 24, 1968. When it discovered there was going to be a protest march, the local IRA unit sent word to the Army Council in Dublin that it wanted to participate. The council unanimously endorsed the request and sent word to all IRA units in the north encouraging the participation of as many people as possible. The northern authorities, with reason, were suspicious of NICRA, claiming it was a Republican plot. The RUC had a habit of arresting southern Republicans and declaring that the arrests were evidence that their trouble was caused by outsiders. Therefore, the Army Council decided that known IRA members from the Twenty-Six Counties could not participate.

Ruairí Ó Brádaigh supported the IRA's involvement with NICRA and he supported the participation of IRA members in the march from Coalisland to Dungannon. For personal and political reasons, he did not attend the march. His private life was complicated. He was now the father of five young children; Patsy had given birth to another daughter, Eithne, in May 1968. He was also enrolled in a graduate course at University College Galway, studying for his Higher Diploma in Education. Cathal Goulding also missed the march. The most prominent Republican in attendance was Tomás Mac Giolla who, as president of Sinn Féin, was publicly identified as a politician. The movement provided the trucks, the loudspeakers, and the stewards. And, according to Mac Giolla, the turnout was "fantastic."

Between 2,500 and 3,000 people set out from Coalisland, whose population was only about 1,250. The marchers included Betty Sinclair, MP Gerry Fitt, and a young Queens University student, Bernadette Devlin. On the outskirts of Dungannon they ran into a police blockade and learned that they had been banned from the center of town, Market Square. Behind the police barricade were Unionist and Protestant counterdemonstrators (Paisleyites), many of whom were armed with clubs, chatting with police officers. There were minor scuffles with the police and some marchers wanted to push through the blockade. Tomás Mac Giolla, among others, worked to ease the situation; it was a peaceful civil rights march. As Mac Giolla remembers it, there was a bit of a row between those who wanted to push on and those who did not. Once things were calm, a lorry was put in place and used as a platform for speakers. Microphones were set up and the marchers sat and listened to speeches from Austin Currie, Betty Sinclair, Gerry Fitt, and others. The meeting ended with the singing of "We Shall Overcome."

What had started as a minor protest march had brought forth, if in microcosm, a variety of political forces in Northern Ireland: civil rights protesters, counterdemonstrators, Nationalists, Republicans, Unionists, university students, and the police. The march from Coalisland to Dungannon was the beginning of the end of peace in Northern Ireland for more than a generation.

10

The Provisionals

CIVIL RIGHTS ACTIVISTS set their sights on Derry, where, even though the majority were Nationalist and Catholic, Unionists and Protestants controlled the city through gerrymandering. NICRA set Saturday, October 5, 1968, as the date for their second march. The minister of home affairs at Stormont, William Craig, banned it. The ban was ignored, but only about 500 people participated. The march's intended route crossed the River Foyle, went through a gate of the walled city, and ended in the city center, the Diamond, a symbol of Protestant supremacy. The RUC stopped the march on Duke Street, outside the city's gate. As organizers appealed for peace, the RUC attacked with batons. The assault was recorded on film, was broadcast on television that evening, and is included in most documentaries on the conflict in Northern Ireland. Eighty to ninety people were treated for injuries; MP Gerry Fitt was hospitalized. Some marchers made their way to the Diamond, where a crowd of supporters was waiting. The crowd jeered the police, who attacked with batons and pushed them out of the Diamond and into the Bogside ghetto. A major riot developed.

The police assault was a watershed for the civil rights movement and sparked a new era in Irish politics. In Derry, riots and battles with the police continued into the next week. To protect their neighborhoods from the police, people erected barricades. In Belfast, students marched in protest to Craig's home; he dismissed them as "Silly bloody fools." At midweek, they formed their own civil rights group, People's Democracy. The police assault mobilized the general Nationalist population, and protests continued throughout the fall. The Nationalist Party withdrew from Stormont. In November, 15,000 people turned up for another march in Derry. The marchers were not assaulted, but they were kept out of the Diamond.

Republicans viewed the assault in Derry as predictable. They remembered RUC attacks on Fermanagh festivals in the 1950s. The political climate in Ireland—and the world—had changed, however. In 1955, the media reported and Dublin politicians condemned police attacks, but that was it. In 1968, the attack in Derry divided the Unionist Party, mobilized Nationalists, and horrified London. Northern politics were transformed and this influenced the IRA and Sinn Féin. At the IRA convention late in the fall, a vigorous debate on abstentionism again led to nothing. The IRA was fairly evenly split on the issue, and it was clear that Ruairí Ó Brádaigh, Seán Mac Stiofáin, and Paddy Mulcahy, or people like them, would remain on the Army Council. Cathal Goulding sought a way around them and introduced two resolutions designed to increase the chief of staff's influence. The Army Executive serves as a check on the Army Council; by calling a convention, the Executive can sack the council. The first resolution eliminated the Executive. The delegates rejected the resolution, as it went too far. The second resolution, which on the surface was designed to increase the number of people involved in making decisions, increased the Army Council from seven to twenty members and changed its election procedures. Under a new scheme, seven council members would be elected by the Executive, while eight others would be elected at provincial meetings of regional commanding officers. The other five would be co-opted by the fifteen. Because commanding officers are appointed by general headquarters, which is under the control of the chief of staff, Goulding could pack the council; no matter what, eight of his people could outvote the seven people elected by the convention. This resolution passed.

At the Sinn Féin Ard Fheis in December, northern events influenced the discussion. In his presidential address, Tomás Mac Giolla commented, "For the first time the mass of the underprivileged people in the North realise the power that lies in their own organized strength, so long as they remain united and disciplined." The leadership, aware that in the charged atmosphere a heated debate on abstentionism could lead to a split, worked around the abstentionists. They began by isolating Ruairí Ó Brádaigh. For the fourth year in a row, Goulding and Mac Giolla asked him to chair the Ard Fheis. He agreed to do it but suspected he was being used—as chair, he would not actively participate in the debate.

Motion 17 on the agenda called for the end of abstention from Leinster House. Before the debate could begin—and by prior arrangement—Seán Garland proposed an amendment that would "set up a commission of the persons representing both branches of the movement" to examine how the new political situation "may be turned to the advantage of the movement." If the commission's report called for "fundamental change," it would then go before an extraordinary Ard Fheis. Séamus Costello seconded the amendment. In doing so he went too far, attacking abstentionism so hard that some suspected the commission would be a sham, its findings already decided. Still, the Garland amendment passed. People in the IRA, including Ó Brádaigh, Mulcahy, and Mac Stiofáin, knew that Goulding controlled the new 20-person Army Council and through it would influence the commission. It seemed certain that Sinn Féin and the IRA were headed for significant change.

Soon after the Ard Fheis, more violence in the North set in motion a series of events that preempted the leadership's plans. The day after the Ard Fheis, December 9th, Terence O'Neill, prime minister at Stormont, went to the people of Northern Ireland, appealed for restraint, and asked "men of goodwill to come together." Moderates responded positively. NICRA called for a truce period without marches or rallies. The students in People's Democracy were radicals and wanted to keep pressure on O'Neill and NICRA. On January 1, 1969, a small group of students set out on a four-day civil rights trek from Belfast City Hall to Derry. They expected trouble and got it. They were harassed repeatedly, by the police, by the B Specials, by Loyalist extremists, and by Paisleyites, culminating with two major confrontations on the 4th. At Burntollet Bridge in County Derry, a mob supported by the RUC attacked them with stones and sticks studded with nails. When they reassembled and marched into Derry, the RUC blocked them and allowed counterdemonstrators to shell them with bricks, stones, and bottles. A major riot developed in the city center. That night, after the rioting, members of the RUC entered the Bogside, beat people up, and threw stones through windows.

Hard-line Unionists had been upset with Terence O'Neill for years. Civil rights marches and social unrest upset them more. When O'Neill endorsed reform, Unionist critics said he was too soft and civil rights supporters said it was not enough. London was putting pressure on him to resolve the situation. In February, hoping to strengthen his position, O'Neill suspended his government and called an election. It was a disaster. He was returned as prime minister, but his Unionist critics were also re-elected, including William Craig and Brian Faulkner. And several civil rights candidates were elected, including John Hume, the vice chairman of the Derry Citizens' Action Committee. Things got worse. In April, 21-year-old Bernadette Devlin was elected to Westminster in a Mid-Ulster by-election; she is the youngest person ever elected to that body. A leader in People's Democracy, she was energetic, articulate, a fiery speaker, and a

Republican at heart. A fortnight later, O'Neill gave up and resigned as prime minister. He was replaced by Major James Chichester-Clark of the Unionist Party. The change did not bring relief. Civil rights advocates continued their protests, riots became common, and confrontation with the police became deadly. Two Nationalists, Francis McCloskey and Sammy Devenny, died in July from wounds received from RUC batons.

Goulding's supporters believed their plan was working. In an incredibly short period of time, civil rights agitation had brought worldwide attention to the discriminatory practices of the Northern state, had forced reforms, and had split the Unionists. Some Republicans viewed Devlin's election as a lost opportunity. Because of abstentionism they would not contest the election, so they arranged for her to be the only Nationalist candidate. If abstentionism had been dropped, one of their own might be attending Westminster, influencing events, instead of Devlin. Those opposed to constitutional politics, the purists and the traditionalists, had a different perspective. There had been no real social change, and Northern Ireland was still firmly in the United Kingdom. And Nationalists were under attack from the police and mobs. Seán Mac Stiofáin and Ruairí Ó Brádaigh led the traditionalist challenge. At the Army Council meeting after Burntollet, Mac Stiofáin urged Goulding to sanction attacks on the RUC. Goulding refused. Mac Stiofáin also asked that the IRA create auxiliary units for defense, especially in Derry. Seán Keenan, an IRA veteran from the 1940s, was chair of the Derry Defence Association; it was a natural recruiting ground for the IRA. Goulding refused. Keenan's reputation as a staunch abstentionist did not help Mac Stiofáin's argument.

The situation in Belfast was discussed at a large IRA meeting in May 1969 that included the Army Council and representatives from northern units. The city, everyone knew, had a history of sectarian violence. Ó Brádaigh remembered his mother's aunt, who had been burned out of her Belfast home in 1920, and argued it was irresponsible for the IRA to sit back and allow the civil rights movement to increase the pressure and not be ready "to meet the logical consequences." He felt that "it was quite obvious that there would be shooting soon," and he wanted the IRA to be ready for it. From Paddy McLogan he knew that the Belfast IRA had established defense committees in the 1920s; he wanted them reestablished. To his amazement, Goulding countered with, "It is not our job to be Catholic defenders. When the time comes, we'll put it up to the official forces, the British Army and the RUC, to defend the people." Goulding assumed that the British, embarrassed by events, would protect Nationalists from the RUC, which would also drive a wedge between British and

Unionist politicians. Ó Brádaigh rejected this and, "disgusted," made that clear. He asked rhetorically, "And what if they don't do it?" Concerned about defense, he continued, "I'd like to ask a further question. What arms are available in Belfast?" Goulding looked to Billy McMillan, the Belfast commanding officer, who replied, "Enough for one job or one operation." Ó Brádaigh sarcastically replied, "Whatever that means." In practice, he knew, it probably meant enough for training—that is, one pistol, one revolver, one rifle, one submachine gun, and some ammunition.

In July, the British government gave the traditionalists an opportunity to publicly challenge the IRA leadership. After a successful campaign to repatriate Sir Roger Casement, who was hanged in Pentonville Prison in 1916 and was Ó Brádaigh's namesake, his remains were reinterred in Irish soil in 1966. Soon thereafter, The Barnes and McCormack Repatriation Association was formed in Mullingar, County Westmeath. Its goal was to inter in Irish soil the bodies of Peter Barnes and James McCormack, the two IRA members hanged in Birmingham in 1940. One of Ruairí Ó Brádaigh's earliest political memories is his father's reaction to their execution. The committee's secretary was Caitlín Uí Mhuimhneacháin (Kate Moynihan), a Cumann na mBan veteran of the 1940s, a friend of the McCormack family, and a staunch abstentionist. The committee became a center for those opposed to Goulding and his followers. Other committee members included Ruairí Ó Brádaigh, Caoimhín Mac Cathmhaoil (Kevin Campbell), and Seamas Ó Mongáin, both from County Mayo, and Jimmy Steele, Jimmy Drumm, Billy McKee, and Joe Cahill, each from Belfast. Their campaign was successful and the bodies were flown to Dublin on Friday, July 4, 1969. Casement, a hero of the Easter Rising, had been given a large state funeral. Barnes and McCormack, enemies of the state who had been executed in 1940, were not. Yet on Sunday, July 6, thousands attended the funeral at Ballyglass Cemetery outside of Mullingar.

It was Irish Republican tradition at its finest. At the graveside, a group of IRA volunteers removed their jackets, drew their pistols, and fired a three-volley salute. Buglers from Fianna Éireann, the Republican youth group, played the Last Post. Five decades of the rosary were recited. The speakers included James O'Regan of Cork, a veteran Republican and socialist who was expected to support the new political direction, and Jimmy Steele. The traditionalists, abstentionists, and other dissidents were there to hear Steele, a living legend in the Belfast IRA. A milkman by trade, he had joined Na Fianna Éireann at an early age, graduated into the IRA, and stayed involved. He was first arrested in 1923, was a prison escapee in the 1940s, and was a stalwart in the 1950s and 1960s; he had spent more than twenty years in prison for the cause. And he was primed. The Belfast people knew what was coming. As Steele rose to speak, Jimmy Drumm, another 1940s veteran, leaned over and suggested that Ó Brádaigh listen carefully. In his remarks, Steele avoided the civil rights movement and recent political developments. Instead, he defended the militarism of the IRA. It was the antithesis of Cathal Goulding's address at Bodenstown in 1967. Steele spoke of Barnes and McCormack, "Our two martyred comrades whom we honor today." They "went forth to carry the fight to the enemy, into enemy territory, using the only methods that will ever succeed, not the method of the politicians, nor the constitutionalists, but the method of soldiers, the method of armed force." To shouts of "hear, hear" and applause, he added, "The ultimate aim of the Irish nation will never emerge from the political or constitutional platform. Indeed one is now expected to be more conversant with the teaching of Chairman Mao than those of our dead patriots." Steele stole the show. Tomás Mac Giolla, who was sitting on the platform, "could feel the tension." Steele was summarily dismissed from the IRA; his remarks were contrary to army policy.

On Tuesday, August 12th, the "logical consequences" of continued agitation in the North were made manifest. The Stormont government had banned NICRA marches, but the Apprentice Boys of Derry—who celebrate Protestant domination of the city—were allowed to march. Another riot developed. At first, the RUC pushed Nationalist rioters into the Bogside ghetto. But the large crowd turned, stopped the advance, and pushed the RUC out. The police doused the area with teargas and tried to clear out barricades; they were kept back by showers of petrol bombs and stones from the top of Rossville Flats, a nearby high-rise housing estate. In the thick of the fighting, to the delight of her constituents, was Bernadette Devlin, MP. She was later convicted of incitement to riot and riotous behavior and sentenced to six months in prison. In support of Derry, Nationalists held rallies in other northern cities; they also became violent. Crowds attacked RUC stations in Coalisland, Newry, and Strabane. On Wednesday, there were fires in Dungannon and Dungiven, roads were blocked in Newry, and RUC stations in Belfast were attacked. On Thursday, there was rioting in Belfast and in Armagh the B Specials shot dead a Nationalist.

There were no fatalities in Derry. From August 12th to 14th, Derry's Bogside—Free Derry—was under police attack. The RUC never entered the area; every attempt they made was countered with petrol bombs and stones. Belfast, where Nationalists were in the minority, was another story—between August 12th and 15th, more than 150 people were injured by gunfire and 150 homes were burned out. On August 14th, there were riots throughout the city and vigilantes attacked Catholic neighborhoods, burning people out. Five people were killed; a vigilante was shot dead by IRA defenders and four Nationalists were shot dead by the RUC. Two people died on the 15th, including 15-year-old Gerald McAuley, shot by Loyalist paramilitaries. McAuley, a member of Na Fianna Éireann, was the first Republican to die in the current Troubles.

Among the Nationalists' Belfast defenders were several IRA veterans, including Billy McKee, Séamus Twomey, Leo Martin, Liam Burke, and Joe Cahill. Cahill, who had left the IRA in 1965, reported back on August 14th. It was on the 14th that the British government, believing the situation was out of control, sent British troops onto the streets of Northern Ireland. In Derry, then Belfast, and then in other locations, troops replaced the RUC and the B Specials, bringing an end to overt conflict.

Southern Ireland rallied in support of northern Nationalists. Jack Lynch of Fianna Fáil had succeeded Seán Lemass as Taoiseach in 1966. With Derry under siege, Lynch addressed the country on Irish radio, stating that "the Stormont government is no longer in control of the situation" and "the Irish Government can no longer stand by and see innocent people injured and perhaps worse." He announced that the Irish government had requested a United Nations peacekeeping force for Northern Ireland and that the Irish Army was opening field hospitals along the border for refugees. On August 14th, the Connacht directorate of Sinn Féin announced a series of meetings in solidarity with the people of the Bogside that would conclude with a teach-in at the County Hotel in Carrick-on-Shannon. Those involved included Tom Mitchell, John Joe McGirl, and Ruairí Ó Brádaigh. Privately, some southern Republicans offered more direct support. Disenchanted Belfast Republicans went around their local leadership and asked the Dublin leadership for weapons. Dublin said no, fearing that more guns would lead to more bloodshed. The network of people associated with the reinterment of Barnes and McCormack then came in handy; the Belfast dissidents knew where to turn. Teams led by Joe Cahill, Jimmy Drumm, and Leo Martin went south looking for weapons. On Sunday, August 17th, Cahill's team picked theirs up from John Joe McGirl in Leitrim. That same day, Seán Mac Stiofáin organized and led an attack on an RUC station in Crossmaglen, County Armagh.

Others were also interested in more direct support. Charles Haughey, Seán Lemass's son-in-law and the Fianna Fáil minister for justice who had introduced military tribunals in 1961, was Lynch's minister for finance. His father had been second in command of one of the IRA's County Derry battalions in the early 1920s. It is reported in the pamphlet *Fianna Fáil and the I.R.A.* that on August 17th, Haughey's brother, Pádraic Haughey, met Cathal Goulding in London and gave him £1,500 to purchase weapons. Goulding was told that another £50,000 would follow, but there were strings attached. Among other things, the Fianna Fáil people wanted the Republicans to cease all political activity in the south. The Dublin-based IRA leadership rejected the offer. Dissidents in Belfast, who heard about the offer, did not. A week later, Jimmy Steele, Billy McKee, Jimmy Drumm, Joe Cahill, John Kelly, and Séamus Twomey met with Fianna Fáil people. It is reported by those close to Goulding that they were willing to meet Fianna Fáil's conditions, which included overthrowing the IRA's Belfast staff and setting up an independent northern command. And, it is alleged, Seán Mac Stiofáin supported them.

Whether or not they were inspired by Fianna Fáil, the dissidents staged a coup on September 22nd. Billy McMillan and his adjutant, Jim Sullivan, were conducting a brigade meeting when several people—including Billy McKee, Jimmy Steele, Leo Martin, Joe Cahill, Séamus Twomey, and John Kelly—arrived. They produced weapons and informed McMillan that they were taking over. One suspects that McMillan and Sullivan viewed them as apolitical militarists. J. Bowyer Bell describes McKee, Twomey, and Cahill as "typical Belfast Republicans, working class, parochial in experience" who "believed in physical force." McMillan and Sullivan knew that Twomey had not been in the IRA since the 1940s; that Cahill had left in the mid-1960s; and that Steele had been dismissed a month earlier. McKee, who had been involved through the 1960s, had opposed the civil rights movement. From his perspective, "as a Republican, we didn't ask or plead for civil rights, we demanded them. And if we didn't get them, we took them." McMillan brokered a compromise that kept him as commanding officer but added some dissidents to the brigade staff. Other conditions included breaking with Dublin and setting up a northern command; abandoning socialist policy, which was interpreted as any political involvement; not attending the next IRA convention; and removing some people from the Army Council, including Cathal Goulding. Ultimately, McMillan stayed in contact with Goulding and no one left the Army Council.

The IRA soldiered on, without Belfast and with difficulty. Goulding and his supporters focused on developing political opportunities. In October, the Hunt Commission, which was examining the disturbances in

Derry the previous October, recommended major changes in Northern Ireland, including disarming the RUC and disbanding the B Specials, which were to be replaced by a regiment of the British Army. Civil rights advocates welcomed the report; the Unionist community rejected it. Widespread rioting in Belfast left three people dead, including RUC constable Victor Arbuckle. With even the Unionist community attacking the forces of the state, all sorts of political change seemed possible. Goulding wanted to influence that change. He described the plan in an interview with Sam Dowling that was published in *This Week* in July 1970: "After a period of agitations, demonstrations and frustrations in line with the political phase of the struggle, people would see that they couldn't really develop political ACTION itself without actual political PARTICIPATION" (emphasis in the original). Electing people to Stormont, Leinster House, or Westminster could have an impact; in his words, Republican representatives could "refuse to attend Parliament on a critical issue in which the Government would have a bare majority, or in other cases where our one or two or three deputies would swing the vote against them, we could send our men in to speak on the issue, to vote and to beat them on it."

From the perspective of the abstentionists on the expanded Army Council—Ó Brádaigh, Mac Stiofáin, Paddy Mulcahy, and Dáithí O'Connell—this was nonsense. Goulding wanted to reform a Parliament —Stormont—that was subservient to the mother of imperialism—London. It made more sense to push for the abolition of Stormont, which seemed possible, as the British were clearly frustrated by continued violence and the slow pace of reform. Once Stormont was gone, the movement could directly confront the British on Irish soil—a return to the situation in the 1920s. At a minimum, the power of local elites would be diminished. The abstentionists were also worried that while Goulding played politics, Belfast would again go up in flames. The IRA had to be ready for this. Ó Brádaigh and other veterans of the 1950s also believed that the ground was being laid for a full-scale guerrilla campaign. In the original 1956 plan, the campaign was to follow a period of social agitation and passive resistance, which would mobilize people. The campaign skipped this phase and failed. The civil rights movement had mobilized people. If it was built on the back of this mobilization, an IRA campaign might succeed.

Ó Brádaigh, Mac Stiofáin, Mulcahy, and their supporters did their best to stay in the fold, but the movement was destined to split. They wanted to be there when it happened and take as many people with them as possible. Ó Brádaigh saw it as "maximizing" his position. That fall, Goulding drafted a document on the movement's policies to distribute to

Irish-American supporters. Ó Brádaigh and Mac Stiofáin signed off on it, even though they objected to its contents. If they had not signed, Ó Brádaigh suspected, Goulding would have said they opposed official policy and suspended them. That would have kept them from the upcoming IRA convention. Not everyone was so patient. In Donegal, the general headquarters representative—Ó Brádaigh believes it was Séamus Costello— refused to let Frank Morris, a long-term Republican, attend the unit convention, arguing that Morris had left the IRA. Dáithí O'Connell, the Donegal unit's commanding officer, walked out of the unit convention in protest and was suspended from the IRA. Ó Brádaigh sympathized with O'Connell and Morris, but he also believed that O'Connell had made a mistake. O'Connell, who was known as a top soldier in the 1950s, was much more than that. He was bright and articulate and thought strategically. Leo Martin remembers him as brains, strategic thinking, and leadership "all combined into one person." O'Connell would be missed at the general convention.

After unit conventions, the general headquarters representatives report back to the chief of staff. General headquarters and the chief of staff then make arrangements for the general convention. When Ó Brádaigh, Mac Stiofáin, and their colleagues received word about the convention details—it was to be held in mid-December in North Roscommon—they figured that Goulding had won. If the reports from the unit representatives had been negative, he would have put off the convention. The IRA was a conspiratorial clan at this time with few members and fewer leaders. People knew each other well and knew who was on which side. The pro-abstentionist delegates began planning for a showdown. Security issues prevented them from walking out of the convention. They agreed that if abstentionism was dropped, they would stay to the end, meet afterward at a prearranged location, and then set a course of action.

When they arrived at the convention, they saw that Goulding had also been planning. As agreed at the September coup, Belfast was not represented. But delegates from Clare, Tipperary, and Limerick who supported abstentionism—including Paddy Mulcahy—were also missing. Séamus Costello left them in Mullingar, waiting for a ride. And County Tyrone was overrepresented by persons opposed to abstentionism. The plots of both sides were complemented by personality clashes. For Ó Brádaigh, the movement had become "like a bad marriage" that was unraveling. Goulding and company had been caught unprepared in August and had never recovered. Going into the first Army Council meeting after August, Goulding looked at Ó Brádaigh and said, "Don't say 'I told you so.'" In November, Roy Johnston irritated a number of people by lecturing that "[i]t's important to realise that we don't have a revolutionary situation here. What we have is an opportunity for education." Goulding replied, "Look here, Roy, we were caught out once. If we're caught out again, the people will rise up and destroy us." People were tired of each other and of hearing the same arguments year after year. Goulding saw Seán Mac Stiofáin as a "petty minded conspirator" who was "continually trying to prove that he was as much an Irishman as anyone else." Ruairí Ó Brádaigh, who rarely speaks ill of anyone, describes Séamus Costello at this time as "very arrogant."

On the agenda were two controversial motions. The first called for the IRA to enter a national liberation front with "radical left" groups. This required only a majority vote. The second called for the IRA to recognize Leinster House, Stormont, and Westminster. The abstentionists opposed the creation of the national liberation front and lost. The debate on the second motion must have sounded like a broken record. Ó Brádaigh and Mac Stiofáin were the primary opposition; Mac Stiofáin spoke last. When Ó Brádaigh spoke he argued that the issue was not politics but *constitutional* politics. He repeated his argument that with constitutional politics the revolutionary becomes part of the status quo: "You become part of the machine." Then, in defending that machine from people like him, the former revolutionary joins with those opposed to revolution to quell dissent—to repress former comrades. "[B]ecause there's a crowd of madmen like us loose—because you're under a blitz from the crowd you have left and you seek refuge with the others." It was inevitable, it was what had happened to Mick Collins, Seán Mac Eoin, Éamon de Valera, Seán Lemass, and others. He argued: "Parliament is a replacement for civil war. You talk it out, instead of in the streets. But if you think you can keep one leg in the streets and the other leg in Parliament, you've a bloody awful mistake." He also challenged them: "What are you going to do with us, how are you going to cope with us?" He never got an answer. Based on his reading of history, he suspected that the answer was "Put us against the bloody wall and behind the barbed wire and six feet under."

His argument was that the system corrupts. His evidence was Irish history. Goulding, Costello, and Garland and their supporters felt that their sincerity was being questioned. In their view, Collins, Mac Eoin, de Valera, Lemass, and their cohorts had been weak and insincere. They believed themselves to be different. They thought they were doing something new. Ó Brádaigh asked them to not repeat the mistake of the past.

The final vote—by a show of hands—was twenty-eight for dropping abstentionism and twelve opposed. Goulding had his two-thirds majority, but it must have been anticlimactic. There were no angry confrontations and no one stormed out. The only indication that there was a problem was that the abstentionists did not allow their names to be put forward for the required election to the new Executive, which preceded the convention's end. They did not vote, either; they took no further part in proceedings. Immediately after the convention, the minority delegates rendezvoused for another meeting. There, they agreed on three basic points: the convention had been rigged and was illegitimate; those who had voted in favor of ending abstentionism had forfeited their membership in the IRA; and they needed to organize another convention that would repudiate the first. They distributed responsibility for contacting people who had been excluded from the convention and split up. Mac Stiofáin left for Belfast. Ó Brádaigh contacted, among others, Dáithí O'Connell. When O'Connell asked him, "What's going to happen?" Ó Brádaigh replied, "The minority is going to expel the majority." Key people met a week later at Mary Delaney's—Ó Brádaigh's sister's—house. It was centrally located in Athlone, and she was happy to loan it out for a meeting of Republicans. There they checked on their progress and made final arrangements for the second convention, which followed a few days later.

Twenty-six people—thirteen delegates and thirteen visitors—attended this second IRA convention, including the twelve minority delegates from the first convention; the missing Clare, Tipperary, and Limerick delegates; representatives from Belfast; and others, including Dáithí O'Connell. First on the agenda was electing a chairman. The natural choice was Seán Mac Stiofáin. He had been at the earlier convention, he had been on the Army Council for five years, and he had fought the old leadership from the beginning, in public and in private. He was very active in organizing the second convention and he wanted the position.

Over two days the delegates sorted out their priorities and what they were. Defense of the north was their primary concern. The old leadership had failed Belfast in August; this group would not. They also had to deal with the fact that there would now be two IRAs. Dáithí O'Connell, who had a flair for such things, suggested they were the "Provisional" IRA— the 1916 Proclamation had declared a provisional government, so they could be the provisional leadership until a proper IRA convention was organized. They also had to elect leaders. In 1968, the Army Council had been expanded to twenty members. The Provisionals returned to the previous arrangement of electing an Executive that then elected a sevenmember Army Council. Patrick Bishop and Eamonn Mallie, in *The Pro visional IRA,* were the first to identify those elected to the Army Council: Ruairí Ó Brádaigh, Seán Mac Stiofáin, Dáithí O'Connell, Paddy Mulcahy, Seán Treacy, Joe Cahill, and Leo Martin. Mac Stiofáin was the unanimous choice as the first chief of staff of the Provisional IRA. In politics, he was an ardent abstentionist. In military matters, he was a hawk. In IRA circles, ambition is often viewed with suspicion. Mac Stiofáin was ambitious, but he was clearly motivated by his passion for the movement. Ó Brádaigh believed him perfect for the position. The convention and election were over by Christmas.

In the popular imagination, guerrillas and terrorists are hot-headed young men who are itching for action. The Provisional Army Council was anything but. They were middle-aged family men with jobs and responsibilities. Ó Brádaigh and his family had moved to a larger house, with a larger mortgage, on July 1, 1969. He and O'Connell were teachers, Mac Stiofáin lived in Navan in County Meath and was still working for Conradh na Gaeilge. Cahill was a construction foreman. The oldest, at 53, was Paddy Mulcahy, an insurance agent in Limerick. O'Connell, at 31, was the youngest. Ó Brádaigh, 37, was in the middle. On the surface, they were a pretty ordinary group. Their Republican beliefs made them unique. All save Mac Stiofáin had grown up in Republican households. At one point or another, each had put his life on hold for the Republican Movement. Ó Brádaigh had not taught between 1956 and 1962. O'Connell had delayed marriage until he got out of jail. Cahill's situation was a classic example of Irish Republican family planning. In prison in the 1940s and again in the 1950s, he married late and had his children during the peace years—including six daughters born between 1962 and 1970. Collectively, the Provisional Council had more than a century of experience as members of a guerrilla army. Ó Brádaigh, Mac Stiofáin, Mulcahy, and O'Connell had leadership experience; Ó Brádaigh had been on the Army Council since 1956 (except for when he was a guest of the state). It was not clear at the time, but Ruairí Ó Brádaigh had joined Larry Grogan as one of only two people to serve on the IRA's Army Council at the start of two campaigns.

In their personal characteristics, the Provisionals were similar to those who remained in the "Official" IRA. Goulding and his colleagues had families, had interrupted careers, had made personal sacrifices, and had years of experience. The two groups were different in where they lived and their attitude on abstentionism. The core of the Provisionals were southern Republicans living in the west and in rural areas: Ó Brádaigh in Roscommon, Mulcahy in Limerick, O'Connell from Cork and living in Donegal, Mac Stiofáin from London and living Meath, and Treacy in County

Laois. The Official IRA leadership was based in Dublin, and most in Dublin stayed with the Officials. The Provisionals were the traditionalists in the countryside. They were in touch with each other and their rural constituency. They had not personally experienced August 1969. Defense in the north was important, but not important enough for them to join Belfast in a split in September. Abstentionism was the key for them. It was also very important for Leo Martin, as demonstrated by another split in 1986. The exception, it would seem, was Cahill, who later claimed that the 1969 split was "was over the failure of the IRA to defend the people of the North. . . . Albeit, abstentionism was used as a vehicle for the split, if you like." But his remark was made much later.

The first public indication of a split was on the morning of December 28th with a report in the Dublin-based *Sunday Press*. At a meeting that afternoon, "the Provisional Army Council" drafted a response deploring "the inspired leaking of confidential matters," stating it was "a clear attempt to prejudice the decision" of the upcoming Sinn Féin Ard Fheis. They repudiated the unrepresentative IRA convention and the dropping of abstentionism, acknowledged the second convention, and declared "allegiance to the 32-County Irish Republic, proclaimed at Easter 1916, established by the first Dáil Éireann in 1919, overthrown by force of arms in 1922 and suppressed to this day by the existing British-imposed Six-County and 26-County partition states." It was probably at this meeting that three decisions were made: the Provisionals decided they needed their own newspaper; Dáithí O'Connell was appointed the IRA's director of publicity; and, at O'Connell's suggestion, the statement was released under the name of "P. O'Neill." To this day, Provisional IRA statements are released under this nom de guerre. They named the paper *An Phoblacht* (The Republic), the title of the IRA's paper in the 1920s and 1930s.

A few days later, Ó Brádaigh visited 77-year-old Tom Maguire at his home in Cross, County Mayo. Maguire's opposition to Leinster House had not wavered. The Irish Civil War had prevented formal dissolution of the Second All-Ireland Dáil. Its successor, the Third (26-County) Dáil, was therefore illegitimate. On December 31st, as "the sole surviving member of the Executive of Dáil Éireann, and the sole surviving signatory of the 1938 proclamation" that delegated the executive powers of government to the IRA Army Council, Maguire released a statement that declared the resolution ending abstentionism illegal. He stated that "the governmental authority delegated in the Proclamation of 1938 now resides in the Provisional Army Council and its lawful successors." The statement confirmed the legitimacy of the Provisionals, the moral and legal heirs of the government of the All-Ireland Republic. As such, their use of physical force defending that republic would be legal and just. For the Officials, who rejected sentimentalism and saw traditions as dead weight, the Third Dáil—whether it was legitimate or not—had taken office forty-seven years earlier. The vast majority of the Irish people recognized it, its successors, and the state. The time had come to recognize reality.

The Officials waged their own propaganda campaign in *The United Irishman,* offering "the most comprehensive statement in the past decade on the aims, objectives and methods of the Irish Republican Army." They had rejected abstentionism, not physical force. "Those who think that political means alone are sufficient for the Re-Conquest of Ireland are closing their minds to the lessons of history, not alone in Ireland but in every other country struggling for national liberation." The Officials were combining revolutionary politics with revolutionary armed struggle, with the result that "[t]his time we can win—because this time it will be a revolutionary struggle of the Irish people and not a military challenge by a small heroic section." They also used the formal apparatus of the IRA to make their case. Immediately after the first convention, Goulding sought meetings with his regional commands. As their commanding officer, Ó Brádaigh allowed Goulding to address the Galway-Roscommon volunteers. Goulding presented his argument and questions and answers flowed. A few volunteers indicated that they agreed with Goulding, but most of them, and most volunteers in the west in general, sided with the Provisionals. Toward the end of the meeting, Goulding addressed Tommy McDermott. Goulding looked at him and said, "Tommy, we were in the Curragh together in the 1940s. You've listened to the discussion, but you haven't said anything." McDermott, who had been through the splits of the 1920s, calmly but with deadly seriousness, responded with, "I was in the Curragh with you, and if I had my way I'd put you up against a wall and shoot you, because you're nothing but a traitor." Goulding, startled, kept his composure. In order to save face, he remained through a break for tea and then set off in a car for Dublin. It was an encounter Ó Brádaigh will never forget.

On Sunday, January 11th, the pre–Ard Fheis lobbying and politicking was played out at the International Hotel in Ballsbridge, Dublin. The press was excluded, and for four hours the delegates debated a motion ending abstentionism from Leinster House, Stormont, and Westminster. In his report on the Ard Fheis, Séamus Ó Tuathail, editor of the *United Irishman,* commented: "The fate of Cumann na nGael, Fianna Fáil and Clann na Poblachta was mentioned with effect again and again" and "The

Republican dead were paraded before the assembled delegates and their names invoked frequently in defense of abstention." When the vote was finally called, it was 153 in favor and 104 opposed; Mac Giolla and Goulding were nineteen votes short of the two-thirds majority required to change the Sinn Féin Constitution. In an interview with the *Irish News* twenty years later, Goulding remembered the event "with some bitterness." After the IRA convention, the Officials had relaxed while the Provisionals had mobilized. Both sides were guilty of extra-parliamentary activities, Goulding charged, but the Provisionals had done a better job of it. Some Officials went too far and alienated supporters. Goulding was particularly upset with Séamus Costello, who left the Ard Fheis debate to watch Bernadette Devlin participate on a television program. (Costello was a big fan of Devlin's.) Goulding thought it was "the height of arrogance."

A tea break was scheduled to follow the vote. Instead, a delegate from Armagh City quickly stood up and proposed a vote of allegiance to the Official Army Council. The motion was seconded. It only required a majority vote, and it was guaranteed to pass. Because the Sinn Féin Constitution deemed recognizing Leinster House, Stormont, or Westminster as "an act of treachery," the abstentionists believed that the motion and vote were unconstitutional. Technically, those opposed to abstentionism should have first removed the embargo on even discussing the subject. The delegates who voted to drop abstentionism, therefore, had forfeited their membership in Sinn Féin. When the motion was seconded, Ruairí Ó Brádaigh got up and started walking out of the room. Someone struck him in the chest, but he kept going. Simultaneously, Seán Mac Stiofáin made his way to a floor microphone. As Mac Stiofáin pledged his allegiance to the Provisional Army Council and said, "Now lads, it is time for us to leave," others made their way to the door. Séamus Ó Tuathail described the scene:

> The final parting had all the quality of tragic drama. MacStíofáin precipitated events by pledging his allegiance to the Provisional Army Council. A delegate suddenly attacked him as he was making his way out and uproar ensued punctuated by appeals for calm and an end to the struggles on the floor. The doors flew open as the walk-out started.

> Joe Nolan was quick to underscore the emotional confusion of the moment. Grabbing a floor microphone, he announced that 'Seosamh Ó Cléirigh [Joe Clarke], the 1916 veteran is now leaving'. And so he was. Councillor Peter Duffy of Dundalk was on his feet haranguing Tom Mitchell in the Chair but could not be heard. Both had spent seven years in Crumlin Road Prison.

Now Peter was leaving. Éamonn Mac Thomáis was the last to leave after a brief protest looking regretfully over his shoulder like Lot's wife. A very subdued Ard-Fheis adjourned for tea.

After tea, Goulding made sure that the motion was voted on; it passed.

Because the walkout was anticipated, the abstentionists had arranged a place to reassemble. Tony Ruane, an IRA general in the 1920s, had rented the basement of Kevin Barry Hall, located at 44 Parnell Square. The building has been used by Republicans throughout the years; in 1951, Ruairí Ó Brádaigh had taken the declaration of an IRA volunteer there. Perhaps 100 people drove, took taxis, or walked through central Dublin and across the Liffey to the hall. Depending upon their route, some of them passed the Gardiner Place headquarters of what was now "Official" Sinn Féin. Among those who walked out were several women active in Sinn Féin and Cumann na mBan, including Caitlín Uí Mhuimhneacháin. As they reassembled, the mood, according to Seán Ó Brádaigh, was "solemn." People had an attitude of "God help us. This is what is left of us." Des Long, a member of the Ard Chomhairle, remembers that the split "was inevitable, but it wasn't a thing that we liked." Yet walking out "was easy because people already knew that there would be an army." Frank Glynn remembers discussing finances with John Joe McGirl; a collection that night netted a bit more than Ł90. For Ruairí Ó Brádaigh, the split was regrettable and it could have been avoided. His view was that Goulding and the others would have been better off starting a new organization, even a constitutional party, to say "if you're tired, Jesus, like, just opt out." This would have avoided bitterness. Instead, they tried "to convert the Republican Movement into what it's not. Something which is contrary to its nature." The result was an upheaval which hurt the movement and led to lasting bitterness on both sides.

Other than renting the room, the walkouts had no agenda; the only handout was a flyer announcing that *An Phoblacht* would be forthcoming. Because it was the second time in a month that essentially the same people were creating a new organization, they knew what they had to do—elect a temporary leadership until a proper Ard Fheis could repudiate what had just happened. The leadership developed naturally. Ruairí Ó Brádaigh found himself "put in the chair." Just as Mac Stíofáin was perfect for the position of chief of staff; Ó Brádaigh was the perfect chairman of the caretaker executive. His politics were sound; when he had been elected to Leinster House in 1957, he had not been tempted to enter that Assembly. He had been on the Ard Chomhairle in the 1950s, had been a Sinn Féin

Seán Ó Brádaigh, circa 1970.
Seán Ó Brádaigh Collection.

candidate in Fermanagh–South Tyrone in 1966, and had chaired four successive Ard Fheiseanna. And, and this was important for many people in the room, he was an established figure in the IRA. Most important, Ó Brádaigh was willing to serve. The army already was in good hands, and he was increasingly interested in the movement's politics. It was his opportunity to keep the movement abstentionist, "Republican," but at the same time develop its political program.

Other members joined the caretaker executive in a similar fashion; the people in the room knew each other and their talents. Seán Ó Brádaigh became director of publicity, Walter Lynch of Dublin became party secretary, and Tony Ruane became the treasurer. Following a pattern that had held for years, the IRA was well represented, by Ruairí Ó Brádaigh, Seán Mac Stiofáin, and Paddy Mulcahy, among others. In all, twenty people were elected to the Executive. Seventeen of them had been born and raised in the Twenty-Six Counties. Like their Provisional IRA counterparts, abstentionism was the key to their walkout. At the conclusion of the meeting, they issued a statement to the press: "The delegates here tonight consider themselves to be the adjourned Ard-Fheis of Sinn Féin. . . .

We adhere to the Sinn Féin Constitution as upheld by the Ard-Fheis, but those who remained in the Intercontinental Hotel stated that they did not accept the Constitution and rules of Sinn Féin in so far as these preclude recognition of the three parliaments. A Caretaker Executive was appointed from members of the new Ard-Chomhairle and Sinn Féin public representatives in attendance. A full Ard-Fheis will be held in due course."

The caretaker executive rented offices on Kevin Street, on Dublin's near south side, and scrambled to get out the first issue of *An Phoblacht* under the editorship of Seán Ó Brádaigh. It was financed through a £500 loan he procured from a sympathetic Dublin businessman, to be paid off in five monthly installments. The paper hit Dublin's streets on January 31st, a day ahead of schedule. It was an amalgamation of press releases—including Maguire's statement—pledges of support from around the country—including North Kerry and "the Roscommon and Galway units of the Irish Republican Army"—and the firm statement that they, the caretaker executive, were "standing on 'The Rock of the Republic,' and from that position we refuse to budge." The Provisionals' founders are often described as personal and political conservatives who were militarists uninterested in politics. Fairly or not, Seán Mac Stiofáin is the standard example cited. The Ó Brádaighs and people like Éamonn Mac Thomáis were interested in progressive politics and they used the first edition of *An Phoblacht* to illustrate their point. There was a lengthy two-part article by Séamas Ó Mongáin on the Irish tradition of Comhar na gComharsan (translated as "the neighbors' cooperation"). Collectively, the caretaker executive rejected communism but not socialism. Developing Comhar na gComharsan would be "one of the foundations of a just social order in Ireland." The paper met a receptive audience and the first run of 14,000 sold out quickly. A second run of 6,000 also sold out. The next month, 25,000 copies were printed. The loan was paid back on time.

By May, the dust had settled and it had become clear that the IRA and Sinn Féin had each pretty much split in half. *This Week* reported that the Provisionals had "fairly strong support" in Limerick, Kerry, Cork, and Waterford and "claim to have 50 per cent of Derry." They were strongest in Meath, Louth, Monaghan, and Belfast. In Belfast, they had "swung 60 per cent of the original IRA-Sinn Féin men." Cumann na mBan also sided with the Provisionals. In June and July, the Provisionals began flexing their muscles. On Saturday, June 27th, there was rioting across Belfast, suggesting a repeat of the previous August. The Short Strand is a small Nationalist enclave in East Belfast; a focal point for the community is the local Catholic Church, St. Matthew's. A Loyalist-inspired mob threatened the church with petrol bombs. Local people appealed to the British Army for assistance but were refused. It was busy elsewhere and did not have the personnel. Into the breach and into Irish Republican legend stepped Billy McKee, the Provisional IRA's Belfast Commander.

McKee, a "single, slightly-built and mild-mannered" bachelor and a "passionate Catholic," organized the defense of St. Matthew's. Two attackers were shot dead on the scene and two others were mortally wounded. One defender, Henry McIlhone, was shot dead. McKee was shot twice, once in the arm and once through the back and out his neck. He was hospitalized overnight and then some of his "boys" lifted him and sent him south for recuperation. In the words of Raymond Quinn in *A Rebel Voice: A History of Belfast Republicanism, 1925–1972*, it was "a classic example of the traditional role of the I.R.A. in Belfast." The next Friday, the British Army—which had been unable to help out at St. Matthew's—raided the Lower Falls area of West Belfast. There had been riots and shootings in the area, but there had been the same in Protestant areas. Protestant areas were not raided; the Lower Falls was. Rioting broke out and the troops responded with teargas. The area was an Official IRA stronghold and it fired on the troops. The British responded in kind. The British placed the area under a curfew and then, as described by J. Bowyer Bell in *The Irish Troubles: A Generation of Violence,* "House by house the soldiers smashed down front doors, tore away walls and floorboards, looking for arms or documents or something, smashed by accident and by design the furnishings, insulted the owners, who insulted them, cursed their lot and the people, who cursed them, took advantage and took liberties." The curfew remained in force until Sunday morning, when a group of women and children filled prams with food and supplies and marched through the British lines. They were led by Máire Drumm, Jimmy's wife and a Cumann na mBan veteran. Four people in the Lower Falls died that weekend. Three were shot dead by the British Army, the fourth was run over by a British armored vehicle. None of them were Republicans. If it had planned it, the British Army could not have done a better job of alienating the Nationalist community in Belfast; it made IRA recruiting—both Official and Provisional—that much easier.

Through the spring, Ruairí Ó Brádaigh had worked as much as he could to promote the caretaker executive. In June, with school out and conflict again developing in the north, things got especially busy. On the 14th, he was chief marshal at Bodenstown. Five thousand people turned out to hear Dáithí O'Connell lambaste constitutional politicians and the Official IRA and make an appeal to northern Protestants. O'Connell reminded them that Wolfe Tone had "proved that Catholic and Protestant could work together for their mutual benefit." On the 18th, Ó Brádaigh appeared on an Irish television marathon that was covering the British general election. The Conservatives, under Edward Heath, were returned to power in London. Among those re-elected in Northern Ireland were Frank McManus in Fermanagh–South Tyrone and Bernadette Devlin in Mid-Ulster. McManus, an Independent Republican, was the brother of Pat McManus, who had been killed in the IRA's 1950s Border Campaign. Also on the RTÉ (Radio Telefis Éireann) program was Tom Mitchell of Official Sinn Féin. Conor Cruise O'Brien, another participant, was surprised to see that Ó Brádaigh and Mitchell had remained friends. O'Brien, a Labour TD in Leinster House who would become the most prominent Irish intellectual over the next thirty years, recorded his impression of Ó Brádaigh in the book *States of Ireland*. He found him "rather disconcerting." He was "a very gentle, quiet, good-humoured man, who seemed more interested in preventing violence than on starting it." Intrigued, O'Brien invited him to lunch at the National Gallery in Dublin. In his notes on this meeting, O'Brien quoted from Yeats's "Meditations in Time of Civil War" and described Ó Brádaigh as "'an affable Irregular' strongly rather than heavily built. Refuses wine. Pleasant open face." Perhaps saying as much about himself as about Ó Brádaigh, O'Brien was one of very few people to question the sincerity of Ó Brádaigh's presentation of self, adding, "Smiles a lot. Too much? Believed to be the leader of the Provisionals." Over lunch, Ó Brádaigh explained the split, denied that it was inspired by Fianna Fáil, and rejected the view that the Provisionals were promoting sectarian violence in the North; they were defending people, as at St. Matthew's.

For the rest of the summer Ó Brádaigh and everybody else on the Caretaker Executive took every opportunity to present the movement's case. On August 9, 1970, 63-year-old Jimmy Steele died of natural causes. A member of the Provisionals' Army Executive, he had founded the Belfast-based newspaper, *Republican News,* in June. By August its circulation was 15,000 copies a month. Ó Brádaigh and Mac Stiofáin drove together to Belfast for the funeral. Mac Stiofáin delivered an oration to an estimated 20,000 people; among the mourners was Billy McKee, who was mending nicely. At the funeral, Ó Brádaigh approached Máire Drumm and asked if she would be interested in joining the Caretaker Executive. It was the beginning of a relationship that led him to refer to her as his "political wife." A few days later, with Liam Slevin and Joe O'Neill, he addressed a public meeting in Donegal Town in support of Roddy Carlin of Derry. Carlin had been arrested in the "Republic," a victim of "collaboration" between Dublin, London, and Belfast. He reminded the crowd of Lynch's August 1969 pledge of support for Derry and added, "Mr. Lynch has gone over to the side of the Crown Forces by jailing a Derry defender."

In mid-August and then a week later, *This Week* published a two-part interview with Ó Brádaigh and an unidentified "official spokesman of the Provisional Army Council for the IRA." It was Mac Stiofáin. He spoke on military issues. Ó Brádaigh spoke on politics. In May 1970, the Arms Crisis had rocked Lynch's government. The meetings that occurred in 1969 between Republicans and members of Fianna Fáil had become public amid allegations that two members of Lynch's cabinet, Charles Haughey and Neil Blaney, were involved in gun-running. Lynch dismissed them while a third cabinet member, Kevin Boland, resigned. (Haughey was later acquitted and the charges against Blaney were dismissed.) The Arms Crisis led to the rumor that the Provisionals were the result of a Fianna Fáil plot, which Ó Brádaigh flatly rejected. He had suffered "personally at the hands of the Fianna Fáil Government." He reminded the interviewer, Sam Dowling, that a Fianna Fáil government had interned him in the "concentration camp in the Curragh."

By September, it was time to end the "Provisional" period. A general IRA convention, held "in accordance with the provisions of the Constitution of Óglaigh na hÉireann," brought together delegates from each of Ireland's thirty-two counties. Tom Maguire, a special guest, also attended. In his biography of Maguire, *Dílseacht,* Ó Brádaigh describes him at the convention as "an imposing and erect figure with an obvious military presence." When Maguire entered the hall, the chairman—presumably Ruairí Ó Brádaigh—brought the delegates to attention. The chair "exchanged salutes with Comdt-Gen Maguire and introduced him to the meeting." Maguire told the delegates that "the authority of the last sovereign parliament for all Ireland now rested with them."

The convention proceeded smoothly; its organizers and the delegates were of a like mind on the big issues. Militarily, the most pressing issue was defense in the north. Politically, they sought "a Democratic Socialist Republic based on the Proclamation of 1916." Organizationally, they kept the twelve-person Executive, electing a seven-person Army Council, with one important change. Under its Constitution, the IRA is a participatory democracy. Since 1932, members of the Executive had been allowed to sit on the Army Council. This helped limit the number of people in leadership positions; when the army is small, leadership delegates might outnumber regular delegates at a convention. Given recent events, the convention delegates wanted as broad a leadership as possible. The IRA was growing again, so they separated the Executive from the Army Council. After 1970, people on the Executive relinquished their seats if they went onto the Army Council. The convention ended with an election to the Executive. The Executive then elected its Army Council, with some changes from the previous December. Paddy Mulcahy and Seán Tracey were replaced by Denis McInerney and Billy McKee. They were joined by Seán Mac Stiofáin (who remained chief of staff), Ruairí Ó Brádaigh, Dáithí O'Connell, Joe Cahill, and Leo Martin.

The (Provisional) Sinn Féin Ard Fheis came next in Liberty Hall, Dublin, the weekend of October 24–25. Described as one of the "most enthusiastic" Ard Fheiseanna in years, it attracted almost 300 delegates from all thirty-two counties of Ireland, representing 130 Sinn Féin Cumainn and Comhairli Ceantair. "Exiles" living in England, Scotland, and Wales also sent delegates. The temporary caretaker executive was dissolved and the delegates elected a regular Officer Board and Ard Chomhairle. There was no controversy, and the transition from temporary to regular leadership went smoothly. Ruairí Ó Brádaigh, who had performed admirably as chairman of the Caretaker Executive, was elected, unopposed, as president of Sinn Féin. Other officers on the Caretaker Executive were elected to the Sinn Féin leadership, including Seán Ó Brádaigh as director of publicity, Walter Lynch as secretary, and Tony Ruane as treasurer. The veterans of 1916–1923, Joe Clarke and Larry Grogan, were elected as vice presidents. Several people on the Caretaker Executive were elected to the Ard Chomhairle, including Seán Mac Stiofáin and Máire Drumm.

The high point of the Ard Fheis was the presidential address, Ó Brádaigh's first. The situation called for a speech demonstrating their legitimacy; they were not new. *They* were Sinn Féin. He began in Irish,

Sibh-se na fíor-Phoblachtánaigh, a d'fhan seasamhach i gcosaint na Poblachta in aghaidh an ionsaithe a rinneadh uirthi roinnt mhí ó shin, tá meas agus buíochas mhuintir dhílis na Poblachta anseo in Éirinn agus ar deoraíocht a dhul daoibh. Rinne sibh ath-riaradh oraibh fhéin sna heagraíochtaí éagsúla agus tá Gluaiseacht na Poblachta in a dhún daingean arís. Buíochas mór le Dia. [You, the true Republicans who stood steadfast in defense of the Republic against the attack made on it some months ago, are entitled to the respect and appreciation of the loyal Republican people here in Ireland and in exile. You reorganized yourselves in the various organizations and the Republican Movement is once more a sturdy stronghold. Thanks be to God.]

Shifting to English, he continued, "On Behalf of the Caretaker Executive I wish to extend a hearty welcome to all delegates and visitors to this—the 66th Annual Ard-Fheis of Sinn Féin." In January, they had "pledged our allegiance to the Constitution of Sinn Féin" and "appointed a Caretaker Executive to carry on the affairs of the organisation on the basis of that Constitution and to convene a representative Ard-Fheis in due course." That convention had assembled and a new leadership had been "regularised." He therefore asked the media to "acknowledge who is the true and official Sinn Féin, upholding the Constitution of the organisation and having the allegiance of the vast majority of Irish Republicans." Because they were Sinn Féin, there were no changes in party policy to announce. The party remained concerned about economic problems in the south and the threat of economic integration with Britain and the European Economic Community. There was also the traditional concern that Dublin was collaborating with London and Belfast. Ó Brádaigh commented that British and Irish forces had recently joined "in the hunt along the Border."

They knew who they were. Where they were going, no one knew. The one sure thing was that everything had changed. Ó Brádaigh, and the movement, were going to capitalize on it. Ó Brádaigh continued:

> The great re-awakening in British-occupied Ireland which dates from October 5, 1968, in the city of Derry, is still with us. The changes which began that day are being hurried along by a new generation, impatient to see the old order gone for ever. The repercussions of that great struggle and the suffering it involved for so many ordinary Irish people have spread south of the Border and even into high places—the places of the would-be mighty who are disturbed as they have never been for 50 years. Nothing has been quite the same ever since that brutal baton-charge in Duke Street.

In a two-year span, Irish politics had been transformed. The Republican Movement, which had been dormant to the external observer since 1962, was again relevant. Within two more years, the IRA, led by Mac Stiofáin, would bomb Stormont out of existence and force the British government into a bilateral truce. And Provisional Sinn Féin, led by Ruairí Ó Brádaigh, would develop a political program that proposed a united Ireland with safeguards for the integrity and culture of the Protestant and Unionist community in Northern Ireland.

11

The Politics of Revolution

ÉIRE NUA, NOVEMBER 1970–DECEMBER 1972

THE END OF THE 1970 Ard Fheis marked the beginning of the most intense period of Ruairí Ó Brádaigh's life. For the next two years the political and the personal were intimately intertwined as he and Dáithí O'Connell charted a course for the movement's politics that held until the early 1980s.

In mid-1970, Irish Press journalist Tim Pat Coogan published *The IRA* and American academic J. Bowyer Bell published *The Secret Army: The IRA from 1916–*. Both histories were well received and had a natural market because of the developing conflict in the north. Ó Brádaigh was interviewed for Bell's book and subsequently reviewed it for the *Irish Press*. Both books correctly identified him as chief of staff at the end of the 1950s campaign. People assumed that he was again chief of staff. He denied it, saying he was too busy running Sinn Féin, but few people believed him. At one point, a journalist, trying to goad him into revealing more than he wanted, called him a "God-damned liar." Ó Brádaigh let it pass, but it was irritating.

The assumption that he was chief of staff had consequences. Patsy gave birth to their sixth and final child, Colm, in December 1970. Late one afternoon, with Patsy and Colm still in the hospital and with his mother-in-law and five children in the house, there was a knock at the front door. He opened it to Cathal Goulding and Mick Ryan of the Officials, standing in a cold hard December rain. Goulding asked, "Can we come in?" Ó Brádaigh, who is almost always polite, replied, "No." In the rain, Goulding explained that their plan had been to pick up John Joe McGirl and drive to Roscommon, where the four of them could discuss a recent development. McGirl was not home, so they had traveled on to Ó Brádaigh's. Goulding, chief of staff of the Official IRA, assumed that

Ó Brádaigh was his counterpart. He explained that there was trouble between "your men in Belfast" and some of the Officials there. Ó Brádaigh responded, "They're not my men. All I can do is pass on the message." Goulding then stepped up onto the small porch, stretched his short frame to the limit, looked Ó Brádaigh in the eye, and said, "You know, it could spread down here." Ó Brádaigh replied, "I think it's time you gentlemen are going" and shut the door. The visit and thinly veiled threat did not bode well.

Accusations of being chief of staff aside, Ó Brádaigh was interested in Republican politics. With Seán Ó Brádaigh and Dáithí O'Connell, he was working on a social and economic program, Éire Nua (New Ireland). The program, which was formally launched on January 17, 1971, had origins in the mid-1960s. Roy Johnston and Seán Ó Brádaigh drafted the original program, but it had never been put to an Ard Fheis. The Ó Brádaighs and O'Connell "took it down from the shelf," updated it, and made it the program of Provisional Sinn Féin. They began with Wolfe Tone, who sought "[t]he rights of man in Ireland. The greatest happiness of the greatest number." Onto this they grafted a version of socialism that fell between "the Western capitalism of the U.S.A. with its 30,000,000 poor and hungry amid plenty" and Soviet "state capitalism" with "its denial of freedom and human rights." They were influenced by the Brehon laws of ancient Ireland, under which property was communally owned, Comhar na gComharsan, which called for cooperative ventures, and the African socialism of Julius Nyerere, president of Tanzania. Nyerere, a former schoolteacher, had charted an independent course for Tanzania that rejected both the West and the Soviets, nationalized key industries, and promoted collective farming. Under Éire Nua, industries such as commercial banking and mining would be nationalized and worker-owned cooperatives would be established in manufacturing, agriculture, and fishing.

Concurrent with Provisional Sinn Féin's development, the Provisional IRA was moving from defense to offense. The Provisionals started an economic war and bombed businesses throughout the north. They also confronted the British Army. On Saturday morning, February 6, 1971, the Provisionals shot dead Robert Curtis of the Royal Artillery; he was the first British soldier killed by the IRA since the 1920s. At about the same time, the British Army shot dead James Saunders of the Belfast IRA and Bernard Watt, a Nationalist civilian. Describing the situation, Prime Minister Chichester-Clark stated on television that "Northern Ireland is at war with the Irish Republican Army Provisionals."

As the Provisionals grew, there was more trouble in Belfast, and

Ó Brádaigh and Tomás Mac Giolla, president of Official Sinn Féin, got into a war of words in the press. In mid-February, Mac Giolla claimed that his organization had sought cooperation, only to receive "bitter public attacks, distortion of our policies and objectives, many deliberate lies in regard to our members and our organisation, and a refusal even to speak to us." He charged that the caretaker Executive's director of publicity— Seán Ó Brádaigh—was "foremost in building up the bitterness." Ruairí Ó Brádaigh publicly dismissed the charges, referring to Mac Giolla as the "National Liberation Front" leader and stating that he was engaged in "a frantic effort to avoid political eclipse." Mac Giolla responded by likening the publicity campaign of the Provisionals with "Goebbels' propaganda in Germany." He also warned: "Our verbal restraint in the face of the Caretaker publicity officer's McCarthyite communist witchhunt campaign has reached breaking point." Ó Brádaigh responded that the Officials were "behaving as a splinter group" and included a political dig: "We have published our social and economic programme, something which Gardiner Place have yet to do."

The dispute became deadly. Each IRA had its strongholds, and each discouraged the other from operating inside them. When the Officials attacked a British base in a Provisional area, the Provisionals assaulted the Officials' commanding officer. The British Army stood by and watched a feud erupt. It climaxed on March 8, 1971, when Charlie Hughes of the Provisionals was shot dead. Hughes, who was from a respected Belfast Republican family, had many friends, and his death was a wake-up call. A truce was negotiated, but tension remained; a number of people never forgave the Officials for killing Hughes. Hughes's death was also noteworthy because a group of British soldiers were photographed saluting the cortege as it passed by. In the press, Mac Giolla and Ó Brádaigh continued to trade insults. In April, Official Sinn Féin registered as a political party in the Twenty-Six Counties and Ó Brádaigh commented, "It is laughable that the Mac Giolla group who are supposed to be opposed to the machinery of this State and want to tear it down are using that same machinery to get registration as a party."

The day after the Hughes shooting, on March 9th, the Belfast Provisionals demonstrated how serious they were. They lured John McCaig, 17, his brother Joseph, 18, and Dougald McDonald, 23, British soldiers in the Royal Highland Fusiliers, from a Belfast bar and shot them. Their half-full beer glasses were propped up in their hands. Their ages and off-duty status shocked the community. Unionist politicians called for increased security measures, including internment, and Chichester-Clark flew to London seeking help. The British sent over additional troops, but not enough for Chichester-Clark, who resigned. Two potential successors emerged, William Craig and Brian Faulkner. Faulkner, who as minister for home affairs at Stormont had introduced internment in 1956, was viewed as the more moderate of the two, received more support from his Unionist Party colleagues, and was elected prime minister.

Faulkner inherited a deteriorating situation. In early June, General Harry Tuzo, the British Army general commanding officer in Northern Ireland, admitted that the army could only achieve a "gradual ascendancy" over the IRA. He also stated that a "permanent solution" could not be achieved by military means. Faulkner, recognizing the same, tried to foster cross-community politics and undercut support for the Republicans. In 1970, a mix of Nationalist politicians and civil rights activists, including Austin Currie, Paddy Devlin (a former Republican), Gerry Fitt (the first leader of the party), and John Hume, had formed the Social Democratic and Labour Party (SDLP). They viewed themselves as progressives, rejecting both the conservatism of the Nationalist Party and the physical force of the Republicans. They advocated the reunification of Ireland by peaceful means and took their seats at Stormont. Brian Faulkner courted their support. In June 1971, he proposed all-party involvement in parliamentary committees. It was a radical departure from the traditional one-party rule in Stormont, and it was welcomed by the SDLP. It seemed that there might be an alternative to the half-century of Unionist domination that bred Nationalist discontent, Republican physical force, and Unionist repression.

The opportunity was lost in July. On Thursday, July 8th, after four nights of rioting in Derry, the British Army shot dead Séamus Cusack, a Nationalist civilian. They claimed he had a rifle; witnesses denied it. There were mourning processions and riots on Friday and the British Army killed a second civilian, Desmond Beattie. They claimed he was preparing to throw a nail bomb; witnesses again denied it. Beattie and Cusack were buried on Saturday. With Derry in an uproar, Ó Brádaigh and Sinn Féin seized an opportunity. More than 1,000 people showed up for a Sinn Féin rally on Sunday to hear Seán Keenan, Walter Lynch, Gerry O'Hare, Máire Drumm, and Ruairí Ó Brádaigh offer their interpretation of events. Keenan stated bluntly what most felt, that Beattie and Cusack had been murdered. Máire Drumm pushed the crowd to avenge their deaths. The people of Derry had risen. As people cheered, she shouted, "For Christ's sake, stay up." Pulling no punches, she continued, "I would personally prefer to see all the British Army going back dead." And, with the sound bite for which she is remembered, she summed up her attitude, "It is a waste of time shouting, 'Up the IRA!' The important thing is to join." To cheers and applause she ended with "God bless you all, long live Free Derry and God save Ireland."

Ó Brádaigh spoke last, and he placed the other speakers' comments in a context. They were assembled "in just and righteous anger to illustrate to the world just how the people felt, and what their aspirations were at this time." Although the UN Declaration of Human Rights guaranteed equality in dignity and rights, in Derry "there are double-standards in high places" that allowed the British Army to get away with murder. Derry was an outpost in a colonial empire and these outposts "tread on the bodies and lives of ordinary people." It was time for those people, the "wonderful" people of Derry, to lead the way so that all Irish people "get off their knees and follow." He offered his own call to action, shouting, "Are we going to go on another ten years? This is my own second time round." The crowd shouted back, "No, no." He ended with, "We're going to finish this this time. We're on the high road to freedom, and what we need to do is to rock Stormont and to keep rocking it until Stormont comes down. Hands off, John Bull!" In the crowd, the Derry IRA was literally signing recruits up on clipboards.

The positive response to the Republican message threatened the SDLP. Pat Walsh, in *From Civil Rights to National War*, states that "after a visit to Derry by Ruairí Ó Brádaigh, the Sinn Féin leader, [John] Hume lost his nerve and called a meeting of the SDLP." Hume announced that the party would withdraw from Stormont unless there was an immediate inquiry into the shootings. The British Ministry of Defence rejected his call, and the RUC arrested Máire Drumm for seditious speech. The SDLP, rebuffed, withdrew from Stormont and announced that they would set up their own "non-sectarian, non-unionist assembly." It did not help Máire Drumm. She was found guilty and sentenced to six months in prison.

Probably inspired by the rally in Derry, John Rooks of the *Belfast Telegraph* traveled to Roscommon and interviewed "Rory Brady." The interview is revealing, for it gives Ó Brádaigh's political perspective in July 1971, when there was probably still a chance that the Troubles could be short-circuited, a chance that was lost in August. Rooks was especially interested in Ó Brádaigh's opinions on Northern Ireland's Protestant community. Critics, including Official Sinn Féin, were charging that the IRA's bombing campaign was sectarian, targeting that community and its businesses. Ó Brádaigh disagreed. He viewed the conflict in political, not religious, terms; the conflict was with the British government. He, and the movement, did not want to dominate Protestants in a Catholic state. Instead, they wanted to build a pluralist society, with "all sides in a 32-county democratic socialist republic." Rooks, and many others, wanted to know Ó Brádaigh's thoughts on the consequences of IRA success, asking "If the British withdraw, do you imagine that the Protestant people will not arm and fight?" Ó Brádaigh did not want, or expect, such a response. Ó Brádaigh believed that the result of the 1920 gerrymandered political outcome inevitably guaranteed continued conflict which successive British governments used as an excuse for remaining in Northern Ireland, claiming they were there to keep the peace and prevent civil war. Because the British guaranteed Unionist domination, Unionists had never needed to work with Nationalists. But, Ó Brádaigh argued, if the British withdrew, "the majority of the Protestant people are hard-headed, sensible, very realistic, and they would come to realise that the best thing to do would be to participate in the building of the new Ireland. We would invite them to do that; they have a very real contribution to make." Rooks also asked about Ó Brádaigh's "military boss." Ó Brádaigh gave his standard response, "I am head of the political wing. Military questions, as such, I am not competent to answer." But Ó Brádaigh did comment on General Tuzo's remarks and the IRA, stating, "I cannot imagine the IRA driving the British Army into the sea, or anything like that, but I think it would be possible to force the British authorities to the conference table." It was a prescient comment.

The SDLP's withdrawal from Stormont limited Brian Faulkner's options; there was no group with which he could cultivate a middle ground. After consulting Prime Minister Heath, and against the recommendation of General Tuzo, Faulkner turned to internment. It had worked in the past; it might work again. Early Monday morning, August 9th, British troops raided homes and detained more than 340 people. The Nationalist community, following three years of civil rights protests, was outraged. In spite of substantial pro-Unionist violence, only Nationalists were interned. Adding to the outrage, it became public that several internees had been brutalized by the British Army and the RUC while in custody. The SDLP asked for the immediate suspension of Stormont and called on the public to withhold rents paid for state-owned houses and rates paid for services to the houses. Practice raids had tipped off Provisional and Official activists. Only a few of them were interned, and each IRA went to war, confronting the British Army with pitched gun battles in several areas. Recruits joined en masse. Barricades went up in Derry's Bogside and in areas of Belfast, creating "no-go" areas controlled by Republicans. Only the British Army, in force and at risk, could patrol them.

At the end of the week, the British Army organized a press conference and claimed that internment had been a great success, that several IRA personnel had been killed or interned. At almost the same time, the Provisional IRA's Belfast commanding officer, Joe Cahill, met with correspondents and photographers and offered the Republican interpretation of internment. The British Army had shot dead eighteen people, including a Catholic priest, but only two of them were Provisionals—Séamus Simpson and Paddy McAdorey. Hundreds of people had been interned, but only thirty or so were Provisionals. From Cahill's perspective, things were going well, although the Provisionals needed more ammunition. Cahill was instantly famous and the British Army's credibility was sorely undermined. And there was no letup. That August there were more than 100 explosions in Northern Ireland. At the end of the month, Ó Brádaigh, who had been invited over for a lecture, was excluded from Britain and Cahill was denied entry into the United States, but these seemed like minor setbacks. Things were going so well that in early September the Provisionals felt strong enough to offer a suspension of operations if five conditions were met: the British Army stopped all action, Stormont was abolished, there was a guarantee of a free election in the Six Counties, all political prisoners were released, and compensation was guaranteed for those who had suffered from British violence. A Stormont spokesman replied, "We do not do deals with murderers or comment on their actions."

Prior to internment, the movement had been growing, and its demands on Ó Brádaigh had been increasing. After internment, things were so hectic that he realized there was no way he could keep up his political commitments and return to teaching in the fall. He discussed the situation with Dáithí O'Connell, who faced the same choice, and with Patsy, whose life would be most affected. O'Connell agreed that there was no way they could teach and run Sinn Féin. Patsy agreed that with some effort they could afford it if Ruairí took a leave of absence. The Ard Chomhairle gave him a small stipend and she could probably find work teaching part-time. In late August, Ó Brádaigh asked the Roscommon Vocational Education Committee for an open-ended unpaid leave of absence. It was granted by the committee, but it was not endorsed by the minister for education.

O'Connell also took a leave of absence and started making plans to move to Dublin. Living in Ballyshannon, Donegal, he was very much removed from things. Ó Brádaigh also considered moving to Dublin but decided against it. Three of the children were in primary school and he did not want to uproot them. He also wanted to stay near his mother, who was in a nursing home in Longford. There were also political considerations. The Vocational Education Committee, and Roscommon in general, had openly supported him over the years, including people who disagreed with his politics. He also knew every police officer—uniformed and plain-clothed, friendly and unfriendly—in the area. Most important, a move to Dublin would not help his family life. He was constantly on the road in and out of Roscommon and Dublin. His choices were to be gone constantly from a Dublin home or from a Roscommon home. He chose Roscommon. The decision also made his life, and his family, safer. Everyone in the area pretty much knew everyone else and, to a degree, their business. This level of knowledge could work to protect Ó Brádaigh and his family. In the spring of 1972, Loyalists sent letter bombs to four prominent Republicans. Cathal Goulding defused his. Tony Ruane was badly burned when his went off in the Provisional Sinn Féin head office, and Seán Mac Stiofáin was injured in his left eye when his went off as he inspected it at home. Ó Brádaigh's was intercepted by the Roscommon post office.

The SDLP call for an alternative to Stormont echoed a sentiment held by many people. Ó Brádaigh and Dáithí O'Connell had for some time been interested in the Swiss political system, where regional parliaments brought a diverse population into an integrated whole. With this as a model, they considered a regional parliament for all of Ulster—the Six Counties of Northern Ireland plus Cavan, Donegal, and Monaghan. They invited representatives from a number of political perspectives, including the SDLP and the Unionists, to a convention in Monaghan town on August 21st; the risk of internment precluded siting the convention in Northern Ireland. The SDLP, which had called for its own assembly, did not attend. Unionists, who wanted a return to Stormont and were not interested in talking with the Provisionals, also did not attend. However, a variety of Nationalists did, including Jimmy McElwain, a Sinn Féin county councilor in Monaghan; representatives from Peoples' Democracy; Frank McManus, the MP at Westminster for Fermanagh–South Tyrone; Frank Gogarty and Aidan Corrigan of NICRA; and Paddy Kennedy, an MP at Stormont and the person who had introduced Joe Cahill to the press. The delegates debated two proposals. The first, put forward by the Provisional IRA Army Council, called for the establishment of Dáil Uladh, "a regional parliament for the historic province of Ulster." This was passed unanimously. The second called for an election to Comhairle

Uladh, a council for Ulster, which would be charged with implementing the first proposal. This also passed unanimously, and twenty-four people were elected to that body. The council was charged with drafting a Constitution, an office was opened in Monaghan, and plans were made to open offices in Belfast, Omagh, and Enniskillen. At Comhairle Uladh's second meeting, in October, 147 delegates discussed a draft Constitution for Dáil Uladh.

Des Fennell was an observer at the Monaghan convention. In a prominent article published in the *Sunday Observer,* Fennell had proposed self-government for Northern Ireland under the joint control of London and Dublin. He had also written a series of articles arguing that the west of Ireland had suffered because political power was entrenched in Dublin. Fennell's work caught the attention of Ó Brádaigh and O'Connell, and they invited him to the Monaghan convention. Fennell became an important non-Republican resource. One of his first acts was to help organize a conference on regional government for Connacht. The conference, which was held in Tuam, County Galway, attracted more than 200 delegates. They elected a Comhairle Chonnacht and, as delegates had with Comhairle Uladh, they charged it with establishing Dáil Chonnacht. In his remarks to the conference, Ó Brádaigh referred to Dáil Chonnacht as the second step in creating new political structures for all of Ireland. The region needed self-government because the current system, which was inherited from the British, had failed. While Dublin had prospered, the population in the west had been declining for years. A regional parliament would be more efficient and it would allow the people of the region to manage their own affairs. Several Republicans, including Ó Brádaigh; Frank Glynn, a Sinn Féin county councilor in Galway; and John Joe McGirl, a Sinn Féin county councilor in Leitrim, attended the conference. But there was also substantial non-Republican involvement. Because of a large Irish-speaking minority and the region's traditional underdevelopment, there was a significant base of potential supporters of Dáil Chonnacht. Comhairle Chonnacht was launched via fifty public meetings, ending with a meeting at University College Galway (today the National University of Ireland, Galway), with speakers that included Fennell, Dáithí O'Connell, and Michael D. Higgins, a member of the faculty. Higgins was later elected Labour TD at Leinster House and served as minister for arts, culture and the Gaeltacht in a Fine Gael–Labour coalition government in the 1990s.

In 1971, concerns about security precluded an IRA convention. Comhairle Uladh and Comhairle Chonnacht were under way by the time

Sinn Féin held its Ard Fheis the weekend of October 23–24. More than 1,000 delegates crammed into Liberty Hall, headquarters of the Irish labor movement in Dublin. Some British journalists had been excluded; the British press, especially the tabloids, had been hammering the movement, smearing Republicans as murdering terrorists but treading lightly when it came to the security forces. Prominent victims included Joe Cahill, who was described in the *Daily Mail* as a "terrorist leader," and Ó Brádaigh, who was still reported to be chief of staff and whose comments on the death of Angela Gallagher had been used against him, as noted in the introduction to this volume. *An Phoblacht,* probably taking direction from Ó Brádaigh, explained the exclusion, "Comment is free but facts are sacred, and as long as any press group play the part of propagandists they are not welcome in our midst." This remains his approach to journalists and academics.

The war in the north cast a long shadow that weekend. Early Saturday morning, Dorothy Maguire and Maura Meehan, sisters and members of Cumann na mBan, were shot dead in Belfast under disputed circumstances by the British Army. The tricolor over Liberty Hall was flown at half mast and the Ard Fheis passed a number of motions supporting "the freedom fighters of the I.R.A." There were no controversial motions and there was no real change in Sinn Féin's leadership. Ruairí Ó Brádaigh was re-elected president, Dáithí O'Connell and Joe Clarke were elected vice presidents, and people such as Máire Drumm (who was in and out of jail in this period), Larry Grogan, and Seán Ó Brádaigh remained on the Ard Chomhairle. The highlights that weekend were the "Army Statement" offered by Seán Mac Stiofáin and Ó Brádaigh's presidential address. Mac Stiofáin described the IRA's growth. Its struggle had changed "from a defensive role to defence and retaliation and then eventually to an offensive campaign of resistance in all parts of the occupied area." This included an "economic war" in which IRA bombs would wreck the Northern Irish economy. Internment had failed, and the IRA was now "battle hardened, ready to face up to the hardships of the final phase which of course will be more intensive than anything experienced thus far." Things were going very well.

By the time Ó Brádaigh began his presidential address, the delegates had heard of more losses in Belfast. The RUC had shot dead IRA volunteer Martin Forsythe and seriously wounded Pat Murray of Cumann na mBan as they planted a bomb. The mood was somber as Ó Brádaigh described the previous year as "an eventful one for the country and for our Movement." He reviewed the political highlights, including the publication of the political program Éire Nua, the establishment of Comhairle Uladh and Comhairle Chonnacht, and the potential of Dáil Uladh. Comhairle Uladh would "build an alternative administration among the people at ground level." Based on existing voting patterns, Dáil Uladh would place former Unionists in a working majority, but there would also be "a good strong [Nationalist] opposition within reach of government." As a result, Unionist excesses would not be possible, but the regional parliament would protect Unionists from "being swamped in a 32-County Ireland." Maximum devolution to strong regional and powerful local councils would give control to local majorities.

Ó Brádaigh also laid out the movement's strategy for the north. The IRA would defend the people and Sinn Féin would give leadership to the civil resistance campaign. The goal was "to bring down Stormont by making the area ungovernable." This would be followed "by an all-out effort to force British evacuation and disengagement." With the British gone, and perhaps with a neutral peacekeeping force in place, they would be able to "go to all people North and South, Unionist and Nationalist with our Social and Economic programme and ask them to join with us in building the Democratic Socialist Republic." He ended dramatically, melding politics, the future, and commitment to the cause:

> We stand on the threshold of a new era in Irish history. Great is the responsibility which events have thrust upon us. We must not stand idly by, we must not be content merely to reflect on the past or pay lip service to the present.
>
> We must not fail our struggling people striving to be free of social, economic, cultural and political servitude; we dare not fail our dead—and there have been so many to make the supreme sacrifice in the past year—who made an act of faith in us, their comrades. Our oppressed and harassed people in the streets and the countryside, our menfolk being subjected to unspeakable degradations in the torture mills, our women and men in the concentration camps and prison cells, our exiled kith and kin, all look to us.
>
> Let us turn outwards not inwards on ourselves and face the opposition. There is unlimited hard work to be done. To do it is at once our duty—and our privilege.

The Ard Fheis concluded with a march from Liberty Hall to the British embassy in Merrion Square, where a letter was submitted that protested murder committed by British troops in Ireland. Joe Cahill addressed the crowd, which then marched to the GPO and observed a minute's silence in prayer for those killed by the British that weekend.

As planned, the north was becoming ungovernable, but not just because of the Provisionals. In September 1971, opposition to moderates in the Unionist Party coalesced around Rev. Ian Paisley and Desmond Boal, both MPs at Stormont. Paisley, who also held a seat at Westminster, had founded the Democratic Unionist Party, which, in contrast to the "Official" Unionists, gave a public voice to hard-liners who wanted more action against Republicans. At a rally in October, Paisley threatened that "Ulster will have to go it alone." Complementing the Paisleyites, militant Protestants formed the Ulster Defence Association, a legal body that fronted the Ulster Freedom Fighters, a Loyalist paramilitary organization. In late September, the Four Step Inn, a Protestant bar, was bombed in Belfast. Both IRAs denied responsibility, but the Ulster Freedom Fighters bombed a Nationalist bar, the Fiddlers House, in retaliation. There were a number of pub bombings, and other Loyalist paramilitary organizations developed, including a revived Ulster Volunteer Force. In December, the Official IRA increased the tension by assassinating a Unionist politician, John Barnhill. Complementing the political violence was an ongoing civil disobedience campaign. By December, 23,000 Nationalist homes were participating in the anti-internment rent and rates strike. Gas and electricity bills also remained unpaid.

The unrest continued through January 1972. On Sunday, January 30th, NICRA sponsored an anti-internment march in Derry. Stormont banned the march, and a wire barricade, keeping marchers out of the city center, was erected. Thousands ignored the ban and marched from the Bogside to the barricade and back to the Bogside, where a rally was scheduled. As the march wound down, an RUC station was stoned and teargas was fired in response, which was routine. Then, inexplicably, British troops fired live rounds at marchers. In roughly twenty minutes, thirteen civil rights marchers were dead and seventeen were wounded; one of the injured later succumbed to his injuries. Major-General Robert Ford of the British Army claimed that the soldiers had faced nail bombs, petrol bombs, acid bombs, and a "hail of bullets." Everyone but the British Army contradicted him.

What became known as Bloody Sunday changed everything. The event marks the end of the civil rights era—instead of going on marches, young Nationalists joined the IRA in droves. Unionists, recognizing that the British were likely to respond with a political initiative, feared the end of Stormont. William Craig organized a series of rallies in defense of the Union, pledging "God help those who get in our way, for we mean business." The Lynch government was caught between a public that sought retribution and the fear that northern violence would spread south. The day of the funerals of the victims of Bloody Sunday, a huge crowd gathered at the British embassy in Dublin. Feelings were so high that there was little the Gardaí could do but watch as people—with help from the IRA—threw petrol bombs at the building; it was a total loss. Later in the month, a Republican march in Dublin drew 12,000 people, Seán Mac Stiofáin described it "as the biggest held by the Republican movement in Dublin since the 1920s." Joe Cahill, to the consternation of the authorities, informed the crowd that "[t]he Provos are the force in Ireland today." The IRA was not actively confronting the southern state, but the implications of the rhetoric were serious and given the emotions of the time, introducing internment or some other measure to counter the rhetoric was not an option.

Through February and into March there were daily bombings and shootings and there was a perception, which was fostered by the media, that things were out of control. On Saturday, March 4th, a Provisional IRA bomb exploded in the Abercorn Restaurant in Belfast, which was crowded with people out for a day of shopping. Two people were killed and another 130 were injured. The media portrayed it as more work by mindless bombers. The Provisional Army Council met and decided to counter the propaganda. It was agreed that Seán Mac Stiofáin would approach Frank McManus and ask him to read a Provisional IRA statement into the record of the House of Commons and then withdraw as an abstentionist. McManus turned Mac Stiofáin down. The council then sent an emissary to John O'Connell, a Dublin physician and Labour TD at Leinster House. O'Connell, who had contacts in the British Labour Party, agreed to deliver a written message to Harold Wilson, the leader of Labour's opposition at Westminster. The message reiterated the movement's demands—a withdrawal of British forces from the streets, a promise that those forces would eventually be evacuated, acknowledgment of the right of the Irish people as a whole to determine their own future, abolition of Stormont, and amnesty for political prisoners—but it also contained welcome news. As a sign of their sincerity and evidence that they could control their soldiers, the Provisionals announced that they would unilaterally suspend all activity for seventy-two hours, beginning midnight, Friday, March 10.

Wilson passed the message to the prime minister and, with Edward Heath's permission, sought a meeting with the IRA. John O'Connell delivered this news to the Republicans. Mac Stiofáin was opposed because Wilson was only leader of the opposition, but he was outvoted by the others on the Army Council. As promised, the cease-fire went into effect at midnight on the 10th. On Monday evening, the 13th, Dáithí O'Connell, Joe Cahill, and John Kelly met with Harold Wilson, Merlyn Rees (Labour's "shadow minister" on Northern Ireland), and two others at John O'Connell's home in Dublin. There was no set agenda; Wilson wanted to learn more about the Republicans and the Republicans wanted to demonstrate that their motives were political. Dáithí O'Connell, taking the lead, described the movement's politics, including Éire Nua and Dáil Uladh. Wilson later remarked to John O'Connell that he was very impressed with Dáithí O'Connell. The meeting ended late in the evening. The British delegation left, but the Provisionals stayed for tea, and John O'Connell saw in person how much the leadership controlled its soldiers. The cease-fire ended at midnight. At 1 AM, Joe Cahill took out a pocket radio, tuned in the BBC, and listened to the news. The campaign had resumed with a bang. As a series of bombings was announced, Cahill quietly checked each one off a list he had.

Two weeks later, the cease-fire and meeting with Wilson bore fruit. Edward Heath informed Brian Faulkner that he was making a number of changes, including the transfer of responsibility for law and order to Westminster and the selected release of internees. Faulkner consulted with his cabinet and informed Heath that they would resign first. Heath accepted the resignations, went to the House of Commons, and announced that Stormont was suspended for a year. William Whitelaw, leader of the Commons, was appointed secretary of state for Northern Ireland. Brian Faulkner commented that people would "draw a sinister and depressing message from these events—that violence can pay and that violence does pay." This was certainly the Republican interpretation.

In the Sinn Féin offices in Dublin, Ruairí Ó Brádaigh and Maria McGuire, his administrative assistant, listened to RTÉ radio coverage of Heath's historic address. McGuire, a college student, had been brought into Sinn Féin by Seán Ó Brádaigh; she was bright and energetic and he put her to work. Over time, she became Ruairí's unpaid assistant. The IRA also put her to work. She was fluent in several languages, and in October 1971, she joined Dáithí O'Connell in an attempt to purchase arms on the continent. The attempt, which was leaked to the press, failed, but in the process she had become prominent. In her memoir, *To Take Arms: My Year with the IRA Provisionals,* she describes the fall of Stormont. As she and Ruairí were "furiously scribbling down" Heath's statement, focusing on the most important achievement of the Republican Movement in more than fifty years, the phone rang. It was a collision of the dramatic with the mundane. Ó Brádaigh, figuring it was something exceptionally important, grabbed the phone, only to discover it was a Sinn Féiner in Kerry who wanted to know why the Easter lilies he had ordered for the upcoming 1916 commemorations had not yet arrived. He told the caller, "Stormont is coming down after fifty years and you want your Easter lilies? I'll get back to you."

Seán Mac Stiofáin, who also heard the news, immediately issued a statement on behalf of the IRA. Speaking to his troops, he said the campaign would continue until *all* of their demands were met. Ó Brádaigh, on behalf of Sinn Féin, was more conciliatory. Heath's statement was "an advance on previous British Government attitudes" and suspending Stormont went "part of the way" to meet the Republican demands. He wanted all of the demands met, but he also called for "a cool appraisal of the entire situation followed by a determined movement forward toward the realisation of these goals." According to Maria McGuire, Ó Brádaigh's statement was aired on the radio and the phone rang again. This time it was Mac Stiofáin, who yelled at Ó Brádaigh for taking too soft of a line. According to Ó Brádaigh, McGuire read too much into the phone call. Mac Stiofáin may have yelled at him (Ó Brádaigh does not remember that part one way or the other), but he also notes that "[p]eople think that people working together in this type of thing never shout at each other. I am sure I have shouted at people and I am sure Mac Stiofáin had shouted at me and shouted at a lot of other people as well." It was an intense period. Mac Stiofáin's role, as chief of staff, was to be the hard man. Ó Brádaigh's role, as president of Sinn Féin, was to be an "enthusiastic person who is putting forward alternatives and assessing situations and so on." From Ó Brádaigh's perspective, the president of Sinn Féin and the chief of staff of the IRA did not have to agree on everything; in fact, occasional disagreement was healthy.

But Ó Brádaigh confirms that there was tension developing between himself and Dáithí O'Connell on one side and Mac Stiofáin on another. Ó Brádaigh and O'Connell were very close and had been for years. As president and vice president of Sinn Féin, they were collaborating on a new Sinn Féin program, Éire Nua II. Mac Stiofáin, in contrast, was focusing almost exclusively on the IRA; he was so busy that he had stopped attending Ard Chomhairle meetings. As a contributing factor, Mac Stiofáin's ego was growing with each IRA success. There was no major conflict, however, and Ó Brádaigh publicly defended him. On Easter Sunday, Cardinal William Conway, primate of all Ireland, complained that the IRA had not called a cease-fire after the fall of Stormont and indicated that if he could speak with Mac Stiofáin he would say that to him directly. Ó Brádaigh condemned the cardinal's "peace at all costs" approach. The same approach by the Catholic hierarchy in 1922, he charged, had "sown the seeds of recurring cycles of repression, violence, death and destruction on a massive scale." He called the cardinal a hypocrite and revealed the cardinal's refusal to meet with Belfast Sinn Féin; Ó Brádaigh, Mac Stiofáin, or both would have attended such a meeting.

Soon after condemning the cardinal's approach, Ó Brádaigh paid his first visit to the United States, in March 1972. In 1970, three IRA veterans of the 1920s who were living in the United States, Michael Flannery, John McGowan and Jack McCarthy, had formed Irish Northern Aid (Noraid), a charitable organization that supported the families of IRA prisoners. They sponsored tours by a number of people, including Seán Keenan, Dáithí O'Connell, and Ó Brádaigh. Ó Brádaigh remembers the trip, which included stops in Boston, Cleveland, New York, Philadelphia, and Washington, for several reasons. In Cleveland, he was given the Freedom of the City. In New York, one of Noraid's founders, whom Ó Brádaigh will not identify, took him aside and said, "Look here sonny. Don't mention that goddamn word socialism when you're here." Ó Brádaigh, amused that "sonny" was 40 years old, thought about it and found a way to accommodate the gentleman and still not compromise his own politics. He replied, "I will give the same speech as I give in Ireland but I won't use the word socialism." This was accepted, and his presentations were well received.

In Boston, on a second trip in April, Ó Brádaigh met William Craig. They were participants in a televised debate on Northern Ireland. At a reception afterward, John Hume introduced Ó Brádaigh to Craig, who offered his hand. Ó Brádaigh shook it, and the crowded room went quiet. After some small talk, the discussion moved to politics. Ó Brádaigh asked Craig what would happen if the British suddenly withdrew from the North. "U.D.I. [a unilateral declaration of independence] is on," replied Craig. It was not a surprise; Craig, Paisley, and others had been threatening UDI for months. What, Ó Brádaigh asked, would happen if that was not feasible, if the Six Counties could not make it alone? Craig then brought up a system of regional governments "with the richer areas helping the poorer ones." Although Craig saw things in a British context and Ó Brádaigh saw them in an Irish context, they agreed that regional governments might work. They also agreed that there was too much violence in the north and that a civil war would be a disaster for everyone.

The conversation with Craig was satisfying because it suggested that some Unionists might take the Republican political initiatives seriously, including Dáil Uladh. Unfortunately, IRA activities made continuing the dialogue highly unlikely as conditions deteriorated and some volunteers engaged in attacks that were contrary to Republican ideology. The movement's founders, the United Irishmen of the 1790s, were enlightened Protestants pursuing a secular Republican philosophy. Those founders include Wolfe Tone, a Dubliner and member of the Church of Ireland, and several Belfast merchants who were Presbyterians. Ó Brádaigh embraces the historically nonsectarian policy of the IRA; his interpretation of the conflict is that it is not between Catholics and Protestants in the Six Counties, but between the Irish Republican Army and the British government and its security forces. During the 1950s campaign, when the IRA was small and most of its members came from Republican backgrounds, Tony Magan, Seán Cronin, and Ruairí Ó Brádaigh, as chiefs of staff, kept the IRA focused on the security forces. However, because these forces were almost exclusively Protestant, many Unionists interpreted the attacks as sectarian.

August 1969, the attack on St. Matthew's, widespread rioting, internment, and other incidents generated large numbers of IRA recruits; by mid-1972 there were more than 1,000 volunteers in Belfast alone. The sheer number of recruits created problems. The bulk of the fighting was being done by young northerners, some of whom were beginning to resent what they saw as control from Dublin. IRA policy allowed only defensive action in the case of sectarian attacks (such as the attack at St. Matthews). But some IRA personnel were willing and able to retaliate. In mid-May, Loyalist paramilitaries bombed and shot up Kelly's Bar in West Belfast, killing four civilians and a British soldier. In apparent retaliation, the Bluebell Bar, located in Sandy Row, a Protestant area, was car-bombed. A few days later, members of Na Fianna Éireann, the IRA's youth group, fired on Protestant workers as they made their way home through a Nationalist area in West Belfast. Unionists interpreted IRA attacks on the RUC and the Ulster Defense Regiment (which had replaced the B Specials) as sectarian. The IRA's defense was that they only targeted uniforms—they did not know or care about the religion of the person wearing the uniform. Attacks on Protestant bars and workers, however, was not only indefensible, it also worked to increase the division between Unionists and Nationalists. Richard English, in *Armed Struggle: A History of the IRA,* describes this effect: "They wanted to end sectarianism, but their violence helped to ossify and to bloodstain sectarian division in the north."

Ó Brádaigh was adamantly opposed to such activity. It undercut the concept of Dáil Uladh, which was designed to make a united Ireland palatable for the Unionist community, and it gave critics a propaganda weapon. The IRA claimed it was fighting a war of national liberation. Attacks like these made it look like they were in a tit-for-tat feud between Catholics and Protestants. As president of Sinn Féin, Ó Brádaigh was asked about the shooting. He replied that he did not understand "what contribution it could make." Asked if the IRA was "prepared to bomb a million Protestants into what the I.R.A. saw as their proper place in the community," he replied, "I don't think so." Because some Republicans believed the IRA was beyond reproach, some of his own people were upset with his remarks.

About the only good news from the north came on May 29th, when the Official IRA announced "an immediate suspension of all armed offensive operations in Ulster." The Provisionals welcomed the news because it cleared the way for them; *they* were the army of liberation. It also confirmed their analysis; the Officials had tried to wed constitutional politics with revolutionary action and had failed, as had Fianna Fáil in the 1930s and Clann na Poblachta in the 1950s. The announcement also condemned the Provisionals' bombing campaign because it might "provoke civil war in Northern Ireland." This was troublesome, as the Officials were also guilty of blatant sectarian attacks. In December, they had assassinated Stormont senator John Barnhill and in February they had tried to kill another Unionist politician, John Taylor. The Barnhill attack prompted Roy Johnston to publicly resign from Official Sinn Féin. Ó Brádaigh, who had been threatened by these former comrades, understood the bitterness that his parents' generation felt toward de Valera. The Officials were traitors.

Two days later, de Valera's political heirs raided the Sinn Féin headquarters in Dublin and arrested Joe Cahill. The head office phoned Ó Brádaigh in Roscommon with the news. He had hung up the phone and started working on a statement when some of the children rushed in and said that the police were at the back door; they came in the front and the back and started searching the house. Patsy kept a nervous eye on them while Ruairí phoned the press. He was reporting to the *Irish Times* that "my own house is being raided" when a Garda superintendent took the phone and hung it up. Another officer reported that he had found "incriminating documents" indicating Ó Brádaigh's membership in the IRA. Ó Brádaigh, incredulous, asked "What documents?" The officers ignored him, placed him under arrest, and carted him off to the local Garda station. Ruairí found out later that Seán Ó Brádaigh's home had been raided and that he too had been arrested. The next day, Ruairí, Seán, and Cahill were brought together in Mountjoy in Dublin.

The previous fall, the leadership had agreed that if they were arrested on trumped-up charges they would go on a hunger strike to demand their release. A hunger strike would either force their release or compound a miscarriage of justice by creating another Republican martyr. At the time, Mac Stiofáin had declared that his would be a hunger and thirst strike. The Ó Brádaighs and Cahill informed the authorities that they would consume only water and salt and joined about twenty IRA prisoners, led by Billy McKee, who were on hunger strike in Crumlin Road Prison, Belfast. The Crumlin Road prisoners, who had been sentenced in a court of law, were demanding political status. On the first in night in Mountjoy the warders left bread and tea in the cells. Ó Brádaigh remembers being able to smell the crust of the bread.

Even as they were taking Ruairí away, Patsy started making plans to visit him; she knew the routine. Although she was again a single parent—this time with six children—her first worry was Ruairí. She feared for him, because she knew he would see the hunger strike to the end. She also fully supported his decision. On her visit, they met in a private room, supervised by a warder. To his surprise and delight, she told him that she and his sister Mary were making arrangements to go on their own hunger strike in support of him, Seán, and Cahill. They were planning to rent a caravan (a small mobile home) that would be parked just up the road from Mountjoy, and Cumann na mBan was willing to send its volunteers to Roscommon to watch the children. When the visit ended, they stepped into a corridor and separated—Patsy walked in one direction while prison officers snatched Ruairí and took him to an adjoining room. The prison governor and other officials, assuming he would be at a low point, started to berate him with statements such as "You're an irresponsible man for doing this to your family." He sat there and listened until one of them asked, "What does your wife think of all this?" "Well," he answered, "she and my sister are starting a hunger strike outside. Immediately." The man shouted, "Oh my God!" and the others threw up their hands. A quick, "Get him out!" sent Ruairí back to his cell.

The prison authorities moved the Ó Brádaighs and Cahill to the hospital wing, isolating them from other Republican prisoners. They also lost all privileges, including visitation rights. And the strike took a toll. They had been arrested wearing summer clothing. In the dank prison, they were constantly cold. Warmer clothes were sent in, but Ruairí found that he could not keep his toes warm. He also dreamed about food; he would wake up just as he was about to take a bite of a juicy steak. As they became weaker, their balance became compromised. In the hallways, an "ordinary" prisoner would sometimes bump into one of them. Normally, it would not have been an issue, but after five days without food, even a slight bump knocked them over. As a safety precaution, they started avoiding groups of ordinary prisoners. They also spent much of their time writing out, with difficulty, statements for their court appearances.

A week later, on Tuesday, June 6th, Ó Brádaigh was handcuffed, put in a police van, and driven ninety miles to Roscommon. Outside the courthouse, 150 or so supporters, led by the local Sinn Féin *cumann,* awaited his arrival. So did a number of police officers. In court, he was charged with membership in an illegal organization and possession of "incriminating documents"; he still had no information about the documents. And the strike was taking a toll. Maria McGuire reports that he "looked drawn, his skin was yellow, and his hands were trembling." The prosecution, still assembling the "evidence," asked for a delay until June 13th. As usual, Ó Brádaigh refused to recognize the court, but he voiced several objections. He asked for a copy of the deposition and he complained that he had not been allowed to attend Mass the previous Thursday. He was given a copy of the deposition.

Ó Brádaigh asked about the evidence. If there was none, then his arrest was "not lawful." Roscommon Garda superintendent O'Flaherty defended the arrest and stated that the evidence was just "not yet ready." Suspecting there was no evidence, Ó Brádaigh pressed, "If not, how many witnesses' statements are involved?" The superintendent lamely replied, "I cannot say at the moment."

Ó Brádaigh persisted: "How many of these statements had you available when the arrest was carried out?"

O'Flaherty: "I cannot say."

Ó Brádaigh: "On what grounds then did you base my arrest?"

O'Flaherty referred to the deposition. The deposition only listed the law under which he was being held, Section 30 of the Offenses Against the State Act, which made membership in the IRA illegal. Ó Brádaigh continued: "It's not sufficient to say that. On what grounds against Section 30 of the Act was I arrested?"

O'Flaherty stuck to his facts. He had arrested Ó Brádaigh under Section 30 of the Offenses Against the State Act. Ó Brádaigh asserted that there had been "a breach of faith." He had been promised a chance to view the incriminating documents but they had not been delivered. Court was adjourned for fifteen minutes and he finally saw the "evidence"—a draft of a statement written by Seán and a copy of a statement from the Republican publicity office that had been circulated in March, announcing the IRA's cease-fire. Neither document contained anything incriminating and everyone involved knew it.

When court resumed, Ó Brádaigh made the best of the situation. He asked that the documents be "placed on record" and he asked for permission to read out his prepared statement. The justice granted both requests and with a strained voice Ó Brádaigh explained that the "evidence" against him was only a press release that "had appeared in papers all over the world" and a draft of another statement that would be released after minor alterations. He protested his arrest, which was "capricious," and complained that dozens of Republicans, including Seán, had suffered the same fate, all in the cause of a "lasting and just peace for all time." Surprisingly, he ended with kind words for Roscommon's police officers, who, he was sure, found their involvement "distasteful." The justice remanded him back to Mountjoy to appear in Elphin Court on June 13th. Ó Brádaigh thanked the justice for allowing him to read his statement and asked if he could have the handcuffs removed for the return trip, adding, "I couldn't escape if I tried." The justice replied, "I assure you, you will get the same treatment as anybody else," and he was handcuffed. As he left the courthouse, his supporters staged a rally. When she was interviewed by the press, Patsy commented that after a checkup from her physician, she was going on a hunger strike. A caravan was rented and placed outside of Mountjoy. Two days later, on Thursday, the case against Seán collapsed and he was released. On Saturday, with Ruairí still in Mountjoy, Patsy and Mary Delaney began their fast. They continued for three days, until Ruairí's anticlimactic final court appearance. There was no real evidence and he was cleared of all charges. The case against Cahill collapsed less than a week later.

Ó Brádaigh's supporters cheered as he left the courthouse. Relieved, but numb and starving, he wanted food. The crowd, to his consternation, enthusiastically demanded a statement from him. From a makeshift podium he quickly thanked them for their support and offered a few more remarks. Then he was taken to the nearby home of a local teacher for his first food in fourteen days. He remembered his history. In breaking his fast in 1923, Peadar O'Donnell had avoided solid foods and ordered an egg flip and brandy. Ó Brádaigh skipped the brandy, but ate the egg flip. Exhausted, he was then driven the seventeen miles to Roscommon, where there was another rally. A parade that included several former students and some of his children marched from the center of town and returned him to his front gate; "back from where they took you," in the words of the

Released from Elphin Court, County Roscommon, June 13, 1972. From left: Deirdre Ó Brádaigh (daughter), Patsy Ó Brádaigh, Ruairí Ó Brádaigh, and Mary Delaney (sister). Ó Brádaigh family collection.

chief marshal, Sylvester Fitzsimons. Finally back home, he ate again, rested, and visited with Patsy and his family.

The day Ó Brádaigh was released, Seán Mac Stiofáin, Dáithí O'Connell, Séamus Twomey, and Martin McGuinness (the IRA's Derry commander), who were widely perceived to be the IRA's leadership, held a highly publicized press conference in which they offered another truce if their demands were met. The demands were rejected outright, but William Whitelaw found a way to respond positively. The Crumlin Road hunger strikers had been fasting for thirty days and the situation was becoming serious; on the day of the press conference, a rumor that Billy

Provisional IRA press conference in Derry, June 13, 1972. From left: Martin McGuinness, Dáithí O'Connell, Seán Mac Stíofáin, and Séamus Twomey. Victor Patterson/Linenhall Library.

McKee had died set off rioting in Belfast. Whitelaw granted Republican and Loyalist paramilitary prisoners "special category status," political status in all but name. He later agreed to release Gerry Adams, an important figure in Belfast, who was interned in Long Kesh, a former RAF base outside of Lisburn. The IRA then announced that it would suspend operations if the British government would do the same. Whitelaw, in the House of Commons, stated that Her Majesty's forces would "reciprocate" and at midnight, June 26th, an open-ended bilateral IRA–British Army truce went into effect. What was not known was that the contacts between the IRA and the British had continued since March, often with John Hume or John O'Connell serving as a liaison. As part of the truce, the British had secretly agreed to meet an IRA delegation. While the Republican leadership prepared for their meeting with Whitelaw, Loyalist paramilitaries took to the streets. On Wednesday, June 28th, almost 1,000 Ulster Defence Association members marched through Belfast in battle dress in a funeral parade. Over the weekend, Loyalist paramilitaries killed five Catholic civilians in Belfast.

Throughout all of this activity Ó Brádaigh and O'Connell had been working on Sinn Féin's program. Ó Brádaigh, who had earned his Higher Diploma in Education from University College Galway in 1968, knew members of the faculty and brought them into the discussion. A committee of academics at the university had finished a draft with an outline of the structures of a proposed federal government for Ireland, which would meet at Athlone. Thus, also on June 28th, the Republicans revealed their solution to the conflict. Ó Brádaigh recalls the day for its irony, for it was the fiftieth anniversary of the beginning of the Irish Civil War. At a press conference in the Ormond Hotel, just up the quays from the Four Courts where the Civil War started, Dáithí O'Connell unveiled Éire Nua II, which melded Éire Nua's democratic socialism with a federal scheme that was based on the historic provinces of Ulster, Leinster, Munster, and Connacht. Éire Nua II had three main features: a new constitution and charter of rights for a united Ireland, a federal government based on the four provinces, and an updated social and economic program. The underlying theme was the creation of a secular united Ireland that safeguarded the rights and traditions of both the Unionist and Nationalist communities. Freedom of religion was a basic right in the new constitution: "Every person has the right to freedom of conscience and religion and the open practice and teaching of ethical and political beliefs."

It was a complex scheme that proposed a three-tiered political system: federal, provincial, and local. Nationwide, anti-Unionists would be in the majority, but safeguards in the constitution and proposed political structures would protect Unionists. In a federal parliament of approximately 150 deputies, half would be elected directly and the other half would be sent forward in equal numbers from the provincial parliaments. At the provincial level, the cornerstone would be Dáil Uladh. In Northern Ireland, the gerrymander of 1920 had guaranteed Unionist domination through Stormont. Dáil Uladh would include Cavan, Donegal, and Monaghan and change the demographics. Unionists would still have a majority over Nationalists of about 5 percent out of a total population of perhaps 1,700,000. There would be a credible opposition and, with relatively limited cross-community voting, Nationalists might even achieve power at the provincial level. At the community level, local government would be Unionist or anti-Unionist/Nationalist according to the local population. The result was a system of checks and balances; local power according to the local community, provincial power according to the provincial majority, and national power according to the national majority.

In the IRA, the Provisionals were working on who would represent them in their meeting with William Whitelaw, which was scheduled for

Friday, July 7th. Patrick Bishop and Eamonn Mallie report that Ó Brádaigh had been excluded from the delegation because he had "fallen foul" of Mac Stiofáin, but he was in fact left off of the team for legitimate reasons. The IRA, not Sinn Féin or the movement in general, had entered into the bilateral truce and the delegation would represent only the IRA. Mac Stiofáin's memoirs add that he did not wish to link Sinn Féin with the meeting. If things went well, Sinn Féin and Ó Brádaigh could participate in future meetings; if things went poorly, Sinn Féin would not be implicated in any fallout. There were also practical concerns. Ó Brádaigh was still recovering from his hunger strike. He was considerably weakened; it took him three months to fully recover. For the first time in his life he felt physically vulnerable—he used the train to get about because he could not drive long distances. In the end, the IRA delegation was a mix of veterans and relatively recent recruits. Veterans Seán Mac Stiofáin; Dáithí O'Connell; Séamus Twomey, commanding officer Belfast; and Ivor Bell, a Belfast commander; were joined by Martin McGuinness and Gerry Adams. McGuinness, 22, was from a Nationalist family in Derry and was widely perceived as a guerrilla boy wonder. Under his leadership, the Derry Provisionals were bombing the commercial center out of Derry with minimal civilian casualties. Adams, 23, was from a prominent Republican family in West Belfast. He was perceived as having a keen political mind. Although he was allegedly an IRA leader prior to his internment, Adams maintains that he never joined the IRA. The final member of the team was Myles Shevlin, an attorney and Sinn Féin member, who was sent as an observer and legal advisor.

The delegation was flown by the RAF to London, where they met Whitelaw and other civil servants. O'Connell gave Whitelaw a copy of Éire Nua II and laid out the movement's political program, but, led by Mac Stiofáin, the IRA team pushed for a declaration that the British would withdraw from the North. The Irish people, "acting as a unit," would determine their own future. It was not an option for Whitelaw. Nothing was resolved, but a reply to the demands was promised. Three days later, it all fell apart. There had been a number of altercations between Loyalist paramilitaries, Nationalists, and the IRA. The day of the meeting in London, Nationalist families who had been intimidated from their homes sought housing in Lenadoon, a mixed area in West Belfast. The homes had been abandoned by Protestant families and the British housing executive allocated them to the Nationalists, but the Ulster Defence Association refused to allow them to take possession. A stalemate, monitored by the British Army, developed. On Sunday afternoon, people tried to unload furniture from a van. A British Army vehicle rammed the van and a riot developed. At about 5PM, gunfire erupted between the IRA and the British Army; by 9 PM the IRA had announced that the cease-fire was officially over. That evening, British marksmen shot dead five people in Lenadoon, including a 13-year-old schoolgirl and a Catholic priest giving her last rites.

The fallout was intense. The Provisionals made public their meeting with Whitelaw. Whitelaw defended the British Army and admitted in Parliament that he had met with an IRA delegation. Some of his Conservative colleagues, including Enoch Powell, criticized him for the meeting. Cardinal Conway called for peace and asked those responsible to have mercy on the innocent. Conor Cruise O'Brien blamed the Provisionals, claiming they had made a tactical decision that allowed them "to recover support among the Catholic population." Ó Brádaigh blamed a one-sided British policy, arguing that the British Army was implementing Ulster Defence Association policy at Lenadoon. Whitelaw, he reported, had promised Dáithí O'Connell an end to sectarian killing. He had "not delivered the goods." Ó Brádaigh also had choice words for Cardinal Conway, who had exonerated "the British Government and sectarian Unionist forces of all blame." He had not given up hope for another truce, but it would have to be, in his words, a "realistic one."

There was still formal and informal contact between the British and the IRA. Merlyn Rees in Dublin was called to London for another secret meeting with the Provisionals. John O'Connell, who was also in Dublin, offered to pick him up at the Shelbourne Hotel and drive him to the airport. When O'Connell arrived, Rees got in the back seat, only to discover that Ruairí Ó Brádaigh was the passenger in the front seat; O'Connell was giving him a lift to the Sinn Féin offices on Kevin Street, just around the corner off St. Stephen's Green. Ó Brádaigh was a very public figure, but Rees states in his memoir that he did not know who the "stranger" was until after he left the car. It was "a cloak-and-dagger situation that I found very unpleasant," he wrote. Ó Brádaigh remembers the ride with a laugh. He and John O'Connell had been at a meeting. When it broke up, O'Connell offered him a lift to the Sinn Féin office. When they picked up Rees, there were no introductions, but the three of them shared jokes. O'Connell stopped at the Sinn Féin office and Ó Brádaigh remembers Rees saying something like, 'Where are we? What is this place?' He replied, "Well, this is the place that counts." Things went less well at the secret meeting. According to Rees, the British wanted the Provisionals to see "political reality" and return to a cease-fire, but "we were wasting our time." In mid-July, Harold Wilson met with Joe Cahill with a message from Prime Minister Heath: "the answer was no."

Any chance of a quick return to a truce ended when the IRA, with a "bomb blitz to show the cost of further war," went too far. On July 21st, the Provisionals set off thirty-six bombs in Northern Ireland, twenty-two of them in Belfast. The IRA telephoned warnings, but there were too many bombs and not enough police, soldiers, and firefighters to cover them. Nine people were killed in Belfast—two British soldiers and seven civilians, including three teenagers, William Irvine, 18, William Crothers, 15, and Stephen Parker, 14. Initial reports put the death toll higher, as several bodies were dismembered. Another 130 people were injured. The date is remembered as Bloody Friday—the Provisional IRA complement to Bloody Sunday. For the Belfast brigade, it was an operation gone awry, and it accepted responsibility for the explosions. For the victims, their families and virtually everybody but the Provisionals, it was terrorism, plain and simple. The event is often included in terrorism chronologies. Criticism of internment and Bloody Sunday had limited the British military response in the North. Bloody Friday changed the scene again. More troops were sent over, bringing the total to 21,000, and early on the morning of July 31st, they saturated the Nationalist areas in Belfast and Derry and cleared the "no-go" areas, with 50-ton tanks in the case of Derry. The IRA, who had anticipated what was known as "Operation Motorman," offered no resistance. July 31st, 1972, is also remembered for three car bombs that exploded in Claudy village in County Derry. Six people were killed outright and three more died over the next few days. It was a bloody end to the bloodiest month of the Troubles. Ninety-five people were killed in Northern Ireland that July.

12

International Gains and Personal Losses

JANUARY 1973–NOVEMBER 1974

THE PROMISE OF June was lost in July 1972, and time would tell that the disruption caused by the IRA's campaign had peaked. But August 1969, the Lower Falls curfew in West Belfast, internment, and Bloody Sunday guaranteed that the IRA would always have a base of support. Sinn Féin was still growing. *An Phoblacht* acquired new offices at 44 Parnell Square and moved from monthly to biweekly publication.

In August 1972, William Whitelaw, secretary of state for Northern Ireland, challenged Sinn Féin to participate in upcoming local elections. Ó Brádaigh wanted to participate, but on a footing equal to that of other political parties. He replied with his own challenge: drop the ban on Sinn Féin, end the harassment of party members, and drop the requirement that candidates sign an oath of allegiance to the Crown. Otherwise, Whitelaw was a hypocrite. Ó Brádaigh's challenge went unanswered. Led by people in Belfast, Sinn Féin decided not to contest the elections. As that would play out, Belfast would be wary of politics for another decade. Meanwhile, there was more fallout from Bloody Friday.

Maria McGuire left the movement after the bombings. In September, the *Observer* published two articles, "IRA Gun Girl Flees" and "I Accuse Seán Mac Stiofáin," based on interviews with her. She claimed to have been in the IRA and offered a number of juicy revelations. She described Mac Stiofáin as a "bigoted murderer," claimed she had had a "public" affair with Dáithí O'Connell, and said that Mac Stiofáin had reduced Ó Brádaigh to a figurehead as president of Sinn Féin. Sinn Féin released a statement rejecting her accounts, and at a press conference Ó Brádaigh said that her allegations were "utter nonsense." She had previously denied rumors of a relationship with O'Connell. At the press conference, Dáithí O'Connell quoted her previous statement, "I wish to put it categorically on the record that there was nothing improper in my association with Mr O'Connell and I wish to pay tribute to him as a man of integrity and courage." The articles and McGuire's subsequent book, *To Take Arms: My Year with the IRA Provisionals,* had long-term consequences. For years, journalists and academics accepted without question her portrayal that leading Republicans, especially Seán Mac Stiofáin, were openly anti-Protestant.

Publicly, the leadership denied the gossip; privately, they realized that security had been breached. McGuire had traveled throughout Ireland, had met a number of Republicans, and had picked up bits and pieces of information along the way. She reported that O'Connell and Ó Brádaigh had discussed assassinating Mac Stiofáin, which was not credible. But it was true that they were not getting along with Mac Stiofáin and his auto-cratic style. Mac Stiofáin, she reported, tried to court-martial Ó Brádaigh for not accounting for funds properly. Ó Brádaigh confirms that there was a court of inquiry. Ó Brádaigh, who taught accounting, produced the appropriate records and the charges were dropped. To this day he does not know why Mac Stiofáin brought the charges against him. He may have truly believed that Ó Brádaigh was being careless with the movement's money, or he may have been trying to show him who was in charge. Either way, Ó Brádaigh continued to work with Mac Stiofáin, but he also watched his back. There was no time to dwell on it, because he had to defend himself from the Lynch government next.

When Ó Brádaigh took his leave of absence, the Roscommon Voca-tional Education Committee had replaced him with a temporary teacher. In a letter to the committee, the minister for education noted that his office had not authorized Ó Brádaigh's leave of absence. The minister in-formed the committee that "Mr. P. R. Ó Brádaigh" had "vacated his post" and that his position should be filled. The implications were serious. Ó Brádaigh, who received a photocopy of the letter, was potentially out of a job, and any money he had paid into the retirement or pension fund was forfeited. The committee discussed the letter but forestalled a decision until they heard from him. Ó Brádaigh informally discussed the situation with some committee members and then sent a letter notifying the com-mittee that although he wanted to keep his job, he could not give them a date on which he would return to work. As it had in 1962, the committee found a way to support him. They simply ignored the directive; over the years, the position was filled by temporary replacements.

In early October, Jack Lynch's government went after Sinn Féin. The Special Branch raided the party headquarters in Dublin, arrested Walter

Lynch, the party secretary, and confiscated boxes of literature, including resolutions for the upcoming Ard Fheis. The Dublin city office was treated likewise. A three-month closure order was nailed to the door. Ó Brádaigh accused Jack Lynch of taking instructions from British prime minister Edward Heath, adding, "Your actions in the current campaign for the national liberation of the Irish people will go down in history as the actions of a quisling, a coward and a traitor." Undeterred, Sinn Féin went ahead and established Comhairle na Mumhan (Munster Executive) and Comhairle Laighean (Leinster Executive), the beginnings of Dáil na Mumhan and Dáil Laighean. In his address to the Comhairle na Mumhan delegates, Ó Brádaigh said that Dáil na Mumhan was "a revolutionary weapon" and a means of going forward against the current state and toward "the building of a new Ireland." In his remarks to the Comhairle Laighean convention, he focused on what decentralized government had done for Switzerland, "a nation divided into three ethnic groups, with four languages and two major religious persuasions and which has survived for over 500 years and is a witness to true democracy at work."

The 1972 Ard Fheis was again held in Liberty Hall, Dublin, on October 28–29. The press, including British journalists, were allowed in, but because of two bomb scares everyone was searched. Outside the venue, the Special Branch kept tabs on all who entered. The agenda reflected growth in Sinn Féin. New people, especially northerners, brought new ideas. A controversial resolution, which was supported by several northerners, allowed membership to persons who had signed the "oath of allegiance" required of candidates in local elections and occupants of some jobs in the Six Counties. The resolution was amended such that membership was allowed to people who repudiated the oath or no longer held the position that required the oath; it passed. Most important, the principal components of Éire Nua—that Sinn Féin sought a united democratic socialist and federal Ireland—were written into the party Constitution.

In his presidential address, Ó Brádaigh set a serious tone. They were assembled "with a great sense of high purpose . . . deeply conscious of the tremendous responsibility for the future of our country, for the generations yet unborn, which is thrust upon us at this time." In March, they had achieved their greatest success, "the down-fall of the puppet parliament in Belfast after 50 years of tyrannical power." Since then, they had faced opposition from every quarter: the Whitelaw regime and its "massive propaganda war mounted throughout the world"; Ulster Defence Association "pressure on Nationalist communities with the connivance of the British Army"; the Catholic hierarchy and their "peace-at-all-costs" perspective; and the Twenty-six-county government, "who have failed the people." Yet they had carried on. Service had been rendered "in heroic measure, on the streets, in the jails and prison camps and on the hillsides. The men and women, boys and girls and the mass of ordinary people participating in the fight, we assembled here today salute as the glory of their generation." Ó Brádaigh was interested in more than the war. He called on Republicans to be active in local economic issues "so that Irish workers may experience at first hand our concern for their interests and in order that our members may have an opportunity of implementing part of our Social and Economic Programme now." If they did not get involved, he warned, Sinn Féin was in danger of becoming only a "support group for the struggle in the North." He also appealed to the Unionists: "Let us repeat once more; we do not wish to submerge the Unionists of the North-east in an All-Ireland state; we offer them very real powers in majority control of a greater Ulster through the Dáil Uladh plan; incorporation of all nine counties will give a healthier balance of population with a credible opposition—something the Six-County state of Northern Ireland has always lacked. We would never ask you to join the 26-County State—we are trying to escape from it ourselves!"

His conclusion called for revolutionary change: "To all the people of Ireland we say; let us wipe the slate clean and start anew, 'abolishing the memory of past dissensions' [quoting Wolfe Tone]; regional government will correct economic imbalance and bring power nearer to the people, giving them greater say in decisions affecting their own lives; Éire Nua will restore the wealth of Ireland to the people of Ireland with a more just distribution of the goods of this world, worker-ownership and participation in decision making in industry." The result would be "a new life, a better life, a more human life for all of our people." They were part of the march of history. They had wedded the principles of the Enlightenment to democratic socialism and they were "spiritually, at least, part of a world-wide movement to increase the dignity of man now threatened with being submerged by the consumer society. Our struggle is for weak and oppressed nations and peoples—but in the first instance for our own people now enduring all that Imperialism can inflict." He ended: "The heroism, the sacrifices, the terrible price paid over the past year all compel us to one conclusion: we must not fail—not now after all that has happened."

It was a speech given by a committed revolutionary to a crowd of people engaged in a political and military struggle against the mother of imperialism. The delegates gave him a ten-minute standing ovation. The rest of Ireland was less enthusiastic about the Republican dream. An *Irish Independent* editorial wondered if it was worth the cost: "[T]here is no sin in accepting that imperfection is here to stay—indeed, there may be grave irresponsibility in pretending that it can be eradicated, especially if such pretence could lead people to jeopardise their lives." The *Irish Times,* in a generally positive review, noted the "tragic irony in Ruairí Ó Brádaigh's appeal from the Ard-fheis of Provisional Sinn Féin, for the slate is smeared with the blood of victims of the Provisional I.R.A.'s bombing campaign."

The Lynch government, whose slate would be wiped clean, stepped up its pressure. Having failed to put away the Ó Brádaighs and Cahill in June, the minister for justice, Des O'Malley, began work on an amendment to the Offenses Against the State Act that would make it easier to convict people for membership in the IRA. The Lynch government decided to rein in Seán Mac Stiofáin. Kevin O'Kelly, of RTÉ radio, taped an interview with Mac Stiofáin early Sunday morning, November 19th. After the interview, Mac Stiofáin and Joe Cahill were driving away when they were stopped and Mac Stiofáin was arrested. Mac Stiofáin was taken to the Bridewell, where he immediately began his promised hunger and thirst strike. This put pressure on everyone concerned, for, at most, he would last twenty days. By noon, Sinn Féin had a continuous picket outside the prison. At a "monster rally" at the General Post Office in Dublin the next day, Ruairí Ó Brádaigh, Dáithí O'Connell, Éamonn Mac Thomáis, John Kelly, Séamus Twomey, and Marie Moore spoke in support of Mac Stiofáin. Ó Brádaigh, ignoring any differences between them, deplored the arrest "as a blatant act of collaboration with the British troops of occupation in Ireland." The name Seán Mac Stiofáin, he told the crowd, "would long be remembered—long after the O'Malleys and the Lynchs have long been forgotten."

On Friday, November 24th, a rapidly deteriorating Mac Stiofáin appeared before the Special Criminal Court—three judges, no jury. The primary evidence against him was the taped interview. The speaker was a member of the IRA; the question was whether or not it was Mac Stiofáin on the tape. The prosecution asked for a transcription, which delayed the hearing until Saturday. The delay was granted, but the interview became a major news item. RTÉ aired the interview and the government sacked its chairman and entire board of governors. On Saturday, Mac Stiofáin sat in court in obvious pain, wrapped in blankets, a hot water bottle on his stomach. O'Kelly, who was called by the prosecution, refused to identify the voice on the tape. He was sentenced to three months for contempt. A Garda detective then testified that in his opinion, it was Mac Stiofáin's voice. This was enough for the court, and Mac Stiofáin was sentenced to six months in prison for membership in the IRA. After the sentence was passed, he shouted, "It may as well have been six years. I will be dead in six days." A judge replied, "Unfortunately, that is something over which we have no control." Mac Stiofáin retorted, "I'll see you damned in hell before I submit."

Events appeared to spiral out of control. A hundred journalists walked off their jobs in support of O'Kelly, and Irish radio and television went off the air for two days. That evening, a bomb exploded in Dublin's city center, injuring about forty people. The next day, shots were fired as the IRA tried to liberate Mac Stiofáin from the Mater Hospital. But the Dublin government held firm. Mac Stiofáin was transferred by helicopter to the more secure Curragh Camp hospital, and the details of the amendment to the Offenses Against the State Act were made public. Although it was flimsy, Mac Stiofáin's conviction rested on physical evidence—the O'Kelly tape. Under the amended act, the *opinion* of a senior police officer that an individual was a member of an illegal organization would be enough for conviction.

When Sinn Féin's head office was closed, supporters loaned the organization the use of two offices in the center of Dublin. As Mac Stiofáin was being helicoptered to the Curragh, Ó Brádaigh was in one of them giving an interview to Brian Park, of the *Daily Mail*; the helicopter literally flew overhead during the interview. Ó Brádaigh, upset at Mac Stiofáin's treatment and the new legislation, was gearing up for a massive challenge to the Dublin government. He condemned "this brutal treatment of a dying man" and warned, "This, together with the new laws Lynch is bringing against us, means the South will soon be experiencing what the North has gone through in recent years." The ground was being laid for Mac Stiofáin's death to be the southern complement to internment and Bloody Sunday, creating a revolutionary situation. The four regional parliaments of the Provisionals might provide the basis for an alternative government. It did not happen. On the tenth day of the strike, Father Seán McManus, brother of MP Frank McManus and Pat McManus, the IRA leader killed in the 1950s, visited Mac Stiofáin in the Curragh. Father McManus told Mac Stiofáin that his death would lead to rioting and bloodshed. Mac Stiofáin, fearing this would rebound against the movement, abandoned his thirst strike. This relieved the pressure on the state and undercut a huge number of people who had rapidly mobilized in his support. Mac Stiofáin had presented himself as the most uncompromising of Republicans. Yet he compromised. Even though he remained on hunger strike, the change in stance began the process of destroying his credibility; having gone to the brink and blinked, he might do so again. Protests continued, but with less urgency.

After sidelining Mac Stiofáin, Fianna Fail presented the amended Offenses Against the State Act at Leinster House. The legislation was a clear infringement on civil liberties, and several opposition TDs were opposed; a Fine Gaeler equated it with legislation in South Africa. As the debate flowed, two bombs exploded in Dublin; two people were killed and eighty more were injured. It was either the IRA moving south, which many feared but was unlikely, or the IRA's enemies showing what could happen if the southern government did not act against the IRA. Sinn Féin immediately condemned the bombs, to no avail. Fine Gael opposition to the amendment faded and the amended act was passed. It was signed into law by Éamon de Valera, the 90-year-old President of the Irish Republic. His government had introduced the original act in 1939.

It was only a matter of time before the state used the new legislation. With Mac Stiofáin in prison (and still on hunger strike), their first target was Dáithí O'Connell. On December 17th, O'Connell chaired the inaugural meeting of the Irish Civil Rights Association in Dublin; sponsors of the event included Ó Brádaigh, Frank Gogarty of NICRA, Bernadette Devlin, and the author Edna O'Brien. Following the meeting, a Special Branch officer tried to arrest O'Connell—Deirdre O'Connell, who was also at the event, stepped between them and confronted the officer, giving her husband the opportunity to slip away. After Christmas, the government targeted Ó Brádaigh. On December 28th, Loyalist paramilitaries set off bombs in the border towns of Clones, County Monaghan; Belturbet, County Cavan; and Pettigo, County Donegal, killing two and injuring several others. As usual, Ó Brádaigh wrote a statement for the press; he accused the perpetrators of trying to blackmail Jack Lynch "into implementing his new totalitarian legislation against northern political refugees and Irish Republicans generally." At about 8 PM, he set off with Gabriel Kennedy, an Irish-American, to find a phone and then dinner. Kennedy stopped by a public phone not far from the Sinn Féin Head Office, which was still closed, and Ó Brádaigh called papers with the statement. He was about to get back in the car when three Special Branch Officers intervened; one said, "I am a police officer and I am arresting you." They dragged him off to the nearby Bridewell, where he could be held without charge for forty-eight hours. Under the amended Offenses Against the State Act, he could be sent to jail without any evidence.

In the Bridewell, the first thing he did was to phone Patsy, who started making arrangements for a visit. The next day, December 31st, the arresting officer formally asked him if he was a member of the IRA. He replied, "No comment." Chief Inspector Patrick Doucy then informed him that he was being charged with membership in the IRA. That evening, under tight security, he was taken by underground tunnel to Green Street Courthouse, site of the three judge, no jury Special Criminal Court. A few members of the press were admitted but the public was not. Ciarán Mac An Ailí, a well-known solicitor, was also there acting as a consultant for the Ó Brádaigh family. Chief Inspector Doucy informed the court that he had been directed by the state's attorney general, Mr. Colm Condon, to have Ó Brádaigh charged before the Special Criminal Court. The court president, Justice Aindrias Ó Caoimh, asked, "Was the direction from the Attorney General himself?" Doucy replied, "Yes, my lord." The court registrar then read the charges: membership in the IRA on two specific dates, September 23rd and November 26th, 1972.

The *Sunday Times* described Ó Brádaigh as "quite composed during the half hour hearing." He did not recognize the court but asked Ó Caoimh if he could offer a statement. Ó Caoimh assented, and he "quietly and unemotionally" informed the court that he had faced a similar charge earlier in the year. "How often can a person be subjected to arrest and prosecution on the same charges and still be regarded as a free citizen?" he asked. He described the political work he had been doing and said that stopping his political commentary was "the real purpose for my arrest." He also quoted from a statement by Minister for Justice Des O'Malley. In the Dáil debate on the Offenses Against the State Act, O'Malley had argued that the bill did not shift the burden of proof onto defendants; that even if a senior police officer testified that someone was a member of an illegal organization and the defendant offered no evidence to the contrary, the bill did not require the courts to convict the defendant. "Accordingly," said Ó Brádaigh, "I do not wish to make any comment on the charges preferred."

Ó Caoimh turned to the prosecution and asked when they would be ready. The prosecutor, Mr. Farrell, asked for a court date of January 12th. Ó Caoimh noted that the charges "did not arise yesterday" and suggested that delay would unfairly deprive Ó Brádaigh of his "liberty." Farrell pleaded that he was at the mercy of the Gardaí, who supplied him with his evidence, and pointed out that Ó Brádaigh could apply for bail. It was a familiar game. Ó Caoimh asked Ó Brádaigh about bail. He replied that it was well known that Sinn Féin did not allow its members to post bail. Ó Caoimh gave him a break of one day; he was remanded to Mountjoy and the trial was set for January 11th. Ó Brádaigh spoke briefly with Ciarán Mac An Ailí, smiled and waved to reporters, and was then escorted back down the stairs and into the tunnel.

He spent New Year's Day 1973 in Mountjoy; it was his fourth New Year as a guest of the state, his second in Mountjoy. The commanding officer was Joe O'Neill, an old friend from the 1950s. As one of the senior Republicans, he made himself available to the younger prisoners, including Martin McGuinness, who had been arrested in Donegal with Joe McCallion. Ó Brádaigh remembers McGuinness with a smile. It was the first time McGuinness, a very likeable person and an extremely dedicated Republican, had faced charges. McGuinness and McCallion were charged with IRA membership and possession of explosives that were found in a car near the site of their arrest. The membership charge would be hard to beat, but Ó Brádaigh went over the book of evidence and noticed contradictory police accounts on the color of the car and its license plate number. If they raised this in court, Ó Brádaigh pointed out, the explosives charge could not be sustained. Even though the IRA allowed volunteers to cross-examine witnesses and make unsworn statements, McGuinness was upping the standard. *He* would not recognize the court and *he* would not ask any questions. Ó Brádaigh thought it naive and similar to Mac Stiofáin's insistence on a hunger *and* a thirst strike. Ó Brádaigh, who was getting ready for his fourth court case, pointed out that Republicans could cross-examine witnesses and make statements and still not recognize the court and that four or five questions would probably make a difference between six months and six years in sentencing. McGuinness held firm, adamant he would accept the consequences of not making any statements in court.

In Ó Brádaigh's own case, security was tight on January 11th, but some members of the public were admitted. As he entered the room, he waved to Patsy, Deirdre O'Connell, and Máire Drumm, who was serving as acting president of Sinn Féin in his place. The prosecution began by offering evidence from public statements that they claimed indicated Ó Brádaigh's IRA membership. A police officer had taken notes of Ó Brádaigh's description of the IRA to a crowd at the General Post Office on September 23rd as the "only shield" for the people of the north; he had asked people to join the movement's "political wing," Sinn Féin, because when the "military wing" was finished "it would be necessary for the political machinery to keep things going and to establish a 32-County social republic." In his cross-examination, Ó Brádaigh argued that the officers were taking lengthy speeches and reducing them to forty- to sixty-second inaccurate summaries. He denied using the phrase "military wing" in the

September 23rd speech and he pointed out that he *always* referred to Sinn Féin's goal as a 32-county *democratic* socialist Republic. The officer who testified accepted this, saying, "Now that I recall, I wrote down 'socialist republic,' but I can see your point that you did not use the phrase."

The key prosecution witness was Chief Superintendent John Fleming, head of the Special Branch. The prosecutor asked for his opinion on Ó Brádaigh's IRA status on September 23rd. Fleming replied, "I believe he was a member of the I.R.A. on that date." In cross-examination, Ó Brádaigh asked Fleming if his opinion was based on personal knowledge. Fleming replied that it was not, that it was based on reports and on confidential information. Ó Brádaigh, who had prepared for this moment, brought up previous examples where Fleming had admitted that his information and opinion were suspect. In court a month earlier, he pointed out, Fleming had said "he could be fed inaccurate information once or twice, but never more than that." Fleming acknowledged the statement. Ó Brádaigh put it to Fleming that his evidence was not always correct, and he produced the official record of a public inquiry related to the Arms Crisis, in which Fleming claimed that Ó Brádaigh had met Captain James Kelly of the Irish Army in a hotel in Monaghan in 1969. Ó Brádaigh asserted that he had not met Captain Kelly until 1972, at the Mac Stiofáin trial. Making his point, he asked Fleming if his sources were infallible and free of prejudice. Fleming honestly replied, "Not always." Continuing, he asked if Fleming's opinion was influenced by "political prejudice." Fleming denied this.

After the cross-examination, Justice Ó Caoimh asked Ó Brádaigh if he wished to give evidence under oath, remain silent, or make an unsworn statement. He made an unsworn statement. Because he was president of Sinn Féin, he said, both he and his party were on trial. Sinn Féin's offices had been closed, Sinn Féin members had been banned from RTÉ, and Sinn Féin's leaders had been harassed and arrested. He challenged the police officers' accounts: "I submit that there is no evidence against me. What I said in O'Connell Street was a political commentary." He argued that the only thing against him was Fleming's opinion and that membership in Sinn Féin did not mean membership in the IRA. He concluded by saying that it was his "fame, or notoriety, whichever one wishes" that had him in court and nothing else.

The court broke for lunch and the justices considered the evidence. When they reconvened, Justice Ó Caoimh quickly laid out their conclusions. They agreed with Ó Brádaigh; his speeches were political commentary and only demonstrated that he was prominent in Sinn Féin. Fleming's testimony was another issue. Although Ó Brádaigh had shown that Fleming's opinion might not be reliable, the justices were concerned that he had never denied membership in the IRA. This, in conjunction with Fleming's opinion, was enough to convict him. He was sentenced to six months in prison for membership in the IRA. As Ó Brádaigh had suspected all along, the burden of proof had shifted to the defendant. It was a test case, and the state had won. As he was escorted from the courtroom, he turned to the press and said, "That is the way it is done." An editorial in the London *Times* stated, "The most articulate member of the Provisional Sinn Féin is now in the Curragh detention centre. And that, from Mr Lynch's point of view, must be worth having a good number of his lesser Republican opponents out of circulation."

Ó Brádaigh joined about forty Republicans in the Glasshouse in the Curragh. Most of them were young northerners, but the commanding officer, Dan Hoban from Mayo, was a 1950s veteran. Ó Brádaigh became Hoban's adjutant. Another prisoner was Richard Behal, who had been exiled in 1966. He returned to Ireland as an independent and was now with the Provisionals. Seán Mac Stiofáin soon joined them. The Army Council ordered him off his 59-day hunger strike, during which he had lost fifty-six pounds; amid rumors that he was not keeping strictly to the fast, the leadership had decided the strike was a distraction. When Mac Stiofáin was transferred in from the military hospital, Ó Brádaigh was pleased to see him. The two of them had much in common, including young families and fluency in Irish. At the end of the month, Martin McGuinness and Joe McCallion arrived from Mountjoy. In court, both men had asked questions and drew six months each. McGuinness also told the court, "I am a member of the Derry Brigade of Óglaigh na hÉireann and am very, very proud of it."

When he first arrived at the Curragh, Ó Brádaigh was exhausted. From August 1971 through his trial, the demands on him had been constant; he put 30,000 miles on his car in 1972. He did not welcome prison, but the chance to rest was nice. It was also frustrating. On the outside, he would have been involved in and commented on a number of political developments. On January 1st, Ireland, Great Britain, and Denmark became members of the European Economic Community. In February, for the first time, Protestant paramilitaries were interned in Northern Ireland; it led to a one-day strike by utility workers and blackouts in some areas and five people were killed in unrest in Belfast. In March, a British white paper, "Northern Ireland Constitutional Proposals," proposed a new Northern Ireland Assembly and a Council of Ireland for the island as a whole.

The assembly was designed to foster cross-community politics—the prime minister's cabinet would include the opposition (Nationalists), while the proposed Council of Ireland would foster cross-border cooperation. Hard-line Unionists, fearing that the Council of Ireland was a step on the road to a united Ireland, rejected the proposals; William Craig called them "absurd." Moderates, led by Brian Faulkner, the likely prime minister of the new assembly, welcomed them. So did the SDLP. Because it viewed internment as an attack on the Nationalist community, the party had vowed to remain out of Stormont until internment was ended. Instead, and perhaps because Protestants were being interned, the SDLP remained opposed to internment but agreed to participate in the assembly. Ó Brádaigh wanted Sinn Féin to contest the election for the proposed assembly, albeit as abstentionists. It was an opportunity to develop the movement's political base and to challenge the SDLP; otherwise, the SDLP would remain unchallenged and continue to grow in the Nationalist community. He was on the sidelines, however. Séamus Twomey, who feared that fighting an election would take resources away from the IRA, and Máire Drumm, who feared that Sinn Féin might be humiliated, successfully argued that the election be boycotted.

Sinn Féin also passed when Jack Lynch called an election for the Dáil (Leinster House) for late February. The conflict in the north, the Arms Crisis and resignations of Haughey and Blaney, the Dublin bombings, and the fact that the party had been in power since 1957 all worked against Fianna Fáil. Lynch was re-elected to the Dáil, but a coalition government replaced Fianna Fáil. Liam Cosgrave, Garret FitzGerald, Paddy Cooney, and Declan Costello, all of Fine Gael, became, respectively, the Taoiseach, the minister for foreign affairs, the minister for justice, and the attorney general. Brendan Corish of Labour became the Tánaiste (deputy prime minister), and Conor Cruise O'Brien became minister for posts and telegraphs. In the Curragh, Ó Brádaigh must have watched this unfold and pondered how little things had changed over the years. In 1921, William Cosgrave, Liam's father, had been a revolutionary Sinn Féiner; he had signed the order giving sanction to May Caffrey, Ruairí's mother, for her job in Longford. Cosgrave, who was later pro-treaty, became president of the Irish Free State. Desmond FitzGerald, Garret's father, had been in the senior Cosgrave's cabinet. When the IRA split in 1922, Longford's Seán Mac Eoin had become one of the Free State's top generals. Paddy Cooney was his nephew-in-law (Cooney's aunt had married Mac Eoin). John A. Costello, who served in a Cosgrave cabinet and was Taoiseach in 1956 when the IRA launched the Border Campaign, was Declan Costello's father. Like their pro-Treaty predecessors, they took a hard line against the Republicans. In his autobiography, *Memoir: My Life and Themes,* Conor Cruise O'Brien writes that he, Cosgrave, and Corish viewed the IRA as the greatest threat to the state's security.

Ó Brádaigh has spent his political career writing letters to the editor, election manifestos, Sinn Féin policies, and so forth. Prior to his arrest he was working on a small book called *Our People, Our Future: What Éire Nua Means.* It was to be a collection of essays, letters, and presidential addresses that laid out the political development of Sinn Féin since 1970. When he was arrested, he was working on a lengthy essay, "A New Democracy." Once he was settled in at the Curragh, he continued to work on the essay, although the primitive conditions slowed his work. Too many people were crammed into the Glasshouse and the craft area was located by an open toilet. There was also tension between the prisoners and the staff. Visitors were often delayed, which cut into their allocated time, and when a prison officer stuck a baton between one prisoner and his wife who were trying to kiss goodbye, a fight broke out. To highlight their situation, the prisoners announced in March that they would no longer accept visitors. It generated some publicity, but the confrontation also interrupted Ó Brádaigh's work.

Conditions in the Curragh were unchanged two months later when, on the morning of May 14th, he was strip-searched, led to the gate, and released. Awaiting him were Patsy, his brother Seán, and his sister Mary. The *Belfast Telegraph* described him as "obviously undaunted." At a press conference, he said of the white paper that "it served no useful purpose at all and could, at best, provide only a short peace." Asked if he was repentant, he quoted Fenian O'Donovan Rossa: "I have been an Irishman since the day I was born and I am not dead yet." After a few more questions, they set off for Naas and thence to Roscommon. From there, he reported back for service to Sinn Féin's headquarters, which had been allowed to reopen.

At the first Ard Chomhairle meeting after his release, he was reinstalled as president of Sinn Féin. His status in the IRA was less clear. As it had been during the 1950s campaign, membership on the Army Council was fluid. From 1970 through 1975, a group of perhaps ten to fifteen men, including Seán Mac Stiofáin, Joe Cahill, Denis McInerney, Billy McKee, Kevin Mallon, Leo Martin, Dáithí O'Connell, Éamon O'Doherty, J. B. O'Hagan, Séamus Twomey, and Ruairí Ó Brádaigh, served on the council. Mac Stiofáin's credibility was destroyed by the hunger-strike episode. After his release from prison he returned to the movement but never the leadership. Several of members of the council, however—including Cahill, Mallon, McKee, O'Hagan, and Twomey—were arrested, served their time or escaped from jail, and were then reappointed to the council. Cahill succeeded Mac Stiofáin as chief of staff and held the position until March 1973, when he and Denis McInerney were arrested off the coast of Waterford on a ship loaded with Libyan arms. Cahill was succeeded by Séamus Twomey, who was arrested in September 1973. Éamon O'Doherty of Tipperary replaced Twomey until his own arrest in October 1974, at which point Twomey was again appointed chief of staff. Twomey was available because of a dramatic escape he had made with J. B. O'Hagan and Kevin Mallon from Mountjoy in October 1973; a helicopter landed in the prison yard, picked them up, and delivered them to a prearranged location in North County Dublin. Mallon was rearrested but escaped again; in August 1974, he and eighteen other Provisionals used smuggled explosives to blow a hole in a gate of Port Laoise Prison.

It is highly likely that Ó Brádaigh was reappointed to the Army Council after his release from the Curragh. Even if he was not on the council, the Dublin government assumed he was and treated him as such. The police followed him constantly. When they felt like it, they would force his car to the side of a road for a detailed search of him and the car. It was especially bad after the Twomey-O'Hagan-Mallon escape. Instead of letting the harassment slow him down, he called a press conference and invited journalists to travel with him. For a time, the editor of the local *Roscommon Champion* joined him regularly, which eased the situation. In January 1974, the coalition minister for education, Richard Burke, went after his job. A letter from the minister informed the County Roscommon Vocational Education Committee that because of Ó Brádaigh's conviction on the IRA membership charge, he had been dismissed. The committee, which had ignored the Fianna Fáil minister for education in this regard, also ignored the coalition minister. They replied that Ó Brádaigh had been on unpaid leave when he was convicted. As such, he was not their employee and they could not dismiss him. Even when the minister insisted, they refused.

The one person constant in the leadership through this time was Dáithí O'Connell. As IRA director of publicity, he made a number of public appearances and was assumed to be chief of staff. At Easter 1973, while British troops combed the area, O'Connell slipped into Milltown Cemetery in Belfast, gave the oration at the Republican plot, and then slipped away. At the Sinn Féin Ard Fheis in October 1973, while the police watched the Mansion House, O'Connell slipped in, offered the army statement, and slipped away again; the incident delighted the delegates and embarrassed the government. At Easter 1974, he slipped into Derry for the Easter Commemoration. The IRA shot dead a plainclothes British soldier photographing him. He became the most wanted man in Ireland but managed to avoid arrest until July 1975; a Special Branch unit dedicated to finding him finally caught him in a journalist's home.

There were a number of strong personalities in the leadership—Séamus Twomey was nicknamed "Thumper" because he would bang the table to get people's attention—but it was a collective leadership of people who had known each other for years: Cahill, McKee, and O'Hagan had been in the IRA for more than thirty years. Twomey had missed the 1950s campaign but was a veteran from the 1940s. The "younger" people—Ó Brádaigh, O'Connell, Denis McInerney, Éamon O'Doherty, and Kevin Mallon—had been involved since the 1950s. If anything, the leadership was dominated by the Northerners. O'Hagan was from Lurgan, Mallon was from Tyrone, and Cahill, Martin, Twomey, and McKee were from Belfast. Publicly, Ó Brádaigh and O'Connell became the dominant figures in the movement and it was widely, but incorrectly, assumed that they also dominated behind the scenes. The leadership was actually collective and more broad.

The most important change in the movement while Ó Brádaigh was in prison involved the extension of the IRA campaign to England. In March 1973, an IRA unit planted four bombs in London; two exploded, killing one person, who had a heart attack, and injuring another 180. In August and September, IRA units bombed Harrods department store in London and two railway stations. In the fall, an IRA engineer from Derry, Shane O'Doherty, undertook what may be the most efficient terrorist campaign ever. O'Doherty developed and delivered letter bombs that wreaked havoc on the mail system in London. His bombs went off at the Stock Exchange, the Bank of England, the House of Commons, and the British embassy in Washington; the latter blew the hand off of a Galway-born secretary. Another of his bombs was delivered to 10 Downing Street, the prime minister's residence, but failed to explode.

With the new military front came more political prisoners. Sisters Marion and Dolours Price and Gerry Kelly and Hugh Feeney, all of whom were from Belfast, were convicted for their involvement in the March 1973 London bombings and given stiff sentences. The bomb linked to Kelly was defused, but he was given two life sentences plus twenty years; in Belfast, he would have probably received ten years. All four went on hunger strike, demanding repatriation to Northern Ireland, where they would have political status. Their demand was rejected, and two other prisoners, Michael Gaughan and Frank Stagg, both from County Mayo, joined the hunger strike.

After about twenty days, the authorities began force-feeding them, which generated international interest in their cause. Marion Price, in a letter to her family, described the force-feeding: "My head was held and my nostrils blocked in an attempt to open my mouth for air. I opened my lips to breathe but kept my teeth tightly clenched together. . . . At this stage I was blind-folded and a metal clamp was used to prise my teeth apart, the wooden gag was then placed in my mouth and the plastic tube shoved down my stomach." Gerry Kelly described his experience in the booklet *Words from a Cell.* Six to eight warders would pin down his arms and legs and pull his hair to stretch out his neck. If they could not pry open his mouth, "forceps were sometimes run violently along my gums to get me to open my teeth." When this no longer worked, a hard plastic tube was pushed up his nose. When it hit the back of his throat he would "dry-retch," allowing them to put a clamp between his teeth. When he overcame the urge to vomit, the tube would be rubbed against tissue at the back of his nose, causing intense pain, "like a hot knitting-needle being pushed in between my nose and eye."

In early June 1974, Michael Gaughan died of pneumonia caused by complications from force-feeding; the tube deposited liquid in his lungs, not his stomach. He was the first Republican to die on hunger strike since Seán McCaughey in 1946, and Republicans in Ireland and England were outraged. Ó Brádaigh referred to it as "callous, brutal and premeditated murder by the British Government." The *Daily Mirror,* in response, accused him of "double-think" and argued that while IRA victims had no choice, Gaughan had chosen to die. His funeral caught the British and Irish governments off guard. A Republican guard of honor escorted the remains from Parkhurst Prison on the Isle of Wight to London, where Mass was celebrated at Christ the King Church in Kilburn; it was the same church where Ó Brádaigh had gone to confession prior to the Arborfield raid. The body was then flown to Dublin, where it was met by Ó Brádaigh, O'Connell, Máire Drumm, and others. It was escorted across Ireland to another funeral Mass in Ballina, County Mayo. The coffin was draped in the same Irish flag that had draped the coffin of Cork lord mayor Terence MacSwiney, who had died on hunger strike in London in 1920. During Mass, the priest questioned the wisdom of the IRA's campaign, and Ó Brádaigh, O'Connell, and several others walked out. At the cemetery, O'Connell addressed a crowd of 10,000 people. Representing the IRA, he said that Gaughan had "taken up the struggle against British oppressors, the well-heeled politicians in the south, the hired scribes and venal churchmen. He had been tortured in prison by the vampires of a discredited empire, who were joined by decrepit politicians who were a disgrace to the name of Irish men." He ended: "Your body is joined to Ireland. You are Ireland." Gaughan's death had not been in vain. Prison physicians refused to continue the force-feedings and the British authorities promised that the prisoners would be repatriated. After almost 170 days of force-feeding, the Price sisters, Kelly, Feeney, and Stagg ended their protest.

Throughout this period, Ó Brádaigh worked to get Sinn Féin's message to the public. He was banned from Irish television and radio and therefore focused on Irish print media and public presentations. In the summer of 1973, he finished *Our People, Our Future,* which reviewed the development of Sinn Féin and defined the party's democratic socialism. The slender paperback book was launched at a press conference in Athlone, which had been designated by the movement as the future capital of Ireland under Éire Nua. It was sold in Sinn Féin bookstores and sent to libraries and other interested parties throughout the Western world. The first 2,000 were distributed quickly, and in December 3,000 copies of an expanded edition were printed. The Ard Fheis, which was always covered in the press, was another opportunity for him to promote the cause. In October 1973, his presidential address attacked southern Irish politicians, who "resist change; they oppose the inevitable. They stoop to such practices as collaboration with the invading British forces, the operation of non-jury courts, the jailing and general harassment of those who promote change, who seek a new and better Ireland." He was quick to point out the hypocrisy endemic in Irish politics. Several members of the Labour Party, who were the voice of liberal Ireland when they were out of government, had opposed the amendment to the Offenses Against the State Act the previous December. Once in government, they did not question the act's operation. Ó Brádaigh was especially critical of Conor Cruise O'Brien, who as minister for posts and telegraphs oversaw the operation of Irish radio and television. When he was in the opposition, O'Brien criticized Fianna Fáil for censoring Republicans. As minister, he enforced the RTÉ ban on Sinn Féin. He was widely perceived to be pro-British and Unionist. In February 1974, he proposed that BBC1 be rebroadcast in Ireland on a second Irish channel, RTÉ2. Ó Brádaigh described it as an

Cumann na mBan dinner in Limerick, early 1970s. Seated, from left: Máire Drumm, Patsy Ó Brádaigh, Susie Mulcahy, Annie Cahill, Marie Quinlivan, and Líta Ní Chathmhaoil. Standing from left: Paddy Mulcahy, Ruairí Ó Brádaigh, Jimmy Drumm, and Joe Cahill. Ó Brádaigh family collection.

example of "the dictatorial zeal of a warped pseudo-intellectual who, having got the taste of power, wants to mould the national broadcasting service in his own image and likeness."

Ó Brádaigh also met with individual journalists. Just after the 1973 Ard Fheis, Mary Gaffney of the *Sunday World* interviewed him in Roscommon, asking for his thoughts on "violence" and the Catholic Church. "The British presence in Ireland for the past 800 years," he said, "is the first violence." He reminded her that the current round of violence began in Derry when the RUC attacked peaceful marchers, which was followed by the "mob violence" of August 1969. Northern Nationalists had to defend themselves: "It was thrust upon us. We had no alternative." Asked to comment on the Catholic Church, he drew on his recent stint in the Curragh: "[T]he lads in the Curragh ask simply, 'Didn't Cardinal Spellman go to Vietnam and tell the [U.S.] troops they were the Army of God while their planes were unloading thousands of bombs, destroying the countryside and burning men, women and children to death by the thousand?" Yet the Irish hierarchy condemned the Provisionals and their much smaller level of violence—there was a double standard. The prisoners had also noted, bitterly, that prior to 1969 the Irish Bishops had ignored widespread poverty and unemployment in Belfast and Derry. Ó Brádaigh summed his attitude by saying, "The bishops and clergy have their own political views and as human beings they are entitled to them. But their political views are not the word of God." Ó Brádaigh believes that the Church hierarchy will almost always support law and order over morality. Although he is a practicing Catholic and all of his children were raised as Catholics, he views the clergy as important but not essential for his faith. This probably reflects his Protestant heritage, and it is something he has thought about seriously. In his view, the clergy are "middlemen" who may be bypassed; this is why Maria McGuire described Ó Brádaigh as someone "who believed he had direct contact with God."

He also pushed the Republican agenda outside of Ireland. On an Irish Northern Aid tour in July 1973, he visited Baltimore, Boston, Hartford, New York, and Philadelphia. At a press conference in New York City, he repeated his view that the conflict was not about religion but was "a war of national liberation—a colonial war—with social and economic factors." With him was Father Seán McManus, who criticized the British Army's use of plastic bullets for crowd control. The bullets, which were manufactured in the United States, had killed three people, including an 11-year-old child, Francis Rowntree. In October 1973, Ó Brádaigh and Frank McManus, the Fermanagh–South Tyrone MP and Seán's brother, flew to Washington. They held a press conference on Capitol Hill and then testified before a subcommittee of the Foreign Relations Committee of the House of Representatives that was investigating the international protection of human rights. They described the Special Powers Act in the north and the Offenses Against the State Act in the south. They were then guests of honor at a reception in the Rayburn Building hosted by Thomas P. O'Neill, Democrat from Massachusetts and House majority leader, and Silvio Conte, a Republican from Massachusetts. More than 60 congressmen attended the reception. The testimony and reception generated a good deal of publicity for the movement, including a photograph of Ó Brádaigh and McManus flanked by O'Neill, Conte, and Bishop Thomas Drury of Corpus Christi, that was printed in the *Irish Press.*

The success of the August and October trips spurred Irish Northern Aid to invite Ó Brádaigh to be the keynote speaker for their 1974 annual testimonial dinner. He booked a flight with Aer Lingus for January 16th from Shannon to New York. The U.S. State Department, however, had taken notice of him. When Ó Brádaigh was in Washington, Henry Kissinger, the secretary of state, had sent a telegram to the U.S. embassy

Ruairí Ó Brádaigh in Boston, July 1973. Seated at his left is Michael Flannery.
Ó Brádaigh family collection.

in Dublin, seeking information on him. The embassy checked with the Irish Foreign Office and responded that "[b]ecause of Ó Brádaigh's continued involvement in top-level planning of Provisional Sinn Fein/IRA, he . . . bears heavy responsibility for a serious and sustained campaign of terrorism." The embassy, believing he would use this trip to raise money for "Irish violence," recommended that steps be taken to prevent it. As he was preparing to drive to Shannon, his travel agent phoned with the news that the State Department had revoked his visa. But Patsy still had hers. The younger children were quickly sent to stay with her mother in Galway and she was off on her first trip to the United States. Supporters met her at JFK and drove her to directly to the Astoria Hotel in Queens, where she entered a packed room to the "skirl of bagpipes and a standing ovation." The toastmaster was Paul O'Dwyer, the Mayo-born president of the New York City Council. One of the speakers was New York congressman Ogden Reid, who was seeking the Democratic nomination for governor of New York. In her remarks, Patsy focused on prisoner issues, noting in particular the Price sisters, who were enduring their force-feeding.

Now excluded from Britain and the United States, Ruairí Ó Brádaigh

looked to the Continent. At the 1973 Ard Fheis, the delegates endorsed
the creation of an international office for Sinn Féin. The Ard Chomhairle
appointed Richard Behal to head the office. Behal chose Brussels as the
site, and from this base he traveled far and wide publicizing the cause.
Over the years, he organized tours of Europe and beyond. In July 1974,
he secured an invitation for Sinn Féin to the International Conference on
Minorities in Trieste, Italy. Behal and Ó Brádaigh turned the invitation
into an nine-day tour of Western Europe, with press conferences and television appearances in Trieste, Paris, Brussels, and Zurich. In Trieste, they
passed out literature and offered a public presentation in Irish on three
Irish minorities: Nationalists in the Six Counties, Irish-speakers in the
west; and Unionists in Ireland as a whole. It was Ó Brádaigh's first trip to
the Continent and he enjoyed himself immensely; he was among his own
kind in an international context. More than 600 delegates representing
more than twenty different minority groups, including Kurds, Basques,
Catalans, Scottish, Welsh, and Bretons, discussed how governments address minority problems. Regionalization and federalization featured prominently in the discussion. His presence with Behal was well received. The
Scottish group circulated a petition expressing solidarity with Provisional
Sinn Féin. The mayor of Trieste said that the city was honored to have
representatives from the only national minority in Europe that was "actually fighting for its existence." In reply, Ó Brádaigh pointed out that it was
not the first time Trieste had expressed sympathy with the Republican
struggle. In the 1919–1923 period Trieste, then an independent state, was
alone in granting full diplomatic recognition to the revolutionary Dáil
Éireann.

Underlying all of Ó Brádaigh's activity was the promotion of Éire
Nua, the Republican solution to Ireland's problems. Unfortunately, the
Unionists in the north were still focused on a return to Stormont. For the
most part they wanted nothing to do with the Social Democratic and
Labour Party, let alone the "men of violence": Sinn Féin was still a proscribed organization in the north. In the south, established politicians
were not interested in changes that might diminish their authority. Des
Fennell, in *Beyond Nationalism,* comments that TDs in Dublin, whose
"role was in effect that of intermediaries between the people and the distant, mysterious bureaucracy," were threatened by "arrangements which
would render government unmysterious, easily accessible, and subject to
local control." The British ignored Éire Nua and instead offered their
own solution to the conflict. If their proposed assembly led to a cross-
community Unionist-Nationalist government, it might bring peace and

then London could relinquish direct control. The assembly elections, which were held in June of 1973, went well from the British perspective. Moderate Unionists led by Brian Faulkner and the SDLP won more than half of the 78 seats, which meant that intransigent Unionists, led by a William Craig–Ian Paisley coalition, might cause trouble, but they could not block all progress. The elected representatives set a target date of January 1, 1974, as the day they would take office, and they met through the summer and into the fall to prepare. Brian Faulkner was chosen as the chief executive and the representatives selected a Northern Ireland Executive that included some SDLP members. Simultaneously, the British courted the Dublin government.

In early December 1973, Prime Minister Edward Heath, Taoiseach Liam Cosgrave, Chief Executive Brian Faulkner, assorted British and Irish civil servants, and other members of the Northern Ireland Executive met at the Civil Service Staff College at Sunningdale in England. On Sunday evening, December 9th, they issued a communiqué that had significant political ramifications. The Dublin government had accepted the position that until the majority of the people desired it, Northern Ireland's status would be unchanged. The London government, in turn, affirmed that Northern Ireland was part of the United Kingdom but added that if a majority of the people there desired unification with Ireland it would support it. The two governments also agreed to establish a Council of Ireland that would enhance cross-border cooperation, including measures that would make it easier for Dublin to prosecute persons accused of crimes committed in Northern Ireland.

As far as Republicans were concerned, Cosgrave and the coalition government had given the Unionist minority in Ireland a veto over the wishes of the overall majority of Irish Nationalists. Ó Brádaigh described the agreement as a "step backward." Hard-line Unionists and Loyalist paramilitaries also rejected the Sunningdale agreement. Many of them viewed the SDLP, which advocated the peaceful reunification of Ireland, as traitors on a level with Republicans. The hard-liners rejected power-sharing and suspected that the Council of Ireland would be a stepping-stone to a united Ireland. Ironically, some of them turned to political alternatives that were consistent with Éire Nua. Desmond Boal, a former chairman of the Democratic Unionist Party and an associate of Rev. Ian Paisley, feared that Unionist power would decline over time and that a united Ireland was inevitable. On January 1st, 1974, the British formally turned a number of the powers of government over to the Northern Ireland Executive. On January 6th, in a highly publicized interview with the Belfast *Sunday News,* Boal argued that in order to secure the best deal possible it was time for Unionists to negotiate with the Dublin government. He proposed a federal Ireland on a Six–Twenty Six-County basis with a provincial parliament for the north. Paddy Devlin of the SDLP said it was a "courageous gesture." The Republicans embraced the proposal insofar as it included British disengagement. Ó Brádaigh described it an alternative to Sunningdale and said "it could be the big breakthrough," but added that the four-province model was more workable. Some Loyalist paramilitaries in the Ulster Defence Association and the Ulster Volunteer Force indicated interest in the proposal. Mainstream Unionist politicians rejected it. Ian Paisley and William Craig immediately dissociated themselves from Boal. And in a prominent critique that appeared in the *Belfast Sunday News,* David Trimble, then a young attorney, argued that if the union with Great Britain was broken, Northern Ireland would be better off independent than in a reunited Ireland.

The Northern Ireland Executive and the Council of Ireland had potential, but the initiative floundered when British politics intervened. Edward Heath, faced with a deteriorating economy and labor unrest, called an election even though the SDLP strongly argued against it. In Northern Ireland it became a referendum on the Executive. In Britain, Heath and the Conservatives were replaced by a Labour government under Harold Wilson. In the north, the Executive's opponents, including Craig and Paisley, formed the United Ulster Unionist Council, won 51 percent of the vote, captured eleven of the twelve Northern Ireland seats at Westminster, and destroyed the Executive's credibility. The only winner for the moderates was the SDLP's Gerry Fitt, who retained his seat in West Belfast. The United Ulster Unionist Council, arguing they had a mandate from the people, immediately called for new elections to the Northern Ireland Assembly under the assumption that they would repeat their success and put an end to power-sharing. Merlyn Rees, the new secretary of state, refused, supported the Executive, and charted a course in which he tried to balance calls for increased security with a desire to bring paramilitaries into mainstream political dialogue.

It was a difficult position to take, and the result was that Rees sent mixed signals throughout his tenure. In April 1974, he lifted the proscription on the Ulster Volunteer Force and Sinn Féin and announced that internment would be phased out. But two weeks later, while John Joe McGirl was in Belfast to deliver the Easter Commemoration address at

Milltown Cemetery, the police, believing he was Séamus Twomey, arrested him. McGirl, a citizen of the Irish Republic who was not wanted for any criminal activity north or south, was subsequently interned in Long Kesh. Ó Brádaigh commented that "[f]reedom of political action or 'freedom to act politically' to use Mr. Rees' terminology does not exist in the Six Counties as far as Sinn Féin is concerned." Loyalist paramilitaries were also wary. That April, the Ulster Defence Association published a document indicating that it had just two options, civil war or talks with the Provisionals. The document and Rees's lifting of the proscription on Sinn Féin and the Ulster Volunteer Force brought together an unlikely group of people: Ruairí Ó Brádaigh, William Craig, and Sammy Smyth, the Ulster Defence Association's press officer. In Dundalk they taped an edition of the London-based television show *Weekend World*. Smyth and Ó Brádaigh, it turned out, agreed on several things. Both were alienated from mainstream politics, both distrusted the British, and both agreed that a federal Ireland might provide a permanent peace. Ó Brádaigh, for his part, stated that the Provisionals wanted a planned, phased, and orderly withdrawal that would allow for political structures to be put into place. In 1960, Belgium had pulled out of the Congo and left behind a political morass that degenerated into widespread violence, the secession of the Katanga province, and the assassination of Premier Patrice Lumumba. Ó Brádaigh wanted to avoid a "Congo situation."

After the taping, as he had with William Craig in Boston in 1972, Ó Brádaigh took advantage of an opportunity and discussed Éire Nua with Smyth. If it was not possible to bring back the old Stormont system, Ó Brádaigh asked, what was his preferred option? Smyth replied, "A federal Ireland." Indeed, Smyth had authored an Ulster Defence Association position paper titled "Fight, Compromise, or Fade Away: Your Choice," which examined the Swiss federal system. Like Ó Brádaigh and Dáithí O'Connell, he found much to admire in the system and wrote that "the power given to regions or 'Cantons' . . . would, if applied in a similar way to Northern Ireland, undoubtedly, in our view, be satisfactory to all the present citizens in Northern Ireland." Smyth did express some concerns, notably that the traditionally higher birth rate of Catholics suggested that a Protestant majority under Dáil Uladh would not last. What was important, for Ó Brádaigh, was that Éire Nua and Dáil Uladh might be a basis for continued dialogue and a resolution to the conflict. Opportunities to continue the dialogue were few and far between, however. As Boal had learned, Unionist political leaders who entertained federalist ideas in public would be dropped.

In May, frustration in the Unionist community over the Northern Ireland Executive and the Council of Ireland reached the breaking point. In the Northern Ireland Assembly, a motion condemning power-sharing failed. In response, the Ulster Workers Council, a coalition of politicians, including Craig and Paisley, and paramilitaries, including the Ulster Defence Association and Ulster Volunteer Force, called a general strike. Workers cut power to utilities and Loyalist paramilitaries set up roadblocks allowing only "essential workers" through barricades. As everyone in Ireland and Britain watched, workers were prevented from getting to their jobs, factories were closed, violence flared in Belfast, and Northern Ireland ground to a halt. The trouble spread south on May 17th. Three car bombs went off without warning in Dublin, killing twenty-six people and injuring another hundred. A couple of hours later, another car bomb went off in Monaghan, killing seven more people and injuring twenty. Although no one claimed responsibility for the bombs, the cars involved had been stolen from Loyalist areas of Belfast and Portadown, and it was assumed that these actions were taken either in retaliation for IRA activity or a warning of what would come if Dublin interfered in the north. Sammy Smyth was quoted as saying "I am very happy about the bombings in Dublin. There is a war with the Free State, and now we are laughing at them." On May 25th, Harold Wilson described the strike as "a deliberate and calculated attempt to use every undemocratic and unparliamentary means for the purpose of bringing down the whole Constitution of Northern Ireland so as to set up a sectarian and undemocratic state, from which one-third of the people would be excluded." He described the strike's organizers as "thugs and bullies," but no direct action was taken against them. On the 28th, with more power cuts looming, Brian Faulkner and his Unionist supporters withdrew from the Northern Ireland Executive, effectively ending it and the Council of Ireland. Merlyn Rees assumed political responsibility for the province and the strike was ended.

Liam Cosgrave blamed the collapse of the Executive on the IRA, charging that "the campaign of the IRA has sparked a massive sectarian backlash." Ó Brádaigh replied that Cosgrave was looking for a scapegoat and called on the British to make a declaration of intent to withdraw and to begin the phased withdrawal of British troops over a period of years. And he again offered Dáil Uladh as a solution to the conflict; the *Irish Independent* reported him saying that "Unionist domination made the north basically ungovernable, but power sharing could still work if it was made a nine-county state by the addition of Monaghan, Cavan and Donegal and administration carried out by district councils as advocated by Sinn Féin." In support of Éire Nua, Sinn Féin was focusing its attention on the upcoming local elections in the south, which were scheduled for June.

The 1974 local elections, the first since the war started, gave Sinn Féin a chance to gauge support in the Twenty-Six Counties. Banned from RTÉ, and in spite of harassment from the police, Sinn Féin distributed 100,000 copies of an election manifesto that called for a national housing fund to finance home purchases, comprehensive free medical service, and more local control over educational facilities. The manifesto also called for self-government for the Gaeltacht. The status quo was not threatened, but Sinn Féin's representation grew from twelve representatives in nine counties to twenty-six representatives in fourteen counties. At the county council level, Frank Glynn and Paddy Ruane in Galway and Jimmy McElwain in Monaghan were re-elected. And John Joe McGirl, Fra Browne, and Seán Lynch and Michael Nevin were elected in Leitrim, Louth, and Longford, respectively. McGirl, who was still interned in Long Kesh, topped the poll in Leitrim. Ó Brádaigh sent a congratulatory telegram to McGirl and another to Merlyn Rees, demanding McGirl's release so he could "serve the people of Leitrim"; McGirl was still in Long Kesh in October 1974 when the internees set fire to several of their huts in protest, and he was not released until early 1975. Ó Brádaigh was especially pleased with the election results in Longford. Michael Nevin was a distant cousin and Seán Lynch was the son of his father's old comrade, Seán F. Lynch, who had remained on the County Council until his death in 1969. Seán Lynch, whose home was raided the morning of the election, reclaimed the seat for Sinn Féin. Ó Brádaigh, who was in Longford for the count, said, "I look forward to seeing the Sinn Féin councilors putting the Éire Nua policies before the people. I regard their achievements as a victory for the small man over the all-consumer society of big business and the gigantic forces of the E.E.C."

Unfortunately, the Ó Brádaigh family and Republican Longford also experienced a significant loss not long after the election as time took its toll on the veterans of the 1916–1923 era. Seán F. Lynch's death in 1969 was followed by the death in Dublin of Seán Mac Eoin in July of 1973. Mac Eoin, a hero from the War of Independence and twice Fine Gael's candidate for president of Ireland, was given a massive state funeral. The Ó Brádaighs rejected the state but not Mac Eoin, who had saved their father's life and had remained on good terms with the family. Seán Ó Brádaigh attended the removal of the remains from a military hospital in Dublin. Journalists, unaware of the family's history, were surprised. Ruairí joined a huge crowd attending the funeral Mass in Ballinalee. The *Irish Press* ran a photograph of him, Seán Lynch, and Frank Quinn, another Longford Sinn Féiner, with the caption, "A face in the crowd."

A year after Mac Eoin's funeral, Longford buried an anti-treatyite, May Brady Twohig. She had held firm for the Republic from 1922 until her death on August 12, 1974, at the age of 75. She was the mother of Sinn Féin's president and its director of publicity and was a veteran of Cumann na mBan. Cars arriving for her funeral were stopped and searched and their occupants were forced out onto the roadside. After Mass at St. Mel's Cathedral, the family, including Ruairí, Seán, and Mary, and their families, and May's Twohig stepchildren, Paddy, Moira, and Anna and their children and grandchildren, watched as Sinn Féiners, wearing black berets, carried the tricolor-draped coffin to the hearse and marched alongside military style for three miles as it made its way to Ballymacormack Cemetery. She was laid to rest between Matt Brady and Patrick Twohig. Prominent among the 1,000 or so mourners were Máire Drumm, Seán Keenan, Joe O'Neill, and Éamon Mac Thomáis. The gravesite was filled with wreaths from Sinn Féin's Ard Chomhairle and *cumainn* from throughout the country.

Under the watchful eyes of the Gardaí and Special Branch, and in a driving rain, Seán Lynch, Sinn Féin county councilor, gave the funeral oration. Lynch, who through his father knew May Brady Twohig well, referred to her as a "truly great woman" and offered a brief life history. He concluded his remarks with "May this great woman, who embodied all that was best in Irish culture, public service and true patriotism, serve as an example to us all as we strive to free the nation she loved and served so well. *I measc Naomh is Laochra na h-Éireann go raibh a h-anam uasal* [Among the saints and heroes of Ireland may her noble soul rest]."

She had been a role model for her family, someone who led by example. Because of Matt Brady's politics and Ruairí Ó Brádaigh's age when his father died, it is tempting to conclude that his father was the major influence on his life. Ó Brádaigh acknowledges his father's importance, even saying, "They say that a parent has the most influence over a child between the ages of eight and twelve, and I was ten [when Matt Brady died]." But to understand Ruairí Ó Brádaigh is to also acknowledge his mother's tremendous influence on him and his siblings. When it came time to make difficult choices—whether to pursue a career as a teacher or how to respond to the condemnation of the IRA by the clergy—his father could not be there. He sought out her advice, and she supported his choices. Of Ruairí Ó Brádaigh's parents, hers is the model for his life. Like her son, May Brady Twohig successfully balanced raising a family, pursuing a career, and keeping the Republican faith. Among the many condolences that he received after his mother's death was a letter from Seán Cronin in Washington, in which Cronin described her as "a liberated woman of the first Dáil period." It is a compliment Ó Brádaigh has not forgotten.

13

The Responsibilities of Leadership

NOVEMBER 1974–FEBRUARY 1976

SINN FÉIN'S MODERATE success in the southern local council elections, and the IRA's continued ability to mount an effective campaign were reasons for optimism among the Republican leadership as the summer of 1974 moved into the fall. *An Phoblacht's* circulation was 40,000; the paper had been published weekly since March 1973. After five years in the field, the IRA was stronger and more active than at any time since the 1920s. The campaign in England continued. During 1974, bombs exploded in London in June and in London, Birmingham, and Manchester in July. Northern Ireland was not ungovernable, but neither was it a model of Western democracy. The SDLP had secured its place as the party of moderate Nationalists, but confrontation with the security forces on the streets of Belfast and Derry brought the IRA new recruits and continued support. Only with significant support from the British Army could the RUC patrol Derry's Bogside and parts of Nationalist Belfast. The countryside, especially in South Derry, mid-Tyrone, and along the border, was also dangerous for the security forces. And in South Armagh, the IRA had created the liberated area that it had hoped to create in Fermanagh during the Border Campaign. The movement's leadership, who had lived it, were well aware that their army was light years removed from the 1950s.

With an almost exclusively Nationalist population and a history of resistance to the Crown, South Armagh was a natural haven for IRA guerrillas. For the British Army, it had become the most dangerous place to serve in Northern Ireland; the roads were so dangerous that they were forced to helicopter in supplies for their base at Crossmaglen. By the time the first IRA volunteer was killed in action in South Armagh, Michael McVerry in November 1973, the South Armagh IRA had killed twenty-two British soldiers. A year after McVerry's death, an estimated crowd of

10,000 people attended the unveiling of a garden of remembrance in his honor in his home village of Cullyhanna. The keynote speaker, Ruairí Ó Brádaigh, described McVerry as "tireless, fearless, dedicated to the cause" and the area as "liberated" and cleared of Crown forces. He also looked to the future and victory, stating, "We can only talk war in times of war but when the British Government declares its intention to get out of Ireland, we must ensure that we are skilled in the art of negotiating the peace built upon justice and freedom."

Ó Brádaigh's talk about British withdrawal was not political dreaming. Since the British-IRA truce in 1972, the Republicans had remained in contact, through intermediaries, with British representatives in the Northern Ireland Office in Belfast; these included James Allan of the Foreign Office and Michael Oatley of British Intelligence. There was nothing concrete, but there were "vibrations" that the British, having failed with the assembly, were considering a withdrawal. At the 1974 Ard Fheis in September, Ó Brádaigh spoke directly to London, saying, "You know you have failed to break the people's resistance and crush the Republican Movement. We all know that you are beaten and that you may secretly be preparing to go home." He called on the British to admit this publicly. Non-Republicans were also concerned about the situation. The U.S. embassy in Dublin monitored the Ard Fheis and sent a summary to the State Department. It included the following on Ó Brádaigh's speech, "Fact that he reiterated request at convention does not mean that Sinn Féin is going soft on [B]ritish. It does show, however, that Sinn Féin seriously believes British may decide to abandon Northern Ireland in a hurry in fairly near future. *This is one of very few points on which Sinn Féin and GOI [Government of Ireland] agree*" (emphasis added).

The IRA stepped up the campaign in England. On Saturday night, October 5th, 1974, no-warning bombs were placed in pubs frequented by military personnel in Guildford, England. Five people, including four soldiers, were killed and fifty more were injured. In early November, another no-warning bomb at another pub frequented by British soldiers in Woolwich killed two people. In mid-November, Dáithí O'Connell secretly taped an interview with Mary Holland, an Irish journalist, that was broadcast on the British television news show *Weekend World*. O'Connell promised more attacks and ruled nothing out. Political assassination was possible and military targets would be bombed without warning. Calmly, and with calculation, he said, "I bring it home to the British Government that the consequences of war are not going to be kept solely in Ireland; they are going to be felt on the mainland of Britain." A few days later, the threat became real. On November 21st, two pubs in Birmingham were bombed, killing 21 people and injuring another 182. It was not a military target, but the warnings came too late to prevent the slaughter.

It was not what O'Connell had intended. The IRA leadership was horrified, as were their supporters. Ó Brádaigh was personally outraged. He believed the bombing was inappropriate, no matter who carried it out. He made inquiries and confirmed that the IRA leadership had not sanctioned the bombs; it was not policy to bomb civilians in England. When the IRA, through Dáithí O'Connell, denied that it was their work, he believed it. No one else did, however, and the historical record shows that the two bombs in Birmingham resulted in the highest Provisional IRA death toll for a single day. When O'Connell announced that six people charged with the bombings—the Birmingham Six—were not affiliated with the Republican Movement, no one believed that, either. History would show that O'Connell was correct.

The Provisionals faced worldwide condemnation. Blowing up civilians in a crowded pub on a Saturday night was terrorism, not a war for national liberation. British reaction was swift. Forty-eight hours after Birmingham, Westminster passed the Prevention of Terrorism Act (1974), which allowed arrest without warrant, detention without trial for up to seven days, and the expelling of suspected terrorists from the UK. A suspected terrorist from Northern Ireland, a citizen of the UK, could be arrested in England without warrant, held for a number of days, and then exiled back to Northern Ireland. The home secretary, Roy Jenkins, described the powers as "draconian" but justified. The act became law four days later. The first person arrested under the PTA was Paul Hill from Belfast. Hill and ten other people—the Guildford Four and the Maguire Seven—were convicted in connection with the bombings. Like the conviction of the Birmingham Six, these convictions would be overturned many years later, in 1990–1992.

Soon after Birmingham, the Provisionals got a break. Various Republicans had been in a dialogue with several Protestant ministers who were searching for a way to bring about a cease-fire. Through Rev. William Arlow, deputy secretary of the Irish Council of Churches, the ministers had requested a meeting with the movement's leadership. The leadership, who knew that Arlow had contacts in the Northern Ireland Office, took the invitation seriously. A meeting date was set for December 10th at Smyth's Village Hotel in Feakle, County Clare. The evening before, eight Protestant clergymen arrived at the hotel, including Arlow; Rev. A. J. Weir, clerk of the Assembly of the Presbyterian Church in Ireland; Bishop

Arthur Butler of the Church of Ireland; and Stanley Worrall, former head-master of Methodist College, Belfast, and chairman of the New Ulster Movement. They were complemented by a high-level Republican delega-tion: Ruairí Ó Brádaigh, Máire Drumm, Séamus Loughran, Kevin Mal-lon, Dáithí O'Connell, J. B. O'Hagan, Séamus Twomey, and Billy McKee. McKee had only recently been released from prison. They described them-selves as the "political and military leadership of the Republican Movement."

The two sides met for an informal drink, and the clergymen were surprised at what they found. Rev. William Arlow later stated, "I thought I was going to meet a group of mindless monsters because that is how the media was projecting them at the time." All but one of the ministers took a drink; only Dáithí O'Connell of the Republicans did so. O'Connell was also the only Republican who smoked cigarettes. The meeting the next day went well. Bishop Butler later commented, "We were all most im-pressed by their attitude, with their fair-mindedness, and we were so pleased to find that they were talking seriously and deeply and with great conviction and had listened very carefully to what we had to say." The clergymen were seeking Republican input on a position paper they had drafted that laid out a cease-fire between the IRA and "Her Majesty's Government." In the discussion that followed, the Republicans impressed on them that a cease-fire was possible, but only if it would lead to a British declaration of intent to withdraw. At about four o'clock in the afternoon, after the clergymen had withdrawn to an upstairs room to work on the proposal, the Republicans received word that the Gardaí were about to raid the hotel. They passed this on to the clergymen and told them that O'Connell, Mallon, Twomey, and O'Hagan, who were on the run, were leaving. The clergymen, aware of how careful they had been to keep the meeting secret, were dubious and suggested it was an excuse to stop the meeting. They returned to their caucus while Ó Brádaigh, McKee, Drumm, and Loughran sat by the downstairs fire and chatted. About 4:30 in the afternoon, the police came in en masse. Spotting Ó Brádaigh and company, they asked where the others were. McKee replied, "Upstairs." Loaded with submachine guns and assuming they had captured the lead-ership of the Republican Movement in one swoop, they raced up the stairs, lined the clergymen up against the wall, and learned their identities. Ó Brádaigh, McKee, Drumm, and Loughran were highly amused. The police left without arresting anyone.

When the public learned of the meeting, it helped undercut the fall-out from the Birmingham bombs. Ó Brádaigh says that "[we were] found out to be doing good." When journalists called for interviews, he described the talks as "amicable" and "fruitful." An interview with RTÉ radio went very well and he was asked to drive to Dublin to tape an interview for the television news program *Seven Days*. He was more than willing and set off for Dublin. He arrived at the studios only to learn that the taping was canceled by order of a "higher authority." It was a minor irritant in a much bigger process that was unfolding.

After Feakle, the Army Council met over a two-day period and developed a response to the clergymen's proposals. They forwarded this to the clergymen, who had set up a meeting with Merlyn Rees. The clergymen, with the Republicans' blessing, gave a copy to Rees. Rees, who knew that members of his staff were already in contact with Republicans, was intrigued. The Provisionals wanted the people of Ireland to elect a constituent assembly that would draft an all-Ireland constitution with a "provincial parliament for Ulster (nine counties) with meaningful powers," a public commitment from the British that they would withdraw within twelve months of the adoption of the constitution, and amnesty for all political prisoners and for those on the "wanted list." To facilitate the transition, they welcomed "tripartite talks with loyalist and British army forces to secure their co-operation in the implementation of the cease-fire and the maintenance of community peace." In the meantime, as a sign of good faith, and if the British were willing to stop "army raids, harassments and arrests," if there was "no show of provocation" from crown forces, and if the RUC was not reintroduced "into areas in which they are not acceptable," then the Provisionals were willing to declare "a temporary cessation of activities" from December 22, 1974 through January 2, 1975. They asked for a response from the British by December 28th.

Since the fall of the Northern Ireland Assembly the previous May, Rees had been trying to develop a plan for self-government of Northern Ireland that included power-sharing. His solution, which had been announced in a British white paper in July, was a constitutional convention for Northern Ireland in which elected delegates would be charged with developing governmental structures. In his memoir *Northern Ireland: A Personal Perspective*, Rees records that on seeing the Provisional IRA's response to Feakle he surmised that the "political wing" of the Provisionals realized "there was no possibility of a military victory" and, on the heels of the Birmingham bombings, wanted to participate in the convention. He records that he told the clergymen he would not negotiate with the Republicans but said that "[i]f there were to be 'a genuine and sustained cessation of violence' it would create a new situation." Also, the cease-fire had to include Great Britain.

The clergymen flew back to Dublin from London and Arlow reported Rees's response to the Republicans. An IRA statement on December 20th suggests that Rees offered more than a "new situation." It began, "As a result of the Feakle meeting the leadership of the Republican movement have ordered a suspension of offensive military action in Britain and Ireland over the Christmas period." The statement repeated the conditions for the cease-fire and hinted that something more was in the offing: "The truce is also designed to give the British Government an opportunity to consider the proposals for a permanent cease-fire. The suspension of operations has been ordered on the clear understanding that a positive response will be forthcoming from the British government." Rees, who welcomed the statement, stated that "that there was no question of the British Government giving a specific undertaking." The Republican leadership did not know what "specific undertaking" he referred to and interpreted this as "Rees double talk."

In response to the announcement, RTÉ taped an interview with Ó Brádaigh for *Seven Days.* The program broadcast the interview and then allowed Austin Currie of the SDLP and John Laird of the Official Unionists to comment on Ó Brádaigh's remarks. In the interview, Ó Brádaigh said that he was optimistic that the cease-fire could hold and that a permanent peace would have to be based on justice. It would require a British declaration of intent to withdraw, the terms of which were negotiable. Once this was done, it would be possible to enter an arrangement whereby Loyalists would accept a nine-county Ulster. Currie and Laird were less optimistic. Currie, who noted that Ó Brádaigh was "trying to be reasonable," pointed out that the people of Cavan, Monaghan, and Donegal had not been consulted. Laird accused Ó Brádaigh of living in "Cloud Cuckoo-Land." The next day, at home in Roscommon, Ó Brádaigh told the *Irish Press* that the Dublin government could help the situation by giving Sinn Féin total freedom of the media, adding that he had not been afforded the right of reply. There was no response from Dublin.

To Ó Brádaigh's surprise, the British government's response to the IRA's proposals came on Christmas Day. He was at home with his family when he looked out the front window to see that he had a visitor—one of the persons acting as an intermediary between himself and the Northern Ireland Office. The man had a message to deliver—a letter, dictated by the British and in the intermediary's handwriting, requesting a meeting in order to establish structures for a British withdrawal from Ireland. Ó Brádaigh, "astonished," thanked him and contacted the Army Council. The council was interested but wary. On December 31st, Ó Brádaigh introduced the intermediary to the council and vouched for his credibility; the council was not introduced to the intermediary. After some questioning, Billy McKee asked, "Well, what's on the agenda?" The reply: "Withdrawal." The intermediary explained that the British had asked him to help arrange a meeting between Michael Oatley of the Northern Ireland Office and Billy McKee, who the British knew was highly regarded among Republicans. He did not realize that McKee, who was not a public figure, had asked the question. Séamus Twomey asked McKee if he was willing to meet with Oatley. McKee said he would, but not without a witness. Twomey accepted this and the intermediary reported it back to Oatley. To give the British some time, the council also agreed to extend the cease-fire to midnight, January 16, 1975.

On the day the council met the intermediary, Merlyn Rees announced the release of fifty-three internees and prisoners and said that the British would not be found wanting if the cease-fire held. The next day, January 1st, Ó Brádaigh and Máire Drumm led a "Peace with Justice" march through Dublin's streets. Wreaths were laid at the scene of the Dublin bombings and a Sinn Féin rally that attracted 500–600 people was held at the new British embassy in Ballsbridge. Ó Brádaigh's audience was the marchers, but he spoke to the British. He called the releases a "positive response" that was "almost too late and certainly too little" and added, "There has got to be political movement and there has got to be a political response." On January 2nd, the Provisionals announced that the cease-fire was extended to midnight the 16th. On the 7th, McKee and his witness met in secret with Michael Oatley in Derry. When McKee again asked about the agenda, Oatley replied, "Withdrawal." But, Oatley explained, the British wanted to avoid a "bloodbath" and needed help from the Provisionals. Nothing definitive resulted from the meeting, but that day Rees announced that twenty more internees would be released. That evening, Ó Brádaigh told the press he was "cautiously optimistic" that the cease-fire would hold. A week later, Rees went before the House of Commons to deliver a major speech on the cease-fire situation. He acknowledged that his staff had met with members of Sinn Féin and also with members of the Ulster Defence Association and the Ulster Volunteer Force. He encouraged all three organizations to "take part in genuine political activity within the law," including participation in the constitutional convention. Concerning the cease-fire, he said that with a "genuine and sustained cessation of violence," the army would "make a planned, orderly and progressive reduction in its present commitment" if the RUC "was in a position to take over the major law and order role." He concluded: "The question being asked throughout the whole community is 'Can there be peace?' The people of Northern Ireland say 'Yes'. The government have responded positively and will continue to do so. We await a similar response from the Provisionals and the other paramilitary organisations."

The Provisionals wanted concrete actions, not promises. Based on their response to the clergy in December, Rees knew that giving the RUC a major role in law and order would be unacceptable. In an interview with the *Irish Press*, Ó Brádaigh described himself as "depressed" by the British attitude and stated, "They have been stringing the thing along throughout until the final moment, and then making a move. That is no way to do business in these circumstances." At midnight on the 16th, the cease-fire ended and the IRA went back to war. Rees denounced them, stating, "I will not be influenced by any views which are backed by the bomb and the bullet." What the public did not know is that at 2 AM on the 17th, prior to Rees's statement, Ó Brádaigh was awakened by a phone call that told him to contact the intermediary immediately. Assuming his own phone was tapped, he dressed and went to a public telephone and placed the call. The intermediary informed him that although the cease-fire was off, the British wanted to maintain contact and discuss the possibility of another cease-fire.

The conversation had not gone much further when the Gardaí arrived at the public phone booth. This confirmed Ó Brádaigh's suspicion that his phone was tapped and that his movements were being monitored. He hung up the phone and was held only briefly, but it was not until 7 PM that evening that he again reached the intermediary. He was told that not only did the British want to continue the dialogue, but they specifically requested that he be involved. Prior to this, he was told, they had considered him "too prominent." He thanked the intermediary for the information and said he would be back in touch. Then he contacted the Army Council, from whom he received explicit instructions. He was to deliver two messages to the intermediary. The movement was prepared to send two representatives to meet two British representatives and negotiate the terms of a bilateral truce. And it was prepared to have its representatives negotiate the implementation of its three demands—a British declaration of intent to withdraw from Ireland, amnesty for political prisoners, and self-determination for the Irish people "acting as a unit." The British evidently accepted the approach, because on January 20th, in Derry, Ruairí Ó Brádaigh, Billy McKee, and one other representative met with the two British representatives, Michael Oatley and James Allan.

This was the first of more than twenty "formal meetings" between

Ó Brádaigh, McKee, and the third Republican and five different British civil servants, including Oatley, Allan, and Donald Middleton of the Foreign Office. They reported to Frank Cooper, later Sir Frank Cooper, who was serving, under Merlyn Rees, as the permanent undersecretary for Northern Ireland. Oatley was involved in the meetings until February, while Allan attended meetings into the summer. Oatley's replacement was Middleton. When the two sides were not meeting they continued to exchange information through the intermediary. Each meeting was in Derry, which provided easy access over the border for the Republican team. It also allowed them to consult with the Army Council, primarily Dáithí O'Connell and Séamus Twomey, who would move up to the border to make themselves available as needed. Perhaps most important, Ó Brádaigh kept a record of the meetings. They were not minutes per se but rather his own detailed handwritten record of each meeting. He also kept notes on the instructions that he and the team received from the Army Council, which was consulted regularly, and on the discussions that he had with the intermediary.

At the first formal meeting, the group discussed ways to avoid another breakdown in the dialogue, the terms of future meetings, and arrangements for a truce. Ó Brádaigh felt a heavy responsibility. The Army Council had developed terms for a bilateral truce, which the team presented to Allan and Oatley. They included: "Freedom of movement for all members of the Republican Movement," the right for some Republicans to "carry concealed short arms" for self defense, agreement on an effective liaison system between British and Republican forces, the withdrawal of British troops to their barracks when the truce was implemented, and confirmation that the meetings would continue "towards securing a permanent ceasefire." As the dialogue continued, so did the IRA campaign. Between January 17th and the end of the month, the IRA killed a British soldier in West Belfast, an RUC man in Tyrone, and a Catholic civilian (in an accidental explosion) in Armagh. On January 27th, 1975, the IRA also set off bombs in London and Manchester. They also lost three volunteers: Kevin Coen was shot dead by the British Army in Fermanagh and John Stone and John Kelly were killed in a premature explosion in Belfast.

The Army Council, upset by the loss of the three volunteers and concerned that the British were "evading agreeing to practical arrangements," met on January 23rd and gave their representatives instructions on three issues. First, they were to demand freedom of movement for their personnel. In the words of the Army Council, the truce would "rise or fall" on this issue. Second, the RUC would not be allowed back into the Nationalist areas from which they had been excluded; Republicans, with help from the clergy, if necessary, would police those areas. Finally, some Loyalists and some members of the Official IRA had permits to carry personal weapons. The IRA would become more public during a truce, making sectarian assassination that much more possible. Therefore, the team was instructed to push for weapons permits. The British response was positive, and over a two-week period a twelve-point agreement was worked out. As recorded by Ó Brádaigh, the British agreed to the following (this may be compared with what the Republicans agreed to; see page 230):

1. In a situation of genuine and sustained cessation of violence no existing organisations would be proscribed. There would be no restrictions on freedom of movement and there is no question of those wishing to return home to live in peace being harassed by the Security Forces.
2. In a situation of genuine and sustained cessation of violence and an agreed cease-fire in operation no action by the Security Forces would be authorised which could be interpreted as harassment of the civilian population.
3. The action of the Security Forces is related to the level of any violent and hostile activity which may occur. If there is no such activity there will be no operations other than against law-breakers.
4. The only arrests will be arrests of people breaking the law. Interim Custody Orders [Internment Orders] will not be signed if there is no violence.
5. Following a genuine and sustained cessation of violence, screening, photographing and identity checks will be ended.
6. The law provides for permits to be granted for people to carry arms for self-defence. The issue of firearms permits will take account of the risk to individuals. The need to protect individuals who may be at risk of assassination is recognised. *(Additional message confirmed)*.
7. There is no question of the Security Forces undertaking provocative displays of force.
8. The preservation of the peace is in everyone's interest. Policing and community peace-keeping if they are to be effective must be achieved by co-operation area by area over a period of time.
9. In a sustained ceasefire misunderstandings must be avoided between the Security Forces and others to ensure that it did not break down. This will require practical and effective arrangements.
10. If there is a genuine and sustained cessation of violence and hostilities the Army would gradually be reduced to peace-time levels and withdrawn to barracks.
11. Discussion will continue between officials and representatives of Provisional Sinn Féin and will include the aim of securing permanent peace.

12. A genuine and sustained cessation of violence would require the ending of all offensive operations and hostilities such as the following:
    a. A Cessation of the intimidation of the public and of murders, woundings, kneecappings, kangaroo courts and all other assaults on the person.
    b. A cessation of armed robberies and hi-jackings.
    c. A cessation of the illegal purchase, manufacture and holding of arms, ammunitions and explosives.
    d. Once violence has come to a complete end, the rate of release will be speeded up with a view to releasing all detainees.

Three issues were never resolved. The Republican representatives always rejected the term "violence" and referred to "hostilities." The second issue concerned point 6 and the weapons permits, which were not issued immediately. The British side later reported that they had received a "personal assurance" from Frank Cooper that "we shall find a way round that difficulty." Thus, Ó Brádaigh added: "Additional message confirmed." The third issue concerned point 12. The Republicans said that they "noted" subpoints a through d, but they did not agree to them (and they do not appear among the Republicans' terms). The British accepted that there was disagreement on the point but it was not a deal-breaker. Ó Brádaigh was cautious but felt there was a possibility of progress. Both sides agreed to go forward with a truce, although nothing was signed. Soon after the truce went into effect Merlyn Rees stated, honestly, "There have been no signed documents." Neither side disclosed that they had kept a record of a twelve-point truce agreement that, in spite of its differences, was referred to in subsequent meetings.

On February 8th, the two sides met to finalize the "practical and effective arrangements" (point 9) that would sustain the truce and to work on the public statements that the IRA and Rees would make announcing the agreement. In the early 1970s, the British routinely raided homes, harassed people at roadblocks, and arrested Republicans. If such activity continued, the truce would fail, quickly. They agreed to establish "truce incident centres" in Nationalist areas of North and West Belfast, Armagh, Derry, Dungannon, Enniskillen, and Newry. They were staffed by Republicans who monitored the situation in the area, taking reports from local people. In North and West Belfast, the centers were located in Sinn Féin offices. In Dungannon, the incident center was located in a private home and was staffed by IRA personnel on the run but with passes that kept them from being arrested. At each site the British installed a direct phone

INSTRUCTIONS   20. 1. '75.

TERMS   FOR   BI-LATERAL   TRUCE

1.   Freedom of movement for all members of the Republican
     Movement.

2.   A Cessation of all harassment of the civilian population.

3.   A Cessation of all raids on lands, homes and other buildings.

4.   A Cessation of arrests of members of the Republican Movement.

5.   An end to screening, photographing and identity checks.

6.   Members of the Republican Movement reserve the right to
     carry concealed short arms solely for the purpose of self-defence.

7.   No provocative displays of force by either side.

8.   No reintroduction of R.U.C. and U.D.R. into designated areas.

9.   Agreement of effective liaison system between British and
     Republican Forces.

10. A progressive withdrawal of troops to barracks to begin with
     the implementation of the bi-lateral truce.

11. Confirmation that discussions between representatives of the
     Republican movement and H.M.G. will continue towards
     securing a permanent ceasefire.

12. In the event of any of these terms being violated, the
     Republican Movement reserve the right of freedom of action.

ENDS

Scanned copy of Provisional Irish Republican terms of the truce agreement,
January 20, 1975. Ruairí Ó Brádaigh Truce Notes.

line connecting the Northern Ireland Office in Belfast and the incident center—if the phone rang on either end it signaled that there was a problem. The goal was to have complaints worked out at the local level. If this was not possible, Jimmy Drumm and Proinsias Mac Airt, as liaisons between the incident center and the Northern Ireland Office, would either work out the problem over the telephone or in person with Northern Ireland Office officials.

On February 9th, the IRA announced that "[i]n the light of discussions which have taken place between representatives of the Republican Movement and British Officials on effective arrangements to ensure that there is no breakdown of a new Truce," operations would be suspended on February 10th. Rees, who never acknowledged that his staff members were meeting with the IRA, then put out a statement indicating that meetings with members of Provisional Sinn Féin had produced the ceasefire and announcing that truce incident centers would be opened "to allow for rapid communication about potential incidents." On the 10th, there was no IRA activity. The incident centers opened on the 11th. In practical terms, for the first time Sinn Féin was active on the ground in the north. For several young Republicans, including Tom Hartley and Danny Morrison in Belfast and Martin McGuinness in Derry, working the centers was their first real experience in community politics. The Sinn Féin leadership hoped that the incident centers and Sinn Féin advice centers would establish links in the communities and translate into electoral support if and when the party contested northern elections.

The Army Council knew they were taking a gamble by entering the truce. They were negotiating with people who publicly denied that the negotiations even existed, and British policy seemed to be following divergent paths. While Oatley was talking about a British withdrawal the Gardiner Report, which was released January 30th, suggested they were planning to stay. The report recommended the building of a new prison at the Long Kesh site and ending "special category status" (political status, won by the McKee-led hunger strike of 1972). New prisoners would be treated as ordinary criminals and housed in the new prison. Prison construction began almost immediately. At a formal meeting, Ó Brádaigh, with his sense of history, warned the British that they were heading into a crisis in the prisons and on the outside. He recounted at length the history of IRA prisoners who refused to be criminalized, including the 1940s strip strike in Port Laoise Prison that had lasted seven years.

The Army Council was aware that Rees's constitutional convention could lead to two very different outcomes. If moderate Unionists and the

SDLP did well in the elections, the convention might lead to an effective power-sharing assembly. This could undercut support for the paramilitaries, making it harder for the IRA to return to war. If Rees could get the Republicans and the Loyalists to participate in the convention, it would be that much more likely to succeed. But if the convention failed, it might strengthen the Republican argument that a united and free Ireland was the only solution. At the least, the British would probably reassess their options, including withdrawal. The IRA, which would be strengthened by the rest period and the return of internees to its ranks, would be better able to push the British in that direction. Rees evidently assessed the situation in the same way. In April 1975, he met with Garret Fitzgerald, the Irish foreign minister, in Dublin. He indicated that he was not optimistic about the convention and "feared that if it failed, pressure in Britain for a withdrawal from Ireland might mount."

The Republicans were also aware that the truce had implications for parties that were beyond British control. The Dublin government would remain troublesome. The Army Council itself was disrupted in January when Kevin Mallon and J. B. O'Hagan were arrested; it is not known who replaced them on the council. After Mallon's arrest, Ó Brádaigh accused the Dublin government of trying to "sabotage the peace initiative" because peace with justice "would lead to an entirely new political situation in Ireland, new alignments and a new type of politics." There was also trouble in Port Laoise Prison. In February, hunger-striking prisoners had achieved better conditions, but after forty-five days, one of them, Pat Ward, had suffered permanent physical damage. In March, IRA prisoner Tom Smith was shot dead in disputed circumstances. Police officers in riot gear attacked those attending his funeral. Finally, Loyalist paramilitaries, suspicious that the British and the IRA had cut a deal, stepped up their campaign. On February 10th, they shot dead three Nationalist/Catholic civilians, one in Belfast and two in Tyrone. On the 19th, another Nationalist/Catholic civilian was shot dead in North Armagh. Still, the Army Council agreed to the Truce.

Ó Brádaigh will not discuss council membership, but he does state that all decisions on the truce were unanimous, with no dissent. There was too much at stake for the movement to have it any other way. Ó Brádaigh felt that it was "a moment in history . . . it was a feeling of responsibility that people had to make the very most of this. If there was a way out of this centuries old conflict. [If] there was a way of getting British withdrawal in whatever manner." In the view of the leadership, the war had not been won or lost, it had moved to another front. It was possible that this was the beginning of the end of the conflict with the British. It was their responsibility to pursue it.

In his pursuit of peace, Ó Brádaigh entered another extremely busy period in his life. In March, in an interview with John Donlon of the *Longford Leader*, he commented that he saw little of Roscommon "except the house, the garage, and church." To keep up with the family and to pick up his messages, he phoned Patsy every day. As he pointed out to Donlon, "It has taken a lot of courage on her part to put up with this. It's not every woman who would do so."

The truce was on, the incident centers were operating, and Ó Brádaigh and McKee and the third representative met regularly with their British counterparts. From the beginning, the Republicans wanted evidence of progress, while the British moved slowly. The negotiations were complicated by continued Loyalist violence and a feud that erupted among Republicans. Seámus Costello was a vigorous opponent of the Official IRA cease-fire, and the Officials expelled him. In December 1974, he formed the Irish Republican Socialist Party (IRSP) and the Peoples Liberation Army, later renamed the Irish National Liberation Army (INLA). It attracted other disgruntled members of the Official IRA. On February 20th, the Officials shot dead an IRSP member, which provoked INLA retaliation and more bloodshed. The most prominent victim was Billy McMillan, the long-term Official IRA commanding officer in Belfast. On February 26th, there was also an incident in London involving the Provisionals. Police officers spotted a man acting suspiciously and pursued him. An off-duty officer, Stephen Tibble, joined the pursuit, confronted the individual, and was shot dead. Investigation of the area uncovered an IRA bomb factory. Ó Brádaigh's notes on the background for the meeting immediately after this stated "Truce in acute danger." The British representatives were outraged at the shooting of an unarmed man. Yet the meetings continued. Through February and March there were tough negotiations and very slow progress. On February 19th, the British indicated that the Price sisters were scheduled for repatriation. On the 28th, the British agreed to issue passes to about two dozen members of Sinn Féin that would keep them from being searched by the British Army. It was part of a "parallel scheme" that resulted in weapons permits, which were never used.

In March, the British focused on the convention, claiming it was a "sign that H.M.G. no longer wants to dictate events in Ireland," that it wanted to turn control over to the Irish. The convention was an opportunity for Sinn Féin to participate in events, even to use the convention to "advocate an all-Ireland convention." In this way, the British argued, the convention itself might "produce ideas which would lead to agreement." The Republicans replied that that was unacceptable—any subject matter that might be raised in the convention was confined to six of the thirty-two counties of Ireland and the British Parliament would have the last word. The British representatives were obviously disappointed. They also expressed their concern about a lack of progress in the negotiations. On March 10th, the Army Council sent a formal communiqué that complained that "[a]fter four weeks of genuine and sustained suspension of hostilities by Óglaigh na hÉireann the response by the British Government is considered unsatisfactory by the Army Council." They demanded the initiation of talks on a realistic basis and noted violations of the truce agreement: the RUC was harassing people, and three Republicans in Armagh had been arrested. At formal meetings on March 13th and 16th, the British were conciliatory and begged for patience: "The patience in negotiation and the discipline of R.M. [Republican Movement] are acknowledged by H.M.G.," Ó Brádaigh recorded. The British government could not "interfere in the processes of law once law-breakers are arrested," but its representatives noted that 160 internees out of 570 had been released since Christmas and promised positive news on prisoner issues the next week. On March 18th, the Price sisters were transferred to Armagh Women's Prison.

While the British tried to entice Sinn Féin into contesting the upcoming election to select representatives who would attend the constitutional convention, the press speculated that the party might actually participate in the body if it was elected. It would not be a legislative assembly, and participation would not be a breach of abstentionism, the press alleged. However, when Prime Minister Harold Wilson announced that the convention election would be held on May 1st, Sinn Féin called for a "32-county convention with a provincial parliament for Ulster" and announced a campaign to boycott the election. Ó Brádaigh toured the north and met with the eleven Comhairlí Ceantair (district councils) of Sinn Féin there. He was in Derry at Easter, March 30th, and unveiled a memorial to twenty-nine Provisional IRA members who had died in the city. To a crowd of about 3,000 people, including Martin McGuinness, he described the convention as a "sectarian body" that could not produce peace with justice. He described the truce as "uneasy" and said it had been condemned by "the Dublin Government, the U.U.U.C., Brian Faulkner, the RUC and SDLP" because "they fear the ideal of a new Ireland and a new coming together of Catholic and Protestant." At the Easter Commemoration at Milltown Cemetery in Belfast, Séamus Twomey warned that until the British met the movement's three demands, there would be no permanent cease-fire. These speeches were combined with military action. On April 2nd, the date of the next formal meeting, the Provisional IRA bombed a travel agency in Belfast. An IRA statement explained it was the first Provisional IRA violation of the truce and that it was in response to repeated violations by the security forces.

The April 2nd formal meeting was difficult. In essence, according to Ó Brádaigh's notes, the British tried to placate the Republicans. They complained that "the bombing and statement . . . were not helpful" but noted that the "acceptability of R.M. as a respectable movement has greatly increased" and would be lost if the IRA returned to war. The preferred alternative was "to accept a rate of progress which is slow but will increase as it goes along." Twomey's suggestion of a declaration of intent was "*totally and absolutely*" out of the question (emphasis in original). A declaration, they argued, would result in such chaos that it would prevent them from withdrawing. Echoing Oatley's statement in January to Billy McKee, they asked for help in creating "*circumstances out of which the structures of disengagement can naturally grow*" (emphasis in original). They offered evidence that disengagement was under way, albeit slowly. Harland & Wolff, the huge shipbuilding concern in Belfast, had been nationalized, but it had been retained separately from other British nationalized industries. The Republican representatives were unimpressed and charged that there had been additional violations of the truce agreement. At one point, Ó Brádaigh interjected, "Then you have deceived us." But again, there was some progress. On April 8th, Hugh Feeney and Gerry Kelly were secretly transferred from English prisons to Long Kesh. And the election to the convention lay ahead. Strategically, it made sense for each side to continue the meetings.

The convention election went as the Republicans expected. Opponents of power-sharing, organized as the United Ulster Unionist Council, won forty-seven of seventy-eight seats. Even in combination, the moderates in the SDLP, Faulkner's Official Unionists, and the Alliance Party were outnumbered. *An Phoblacht* declared the result a victory for Sinn Féin; of an electorate of 1 million people, 356,000 voted for the United Ulster Unionist Council (and against the British plan), 302,000 voted for the moderates (for the plan), and 368,000 had boycotted. By their calculation, 70 percent (368,000 plus 356,000) of the electorate opposed the convention. *An Phoblacht* overestimated the impact of the boycott, but it did cost the SDLP two seats, one in South Armagh and one in South

Press conference in Belfast, April 1975. From left: Marie Moore, Ruairí Ó Brádaigh, Máire Drumm, and unidentified. The posters in the background call for a boycott of the convention election. Victor Patterson/Linenhall Library.

Derry. All political observers agreed that the results were not promising. Still, the convention went ahead. The elected representatives worked on procedural issues until July, when they recessed for the summer.

The day the constitutional convention opened, May 8th, the RUC arrested Shane O'Doherty, the London mail-bomber. O'Doherty was wanted in the North and in Britain. For years the RUC had searched his parents' trash for signs that he had returned to Derry. He had assumed that as long as the truce held, it was safe for him to return home. Local units had been instructed to react to breaches of the truce. The Derry IRA retaliated on May 10th. Paul Gray, a 20-year old RUC constable, was shot dead as he patrolled the city's walls. At the next formal meeting, May 14th, the British representatives stated it "was a totally disproportionate action to the arrest of Shane Doherty." The shooting "put a stop to progress," and the two sides did not meet again until June 4th, by which time there were serious problems.

The talks with the British were on hiatus, but Ó Brádaigh was no less busy—he spent three straight weeks in the north at one point in this period. In June there was a referendum in Great Britain and Northern Ireland on UK membership in the EEC. It was evident that the referendum would be endorsed by the rest of the United Kingdom but not necessarily in Northern Ireland. For years, Sinn Féin had opposed Irish membership in the organization, viewing it as a threat to Irish culture and as a new form of imperialism. The SDLP supported continued membership. The Unionists were split. Ian Paisley and the Democratic Unionist Party advocated a "No" vote, the moderate Ulster Unionist Party was neutral, and William Craig's Vanguard Party supported staying in the EEC. Ó Brádaigh believed that a successful "No" vote would send the message that the kingdom was not so united, but his canvassing was laden with difficulty. Sinn Féin had been boycotting elections since 1970; now he had to convince people to vote. There was also the curious situation of supporting the same vote as Paisley. His answer was that Paisley rejected the EEC because it threatened traditional British imperialism, while Ó Brádaigh and Sinn Féin rejected it because they opposed both the old imperialism of Britain and the new imperialism of the EEC. The exercise was frustrating and unsuccessful.

Behind the scenes, Ó Brádaigh was involved in meetings with Loyalists. In an attempt to curtail the continuing assassination of Nationalist civilians, the Republicans entered into direct conversation with leading members of the Ulster Defence Association, which was associated with the paramilitary Ulster Freedom Fighters. The meetings lasted until at least late August. They were unsuccessful. The Ulster Defence Association leaders denied that they were involved and claimed the assassinations were the work of former B Specials who were beyond their control. The Republicans doubted this claim. For their part, the Loyalists were interested in what the British had been saying to the Republicans. In general, Ó Brádaigh found them very nervous at the meetings.

As he toured, Ó Brádaigh watched the situation deteriorate first-hand. He was in Belfast on April 28th, the day Billy McMillan was assassinated. In May, Belfast Nationalists clashed with the British Army and, briefly, the incident centers were closed. Between May 18th and June 3rd, Loyalists killed six Catholics and the Irish National Liberation Army killed an RUC member in Derry. In early June, an IRA bomb accidentally killed a Protestant woman in Fermanagh and in South Armagh an IRA ambush killed three people, two Protestant civilians and a part-time member of the Ulster Defence Regiment. And still the British sent signals through the intermediary that they wanted to continue meeting and that they were moving toward withdrawal. On May 20th, the intermediary reported to Ó Brádaigh that he had received a phone call from his British contact, who was "very excited" and told him to "tell the Leadership everyone is agreed; the inevitable position of the British is withdrawal."

But a June 4th meeting complicated the situation. The British stated that unless the Republicans guaranteed that the killings in South Armagh were not the work of the IRA, they would postpone the release of internees. They also expressed a concern that "British Intelligence reports still indicate that R.M. is re-grouping and training." But they also presented a draft of an "economic document" that suggested that the Northern Irish economy would be disentangled from the British economy, presumably as a precursor to a withdrawal. After the meeting, the team reported to the Army Council, which drafted another communiqué that was sent the next day. They accused the British of using internees as hostages and rejected the economic document, stating it was "an academic red herring and puts the cart before the horse, i.e. economic disengagement before military and political withdrawal." They wanted a 32-county Irish government to decide its own economic priorities. The British, in reply, denied linking the internees to the killings, but a breach was looming. At subsequent meetings, the Republicans pushed for the release of more internees, the transfer of prisoners from England—notably Frank Stagg, and for something to be done about the Loyalists. They were especially concerned about the "murder triangle," a small area in Tyrone and Armagh bounded by the towns of Portadown, Pomeroy, and Aughnacloy, where more than forty Catholic civilians were killed in 1975. They were also concerned that the RUC and the Ulster Defence Regiment were being increased in size; the Ulster Defence Regiment situation was especially troubling because of suspicions that its soldiers were colluding with Loyalist paramilitaries. The British did send troops and the Royal Military Police to patrol in Tyrone, but no prisoners were transferred to Ireland, few internees were released, and Loyalist killings continued.

In mid-June, Merlyn Rees stated in the House of Commons that the truce was not complete, genuine, or sustained. It was a breaking point. The Army Council, through the intermediary, sent a third communiqué, dated June 19th, stating this "shows gross insincerity and is tantamount to a repudiation of the Truce agreement." The Council canceled future meetings. At the Wolfe Tone Commemoration three days later, Ó Brádaigh remembers, he no longer defended the truce in conversation with people. He even indicated that it could end and would end if it did not soon show concrete results. In the first week of July, the IRA held an operational meeting in South Armagh. All of the active service units were represented. The participants were told that the truce was as good as over, that it appeared to be leading nowhere, and that preparations should be made to ease gradually into a resumption of the campaign.

While the truce fell apart in earnest, the British sent what can only be described as mixed signals. Through the intermediary, "A. and B." (James Allan and another person) sought additional meetings and continued to talk about withdrawal. But other than promises about prisoner repatriation and internee releases, there was no progress. On the ground, the security forces became provocative. The weekend of June 27–29, there was a major confrontation between British troops and Nationalists in Derry. In mid-July, the British Army shot dead a 16-year-old Belfast Nationalist, Charles Irvine, in disputed circumstances. In Derry, the IRA bombed three Crown buildings in retaliation for army harassment. In South Armagh, an IRA bomb killed four British soldiers. In Parliament, the Labour government renewed the Prevention of Terrorism Act and directed passage of the Criminal Jurisdiction Act (1975), which made cross-border prosecution of the IRA easier. Complicating the situation was the arrest of Dáithí O'Connell. In describing the arrest, Ó Brádaigh said that "the [Dublin] Government have deliberately aimed a deadly blow at the six-month-old truce and, more importantly, at the prospects for a permanent peace in this country." It was a significant blow on a number of levels. Although O'Connell had never met with the British representatives, he had been consulted regularly and was familiar with the ongoing discussions. In late July, he was convicted on the charge of membership in the IRA and received a twelve-month sentence; among those testifying against him was Chief Superintendent Fleming of the Special Branch.

The IRA also lost control of some of its volunteers. Some, who were frustrated on the sidelines, cooperated with or left for the Irish National Liberation Army. Others, viewing themselves as Nationalist defenders, responded to the ongoing Loyalist campaign by targeting Protestants, and a tit-for-tat situation developed. There were individual assassinations, and in Belfast, starting in April, Loyalists and Provisionals again bombed crowded pubs. The most prominent Loyalist attack came in July. It involved the Miami Showband, a popular musical group based in the south. After they had played at an engagement in the north, they were stopped at what seemed to be an Ulster Defence Regiment roadblock. It was, in fact, a joint Ulster Defence Regiment–Ulster Volunteer Force team. As the band members were being questioned, UVF members tried to plant a bomb in the van; it would look like the band was killed transporting explosives. The bomb went off prematurely, killing two UVF men. The others opened fire, killing three band members. The attack confirmed Loyalist–Ulster Defence Regiment collusion.

Sinn Féin, dissatisfied with the British response to the situation, had begun a campaign to force comments from those who had been pressing for peace when the IRA was active but were silent on issues such as collusion and sectarian assassination after the truce started—presumably because they feared Republican political gains. One poster was worded "80 Sectarian Assassinations since February 10—but not a word from the peace campaigners." Some IRA members took direct action. A few weeks after the attack on the Miami Showband, an IRA unit in Belfast carried out a bomb and gun attack on the Bayardo Bar, killing five Protestant civilians and a UVF man.

By this point, Merlyn Rees had lost his credibility with almost everyone. Frank King, general officer commanding of British Forces in Northern Ireland, had publicly questioned the wisdom of the cease-fire and the release of internees. In the House of Commons, Conservatives asked if Rees was bargaining with terrorists and Northern Irish MPs wondered if Séamus Twomey, who had been spotted but not arrested, had been granted immunity from arrest. Rees denied making bargains and granting immunity, but British and Northern Irish politicians had their doubts. So did the Irish government. When Dáithí O'Connell was arrested, the police confiscated truce documents, including the twelve-point truce agreement. Minister for Foreign Affairs Garret FitzGerald sought a meeting with Merlyn Rees, but Rees refused. FitzGerald, who complains in his autobiography of a "wall of silence" around Rees, met instead with James Callaghan, the former home secretary and future prime minister. He expressed his concern that the IRA had been led to believe that the British would declare their intention to withdraw "if and when the Convention talks broke down." In August, an article by Robert Fisk in the *New Statesman* claimed that "[t]he Dublin government has now reached the stage of simply refusing to believe some of Mr Rees's statements."

Against this backdrop of suspicion and violence from all quarters, the meetings between the IRA and the British were renewed on July 22nd and continued until mid-September. What seemed to be a rapprochement began on July 16th with a conciliatory message from the British announcing that all internees would be released by the end of the year (which Rees announced publicly on July 24th) and the sentence "We feel that the efforts by our representatives over the past seven months to achieve a permanent peace in Northern Ireland should be regarded as evidence of our complete sincerity." In these meetings, the Republicans pushed for a British declaration of intent and movement on the issue of prisoners. In return, they were given apologies for specific events, including the shooting by British troops of Charles Irvine; more promises; and excuses for why a declaration of intent would not be forthcoming: they had to give the convention "a chance publicly"; "H.M.G. is waiting for consensus of opinion in Britain"; and concern about "[t]he danger of a Congo-type situation." At one point the Republicans asked some pointed questions: "Why continue to fight in Ireland when withdrawal is on? Is the loss of life justified?" The British replied that "there was no British de Gaulle on the horizon." Much of the discussion involved charges and countercharges. At a meeting in August, the Republicans charged that the British Army had "declared open war on the people." The British countered that their Army was there "to separate the communities." Billy McKee replied that there was television footage of British troops "firing wildly from the hip" and drinking looted beer. The British countered that six of the 262 released internees had been subsequently charged; one of them had been charged in connection with the Bayardo Bar attack. The IRA had entered the situation in a stepwise fashion, with the Christmas cease-fire, the extension of the cease-fire, and then the truce agreement. They removed themselves in a similar fashion. They began with complaints about truce breaches that escalated into retaliation. Then units in England—acting on their own in response to the general situation and an untimely statement by Rees—went into action. In a ten-day period, beginning August 27th, five bombs went off in London, one of which killed a bomb-disposal expert.

Early in September, the previously unheard-of Republican Action Force attacked an Orange Hall and shot dead four Protestant civilians in South Armagh; an IRA unit bombed the London Hilton, killing two people; and the British Army shot dead a 17-year-old Nationalist, Leo Norney, in West Belfast. The violence was complemented by political discord. Over the summer, John Hume and Austin Currie of the SDLP and William Craig had worked out a "voluntary coalition" formula that would allow an emergency government for Northern Ireland. The convention ended its summer recess and, influenced by the killings in South Armagh, United Ulster Unionist Council hard-liners rejected the plan; they insisted on "majority rule." This meant no power-sharing and doomed the convention. Ó Brádaigh's notes for a formal meeting on September 16th record the acknowledgement of the British representatives: "the forecast made by both sides (R.M. and H.M.G.) has proved correct; there is no result." The Republicans pushed for the declaration of intent, stating that "[t]he absence of it is prolonging the agony." The British indicated that they would let the convention run its course, devise a way to govern Northern Ireland "in the short term"—presumably a return to direct rule from London—and then "the transitional period [for withdrawal] will begin." It sounded good, but Ó Brádaigh, McKee, and their compatriot wanted something concrete. Frank Stagg, they believed, was being held hostage by the British and they asked that he be transferred to an Irish prison. The British replied that because of recent bombings in England, public opinion would not allow it. The Republicans believed that the British were refusing to concede anything under pressure. Ó Brádaigh's notes record that "R.M. said that it was not responsible for the bombings and the meeting broke off at this point."

On September 20th, Rees publicly denied that there was or ever had been a bilateral truce. Two days later, the truce was over. The Provisionals set off eighteen bombs in Northern Ireland. Another bomb went off at the Portman Hotel in London. According to Ó Brádaigh, the movement's leadership viewed the British as "clever, scheming politicians who will go to any length to secure their own position. And so on, and snare people." The leadership had felt "duty bound to respond to the offer that was made and to explore it for what it was worth and when it became blatantly obvious that this situation wasn't going anywhere, it was a case of back to war." There was no announcement that the truce was ended, however. Sinn Féin called a press conference on September 25th. Ó Brádaigh, John Joe McGirl, Joe O'Neill, Seán Keenan, Walter Lynch, Marie Moore, and Brendan Magill announced a "Moment of Truth" campaign during which Sinn Féin would distribute 250,000 leaflets. The leaflets described the constitutional convention as "doomed to failure," reiterated the "inevitability of a British withdrawal from Ireland," and demanded the declaration of intent. It called for an All-Ireland Parliament, to be sited at Athlone, and appealed to Unionists: "To the Unionist-minded people we say that an Ulster Parliament for the nine counties will guarantee the rights of all." When questioned, Ó Brádaigh repeated that there was a truce agreement, but when pressed he refused to confirm that it was either a written or oral agreement. Because the talks had been held in confidence, he would not offer any details. Merlyn Rees again denied that there was an agreement. Incredibly, the Republicans were still in contact with the British.

Throughout this period Ó Brádaigh made sure he kept in touch with the rank-and-file Sinn Féin membership, especially in the north. He attended every meeting of the Comhairle Uladh of Sinn Féin, which was held in Coalisland. When he could, he included his older children in his travels. On one trip through Fermanagh, Tyrone, and Derry on the way to open a Sinn Féin bookshop in Buncrana, County Donegal, Ruairí Óg, who was 13, was asleep in the backseat. He remembers waking up at a Ulster Defence Regiment roadblock. Soldiers with flashlights had their weapons trained on the car. Ó Brádaigh wanted to keep the rank and file informed of developments, and he also wanted them to turn out at the upcoming Ard Fheis in late October. Well over 600 delegates attended.

At the Ard Fheis, the leadership remained optimistic. The Army statement reiterated that "[t]he main demand of Óglaigh na hÉireann is for a British declaration of intent to withdraw from Ireland and to give to the Irish people the right to control their own destinies." It also claimed, "Today, Óglaigh na hÉireann are in a very strong position with the ability to win through to final victory—let it be recorded that this is the last phase in Ireland's long fight for freedom." In his presidential address, Ó Brádaigh described the meetings with the British: "In short, what we have been saying to the British is this: if you intend to leave Ireland then we will do everything possible to smooth your path and make it easy for you; but if, on the other hand, you intend to remain in Ireland and to re-structure British rule here, putting a more acceptable and perhaps more human face on it, then if this is your intention make no mistake about it—we will contest every inch of the ground with you. And we shall win, because we regard British disengagement from Ireland now as inevitable." But he also had to address problems in the IRA. A rogue unit had kidnapped Tiede Herrema, the Dutch manager of a factory in Limerick. They hoped to trade Herrema for the release of three IRA prisoners in Portlaoise, including Kevin Mallon. The Irish police cornered the group, still holding Herrema, and a siege that carried through the Ard Fheis followed. The group's activities were an embarrassment. In his address, Ó Brádaigh called for Herrema's release, saying, "Sinn Féin believes that the abduction serves no useful purpose and we call on those responsible to release him." The group was arrested and Herrema freed, but another problem developed.

Since the death of Charlie Hughes in 1970, tension had remained between some Belfast Provisionals and the Official IRA. The Official IRA–Irish National Liberation Army split and feud earlier in the year heightened the tension. Just after the Ard Fheis, another Provisional IRA–Official IRA feud broke out. Between October 29 and November 12, eleven people were killed—one Provisional, seven Officials, and three civilians. Among the dead were Seámus McCusker, who directed the Provisionals' incident center in North Belfast, and 6-year-old Eileen Kelly, who was shot dead by Provisionals who were firing at her father. Ó Brádaigh went to Belfast for McCusker's funeral and stayed on for several days to help sort out a truce with the Officials. He worked with Sinn Féin's Belfast headquarters in the Lower Falls to organize a public response to the situation and gave a press conference in Andersonstown, West Belfast, that was covered by the television press. He described the situation as a "war for the streets." A resolution was finally reached through the intervention of several parties, including Belfast priests Des Wilson and Alex Reid.

Throughout this period, the IRA and the British had maintained a dialogue. The day the Moment of Truth campaign was launched, Ó Brádaigh received a message from a subintermediary. The message complained about "[t]he P.I.R.A. planned and deliberate display of violence, coupled with a public slanging match," but also said that "[t]he Secretary of State's policy . . . has not changed." In delivering the message, the subintermediary asked him, "Should you not think carefully?" The Army Council response, on October 2nd, was pointed. It noted violence by "Crown Forces" prior to the 22nd, including the deaths of Leo Norney and 10-year-old Stephen Geddis, who had been killed by a plastic bullet. It continued, "Mr. Rees' blatant denial of the factual position and his continued assertions that there is merely a unilateral ceasefire by the Republican Movement have not helped matters, to say the least. How can the word of H.M.G.'s representatives be taken in private when the public spokesmen of the British Government deny it?" They were willing to meet again, but only after "full implementation" of the truce agreement and an agreed understanding that "[t]he purpose of the meetings [is] to be the devising of structures of British disengagement from Ireland." In message exchanges that continued through October and into November, the British sent signals that they were considering withdrawal, while Rees took a harder line in public. A message from the British dated October 22nd asked, "In the event of H.M.G. giving the Declaration of Intent—what accommodation could be reached with the Loyalists by the Republican Movement?" and another on November 11th hinted at a "committee system of government in the Six Counties" with "*a Bill of Rights for Roman Catholics*" (emphasis in original). Rees announced that the incident centers would be closed and that persons convicted of "terrorist crimes" after March 1, 1976, would not receive special category status. The Derry IRA closed their incident center and blew up the building. On December 5th, Rees announced the release of the final group of internees.

In his memoir, Rees claims that the talks with "Provisional Sinn Féin" (the story used to cover meetings with the IRA) had concluded by the end of 1975. Ó Brádaigh's notes tell a different tale. In early January 1976, the British requested a formal meeting to discuss the Army Council's message of October 2nd, which said there would be no meetings unless they were to devise "structures of British disengagement from Ireland." The meeting was put on hold by the most blatantly sectarian attack by the IRA during the course of the conflict. On January 4th, the Ulster Volunteer Force attacked two Catholic homes in South Armagh and shot dead six civilians. The next day, paramilitaries stopped a group of workers traveling in a minibus at Kingsmills in South Armagh. Those on board were asked their religion; there were ten Protestants and one Catholic. The Catholic was told to run off. The Protestants were lined up and shot; only one man, who was shot eighteen times, survived. The action was claimed on behalf of the Republican Action Force, but the attack is attributed to the Provisional IRA.

Merlyn Rees and Frank Cooper flew to London to discuss the situation with British Army and government officials; the British sent additional troops to South Armagh. There was widespread condemnation coupled with concern that the tit-for-tat killings would continue and in greater number. Ó Brádaigh publicly asked the Protestant ministers who had attended the Feakle meeting to intervene "to halt the escalation of sectarian murders." They turned him down and issued a statement calling on paramilitary organizations to issue orders "forbidding all acts of aggression or retaliation, at least for such a time as will test the willingness of the other side to do the same." The IRA issued a statement that as far as sectarian killings were concerned, "the question of retaliation from whatever source will not arise," and the Ulster Defence Association issued a statement that because of the situation, the "Protestant citizen" had no option but "to protect himself and his family and ultimately his whole area." On the day of the funerals of the Kingsmills victims, the Protestant ministers welcomed these statements, which "could mean that each body, while stating its readiness to act in a retaliatory or protective role, is in fact indicating a willingness to refrain from offensive or aggressive action as far as sectarian assassinations are concerned, provided the other side does the same." These statements, and the obvious threat that the IRA would respond in kind, effectively ended Loyalist assassinations in South Armagh.

Once things had settled down, a formal meeting was scheduled for February 11th. It started poorly when one of the British team thanked the Republicans for requesting the meeting. Ó Brádaigh sharply replied that "it was entirely the contrary." The British representative responded, "Let's not quibble about such matters" and began a discussion of their long-term plans. They indicated that once there was "an acceptable government" in the north, the withdrawal of the British Army would follow. The Republicans, who were there to discuss a British withdrawal, asked if this was an interim step to a complete withdrawal. The British replied that it was "the first step in a phased and orderly withdrawal procedure," but that they could not commit future British governments to anything. Harold Wilson was considering retirement (he was replaced as prime minister by James Callaghan later in 1976), and Merlyn Rees was to be replaced as secretary of state for Northern Ireland (Roy Mason became secretary of state in September 1976). The best they could promise was to "work for a policy which is leading in that direction." It was not enough. Ó Brádaigh's notes summarize the meeting: "Talks consisted of update by both sides. No concrete result."

In *Fighting for Ireland?*, M. L. R. Smith is highly critical of the Republican leadership's role during the truce. He argues that they had an "exaggerated view" of their military prowess and "fell into the trap of believing that they had forced Britain into the ceasefire, and were, consequently, in a position to exact everything they wanted." Instead, he argues, they should have participated in the convention elections, thereby challenging the SDLP, and turned to peaceful political tactics to keep volunteers busy, thus avoiding the descent into sectarian violence and factional feuds. He complains of the leadership's inability to see their objectives in anything other than black-and-white terms—the granting of their demands or a return to war. The truce, he argues, "revealed the effects of PIRA's political vacuity." Smith, who did not have access to Ó Brádaigh's notes, misses the complexity of the process and the dialogue. Beginning in January 1975, the British sent signals that they were considering a withdrawal—whether or not the British representatives were purposely or accidentally sending these signals, they were real. If Rees was trying to use the truce as a means of enticing the Provisionals to participate in the convention election, he was undercut by the messages delivered by his representatives, which acknowledged the failure of the convention and continued through the resumption of the IRA campaign. Finally, and most important, the Republicans who entered the truce were the same people who had rejected constitutional politics only five years earlier in a split that became bloody. Over these five years they had become so important that twice British representatives, in 1972 and from late 1974 to February 1976, had bargained with them. From their perspective, they were on the right path.

In December 1975, Frank Stagg started another hunger strike, seek-

ing repatriation to Ireland. In a sad denouement to the British-IRA meetings, he died the day after the final meeting, after sixty-two days without
food. Stagg had asked to be buried next to Michael Gaughan. Sinn Féin
planned a repeat of the Gaughan funeral with another procession across
Ireland. The coalition government was having none of it. While Ó Brádaigh, Joe Cahill, and other supporters waited at Dublin Airport, the authorities diverted the plane carrying Stagg's coffin to Shannon. His coffin
was seized and at a government-controlled funeral it was buried in the
cemetery at Ballina, but not next to Gaughan. To keep it there, concrete
was poured over the grave and a guard was placed over it. At a protest rally
nearby, Joe Cahill pledged that at some point they would return and move
Stagg next to his "great comrade, Michael Gaughan," and Ruairí Ó Brádaigh presented Stagg's mother with the black beret and the tricolor that
had covered the coffin in England. Eight months later, once the guard was
removed, a group of IRA volunteers quietly entered the Ballina cemetery
at night and disinterred Stagg's coffin. After prayers from a friendly priest,
Stagg was reburied next to Gaughan. The British and Irish governments
were staying their courses. So were the Republicans.

14

A Long War

IN THE SPRING OF 1976, it appeared that the truce had not affected the Republican Movement. The level of IRA activity had returned almost to its 1974 level, and the leadership, with Seámus Twomey as chief of staff and Ruairí Ó Brádaigh as president of Sinn Féin, was unchanged. They remained optimistic. At Easter, the movement celebrated the sixtieth anniversary of the Rising with a rally at the general post office in Dublin. The event was banned, but a crowd of 30,000 turned up to hear Ruairí Ó Brádaigh, Joe Cahill, Máire Drumm, Seán Keenan, and Dáithí O'Connell, who had recently been released from Port Laoise, pledge to free Ireland. The only person missing was Joe Clarke—the 1916 veteran, Ard Chomhairle member for decades, and honorary life vice president of Sinn Féin—who passed away just before the event, at the age of 94. In its Easter statement, the IRA declared, "The Republican Movement is in fact stronger now than ever." In May, an article in *An Phoblacht* that was based on the economic document that the British had given the Republicans the year before stated, "The economic withdrawal of the British from the Six Counties is more apparent now than at any time in the past 55 years of colonial rule."

While the truce was on, Ó Brádaigh had stayed in Ireland. After the truce ended, he again sought to "raise the Irish struggle onto the world stage." His first opportunity came in June 1976, at "Habitat," a United Nations conference on World Habitation in Vancouver, Canada. With the help of the Vancouver unit of the Irish Prisoner of War Committee, Sinn Féin secured an invitation. Ó Brádaigh and Seán Keenan made the most of the trip. The conference focused on issues such as clean water, recycling, and energy conservation and brought together representatives from a number of organizations and perspectives, including the Maryknoll

Missionaries, the World Council of Churches, pro-life and pro-choice groups, and notables such as Mother Teresa and Margaret Mead. The main attraction was the representatives who attended from liberation organizations that were recognized by the UN, including the Palestine Liberation Organization (PLO), the African National Congress (ANC), and the South West Africa People's Organization (SWAPO). They also met Chileans opposed to Pinochet, Filipinos opposed to Marcos, the Sandinistas of Nicaragua, and members of the FMLN in El Salvador, the Pan-African Congress in South Africa, and liberation movements in Zimbabwe.

They set up a stall and over a two-week period distributed literature, held a press conference and a public meeting in Fisherman's Hall, participated in two live call-in radio shows, and appeared on Canadian television. An ANC representative based in London recognized Ó Brádaigh from BBC TV reports and introduced him and Keenan to members of other organizations. They breakfasted with the PLO and Ó Brádaigh found them "exotic"—they ate bits of beef but no pork. He also found that their approach to politics was similar to his own. Their phrase "The revolution may end, but the struggle continues" summed up his politics; he wanted the British out of Ireland, but he also wanted social and economic justice, which required more than "Brits Out." He also connected with the Africans, who were surprised to learn that imperial Europeans used the same stereotype against the Irish—that they were lazy and stupid—that they used against the Africans. They were also receptive to the argument that the Irish struggle, like theirs, was fighting colonialism and imperialism.

The trip was a success, and Ó Brádaigh would return to Canada several times. Back in Dublin, Ó Brádaigh and Richard Behal approached the Ard Chomhairle and sought authorization for more international trips. Ó Brádaigh had learned that African embassies in Western European capitals often employed representatives of various liberation organizations. They wanted to visit the embassies and build on the connections established in Vancouver. The 1976 Ard Fheis authorized additional embassy visits, ratified a Sinn Féin foreign policy, and formally established a Foreign Affairs Bureau under Behal's direction. The foreign policy visualized action in three concentric circles: a) with the other Celtic countries toward a Celtic League on the lines of the Nordic Council or the Arab League; b) with the stateless nationalities of Europe and the working-class movements in Europe toward "a free federation of free peoples" (which was James Connolly's goal); and c) with the formerly colonized nations and the people still struggling against colonialism through the Non-

Aligned Movement, the Group of 77 at the United Nations, and the Liberation Committee of the Organization of African Unity, which was working toward liberation and non-alignment on a global scale. Over the next several years, Ó Brádaigh, Behal, or both visited Brussels, Lisbon, Madrid, Paris, Rome, and other cities and their respective embassies. The Algerians were very helpful, which led them to Algiers and representatives of other North African countries.

Ironically, as Ó Brádaigh was being welcomed internationally, his ability to operate in Ireland was being restricted. In July 1976, Patrick Cannon, an IRA volunteer from Dublin, was killed in a premature explosion in Tyrone. Several leading Sinn Féiners attended Cannon's funeral in Dublin. That day, July 21st, 1976, the IRA carried out the first of several "spectaculars" that would mark the late 1970s. An IRA land mine in Dublin killed Britain's new ambassador to Ireland, Christopher Ewart-Biggs, and one of his assistants, Judith Cooke. Ewart-Biggs had served the British in Algeria and the Middle East and his appointment was viewed as an indication of increased collaboration between Dublin and London. Later, it was discovered that Merlyn Rees had been scheduled to be in the convoy. The Irish government responded quickly. Dáithí O'Connell and Joe O'Neill were arrested at the Cannon funeral. O'Connell was subsequently convicted of membership in the IRA and sent to Port Laoise Prison. Ó Brádaigh and Seán Keenan were on the road to Magherafelt, County Derry, when O'Neill and O'Connell were arrested. Evidently the Irish police were looking for them and alerted the RUC. Just over the border, outside Lisnaskea, they were stopped at a British Army roadblock. Ó Brádaigh remembers the event with some humor. His driver's license identifies him as "P.R.C. Brady." An RUC officer arrived and asked him to explain the initials. He replied, "You're not going to like it," and gave him his full name, "Peter Roger Casement Brady." They were taken into custody, spent the night in separate cells, and spent the next day being interrogated by Lisnaskea RUC officers about the purpose of their visit—which was to attend the funeral of Derek Highstead, formerly Sinn Féin's organizer in Britain. Keenan was released the next day. Under the provisions of the Prevention of Terrorism Act, Ó Brádaigh was moved to Castlereagh Interrogation Centre in Belfast.

Castlereagh was developing a reputation as a place where prisoners were mistreated, and there were allegations, which were later confirmed, that prisoners there were forced to sign confessions. Ó Brádaigh was harassed in Castlereagh, but because of his prominence, he was not brutalized. He was kept alone in a small windowless cell. There was no clock and the light was turned off and on at irregular intervals to disorient him. Teams of "heavy" and "soft" RUC interrogators took turns questioning him about various subjects, including Patsy and the children, his religion, Sinn Féin policy, links between the IRA and Sinn Féin, and the assassination of Ewart-Biggs. During one session, trying to shake his confidence, they shouted obscenities and verbally abused him. Most of their harassment came in the form of taunts. Máire Drumm had phoned Castlereagh several times seeking information on his status, and the officers suggested that there was something more than politics between them. He ignored police officers who were obnoxious and explained Sinn Féin policy to those who were less so. On occasion, they asked about specific statements he had made. In July 1974, a no-warning bomb had killed a woman and injured several others at the Tower of London. Ó Brádaigh was returning from the Trieste conference, and at a press conference in Brussels he stated his opposition to no-warning bombs. Two years later, the RUC wanted to know if that meant he approved of bombs if they had warnings. He replied that he could not remember everything he had said and that he was frequently incorrectly quoted. They asked why he did not correct such reports and suggested that as president of Sinn Féin he would have a cutting service. He replied that he did not have that luxury.

The situation was unpleasant, but he knew he would eventually be released. There were no outstanding charges against him, he had given them nothing that would lead to a criminal charge, and, unlike the situation with John Joe McGirl in 1974, internment had ended. After nine days in custody he was released and presented with an exclusion order, signed by Merlyn Rees. If he returned to Northern Ireland he would be arrested and face five years in prison. He was pleased to be free and was undaunted by the exclusion order. At a press conference, he informed reporters that neither Merlyn Rees nor the British government had the right to exclude him from any part of Ireland.

The Castlereagh interrogation was one of a series of events that made the work of Ó Brádaigh and the Republican Movement more difficult in 1976. Many people, both Nationalist and Unionist, were disappointed that the truce had not led to a permanent peace. In August, IRA volunteer Danny Lennon was behind the wheel of a car being pursued by a British armored vehicle in West Belfast. Shots were fired, killing Lennon and sending the car out of control. It plowed into a young mother, Anne Maguire, who was out for a walk with her children: Andrew, six weeks old and in a stroller; John, 3; Mark, 7, and Joanne, 9. Mark was ahead of the group and the car missed him. Joanne and Andrew Maguire were killed instantly and John Maguire died in the hospital. Anne Maguire suffered multiple injuries, spent several days unconscious, and never completely recovered. She took her own life in 1980. The event sent shock waves throughout war-weary Ireland and generated a widespread, seemingly spontaneous demand for an immediate end to the Troubles. A thousand women gathered at the accident site for a rosary service, and 20,000 people from across Northern Ireland came together for a peace rally in Ormeau Park, South Belfast. The group called Peace People, which was led by Máiréad Corrigan, the Maguire children's aunt; Betty Williams, a local housewife; and Ciarán McKeown, a journalist with the *Irish Press,* developed out of the demand for peace.

The call for peace resonated with thousands of Irish people, but not with Republicans. The Peace People were selective in their condemnation of violence. Four days after the Maguire children were killed, the British Army shot dead 12-year-old Majella O'Hare in South Armagh. A rally against "crown killings" was organized and the Peace People were conspicuous by their absence. A headline in *An Phoblacht* charged "Crown Murders O.K. to Belfast 'Peace Women.'" In October, Máiréad Corrigan and Betty Williams flew to the United States and urged Irish-Americans to withhold support from the IRA. Sinn Féin launched a campaign against them. At the 1976 Ard Fheis, Ó Brádaigh, who privately referred to them as "peace mongers," attacked the Peace People for supporting the RUC and the British Army. They missed a very important point, he believed; a peace without a resolution of the conditions that generated conflict would not, could not, last. As it transpired, they were a fleeting phenomenon, peaking that November when Corrigan and Williams won the Nobel Peace Prize. Instead of putting the prize money back into their organization, they kept it for themselves. This contributed to internal dissension and alienated many of their supporters, and the organization went into decline. Unlike the Peace People, three other developments that fall had much-longer-lasting effects on the Republican Movement: the "criminalization" of IRA prisoners, the formal banning of Sinn Féin from RTÉ, and the assassination of Máire Drumm.

In January 1975, the Gardiner Report had recommended ending special-category status and the "criminalization" of paramilitary prisoners. Ó Brádaigh, McKee and the third Republican had warned the British that IRA prisoners would not allow themselves to be treated as criminals; they were political prisoners. Merlyn Rees subsequently delayed any announcement on the issue, but the British went ahead and built the Maze, a modern prison facility located next to Long Kesh internment camp. Long Kesh had compounds where groups of prisoners could mix; the Maze has several buildings where two wings with cells are connected by a middle corridor, called the H-Blocks. After the truce fell apart, Rees announced that beginning March 1, 1976, persons convicted of "terrorist" offenses would be treated as ordinary criminals. In September, Belfast IRA volunteer Kieran Nugent became the first prisoner to be convicted under the new system. When he was stripped and given a prison uniform he refused to wear it and wrapped his naked body in a blanket—the first blanketman of his generation. A steady trickle of prisoners followed him into the protest, including the women in Armagh Prison. The prisoners rejected criminalization and the movement rejected the term "Maze"; they continued to refer to the facility as Long Kesh, an internment camp in which they had political status. By December, *An Phoblacht* was publishing photographs of shivering women marching in Belfast, wearing only blankets to protest the prisoners' plight. The prison protest would continue for five long years.

The 1976 Ard Fheis was covered by the print media, and an RTÉ film crew videotaped a portion of the proceedings. Up to this point, the media ban on Sinn Féin was an informal one, and occasionally something like the videotape slipped through. When the videotape was aired, Conor Cruise O'Brien, the minister for posts and telegraphs, used it as an excuse to formally ban Sinn Féin completely from Irish radio and television. He referred to the organization as a "public relations agency for a murder gang." The ban would be in place for the next eighteen years.

The other significant event that fall was Máire Drumm's assassination. Drumm was released from another stint in prison shortly before the Ard Fheis. Exhausted and in poor health, she resigned as vice president of Sinn Féin and sought medical treatment in the United States. She was denied a visa but was admitted to the Mater Hospital in Belfast. Joe Cahill succeeded her as joint vice president. The most prominent of northern Republicans, she was reviled by the establishment and hated by Loyalists. The *Daily Express* described her as "Grandma Venom." Merlyn Rees once compared her to Madame Lafarge, knitting while the guillotine did its business. On October 28, 1976, Loyalist paramilitaries dressed as doctors entered her hospital ward and shot her three times in the chest. She died in the operating room. Her death was a significant blow to the movement and left a void in Sinn Féin in the north that was unfilled until the rise to prominence of Gerry Adams and Danny Morrison. Ruairí Ó Brádaigh lost a good friend and a political ally. He issued a statement describing her as the voice of a "beleaguered people" who suffered from and resisted "British and pro-British terror."

There was widespread speculation that Séamus Twomey, who was described by the *Daily Express* as "the country's most wanted man," and Ó Brádaigh, who was excluded from Northern Ireland, would attend her funeral, which drew an estimated 15,000 people. Twomey was there, but Ó Brádaigh was not. The night before, the RUC set up roadblocks all along the border. Alongside the roadblocks were easels with photographs of prominent Republicans, including Twomey and Ó Brádaigh. Cars were stopped and faces were checked against the photographs. Ó Brádaigh made his way up to the Donegal border, spent the night at the home of a Sinn Féiner, and waited for a prearranged ride the next morning. It never arrived; his driver was scared off by the roadblocks. He tried several times to telephone the driver, but the phone was off the hook. By the time he realized the ride would not come, it was too late to find another ride and it was too risky to hire a taxi. At Belfast's Milltown Cemetery, it was announced that Ó Brádaigh had been "unable to penetrate" the security net. The oration was given by Andréas O'Callaghan, representing the Sinn Féin Ard Chomhairle. Ó Brádaigh, feeling awful, went home to Roscommon and arranged to have his tribute, which praised Drumm as a "fearless anti-imperialist fighter," published in *An Phoblacht*. It was some time before he spoke to his driver again.

In public, the Drumm assassination was presented as another sad event in the Irish conflict and the IRA and Sinn Féin soldiered on. In private, the IRA was undergoing significant change. Most accounts suggest that these changes were inspired by prisoners in Long Kesh, who had watched the truce unfold and believed it was a mistake. A sort of think tank had developed in Long Kesh that was centered on Gerry Adams, Ivor Bell, Brendan Hughes, and Gerry Kelly. They had organized lectures and discussions, and an important topic for examination was the truce. For the prisoners, who were virtually on site as it was built, the Maze was evidence that the British were planning to stay, not withdraw. They were also upset with IRA involvement in sectarian attacks and the feud with the Officials in October 1975; it seemed that the organization had lost its way. In the spring of 1976, Merlyn Rees had announced the policy of "Ulsterisation," by which the RUC and Ulster Defence Regiment would be moved to the fore and the British Army would move to a supporting role. The denial of special status ("criminalization") and the ending of internment, which was an affront to civil liberties, rejected Republican assertions that they were soldiers and that their cause was political. Ulsterization made it less likely that British soldiers would suffer casualties, a fact that shielded the British public from the war. And because the RUC and Ulster Defence Regiment were largely Protestant forces, Ulsterization supported the British view that the conflict was between Irish Catholics and Irish Protestants, with the British as neutral peacekeepers. The overall British objective was what they called "normalisation." It appeared that the British had set in place the final piece of a master plan to reorganize their counterinsurgency, using the truce as a cover.

Some Republicans use the truce to question the abilities of the Republican leadership of 1975, especially Ruairí Ó Brádaigh and Dáithí O'Connell. Joe Cahill has commented that the leadership "fell for a British ploy" and that the truce went on too long. This allowed the British time to reorganize and it allowed a sense of normalcy to penetrate the lives of IRA volunteers. People on the run returned to families and jobs. When this happens and when it comes time to go back to war, Cahill commented, "It's very hard to get them to give that up." The leadership misread the situation, it is argued, because it was based in the south. Ó Brádaigh and O'Connell lived there and Twomey, who was on the run, was based there. Mitchel McLoughlin describes them as "sincere and genuine Republican leaders" who "didn't read [problems with the truce] as early as those people who lived in the war zone." Historical accounts tend to accept such comments uncritically. The analysis has the benefit of hindsight; Ó Brádaigh does not remember Cahill or McLoughlin expressing concerns in 1975.

Ó Brádaigh, O'Connell, Twomey, and McKee were in and out of the north throughout the truce. Ó Brádaigh was there often enough that in August 1975, Gerry Fitt of the SLDP had complained publicly about his "coming here from Dublin." O'Connell went north regularly until his arrest. Twomey was wanted in the south, but not the north. He was in Belfast often enough that Unionists at Westminster loudly complained about the fact that he had not been arrested. McKee was not wanted north or south and as the Belfast commanding officer was there most of the time. More important, the leadership had not experienced the truce in a vacuum. They realized that political status was likely to end and saw that the size of the RUC and the Ulster Defence Regiment was increasing. Ó Brádaigh's truce notes reflect this knowledge. The prisoners came to the conclusion that the IRA was in for a long war. So did the leadership. If the British were not calling it quits, neither was the leadership. Whether or not the truce was successful, the leadership believed that after fifty years in the doldrums, the Republican Movement was still a potent force in Irish politics. The British were not going to withdraw in the short term, but they might in the long run if the IRA kept the pressure on. When the prisoners lobbied for the IRA to reorganize for a long war of attrition, the leadership was receptive. If the leadership had not been receptive, the changes that followed the end of the truce would not have occurred as quickly as they did.

The IRA has survived for decades because of a willingness to adapt to changing circumstances. In 1939, the IRA military campaign started with bombs in England, but by the early 1940s much of its activity was confined to Northern Ireland. To support that campaign, a Northern Command was established. At the start of the Border Campaign, in 1956, the focus was on the countryside and the IRA employed flying columns of volunteers that would operate for extended periods in the countryside. However, early in 1957, and at the urging of Paddy McLogan, the IRA went to smaller battle teams because the flying columns were too cumbersome. In the early 1970s, when there was a massive mobilization of Nationalists in Northern Ireland, a company, brigade, and battalion structure, which dated from the 1920s, was effective. This was especially so in Belfast and Derry, where volunteers could operate behind barricades in no-go areas. The no-go areas, however, were cleared in July 1972 in Operation Motorman. In 1975, the British used the truce to monitor people's movements. And in 1976, Roy Mason, who replaced Merlyn Rees as secretary of state for Northern Ireland, encouraged the RUC to take a much tougher line in interrogations, as the authorities in Castlereagh had done. Because too many people had access to information, the battalion system became a liability.

In response to changed conditions, the IRA reorganized. It adopted a Northern Command and a cell structure. The Northern Command, a liaison between battalion commanders and the Army Council, gave the northern commanders more autonomy. The command first met in November 1976, under the direction of Martin McGuinness. The reorganization into cells ("active service units") was developed in Long Kesh by Ivor Bell. The more secure active service units had four or five members who operated as battle teams with—in theory—only one member in contact with the next level. This reorganization, coupled with the long war strategy, changed the IRA. Active service units required fewer volunteers, which made the IRA smaller. The IRA also scaled back the bombing campaign of its economic war and focused more on killing members of the security forces, which reduced civilian casualties. In 1976–1977, the number of IRA operations declined and then leveled off in 1977–1978, after which it appeared that the IRA could continue forever. A British army intelligence document, "Northern Ireland: Future Terrorist Trends," dated November 2, 1978, which was intercepted by the Republicans, stated that "[t]he Provisionals' campaign of violence is likely to continue while the British remain in Northern Ireland."

A key strategist in all of this was Gerry Adams. In the late 1970s, with his full beard and shoulder-length hair, he looked and acted more like a hip young college professor than a wild-eyed terrorist. By his demeanor and physical presence he was closer to Dáithí O'Connell than Ruairí Ó Brádaigh, though O'Connell chain-smoked cigarettes and Adams smoked a pipe. Adams had been released from Long Kesh to participate in the 1972 IRA-British negotiations and was subsequently rearrested in July 1973 with Brendan Hughes and Tom Cahill (Joe Cahill's brother). Back in Long Kesh, he was in the prison leadership, helped organize lectures and discussions, and wrote a column for *Republican News* under the pseudonym "Brownie." The column developed from his friendship with Danny Morrison, who was interned in Long Kesh for most of 1973. Morrison was working in the West Belfast truce incident center when Billy McKee appointed him editor of *Republican News*. He asked Adams to write a column from the prisoners' perspective. The first Brownie column appeared in August 1975.

The Brownie column is often presented as the beginning of Gerry Adams's quest to undermine the Republican leadership and push his own agenda. However, there was nothing in the column that the leadership found especially troubling. If there had been, McKee would have dropped the column and replaced Morrison as editor. Instead, the column was frequently carried in *An Phoblacht* as well as well as *Republican News*. Brownie's call for action was consistent with and, in a sense, complementary to Sinn Féin policy. In a letter to the *Irish Independent* in December 1970, Ruairí Ó Brádaigh had asked, "What is Republicanism?" In May 1976, Brownie asked, "What then is our definition of a Republican?" Ó Brádaigh's answer drew on Fintan Lalor, who sought to restore the Irish people's "social, cultural and economic heritage"; James Connolly's socialism; and, most important, Wolfe Tone. Quoting Tone, he argued that Republicans sought "[t]he rights of man in Ireland. The greatest happiness of the greatest number." This was the foundation of Éire Nua. Adams's answer to the question, reflecting his Belfast working-class origins, was not a policy statement but a "personal definition" that led to a working-class socialist call to action. His commentary included, "We fight for the people who find it hard to make ends meet, whether they be small farmers being pushed off the land by big ranchers or factory workers being sold out by their Trade Union leaderships. They are our fight and our fight must be based among them." At an education seminar not long after Brownie wrote this, Ó Brádaigh stated, "Our aim is not to reform the present system, not to work towards a more just distribution of the fruits of capitalism. It is to change completely the present system and create a new democratic socialist federal Ireland." Although Brownie tended to focus on class issues in Ireland and Ó Brádaigh tended to place them in an international, anti-imperialist context, there was no disagreement across their politics. What was new, and welcome, was that Brownie was a young northerner.

Ó Brádaigh, and the leadership in general, did not know who Brownie was. They knew who was in Long Kesh, of course, and concluded that Brownie was one of a handful of people, including Adams. For years, the younger people had been too busy fighting the war to worry about Sinn Féin and politics. When Adams was released from Long Kesh in March 1977, one of the first things he did was to meet with Séamus Twomey. Although Adams denies that he has ever been an IRA member, most observers agree that he joined the Army Council soon afterward. While in Long Kesh, Adams was regularly elected to the Sinn Féin Ard Chomhairle. He attended the 1977 Ard Fheis, was again elected to the Ard Chomhairle, and, for the first time in years, was able to attend meetings.

At the Wolfe Tone Commemoration in June 1977, the IRA's change in strategy was revealed to the movement as a whole. The keynote speaker was Jimmy Drumm, Máire's widower and one of the most respected of Republicans. Drumm announced to the crowd that the movement needed politics, especially in the south, that "a successful war of liberation cannot be fought exclusively on the back of the oppressed in the Six Counties" and that the "isolation" of Republicans around "the armed struggle" was dangerous. The movement needed to fight censorship and the traditionally conservative Irish ethos, to develop "a positive tie in with the mass of the Irish people who have little or no idea of the sufferings in the North." Doing so required taking a stand "on economic issues and on the everyday struggles of the people." He boldly acknowledged that "[t]he British Government is NOT withdrawing from the Six Counties (emphasis in original)." The previous year, an article in *An Phoblacht* had argued that the closing of factories in the north was evidence that the British were leaving. Drumm admitted that these were not "symptoms of withdrawal" but were caused by a recession. The British were prepared "for a long haul against the Irish Republican Army."

As he listened to the speech, Ó Brádaigh must have experienced a curious mix of emotions, for Drumm was saying what he had been saying for years. As early as his 1972 presidential address, he had called on Republicans to be active in local economic issues "so that Irish workers may experience at first hand our concern for their interests," and he warned that Sinn Féin was in danger of becoming only a "support group for the struggle in the North." To have Drumm's speech presented as a new departure was frustrating. The acknowledgment that the IRA was in for a long war was not new. Even though Ó Brádaigh had been the most prominent of those claiming that a British withdrawal was inevitable, he had always made it clear that the withdrawal would take place over time. He agreed with Drumm's assessment and said so. The day after the speech, as reported in the *Belfast Telegraph*, Ó Brádaigh said, "He [Drumm] was articulating the view, which we all hold, that a British withdrawal, while not on in the immediate future, is inevitable and that victory is certain in the long run. It is something that we will have to struggle for."

The content of Drumm's speech was important, especially the public admission that the war would be a long one. Voluntary organizations survive because their members are willing to make sacrifices. The Republican Movement was calling for a long-term, high-level sacrifice from its members. The speech is most important because it reached Gerry Adams and Danny Morrison's targeted audience, their peers. Through the early 1970s, new recruits to the movement believed that victory was imminent, and they focused on the IRA's armed struggle. When victory did not come, they asked why. Some of them, no doubt, became disillusioned and drifted away. Others began questioning the abilities of their leaders and came to believe they could do a better job. The speech is seen as a watershed for the movement, a signal that the movement would combine revolutionary military and political struggle. Only later did it emerge that the speech was written by Adams and Morrison and that it was a sign that the old leadership was being replaced by the new—Gerry Adams and Danny Morrison, as it were, for Ruairí Ó Brádaigh and Dáithí O'Connell.

The replacement of Ó Brádaigh with Adams was several years away, however. Ó Brádaigh remained central to the movement, publicly and privately. He was involved in two important initiatives in this period. In the first, between December 1976 and June 1977, the Ulster Loyalist Central Coordinating Committee sent two representatives—John McKeague and John McLure—to meet two Republican representatives, Ruairí Ó Brádaigh and Joe Cahill. The Ulster Loyalist Central Coordinating Committee people represented all of the Loyalist bodies (the Ulster Defence Association, the Ulster Volunteer Force, the Red Hand Commando, etc.). The agenda was how to reconcile the Loyalist policy of an independent six-county state with the Republican policy of Éire Nua, which called for a federation of the four provinces, including a nine-county Ulster, with maximum political devolution to the local level. The four men met several times, and they decided to ask Desmond Boal and Seán MacBride to represent each side. Boal and MacBride agreed to do so. MacBride consulted with and was instructed by the Republicans. He met Boal several times—once in Paris where they both had business—and exchanged a number of position papers. The meetings were discreet and confidential. However, Conor Cruise O'Brien received information that the talks were taking place and criticized them on RTÉ radio, which ended progress. In the second initiative, in 1977, the Republicans were involved in an attempt to establish an anti-imperialist front. Representatives from several organizations, including Sinn Féin and Séamus Costello's Irish Republican Socialist Party, met in Dublin. Richard Behal was one of the Sinn Féin representatives, and at the first meeting he got along very well with Costello. Afterward Ó Brádaigh felt compelled to let him know that this was the same Séamus Costello who eleven years earlier had argued that Behal should be executed for insubordination. Behal is a very direct person. To Ó Brádaigh's amusement, at the beginning of the next meeting Behal asked Costello about events in 1966. Costello handled it well and the meeting in general went well. Unfortunately, one of the parties involved—not the IRSP or the Provisionals—watered down a joint manifesto so much that the project failed. Costello, the Irish National Liberation Army's chief of staff, was subsequently assassinated by an Official IRA member in October 1977. The IRSP and the INLA never fully recovered from this loss. Ó Brádaigh and Charlie McGlade, representing the Sinn Féin Ard Chomhairle, attended Costello's funeral.

In the mid- to late 1970s, Ó Brádaigh was intent on keeping Sinn Féin on a path he had charted since 1970, including the internationalization of the movement. In 1976, Jimmy Carter was elected president of the United States. Traditionally, Democrats have been more interested in Irish affairs than Republicans and Carter had expressed a personal interest in human rights issues. Ó Brádaigh hoped the change in administrations would lead to a visa. Instead, successful lobbying by the British and Irish governments, who had access to Washington, closed the door more tightly.

On St. Patrick's Day in 1977, four prominent Irish-American politicians, Senators Edward Kennedy and Daniel Moynihan, Congressman Tip O'Neill, and Governor Hugh Carey, issued a statement calling on their fellow Irish-Americans not to support the IRA. It was a significant change from the early 1970s, when Kennedy had called for a British withdrawal and O'Neill had been willing to cohost a reception for Ó Brádaigh and Frank McManus on Capitol Hill. Ó Brádaigh had already applied for another visa when he received an invitation to speak at the New York convention of the Ancient Order of Hibernians, which was scheduled for June 1977. He booked a flight on TWA and paid another visit to the U.S. embassy in Dublin, providing details on the invitation and his itinerary. On the morning of June 23rd, the day he was scheduled to leave, he received a phone call with the news that his visa application was denied. In a statement to the press, he commented on the "denial of my right to travel at a time when the Carter administration is expressing concern about the denial of the rights of Soviet Jews to travel." He made do as best he could and participated in a telephone interview with Bob Grant of Radio WOR in New York City.

His difficulties with the U.S. State Department have never been resolved, even with the intervention of United States congressmen. In the summer of 1978, Congressmen Joshua Eilberg of Pennsylvania, and Hamilton Fish, Jr. of New York, who were members of the House Judiciary Committee, investigated the visa denial process. They visited London, Belfast, and Dublin and interviewed various government officials and interested parties. In Dublin, they met with Ó Brádaigh, Joe Cahill, John Joe McGirl, and Joe Stagg (Frank Stagg's brother), each of whom had been denied a visa. Dáithí O'Connell, who was planning to apply for a visa, also participated. The Republicans, who stressed their affiliation with Sinn Féin, described the violation of their human rights; Ó Brádaigh, Cahill, McGirl, and O'Connell had been interned without charge or trial by either the southern or northern governments or, in McGirl's case, both. The opinion of a police officer had been enough to send Ó Brádaigh to prison. Eilberg and Fish were impressed, and their report to Congress states, "The delegation feels that the Department of State may have acted unfairly and unjustifiably in denying or revoking non-immigrant visas to certain Irish nationals desirous of visiting the United States. . . . Considerably more effort should be made to differentiate between political activity and terrorist activity which now appears to be regarded as synonymous." It did not help. In October 1978, Ian Smith, prime minister of the openly racist regime in Rhodesia, was granted a visa to enter the

United States. An article in *An Phoblacht* pointed out the contrast with
the continued denial of Ó Brádaigh's visa. He is still excluded from the
United States.

Banned from Irish radio and television and from the United States,
England, and Northern Ireland, Ó Brádaigh went elsewhere. A natural
audience was the other cultural minorities in Western Europe who were
struggling to maintain their unique identities against the onslaught of
Western imperialism, including Corsicans, Bretons in northwest France,
Catalans in Spain, and Basques in northern Spain and southern France.
He felt a special affinity with the Basques, who had endured a history
similar to that of the Irish. Each nation suffered politically and culturally
at the hands of imperial powers—Britain and Spain. Each nation had
declared a Republic earlier in the century only to lose it in a civil war—the
Irish in the 1920s, the Basques in 1936. In 1936, Irish and Basque soldiers had fought together in defense of the Spanish Republic, as Ó Brádaigh noted on a tour: "Forty years ago Irishmen and Basques fought and
died as comrades [in the International Brigade] for the liberty of both
our countries." In 1959, a Basque militant separatist group, Euzkadi Ta
Askatasuna (ETA), was founded; it was the Basque version of the IRA.
The political party Euskal Iraultzarako Alderia (EIA) developed out of
ETA; it was the Basque version of Sinn Féin. An EIA representative attended the 1977 Sinn Féin Ard Fheis. From this connection, Ó Brádaigh, Richard Behal, and Ted Howell developed very strong links with
Basque separatists. They visited the Basque region regularly between 1977
and 1983.

Ó Brádaigh, Behal, and Ted Howell nurtured ties with other groups.
They attended the first Congress of the Portuguese socialist organization
Oganizacao Unitaria de Trabalhadores (the United Organization of Workers, OUT) in Lisbon, and Ó Brádaigh and Behal attended a conference
organized by the Movimento di Su Populu Sardu (Movement of the Sar-
dinian People) in Sardinia. The Basques, among others, attended the
OUT Congress, and the Basques, OUT representatives, and the Catalans
(representatives from the Front Nacional de Catalunya, the National Front
of Catalonia) were among those in Sardinia. These groups shared a common interest in opposing the EEC, which they saw as an amalgamation
of imperial powers that was destined to wipe out cultural minorities in
Europe. In Portugal, Ó Brádaigh described them as representing "small
nations locked in the life-and-death struggle against imperialism, international capitalism and neo-colonialism." Another common concern was
their victimization at the hands of their oppressors. In April 1979, Sinn

Féin brought them all together for a conference on European Political Prisoners, held in Dublin and Belfast. Delegates from Belgium, Brittany, Denmark, England, Euskadi (Basque), Flanders, France, Italy, Portugal, and Scotland attended sessions on topics such as "Arrest, Interrogation, and Sentencing" and "Conditions of Imprisonment and Treatment." Ó Brádaigh, Richard Behal, Joe Cahill, and Dáithí O'Connell represented Sinn Féin. Other Irish delegates represented the Irish Republican Socialist Party and a new group organized in support of prisoners on the blanket, the Relatives Action Committee. The international links forged during these years are one of Ó Brádaigh's most significant achievements as president of Sinn Féin.

Ó Brádaigh pursued some personal interests on these trips. In the seventeenth century, it was illegal for Catholics to pursue a higher education in Ireland. Those who could do so attended schools on the European continent, including one in Paris. In Paris, he visited the site of the former Irish college on rue des Irlandais; in the mid-1970s it was a college for Polish students. He also indulged his interest in books. In a Barcelona bookshop he purchased a copy of Seán Cronin's *Resistance* that had been translated into Catalan. He investigated cooperatives and cooperative living whenever he had the chance. After the Vancouver conference, he spent the weekend at an Indian reservation on one of the islands off the Canadian coast. The people lived communally, sharing everything, including their living space. In Portugal, Ó Brádaigh, Behal, and Howell, toured cooperative farms in the countryside. As he described it to his hosts, with these cooperatives, "the rural people have seized control of the land and are carving out in freedom their own communal way of life."

Some trips had their humorous moments. In 1977 in Corsica, a young girl translating English to Corsican garbled the phrase "the Third World" so that it came out "the Third World War." Other trips had their bizarre moments. In May 1979, Ó Brádaigh, Richie Ryan of Fine Gael, Glenn Barr of the Ulster Defence Association, Conor Cruise O'Brien, and some British MPs were invited to appear on *David Frost's Global Village,* which was produced by Yorkshire Television in England. The guests, some in the studio and some at remote locations, were connected via satellite. Yorkshire Television tried to arrange for Ó Brádaigh to broadcast from an RTÉ studio, but they would not let him in the building. Belfast and London studios were also closed to him. A studio was found in Paris, and the day of the broadcast he flew there only to find out that it also was not available. Because the show aired late in the evening, there was still time. He was given tickets to Hamburg, via Amsterdam, and sent back to the airport. He was picked up in Hamburg by a non-English-speaking taxi driver who delivered him to the studio in time. The show started and Ó Brádaigh patiently sat in front of a television camera, a microphone clipped to his shirt. He could hear, but not see, Frost and the other guests. When Frost tried to include Ó Brádaigh in the discussion, the Conservative MPs objected immediately and some of them walked off the show. Ó Brádaigh's audio feed was never turned on and for eleven minutes his face was projected onto television screens in Britain and Ireland. The audience could see and hear the others guests revile him, but he could only sit there and listen; as the other studio participants talked away, he was a picture on the wall, beside or over them, always silent. He spent the night in a hotel in Hamburg, cashed in his return ticket the next day, and took a train to the Basque and Catalan areas of Spain.

While Ó Brádaigh was pushing Sinn Féin's politics, Gerry Adams, it seems, was consolidating his power in the IRA. An early victim was Billy McKee. McKee had never forgiven the Official IRA for the death of Charlie Hughes in 1970 and always took a hard line in feuds with the Officials. Adams believed this approach was a mistake because it played into British propaganda that the Provisionals were gangsters, not revolutionaries. When yet another feud developed in 1977, Adams attacked McKee for supporting the Provisionals' involvement. Adams, who was supported by a number of others on the Army Council, won the argument. McKee's influence was in decline when he became ill, was hospitalized, and left the council. In December, Adams's position was further strengthened when Séamus Twomey was arrested in Dublin. Adams, most observers agree, replaced him as chief of staff.

Adams's tenure as apparent chief of staff was short lived. On a Friday night in February 1978, the IRA attacked the La Mon House, a restaurant and hotel on the outskirts of Belfast. A telephone warning did not get through and a firebomb engulfed a room in flames, burning twelve people to death, all of them Protestant civilians. Several others suffered very serious burns. The attack made no sense: it was not a military installation, an establishment frequented by the security forces, or some key economic target. It was simply a hotel packed with guests, and there was widespread outrage. Fianna Fáil was returned to power in Dublin in 1977, with Jack Lynch again as Taoiseach. Lynch referred to the perpetrators as "callous beasts who have no place in society." In the most critical statement he ever offered on a Provisional IRA operation, Ó Brádaigh described the attack as "totally inexcusable" and said that the deaths and injuries "cannot be condoned in any way." In Belfast, the RUC raided Sinn Féin's Belfast offices, smashed up the *Republican News* office, and arrested twenty-one people, including Gerry Adams. Adams was interrogated in Castlereagh, charged with IRA membership, and transferred to Long Kesh, where he was held on remand. He denied the membership charge, threatened to sue reporters who repeated the charge, and applied for bail. Bail was denied and he was transferred to Long Kesh to await trial. Martin McGuinness, it is alleged, replaced him as chief of staff.

It was a fortuitous time for Adams to be in Long Kesh, where about 400 prisoners were on the blanket. Because they refused the uniforms of the criminal population, the authorities had withdrawn exercise facilities, access to reading and writing material, radios, newspapers, and furniture; a prisoner had only a blanket, a mattress, and his comrades. Around the time Adams arrived in Long Kesh, protesting prisoners were being assaulted by guards when they left their cells to wash up or go to the toilet. Beginning in March 1978, the blanketmen refused to leave their cells for any reason, adopting a "dirty" protest—they urinated on the floor and spread their excrement on the cell walls. Several women prisoners in Armagh joined the protest. When he visited Long Kesh in July 1978, Archbishop (later Cardinal) Tomás Ó Fiaich compared the prisoners to poor people living in the sewers of Calcutta and stated, "One would hardly allow animals to remain in such conditions, let alone a human being." Sinn Féin organized rallies for the prisoners and the IRA assassinated prison officers, including Albert Myles, the deputy governor of the Maze (Long Kesh). Adams was awaiting trial and was not subjected to the conditions, but he was able to meet with people who were. The commanding officer was Brendan Hughes, his old comrade and friend, and the second in command was Bobby Sands, whom he knew from his earlier spell in Long Kesh.

The case against Adams went to court in September 1978. The evidence against him was similar to the evidence used against Ó Brádaigh in 1973 and included Brownie articles and the text of a speech he had made at the 1977 Sinn Féin Ard Fheis. In the south, the opinion of a senior police officer would have been enough for a conviction. Northern Ireland did not have an Offenses Against the State Act, and the charges were dismissed. He reported back to the movement and all indications are that he rejoined the Army Council. At the 1978 Sinn Féin Ard Fheis in November, he succeeded Dáithí O'Connell as a joint vice president; O'Connell, for a time, became a joint secretary. Ó Brádaigh respected Adams's intelligence and welcomed his release. In writing his presidential addresses, he liked to consult with people, asking for things to include and exclude. He met with Adams, discussed the situation in Long Kesh, and updated his comments on the prisoners.

Ó Brádaigh was also wary of Adams. In the Republican Movement the ideal member offers service to the cause and expects nothing in return. Self-promoters and people who seek power are suspect. Adams was developing a power base, and Ó Brádaigh wondered what he was up to. Another issue, though not as serious, was Adams's repeated denial that he was a member of the IRA. Ó Brádaigh refused to confirm or deny IRA membership because this gave the authorities no information and was no help in a possible process of elimination. But he also paid a price for this. His refusal to deny membership cost him five months in the Curragh, gave the minister for education a reason to fire him, and gave the U.S. State Department a reason to exclude him. In contrast, Adams's denial was curious.

15

A New Generation Setting the Pace

OCTOBER 1978–AUGUST 1981

GERRY ADAMS HAS a reputation for placing people close to him into key positions in the Republican Movement. One of the people closest to him was Danny Morrison, who edited *Republican News*. They had worked together on Jimmy Drumm's speech at Bodenstown and they were part of a group of young people in Belfast who argued that the movement needed to become more politically relevant. Soon after the charges that Adams was an IRA member were dismissed, he set his sights on *An Phoblacht*. Republicans in Belfast had suggested that the papers be merged. Morrison argued that one paper would be more efficient than two and that, given that the goal was a united Ireland, having two papers was a contradiction. After much discussion the leadership agreed that a merger made sense, but no date was set. In early January 1979, Deasún Breatnach, *An Phoblacht's* editor, decided to move on. Morrison met with Ruairí Ó Brádaigh and Dáithí O'Connell to consider the paper's future and learned that O'Connell was considering becoming interim editor until the merger. Morrison intervened and merged the papers immediately, moving his staff down from Belfast and becoming editor of the new *An Phoblacht/Republican News*. It was a significant change that placed the young northerners in charge of the movement's main propaganda organ.

Ó Brádaigh and O'Connell went along with the merger because they recognized that changes of this kind were inevitable. The war had lasted for almost ten years, longer than any previous Republican military campaign. At some point, as senior people were arrested, younger people would move into the leadership. The same thing had happened during the 1950s when they were the young people. Generational change happened, and Ó Brádaigh accepted it. At the 1979 Easter Commemoration at Milltown Cemetery the scheduled speaker was Gerry Adams. In defiance of his exclusion order, Ruairí Ó Brádaigh emerged from a crowd of about a thousand people and gave the address. In his remarks, he publicly acknowledged that it was the young northerners who bore the brunt of the war. He praised them. On the prisoners he commented, "The courage of the men in the H-Blocks and the women in Armagh in their third year of continual protest for the restoration of Prisoner of War status under the most horrifying conditions, testifies to the great moral strength and fibre of the Republican movement today, as something unequaled in a previous generation." In his conclusion, he figuratively passed the torch from his generation to the next, stating, "No one phase of struggle has gone on for so long, it is not simply the effort to exhaustion of a single generation, for within the present struggle the turn-over of the generations has already taken place. A new generation is setting the pace now. This is the greatest possible acquisition of strength to a revolutionary movement—and the surest guarantee of victory."

Out of the public eye, the transfer was not so smooth. It was one thing to turn over the reins of power to another generation. It was another to sit by and have them dismantle a decade's worth of valuable work. The Ó Brádaighs and Dáithí O'Connell had led the development of policies on a number of topics, including "The Quality of Life in a New Ireland" (1973), "Foreign Affairs" (1974), "Mining and Energy" (1974), "The National Offshore" (1977), a "Local Government Manifesto" (1979), and "Women in the New Ireland" (1980). Not only were the social and economic policies of Éire Nua I and the federalism policy of Éire Nua II, with its nine-county Dáil Uladh, central to Sinn Féin policy, but the Ó Brádaighs and Dáithí O'Connell believed that federalism would be a mechanism that would allow Unionists to enter a united Ireland and still maintain their identity and some political power.

Although elected politicians, north and south, were not interested in working with the Republicans, there was some support for federalism in Ireland. In 1978, the Economic and Social Research Institute (ESRI) in Dublin sponsored a survey of political opinion in the Republic of Ireland. One question offered a list of choices and asked respondents to identify "the most workable and acceptable to you as a solution" to the problem in Northern Ireland. The largest proportion of respondents (41.2 percent) chose uniting Northern Ireland and the Republic of Ireland with one government, but the next-largest group (26.7 percent) chose "Northern Ireland and the Republic to unite in a federal system, that is with strong regional governments for Northern Ireland and the Republic as well as an over-all central government." A federal Ireland was the first or second choice for 57.2 percent of the respondents. In the north, there was less support for a federal solution. The Northern Ireland Attitude Survey, which was conducted at the same time as the ESRI survey, asked the same question. The first choice for Protestants and Unionists was devolution to a majority rule Stormont-like government (37.3 percent), followed closely by devolution to a power-sharing type government, presumably similar to the Northern Ireland Executive of 1974 (34.8 percent). Only 4.4 percent of Protestants chose a federal Ireland, but even fewer chose a united Ireland (1.5 percent). The first choice of Nationalists and Catholics was a devolved power-sharing government (39 percent), followed by a united Ireland (24.9 percent). There was some support for a federal Ireland among Nationalists, however; this was the first choice of 13.9 percent of the respondents. Although Unionists and Protestants were primarily interested in some form of a return to Stormont, the Irish public as a whole had not rejected federalism as a solution. Based on his interactions with people such as William Craig and Sammy Smyth, Ó Brádaigh still believed that Unionists might embrace a federal solution if the British made it clear that they were going to withdraw.

But the young northerners in Sinn Féin rejected federalism. Adams, Morrison, and Tom Hartley, who was also from Belfast, believed that the Ó Brádaighs and O'Connell were out of touch with Irish politics. They began to challenge various Sinn Féin policies, and their chief target was federalism. They had not been involved in developing Éire Nua I or Éire Nua II, and they viewed federalism from a different perspective. They saw no evidence that the people of Cavan, Donegal, and Monaghan wanted to be governed by a regional parliament that would have a Unionist majority. And even if such evidence existed, they believed it would be a mistake. They had personally suffered at the hands of a Unionist-dominated Stormont government. Unionists, they believed, had shown no inclination for cross-community government. From their perspective, Dáil Uladh would sustain Unionist misrule; the IRA might win the war and lose the peace by handing power back to their oppressors. The first issue of *An Phoblacht/Republican News* appeared on January 27, 1979. It announced "One paper, one message, the harnessing of Republicanism in 32 Counties behind our independence and socialist struggle. . . ." The lead article ended: "Victory to the army, victory to the socialist republic." Sinn Féin policy called for a *federal* socialist republic. Seán Ó Brádaigh believed that Morrison was arrogantly ignoring Sinn Féin policy and vigorously complained about the omission at the next Ard Chomhairle meeting, but the paper was already in print. Morrison admits that he was willing to take "certain liberties," but adds that they were "liberties that were following the much stronger current of thinking."

There were other issues. In his autobiography, *Before the Dawn,* Adams states that he and others in the young northern element questioned the handling of the truce and "were disturbed when we couldn't find minutes for the meetings with the British or other records," but "there was little tension as we thrashed out issues." The situation was more tense than he reveals. When Adams asked him for the minutes, Ó Brádaigh was concerned. He saw what he had written as notes rather than minutes, and he was suspicious that they would be used against him. He had them brought to Dublin, but when the issue did not come up again he did nothing further. Adding to the difficulties of the Ó Brádaighs and O'Connell was Joe Cahill, who was very close to Adams and a supporter of the younger Belfast crowd. Part of this had to do with Cahill's leadership style. Billy McKee was very conservative and as the Belfast commanding officer he ran a very tight ship. When Cahill took over Belfast in 1971, he exercised less control. He was in charge when the Belfast IRA greatly expanded at the time of internment. More important, and several people noticed this, Cahill had a tendency to go along with the majority on important issues. After accepting federalism for a number of years, he stated at an Ard Chomhairle meeting in 1980 that "I never believed in federalism. This may come as a surprise to many of you."

Adams, Morrison, and Hartley began pushing for radical change in Éire Nua's social and economic program—change so radical that the Ó Brádaighs suspected it was an attempt to force them from the leadership. One proposal, the "grey document," called for the elimination of all private property in Ireland. To the younger people, who were working-class city dwellers who owned no property, this proposal demonstrated their radical politics. To the older people, who were aware of Ireland's conservative traditions and thousands of small family-owned farms in the countryside, it was ridiculous. The Ó Brádaighs had gone through similar arguments with Goulding and Mac Giolla ten years earlier, and they were prepared. Seán Ó Brádaigh commented that in Vietnam and in Eastern Europe there were still private enterprises. In Hungary, he noted, there was even a privately owned railway. For his contribution he received "dirty looks" and challenges to prove his assertions. When he did prove them, Adams and company were uninterested.

Curiously, the people who argued that Sinn Féin had to become more relevant in Irish political life were also very cautious about testing their ideas with the electorate. There were two important elections in 1979, a

Westminster election in May and the first election to the European Parliament in June. Sinn Féin, which had not contested a Westminster election since 1966, passed again in 1979. This election brought Margaret Thatcher and the Conservatives to power. Thatcher, who was already pro-Union, was influenced by events just before and soon after the election. In March 1979, an Irish National Liberation Army car bomb killed Airey Neave as he drove out of the House of Commons parking lot. Neave, an ardent supporter of the security forces, had engineered Thatcher's rise to the leadership of the Conservative Party. In return, she had appointed him shadow secretary of state for Northern Ireland. They were close, and his death affected her personally. A few months after the election, the IRA pulled off a double spectacular. Lord Mountbatten, the 82-year-old cousin to Queen Elizabeth and uncle of Prince Philip, was vacationing in Sligo in the Republic of Ireland. On August 27th, as his boat pulled out into the Atlantic, an IRA bomb ripped it apart, killing Mountbatten, his daughter's mother-in-law, his grandson, and a local boy piloting the boat. It was international news. Later that day, near Warrenpoint in County Down, an IRA bomb exploded as a British Army convoy passed by, killing six soldiers and wounding several others. The soldiers set up a field base and called for reinforcements. As a helicopter was landing, a second bomb buried beneath the field base exploded, killing twelve more soldiers. It was the British Army's worst day since World War II. The IRA has never had a good relationship with a British prime minister; their relationship with Mrs. Thatcher would be particularly poor.

The Mountbatten and Warrenpoint attacks also affected Ruairí Ó Brádaigh, but in a very different way. Archbishop George Simms of the Church of Ireland and Cardinal Ó Fiaich, the Catholic primate of Ireland, had invited the new Polish pope, John Paul II, to visit their parishes in Armagh in Northern Ireland. The pope accepted the invitation and the trip was scheduled for September. It would be the first time a pope had visited Ireland. After August 27th, the visit to Armagh was relocated to Drogheda in County Louth, where the pope presided over a Mass for 300,000 people and denounced violence in Ireland. He referred to the conflict as a struggle between haters and said that Christianity forbade solutions to injustice "by the ways of hatred, by the murdering of defenseless people, by the methods of terrorism. . . . On my knees I beg you to turn away from the paths of violence and to return to the ways of peace." Ó Brádaigh was extremely disappointed. The leader of his church had denied the validity of an IRA campaign that he believed was consistent with Catholic teaching on a just war. Another papal Mass was scheduled for Galway, and the Ó Brádaigh family had planned to attend it with Patsy's family, who lived near the site of the outdoor Mass. The Ó Brádaighs drove over to Galway, but while Patsy and her family attended the Mass, Ruairí and Ruairí Óg did not. They did not want to be compelled to walk out of the ceremonies if the condemnations were repeated. The pope, who had been politically active against the communist regime in Poland, ignored the national liberation aspect of the Irish conflict. It seemed to Ó Brádaigh that he accepted the concept of a Polish nation but not an Irish one.

In the second election in 1979, for the European Parliament, Ó Brádaigh suffered a significant defeat. The election had been in process for years, and he had repeatedly argued that it should be contested on an all-Ireland basis. The movement's anti-imperialist stance struck a chord with many northern Nationalists whose streets were patrolled by British soldiers. In the south, Sinn Féin's anti-imperialist message had not generated much enthusiasm, but there had been a large (17 percent) "No" vote in the 1972 referendum on EEC membership. It was a chance to build an anti-EEC campaign that would join the anti-imperialists in the north with the anti-EEC people in the south. If anti-EEC sentiment had grown since 1972, a Sinn Féin candidate could potentially win a seat. In that event, the individual would attend the European Parliament once, read a statement, and leave. The representative would become an international anti-imperialist ambassador who would also promote Sinn Féin. At the 1977 Sinn Féin Ard Fheis, Ó Brádaigh advocated contesting the election. The Belfast delegates, led by Gerry Adams, who were opposed, won the debate. Ó Brádaigh persisted and the Ard Chomhairle established a subcommittee to consider participation in the election. Subcommittee members included Ó Brádaigh, Adams, and Dáithí O'Connell. To Ó Brádaigh's disappointment, the people arguing that Sinn Féin was not politically relevant, especially Gerry Adams, opposed contesting the election. They were supported by Dáithí O'Connell, who usually sided with Ó Brádaigh. If Sinn Féin did poorly, they argued, it would slow down political development and hurt the IRA. Critics charged that the IRA had no mandate from the people it claimed to represent. Although Ó Brádaigh believed the support was there, Adams and O'Connell feared it was not, and they won the debate. The subcommittee recommended that Sinn Féin skip the election by a margin of one vote. The Ard Chomhairle agreed and went a step farther—Sinn Féin called for a boycott of the election. The election results suggest that this was a mistake.

When Sinn Féin announced it would not contest the election,

Ruairí Ó Brádaigh delivering the Presidential Address at the 1979 Sinn Féin Ard Fheis (held in January 1980). The Sinn Féin Ard Chomhairle is behind him. First row: Walter Lynch, Dáithí O'Connell, Gerry Adams, Christine Elias, Niall Fagan, Charlie McGlade, George Lynch, and Cathleen Knowles. Second row: P.J. Kearney, Jimmy Drumm, Marie Moore (behind Charlie McGlade), unknown, John Joe McGirl, Richard Behal. Standing in the third row: Gearóid Mac Cárthaigh, George Stagg, Tom Ó Sullivan, Joe O'Neill, and Tom Hartley. Photo Derek Speirs.

Bernadette Devlin McAliskey, the former Mid-Ulster MP, stepped in. She had married, was the mother of three young children, and was very active in the Relatives Action Committee. She used her candidacy to heighten awareness of the situation in Long Kesh and Armagh. In the north, Ian Paisley topped the poll with 170,000 votes. Also elected were John Hume, who had replaced Gerry Fitt as leader of the SDLP, and John Taylor of the Ulster Unionist Party. McAliskey finished seventh, with 34,000 votes. It was a good showing, and if Sinn Féin had not boycotted the election she might have polled substantially higher. But the vote did not directly help the prisoners, who were becoming desperate after three years on the blanket and more than one year on the dirty protest.

The H-Block protest remained an important background issue as Adams and company pursued their agenda. At the 1979 Ard Fheis (which was held in January 1980 because the Dublin Mansion House was being refurbished), a "radical" update of the social and economic program was put before the delegates. It was a marriage between the "grey document" and existing policies. The proposal abolishing private property was omitted, but included was a proposed upper limit on the amount of land an individual could own, which had been policy since 1971. Also included was the statement, "No person shall have the means economically to exploit his fellow man." Ó Brádaigh did not have a significant problem with the radicalization of Sinn Féin. Over his almost thirty years in the organization, Sinn Féin had grown from virtually no politics in the 1950s to the radicalization of the 1960s, which he accepted as long as it did not threaten abstentionism. In the 1970s, he had tried to keep politics relevant when almost everyone else, it seemed, focused on the IRA. In the late 1970s, the movement again lurched to the left, all of which was part of the zig and zag of Republican politics. On behalf of the Ard Chomhairle, he put forward the motion calling on the Ard Fheis to adopt the "radical" proposals, which he described as "unashamedly democratic and socialist in character"; he was seconded by Gerry Adams.

Radicalism was not new for Sinn Féin, but federalism was. Dáithí O'Connell was its principal architect and Ó Brádaigh had traveled extensively to publicize it as the solution to the Irish conflict. The two of them still believed in the policy. By this point, however, Gerry Adams and his supporters controlled the Army Council, and the council had rejected the policy, creating a split between IRA policy and Sinn Féin policy. Instead of trying to bring the two organizations into sync, Ó Brádaigh and O'Connell took a stand. O'Connell, on behalf of the Ard Chomhairle, put forward a motion, seconded by Richard Behal, that proposed that "the present Éire Nua Policy and government structures be retained, promoted and publicised during the coming year as the policy of Sinn Féin." The motion passed easily, but not without pointed comments from its opponents. A delegate from Belfast described federalism as "a sop to loyalism."

At the 1980 Ard Fheis in November, the same motion was again endorsed by the delegates. But that year Ó Brádaigh suffered a personal defeat. Sinn Féin policy called for a planned, phased, and orderly withdrawal of the British from Ireland. He wanted a phased withdrawal which would allow the development of political structures and prevent a civil war, a "Congo situation." He had endorsed this position in television, radio, and press interviews and in his writings countless times. Jim Gibney, who was from Belfast and one of the younger people, disagreed. He argued that a phased withdrawal would give Loyalists time to organize "an unprecedented terror campaign" which would then force the British to stay. He put forward a motion calling for "the immediate and total withdrawal of British troops from Ireland." The motion passed, indicating very publicly that Ó Brádaigh's influence was on the wane.

But even in 1980 Ó Brádaigh had his successes. He is pleased that as president he presented the policy document "Women in the New Ireland" to the delegates. It called for a Women's Department, committed Sinn Féin "fully to equality between the sexes," argued that "safe contraception should be available from family planning clinics," and stated, "We are totally opposed to abortion but we are also opposed to the forces in society which impel women to have abortions." It was a controversial document. Some delegates, mostly men, believed that a Women's Department would shift focus from more important things, including the IRA's armed struggle. Others argued that in spite of the disclaimer, the document would lead the way to a Sinn Féin policy that endorsed a woman's right to choose. Ó Brádaigh is not pro-choice, but he is also the son of a woman ahead of her time. When the debate was closed he went to the podium and endorsed the policy, stating that "men are not the enemies of women, but are the allies of women against their oppression." The document was endorsed by the Ard Fheis.

The most important change in Sinn Féin during this period involved personnel rather than policy. As the younger people were becoming more influential in the organization, some very senior people who were allies of Ó Brádaigh and O'Connell left the scene. Joe Clarke had died in 1976. Larry Grogan, another IRA veteran from the 1920s and a long-term Ard Chomhairle member, passed away in 1979 at the age of 82. Walter Lynch and Seán Ó Brádaigh resigned from the Officer Board in 1980. Lynch, who had been a Sinn Féin joint secretary for almost a decade, was replaced by Cathleen Knowles from Dublin. She was an Ó Brádaigh-O'Connell supporter. Seán Ó Brádaigh, who had been Sinn Féin's part-time director of publicity for almost twenty years, felt it was time to move on. The tension in the movement contributed to his decision—the incident with Morrison over the first issue of *An Phoblacht/Republican News* seemed a repeat of problems of the 1960s that preceded the 1969/1970 split. But the main issue was that the publicity director's responsibilities had become enormous and required a full-time person. He also wanted to spend more time with his children, who were teenagers. His replacement was Danny Morrison, who was available full-time. Mick Timothy, business manager of *An Phoblacht/Republican News,* replaced Morrison as editor. Timothy was an Adams-Morrison supporter.

In the fall of 1980, the internal debate in Sinn Féin and these leadership changes were overshadowed by events beyond the control of Sinn Féin or the IRA. In an attempt to broaden support for the prisoners, Sinn Féin's Smash H-Block campaign joined forces with the Relatives Action Committee to create a more broad-based approach, "The National H-Block/ Armagh Committee." Prominent members of the H-Block/Armagh Committee included Bernadette McAliskey, Jim Gibney, and the two Sinn Féin vice presidents, Gerry Adams and Dáithí O'Connell. The committee formulated five demands that would give the prisoners political status in all but name: the right to refuse to wear prison uniforms; the right to refuse to do prison work; the right to associate freely; full remission of sentences; and the right to receive visits and parcels and use recreational facilities. The committee organized protests, and Cardinal Ó Fiaich met with the prisoners and Northern Ireland Officials who were trying to resolve the situation, but nothing worked. Neither the prisoners nor the authorities would back down. About a month before the 1980 Ard Fheis, the prisoners, led by Brendan Hughes, took matters into their own hands. Hughes resigned as commanding officer and with six others (five IRA, one INLA) went on hunger strike for the five demands. Bobby Sands replaced Hughes as commanding officer. Reluctantly, the leadership went along with it. When asked why they were reluctant, Ó Brádaigh replies quickly, "Who *wants* a hunger strike?" Adams was concerned that it would divert attention from the political development he was pushing.

In spite of these reservations, Sinn Féin supported the strikers. At the Ard Fheis, about twenty foreign visitors were introduced from the stage— all of whom were committed to supporting the hunger strikers. Ó Brádaigh concluded his presidential address with "We join hands with each other, with our comrades throughout the world and our slogans are: Victory to the hunger-strikers! Victory to the Irish people!" After the Ard Fheis, Richard Behal set off to raise support on the continent. Others went to the United States and Canada. Ó Brádaigh, O'Connell, Adams, Morrison, Gibney, and everyone else threw themselves into rallies and protests that supported the prisoners. Adams and Morrison knew several of the hunger strikers personally and became liaisons with the prisoners, the press, the Republican leadership, and Northern Ireland office officials. Because people such as Ó Brádaigh and O'Connell could not go north and were not in direct contact with the prisoners, Adams and Morrison came to be seen as spokespersons for Sinn Féin and they became public figures. Ó Brádaigh knew two of the prisoners personally—Brendan Hughes and Tommy McKearney of Tyrone. He knew Hughes from the early 1970s, when he had toured Belfast. He knew McKearney on several levels. Tom Murray, McKearney's grandfather, was active in the South Roscommon IRA in the 1920s. Murray had moved to Tyrone, but Ó Brádaigh had known the family since the 1950s. Tommy McKearney's sister, Margaret, had worked in the Sinn Féin office in Dublin and Ruairí knew her; Margaret McKearney was good friends with the O'Connells and Deirdre was the maid of honor at her wedding.

The young men who were willing to live in filth and die a painful death because they refused to be criminalized by the British government caught the attention of many Irish people. Nationalist Ireland rallied in support of the prisoners. In an amazing display of political rehabilitation, Charles Haughey, who had been forced out of Jack Lynch's cabinet in 1970 because of the Arms Crisis, replaced Lynch as Taoiseach in 1979. Haughey's government was concerned enough that on December 1st, 1980, he met with Margaret Thatcher and urged her to find a way for the prisoners to save face and end the fast. Thatcher, who believed that the IRA had ordered the hunger strike, refused. On that same day, three women IRA prisoners in Armagh Prison, Máiréad Farrell, Máiréad Nugent, and Mary Doyle, upped the ante and started their own fast. Behind the scenes, Gerry Adams and Martin McGuinness met with British representatives in an attempt to resolve the situation. One of them was Michael Oatley, who had participated in the 1975 talks between the British and the IRA. Ó Brádaigh, who had been central to the discussions with the British in 1975, was not involved in these meetings.

After about fifty days the strike had begun to take its toll; Seán McKenna was dying, slipping in and out of a coma. Brendan Hughes, who had been his commanding officer, promised McKenna that he would not let him die. With the pressure on, northern Irish civil servants gave Hughes and Sands a 32-page document that contained a proposed solution to the crisis. The prisoners would not be granted political status, but they would be allowed to wear their own clothes. Hughes and Sands saw an opening that might lead to an agreement on all five demands, and if they accepted it McKenna's life would be saved. On December 18th, the fifty-third day, Hughes ended the hunger-strike. When the prisoners arranged for their families to deliver personal clothing, the clothes were not allowed in to Long Kesh and the prisoners were informed that they would be issued "civilian style" clothing. The prisoners, believing they had been deceived, protested, the situation deteriorated, and Bobby Sands sent word to the IRA leadership that there would be another hunger strike.

The leadership again was opposed. Gerry Adams feared it would hinder Sinn Féin's political development. Ruairí Ó Brádaigh believed that their supporters had not recovered from the first hunger strike. It would be hard to mobilize them again. And the authorities would not take the strike seriously until at least its fifty-third day. Sands was determined, and the leadership relented. He organized a staggered hunger strike where prisoners began fasting at intervals. This meant that hunger strikers would reach critical stages alone. With each individual more responsible for his own situation and less responsible for the health of other hunger strikers, it would be less likely that there would be a repeat of the situation Brendan Hughes had faced with Seán McKenna. A staggered strike, once people began dying, would also put enormous pressure on other prisoners to continue their fast or join the hunger strike. And if hunger strikers started dying, the specter of death would be constant and the pressure on the authorities enormous.

Sands began his hunger strike on March 1st, the fifth anniversary of the ending of special category status. The next day the prisoners ended the dirty protest; the strike would be a final showdown on political status. On March 5th, Frank Maguire, the Independent MP for Fermanagh–South Tyrone, suddenly died of a heart attack. There was still a Nationalist majority in the constituency, where Phil Clarke had won in 1955. Dáithí O'Connell, the IRA's organizer in Fermanagh in the 1950s, was convinced that Sands would do well in a by-election to replace Maguire. If Sands was the only nationalist candidate, O'Connell believed, he might win. At an Ard Chomhairle meeting he suggested putting Sands forward as an "Anti-H-Block/Armagh" candidate. Ó Brádaigh, who had run for the seat in 1966, agreed with him. The northerners, led by Gerry Adams, were opposed. O'Connell, who argued that they needed to do something to break the prison stalemate, won them over.

O'Connell, who had stayed with the Maguire family when he was on the run in the 1950s, was dispatched to meet with Noel Maguire, Frank's brother and the heir apparent. Noel Maguire agreed to step aside for a prisoner candidate. Jim Gibney was dispatched to meet with Bernadette McAliskey, the other likely candidate. She also agreed to step aside. Ó Brádaigh met with Owen Carron of Fermanagh Sinn Féin, who helped arrange an election convention that brought together the Sinn Féin leadership—Ó Brádaigh, O'Connell, Adams, John Joe McGirl, Jimmy Drumm, and Joe Cahill—and local Republicans. They met in Clones, on the border. Anti-election sentiment was so strong that the locals rejected a Sands campaign. The leadership, believing the opportunity was too important to let it pass, asked them to reconsider. After further deliberations, another constituency convention agreed that Sands would contest the seat and that Owen Carron would serve as his election agent. This placed the SDLP in a difficult position. The party rejected the IRA's methods, but at the grassroots level there was a great deal of sympathy for the prisoners. An SDLP candidate would hurt the prisoners' cause, split the Nationalist vote, guarantee a Unionist victory, and alienate many of their constituents. In a twist, the SDLP boycotted the election. The candidates were Bobby Sands and Harry West, IRA gunman versus Unionist farmer.

The Sands campaign faced enormous difficulties. The candidate could not visit the constituency and Humphrey Atkins, the secretary of state for Northern Ireland, refused to allow journalists into the H-Blocks. Because Ó Brádaigh was banned from the north, he set up election headquarters in Clones. From there he coordinated the work of offices in Enniskillen, Coalisland, and Dungannon and met with people such as Gerry Adams (who ran the Dungannon office), Danny Morrison, Jim Gibney, and Owen Carron, who could meet with the candidate. Republicans from all over flooded the constituency, including Ruairí Óg Ó Brádaigh, a 19-year-old college student. (The next generation of Ó Brádaigh brothers, Maitiú, Ruairí Óg, and, later, Conchúr, had formed a Sinn Féin *cumann* at University College Galway.) As the campaign progressed, Nationalist support was forthcoming and the Sinn Féin leadership realized that O'Connell was right: Sands might win.

Election day was April 9th. Ó Brádaigh remembers dates based on historical events. It was in the middle of Lent: Christ had spent forty days in the wilderness; St. Patrick had spent forty days on Croagh Patrick fasting and praying; and, on the fortieth day of his fast, Bobby Sands was elected MP for Fermanagh–South Tyrone. The British were stunned; Republicans were jubilant. Nationalist Ireland was mobilized to a level not seen since 1972. There were victory parades throughout the country; in Belfast, they ended in riots.

Many believed that the election was a breakthrough, that Margaret Thatcher would not allow an MP to die on hunger strike. In spite of appeals from the Vatican, the European Commission on Human Rights, the Irish Commission for Peace and Justice, Irish members of the European Parliament at Strasbourg, and Taoiseach Charles Haughey, neither Thatcher nor Sands would back down. On May 5, after sixty-six days without food, a deaf and blind Sands lapsed into a coma and died. Belfast erupted in riots. Black flags were flown throughout nationalist Ireland. International interest soared. In Lisbon, Richard Behal was placed at the head of huge march in support of Sands and the other prisoners. In Tehran, the revolutionary government changed the name of the street in front of the British embassy from Winston Churchill Street to Bobby Sands Street. Sands's paramilitary funeral in Belfast drew an estimated 100,000 mourners. And, as Sands had planned, the specter of death continued. IRA prisoner Francis Hughes died on May 12th, sparking more rioting. On May 21st, IRA prisoner Raymond McCreesh and INLA prisoner Patsy O'Hara both died. By the end of May, rioting was constant. And more prisoners joined the strike.

Sands's funeral, which featured an IRA color guard, a volley of shots over the casket, and an oration from Owen Carron, set the standard for funerals of hunger strikers. The leadership asked Ó Brádaigh to deliver the oration for McCreesh. He slipped over the border into Camlough in South Armagh, where he paid his respects to the family and signed a book of condolences. Sixty-three priests participated in the funeral Mass, which was said in Irish. The principal celebrant was Father Brian McCreesh, Raymond's older brother. From St. Malachy's Chapel a huge procession followed McCreesh's tricolor-draped coffin and a lone piper, who played the Irish resistance lament, "Úir-Chill an Chreagáin" ("The Churchyard of Creggan"), to the nearby cemetery. At the graveside, which was filled with wreaths, a minute's silence was observed, two buglers played the Last Post, and a color guard comprised of volunteers from the IRA, Cumann na mBan, and Na Fianna Éireann offered a salute. Ó Brádaigh then emerged from the crowd. With a British Army helicopter hovering overhead to drown him out, he began in Irish and referred to the piper's refrain. The poet was invited by the Aisling (Vision) to "*tír dheas na meala nach bhfuair Galla inti réim go fóill*" [to "journey with her to the sweet land of honey where the English did not yet rule"].

He announced to a crowd of thousands that they had gathered "to perform a last, sad but proud duty for that great Irishman and human being, Raymond McCreesh." He stressed the continuity of the struggle. McCreesh had operated in the same hills "where the men of the 4th Northern Division of the IRA operated sixty years ago." In May 1916, the Easter Rising martyrs were executed, "one by one and two by two." In May 1981, it was "First Bobby Sands MP, then Francie Hughes, then Raymond McCreesh and now Patsy O'Hara." He quoted Terence Mac-Swiney, the hunger striker who died in 1920: "'But not all the armies of all the empires on earth can crush the spirit of one true man, and that one man will prevail.' Such a man, a chairde [my friends], was Raymond McCreesh, your fellow Irishman, your kith and kin, your flesh and blood." Over McCreesh's grave, he promised that the movement would continue until the Republic was achieved: "[W]e pledge that while an Irish heart beats we shall not desist in our efforts until the hands of those who would rob our country of its independence fall nerveless, or a just judge has taken His vengeance." He ended in Irish: "*Leaba i measc na bhFíníní agus i láthair naoimh uile na hÉireann go raibh ag ár gcomrádaí Réamonn Mac-Raois. Go raibh maith agaibh* [May our comrade Raymond McCreesh rest in the midst of the Fenians and all the saints of Ireland. Thank you all]."

The day McCreesh and O'Hara died, another electoral opportunity presented itself. Charles Haughey, hoping to squeeze an election in before another hunger striker died, set an election for June 11th. Sinn Féin had not contested a Leinster House general election since 1961, but Ó Brádaigh proposed that they put forward candidates who supported the H-Block/Armagh Committee. Again, the young northerners had to be convinced. Paralleling Dáithí O'Connell in March, he argued that four hunger strikers were dead and that they had to introduce a new factor to move the situation forward. On May 29th, the Ard Chomhairle agreed to contest nine constituencies. At the end of the meeting, Gerry Adams, who was still concerned that Sinn Féin would do poorly, asked Cathleen Knowles, the general secretary, to record his recommendation that they contest only four of the nine constituencies. Such concerns were swept away when two IRA prisoners, Kieran Doherty and Paddy Agnew, were elected and a third prisoner, the Irish National Liberation Army's Kevin Lynch, missed election by only 300 votes.

Doherty and Agnew were two of several independent TDs elected, and overall the election upset the status quo of southern Irish politics. Doherty and Agnew were elected at Fianna Fáil's expense and Charles Haughey was out as Taoiseach. Garret FitzGerald formed a minority government that was destined to be short lived. The other noteworthy result was the election of Joe Sherlock of Sinn Féin/The Workers Party (formerly Official Sinn Féin). Eleven years after the 1970 split, the party elected its first TD. Still led by Tomás Mac Giolla, the party's approach to Republicanism had changed greatly; it was a vociferous critic of the hunger strikers.

Thatcher refused to bend. When Joe McDonnell died on July 8th, some supporters, caught up in the emotions of the hunger strike, became disillusioned and drifted away. London and Dublin took a harder line. In Belfast, the RUC and British Army attacked those who attended McDonnell's funeral, trying to arrest the IRA color guard. A week later, Gardaí stopped a march to the British embassy in Dublin and a major riot developed. This scared off more people, leaving behind a committed mix of older Republicans and new recruits. And hunger strikers continued to die, including Kieran Doherty, TD. After Doherty's death, Ó Brádaigh released a statement expressing his sympathy to the family and accusing the Haughey and FitzGerald administrations, the Catholic Church, and the SDLP of having "actively or by default . . . linked hands with British imperialism in Ireland, currently personified by Margaret Thatcher." The strike finally collapsed in October when families, at the urging of Catholic clergy, intervened. Prisoners would lapse into a coma and family members—caught between supporting a loved one willing to sacrifice himself for a cause and the indisputable fact that Thatcher would never yield—would order that they be fed intravenously.

It was a Pyrrhic victory for Thatcher. The hunger strike and the elections revitalized the Republican Movement. Recruits flocked to the IRA and Sinn Féin. Money poured in from the Irish diaspora. International sympathy remained high. In December, when Margaret Thatcher rose to address the European Parliament, Italian MEP Mario Cappanna stood up, held aloft a photograph of Bobby Sands, and remained standing throughout her speech. Ó Brádaigh, who was touring Italy, met with him the next day. Even Thatcher's manipulation of the electoral process backfired. When Sands died, his seat had to be filled in another by-election. Westminster passed special legislation so another prisoner candidate could not be nominated. On August 20th, Irish National Liberation Army hunger striker Mickey Devine was the tenth and last to die and Owen Carron, "a proxy prisoner," was elected MP for Fermanagh–South Tyrone. Carron actually received more votes than Bobby Sands. It was an indication of how alienated the Nationalist community had become and the power of elections.

16

"Never, that's what I say to you—Never"

SEPTEMBER 1981–OCTOBER 1986

THE MARCHES, RALLIES, and electoral victories of the hunger strike period brought a huge number of new recruits to the IRA and Sinn Féin from all over Ireland. The new recruits, inspired by northern events, tended to look north for leadership—to Gerry Adams, Danny Morrison, MP Owen Carron, and the like. They were the people who represented the prisoners in the media, and they became identified as the leaders of a new phase of the Republican struggle. This emboldened the young northerners. At an Ard Chomhairle meeting, Francie Molloy of Tyrone suggested that Owen Carron take his seat at Westminster. The suggestion was quickly pushed aside, but it was incredible that Molloy would make it.

For the year of the hunger strike, from October 1980 to October 1981, the tension that existed in Sinn Féin was put on hold. It came back with a vengeance, splitting the Ard Chomhairle into camps—Gerry Adams and company versus Ruairí Ó Brádaigh and company. The younger people tended to vote as a bloc and it was evident that they discussed issues among themselves before meetings. On occasion, they would implement decisions without consulting Ó Brádaigh. When they were confronted, they impugned the motives of the other camp. A standard reply to dissent was that it "was not helpful to the Movement." The trouble in Sinn Féin was made public at the 1981 Ard Fheis, soon after the hunger strike ended. In 1980, the young northerners had pushed through a motion forbidding participation in local elections in the north, which were scheduled for May 1981. Ó Brádaigh, among others, objected and lost the argument. The decision was a major blunder. Bobby Sands went on hunger strike in March, was elected to Westminster in April, and died in early May. It was perfect timing to contest the election and take advantage of the hunger strike mobilization. But there was no time to reverse the decision and anti–H-Block candidates from other organizations, including the Irish Independence Party and the Irish Republican Socialist Party, won twenty-five seats on local political bodies. Having been burned by their anti-electoral zeal of the year before, the young northerners put forward a motion in 1981 that encouraged contesting *any* election. Ó Brádaigh again found himself in the opposition, but from the other direction. The motion went too far and he was very concerned with the volatility of the situation. Again, the vote went against him.

Making matters worse, Gerry Adams proposed, and Danny Morrison seconded, a motion that the federal aspect of the Éire Nua policy be dropped. Morrison referred to the policy as a "sop to Loyalists" and argued that "you will have as much trouble getting the loyalists to accept a nine-county parliament as you will in getting them to accept a united Ireland, so why stop short?" He wanted a unitary state which would be dominated by Nationalists. Journalist Ed Moloney would later comment that it was "the ultimate sectarian analysis." Morrison also asked the rhetorical question for which he is best known, "Who here really believes we can win the war with the ballot box? But will anyone here object if, with a ballot paper in one hand and an armalite [rifle] in the other, we take power in Ireland?" The statement became synonymous with the desire to combine the IRA's revolutionary armed struggle with Sinn Féin's revolutionary politics. Ó Brádaigh, as he had after Jimmy Drumm's speech in 1977, wondered what he had been doing since 1970 if not trying to combine revolutionary armed struggle with revolutionary politics. He defended federalism as best he could. Arguing that no alternative policy had been offered, he countered Morrison with "Don't swop a policy for a slogan." A majority of the delegates supported Adams and Morrison, but not the two-thirds required to change the Constitution, where the word "federal" remained. It was still a significant setback and it created an awkward situation where a majority of Ard Fheis delegates opposed a central tenet in Sinn Féin's Constitution.

In February, Ó Brádaigh lost another debate. Garrett FitzGerald, hoping to strengthen his government, called an election. Ó Brádaigh believed it would be about basics, like the economy, and argued that Sinn Féin should pass. Only one other Ard Chomhairle member, Charlie McGlade, agreed with him. Dáithí O'Connell, who generally took the same position as Ó Brádaigh, favored contesting the election. So did Cathleen Knowles, who also tended to agree with them. The Ard Chomhairle voted to contest seven constituencies in which anti–H-Block candidates had done well in 1981. Adding to Ó Brádaigh's concern, Gerry Adams missed the meeting where this decision was taken. He suspected that Adams was making sure he would not be implicated if contesting the election was a mistake. He wanted to stop Sinn Féin's participation in the election and wondered if Adams's failure to attend the meeting indicated that others were also opposed. He immediately sought a meeting with Adams. The vote took place on a Saturday afternoon. The next Monday evening, Joe Cahill picked him up and drove to a meeting with Adams, Martin McGuinness, and one other person. McGuinness did the talking. The Ard Chomhairle had made a decision and that was it, he told Ó Brádaigh. Ó Brádaigh pointed out that it was local organizations that would implement the decision. The convention in Cavan-Monaghan was that night. Dáithí O'Connell would preside. Ó Brádaigh said he could ring the hotel and have O'Connell abort the selection of a candidate. He was also willing to attend the upcoming convention in Dundalk and have that selection process aborted. Others would follow suit and that would end it. He told McGuinness that unless there was a united front he would bring the Ard Chomhairle's decision to nothing. McGuinness, upset, immediately attacked him with, "Who do you think you are, refusing to represent the people? Do you think you are back in 1922, or what?" Ó Brádaigh was shocked, as much by the comment about 1922 as by the attack. The comment was, for him, counter to the basics of Republicanism and the principled stand against the Treaty and its outcomes from 1922. He replied, "This is Free State talk." No one else said anything and their silence spoke volumes; they supported McGuinness and possibly the recognition of Leinster House. The only thing positive about the encounter, from Ó Brádaigh's perspective, was that he had made it clear he believed it was a mistake to participate in an inevitable defeat for Sinn Féin.

The most revealing piece of the evening was yet to come. On the way home from the meeting he told Cahill that he was shocked and outraged. Later, because of "vibes" coming from Adams and McGuinness, he knew that Cahill had repeated his remarks.

As it turned out, he was correct about the election. Without a hunger strike to mobilize voters and because it was banned from radio and television, Sinn Féin fared poorly; its vote fell to less than half of what it had been the year before and no one was elected. But the losses at the ballot box did not vindicate Ó Brádaigh. Many of the new recruits argued that Sinn Féin had not fully participated in the election and used the loss to fuel their call for additional electoral interventions.

No party did exceptionally well and the result was a minority government in Dublin, led by Charles Haughey of Fianna Fáil. Like the FitzGerald coalition government that it replaced, the Haughey government was destined to be short lived. Ironically, Haughey gave Ruairí Ó Brádaigh one of the few moments in his life when he was proud of the action of an Irish government. The Falklands Islands, off the coast of Argentina, were controlled by Britain but also claimed by Argentina. In the spring of 1982, Argentina seized the islands. Margaret Thatcher demanded that they withdraw, mobilized the British navy, and assembled an invasion force. The United Nations tried to resolve the situation peacefully, but a task force of the British navy sailed and war broke out. The British sank the Argentine cruiser *General Belgrano,* with a loss of more than 300 lives. Haughey's government was strident in its criticism of the British. After the *Belgrano* was sunk, Ireland's ambassador to the United Nations referred to the British as the "aggressor" and called for a Security Council meeting. The British put the Security Council on hold, but Irish criticism of British intentions was well received in Europe. When Ó Brádaigh toured Italy, he was pleased by the number of Italians and activists from Latin America who supported Haughey. The war soured Anglo-Irish relations, and Thatcher did not meet with Haughey during this period in office. Even after Garret FitzGerald and a Fine Gael–Labour coalition returned to power in November 1982, Thatcher did not meet with FitzGerald until March 1983. In the meantime, her government tried to find an internal solution to the Northern Ireland problem.

James Prior, Humphrey Atkins's successor as secretary of state for Northern Ireland, tried, like his predecessors William Whitelaw and Merlyn Rees, to establish a Northern Ireland assembly at Stormont that would have cross-community support. Unlike 1973 and 1975, Sinn Féin contested the election as abstentionists. Ó Brádaigh had wanted to contest the 1973 election but was in prison at the time. Máire Drumm and Séamus Twomey kept the party out of that contest. Ó Brádaigh supported contesting the 1982 assembly election and in announcing the decision stated that they were "giving the nationalist people a Republican voice and alternative." He also crossed the border and helped with the campaign. There was a strong belief among the Sinn Féin leadership that in a northern setting they could repeat the success of 1981. Certainly it would help that one of their candidates, Owen Carron, was an MP at Westminster, albeit an abstentionist MP. The SDLP, concerned that it was being outflanked by Sinn Féin and very aware that many northern Nationalists were still upset over how the hunger strike had been handled, announced they would contest the election as abstentionists. It was an interesting twist caused by Sinn Féin's electoral intervention.

Just before the election in October 1982, Gerry Adams tried to push Ruairí Ó Brádaigh out of the Sinn Féin presidency. Adams, a Sinn Féin vice president and (reportedly) a member of the Army Council, confronted Ó Brádaigh and told him that his continued support for federalism was the source of scandal—that the IRA, the prisoners, and a majority of the delegates at the previous Ard Fheis did not support the policy, yet he persisted in promoting it. It had to stop. Adams demanded that he denounce federalism at the upcoming Ard Fheis. He assumed that Ó Brádaigh, who had accepted the *An Phoblacht/Republican News* merger and several Ard Chomhairle decisions, would acquiesce. Ó Brádaigh, who had been willing to accept inevitable change, drew the line at being told to denounce a policy that he still supported. He told Adams that he would lose all credibility if he suddenly denounced federalism. Adams then revealed his plan. Ó Brádaigh would denounce federalism and step down, becoming a Sinn Féin vice president. This would provide continuity at the leadership level, cushion the blow to his ego, and remove him from being the point person on policy. Adams, of course, was the heir apparent. Ó Brádaigh had dealt with any number of strong personalities, from Paddy McLogan to Séamus Costello to Seán Mac Stiofáin, and he was not about to be cowed by Adams. To Adams's chagrin, he replied that without federalism he was not interested in any leadership position. He informed him that when he met with Unionists and Loyalists he told them that he believed so strongly in the policy that he would resign as president if Sinn Féin dropped it. It was not a false promise. He said, "No way. If you want a new song, you get a new singer." And he went home to Roscommon.

Ó Brádaigh's reaction put Adams in a difficult situation. Ó Brádaigh was widely respected in many quarters, the assembly election was under way, and an Ard Fheis would follow the election. If the party suddenly lost its president because of Adams, it might affect the election, lead to an uproar at the Ard Fheis, and reflect poorly on him. Adams arranged for emissaries to try to persuade Ó Brádaigh to go along with the plan. The first was John Joe McGirl, a one-time supporter of federalism who had been close to Ó Brádaigh for years. McGirl had officiated at the first Republican commemoration Ó Brádaigh attended as an adult in the spring of 1950. But McGirl was also very close with the young northerners. As the Leitrim commanding officer, he often helped them move people and equipment across the Leitrim-Fermanagh border. He had also been interned in Long Kesh with several of them, including Gerry Adams—he had been in Long Kesh when the prisoners set fire to their huts in protest in 1974. McGirl saw the situation in terms of personalities, Ó Brádaigh versus Adams. There was room enough for both of them, and he encouraged Ó Brádaigh to become a vice president, but Ó Brádaigh refused. Séamus Twomey also visited. Twomey, who had recently been released from Port Laoise, was IRA director of security. He suggested that the issue would pass, that although Adams's stature was rising, the day would come for him and his ilk. Ó Brádaigh repeated, "You want a new song, you better get a new singer." Twomey explained that Adams was in a bad position, that having issued an ultimatum he could not back down. Ó Brádaigh asked why *he* should back down and added that Adams should have considered the potential consequences of his behavior. One person who was not sent to visit him was Joe Cahill. After the meeting with McGuinness and Adams, their relationship was strained. Ó Brádaigh says, "He wouldn't need to visit me."

In the face of Ó Brádaigh's steadfast refusal to yield, Adams backed down. An accommodation was reached whereby Ó Brádaigh would return as president for another year and Adams and company agreed to coordinate their activities with his. Then came the assembly election, which was another breakthrough for Sinn Féin. Unionists won a majority of the seventy-eight seats, but Sinn Féin stole the election. Five Sinn Féin candidates—Gerry Adams, Danny Morrison, Martin McGuinness, Owen Carron, and Jim McAllister—were elected, and the party received 64,000 votes—more than 10 percent of the total. It demonstrated that the movement did in fact represent a significant section of the northern community. It also confirmed for the young northerners that they needed to be involved in elections. The practical benefits were clear. The SDLP won fourteen seats and because they, like Sinn Féin, refused to enter the assembly, it was effectively scuttled.

Sinn Féiners were enthused by the election and, in Ó Brádaigh's opinion, Adams and company reneged on their agreement. At the Ard Fheis, Adams and Morrison were better prepared than the year before and federalism was successfully deleted from the Constitution. With it went much of Ó Brádaigh's support. He had already lost Charlie McGlade, an Ard Chomhairle member since the caretaker executive days, who had passed away in September at the age of 72. When federalism was voted out, Richard Behal, Joe O'Neill, Des Long, Tom Ó Sullivan, and other supporters of the policy refused to go forward for re-election to the Ard Chomhairle. Ó Brádaigh, Dáithí O'Connell, Cathleen Knowles, and Mick O'Connell from Clare were left, it seemed, "like rocks when the tide has gone out."

They were subjected to personal attacks. The younger people, clad in blue jeans and dressed informally, commented that Ó Brádaigh and

O'Connell, who wore ties, sports coats, and the occasional suit, but never blue jeans, were middle-aged, middle-class, and out of touch. Nasty rumors were circulated. One had Dáithí O'Connell making a nice living off of the movement; it was not true. Another had Ruairí Ó Brádaigh missing Máire Drumm's funeral because he was afraid to go north; he had missed the funeral because of an unreliable driver and had been north as recently as the 1982 assembly campaign. Christine Elias was an Ó Brádaigh-O'Connell supporter and was closely identified with federalism through a column she wrote in *An Phoblacht* titled "Know Your Éire Nua." A rumor circulated that she was a British agent. She was not, but she was taken into IRA custody, interrogated, and expelled from Sinn Féin.

Ó Brádaigh's input was ignored. Mick Timothy, editor of *An Phoblacht/Republican News,* chaired an Ard Chomhairle subcommittee charged with preparing a report on Sinn Féin's electoral strategy in the Twenty-Six Counties. Ó Brádaigh's contribution was titled "The Effects on the Developing of Such a Strategy of Sinn Féin's Attitudes to, for Example, Armed Struggle, Abstentionism, Social Policy, etc." The key to his argument was this:

> A revolutionary movement either succeeds or fails badly. There is hardly an in-between position. So many things are put at risk that often failure or the possibility of failure can inveigle some participants into reformism in order to "save something from the collapse," as it is put.

He argued that in between was worse than failure, for reform meant being "sucked into and [becoming] part of the colonial or neo-colonial system." Over three single-spaced pages he repeated what he had been saying for years, and what Mick Timothy and the others did not want to hear.

> Abstention from taking part in enemy parliaments has a definite role in maintaining Sinn Féin's nonconformism with regard to such institutions and the system they bolster up and perpetuate. The lesson Sinn Féin seeks to drive home is that switching the personnel operating such institutions or even replacing them with well-meaning and politically educated Republican personnel may ameliorate conditions from time to time but will not and cannot—because of the nature of these institutions—bring about the fundamental changes needed to put the Irish people in control of their own affairs. A big and successful heave to topple and replace is what is needed rather than tinkering with the existing system.

In direct contrast to the direction the movement was headed, he continued, "It is useless for Sinn Féin to have TDs until they can become abstentionists with political clout, that is, until they can be successful on a very big scale" and "electoral interventions can be partially successful in the short-term but highly dangerous for the movement engaging in them." Short of a revolutionary situation, he argued, where large numbers of people rejected the state and embraced revolution, Sinn Féin should not participate in parliamentary elections in the Twenty-Six Counties. Otherwise, "slow growth" would result in revolutionaries who were diverted into reform. Electoral defeat and disillusionment were "preferable to and easier overcome in the long-run than the political surrender which is the proper description for being diverted into reformism."

The perspective is similar to that of Frances Fox Piven and Richard Cloward in *Poor People's Movements: Why They Succeed, How They Fail.* Piven and Cloward's analysis reveals that when weaker parties organize and engage in protest, the benefits they gain stem from disruption of the political process. Government elites respond to this disruption differently depending upon the situation and the parties involved. In some instances, the response is repression and the destruction of protest. If the disruption is especially serious and repression is not an option, another response is to make concessions. The key point is that short of a revolutionary situation, protesters may force a government to respond but they cannot dictate the nature of the response. Especially important is that fact that concessions are "measures to reintegrate the movement into normal political channels and to absorb its leaders into stable institutional roles." A classic example is the SDLP, which supported the anti-internment rent and rates strike of 1971 and promised to never enter a Stormont-like assembly as long as internment was in effect. In 1974, when it was granted seats on the Northern Ireland Executive, the party entered the Northern Ireland Assembly at Stormont and endorsed the collection of overdue rents and rates. A concession brought them into the system, even though internment continued. Ó Brádaigh wanted revolution, not reform. He gave his report to Mick Timothy. Timothy asked for a rewrite. Ó Brádaigh, who was preparing for a trip to Canada, refused. At the very least, he looked forward to getting away from the situation.

In the spring of 1983, he flew from Dublin to Montreal via Paris—there were no direct flights and he could not go through the United States. Although it began slowly, it would be one of his most successful international trips. When he arrived at Mirabel Airport, he was stopped by customs officials. Britain's royal family was touring the Canadian west coast in the royal yacht HMS *Britannia*. The Canadians would not allow him in until she cleared their territory; tired from the trip, he spent an extra five hours in a holding room. Once he got past customs, his first stop was Newfoundland and an engagement organized by Irish-Canadians. In Nova Scotia, he lunched with Bishop Austin Burke of Yarmouth and leaders of the Micmac Indians of Eastern Canada. He and Alberto Gallegas of the Sandinista government were honored at a reception organized by Oxfam Canada. He spent St. Patrick's Day in Quebec City, where he met with Irish activists and Quebecois separatists who sought an independent French-speaking republic. He was in Toronto for most of Holy Week, flew to Vancouver for engagements on Holy Saturday evening and Easter Sunday morning, and then flew back to Toronto for a commemoration that evening.

In Montreal, he was amazed to find people with French Christian names and Irish surnames, like Jean-Luc O'Brien. They were the descendants of children whose parents had died of cholera on famine ships in 1847; arriving at Grosse Ile as orphans, they were taken in by French-Canadian families. Montreal was also interesting because in the midst of North America, there were literally millions of people who spoke only French and were proud of it—including some of the people with Irish surnames. At one function, he ran into a Leitrim native who asked a question in Irish. Ó Brádaigh translated it from Irish to English. A translator then put it into French. Ó Brádaigh then answered the question in Irish and translated that to English. The translator put that into French, and the crowd clapped in approval. It was one of several high points in the six-week trip that ended where it began, at Mirabel Airport. As he had started the trip, he ended it—prior to boarding the plane he was taken into custody by two members of the Royal Canadian Mounted Police. They wanted to speak to him about the Quebecois separatists. Other than saying that they were nice people who were friendly to him, he offered no information. The Mounties, aware that there was a planeload of people waiting to take off, let him go.

Trouble in the movement awaited him. In a Westminster election in June 1983, Margaret Thatcher remained the British prime minister and Gerry Adams solidified his position as Sinn Féin's future. Adams was elected MP for West Belfast. It was a stunning outcome, for he unseated Gerry Fitt, West Belfast's MP since 1966. Just as dramatic, Sinn Féin received 102,000 votes, 13.4 percent of the total. Owen Carron lost his seat, but Danny Morrison almost won in Mid Ulster. About two weeks after the election, Adams was the keynote speaker at the Wolfe Tone Commemoration at Bodenstown. His oration suggested that he was considering what many considered heresy. He argued that Republicans have "to realise that ordinary people, understandably enough, accept Free State institutions as legitimate. To ignore this reality is to blinker republican politics, to undermine the development of our struggle and is to have a basic flaw in our analysis." Ó Brádaigh believed that Adams's remarks signaled acceptance of the 26-county state, but there was not much he could do about it. The subcommittee on electoral strategy in the Twenty-Six Counties had largely ignored his effort. In an attempt to get his point across, he distributed copies of his report to Mick Timothy's committee on electoral strategy at an Ard Chomhairle meeting. When the meeting ended, the Adams crowd left their copies on their chairs. Things were getting so bad that he arranged another trip to Canada in late July and early August, where he lobbied at the World Council of Churches meeting in Vancouver.

By the fall of 1983, Danny Morrison was publicly upstaging him. Morrison's "ballot box and armalite" speech confirmed for many people that Sinn Féin and the IRA were one and the same. The phrase played well among people who argued that armed struggle and electoral politics could be merged. It also undermined a decade's worth of work by people like Ó Brádaigh, who argued that the IRA and Sinn Féin were distinct organizations. At a press conference in Dublin, a journalist asked if he approved of the IRA campaign. Even when pressed, he gave his standard reply that Sinn Féin upheld the right of Irish people to engage in armed struggle, but that was it. Morrison interrupted, said he would answer the question, and then said that he approved of the IRA's campaign. In addition to headaches like this, Ó Brádaigh was struck by an ailment of middle age—kidney stones. They were not serious, but he was briefly hospitalized. Journalists, aware of the tension among the leadership, started speculating that he would step down as president of Sinn Féin, to be replaced by Gerry Adams. Ó Brádaigh suspected that the reports were leaked deliberately.

The Ard Fheis was approaching and the journalists were correct; Ó Brádaigh would not seek re-election as Sinn Féin president. At the last minute, Dáithí O'Connell and Cathleen Knowles added their own wrinkle. O'Connell, who knew of Ó Brádaigh's decision, was planning to step down as a Sinn Féin vice president. O'Connell's health was never great; when he was shot in 1959 he had lost his spleen and his 47-day hunger strike in 1977 had taken a toll. Two days before the Ard Fheis he was ill, and he asked to see Cathleen Knowles. Ó Brádaigh was not going to attend the Ard Chomhairle meeting the next day. O'Connell knew that Knowles would, and he gave her a letter. As general secretary, it was her responsibility to report on correspondence received. The next afternoon, the Ard Chomhairle smoothly went through its agenda until they reached the item of correspondence. Knowles calmly announced that she had a letter from Dáithí O'Connell, produced it, and read, "A Chairde [friends], I wish to confirm that I will not be standing for election to the officer-board or the Ard Chomhairle at this year's Ard Fheis." He offered several reasons for his decision, including the dropping of federalism and his be-lief that "the office of Vice-President was regarded by some as one of a 'titular' nature." He was not "a titular-head, figure-head, or yes-man," and was therefore returning to the rank and file. Adams referred to the devel-opment as a bombshell and asked, "Are there any more people who feel this way?" Knowles replied, "Yes, I am not going forward as General Sec-retary." When asked to explain herself, she replied, "To give you a reason would not be helpful to the Movement." The moment passed and no one else spoke. The group then decided that Phil Flynn, from County Louth, would be their nominee to succeed O'Connell.

On Saturday, November 12th, the Ard Fheis opened amid reports that Ó Brádaigh, O'Connell, and Knowles would resign from the leader-ship, but there was no public announcement from anyone. It was not until Sunday afternoon that Ó Brádaigh stood up and went to the podium to deliver his presidential address. He began by announcing that he would not seek re-election as president. The key issue, he told the assembly, was federalism:

> My departure from the office of President of Sinn Féin became inevitable with the defeat in 1981 by a simple majority of the Éire Nua policy of a new Four-Province Federal Ireland with maximum decentralisation of power and decision-making within a Democratic Socialist Republic. In 1982, by a two-thirds majority, all references to that policy were deleted from the Con-stitution of Sinn Féin. As one who has been closely and personally identified with that policy for ten years, my position as President in the face of a re-peated defeat on a major policy has become untenable.

He had been the voice of a revolutionary movement for fourteen years, leading Sinn Féin through internment, Bloody Sunday, the 1975 truce, and the hunger strikes. With good reason, he continued, "I am very proud of two things: firstly, I regard the period 1969–83 as having marked a high point on the graph of the Irish people's struggle for freedom, ranking alongside the 1798 Rising, the Land War of 1879–82 and the 1916–23 period; secondly, during my 14 years as head of Sinn Féin there were no splits or splinters—long may it remain so, as it will, provided we stick to basic principles." The crowd erupted in cheers, but some knew that it was a warning. The most basic of principles was abstentionism; as long as the new leadership remained abstentionists, they would not have any problems from Ó Brádaigh.

In his presidential address, he focused on the dangers of constitutional politics. Constitutional politicians could not be trusted, he warned. Sinn Féin's victory in 1918 was followed by "the terror of the Black and Tans, the partition of the country and the arming of the forces of reaction North and South to defeat the Irish Republican revolution." He had been elected a Sinn Féin TD, "but the reaction of the new Fianna Fáil government returned in the spring of 1957 was to intern the Sinn Féin public representatives without charge or trial in the Curragh Concentration Camp." When Bobby Sands was elected, the "Thatcher 'democrats' . . . simply change[d] the rules." As was his custom, he ended on a positive note. "Meanwhile, Sinn Féin continues under new leadership. On your behalf I welcome them to their positions and wish them well. I wish all of you a progressive and successful future."

Adams, unopposed, was then elected president of Sinn Féin. By all accounts, he had waited for the moment for years. In his first presidential address, he was humble, reassuring, and gracious. He had not sought the office, he told the delegates: "[I]t will come as no surprise to many of you to learn that I was extremely reluctant to let my name go forward." It was in spite of a heavy workload and his belief that the president should come from the Twenty-Six Counties that he had accepted the position. He also denied speculation that he would lead the party into Leinster House: "On the question of Leinster House: we are an abstentionist party; it is not my intention to advocate a change in this situation." But he left himself an opening: "The retention or rejection of this policy, as with all others, lies with the Ard Fheis and I am happy to abide by party policy on this issue, as on any issue." Of Ó Brádaigh he said, it was a "personal honor to be chosen to fill a position which was administered for so long by Ruairí Ó Brádaigh." And on behalf of the Ard Fheis, he extended his appreciation to Ó Brádaigh, Dáithí O'Connell, and Cathleen Knowles for all that they had done. The rest of his remarks, during which he complained about the sorry state of the Irish economy and the perfidy of the London and Dublin governments, could have been written by Ó Brádaigh.

An article in *An Phoblacht/Republican News* described it as a "harmonious change in leadership," which it was, given the tension in the movement since the late 1970s. Ó Brádaigh was not bitter, and he offered his services if they needed a speaker or some other help. He reported back to his *cumann* in Roscommon and looked forward to being active at the local level. It was too late to teach during the 1983–1984 school year, but he planned to apply for his old job. If all went well, he would join Patsy, who was teaching part-time, on the staff of Roscommon Vocational Technical School the next fall.

It was his most relaxed Christmas since 1968. The younger children, Eithne and Colm, still lived at home, and the older children—Maitiú, who had graduated from college and was teaching Irish in Galway, and Ruairí Óg, Conchúr, and Deirdre, who were attending University College Galway—were home for the holidays. The peaceful family time did not last long. Early in January 1984, Ruairí, Patsy, two of the children, and two friends drove to Dublin for an Irish-language course for children. They were returning home when an approaching car pulled out to pass a line of traffic. Ruairí thought the car would cross his lane and end up in a ditch. Instead, it straightened out and before he could do anything it plowed head-on into the Ó Brádaighs. The other driver, who was in a smaller car, was killed at the scene. Ruairí's chest was smashed by his steering wheel, breaking several ribs. The car's motor was driven back, crushing his right foot. Patsy's neck was broken, but her seatbelt kept her in the car and probably saved her life. The children suffered assorted broken ankles, ribs, and teeth. Ambulances transported parents and children to St. James's Hospital in Dublin.

In Dublin, Patsy's condition was stabilized and her neck was put in a brace. Initially, the doctors worried that Ruairí's chest injuries would lead to pneumonia. Once that threat passed, they reconstructed his ankle as best they could. The older children, assorted family members, and friends looked after the younger children in Roscommon while Ruairí and Patsy slowly convalesced in Dublin. Deirdre and Dáithí O'Connell were regular visitors. John Joe McGirl lived in faraway Leitrim, but his daughter, who was living in Dublin, visited regularly. He remembers Martin McGuinness arriving with a big bundle of flowers. Ruairí asked him to take them down to Patsy. McGuinness, who was a busy man and far from Derry, stayed and visited. Noteworthy by their absence were the Belfast crowd; he has no recollection of Adams, Morrison, or Cahill visiting him in the hospital.

If anything good came of the accident, it was that Ruairí and Patsy, who were already close, recovered together. Back in Roscommon, they were miserable; it was a long slow recovery. Ruairí remembers commenting to Patsy that sympathy is like justice: "[T]here just isn't enough to go around." Bored, Patsy found a hobby in winemaking. She then commented that Ruairí, still a teetotaler, was forcing her to drink alone. He took off his Pioneer Badge and started drinking an occasional glass of wine with a meal. Patsy wore a neck brace into the summer and was never able to return to work. Ruairí spent much of his time with his leg propped up in a chair to help blood circulate through his ankle. In March, he was unable to attend a dinner reception in his and Dáithí O'Connell's honor given by County Louth Republicans; Maitiú attended in his place. He was on crutches when Ronald Reagan visited Ireland and could not attend protests against the visit and against Reagan's support for the Contras in Nicaragua, but his children did. University College Galway conferred an honorary degree on Reagan; Maitiú, Ruairí Óg, and Conchúr represented the Ó Brádaighs at a demonstration where people burned their University College Galway degrees in protest.

In the summer of 1984, he was upgraded to a cane and, following doctor's orders, started walking regularly. He reminded himself of his father. He developed regular routes—into the town, to the train station, and so forth—but progress was slow. He was unable to return to teaching that fall, but he did become active in Roscommon Sinn Féin. He was elected secretary of Roscommon Comhairle Ceantair, and he attended the 1984 Ard Fheis as a delegate. He arrived a little late, made his way into the Mansion House, and took a seat. He was sitting with his injured ankle resting on a chair when Phil Flynn noted his presence. The delegates gave him a standing ovation.

Through the winter, he helped out around the house and was active in Roscommon Sinn Féin. His condition continued to improve enough that he applied for reinstatement to his teaching job. Again there was trouble with a minister for education. His application was accepted by the Roscommon Vocational Educational Committee and forwarded to the minister's office for approval. The office rejected it. The statute of limitations for a leave of absence was seven years; he had been on leave for fourteen years. He could apply for a job, but his old job no longer existed. Because there was a glut of teachers, he really had no chance of finding a regular job. The Roscommon Vocational Educational Committee came through again and offered him a part-time teaching position. In the fall of 1985, for the first time since 1971, he was back in a classroom. By this point, major changes were brewing in the Republican Movement that would lead to another split.

Traditionally, the IRA leads and Sinn Féin follows, even if they are distinct organizations. As Sinn Féin developed its electoral profile, some IRA leaders became concerned that the political struggle would at some point supersede the armed struggle. In this, they were sympathetic to

Ó Brádaigh. In 1985 there was an attempt to oust Gerry Adams from the IRA leadership. Ivor Bell, who at one time was very close to Adams, had been released from prison and was a member of the IRA Executive. Bell pushed for a convention and started to organize against Adams. The Army Council can put a convention on hold, but only for security reasons. The Army Council stalled and Adams outmaneuvered Bell—he was charged with insubordination and dismissed from the IRA.

While Adams was suppressing IRA dissenters, Sinn Féin was pursuing its electoral strategy with even more success. In May 1985, for the first time since the 1920s, Sinn Féin contested local elections in Northern Ireland. Fifty-nine Sinn Féin councilors were elected, including seven in Belfast (compared to six for the SDLP). Even better, when the elected councilors took their seats, Unionists refused to sit with them; seventeen of twenty-six Northern Irish councils were adjourned.

In November 1985, the London and Dublin governments signed the Anglo-Irish Agreement, which gave the Dublin government a role in Northern Irish affairs. It was an attempt to undercut support for Sinn Féin, but Unionists were outraged. Their Westminster MPs, who had not been consulted on the agreement, resigned en masse, forcing by-elections. It was more evidence that Sinn Féin's political development was making Northern Ireland unstable.

The same could not be said of Sinn Féin's development in the south. In the June 1985 local elections, the party did slightly better than it had in 1979, electing thirty-nine councilors. There were some notable successes, including the election of Caoimhghin Ó Caoláin to the Monaghan County Council (he topped the poll) and the election of Christy Burke to the Dublin City Council, but compared to the north it was disappointing. Ever since Jimmy Drumm's speech at Bodenstown in 1977, Gerry Adams and Danny Morrison had argued that the key to success lay in political development in the south. The problem, they believed, was Sinn Féin's abstentionist attitude toward Leinster House.

In October 1985, at the Ard Fheis, the Sinn Féin leadership confronted the policy directly. On the agenda was a motion from the Dublin Comhairle Limistéir (Dublin Executive) that abstentionism "be viewed as a tactic and not as a principle." Danny Morrison, who was clearly associated with Sinn Féin's electoral strategy, addressed the delegates just prior to the debate. He asked that they "debate freely and honestly," but he also reminded them that the IRA supported Sinn Féin's electoral strategy and, sounding like Cathal Goulding in the late 1960s, he asked that people avoid "parading the republican dead before this Ard Fheis." For the abstentionists, it was an insult. From 1922 to 1986, perhaps 100 IRA volunteers had been executed by the Dublin government or shot dead by Dublin's special police. An execution in 1922 was ancient history to someone who had joined the movement in 1969, let alone 1981. But people like Tom Maguire of the Second Dáil Éireann were still around; his brother, Seán Maguire, had been executed by the Free State in 1923. Ruairí Ó Brádaigh had childhood memories of his father attending the funerals of volunteers who had died on hunger strike. Many other middle-aged Republicans had similar memories. Aside from any emotional attachment, these Republican dead were evidence that constitutional politics were corrupt.

The account of the debate in *An Phoblacht/Republican News* notes that the youngest participant was Ruairí and Patsy's third son, Conchúr Ó Brádaigh. Conchúr was an infant when Cathal Goulding threatened Ruairí; fifteen years later, he was a member of Sinn Féin's UCG *cumann* and an abstentionist. He argued that every set of Republicans who entered Leinster House, including Goulding's crowd, ended up enmeshed in the system; thus, he said, "let's not fool ourselves that we are better than they [Officials] were, or Seán Mac Bride, or Fianna Fáil." He also asked, "How can we claim to be a revolutionary organization if we take part in the institutions of the state which we oppose?" His father had taught him well. Gerry Adams did not speak on the issue. In his place, Tom Hartley and Seán Crowe of Dublin argued that abstentionism was a tactic. Hartley pragmatically argued that there was a principle "riding above all principles and that is the principle of success." Crowe argued that those who were corrupted by Leinster House were weak, were people who in reality "were not republicans." By implication, true Republicans, like those leading the movement, were incorruptible. It was the same argument Goulding and others had made.

The motion was voted down, 181 opposed and 161 in favor. On the surface, the drift toward constitutionalism was thwarted. In retrospect, the debate was a test case that showed the leadership how far they were from a chance to enter Leinster House, which would require a two-thirds majority vote at an Ard Fheis. If the numbers were unchanged, there would be 342 delegates (representing 171 *cumainn*) at the next Ard Fheis. To change the party constitution, the leadership needed 221 votes (66 percent), which meant convincing 60 delegates to change their votes. That was unlikely, so throughout 1986, they resorted to extraparliamentary maneuvers. When possible, they forced the opposition out. For example, Des Long was Munster Sinn Féin's representative to the Ard Chomhairle. He argued at the Ard Fheis that there was a creeping constitutionalism in

Sinn Féin. Adams asked him to resign. When he refused, Adams dismissed him from the Ard Chomhairle. In addition one-person *cumainn* were created that existed only on paper and were guaranteed to vote as the leadership wished.

The crowning achievement of the new leadership was an IRA convention, which was held in September 1986. The convention, the IRA's first in sixteen years, was allegedly held in County Meath under the cover of an Irish-language conference. This is not correct; the convention did not meet in County Meath. The 1970 convention was organized by Ó Brádaigh's generation; the 1986 convention was organized and dominated by the young northerners. They put together a compelling argument for dropping abstention from Leinster House. That Parliament, which many northern IRA volunteers saw as a distant, irrelevant government, was separated from Stormont and Westminster. Adams, McGuinness, and their followers were willing to enter Leinster House but pledged to never enter a Stormont Assembly or Westminster. Sinn Féin's strategy was working in the north, they argued, so entering Stormont or Westminster was unnecessary. Leinster House was the problem. The abstentionists argued that the IRA ultimately would suffer if Sinn Féin became a constitutional party. The young northerners countered that there was no IRA campaign in the south to be compromised and pledged to take the IRA campaign to an even higher level. As proof their commitment, Martin McGuinness, who was widely perceived to be the militant complement of the more political Gerry Adams, was placed in charge of the IRA campaign. McGuinness's status as an elected (abstentionist) member of the northern Assembly only added to his image as an uncompromising hard-liner.

The supporters of abstentionism never had a chance. They were outnumbered, they faced a compelling argument, and their primary opponents were supported by hard-line IRA-men—Cahill, McGirl, and J. B. O'Hagan—with impeccable credentials. At the end of the convention, Cahill was probably elected to the Army Council. Séamus Twomey, who with Jimmy Drumm voted against the resolution, was elected to the new IRA Executive and took his seat, in effect endorsing what had happened.

As in 1969/1970, the abstentionists did not walk out of the convention. But the stage was set for a public confrontation and likely walkout at the next Sinn Féin Ard Fheis. In an attempt to prevent a split, Gerry Adams asked for a meeting with Ruairí Ó Brádaigh. Ó Brádaigh was and is willing to meet with anyone at any time. He met Adams and Brendan Hughes at a restaurant in Athlone. Hughes, who had just been released from Long Kesh, was respected as one of the IRA's top soldiers ever.

Ó Brádaigh was pleased to see him but also assumed that his presence was an indication of IRA support for Adams. While Hughes sat at a separate table, Adams briefed Ó Brádaigh on recent developments. The IRA, he revealed, was in the process of receiving significant arms shipments that would allow them to take the campaign to another level; the leadership was going to deliver on the promises made at the convention. Adams hoped that this would keep Ó Brádaigh in the fold. Instead, it upset him. Similar arguments had been made sixteen years before; armed struggle would be wedded with constitutional politics, resulting in victory. It had been a mistake in 1969/1970, and Ó Brádaigh thought it was a mistake in 1986. The Officials' cease-fire in 1972 and their condemnations of the Provisionals and the hunger strikers were proof for him that it was a mistake. Hughes was surprised at how angry the normally mild-mannered Ó Brádaigh became, and the meeting was a bust. Adams and Hughes left for another meeting with another prominent abstentionist, which also did not go well. Ó Brádaigh went back to Roscommon to await further developments.

The Sinn Féin Constitution requires that *cumainn* receive three months' warning if policy changes are to be addressed at an Ard Fheis. An Ard Fheis was scheduled for the end of October. Early in the month, and contrary to the Constitution, Sinn Féin *cumainn* were notified that there would be a motion to delete abstention from Leinster House from the party's Constitution. At about the same time, rumors were spreading that an IRA convention had dropped its ban on Leinster House. On October 14th, the IRA confirmed the rumors with a public statement. That same day, a war of words erupted in the press. In a letter to the *Irish News,* Jim Sullivan, who went with the Officials in 1969/1970, pointed out that at the 1970 Ard Fheis, Gerry Adams "sat in his seat without a word"—it was only later that Adams joined the Provisionals. He questioned Adams's integrity: "What is this move now but an attempt to pave the way for Gerry Adams to take his seat in Westminster? Is that what the last 17 years of violence and destruction have been all about? All the young lives lost and all the lifetimes wasted in jail—to put this man into Westminster?" In another letter, Bob Murray, who went with the Provisionals in 1969/1970, argued that 1986 was a repeat of 1969/1970 and asked, "What happened, Gerry? Where and when did it change?"

When the IRA statement was released, members of the press sought out Ó Brádaigh. He had kept quiet for about a month, but now he went on the offensive: "I would say to everyone opposed to the move to fight it tooth and nail." When asked to respond, Adams commented, "I do not want to be drawn into a public dispute." His press secretary was less restrained. In a reply to Bob Murray, Richie McAuley argued that the 1969/70 split had not been about abstentionism but about "whether or not there was a role for armed struggle—for the IRA." The abstentionists noted that McAuley, one of the young northerners, had not been involved in the decision-making process in 1969/1970. He had also conveniently forgotten an Official IRA military campaign from 1969 to 1972. It was an interesting interpretation of events and a harbinger of things to come. Adding to the sensation that 1986 was a replay of 1969/1970, Ó Brádaigh paid another visit to the County Mayo home of Tom Maguire. Maguire, by then 94 years old and still very sharp, issued another statement: "I do not recognise the legitimacy of any Army Council styling itself the Council of the Irish Republican Army which lends support to any person or organisation styling itself as Sinn Féin and prepared to enter the partition parliament of Leinster House."

Ó Brádaigh also attended a meeting of Connacht Sinn Féin in Strokestown, County Roscommon. There, as he had in 1970, he argued that the motion to enter Leinster House was unconstitutional. According to the Sinn Féin Constitution, persons who advocated entering Leinster House forfeited membership in the organization. To be procedurally correct, he argued, this policy had to be removed before any motion advocating entering Leinster House could be on the agenda. The point was lost on many people. Worse, he found himself debating the virtues of entering Leinster House with a former member of Official Sinn Féin. The individual had gone with the Officials in 1970, had become disillusioned by their cease-fire and their drift into exclusively constitutional politics, and had withdrawn from the organization. Caught up in the hunger strike mobilization, he had joined Provisional Sinn Féin. Now, in Strokestown, the individual was saying the exact same thing that he said in 1968, but to a new generation.

The Sinn Féin leadership pulled out all the stops. In some instances, they manipulated the decision-making process at the *cumann* level. Sinn Féin rules state that an individual must serve three months on probation before he or she is allowed to participate in decisions. When University College Dublin's *cumann* met to consider the motion to drop abstentionism and select its delegates to the Ard Fheis, it allowed three new members to participate. An "observer" from Belfast was present who reminded them that the IRA supported the resolution; by implication, a vote against the motion was a vote against the IRA. The *cumann* voted six to two in support of ending abstention from Leinster House. Some of the Sinn Féin leadership's machinations were petty. Seán Keenan, Derry's veteran Republican, had been voted honorary life president of Derry Sinn Féin. He was one of the most vocal critics of entering Leinster House, and in spite of more than forty years of service, he was not chosen as a delegate to the Ard Fheis. When he arrived at the Mansion House to observe the proceedings, he was denied entry. Tony Ruane, Sinn Féin's national treasurer for decades, honorary vice president for life, and another ardent abstentionist, was also refused admission.

Because the debate on abstentionism would be lengthy, the Ard Fheis opened on Friday night, October 31st. The delegates proceeded through the agenda that evening and through Saturday morning. At lunch on Saturday, the abstentionists were eating in a back room of the Mansion House when they received a message that the "leadership" wanted to meet with Ó Brádaigh, Joe O'Neill, Des Long, and one other person—anyone but Dáithí O'Connell. The interpretation was that the leadership feared the articulate O'Connell, who could counter any argument. Pat Ward attended in his place. Ward, who was from Donegal, had been the Fermanagh IRA's commanding officer in the early 1970s. Ó Brádaigh did not bring his cane, but Ward did. Ward had never recovered from his participation in hunger strikes in the 1970s.

The abstentionists met Gerry Adams, Martin McGuinness, John Joe McGirl, Mickey McKevitt, Kevin McKenna (who was reported to be the IRA chief of staff), and others in another of the Mansion House rooms. Adams, who did most of the talking, wanted to know if they were planning a walkout. They were, but they refused to answer the question. Ó Brádaigh spent most of the meeting with his head down and his fists clenched, trying to avoid a conflict. According to Joe O'Neill, Adams launched a fierce attack on Ó Brádaigh for making statements to the press and trying to organize opposition to the leadership. Ó Brádaigh, who believed he was defending the All-Ireland Republic, defended himself "very well" but refused to comment on his plans. In frustration, Pat Ward stood up and brought his cane down on a table with a loud crack. He was not the man he once was, he told them, but if he was, "I would deal with you traitors." Ó Brádaigh immediately remembered Tommy McDermott threatening Cathal Goulding in 1969. Frustrated himself, Des Long said, "If no one else walks out, I'm walking out if that's passed." Joe O'Neill confirmed that he would do the same. The time to rejoin the Ard Fheis was approaching when someone in the Adams group threatened trouble if they tried to form a rival army. The meeting ended on this sour note.

It was late in the afternoon when Gerry Adams rose to give his presidential address. In a lengthy speech, he said that "unity is strength" and argued that those who withdrew from Sinn Féin would "withdraw solidarity and support from the IRA and the armed struggle." He presented a lengthy analysis of Republican involvement in elections and argued that abstentionism was a tactic rather than a principle and that "republicans should not be dogmatic and inflexible on this question." He was adamant that, one way or the other, abstention from Leinster House was going to end: "You may not do this tomorrow but one thing is certain: as Sinn Féin continues to develop its understanding of the needs of this struggle, you are going to do it, sooner rather than later and your leadership is going to be back here year after year until it has convinced you of this necessity." It was a good speech, and it laid the ground for a coordinated assault on abstentionism led by Pat Doherty, John Joe McGirl, Joe Cahill, and Martin McGuinness.

On Sunday morning, Doherty, on behalf of the Ard Chomhairle, put forward Motion 162, which called for an end to abstention from Leinster House. Aware that Ó Brádaigh would argue that the debate was unconstitutional, he noted that Sinn Féin's Constitution allowed for change. Since it was written by Sinn Féiners "and not by God," Sinn Féiners could change it. He defended Sinn Féin's leadership, whom the abstentionists had publicly accused of selling out. "This is as principled a leadership as any previous leadership," he argued. "They were the people who after the disastrous 1975 Truce moved into middle and national leadership and started to pick up the pieces and push the Movement forward once again." Eleven years after the fact, the abstentionists—Ó Brádaigh and Dáithí O'Connell—were being smeared for the "disastrous" 1975 truce. It was a serious and unanticipated rewriting of history.

John Joe McGirl followed Doherty. He was the only member of the 1970 caretaker executive still on the Ard Chomhairle. His continued presence there assuaged the concerns of a number of people who believed he would never enter Leinster House. In 1985, he had voted that abstentionism was a principle. In 1986, he seconded Motion 162. His task was to explain how embracing abstentionism was right in 1970 but not in 1986. In doing so, he claimed that he had not changed: "My aim today is the same as it always was." What was different was the commitment of the IRA's leadership. In 1969, he claimed, the IRA leadership "had abandoned Irish freedom and the Irish struggle" before entering Leinster House. The current leadership, even after entering Leinster House, would never do that. Abstentionism had become a millstone; without it, the current leadership would lead the movement to victory. An editorial in the *Long-*

ford Leader commented, "The saddest thing about the Sinn Féin betrayal of principles was to see a man like John Joe McGirl row in along with the sellout even though he himself when once elected as a TD refused to take his seat in Dáil Éireann."

Joe Cahill was the only member of the first Provisional Army Council who supported the new leadership. His comments paralleled McGirl's. He too said he had not changed: "The dedication and commitment which brought me to the foot of the scaffold in 1942 is the same in my heart today as it was then, and will be until the day I draw my last breath." He too argued that in 1969 the leadership had sold out before entering Leinster House. He knew this because he was there: "And I make it public now, that on the 17th of August [1969] when, along with other people, a few of us had to leave Belfast and come down here in search of arms, John Joe McGirl was the man who gave me arms in Leitrim." The crowd erupted in cheers. Ó Brádaigh knew it was going to be a long day. Cahill had resigned from the IRA in 1965. He told the delegates that it had been a mistake and he urged the abstentionists to stay and fight their corner.

Most speakers supported Motion 162, and some of those who opposed the motion added that even if it passed, they would not walk out. Ó Brádaigh was next in line to speak when Alex Maskey, a Belfast city councilor, attacked him personally. Maskey, upset with comments Ó Brádaigh had made during an interview with the BBC, told the delegates that he no longer had any respect for the man. Ó Brádaigh ignored him. When Maskey finished, he made his way to the microphone, straightened his papers, and was about to start when he felt a tap on his shoulder. Turning, he saw Gerry Adams's smiling face and outstretched hand. The crowd cheered Adams's magnanimous gesture; Ó Brádaigh, suspecting that Adams was playing to journalists, shook the hand while turning away. He waited for the crowd to quiet down and said, alternating between Irish and English, "I shake hands with everyone and at every time, not just in front of the media."

Given the comments of McGirl and Cahill, Ó Brádaigh could have drawn on his own IRA credentials. He had been on the Army Council longer than anyone in the room and was one of very few people who had attended both IRA conventions in 1969 and the 1970 Sinn Féin Ard Fheis. He could have noted the use of his sister's living room to help organize the second IRA convention in 1969. He could have noted that the weapons McGirl gave Cahill had come from southern abstentionists like himself. He could have noted that Cahill had not attended either the first 1969 IRA convention or the 1970 Ard Fheis. Even though he was

Ruairí Ó Brádaigh addressing the 1986 Provisional Sinn Féin Ard Fheis with a copy of the party constitution in his hand. Behind him, from left: Tom Hartley (partially obscured), Pat Doherty (head down), Joe Cahill, and Gerry Adams. Pacemaker Press.

disappointed in McGirl and upset with Cahill, Ó Brádaigh did not want to attack anyone and believed that bringing the IRA into the discussion was inappropriate. He stuck to politics and delivered a brief, crisp argument in support of abstentionism. It was destined to fail.

With a copy of the Constitution in his hand, he charged that "the discussion is totally out of order if this constitution of Sinn Féin means anything." He referred to Gerry Adams's presidential address, where Adams had argued that the membership could disagree on fundamentals, and asked, "How in the name of heavens can we do that? If there are fundamentals there, we either accept them as in the constitution or we go another road and we disagree with them." Echoing his arguments in the 1960s, he asked "Where are our revolutionary socialists, how do they expect to build a democratic socialist republic out of Leinster House? How can serious social change come out of Leinster House? How can the fundamental change in property relations come out of Leinster House? No way can it do that." These are questions that remain unanswered. He reminded the delegates that only a few years previously the same leadership had denied that they had any intention of leading the party into

Leinster House. If the motion passed, it was the beginning of the end. They would end up in Stormont, in Westminster, and "ultimately in the degradation and shame of collaborating with the British, of handing our political prisoners over to them and running counter to what they originally set out to do." He closed with an impassioned appeal:

> A Chairde [friends], I put it to you this way: we have not been wrong for 65 years, we have not been wrong for all those 70 years—we have been right and we should continue to be right. . . . [I]n God's name, don't let it come about that tomorrow, the next day or the day after, that Haughey, FitzGerald, [Dick] Spring [the Tánaiste], and all in London and Belfast who oppose it so much, can come out and say, "Ah, it took 65 years but we have them at last," and those in Leinster House who have done everything, the firing squad, the prison cells, the internment camps, the hunger strike, the lot, and weren't able to break this movement, that they can come and say "at last we have them toeing the line. It took us 65 years but they have come in from the cold, they have come in from the wilderness and we have them now." Never, that's what I say to you—never."

A few of the delegates stood and applauded, but most just politely sat in their seats.

Martin McGuinness spoke late in the afternoon and was vicious. To shouts from his supporters, he vehemently defended the leadership:

> First of all, I would like to give a commitment on behalf of the leadership that we have absolutely no intention of going into Westminster or Stormont. . . . I reject the notion that entering Leinster House would mean an end to Sinn Féin's unapologetic support for the right of Irish people to oppose in arms the British forces of occupation. That, my friends, is a principle which a minority in this hall might doubt, but which I believe all our opponents clearly understand.

McGuinness attacked the "former leadership"—Ó Brádaigh and O'Connell, the most prominent abstentionists and the public face of the movement through the 1970s. He had a sterling reputation as a military leader, and he lectured the delegates:

> [W]hat you are witnessing here today is not a debate over one issue, but two: abstentionism and the leadership of the republican struggle. The issues should not be confused and those who are considering leaving along with members of the former leadership should consider carefully what I am about to say. The reality is that the former leadership of this Movement has never been able to come to terms with this leadership's criticism of the disgraceful attitude adopted by them during the disastrous 18-month ceasefire in the

mid-1970s. Instead of accepting the validity of our case, as others who have remained have done, they chose to withhold their whole-hearted support from the leadership which replaced them.

McGuinness was reinforcing Pat Doherty's revisionist history. The most blatant error in his speech was the fact that the truce only lasted eight months (February to September 1975). Less obvious, it was debatable that it was a "disaster." More important, Ó Brádaigh and O'Connell had not been the only ones involved. As he sat in the audience, Ó Brádaigh remembered that McGuinness had not complained about anything in 1975. O'Connell had never even met with the British representatives. Séamus Twomey had been chief of staff throughout the truce and actively supported it. O'Connell and Séamus Twomey were standing at the back of the hall. O'Connell slid over to him and suggested that he go up on stage and set the record straight. Twomey declined. He had voted against ending abstention from Leinster House at the IRA convention, but he now supported McGuinness. The vast majority of the delegates accepted McGuinness's statements as fact. McGuinness finished with "If you allow yourselves to be led out of this hall today, the only place you will be going is home. You will be walking away from the struggle. Don't go my friends. We will lead you to the Republic." He was given an enthusiastic standing ovation—by most of the delegates. The five-hour debate closed soon after McGuinness spoke, and the vote was taken.

Before the tally was announced, Gerry Adams made one last appeal that there not be a walkout if the motion passed. He was eloquent, "A walk-out only helps our enemies." Bowing to the inevitable, he asked that those who did walk out be treated with respect. He had not shaken hands with Ó Brádaigh for the sake of the media, he told the crowd, but to set an example. He was also sarcastic: "I can do no more. If I bend over backwards any further I'll go up my own arse." Adams finished and Seán McManus, the convention chairman, announced the result: 429 in favor of dropping abstentionism, 161 opposed. Almost 250 more delegates cast votes in 1986 than had in 1985. Adams had his two-thirds majority. For the second time in his career as a Republican, Ruairí Ó Brádaigh got up from his seat and walked out of a Sinn Féin Ard Fheis and into an uncertain political future. As in 1970, he was joined by Dáithí O'Connell, Des Long, Joe O'Neill, Frank Glynn, and others. Outside, he was stopped by journalists. Sidestepping them, he said, "Come out to the West County [Hotel] and you'll hear it all. We are not going to do it here."

17

"We are here and we are very much in business"

OCTOBER 1986–MAY 1998

By CAR, VAN, and bus, the walkouts made the half-hour trek to the West County Hotel in Dublin's suburbs. Ruairí Ó Brádaigh climbed into the back of Joe O'Neill's van and rode with a group of somber people, frustrated and upset that they had helped build one of the most powerful manifestations of Irish Republicanism only to have it suffer yet another split. By six o'clock in the evening, 130 or so people—"hard-liners," the BBC called them—were reassembled in a banquet room. Joining them were forty or so reporters.

Ó Brádaigh asked the press to leave "until we decide who we are and what we are." As he looked around the room, he saw the same people who had formed Provisional Sinn Féin: his brother Seán, Dáithí O'Connell, Des Long, Frank Glynn, Tommy O'Neill, Denis McInerney, and others—including Tony Ruane and Seán Keenan—who were welcome at this meeting. The only member of the caretaker executive of 1970 who was still involved in Republican politics and was not there was John Joe McGirl. An article in the *Sunday Times* described it as the "Night of the Golden Oldies." Frank Glynn suggested they demand a recount; with a swing of only eleven votes Adams would not have had a two-thirds majority. However, a break had been made and it was deemed best to proceed on a course that was inevitable. Because they were experienced in such things, it did not take long for the group to establish a fifteen-person organizing committee and a six-person Officer Board. Dáithí O'Connell was appointed Cathaoirleach (chairman) and Ruairí Ó Brádaigh was appointed Urlabhraí (spokesperson). The other officers were Des Long, Joe O'Neill, Frank Graham, and Cathleen Knowles. Members of the committee included Pat Ward, Díóg Ní Chonaill (Dáithí O'Connell's daughter), and Maitiú Ó Brádaigh. At the suggestion of Seán Ó Brádaigh, and in order to distinguish themselves from the Provisionals, they adopted the name Republican Sinn Féin—Sinn Féin Poblachtach, in Irish. They took up a collection, netting more than £500, and drafted a statement for the press.

After about an hour the press was readmitted and introduced to the Officer Board of Republican Sinn Féin. Ruairí Ó Brádaigh then stood and read aloud the prepared statement. To the satisfaction of those involved, a live recording of the statement was broadcast twice on radio by the BBC World Service. They pledged "to uphold the basic Republican position enshrined in the Sinn Féin Constitution" and to "pursue the Republican objectives by continuing the organisation of *Republican Sinn Féin* whose object will be to organise the Irish people, at home and abroad, in opposition to British interference in the affairs of the historic Irish nation; to defend the interests of the Irish people against all forms of colonialism and exploitation, political, social economic and cultural; and to devise policies for the emancipation of the Irish people." They were not opposed to the armed struggle of the Provisional IRA or any other Republican organization: "We uphold the historic right of the Irish people to use whatever degree of controlled and disciplined force is necessary in resisting English aggression and bringing about an English withdrawal from our country for ever." Abstention from Leinster House was the issue at hand. In the question-and-answer session that followed, Dáithí O'Connell, as chairman, responded on behalf of the new organization. Asked for their attitude toward "Sinn Féin," those present chanted, "We are Sinn Féin." Asked to comment on Martin McGuinness's remarks at the Ard Fheis, O'Connell said that McGuinness was "dishonest and deceitful." Asked if they had a military organization, he replied, "We have no military organisation at this stage." This statement was probably true that evening, but steps were taken in a matter of weeks to change that.

At the IRA's 1986 convention, the delegates passed a motion that allowed Sinn Féin candidates to take their seats in Leinster House if elected. The delegates voted 75 percent in favor of the motion, 25 percent opposed. But the opposition delegates believed that the vote was gerrymandered by the creation of new IRA organizational structures for the convention, including the combinations of Sligo-Roscommon-Longford and Wicklow-Wexford-Waterford. The Adams group had a clear majority, but without the new structures and their influence on the composition of the delegates, the opposition believed, they probably did not have the two-thirds majority required to change the IRA Constitution. The opposition also believed that changing the IRA's Constitution required *two* conventions. At the first, embargoes specifically forbidding participation in Leinster House, Stormont, and Westminster would have to be removed from the Constitution. Only then, at a second convention, could a motion on entering a parliament be voted on. The opposition believed that the Constitution had been breached. They were supported by the only IRA institution that had rejected the motion, the outgoing Army Executive. This body met and dismissed those who supported the new departure. They co-opted new Executive members, rejected the decision to end abstention, and elected a new Army Council. And they began organizing a rival Irish Republican Army. A delegation from the Adams leadership had approached Tom Maguire, hoping he would support them. Maguire rejected them. He did meet with a delegation from the new group. For the second time he pledged his support to a new army of the Republic. To emphasize the link with the IRA of his day, he christened the organizers the Continuity Army Council.

Other than Maguire's involvement, which was not made public until 1996, very little information is available on those who created the Continuity IRA. Given their relationship with Maguire, an understanding of what happened in 1969/1970, and the creation of Republican Sinn Féin, it is likely that the same people who created the Provisional IRA created the Continuity IRA. Of the seven people who, most observers agree, served on the first Provisional IRA Army Council, four of them—Ruairí Ó Brádaigh, Dáithí O'Connell, Leo Martin, and Paddy Mulcahy—attended Republican Sinn Féin's first Wolfe Tone Commemoration in June 1987. And Billy McKee, who was central to the organization of the Provisional IRA, had also cast his lot with Republican Sinn Féin; he was in attendance at the West County Hotel.

The degree to which the Provisional IRA leadership was aware of the new paramilitary organization is unknown. Ó Brádaigh and Joe O'Neill were told not to start a new military organization, and in the spring of 1987 various people were visited by Provisional IRA representatives and threatened. Ó Brádaigh's visitor was not allowed in the house, just as he'd refused entry to Cathal Goulding seventeen years earlier. To the credit of the leadership of both the Provisional IRA and the Continuity IRA, however, there was no repeat of the Provisional IRA–Official IRA feuds of the 1970s. A Continuity IRA campaign, which would compete with the much larger Provisional IRA and likely cause a feud, did not commence immediately. The abstentionists had charged that recognizing Leinster

House would put the Provisionals on the slippery slope away from revo-lutionary armed struggle and toward reformism. For much of the time that the Provisionals would remain in the field, the Continuity IRA spent its time reorganizing and arming but not engaging in action. This allowed the Provisional IRA leadership, if they knew of the split, to pretend it had not happened.

The split in Sinn Féin was public, and to minimize its impact Adams and company presented the walkouts as a few misguided, if sincere, indi-viduals who refused to accept change. Provisional Sinn Féin's account of the 1986 Ard Fheis, *The Politics of Revolution,* claims that less than thirty delegates walked out; photographs of the event and an examination of those present at the West County Hotel suggest it was closer to 100 dele-gates.

There was also a split in Irish America. A front-page article in the issue of *An Phoblacht/Republican News* published immediately after the Ard Fheis was titled, "Noraid Is United," when it was not. Michael Flan-nery, a Noraid founder, sent a message of support to those assembled at the West County Hotel. He subsequently resigned from Noraid and with George Harrison and Joe Stynes helped found Cumann na Saoirse (Or-ganization of Freedom), an Irish-American support group linked with Re-publican Sinn Féin. Ó Brádaigh, who viewed Flannery in the same light as he viewed Tom Maguire, brought the two men together in September 1987 when Flannery visited Ireland.

People like Ruairí Ó Brádaigh were written out of Republican history. Prior to the split, Provisional Sinn Féin's annual Republican Resistance Calendar included a quotation from his Easter 1979 speech at Milltown Cemetery, Belfast:

> The present struggle contains within it a vital ingredient. This is so for many reasons, not least, its total involvement with the people. But it is distin-guished from all the struggles of previous times in one essential aspect. No one phase of struggle has gone on for so long. It is not simply the exhausting effort of a single generation, for within the present struggle the turn-over of the generations has already taken place. A new generation is setting the pace now. That is the greatest possible acquisition of strength to a revolutionary movement—and the surest guarantee of victory.

After the split, attribution was changed to a "Republican Spokesperson." For their part, Ó Brádaigh and the others were not as bitter as they had been in 1969/1970. It was like a second divorce. The sense of betrayal was

Ruairí Ó Brádaigh and 95-year-old Tom Maguire, Easter 1987. Irish Freedom Press.

significant, but not like the first time. Ó Brádaigh, in describing the first split, has been known to become animated, pace about the room, and use the occasional expletive. The second split evokes no such emotion.

Whatever role Ruairí Ó Brádaigh may have played in the creation of the Continuity IRA, his primary role since 1986 has been as the public face of Republican Sinn Féin. After three years in the background he was again in the political limelight, but the pace was slower. Although they had few material resources, the Republican Sinn Féin leadership had a wealth of experience in running a revolutionary political party. In January 1987, they rented space for a head office and bookshop at 21 Shaw Street in Dublin's center city area. Lita Nic Chathmhaoil and Cathleen Knowles staffed the office on a voluntary basis. A larger office would have been better, but it was a start. Seán Ó Brádaigh, who had worked on the *United Irishman* in the 1950s and 1960s and founded *An Phoblacht* in the 1970s, came in after work and, with Ruairí Óg Ó Brádaigh, helped found *Republican Bulletin*. The first issue, which had only four pages and no photographs, was published in November 1986. It featured the statement written at the West County Hotel, a message of support from Cumann na mBan, and a description of progress already made. In April 1987, *SAOIRSE-Irish*

Freedom, a larger paper with photographs, replaced *Republican Bulletin.* Because Republican Sinn Féin was a small organization, people in the leadership had multiple responsibilities; Ruairí Óg Ó Brádaigh, editor of *SAOIRSE,* also became the party's director of publicity.

At their first Ard Fheis as Republican Sinn Féin in November 1987, the organizing committee was disbanded and the leadership was regularized. The delegates formally elected Ruairí Ó Brádaigh president of Republican Sinn Féin. Joining him on the officially elected Officer Board were Dáithí O'Connell (chairman), Éamon Larkin (vice president), Cathleen Knowles and Líta Ní Chathmhaoil (joint secretaries), Joe O'Neill and John O'Connor (joint treasurers), and Ruairí Óg Ó Brádaigh (director of publicity). Among those elected to the Ard Chomhairle were Des Long, Pat Ward, Gerry McCarthy, and Declan Curneen. After the elections, Ó Brádaigh rose and offered (as far as he and the delegates were concerned) his fourteenth address as president of Sinn Féin. He began in Irish, "*A Chathaoirligh, a Theachtaí is a Chairde uilig, Céad míle fáilte romhaibh ar fad ag an Ard Fheis seo, an 83ú ceann de chuid Sinn Féin*" [Chairperson, delegates and friends, a hundred thousand welcomes to you all at this Ard Fheis, the 83rd of the Sinn Féin organization]. Switching to English, he continued, "A greater welcome than is usual at an Ard-Fheis is extended to you at this our 83rd such event. You represent those who rejected the attempts at the 82nd Ard Fheis last year to subvert the Sinn Féin constitution and make a reformist body out of our revolutionary political organisation." For the fifth time in sixty-five years, an attempt had been made to "accept the British imperialist and colonialist" alternative to the All-Ireland Republic, Leinster House. They were the people with the "moral courage" to reject reform. Based on the Constitution in effect at the time of the split, they were Sinn Féin—the same Sinn Féin founded by Arthur Griffith and subsequently abandoned by Griffith, Éamon de Valera, Tomás Mac Giolla, and Gerry Adams.

He described an eventful year that included establishing the head office, publishing the *Republican Bulletin* and *SAOIRSE,* and engaging in political activities that included a January 1st picket of the British embassy in Dublin and a "No" campaign against the Single European Act referendum (which was supported by the southern Irish electorate). He described the September meeting between Tom Maguire and Michael Flannery as a "proud moment for those present" and described the two men as "the one the living link with the revolutionary All-Ireland Dáil of 1919–22 and the other the pillar of support from Irish-America for over 60 years." The delegates voted Maguire the honorary title of "Patron" of

Republican Sinn Féin. In his conclusion, he offered a response to Martin McGuinness's comments of the year before. "We have not gone home," he said, "We are here and we are very much in business. We have no intention of letting slip now all that has been won by so much sacrifice down the years. We must complete our political education, dedicate ourselves once more, gird ourselves anew, reach out to the coming generation and advance steadily and in a clear-headed way toward the high ground of our goal—the Republic of Pearse and Connolly in modernised form and updated form—and so—right into the 21st century." As evidence that they were "very much in business," Ó Brádaigh, O'Connell, Long, O'Neill, Knowles, and the others spent the next several years issuing statements on Irish political events, organizing a testimonial dinner each year honoring senior Republicans, contesting local elections, organizing an annual commemoration of the 1981 hunger strike in O'Neill's hometown of Bundoran, County Donegal, and, as always, holding the traditional commemorations at Bodenstown, at Easter, and at the graves of fallen IRA volunteers.

Republican Sinn Féin "kept the faith" on the sidelines. The Provisional IRA struggled. In March 1987, eight IRA volunteers who were bombing an empty RUC station at Loughgall in County Armagh were killed when they were ambushed by a joint RUC–British Army team. It was the greatest loss of life for the Provisionals in any single event. Among the dead were several leaders in the Provisionals' East Tyrone Brigade, including Pádraig McKearney, the brother of 1980 hunger striker Tommy McKearney. Six months later, a Provisional IRA bomb in Enniskillen killed eleven people, all Protestant, who were gathered for a Remembrance Day ceremony commemorating persons killed in British military service. At best, it was an accident; at worst, it was a blatant attack on Fermanagh's Protestant community. The Provisionals were widely condemned for the attack; 50,000 people signed books of condolences in Dublin. That same month, French customs officers, working with Irish and U.S. officials, intercepted the *Eksund,* a boat carrying 150 tons of rockets, rifles, and explosives from Libya destined for the Provisional IRA. The weaponry and the Provisionals' most important arms route were lost. The Irish police launched a massive search and seizure operation that uncovered several arms caches that led to more arrests. Because of setbacks like these, the Provisional IRA leadership was unable to deliver on its promise to raise the level of its campaign. Aside from an occasional attack in England or on the Continent, the "long war" consisted of a steady and deadly level of activity in Northern Ireland that was not enough to make the province unmanageable or force a change in British intentions.

Provisional Sinn Féin also struggled. Gerry Adams, anticipating that the transition to electoral politics would take time, said in his 1986 presidential address that "the election after the next one will be the first serious test of our ability to win major support." Adams underestimated how difficult the transition would be. In the first Leinster House election after the split, in 1987, twenty-seven Provisional Sinn Féin candidates—the most Sinn Féin candidates in the south since the 1920s—received only 32,900 votes (2 percent of the overall vote). It was a disappointment. The result was no doubt influenced by the loss of several people to Republican Sinn Féin who would have made excellent candidates, including Frank Glynn, a member of the Galway County Council; Seán Lynch, former chairperson of the Longford County Council; and Joe O'Neill, a member of Bundoran's Urban District Council. Provisional Sinn Féin fared worse in the next two Leinster House elections in 1989 and 1992. In a press statement following the 1992 election, Ruairí Ó Brádaigh commented, "By their abject electoral results with 42 candidates in 38 constituencies losing 40 deposits and totally well short of 30,000 votes, the Provisionals' political organisation has inflicted further damage of the historic Sinn Féin name which they hi-jacked in 1986 when they broke the Sinn Féin constitution."

There were problems in Northern Ireland. In January 1989, Margaret Thatcher's government established a test oath for candidates in Stormont and local elections. Candidates were required to pledge that if they were elected, they would not express support for a proscribed organization or for "acts of terrorism." The Provisional IRA was a proscribed organization, as was Cumann na mBan and Na Fianna Éireann, the youth group. Republican Sinn Féin candidates refused to sign the oath and were denied a place on ballots. Provisional Sinn Féin candidates signed it. An article in *SAOIRSE* described this as a "further sell-out of the Republican position." The crown jewel of Provisional Sinn Féin's electoral success was the 1983 election of Gerry Adams to Westminster; their president was an MP. Adams was re-elected in 1987, but Provisional Sinn Féin's vote fell by almost 20,000 votes. In 1992, their vote fell by another 5,000, and Adams lost his seat to Joe Hendron of the SDLP.

The Provisionals were having trouble with both sides of their "armalite and ballot box" strategy, but behind the scenes they had opened a third front. In the 1987 Leinster House election, Fianna Fáil, with Charles

Haughey as Taoiseach, was returned to power in Dublin. During the 1981 hunger strike, elements in the Adams leadership had established contact with Fianna Fáil and Haughey. Adams, who was quick to criticize people if they engaged in any behind-the-scenes actions but was himself a master at it, had not informed Ó Brádaigh of this contact. After the 1986 Ard Fheis, Adams had a freer hand and reestablished the contact. Adams indicated that the Provisionals were interested in ending their campaign but needed help in creating the necessary conditions. Adams had also been in contact with John Hume in the early 1980s and he reestablished this contact as well. Over the next several years Adams, Mitchel McLoughlin, Danny Morrison, and Tom Hartley were in regular contact with Fianna Fáil, the SDLP, or both. The discussions with the SDLP and Fianna Fáil opened the door to a possible "pan-nationalist" front that would represent a significant majority of the Irish people as a whole and would be more formidable than the Provisionals alone. These discussions mark the beginning of the end of the Provisional IRA's military campaign.

The late 1980s and early 1990s was a period of transition for Ruairí Ó Brádaigh. In his mid-50s, he should have been at the peak of his teaching career. Instead, government cutbacks in 1987 eliminated all part-time teachers. Except for the occasional opportunity to substitute teach or help grade examinations, he joined Patsy in professional retirement. Adding insult to injury, the Department of Education maintained its claim that he had forfeited his pension when he was convicted of IRA membership in 1973. He lost twelve years' worth of payments into the program and any interest accrued. With the support of the Roscommon Vocational Educational Committee, he fought the decision for five years. It was not until August 1993, after several appeals and the successful legal challenge of the relevant section of the Offenses Against the State Act by a Provisional Republican, that he received his pension.

The Ó Brádaigh family in general experienced a period of transition. At the time of the 1986 split, only Eithne and Colm still lived at home. As teachers, Ruairí and Patsy stressed the value of an education to each of their children. The children left Roscommon in succession, pursuing a higher-level education, careers, and their own lives. Beginning with Maitiú's graduation from University College Galway in 1982, the family regularly attended graduation ceremonies, weddings, and christenings. Maitiú married first, in 1984. His daughter, Macha, who was born in 1986 just before the split, was the family's first grandchild. Colm, who enrolled at the Waterford Institute of Technology, left home in 1988 and married in 1999. In between, each of the other children received a university education and all but Ruairí Óg married. Conchúr and Eithne earned doctorates in mechanical engineering (1991) and chemistry (1994), respectively. Deirdre graduated in Irish and history and took a job as a high school teacher and, later, as a librarian. Ruairí Óg received a first-class-honors master's degree in Irish history.

Part of the transition that Ruairí Ó Brádaigh experienced in the late 1980s and early 1990s was a result of the aging process. Paddy Mulcahy, Seán Keenan, Gerry McCarthy, and Tony Ruane, people whose Republican careers had lasted as much as a half a century, all succumbed to natural causes. For some, personal sacrifices contributed to "natural" causes. Pat Ward, who had never recovered from his hunger strike, died in 1988, at 43 years old. Dáithí O'Connell died in his sleep on New Year's Day, 1991. He was only 52 years old. He is listed, as is Pat Ward, on Republican Sinn Féin's Roll of Honour as a hunger strike victim. On the day O'Connell died, Ó Brádaigh released a statement that said, "His was the ablest mind in the Republican Movement for over 20 years." In his funeral oration, he compared him to Cúchulainn, the Irish folk hero–warrior who also died young. Of Cúchulainn, he told the crowd, it is said that "[i]t is better to have short life with honour than to have long life without honour." He continued: "Dáithí O'Connell had honour every day of his life." Ó Brádaigh felt O'Connell's loss deeply, for he had been a friend, confidante, member of his extended family, and comrade in arms and in politics for thirty-five years.

Tom Maguire, the most senior Republican of all, passed away in July 1993, at the age of 101. Ó Brádaigh described him as "epitomising the unyielding Republican resistance to British interference in internal Irish affairs throughout the 20th century." Maguire's funeral was as Republican as they come, with a color party, a piper playing a lament, and a special flag, designed by Dáithí O'Connell, draped over the coffin. A guard of honor led the procession. Dan Hoban of Mayo, who was the commanding officer in the Curragh Glasshouse when Ó Brádaigh was incarcerated there in 1973, chaired the graveside ceremony. Ó Brádaigh delivered the funeral oration and stressed the Maguire family's service to Ireland. An ancestor had fought with the United Irishmen. Maguire's father was a Fenian. Tomás Maguire was the model Republican: "Dignity, integrity and loyalty were Tom Maguire's hallmarks . . . [and] here at his graveside on this historic day we salute his eighty years' service to the All-Ireland Republic, from the day he joined the Volunteers in 1913 up to today, 1993." The oration also contained an element of mystery. He commented: "Tom Maguire's last political will and testament has not yet been pub-

Ruairí Ó Brádaigh at the monument to Roscommon Republicans, Shankill Cross, Elphin, County Roscommon, in the 1990s. At the unveiling of the monument in 1963, he became acquainted with Tom Maguire. Bobbie Hanvey Photographs, John J. Burns Library, Boston College.

lished. Suffice it to say that he agreed with Pádraig Pearse: 'Until the English are at last beaten, the Irish have a duty to put a body of people on guard for the nation and it will be necessary for a band of the Irish to man the gap of danger.'"

During this time, Ó Brádaigh experienced his own health problems and a deep personal loss. His sister, Mary Delaney, was diagnosed with lung cancer, and the prospects were not good. Mary, Ruairí, and Seán had always been very close. They shared their Republican beliefs and their interests were similar enough that each had become a teacher, although Seán taught only briefly. Mary's illness was a significant stressor. Concerned over her health, Ruairí was also caught up in a fight with an insurance company related to the 1984 automobile accident. Patsy was unable to teach after the accident and Ruairí was laid up for a significant period of time. The other driver had been killed, so Ruairí and Patsy sought compensation from his insurance company. They were offered a lump sum payment that they felt was too small. But if they challenged it and a judge ruled against them, they could be held responsible for their own and the insurance company's legal fees, which might be considerable.

Mary's illness, the insurance company situation, and the continued struggle over Ruairí's pension all contributed to a stroke he suffered in September 1989. He was in the hospital for three weeks and recovered slowly. Today, the only visible sign of his automobile accident injuries or his stroke is his ever-present cane; the stroke limited his ability to compensate for the damage to his ankle caused by the accident. In diagnosing the stroke, his physician assumed that his major stressors were political. He explained that his politics were not the problem; he had been in the Republican leadership for more than thirty-five years and it had never caused a problem. His personal situation—his sister, the court case, the pension fight—was the issue. The physician, considering the potential for another stroke, told him to settle with the insurance company within the month, which he did. In January 1990, Mary Delaney passed away at her home in Athlone. She was 60 years old.

Considering the deaths of his sister, Dáithí O'Connell, and other comrades; the struggle for his pension; the fight against the insurance company; and his stroke, Ruairí Ó Brádaigh was experiencing a tough period as he moved into his early 60s. Through it all, he continued as president of Republican Sinn Féin and never wavered in his commitment. He would spend one day a week in Dublin, meeting with other members of the Republican Sinn Féin leadership. From home, with a telephone, fax, and computer, he kept in touch with Ruairí Óg, Cathleen Knowles, Líta Ní Chathmhaoil, Peig King, and others in the head office. Public statements were typed at home, faxed to the head office, and distributed to the press. By telephone he conferred with Des Long, Joe O'Neill, Mary Ward, Geraldine Taylor, Des Dalton, and others in the leadership, as well as Seán Lynch, who was re-elected to the Longford County Council. Sometimes with Patsy and sometimes alone, he traveled about Ireland by car to attend commemorations, funerals, regional meetings, and other events. At times, local Roscommon activists took turns driving him to meetings and events.

Under his leadership, Republican Sinn Féin grew, albeit slowly. He

Ruairí and Patsy Ó Brádaigh in the 1990s. Bobbie Hanvey Photographs, John J. Burns Library, Boston College.

was excluded from the United States, which forced him to miss the ceremony in which Conchúr received his Ph.D. from the University of Delaware, but Ruairí Óg, Des Long, Mary Ward, Joe O'Neill, and others visited Cumann na Saoirse supporters there—though Long and O'Neill were later excluded. He and his compatriots were also subject to the occasional raid, having their car pulled over by the police, and general surveillance from the police. They carried on. Republican Sinn Féin launched the Irish Republican Information Service newsletter, which was mailed worldwide. Dáithí O'Connell, just prior to his death, brought Éire Nua's federal scheme down to the level of local government. With others in the party, Ó Brádaigh built on this and developed the policy document "Saol Nua—

A New Society." It was described as "an alternative vision of Ireland based on a different set of values from the current ones—a blend of republican, democratic socialist, self-reliance and ecological principles" and offered a detailed social and economic program for a new, federal Ireland that would allow "the maximum measure of local participatory democracy." Membership in the European Community had "served to accelerate the forces of transnational capitalism," while the fall of the Soviet Union did not "at all signal the triumph of capitalism or market economics. . . . Both systems have been centralising, impersonal, unecological and unethical." Republican Sinn Féin sought "a new system of economics which would put human beings and human development before the interests of finance and maximisation of profits." The goal was for each district, region, and province of Ireland to be as self-sufficient as possible, with Ireland as a whole viewed as a "Community of Communities." The policy was ratified at the 1992 Ard Fheis.

In many ways, Republican Sinn Féin's politics mirrored that of Provisional Sinn Féin. Each party sought a 32-county democratic socialist republic, supported the right of Irish people to seek that Republic through armed struggle, advocated the development of Gaelic culture, and opposed Irish involvement in the European Community. The two parties differed in that Republican Sinn Féin sought a four-province federal Ireland and refused to recognize Leinster House, while Provisional Sinn Féin sought a unitary state and did recognize Leinster House. They also differed in that Provisional Sinn Féin was associated with one of the world's most formidable "terrorist" organizations. For this they were taken much more seriously than Republican Sinn Féin. Through the late 1980s, the SDLP and Fianna Fáil continued to meet with the Provisionals in secret. In 1990, representatives of the British government also began meeting with the Provisionals in secret.

In these behind-the-scenes dialogues, the Provisionals, the SDLP, Fianna Fáil, and the British representatives communicated with each other but never came together as a group. The Provisional Sinn Féin–SDLP dialogue centered on Britain's interests in Ireland. Adams and the Provisionals believed that the British had strategic and economic interests that kept them there. Hume and the SDLP believed they did not. The SDLP representatives noted that in spite of massive Unionist opposition, the British had upheld the terms of the Anglo-Irish Agreement of 1985, including the permanent presence of Dublin's representatives in the north. In November 1990, at the urging of John Hume, Peter Brooke, the secretary of state for Northern Ireland, stated publicly that "[t]he British government has no selfish strategic or economic interest in Northern Ireland: our role is to help, enable and encourage. Britain's purpose, as I have sought to describe it, is not to occupy, oppress or exploit, but to ensure democratic debate and free democratic choice." That same month, Margaret Thatcher, who was unlikely to ever come to any terms with the Provisionals, resigned as prime minister; she was succeeded by John Major. Thatcher's resignation coupled with Brooke's announcement prompted the first formal Provisional IRA Christmas cease-fire in fifteen years. Brooke, with the support of John Major and Charles Haughey, also established "inter-party talks" involving the SDLP and the two largest Unionist political parties, the more moderate Ulster Unionist Party, led by James Molyneaux, and the more hard-line Democratic Unionist Party, led by Rev. Ian Paisley. The talks themselves did not lead to anything substantial, but behind the scenes it was indicated that if the Provisional IRA declared a cease-fire, Provisional Sinn Féin could be included in such talks, which might lead to substantive political change.

This was important, for it appears that the Provisionals' leadership was coming to the conclusion that they could continue the "long war" forever, but they could not create the Republic. A cease-fire, in combination with their developing relationships with the SDLP and Fianna Fáil, was an interesting alternative. The continuing war allowed Unionist politicians to be as intransigent as they wished—How could they be expected to compromise with Nationalists in the face of an ongoing Provisional IRA terrorist campaign? A cease-fire would force them to come to terms with a "pan-Nationalist front" of the Provisionals, the SDLP, and Fianna Fáil. Most likely, it would split the Unionists into moderates willing to compromise and hard-liners who, cease-fire or not, would never work with Nationalists. With the Unionists split, the Provisionals and their Nationalist sympathizers would be in a stronger position as they negotiated with the British. In the long run, a cease-fire might set in motion processes that would lead to a united Ireland. The Provisionals were also aware of the continued cost of their campaign. In some years in the early 1990s, Loyalist paramilitaries killed more people than the Provisional IRA, and most of their victims were innocent Catholics. The Loyalists stated repeatedly that their raison d'être was defense of their community; a Provisional IRA cease-fire would, in theory, end their campaign. The British were also under pressure. In contrast to Northern Ireland, peace was breaking out in, of all places, South Africa and the Middle East. Nelson Mandela was released from prison in February 1990. This set in motion a series of events that resulted in his inauguration as president of South Africa in

May 1994. In September 1993, Yasser Arafat and Israeli prime minister Yitzhak Shamir signed the Oslo Accords, marking—it seemed—the beginning of the end of conflict in the Middle East. The ongoing conflict in Northern Ireland was an embarrassment.

In 1993, the secret multiparty dialogue generated a peace process. Journalists discovered that John Hume and Gerry Adams had been meeting, and it was front-page news. Hume was condemned for meeting with terrorists, but he responded that he was working for a "lasting peace," which sparked speculation that the Provisionals were thinking of ending their campaign. In the fall, Hume and Adams forwarded a report on their discussions to Albert Reynolds, who had succeeded Charles Haughey as leader of Fianna Fáil and Taoiseach. The Hume-Adams document was not published, but it was reported that in return for a British acknowledgment of the right of the Irish people as a whole to "self-determination," the Provisionals and the SDLP were willing to work with Unionists for a "peaceful and democratic accord for all on this island." Soon after this, the meetings between the Provisionals and the British were discovered, prompting more speculation in the press and putting pressure on the Dublin and London governments to encourage peace. In December 1993, John Major and Albert Reynolds issued a joint declaration. The British reiterated that they claimed no strategic or economic interest in Northern Ireland, and the two governments agreed that while the people of Ireland had a right to self-determination, which might include a united Ireland, it was "subject to the agreement and consent of the majority of the people of Northern Ireland." The terms were vague enough that what became known as the Downing Street Declaration was treated with suspicion but was not rejected outright by the Provisionals or the Unionists.

It was rejected by Republican Sinn Féin. In a statement to the press, Ó Brádaigh noted that in eight of its twelve points the Declaration guaranteed a British presence in Northern Ireland for as long as the majority of the people there desired it. Because of the gerrymander of 1920, the majority of people in Northern Ireland were Unionist. Over all of Ireland, the majority were Nationalist—the minority, 18 percent, was holding the majority hostage, he argued. The exclusion order that prevented him from entering Northern Ireland had not been renewed in 1990. At a press conference in Belfast, he argued that for a peace process to endure it had to begin with a British declaration of intent to leave Ireland. The Continuity IRA's response to the Declaration was given on January 21st, 1994, the seventy-fifth anniversary of the First Dáil Éireann. Continuity IRA volunteers fired a volley of shots in salute over Tom Maguire's grave. A statement and photograph of the event were published in *SAOIRSE,* which sparked speculation that another IRA was lurking. Martin McGuinness, in an article in *An Phoblacht/Republican News,* denied there had been any split in the movement.

Whether or not there was another IRA, the Provisionals benefited from an incipient peace process. Albert Reynolds's government allowed the broadcasting ban on Republicans to lapse, which opened the airwaves to Provisional, and Republican, Sinn Féin. President Clinton, who had been kept abreast of the situation, granted a visa to Gerry Adams. Adams's 48-hour visit made the front page of the *New York Times.* He appeared on *Good Morning America* and *Larry King Live* and, as described in *An Phoblacht/Republican News,* "captured the undivided attention of the massive US media machine." Meetings among the primary players—Hume and Adams, Major and Reynolds—continued, as did statements from various parties. Behind the scenes, the British indicated that peace negotiations would start after a Provisional IRA cease-fire, and Albert Reynolds indicated his government would support the Provisionals in dealing with the British and US governments. In late August 1994, and after years of being excluded, 74-year-old Joe Cahill was granted a visa to enter the United States. It was widely assumed that Cahill was admitted in order to brief the Provisionals' Irish-American supporters that a cease-fire was in the works. On August 31st, while Cahill was in the United States, the Provisional IRA announced "a complete cessation of military operations."

The announcement sparked widespread celebrations throughout Nationalist areas of Northern Ireland. Most of Ireland, and the world, agreed with Albert Reynolds, who stated, "As far as we are concerned, the long nightmare is over." Ruairí Ó Brádaigh and Republican Sinn Féin had a different view. They wanted peace, but a British declaration of intent to withdraw from Ireland had not accompanied the unilateral cease-fire. The September headline of *SAOIRSE* stated: "Provos Halt Campaign but No British Withdrawal." There were issues of morality. If the Provisionals were going to stop short of their goal, then how was their killing in pursuit of a 32-county democratic socialist republic ever justified? In an interview for *SAOIRSE,* Ó Brádaigh asked, "What were the sacrifices of the past 25 years all about?" No doubt his critics questioned the morality of continuing an armed campaign that they believed could not be won. The Irish government took this a step further and, six weeks after the cease-fire, the police raided the homes of sixty Republican Sinn Féin members, though no one was arrested. Another prominent person who questioned the cease-fire was Bernadette McAliskey, who commented that "as far as

Ruairí Óg Ó Brádaigh, editor of *SAOIRSE.* Lance Productions.

the Provisionals are concerned, the war is over and the good guys lost." In the euphoria associated with the cease-fire, such criticism seemed like griping from people left behind by political change. This was especially so after the Combined Loyalist Military Command, which represented the main Loyalist paramilitary organizations, announced its own cease-fire. It was a major difference from the 1975 bilateral truce.

Yet, and similar to what happened in 1975, the promising march to peace quickly slowed. Unionist politicians were united in questioning the Provisionals' sincerity. David Trimble argued that the Provisional IRA and Provisional Sinn Féin were one and the same and demanded that the Provisional IRA decommission its weapons before Provisional Sinn Féin be included in any talks about the future of Northern Ireland. Trimble, who became leader of the Ulster Unionist Party, eloquently stated his position as "no guns, no talks." John Major, whose Conservative government was dependent upon Unionist support, demanded that the IRA declare the cease-fire to be permanent. Provisional IRA prisoners were another concern. Some of them had spent more than two decades in jail. The Provisionals believed they were no longer a threat to anyone, but the British moved slowly on the issue. This contrasted poorly with the June 1995 decision to release Lee Clegg, a British soldier who had been sentenced in 1991 to life in prison for the murder of a Belfast teenager. Clegg's release sparked major riots in Belfast and Derry, but it was not until November 1995 that special legislation was passed at Westminster allowing the early release of a number of Republican prisoners. Even then, the legislation did not apply to prisoners serving life terms.

As the peace process slowed, Ruairí Ó Brádaigh and Republican Sinn Féin stepped up their criticism of the Provisionals. Gerry Adams, who had been granted another visa, toured the White House and again appeared on *Larry King Live,* where he debated with Ulster Unionist MP Ken Maginnis. When asked about Adams being "feted" at the White House, Ó Brádaigh commented, "I haven't changed, I am still saying the things that I was saying down the years. Gerry Adams and those associated with him have changed and these are the rewards for them." In a January 1995 interview with the *Northern Ireland Report,* he described the cease-fire as "the inevitability of gradualism." The ban on Ó Brádaigh's visa was subsequently renewed by the Clinton administration. Through the spring, summer, and fall, in press statements, radio, television, and newspaper interviews and any other means available, Ó Brádaigh and other Republican Sinn Féiners argued that what they had been saying for years was coming true—the Provisionals had traded armed struggle for parliamentary politics and they would end up as reformers in a new Stormont, to the detriment of the Republican cause.

Their interpretation of events resonated with some Republican-minded people. Within days of the cease-fire, some Provisional Sinn Féiners left for Republican Sinn Féin. As the process dragged on, a steady trickle of the disenchanted arrived at its door. With them came more resources, including funds to purchase a permanent headquarters on Parnell Street in central Dublin. The building, named Teach Dáithí Ó Conaill (David O'Connell House), was located around the corner and up the street from 44 Parnell Square, which was still the headquarters of Provisional Sinn Féin. It was officially opened on New Years Day 1996, the fifth anniversary of O'Connell's death. The plaque on the building was unveiled by Deirdre O'Connell. Ominously, there was more evidence but no confirmation that there was another IRA. In May 1995, six people were arrested in Dublin and charged with possession of weapons. One of them was Josephine Hayden, a member of Cumann na mBan and joint general secretary of Republican Sinn Féin. In November, another member of Republican Sinn Féin, Mick Hegarty, was arrested in connection with two bombs discovered in County Monaghan.

With the peace process stalled, there was intense pressure on the Provisionals' leadership to either achieve something quickly or end the ceasefire; doing nothing allowed their most important weapon, the Provisional IRA, to wither. The British and Irish governments, aware of this, developed a "twin track" approach that allowed various political parties to participate in "preparatory" talks while an international body, under the chairmanship of former U.S. Senate majority leader George Mitchell addressed the decommissioning issue. It was hoped that the Mitchell Commission's report would provide a basis for "all party" talks in February 1996.

As a precursor to the report, the Continuity IRA revealed itself. Two statements were released through the Irish Republican Publicity Bureau. The first confirmed the existence of the Continuity IRA: "We are neither Official nor Provisional and rejecting reformism we remain revolutionary as the true Óglaigh na hÉireann, Irish Republican Army." The statement was signed "B. Ó Ruairc"—Brian Ó Ruairc had been the last of the seventeenth-century Irish chieftains to hold out against the English invasion; he died without yielding. The second statement involved a letter from "Comdt General Thomas Maguire." Dated July 25th, 1987, Maguire confirmed the Continuity IRA's legitimacy, "I hereby declare that the Continuity Executive and the Continuity Army Council are the lawful Executive and Army Council respectively of the Irish Republican Army, and that the governmental authority, delegated in the Proclamation of 1938, now resides in the Continuity Army Council, and its lawful successors." This was Maguire's "last political will and testament." For those concerned that the Continuity IRA was the military wing of Republican Sinn Féin, a separate article in *SAOIRSE* noted that although the stated objectives of each "appear to be the same," Republican Sinn Féin "works solely by political means." It is the same careful demarcation that Provisional Sinn Féin had shared with the Provisional IRA under Ruairí Ó Brádaigh.

A fortnight later, it appeared that the impasse holding up all-party talks was resolved and the Continuity IRA would become irrelevant. The Mitchell Commission's report offered six principles that political parties would have to accept prior to entering talks, including a commitment to the peaceful resolution of political issues, a commitment to disarmament, and the renunciation of the use of force to influence all-party negotiations. The commission also suggested the compromise of "parallel decommissioning"—paramilitary weapons would not have to be decommissioned prior to inclusion in all-party negotiations but some decommissioning would occur *during* the negotiations. In a surprise move, Prime Minister

John Major rejected parallel decommissioning and proposed an election to secure a "democratic mandate" for a forum to negotiate the future of Northern Ireland.

On February 9, 1996, the Provisional IRA, in frustration, and perhaps concerned that they were being outflanked by the Continuity IRA, responded with a massive bomb at Canary Wharf in London; two people were killed and there was an estimated £100 million in damages. At the end of February, the British and Irish governments indicated their willingness to go ahead with the peace process without Provisional Sinn Féin. They announced that the Northern Ireland Forum election would be in May and that all-party talks with representation based on the election results would commence in June. Provisional Sinn Féin would be excluded from the talks unless there was another Provisional IRA cease-fire. The Provisionals embarked on their own "twin track" approach of carrying on a paramilitary campaign while demanding that their representatives be admitted to the peace process—it was the kind of logical contradiction that Ruairí Ó Brádaigh had warned, for years, would lead to a compromise on basic principles.

In the Northern Ireland Forum election that followed, Provisional Sinn Féin had its best election results ever, winning 116,000 votes (15.5 percent) and electing 17 (of 110) representatives to the Forum. The Provisionals seemingly had their mandate for inclusion in the Forum. When the talks opened, four representatives from political parties associated with Loyalist paramilitaries, which maintained their cease-fire, were admitted. Because the Provisional IRA refused to declare another cease-fire, Provisional Sinn Féin's representatives were not admitted. A Provisional IRA bomb devastated the center of Manchester.

In July, the Continuity IRA acted in dramatic fashion in response to a major confrontation that developed in Portadown when Orangemen tried to follow a traditional marching route down the Garvaghy Road, which was populated by Catholics and Nationalists. The RUC stopped the march, the Orangemen refused to be rerouted, and a standoff ensued. Maverick Loyalist paramilitaries killed a Catholic taxi driver. Unionist politicians, led by David Trimble and Rev. Ian Paisley, threatened to walk out of the Forum. The RUC relented, the march proceeded, and the police batoned the Nationalists off the road. There was again major rioting in Nationalist areas of the north. Early in the morning of July 13th, 1996, a British Army vehicle ran over and killed a Derry Nationalist, sparking a day of protests. That evening, just after midnight, a bomb wrecked the Killyhevlin Hotel, near Enniskillen, causing an estimated £2–3 million in

Gerry Adams and Martin McGuinness locked out of the Northern Ireland Forum (Stormont), June 1997. Pacemaker Press.

damages. It was the first bombing in the north since August 1994, and the immediate assumption was that it was the work of the Provisional IRA. The Provisionals convincingly denied responsibility. It was only after three weeks of speculation that the Irish Republican Publicity Bureau reported they had been asked to release a statement: "The action near Enniskillen on July 14 was carried out by volunteers of the Irish Republican Army under the direction of the Continuity Army Council. This military action against an economic target was an immediate reprisal for the killing of an Irish citizen by British troops the previous night and the general campaign of terror by British Forces against the Nationalist population at that time." It was the start of the Continuity IRA's public campaign and their direct competition with the Provisional IRA. In October, Jim Cusack, the security correspondent for the *Irish Times,* reported that the Continuity IRA was thought to be small but capable of making large bombs and that "in recent weeks there have been reports of secret contacts between senior Provisional IRA elements in the Border area and RSF figures."

While the Continuity IRA expanded, the Provisionals remained caught in the dilemma of whether to put aside years' worth of work toward peace and continue their military campaign, perhaps indefinitely, or end the campaign and fight for the best deal available through participation in the Forum. The contradiction of waging a paramilitary campaign while demanding entree to a peace process was increasingly evident. In September, Provisional IRA volunteer Diarmuid O'Neill was killed in a Special Branch raid on a flat in London. On the day O'Neill's parents flew to London to identify his body, Gerry Adams launched his much-awaited autobiography, *Before the Dawn.* It was widely reported that Adams would receive £100,000 for the book, which he would keep for himself. In an article in the *Belfast Telegraph* titled "Down through History, the Working Class Has Been Cannon-Fodder in Wars," Belfast journalist Suzanne Breene wrote, scathingly, "Diarmuid O'Neill's life wouldn't have made an international best-seller. . . . The Sinn Féin President visits the White House and parties with Donald Trump, Bianca Jagger and Oliver Stone. He enjoys Hollywood treatment in the US. There is even talk of a film of his life." She charged that the Provisionals had abandoned the "32-County socialist republic" but were afraid to admit it, as "this policy change would threaten the leadership's power base. . . . It's a negotiating tactic to ease Sinn Féin's way into all party talks. . . . If the republican leadership possesses a shred of humanity, it should inform its grassroots of its new position and the compromises entailed."

As Gerry Adams was making appearances promoting *Before the Dawn,* Ruairí Ó Brádaigh was putting the finishing touches on his biography of Tom Maguire. The book is dedicated "In memory of my father and mother, Matt Brady and May Caffrey—Comrades of Tom Maguire in Donegal, Longford, and Dublin—who made me what I am." He chose the title carefully, *Dílseacht: The Story of Comdt. General Tom Maguire and the Second (All-Ireland) Dáil.* "Dílseacht" translates into English as "fidelity, loyalty, sincerity, love." *Dílseacht,* obviously a labor of love, chronicles Maguire's lengthy Republican career. Over eighty years he had been a significant figure in virtually every facet of Irish Republicanism—he directed an IRA ambush of British troops at Tourmakeady, County Mayo, in 1921; was elected to the Second Dáil Éireann; rejected the Treaty; was captured by the Free State but escaped; rejected de Valera in 1926; signed over the executive powers of government to the IRA in 1938; and issued his famous statement legitimizing the Provisionals and later did the same for the Continuity IRA. Ó Brádaigh's respect for Maguire is evident throughout. One of the photographs shows 95-year-old Maguire at Easter 1987 demonstrating a Lee-Enfield rifle captured at Tourmakeady. Maguire had suffered personal hardships because of his beliefs—his brother was executed by the Free State and his father lost his business because of the politics of

Launch of *Dílseacht* in Derry City, 1997. From left: Mrs. O'Doherty, Seán Maguire (son of Tom Maguire), Ruairí Ó Brádaigh, Seán Ó Brádaigh, and Tommy McKearney. Ó Brádaigh family collection.

his sons—but had never wavered. When the book was published in April 1997, it was not accompanied by the media blitz that accompanied Gerry Adams's book. Indeed, Ó Brádaigh had difficulty getting the book into some Irish bookstores and an attempt to launch the book in Derry was hindered by threats from the Provisionals.

While Ó Brádaigh worked through the end of 1996 and into the spring of 1997 finishing the Maguire book, the political situation in Ireland remained in what might be best described as stable flux. Outside the Northern Ireland Forum, the Continuity IRA and the Provisionals kept up their low-level military campaigns. Republican Sinn Féin argued that decommissioning meant surrender, and Provisional Sinn Féin demanded inclusion in the Forum without Provisional IRA decommissioning. Inside the Forum, the Unionist parties demanded decommissioning and squabbled among themselves. Winter turned to spring, no progress was made, and the talks were adjourned for two important elections in June 1997. In a Westminster election, and after sixteen years of Conservative government, Labour won in a landslide. Tony Blair, the new prime minister, was committed to moving the peace process forward. He allowed his new ministers to meet with Provisional Sinn Féin representatives, but he also issued an ultimatum to the Provisionals: "The settlement train is leaving. I want you on that train. But it is leaving anyway and I will not allow it to wait for you. . . . So, end the violence now." Blair also set a deadline of May 1998 for the all-party talks. The other significant development was the rise in Provisional Sinn Féin's vote; Gerry Adams reclaimed his seat in West Belfast and Martin McGuinness won in Mid-Ulster. There was speculation that they might take their seats, but it was unfounded. Three weeks later, in local elections in Northern Ireland, the Provisionals did even better, finishing third in the overall vote, behind only David Trimble's Ulster Unionist Party and John Hume's SDLP. Coupled with the Westminster results, the Provisionals had a definite mandate for inclusion in the Northern Ireland Forum. Two weeks later, their claim was further strengthened in a Leinster House election. Albert Reynolds's government had fallen in the fall of 1994 and was replaced by a Fine Gael–Labour coalition. In the 1997 Leinster House election, Fianna Fáil returned to power in Dublin, with Bertie Ahern as Taoiseach. Ahern quickly developed a close working relationship with Tony Blair. And eleven years after the split, Provisional Sinn Féin candidate Caoimhghin Ó Caoláin was elected in Cavan-Monaghan. He became the first (Provisional) Sinn Féin TD to take a seat in the Dublin Parliament since 1922. In both north and south, it seemed, Nationalists wanted Provisional Sinn Féin included in the Forum talks.

In light of these developments, the British and the Provisionals worked out a deal—in return for a cease-fire, but no decommissioning, the Provisionals could join the Forum. In July, almost three years after the first cease-fire, the Provisionals entered their second unilateral and indeterminate cease-fire. Again, almost everyone in Ireland was pleased. The August headline in *SAOIRSE* stated, "New Ceasefire, Same Sell-Out: Another False Peace." The September headline, which went to press as the talks were about to reconvene, charged, "A New Stormont Is the Only Possible Outcome of the Current Process." Ó Brádaigh paid a personal price for his opposition. He was scheduled to fly to Canada for a commemoration of the 150th anniversary of "Black '47" and the "coffin ships" that fled the famine and landed at Grosse Ile with many of their passengers dead or dying of cholera. He was lifting his luggage onto the wing of a plane at Shannon when an official told him that the Canadian embassy in London (rather than Dublin) had sent a fax indicating he was not allowed to enter Canada and that if he took the flight he would be immediately sent back to Ireland. He was very disappointed. He was also out the price of the ticket, £500 Irish.

The Forum reconvened on September 15, 1997, with the Provisionals in attendance. That day, a 350-pound Continuity IRA bomb exploded outside of an RUC station in County Armagh. Adams, McGuinness, and the other Provisionals ignored the criticism of Ó Brádaigh and people like him, the Continuity IRA bombs that went off in October and November, and even another split in the Provisional IRA that occurred late in the fall. As the deadline for the all-party talks approached in April 1997, each party involved faced difficult choices, including whether or not to secure a deal or waste years of effort and potentially start a slide away from peace and toward war—toward "terrorism." The Provisionals were in a particularly difficult situation. The Provisional IRA had not been fully mobilized for four long years. It would not be easy to restart its campaign. The emergence of another group, the Real IRA, was also a problem. To have allowed their army to wither and suffer another split and end up with nothing to show for the damage done would completely destroy the leadership's credibility.

On April 10th, 1998, the various parties involved in the Forum accepted the Good Friday Agreement, by which government in Northern Ireland would be devolved from London to a 108-member assembly with legislative powers, headed by an executive committee. Like the Sunningdale Agreement of 1973, the Assembly would be complemented by a North/South Ministerial Council. To assuage Unionist fears, the Dublin government agreed to amend the Irish Constitution and recognize that "a united Ireland shall be brought about only by peaceful means with the consent of a majority of the people, democratically expressed, in both jurisdictions of the island." To assuage Nationalist concerns, the British government agreed to repeal the Government of Ireland Act of 1920, which had partitioned Ireland, thereby making it possible to bring forward legislation to create a united Ireland if a majority in Northern Ireland desired it. Long-term SDLP politician Seamus Mallon, an MP at Westminster, described the agreement as "Sunningdale for slow learners." In separate and concurrent referendums, in Northern Ireland the Good Friday Agreement was ratified and in the Republic of Ireland the Constitution of 1937 was amended to accommodate that agreement.

For Provisional Sinn Féin, accepting the agreement required changing the party's Constitution, which forbade involvement in a six-county assembly. The party leadership called an extraordinary Ard Fheis for May 10th, 1998. In attendance were four prominent IRA prisoners, Eddie Butler, Joe O'Connell, Harry Duggan, and Hugh Doherty (Pat Doherty's brother). Dubbed the Balcombe Street Gang, they had been implicated in the Guildford bombings in 1974 and the murder of Constable Tebbitt in

February 1975 during the bilateral British-IRA truce. Sentenced to life in prison in England, they were transferred to Ireland and then paroled to attend the Ard Fheis and lend their support to the Good Friday Agreement. Their presence after twenty-three years in English prisons was tangible evidence of the potential benefits of the agreement; if it were endorsed and implemented, they would be freed. After a lengthy debate, the Ard Fheis delegates voted overwhelmingly to change the Provisional Sinn Féin Constitution.

In 1990, Henry McDonald interviewed Cathal Goulding for an article marking the twentieth anniversary of the 1969/1970 split in the Republican Movement, which was published in the *Irish News*. Comparing that split with subsequent events, Goulding commented, "We were probably right too soon, Adams and company are probably right too late and Ruairí Ó Brádaigh will never be right." Twelve years after saying they would never participate in a six-county assembly, Gerry Adams, Martin McGuinness, Pat Doherty, and Joe Cahill and their supporters had proven Ó Brádaigh right—on that issue. Only time will tell if it will result in a 32-county democratic socialist republic.

Epilogue

RUAIRÍ Ó BRÁDAIGH, who turned 70 in October 2002, has led a complex life. Like many men of his generation, he pursued a professional career. College educated with a degree in commerce, he became a vocational school teacher. With his wife, Patsy, he nurtured and provided for six children; Ruairí and Patsy are grandparents thirteen times over. While pursuing his professional career and raising a family, he also led a political life. In 1957, he was thrust onto the political stage when he was a successful Sinn Féin candidate for Leinster House. He remained on that stage as president of Provisional Sinn Féin and, currently, as president of Republican Sinn Féin. Through it all he also lived a clandestine life. He joined the IRA in 1951 and rose quickly through the ranks, joining the Army Council in 1956. He was chief of staff at the end of the Border Campaign, was on the Army Council through the 1960s, and, presumably, helped found the Provisional IRA. Whether or not he remained in the IRA after his 1973 conviction on membership charges, he continued his clandestine life, representing the Republican Movement in behind-the-scenes events, including the negotiations with the British in 1975 and meetings with Loyalists in 1977.

These four lives—professional, personal/family, political, and clandestine—have been intertwined. His teaching career suffered; he was unable to return to teaching in 1957 because he was arrested, and he took a leave of absence in 1971 because he was so busy. His conviction on IRA membership charges in January 1973 ultimately led to his forced early retirement. His family life also suffered because of his IRA and Sinn Féin activities. After his conviction on the membership charge, Patsy spent the next five months raising six young children by herself. His travels took him away from home on numerous occasions. To the degree that he could, he combined his family life and his political life. Patsy and the children attended commemorations, marches, and other functions with him. When he was excluded from the United States, Patsy traveled there in his place. He continues to work closely with his brother Seán and his son, Ruairí Óg, Republican Sinn Féin's director of publicity.

Today, Ruairí Ó Brádaigh is best known as the leading critic of Gerry Adams, Martin McGuinness, and their supporters and as the most prominent opponent of the Provisionals' involvement in the "peace process." His critics dismiss him as someone stuck in time, wedded to an Irish Civil War–Treaty era mentality—a sort of modern version of Tom Maguire. In the popular imagination, the complexity of Ruairí Ó Brádaigh is reduced to a single issue, abstention from parliamentary politics. This focus on a single issue, albeit important, grossly underestimates him.

Living a complex life came naturally to him. As he says, he was "ready made." His parents, Matt Brady and May Brady Twohig, were veterans of revolutionary organizations. May Brady Twohig pursued a professional career as secretary of the Longford Board of Health. Matt Brady, as a member of the Longford County Council, was a public figure. Along with stepfather Patrick Twohig, his parents instilled in him a love of Irish history, Irish language, and Irish culture—he spent nine summer holidays in succession in the Gaeltacht, the Irish-speaking area, and is fluent in the language. They also made him aware of social justice issues, in Ireland and internationally. Matt Brady's public defense of the Longford IRA in the Richard More O'Ferrall case was as much a defense of the "little guy" against a landlord as it was a defense of the IRA. The Spanish Civil War was a topic for discussion in the household.

Ó Brádaigh built on this foundation over the course of his own life. When he joined Sinn Féin in 1950, he would have never identified himself as a socialist. If he had, the IRA might not have admitted him in 1951. Today he openly embraces socialism, as do most Republicans. His socialism, and his lengthy involvement in the cooperative movement, developed out of the general politicization of the Republican Movement in the late 1950s and through the 1960s. Like Cathal Goulding and Tomás Mac Giolla, Ó Brádaigh recognized that the approach of the movement's leaders in the 1950s—Tony Magan, Paddy McLogan, and Tomás Mac Curtáin—was too narrow and too focused on the physical force of the IRA. He endorsed the move to the left in the 1960s and drew on these ideas to help develop Provisional Sinn Féin's social and economic program.

Ó Brádaigh also developed broad international interests. His involvement in the IRA's 1950s campaign led him to examine political movements in places such as Algeria, Cuba, Cyprus, Hungary, Kenya, and

Vietnam. In the 1960s he became interested in African anticolonial movements, especially that associated with Julius Nyerere and Tanzania. This interest is reflected in Provisional Sinn Féin's social and economic program, which rejected Western capitalism and Soviet imperialism, seeking a third path for Irish economic development. These ideas remain in Republican Sinn Féin's current program. The movement's federalism policies, a joint product of Dáithí O'Connell and Ó Brádaigh, were influenced by his international interests. Through the 1970s and into the 1980s he traveled extensively, promoting the movement's cause and examining alternative political arrangements that might help broker a solution to the conflict in Ireland. He laid the foundation for the international support that Provisional Sinn Féin has today.

He follows international politics, but while some of the European Union's onetime opponents, such as Tony Blair, now accept it, Ó Brádaigh views the European Union of today through the same lens as he viewed the European Economic Community that Ireland joined in 1973—it is the manifestation of "new imperialism" whose goal is to evolve into a superpower that can compete economically and militarily with other capitalist economies. Ireland has benefited, in terms of European investment in infrastructure such as roads, but this does not compensate for the massive destruction of small farms across Europe and the development of huge agribusinesses that employ relatively few people. After thirty years of membership, the border has not "withered," and traditional Irish neutrality is still threatened. For some, the fall of the Soviet Union was a triumph of capitalism; for Ó Brádaigh, the problems associated with capitalism remain.

At the core of Ruairí Ó Brádaigh's politics, undeniably, is a rejection of participation in parliamentary politics at Westminster and the partition system in Ireland. This too originates with his parents and their rejection of the 1921 Anglo-Irish Treaty. The central tension in the Republican Movement since 1921 has been whether or not the "Republic" can be achieved through parliamentary politics. The issue split the movement in 1922, 1926, 1946, 1969/1970, and 1986. Ó Brádaigh consistently, firmly, places himself among those who believe that involvement in constitutional politics will divert the Irish Republican Movement into reform, not revolution. In his words, "[I]f you think you can keep one leg in the streets and the other leg in Parliament, you've a bloody awful mistake." He accepted the leftward politicization of the Republican Movement by Cathal Goulding and others in the 1960s and by Gerry Adams and others in the late 1970s, but only so long as it did not threaten abstentionism.

Twice, in 1970 and 1986, he led the opposition to ending abstention from participation in parliamentary politics.

There is a temptation, spurred on by his critics, to reduce this passionate defense of abstentionism to an emotional commitment to "the Republican dead," the memory of his parents, or a commitment to people such as Tom Maguire. This view misunderstands the man. He loves Irish history and the memory of his parents, and he has great respect for Tom Maguire, Joe Clarke, Tony Magan, Paddy McLogan, Tony Ruane, and others who rejected parliamentary politics. But Ó Brádaigh's refusal to countenance involvement in parliamentary politics is based on his interpretation of historical evidence, not emotions. He is a pragmatist, as would be expected of a man who taught business skills to secondary-level students at a vocational school.

It is ironic that in 1992, only two years after Cathal Goulding said "Ruairí Ó Brádaigh will never be right," the Workers' Party (formerly Official Sinn Féin) split again. And the split was in part generated by continued accusations that the constitutional party still had a military wing, the Official IRA, that was still engaged in illegal activities. Six of the party's seven TDs, led by Proinsias de Rossa, who had been an internee in the Curragh in the 1950s, and two-thirds of its local councilors formed a new party, Democratic Left. The lone Workers' Party TD who remained, Tomás Mac Giolla, lost his seat in the next election. The Workers' Party never recovered from this split (though it still exists). Democratic Left participated in the "rainbow coalition" government (from December 1994 to June 1997) led by Fine Gael and the Irish Labour Party and then merged with the Irish Labour Party in January 1999, vanishing from the Irish political scene. It was an interesting end to Official Sinn Féin's quest, as led by Goulding and Mac Giolla, to combine a revolutionary program with constitutional politics and achieve a democratic socialist 32-county united Ireland. For Ruairí Ó Brádaigh, its demise is just that much more evidence that he was right after all.

What is most important in understanding Ó Brádaigh's perspective on constitutional politics is that for him, people such as Mick Collins, Éamon de Valera, Seán Mac Bride, and Cathal Goulding were unable to reunite Ireland because they were trying to do something that cannot be done. It is not that they were insincere, lacked character, or were not "true" Republicans. With a goal of bringing about revolutionary change, they entered parliamentary bodies as weaker parties, facing the weight of the London and/or Dublin Parliaments. The result was they were absorbed into the existing system. As minority parties, they were forced to choose between compromise or irrelevancy. With respect to the question of a united Ireland, they settled for a compromise. Worse, they defended their compromises by turning on former comrades who questioned their choices. The history of Irish Republicanism is littered with examples of compromises turning into betrayal: the executions by the pro-Treaty government in 1922/1923; de Valera and Fianna Fáil's willingness to execute and allow IRA hunger strikers to die in the 1940s; the Official IRA shooting of Charlie Hughes in 1970 and the two later Official IRA–Provisional IRA feuds in the 1970s; and Official Sinn Féin/The Workers' Party refusal to support the hunger strikers in 1980 and 1981. In 1986, Ruairí Ó Brádaigh had every reason to question Gerry Adams's attempt to combine revolutionary struggle with constitutional politics.

At the 1986 Provisional Sinn Féin Ard Fheis, Martin McGuinness stated, "I can give a commitment on behalf of the leadership that we have absolutely no intention of going to Westminster or Stormont." He also said, "Our position is clear and it will never, never, never change. The war against British rule must continue until freedom is achieved." Yet since 1986, the Provisionals have compromised repeatedly. In spite of promises to the contrary, the Provisional IRA ended its campaign short of the Republic. In June 1998, Provisional Sinn Féin contested the election to the new Northern Ireland Assembly, sited at Stormont. In 1999, McGuinness accepted the position of minister for education in the assembly. Throughout the peace process, Unionists have called on the Provisional IRA to decommission their weapons; the Provisional IRA declared, repeatedly, that it would never happen. In October 2001, with the Northern Assembly in a crisis because Unionists refused to work with Provisional Sinn Féin (and after the attacks of 9/11 made it that much more important that Provisional Sinn Féin distance itself from "terrorism"), the Provisional IRA did destroy some weapons. Ó Brádaigh referred to it as "nothing short of treachery"; other Republican critics of the Provisionals agreed with him. The Provisional IRA destroyed more weapons in April 2002, but it was not enough to satisfy its critics, and in October 2002 the Northern Ireland Assembly was suspended indefinitely. More weapons were destroyed in October 2003, and in July 2005, with the assembly still suspended, the Provisional IRA issued a formal statement ending its campaign and ordering all units "to dump arms." Its representatives were authorized "to verifiably put its arms beyond use in a way which will further enhance public confidence and to conclude this as quickly as possible." Volunteers were instructed "to assist the development of purely political and democratic programmes through exclusively peaceful means."

The Provisionals have turned on former comrades. Provisional Sinn

Féin did well in the June 1998 Assembly election, winning 18 (of 108) seats. After the election, members of the Provisional IRA assaulted Michael Donnelly, a former internee in Long Kesh and a critic of Provisional Sinn Féin. They claimed that Donnelly's active criticism of Provisional Sinn Féin's participation in the election had cost it a seat. It was the first of several post–Good Friday Agreement intimidations by the Provisionals. In August 1998, a Real IRA bomb exploded in Omagh, killing twenty-nine people; it was the second worst incident, in terms of loss of life, of the post-1969 Irish conflict. The Real IRA was condemned worldwide, and the bomb effectively destroyed the organization's potential. Many Republicans condemned the bombing. Ó Brádaigh stated that it was unjustified and rejected "the absolute inhumanity of it." Martin McGuinness stated that he was "appalled and disgusted" and that it was "an indefensible action." The Provisional IRA took the condemnation a step further. On September 1, Provisional IRA volunteers visited the homes of several "dissident" Provisionals and the homes of several supporters of the 32-County Sovereignty Committee (which is associated with the Real IRA). They read out a statement from the Provisional IRA Army Council indicating that action would be taken if they did not cease and desist. The "dissidents" were specifically warned to stop speaking against the peace process. A Republican Sinn Féin spokesperson charged that "the Provisionals are now trying to eradicate resistance to the British occupation of Ireland" and suggested that the Provisionals had bought into the "new colonial regime in the Six Counties." The spokesperson asked, "Are they now prepared to kill for it?"

After a cessation period of about a year, the Real IRA reemerged and there was more trouble with the Provisionals. In October 2000, Real IRA volunteer Joe O'Connor was shot dead on a West Belfast street. It is alleged that the shooting, which took place in the middle of the day and in front of witnesses, was carried out by members of the Provisional IRA. The Provisionals' denial of responsibility was questioned in several quarters. A group of former prisoners that was clustered around Anthony McIntyre, Brendan Hughes, Tommy McKearney, and Tommy Gorman, who do not support the Real IRA but who do question the Provisionals' strategy, was particularly vocal. Provisional Sinn Féin organized a picket of McIntyre's and Gorman's homes; McIntyre was assaulted on the street. Marion Price, the former hunger striker, gave the oration at Joe O'Connor's funeral. She described the Provisional IRA as the "armed militia of the British state." She, too, was subjected to harassment from the Provisionals.

Even if the Provisionals have been forced to compromise, the peace process has been good for Northern Ireland. What was a society under siege has been transformed. Sectarian attacks continue, but not on the level seen in the early 1990s or during the truce in 1975. Guerrilla organizations persist, including the Continuity IRA, but the worst paramilitary violence in the post–Good Friday Agreement era pales when compared to the least violent periods of the previous three decades. The Provisionals' compromises have generated significant reforms. For decades the Nationalist community had demanded another inquiry into Bloody Sunday, believing the result of the first inquiry, the 1972 Widgery Report to be a whitewash. The demand was met in January 1998, and there have been significant revelations from the second inquiry, directed by Lord Saville. A Parades Commission has been established to try to broker a compromise between organizations such as the Orange Order, which demands the right to march along traditional, often controversial, routes, and Nationalists, who are subject to triumphalist marches through their streets. An independent commission on policing in Northern Ireland, the Patten Commission, a result of the Good Friday Agreement, recommended a number of reforms for the RUC, and they have been largely implemented. The force's name was changed to the Police Service of Northern Ireland, a new Police Board was instituted, and each group of new recruits must have an equal number of Protestants and Catholics. After the IRA statement of July 2005, the British began dismantling a military base and two watchtowers in South Armagh. These reforms may be the start of real change in Northern Ireland, change that will result in a just and lasting peace. Provisional Sinn Féin has benefited from the peace process; it is the second-largest political party in Northern Ireland, exceeding the SDLP's vote in recent elections.

If Gerry Adams is able to chart a course that leads to a 32-county democratic socialist republic, Ruairí Ó Brádaigh will be delighted. Asked to consider the possibility that Adams is right, he replies, "Ireland is free! Hurray! Joy in excelsis. I'd die a happy man!" However, he believes that there is enough compelling evidence to conclude that Adams has made a "bloody awful mistake." In this, Ó Brádaigh's perspective echoes classic political theorists such as Robert Michels and Rosa Luxemburg. In *Political Parties,* Michels argued that the radical leadership of the socialist parties of the early twentieth century were victims of an "Iron Law of Oligarchy." Organization, by its nature, leads to compromise and working with the status quo. Leaders, no matter how radical they once were, become more interested in maintaining their institutionalized position than they do the radical goals of their party. In *Revolution or Reform,* Rosa Luxemburg argued:

> The secret of historic change through the utilization of political power resides precisely in the transformation of simple quantitative modification into a new quality, or to speak more concretely, in the passage of a historic period from one given form of society to another.
>
> That is why people who pronounce themselves in favor of the method of legislative reform *in place of and in contradistinction to* the conquest of political power and social revolution, do not really choose a more tranquil, calmer and slower road to the *same* goal, but a *different* goal. Instead of taking a stand for the establishment of a new society they take a stand for the modification of the old society. (Emphasis in original)

Ó Brádaigh believes that involvement in constitutional politics will result in compromise, reform, and the achievement of a goal different from a 32-county democratic socialist Irish Republic. It is not that he enjoys being a revolutionary or that he believes the road to the Republic is easiest through the use of physical force and nonconstitutional politics. It is a choice between guaranteed failure or the prospect that, at some point, a revolutionary situation—like the one that existed in the 1920s—will allow real transformation of political power in Ireland.

Time will tell if Adams or Ó Brádaigh is correct on the issue of reform versus revolution. In the meantime, Ó Brádaigh continues as president of Republican Sinn Féin, visiting the head office in Dublin each week, issuing statements, attending commemorations, planning events, and putting up with harassment from the police—"business as usual." Part of the usual business is an unwavering support for the right of Irish people to employ physical force in pursuit of the Republic. In this he is much the same man who as chief of staff accepted the IRA's killing of Constable Norman Anderson in 1961 as the assassination of a cross-border spy and accepted the Derry Provisional IRA's assassination of Constable Paul Gray in 1975 as a justified response to breaches of the truce agreement that included the arrest of Shane O'Doherty. He is pleased that Republican Sinn Féin continues to grow; it has opened another office in Belfast. Some activities are particularly enjoyable because they link his early career with more recent events. In 1963, Tom Maguire unveiled a monument for Republican dead at Shankill Cross, County Roscommon. Ó Brádaigh was there, and out of the event the two men developed a lasting friendship. Forty years later, in October 2003, a Roll of Honour memorial was added to the monument. Ó Brádaigh was among those involved in the project, which was unveiled by Dr. Seán Maguire, Tom Maguire's son. In 2005, for only the second time in his career, he delivered the key oration at Bodenstown.

He is persistent, but he is not bitter. He was deeply disappointed in John Joe McGirl, yet they continued to speak with each other and he attended McGirl's funeral in 1988, paying his respects in the midst of the Provisional leadership. He also remained friendly with Seán Mac Stiofáin, even though Mac Stiofáin brought charges against him in 1972. When Mac Stiofáin passed away in 2001, Ó Brádaigh described him as "a giant of a man in the Republican Movement" and stated that "he will be remembered as an outstanding IRA leader during a crucial period in Irish history." One of the persons who helped with the Shankill Cross Roll of Honour project was Tom Mitchell, who remained friends with Ó Brádaigh in spite of the split with the Officials in 1969/1970. His major regret is that Adams and company settled for an outcome, the Good Friday Agreement, that he believes was available in 1973 with Sunningdale. The twenty years between 1974 and 1994 saw a significant amount of death and destruction—"For what?" Ó Brádaigh asks.

Through fifty-plus years of trials (literally and figuratively), tribulations (two splits in the movement), successes (the fall of Stormont), and disappointments (the Good Friday Agreement), he has also kept his sense of humor. A favorite story begins in 1972. Joe O'Neill had been arrested and there was a protest outside a Donegal courthouse. The crowd became unruly as the prisoner was being removed and a man started yelling, "My watch, my watch! Don't step on my watch!" Ó Brádaigh calmed the immediate area and the man bent down and retrieved his watch. Standing back up, he thanked Ó Brádaigh, shook his hand, and moved off. The protest continued and Colmán Doyle, a prominent Irish photographer, walked up to Ó Brádaigh and complained that he had just missed a classic photograph—for the unidentified man was Inspector Patrick Doucy, of the Irish Special Branch. Ó Brádaigh had not recognized Doucy, who was famous as the police officer who arrested two members of the Irish Cabinet, Charles Haughey and Neil Blaney, as part of the Arms Crisis in 1970.

A year or so later, they met again. Ó Brádaigh was arrested in December 1972 and placed in a holding cell at Green Street Courthouse in Dublin. Following standard procedure, two police officers appeared at his cell. The junior officer identified himself and his companion, Inspector Patrick Doucy. Doucy read the charges aloud and asked, "What do you have to say?" Ó Brádaigh looked at him and replied, "How is your watch keeping?" Doucy laughed, turned immediately, and left the cell. They met again eighteen years later. In January 1990, Republican Sinn Féin staged

Ruairí Ó Brádaigh, at the Annual Wolfe Tone Commemoration, Bodenstown, 2005. Behind him on the platform are Des Long, Chairperson (holding notes) and Seosamh Ó Maoileoin, Chief Marshall. Photo by the author.

a March for All-Ireland Democracy, starting from Tom Maguire's County Mayo home and ending at the Mansion House in Dublin. The march ended on January 21st, the anniversary of the first meeting of Dáil Éireann. Ó Brádaigh joined the demonstration several times along the route and met the marchers in Dublin, who also planned to deliver an anti-EEC petition at Dublin Castle, the site of an EEC Summit. When they arrived at the castle gate, he asked the police officers on duty if he could personally deliver the petition. This request was denied and a bit of a standoff ensued. Patrick Doucy, now a chief superintendent, again entered the picture. He arrived on the scene, spotted Ó Brádaigh, and told the guards "Let this man in." The crowd was treated to the strange sight of a chief superintendent and the president of Republican Sinn Féin laughing together as they walked up to the castle offices to hand in the petition. The laughter started when Ó Brádaigh commented, "I've been telling that watch story for years." Doucy replied, "I've been telling it, too."

Ruairí Ó Brádaigh has also kept his principles. At various points in his Republican career he had opportunities to take the easy way out, to compromise. When he was first arrested at the border in 1957, a police officer offered to let him go free if he would pass on information on the whereabouts of other members of his column. From 1957 to 1961 he could have accepted a seat in the Dublin Parliament. During the 1960s, he was approached by a Labour Party councilor and even by Fianna Fáil members to stand as a candidate for Leinster House. In 1970, along with many other people, he was willing to give up the movement's buildings and newspaper rather than recognize Leinster House, Stormont, and Westminster. In 1982, Gerry Adams offered him a Provisional Sinn Féin vice presidency if he would condemn federalism. In 1986, along with virtually the same people as in 1970, he again gave up the movement's buildings and newspaper rather than recognize Leinster House. He rejected each opportunity for compromise. With each rejection, he remained true to what he believed was the correct Republican path. Ruairí Ó Brádaigh's life may be summarized in one Irish word, found in the title of his biography of Tom Maguire, "*dílseacht*"—"fidelity, loyalty, sincerity, love." For better or for worse, this best describes his ongoing relationship with the Republican Movement.

NOTES ON SOURCES

I have tried to gather as much information on Ruairí Ó Brádaigh as possible from as many and as varied sources as available. The core of this biography involves hours of interviews with Mr. Ó Brádaigh. Most of the interviews were conducted at his home in Roscommon. Over time, questions were answered via telephone calls and letters and notes were exchanged. We took the agreed-on approach that facts are sacred, interpretations are my own. For almost every question I had, he provided a detailed description, from his perspective, of an event, a plan, a person, and so forth. Most important, where I or the historical record had a fact wrong, he corrected it. There were, of course, a few questions that he did not answer, but these were few and far between, and they typically involved implicating someone besides himself in an event or activity. He will not discuss post-1969 membership on the IRA's Army Council.

Although he has a remarkable memory—J. Bowyer Bell described him as the kind of person who not only remembers an event but also remembers the color of the tie he was wearing that day—his accounts were not taken at face value. No one, intentionally or not, remembers everything correctly. The accuracy of the information in the Ó Brádaigh interviews was checked with information from two other sources: additional personal interviews and the public record. I have interviewed a number of people, noted in the text and below, who were or still are Ó Brádaigh's contemporaries. Some of them still have friendly relationships with him, some do not. The respondents include family members, colleagues in the Republican Movement, Republican colleagues who chose a different path from his, and political observers who have never been associated with the Republican Movement. In addition to interviews, people answered questions via e-mail, over the telephone, and with letters. For the most part, persons approached for an interview willingly participated in the project. The exception to this involves persons in the leadership of Provisional Sinn Féin in the late 1970s and early 1980s who did not leave for Republican Sinn Féin in 1986. Repeated attempts to interview Gerry Adams and others were unsuccessful. I must note, with great thanks, that Danny Morrison, who was as important as anyone in Provisional Sinn Féin in the late 1970s through the 1980s but is no longer directly active in the organization, graciously agreed to an interview.

Most interviews were tape-recorded. Interviews were conducted in peoples' homes and offices and other locations. One was conducted in an automobile as the respondent drove through the streets of Dublin. Perhaps the most interesting location was in a hotel room in Cork. Participants in The Future Developments in Terrorism Conference, March 3–5, 1999, organized by Max Taylor and John Horgan of University College Cork, stayed at the hotel. The conference attracted an international array of academics and representatives of police agencies, including Paul Wilkinson, the leading British terrorism expert and no friend of the IRA. Prior to conference sessions one morning, as the "terrorism experts" went about their business, I had the privilege of interviewing Kitty O'Brien, Mick Fitzgibbon, and Mick McCarthy. They were, depending upon one's perspective, veteran Irish Republican "terrorists" or a very nice lady and two very kind gentlemen who were willing to discuss their political careers and offer their impressions of a young Ruairí Ó Brádaigh.

I have tried to locate as much of the public record of Ó Brádaigh's life as possible. The historical record, as presented in newspapers, books, and other sources, has been an invaluable source for documenting his public statements and confirming his description of events. Information on Matt Brady's career was found, with the help of Father Ignatius Fennessey, in the papers of Seán Mac Eoin, which were in the Franciscan Library at Dún Mhuire in 1996 (the papers are now held by University College Dublin). Another important source was a scrapbook of newspaper clippings that Seán Ó Brádaigh kept. The Political Collection at the Linenhall Library in Belfast and the National Library of Ireland in Dublin were important sources for newspaper articles, pamphlets, and other materials. Newspaper clippings of the Northern Ireland Office now in the Political Collection were very helpful in terms of time saved and coverage of events. The Political Collection's staff answered a number of queries via e-mail, for which I am most thankful. For recent events, the CAIN (Conflict Archive on the Internet) Web service (http://cain.ulst.ac.uk) is an excellent source that provides a chronology of events as well as in-depth summaries of topics. Finally, Fred Burns O'Brien graciously provided copies of various documents related to Ruairí Ó Brádaigh.

Ruairí Ó Brádaigh's accounts have been compared with the oral and print accounts of others. The result is a detailed and, to the highest degree possible, accurate presentation of the political life of a person who is simultaneously the typical man next door—a middle-class high school teacher and father of six—and one of the key figures of modern Irish Republicanism.

The following individuals were interviewed for this project. The location of the interview is indicated. In some instances, the interview was followed by a telephone conversation or some other communication, such as e-mail: Richard Behal, Killarney; Líta Ní Chathmhaoil, Dublin; Anthony Coughlan, Dublin; Seán Cronin, Washington, D.C.; Joe Dillon, County Dublin; Des Fennell, Dublin; Mick Fitzgibbon, Cork City; Sir Timothy Garden, Bloomington, Indiana; Frank Glynn, Tuam, Galway; Tommy Gorman, Belfast; Brendan Hughes, Belfast; Roy Johnston, Dublin; Cathleen Knowles McGuirk, Dublin; Des Long, Dublin; Seán Lynch, Mostrim; Leo Martin, Belfast; Mick McCarthy, Cork City; Tomás Mac Giolla, Dublin; Denis McInerney, Ennis, Clare; Anthony McIntyre, Belfast; Tommy McKearney, Belfast; Billy McKee, Belfast; Seán Mac Stiofáin, Navan, Meath; Danny Morrison, Belfast; Fred Burns O'Brien, telephone interview. Conor Cruise O'Brien, Dublin; Patsy O'Connor Ó Brádaigh, Roscommon; Ruairí Óg Ó Brádaigh, Dublin; Seán Ó Brádaigh, Dublin; Kitty O'Brien (nee Ó Callaghan), Cork City; Deirdre Caffrey O'Connell, Dublin; Nollaig Ó Gadhra, County Galway; Joe O'Neill, Dublin; Séamus Ó Tuathail, Dublin; Seán Scott, County Galway; Mary Ward, Chicago; Betty Williams, telephone conversation.

Sources

"RÓB IVs" indicates information from the taped interviews with Ruairí Ó Brádaigh (RÓB). Other interviews are indicated by the respondent's name, such as "Patsy Ó Brádaigh interview." "RÓB Notes" refers to responses to questions and other written comments from Ruairí Ó Brádaigh. "RÓB Truce Notes" refer to notes that he made of meetings with British representatives during 1975 and 1976.

Introduction

xxi A note on the text: In Ireland, military titles follow a different convention. "Chief of Staff" is abbreviated as "C/S" and "Commanding Officer" is abbreviated as "O/C" (Officer Commanding). Standard American English is followed here.

xxi September 3, 1971, Provisional IRA activity: see David McKittrick, Séamus Kelters, Brian Feeney, and Chris Thornton, *Lost Lives: The Stories of the Men, Women and Children Who Died as a Result of the Northern Ireland Troubles* (London: Mainstream Publishing, 1999), 96–97; "Baby and Sentry Slain in Ulster," *New York Times,* September 4, 1971, 1.

xxi Ruairí Ó Brádaigh and the Angela Gallagher shooting: see Michael Hall, *20 Years: A Concise Chronology of Events in Northern Ireland from 1968–1988* (Newtownabbey, Northern Ireland: Island Publications, 1988), 29; Richard Deutsch and Vivien Magowan, *Northern Ireland 1968–1973: A Chronology of Events,* vol. 1, *1968–1971* (Belfast: Blackstaff Press, 1974), 124; "What Mr. Brady Told Pressmen," *Irish News,* September 8, 1971. Jack Lynch and Frank McManus quotations: "New Horror as IRA Rethink," *Irish Press,* September 4, 1971. David Bleakley quotation: "The Price of Hate . . . a Baby," *Daily Mirror,* September 4, 1971. Quotation from Pope Paul VI: "The Pope Condemns Shooting of Baby," *Daily Mirror,* September 6, 1971. Official IRA quotation: "Official I.R.A. Deplores Death of Baby," *Irish News,* September 6, 1971. See also "Lynch 'Yes' to Summit," *Daily Mirror,* September 9, 1971; Tomás Mac Giolla interview, 1997.

xxii The other side of Ruairí Ó Brádaigh: Ruairí Ó Brádaigh interviews (henceforth RÓB IVs); "What Mr. Brady Told Pressmen," *Irish News,* September 8, 1971; Patrick Bishop and Eamonn Mallie, *The Provisional IRA* (Aylesbury Bucks, England: Corgi Books, 1989), 83–84.

xxiii Paula Backscheider, *Reflections on Biography* (Oxford: Oxford University Press, 2001), xvi.

Chapter 1

1 Brady family history: RÓB IVs.

2 History of County Longford: "Heritage of County Longford," Midlands-East Tourism, Ireland; Jude Flynn, "Old Longford Town," "Longford Coats of Arms," and Peter Keenan, "Longford—A Garrison Town for Almost 200 Years," all found in *Exploring Family Origins and Old Longford Town,* published by the *Longford Leader,* n.d.

2 Battle of Ballinamuck: Seán Ó Brádaigh, ed., *The Battle of Ballinamuck: A Traditional History by James O'Neill of Crowdrummin* (Seán Lynch, Cleenrath, Aughnacliffe, County Longford on behalf of the County Longford Branch of the National Graves Association, n.d.), see 2–3 for Seán Ó Donnabháin quotation; "Ballinamuck—Its Page in Ireland's Story," *Longford Leader,* March 11, 1939, 8; "The French Revolution and the Irish Struggle," based on a lecture delivered by Seán Ó Brádaigh, Dublin, January 21, 1989, the seventieth anniversary of the founding of the First (All-Ireland) Dáil Éireann.

2 Matt Brady's move to Longford town in 1913: article in *Longford Leader* on the new courthouse, October 9, 1937, 3.

3 1916 Easter Rising: P. S. O'Hegarty, *The Victory of Sinn Féin: How It Won It and How It Used It* (Dublin: Talbot Press, 1924), 2–3; F. S. L. Lyons, *Ireland since the Famine* (London: Fontana, 1973), 329–380; J. Bowyer Bell, *The Secret Army: The IRA from 1916–* (Dublin: Irish Academy Press, 1979), 3–15.

4 Frongoch and Longford internees: Seán O'Mahony, *Frongoch: University of Revolution* (Killiney, County Dublin: FDR Teoranta, 1987).

4 McGuinness election: "Sinn Féin Meeting at Tang," *Longford Leader,* May 12, 1917, 1; Tim Pat Coogan, *Michael Collins* (London: Arrow Book, Limited, 1991), 67; "Granard Notes," *Longford Leader,* May 12, 1917, 1; Pádraic O'Farrell, *The Blacksmith of Ballinalee: Seán Mac Eoin,* rev. ed. (Mullingar: Uisneach Press, 1993), 21; "The Election," *Longford Leader,* May 12, 1917; Marie Coleman, *County Longford and the Irish Revolution, 1910–1923* (Dublin: Irish Academic Press, 2003).

5 Activities in Longford after the McGuinness election: Thomas Ashe; "Sinn Féin Demonstration in Longford," *Longford Leader,* July 28, 1917, 5; "Sinn Féin Meeting in Granard," *Longford Leader,* August 4, 1917, 5; "Death of Mr. Thomas Ashe," *Longford Leader,* September 29, 1917; "The Inquest," *Longford Leader,* September 29, 1917; "Public Board's Sympathy," *Longford Leader,* September 29, 1917; "Granard Aeridheacht: Sinn Féin Speeches," *Longford Leader,* September 29, 1917; Ernie O'Malley, *On Another Man's Wound* (1936; repr., Dublin: Anvil Books, 1994), 60–61.

5 Matt Brady joins the IRA and participates in the Thomas Ashe funeral: RÓB IVs; Matt Brady's military service record in the IRA is found in his pension application, among the papers of Seán Mac Eoin. Originally held in Dún Mhuire Friary, Killiney, Ireland, the papers have been moved to University College Dublin. Quotations concerning Matt Brady's IRA activities are taken from his account as presented in the pension application. Collins quotation: Lyons, *Ireland since the Famine,* 366, 387, 388; Coogan, *Michael Collins,* 66, 73–74.

6 May Caffrey family history: RÓB IVs; see also "Mother of Sinn Féin Chief Dies," *Republican News,* August 17, 1974, 7.

6 Growth of Sinn Féin and the IRA: see Lyons, *Ireland since the Famine;* Coleman, *County Longford and the Irish Revolution.*

6 Mick Collins and John Joe O'Neill arrests: "Sinn Féin Arrest," *Longford Leader,* March 30, 1918, 1; "Unlawful Assembly," *Longford Leader,* March 30, 1918, 1; "Sinn Féin Prosecution," *Longford Leader,* April 6, 1918, 1; "More Arrests and Prosecutions in Longford," *Longford Leader,* April 20, 1918, 5; "Visit of Mr. Collins," *Longford Leader,* April 27, 1918, 1.

7 Longford anticonscription meeting: "No Conscription," *Longford Leader,* April 27, 1918, 1.

7 Seán Mac Eoin, Mick Collins, the Longford IRA, and conscription: O'Farrell, *The Blacksmith of Ballinalee,* 21–23; Coleman, *County Longford and the Irish Revolution.*

7 1918 Westminster election: "Sinn Féin M.P.s: Biographical Sketches of Successful Candidates," *Longford Leader,* January 4, 1919, 5; "The General Election," *Longford Leader,* January 4, 1919, 5; Lyons, *Ireland since the Famine.*

7 Dáil Éireann and developing IRA activity: Bell, *The Secret Army,* 16–28; Lyons, *Ireland since the Famine;* Dorothy Macardle, *The Irish Republic,* rev. ed. (New York: Farrar, Straus and Giroux, 1965), 292–293.

8 Shooting of Matt Brady: RÓB IVs; Seán Lynch interview; O'Farrell, *The Blacksmith of Ballinalee,* 24; "Columbkille 'O'Rahilly' Sinn Féin Club," *Longford Leader,* March 29, 1919, 1; "See Under Separate Chapter—Shooting of Brady and McNally by RIC at Rathmore, 1919, after County Council, IRB, and Brigade Council Meeting at Aughnacliffe," in the Seán Mac Eoin papers; "Granard Notes: Columbkille Sensation," *Longford Leader,* May 3, 1919, 1; "North Longford Shooting: Critical Condition of One of the Wounded Men," *Longford Leader,* May 3, 1919, 4; "Two Men Shot by Police: County Longford Sensation," *Longford Leader,* May 3, 1919, 4; "Shooting," *Longford Leader,* April 30, 1919; "The Columbkille Shooting," *Longford Leader,* May 10, 1919, 1. Fleming and Clarke claimed that they were confronted by a crowd of forty to fifty people who demanded their rifles in the name of the Irish Republic. Brady and McNally, who faced criminal charges, claimed that they had met the two police officers "who after a slight altercation fired on them." The two bullets in Brady's chest exited from the same wound in the back. A British physician who examined him published an article, describing this as a "freak" of the Irish Troubles. The incident made national news: see "Longford Sensation: Alleged Shooting by RIC," *Irish Independent,* April 29, 1919, 2.

9 Seán F. Lynch, Lord Cavan's physician, and Seán Mac Eoin: RÓB IVs; Seán Lynch interview.

9 T. W. Delaney: Longford Brigade Committee, Pension Papers, M.S.P. (Military Service Pensions), A–C, Bosca 8, Seán Mac Eoin papers.

9 False story: "Shocking Accident in Longford," *Longford Leader,* May 10, 1919, 1.

10 IRA active in Cork, Tipperary, Clare, Limerick, Roscommon, and Longford: Joost Augusteijn, *From Public Defiance to Guerrilla Warfare: The Experience of Ordinary Volunteers in the Irish War of Independence 1916–1921* (Dublin: Irish Academic Press, 1996), 19; Coleman, *County Longford and the Irish Revolution.*

10 Seán Mac Eoin's exploits: O'Farrell, *The Blacksmith of Ballinalee;* Seán Mac Eoin, *With the IRA in the Fight for Freedom: 1919 to the Truce* (Tralee: The Kerryman Ltd.), 71, 106, 113, see especially "The Constitutional Basis of the National Struggle," 13–25; Coleman, *County Longford and the Irish Revolution.*

10 Black and Tan War: British troops were quickly mustered to support the RIC. Their khaki uniforms were complemented by the black-green caps and belts of the RIC, hence they were referred to as "Black and Tans."

11 Matt Brady and May Caffrey in Dublin: RÓB IVs; Matt Brady's pension application.

12 Anglo-Irish Treaty (1921), Irish Civil War, and the Free State executions: Macardle, *The Irish Republic,* 984–985; J. J. Lee, *Ireland, 1912–1985: Politics and Society* (Cambridge: Cambridge University Press, 1969), 68–69; Bell, *The Secret Army,* 29–39; Ruairí Ó Brádaigh, *Dílseacht: The Story of Comdt. General Tom Maguire and the Second (All-Ireland) Dáil* (Dublin: Cló Saoirse [Irish Freedom Press], 1997), 25.

14 Seán Mac Eoin and the executions: Pádraic O'Farrell, *Who's Who in the Irish War of Independence* (Dublin: Lilliput Press, 1997), 97–98; *The Last Post,* 3rd ed. (Dublin: National Graves Association, 1985), 159.

14 Seán Mac Eoin and Seán F. Lynch: O'Farrell, *The Blacksmith of Ballinalee,* 74.

14 Irish civil war ends, Éamon de Valera statement: Bell, *The Secret Army,* 37–40; Tom Brady's status: RÓB IVs. Casualty estimate: Lee, *Ireland, 1912–1985,* 69.

15 Caffrey family opposition and "fullest consideration" quotation: letter to Seán Mac Eoin from an official with the Department of Local Government and Public Health, June 24, 1925. See also a letter from Mac Eoin to the Minister for Local Government Buildings, June 19, 1925. In an August 7, 1926, letter to Mac Eoin, May Caffrey commented, "If I had not perfect confidence in you I would not go on with the matter as I am doing in spite of the opposition of my father, who always looked at the worst side of things anyway." All in Seán Mac Eoin's papers.

15 Matt Brady and May Caffrey relationship, marriage, and honeymoon: RÓB IVs; Seán Ó Brádaigh interview.

Chapter 2

17 Political division in Ireland in the 1920s and 1930s: Brian Hanley, *The IRA: 1926–1936* (Dublin: Four Courts Press, 2002), 93; Bell, *The Secret Army;* Ó Brádaigh, *Dílseacht,* 28–30; Lee, *Ireland, 1912–1985,* 176–181; Lyons, *Ireland since the Famine.*

18 Seán Mac Eoin, the Blueshirts, and Seán F. Lynch letter: Seán F. Lynch letter to the editor, *Longford Leader,* June 9, 1934, 6.

18 Military pensions: Although the IRA opposed pensions, veterans who were "incapacitated in the fight" were permitted to accept them and remain in good standing with the organization. "Memorial to Lieut. Kelleher: Large Hosting at Unveiling Ceremony, Speaker and I.R.A. Pensions," *Longford Leader,* October 27, 1934, 1. After Matt Brady's death, a Black and Tan War service medal was sent to his home: RÓB IVs.

19 The United Ireland Party: in September 1933, Cumann na nGaedheal, the Centre Party and the Blueshirts amalgamated as the United Ireland Party (in Irish, Fine Gael—the tribe or family of the Gaels); Lyons, *Ireland since the Famine,* 529–530.

19 IRA demonstration in Longford: "Republican Rally in Longford," *Longford Leader,* June 16, 1934, 2, 9.

19 Seán F. Lynch, Tom Brady, and Matt Brady in the crowd: see "Sinn Féin Re-Enters Local Election Contests," *SAOIRSE,* Meán Fómhair/September 2000, 14. A number of IRA/Republican veterans held elected positions in the 1920s and 1930s.

19 The *Irish Press* and Matt and May Brady: The Earl of Longford (Frank Pakenham) and Thomas O'Neill, *Éamon de Valera: A Biography* (Boston: Houghton-Mifflin, 1971), 270; RÓB IVs; Ruairí Óg Ó Brádaigh interview.

20 Roger Casement: When the extracts of the diaries were released, Casement was disgraced and many of his supporters withdrew. Others insisted the diaries were forgeries. They have been controversial since 1916. In 2002, forensic tests concluded that they were "exclusively the work of Roger Casement's hand." See Paul Tilzey's BBC article, "Roger Casement: Secrets of the Black Diaries," available online at http://www.bbc.co.uk/history/society_culture/protest_reform/casement_print.html.

20 Silchester: Lord Longford, to whom ground rent was payable, was titled Earl of Longford and Baron Silchester. Silchester was a place in England; RÓB Notes.

20 Matt Brady 1934 election address: "To the Electors of Ballinalee County Electoral Area," *Longford Leader,* June 23, 1934, 10.

21 1934 County Council election: "Co. Council Elections: List of Nominations," *Longford Leader,* June 16, 1934, 5; "Fianna Fáil Victory in County Council Elections," *Longford Leader,* June 30, 1934, 1.

21 First meeting of the Longford County Council: "Scenes at Council Meeting," and "County Council Chairmen," *Longford Leader,* July 14, 1934, 1; "Longford Co. Council: Fianna Fáil Chairman Elected, No Fine Gael Nomination," *Longford Leader,* July 14, 2–3.

21 Seán F. Lynch, Matt Brady, and the 1937 Leinster House election: "The Election," *Longford Leader,* May 29, 1937, 10; "Independent Republican's Campaign," *Longford Leader,* June 12, 1937, 7.

21 Edgeworthstown dispute: "Landlordism Assailed in Edgeworthstown," *Longford Leader,* December 8, 1934.

21 Violence in Longford in the 1830s: Fergus O'Ferrall, "The Ballinamuck 'Land War' 1835–39," *Journal of the Longford Historical Society/Cumann Seanchais Longfoirt* 11, no. 2 (March 1983): 104–109.

22 Shooting of Richard More O'Ferrall: "Sensational Shooting Outrage at Edgeworthstown," *Longford Leader,* February 16, 1935, 1; Frank Columb, *The Shooting of More O'Ferrall* (Cambridge: Evod Academic Publishing, 1996).

22 Longford County Council resolution and quotations: "Angry Words in the Dáil," *Longford Leader,* March 16, 1935, 1; "Lively Council Scene," *Longford Leader,* March 16, 1935, 1, 5.

22 More trouble at Edgeworthstown: "Edgeworthstown Evictions," *Longford Leader,* May 18, 1935, 1.

23 Trial and release of those accused in the death of Richard More O'Ferrall: "Released Prisoners Welcomed," *Longford Leader,* December 21, 1935, 1–2, 8; Bell, *The Secret Army,* 126–127; Columb, *The Shooting of More O'Ferrall.*

23 IRA proscribed, Bodenstown banned: "Ruled Out of Order," *Longford Leader,* June 27, 1936, 1.

24 New Irish Constitution: Upon effect, the Constitution immediately deproscribed the IRA. This was short lived, as the organization was proscribed again in June 1939. After the amendment of Articles 2 and 3 in favor of the Belfast Agreement in 1998–1999, the right to exercise jurisdiction was confined to the Twenty-Six Counties only; see Lee, *Ireland, 1912–1985,* 201–217.

24 Ballinamuck commemoration: "Heroes of Ballinamuck Battle Honoured," *Longford Leader,* September 17, 1938, 1, 3; RÓB IVs.

26 Delegation of the powers of government to the IRA: Ó Brádaigh, *Dílseacht,* 36–39; Bell, *The Secret Army,* 154.

26 Protest against the Treason Bill: "Government Has a Duty" and "Ordinary Law Is Not Enforced," both in *Longford Leader,* March 18, 1939, 1; "General Mac Eoin and Treason Bill," *Longford Leader,* March 18, 1939, 8; Longford County Council to Seán Mac Eoin, March 3, 1939, Box 9/10, Loose Biographical Notes, Seán Mac Eoin Papers; Lyons, *Ireland since the Famine,* 534; Lee, *Ireland, 1912–1985,* 219–224.

27 Coventry explosion and executions of Peter Barnes and James McCormick: RÓB IVs; Bell, *The Secret Army,* 161–162, 171–172; "Longford in Mourning for Executed Irishmen," *Longford Leader,* February 10, 1940, 1; "Protests Against Executions," *Longford Leader,* February 24, 1940, 1. Quotation at the Mullingar Mental Health Committee: "Mullingar Committee's Resolution," *Westmeath Independent,* February 10, 1940, 5.

28 IRA campaign and Fianna Fáil response, military tribunals, Tony D'Arcy and Seán McNeela hunger strikes, deaths of Richard Goss and Barney Casey: Bell, *The Secret Army,*

145–238, see especially 156, 171–178; Tim Pat Coogan, *The IRA,* (Glasgow: Fontana Collins, 1987), 187–191; "Drumlish Shooting Described in Military Court," *Longford Leader,* August 2, 1941, 1, 4; Ruairí Ó Brádaigh, *Longford Remembers,* (Cleenrath, Aughnacliffe, Co. Longford: Seán Lynch on behalf of Co. Longford Branch of the National Graves Association, 1990); "Tom Harte and His Comrades of the Forties: A Tribute to the Republican Soldiers of the Forties," no author or publisher listed, September 1949 (in author's possession); no author, "Ómós Do Tony D'Arcy Galway agus Seán Mac Neela Mayo," Foilsithe ag Coiste Cuimhneacháin Dhomhnach Phádraig, 1990 (in author's possession); Rory Brady quotations: RÓB IVs.

29 Death and funeral of Matt Brady; RÓB IVs; "Co. Surveyor Suspended by Council, Resigns," *Longford Leader,* March 14, 1942, 1; "Health Board's Tribute to Late Mr. Brady," *Longford Leader,* June 13, 1942, 1; "Death of Mr. Matthew Brady," *Longford Leader,* June 13, 1942, 3; "Ballymacormack Cemetery Inscriptions," in *Exploring Family Origins and Old Longford Town* (Westmeath: Westmeath Examiner, 1986). Matt Brady's death was also reported in the *Irish Press:* "Mr. M. Brady, Co. Councillor," *Irish Press,* June 10, 1942, 3.

30 Matt Brady's support for the Irish language and culture and changing the name from Edgeworthstown to Mostrim: letters to the editor, E. R. J. O'Farrell, and Rosa Montagu, *Longford Leader,* December 21, 1935, 8; "Changing a Name: Edgeworthstown or Mostrim, Correspondence from Councillors," *Longford Leader,* January 4, 1936; "Why Mostrim Was Called Edgeworthstown," *Longford Leader,* November 5, 1937, 9. On attending an Irish-language lecture: "Irish Language—Must Be Saved Now," *Longford Leader,* November 5, 1938, 1, 3. Support for the IRA: see resolution of sympathy for James Reynolds and quotations in "Explosion Tragedy Recalled," *Longford Leader,* December 24, 1938, 6; see also *The Last Post,* 75.

30 May Brady at the time of Matt Brady's death: RÓB IVs; Seán Ó Brádaigh interview; "Pádraic Colum: The Longford Poet," text of a lecture given by Mrs. M. Twohig under the auspices of the Longford Tostal Committee at Longford Technical School on May 6th, 1954, Ó Brádaigh family document. May Brady and the Longford County Council: "Health Board's Office Work: Secretary Wants Complete Control," *Longford Leader,* September 15, 1934, 1. May Caffrey's Belfast origins: RÓB IVs. Information on Father Michael O'Flanagan may be found in Denis Carroll, *They Have Fooled You Again: Michael O'Flanagan (1876–1942) Priest, Republican, Social Critic* (Blackrock, County Dublin: Columba Press, 1996).

31 Brady household after the death of Matt Brady: RÓB IVs; Seán Ó Brádaigh interview; Ruairí Ó Brádaigh letter to the editor, "The Long Arm of the Indian People," *SAOIRSE,* Lúnasa/August 1996, 12.

31 Patrick Twohig's background: RÓB IVs; Seán Ó Brádaigh interview.

32 Attending St. Mel's: Eugene McGee, *St. Mel's of Longford* (Longford: St. Mel's Diocesan Trust, 1996); Maria McGuire, *To Take Arms: My Year with the IRA Provisionals* (New York: The Viking Press, 1973), 77. Ruairí and Seán Ó Brádaigh reject McGuire's account and note that there was no more conflict between Rory and Patrick Twohig than that between most teenagers and parents. The Pioneer Total Abstinence Association of the Sacred Heart was founded in 1898 by Father James Cullen. See http://www.pioneertotal.ie. Accessed March 20, 2005.

34 John Devoy, the Fenians, and the Catholic Church: John Devoy, *Recollections of an Irish Rebel* (Shannon, Ireland: Irish University Press, 1969), 118–127.

34 *Wolfe Tone Annual:* see Brian O'Higgins, "My Songs and Myself," *Wolfe Tone Annual 1949* (Dublin: Wolfe Tone Annual, 1949), 16–17.

35 Clann na Poblachta: see Kevin Rafter, *The Clann: The Story of Clann na Poblachta* (Dublin: Mercier Press, 1996).

Chapter 3

36 RÓB moves to Dublin and changes the spelling of his name: RÓB IVs. University College Dublin moved to its present campus in the 1960s. Several Republicans adopted the

Irish form of their names during the 1950s, including Tom Gill (Tomás Mac Giolla) and John Stephenson (Seán Mac Stiofáin).

36 RÓB attends first Republican event in Dublin: RÓB IVs.

36 1950 Sinn Féin Ard Fheis: "Ard-Fheis of Sinn Féin and Others," *SAOIRSE,* Samhain/November 2000, 14.

37 On Margaret Buckley: *The United Irishman,* September 1962, 1, 9.

37 Paddy McLogan, Tony Magan, and Tomás Mac Curtáin: "the austere plotter from a previous generation" and "a hard man," Bell, *The Secret Army,* 245–248; "Ard-Fheis of Sinn Féin and Others," *SAOIRSE,* Samhain/November 2000, 14; Uinseann MacEoin, *The IRA in the Twilight Years, 1923–1948* (Dublin: Argenta Publications, 1997), 495–516 (especially 509), 617–632, 674, 875–877; Coogan, *The IRA* (1987 ed.), 324–329. On conditions in Port Laoise in the 1940s, see Bell, *The Secret Army,* 179–181; Coogan, *The IRA* (1987 ed.), 257–259.

37 Takeover of Sinn Féin by the IRA: According to an internal IRA document, "In the late 20's differences arose between the I.R.A. and Sinn Féin so that the two organizations drifted apart. Following the re-organisation of the I.R.A. after the Second World War, approaches were made to Sinn Féin to re-constitute the old co-operation and to work together again. This plan was adopted at the Sinn Féin Ard-Fheis in 1949, with one proviso only—that Sinn Féin recognised the fact that the Army Council now held the powers of government of the Second Dáil and was, consequently, the supreme authority in the Republican Movement. They also realised that their future policy would have to conform with Army policy. If it did not, the co-operation between the two organisations would cease and Sinn Féin would have to take its separate road again." The document says at the top: "The following is a factual outline of the lead up to the crisis which developed on the leadership of the civil wing of the Republican Movement following the stopping of the resistance campaign" General Headquarters memo, Oglaigh na hÉireann–IRA Department of Publicity, April 1964 (henceforth, GHQ memo) (photocopy in author's possession).

38 RÓB seeks membership in the IRA and General Army Orders: RÓB IVs; Bell, *The Secret Army* (1987 ed.), 271n9; and Coogan, *The IRA* (1987 ed.), 327.

39 RÓB as a typical IRA recruit: Bell, *The Secret Army,* 257.

39 RÓB background and quotation: interview with Mick McCarthy, Kitty O'Brien and Mick Fitzgibbon.

40 RÓB's early IRA career, Easter Commemorations: RÓB IVs.

40 Matt Casey at Easter Commemorations: Republican Sinn Féin Cabhair Testimonial, 1991 (in author's possession).

41 "Long may his memory and his ideals live in the hearts of his countrymen": Untitled article, probably from the *United Irishman,* May 1951, in Seán Ó Brádaigh's clippings.

41 1954 Longford Easter Commemoration: "I.R.A. Heroes Honoured," *Longford Leader,* April 24, 1954; RÓB IVs.

41 RÓB as IRA section leader; first IRA convention; RÓB as commanding officer Longford: RÓB IVs.

42 "co-opted" onto the Executive: When an unexpected opening arises on the Executive, members of the body will approach a potential replacement. If the person is agreeable, someone will propose that he or she join the Executive at a meeting. If the motion is seconded, a vote is taken and the person formally joins the body. The Army Council and other bodies also follow this procedure.

43 RÓB academic career, University College Dublin boxing club, takes job in Roscommon: RÓB IVs. In Roscommon, Ó Brádaigh rented lodgings where one of the other roomers was a Garda chief superintendent. The superintendent would let Ó Brádaigh in when he arrived late after an evening of IRA activities. Ó Brádaigh discussed politics with the man, but limited it to events that predated his birth in 1932. Death of Patrick Twohig: *Longford Leader,* March 24, 1951, 10.

44 Tommy McDermott, RÓB as training officer: RÓB IVs; Seán Scott interview; interview with Belfast IRA veteran.

Chapter 4

47 Northern Ireland: Republicans refer to the area as the Six Counties, rejecting the British label of Northern Ireland.

47 Arms raids; the Felstead raid: Bell, *The Secret Army,* 240–241, 258–265; Coogan, *The IRA* (1987 ed.), 336–337; Seán Mac Stiofáin, *Memoirs of a Revolutionary* (Letchworth, Hertfordshire: Free Ireland Book Club, 1975).

49 General Army Order No. 8: Bell, *The Secret Army,* 266.

49 "Just distribution and effective control of the Nation's wealth and resources": Coogan, *The IRA* (1987 ed.), 330–331.

50 1955 Westminster election: "The Petition," *Irish Times,* September 3, 1955; see also Michael Farrell, *Northern Ireland: The Orange State* (London: Pluto Press, 1980), 209–211.

50 Mitchell and Clarke disqualifications: Bell, *The Secret Army,* 268–270; "Court Unseats Sinn Féin MP: Unionist Candidate 'Elected,'" *Irish Independent,* September 3, 1955.

51 Fermanagh Feis: "16 Injured in Clashes at Newtownbutler," *Irish Independent,* July 25, 1955.

51 1955 IRA convention: Bell, *The Secret Army,* 268–270.

52 Arborfield raid: Bell, *The Secret Army,* 272–275; RÓB IVs; Frank Skuse to the author, December 10, 1997; "Anonymous" [RÓB], "The Arborfield Raid, by One of the Volunteers Who Took Part in It," *United Irishman,* Samhain/November 1955, 1–2.

55 Aftermath of Arborfield: "50,000 Men Hunt Raiders: 'Boats Awaiting Arms at Plymouth' Report," *Irish Press,* August 15, 1955. Burglars use "jemmys" for prying open things like windows. The incident reminded him that two years earlier he had visited London with student friends. They were trying to find Westminster and he asked a police officer for directions. The officer replied, "What do you want to do, Paddy, blow up the ruddy place?" He wanted to say "Bloody sure," but instead acted embarrassed and got the directions.

55 Hoax raid in Wales: "Second Arms Raid Fails, Emergency Meeting of British Cabinet," *The Irish Press,* August 16, 1955, 1, 6.

55 Finding the Arborfield weapons: "British Police Recover Arms Stolen by Irish in Raid," *New York Times,* August 17, 1955, 1–2.

55 Arrest and conviction of Murphy, Murphy, and Doyle: Bell, *The Secret Army,* 274–275; "Arms Raid Charge, Three Irishmen Again Remanded," *Irish Press,* September 6, 1955.

56 Seán Cronin and Operation Harvest: Coogan, *The IRA* (1987 ed.), 369–370; Bell, *The Secret Army,* 276.

56 John Costello speech: "Government Resolved to Curb Militant Organisations," *Irish Press,* December 1, 1955.

56 Catholic hierarchy condemnation: see "Statement by Dr. Kinane on Collections for Prisoners," *Irish Press,* January 28, 1956; RÓB, discussion with May Brady Twohig; RÓB IVs. A similar condemnation was given by Cardinal D'Alton, the Catholic primate of Ireland, on Christmas Eve 1954. The cardinal stated that it was a "mortal sin for a Catholic to become or remain a member of an organization or society which arrogates to itself the right to bear arms and use them against its own or another state." See John Biggs-Davison and George Chowdharay-Best, *The Cross of St. Patrick: The Catholic Unionist Tradition in Ireland* (Bourne End, Buckinghamshire: Kensal Press), 369–370.

57 RÓB on the clergy: RÓB IVs.

57 Seán Cronin writes *Notes on Guerrilla Warfare* and battle lectures: Bell, *The Secret Army,* 286; see also *Handbook for Volunteers of the Irish Republican Army: Notes on Guerrilla Warfare* (IRA General Headquarters 1956; repr., Boulder, Colo.: Paladin Press, 1985), 12–16, probably written by Seán Cronin.

57 No dilemma for Stormont government: *Irish Press,* December 1, 1955.

57 Ban of processions associated with the Fermanagh Feis scheduled for July 22, 1956: "Outcry over Ban on Newtownbutler Feis," *The Sunday Press,* July 22, 1956; and "RUC Mass in Feis," *Irish Press,* July 23, 1956.

57 Decision for a campaign, July 1956: RÓB IVs; Bell, *The Secret Army,* 277. It was the second time Larry Grogan, who had been a member of the Army Council in 1938–1939, had voted to start an IRA campaign.

58 The Christle split and November attacks: Bell, *The Secret Army,* 279–280; "6 Posts Wrecked On Irish Border," *New York Times,* Monday, November 12, 1956, 22.

58 RÓB and Christle's group: RÓB IVs; Seán Cronin interview; Bell, *The Secret Army,* 277–278.

58 Start of the campaign: "Revolt in the North, 1956–62," *SAOIRSE,* Eanáir/January 1997, 8–9.

58 Decision to exclude Belfast: Bell, *The Secret Army,* 285, 287–288n17, 290–291 and 307nn1 and 2; Henry Patterson, *The Politics of Illusion: A Political History of the IRA,* rev. ed. (1989; London: Serif, 1997), 92–93. Patterson states that it is unclear if Belfast was excluded because of a desire to avoid sectarian conflict or because of security issues. Ó Brádaigh, who was on the Army Council at the time, states that Belfast was excluded because of Doyle's arrest. Major security sweeps netted most of the Belfast IRA, leaving no one to organize anything. Patterson claims that in order to avoid "sectarian animosities" there was an order from general headquarters that "all possible steps had to be taken to avoid shooting members of the part-time Protestant constabulary"; that is, the B Specials. Ó Brádaigh does not remember this and notes that the statement announcing the campaign called on members of the RUC and B Specials to either step aside or join the IRA. They did not step aside, and on the first night of the campaign, an RUC officer in Armagh City was shot. On the third night, the IRA attacked RUC barracks at Lisnaskea and Derrylin.

59 December 12th activities: "Terrorists Raid In Northern Ireland: Radio Unit and a Courthouse Are Wrecked—Attack on Barracks Is Beaten Off," *New York Times,* December 12, 1956, 19:3.

59 December 14th activities: "Disorder Grows In North Ireland: 2 Police Stations Attacked—Navy Base Escapes Harm as Bomb Fails to Explode," *New York Times,* December 14, 1956.

59 Reaction to the campaign: "North Ireland Sets Firm Terror Curbs," *New York Times,* December 15, 1956; "Dublin Regime Pledges Action," *New York Times,* December 15, 1956; "North Ireland Gets British Army's Aid," *New York Times,* December 16, 1956, 1, 24.

59 "Dusk-to-dawn curfew": "Belfast to Impose Curfew," *New York Times,* December 21, 1956.

59 British Army engineers destroy bridges: "Border Roads Cut by North Ireland," *New York Times,* December 22, 1956, 4.

59 Police round up thirty Republicans: "Belfast Seizes 30; British Cut Road," *New York Times,* December 23, 1956. After the ban was imposed, anyone who tried to contest an election as a Sinn Féin candidate was subject to arrest. Until 1973, Sinn Féin candidates ran as "Republicans." Later, Sinn Féin *cumainn* were organized as Republican Clubs.

59 Sinn Féin banned: "Ban on Sinn Féin," *United Irishman,* Bulletin, January 5, 1957.

60 Irish police and army personnel arrest suspected IRA activists along the border: "Irish Units Hunt Border Raiders," *New York Times,* December 17, 1956, 15.

60 John Costello urges Anthony Eden: "Costello Bids Eden: End Irish Partition," *New York Times,* December 24, 1956.

60 RÓB misses start of the campaign: RÓB IVs.

Chapter 5

61 Teeling Column: "Revolt in the North, 1956–62," *SAOIRSE,* Eanáir/January 1997, 8–9. The full complement of the column was Noel Kavanagh, Dublin, commanding officer; Ruairí Ó Brádaigh, second in command; Charlie Murphy, general headquarters staff; Pat McManus, Fermanagh; Paddy Duffy, Cavan; Pat McGirl, Leitrim; John Joe Ruane, Galway;

Paddy Hanniffy, Galway; Willie Folan, Galway; Peadar Murray, Mayo; and Joe Daly, Leo Collins, Dermot Blake, and Des Clarke, Meath.

61 Derrylin raid: Bell, *The Secret Army,* 295–297. RÓB's reaction to being under fire for the first time: RÓB IVs; RÓB to the author, October 10, 1998. See also "Inquest on Shot Constable, Sympathy," *Irish Press,* January 1, 1957, 1, 5; "Hunt Goes on for Derrylin Attackers," *Irish Press,* January 1, 1957.

63 Responsibility for shooting Constable Scally: Joe Jackson, "Soldier of Destiny," *Hot Press* 15, no. 7 (April 18, 1991): 16.

63 Derrylin arrests: "Seven Men Arrested in Cavan," *Irish Press,* January 1, 1957; "Men's Arrest in Cavan Described: Six Are Sentenced," *Irish Press,* January 15, 1957; "May Be Charged Today in Dublin," *Irish Press,* January 2, 1957.

64 Offer of amnesty: RÓB to the author, February 20, 1998. Ó Brádaigh states that "Kelly attempted to trade the dropping of charge re. ammo for info. on other comrades' whereabouts."

64 Brookeborough raid: "Two Irish Extremists Killed during Raid," *New York Times,* January 2, 1957, 3:6; Bell, *The Secret Army.*

65 Brookeborough raid; Seán South and Fergal O'Hanlon and nationalism: Bell, *The Secret Army,* 297–300.

65 Court appearances of Derrylin raiders: "Justice Dismisses Cases against Seven Men, Inspector: No Evidence of a Proclamation," *Irish Press,* January 3, 1957; "Offenses Against the State Act," *Irish Press,* Friday, January 4, 1957; Untitled article about the Geneva Convention, *United Irishman,* Bulletin, Eanáir/January 5, 1956, 7; "17 Are Remanded: Three Groups Charged in Dublin District Court," *Irish Press,* January 11, 1957.

66 Justice Lennon: RÓB IVs; "District Justice Lennon Resigns: Judge's Report Is Issued," *Irish Press,* May 25, 1957.

67 Prisons filling: "More Men Arrested in Belfast," *Irish Press,* January 14, 1957; "R.U.C. Arrest 38 More in Early Morning Swoop," *The Sunday Press,* January 13, 1957; "Speeches at College Green Meeting," *Irish Press,* January 13, 1957; Bell, *The Secret Army,* 300–301; "Five I.R.A. Leaders Sentenced to Jail," *New York Times,* January 30, 1957, 7:16; "District Justice Orders Return of Ammunition," *Irish Times,* January 24, 1957; "Inquiry into D.J.'s Conduct," *Irish Press,* January 24, 1957; "Two Men Are Sentenced: Detective Tells of Plan Attack Found in Flat," *Irish Press,* January 18, 1957.

70 Life in Mountjoy: RÓB IVs; Bell, *The Secret Army,* 178–180. In the 1940s, Larry Grogan, a member of the Army Council, entered the Curragh and assumed that his rank on the outside would be respected on the inside, which contributed to difficulties in the prison. The 1950s leadership made sure to avoid a repeat.

72 Dáithí O'Connell: Republican Sinn Féin Cabhair Testimonial, 1991, Díóg Ní Conaill notes; Mick McCarthy interview.

72 Family visits: RÓB IVs; Deirdre Caffrey O'Connell interview. May Brady Twohig, who began her career before 1935, was able to keep her job although she was married.

74 1957 Leinster House election: Bell, *The Secret Army,* 304, 309; RÓB to the author, February 20, 1998.

75 Election results and de Valera comments: "To Try to Avert Need to Emigrate: Mr. de Valera," *Irish Press,* March 9, 1957; "How the First Preference Votes Were Cast," *Irish Press,* March 3, 1957; "Inter-Party Defeated, Mr. Carter Loses Seat to Sinn Féin," *Longford Leader,* March 9, 1957; Ó Brádaigh letter: "Sinn Féin Victory Rally: Jailed Deputy's Letter," *Longford Leader,* March 16, 1957.

Chapter 6

77 Human rights letter: "Jailing of Ruaidhrí Ó Brádaigh, T.D.," *The United Irishman,* Meitheamh/June 1958; RÓB IVs. For information on the Lawless case, see Coogan, *The IRA*

(1987 ed.), 411–412. The European Convention on Human Rights and Fundamental Freedoms was adopted by the 21-nation Council of Europe in 1949. With Seán Mac Bride as the minister for external affairs, the Dublin government was the first to accept the jurisdiction of the European Court of Human Rights. Ó Brádaigh, with Tony Magan, prepared a brief for the convention. The Dublin government replied that it had "derogated from the Convention" because of the emergency situation; that is, the IRA's campaign. Ó Brádaigh countered that there was no emergency because "a hand had not been raised" against the government. In 1961, the human rights commission finally ruled that Ó Brádaigh's case was inadmissable. However, the ruling vindicated the right of the commission and the Court of Human Rights to intervene. A second case, by Gerry Lawless, also went to the Court of Human Rights. Even though Lawless had left the IRA at the time of the Christle split in 1956, he still was interned. His attorney filed an application with the European Commission on Human Rights, seeking his immediate release. He signed an "undertaking" indicating that he would refrain from further activities and was subsequently released. In July 1961, the Court of Human Rights found that the "undertaking" had no legal status but also determined that the court had the right to question a country's decision to adopt measures such as internment. This gave the court the ability to rule on the legality of extreme measures that might be adopted in a crisis.

77 Tony Magan returns to the IRA: Bell, *The Secret Army,* 304.

77 Crossmaglen ambush: "Irish Terrorists Slay Policeman," *New York Times,* July 5, 1957, 3:7; see also Bell, *The Secret Army,* 305.

78 Police raids in July 1957: "63 Men Arrested in Raids by Civic Guards President of Sinn Féin Held in Swoop on Dublin Meeting," *Irish Times,* July 8, 1957.

78 Internment in the South: "Government Establishes Internment Camps at Curragh: Many Arrested Persons Transferred," *Irish Times,* July 9, 1957; "Indication of Courts' Inadequacy," *Irish Times,* July 9, 1957; "Mountjoy Prisoners May Be Sent to Curragh," *Irish Times,* July 10, 1957. Under internment, persons who, in the opinion of an Irish government minister, are involved in activities which threaten the peace or the security of the state may be arrested and detained without trial. Internees have the right to apply to a commission for release. Unless reasonable grounds for continued detention are presented, applicants must be released. None of the total of 200 Republican internees applied for release.

78 *Irish Times* editorial: "Special Powers," *Irish Times,* July 9, 1957.

78 RÓB expecting internment: RÓB IVs. Ó Brádaigh remembers saying to a fellow internee, "If one TD could be interned, then could not a majority—80 TDs—likewise be interned!" Erskine Childers, the Fianna Fáil minister for lands and a TD for Longford-Westmeath, publicly attacked Sinn Féin on a number of occasions. In a letter to the press dated May 23, 1957, which the prison governor refused to send out, Ó Brádaigh suggested that Childers should exercise "more constructiveness and restraint" and, predicting internment, stated, "A more sinister aspect of all this is the probability that Mr. Childers may be engaged in preparing the ground for Coercion of a more ruthless and savage type, timed to follow on the release next July of the 30 Republicans here in Mountjoy." RÓB, letter from Mountjoy Prison, 23/5/57 (photocopy in author's possession).

79 The London *Times* statement; "Well Done Mr. de Valera!" *The United Irishman,* Lúnasa/August 1957, 5.

78 Indications that prisoners would be interned: "Mountjoy Prisoners May Be Sent to Curragh," *Irish Times,* July 10, 1957.

79 RÓB interned: RÓB IVs; "15 Released—Then Interned: Rearrested Outside Jail," *Evening Press,* July 13, 1957.

79 Life in the Curragh: RÓB IVs; "115 Are Held in Curragh," *The United Irishman,* Meán Fómhair/September 1957, 8.

80 Discussions in the Curragh; Gandhi: RÓB IVs; "Big Longford Demonstration," *The United Irishman,* Deireadh Fómhair/October 1957, 7.

80 Political discussions in the Curragh: RÓB IVs; Tomás Mac Giolla interview.

81 The Flags and Emblems Act: Deutsch and Magowan, *Northern Ireland: A Chronology of Events,* 1:153.

82 Visit of Ó Brádaigh's Swiss cousin; the International Red Cross: RÓB IVS. The Longford demonstration: RÓB IVs; Seán Ó Brádaigh interview; RÓB Notes, n.d. Also, in October 1957, Ó Brádaigh was granted one week's parole to attend the funeral of his stepbrother, John Twohig, who was drowned at sea.

82 Exercising with Dáithí O'Connell: McGuire, *To Take Arms,* 76; RÓB IVs.

83 One hundred sixty Republicans in the Curragh in July 1958: "Editorial," *The United Irishman,* Iúil/July 1958, 12.

83 Relationship between the camp leadership and the IRA leadership: RÓB IVs; Bell, *The Secret Army,* 323.

83 Ó Brádaigh-O'Connell escape: RÓB IVs; Seán Cronin interview; Tomás Mac Giolla interview; Bell, *The Secret Army,* 322–323; "Two Internees Escape from the Curragh," *Belfast Telegraph,* September 25, 1958; "2 Internees Escape from Curragh," *Irish Press,* September 26, 1958; "Army Inquiry into Curragh Escape: Two Men Still at Large," *Irish Independent,* September 26, 1958; "Day-Long Search after Two Men Escape from Curragh: Sinn Féin Deputy and Companion," *Irish Times,* September 26, 1958. Frank Skuse arrived in the Curragh the day before the escape. According to Skuse, Tony Magan handpicked Ó Brádaigh because he "was best suited to carry on the policies of the old guard Republicans." J. B. O'Hagan sent to the Curragh: *The United Irishman,* Feabhra/February 1958, 8; Frank Skuse to author, December 10, 1997.

84 John Joe McGirl as chief of staff: Bell, *The Secret Army,* 322.

84 RÓB becomes chief of staff: RÓB IVs; Bell, *The Secret Army,* 322–323.

85 Changes in the IRA leadership since 1956; importance and death of Pat McManus: RÓB IVs; Bell, *The Secret Army,* 322; Seán Cronin, "Notes" (typed manuscript, January 1968), referred to in Bell, *The Secret Army,* 309; RÓB to the author; *The Last Post,* 173; "Funeral of Patrick McManus: Last Respects Paid By Thousands," *The United Irishman,* Lúnasa/August 1958, 3. McManus was close with the Ó Brádaighs. May had used her home as a safe house for him and Seán gave the oration at the funeral.

86 Continuing dissension in the Curragh: Bell, *The Secret Army,* 324; "The Following is a Factual Outline of the Lead Up to the Crisis Which Developed on the Leadership of the Civil Wing of the Republican Movement Following the Stopping of the Resistance Campaign in February '62," GHQ memo.

86 Mass escape: "16 Flee Irish Prison: 44 Others Balked in Attempt at a Mass Escape," *New York Times,* December 3, 1958, 7:1; Bell, *The Secret Army,* 325; Tomás Mac Giolla interview.

87 Escapees rejoin the IRA: RÓB IVs; Bell, *The Secret Army,* 324–325.

87 De Valera; Lemass; changes in the Irish economy: Lyons, *Ireland since the Famine,* 583–585; Lee, *Ireland, 1912–1985,* 329–410, especially 359–360. It is an interesting twist of Irish politics that Seán Mac Eoin, who in 1921 nominated Éamon de Valera for the presidency of the Irish Republic, was the opposition presidential candidate almost forty years later.

87 Meeting of the old and current IRA leadership; RÓB drafts statement: RÓB IVs; Bell, *The Secret Army,* 326–327.

88 Charlie Murphy dismissed: Bell, *The Secret Army,* 327–328; RÓB IVs.

89 1959 IRA convention: RÓB IVs; Bell, *The Secret Army,* 327–328; GHQ memo.

89 Rallies in Mullingar, Longford, and Roscommon: "No Apology for Teaching Fenian Faith—Rory Brady," *Roscommon Champion,* June 19, 1959; "Rory Brady Makes His First Public Appearance," *Roscommon Champion,* June 12, 1959.

90 1959 Wolfe Tone Commemoration: "Pilgrimage to Wolfe Tone's Grave," *Longford Leader,* June 27, 1959.

Chapter 7

92 1959 Westminster election: "Unionists Jubilant over Sinn Féin Move: Imprisoned Men Nominated for Two Areas," *Sunday Independent,* Belfast, September 27, 1959; "Allegations by Sinn Féin, 'Men Held Often Beaten,' *Sunday Review,* September 27, 1959; "Sinn Féin Selects Candidates," *Irish Times,* September 26, 1959; "Sinn Féin's Flat Feet," *Irish Times,* September 26, 1959; RÓB IVs; "Mr. Macmillan on Tory Party's Victory," *Irish Independent,* October 10, 1959; "Loss of Seats Deplored by Nationalists," *Irish Press,* October 10, 1959; "Unionists Retain All 12 Seats," *Irish Times,* October 10, 1959.

92 RÓB's personal life and marriage: RÓB IVs; Patsy O'Connor Ó Brádaigh interview; "Rory Brady Has Not Yet Asked for His Post Back," *Roscommon Herald,* March 28, 1959; "Sinn Féin T.D. Weds," *Sunday Review,* October 4, 1959.

93 Dáithí O'Connell shot; IRA confined to the border: "Shot Cork Man Still Very Ill," *Irish Independent,* November 12, 1959; RÓB to the author, n.d. [1997]; Bell, *The Secret Army,* 328–329. Joining O'Hagan and Devlin in Crumlin Road: *The United Irishman,* Nollaig/ December 1959, 6, 8; "Corkman Sentenced to Eight Years: Illegal Possession of a Gun," *The Irish Times,* March 25, 1960.

94 RÓB arrested: "Arrest of T.D. in Roscommon," *Roscommon Herald,* November 27, 1959, 1, 7; "Arrest of Sinn Féin Deputy," *The United Irishman,* Nollaig/December 1959, 1.

94 RÓB's court appearances: "Sinn Féin T.D. Is Sentenced: A Sop to British Government," *The United Irishman,* Eanáir/January 1960, 8; "Arrest of Sinn Féin Deputy," *The United Irishman,* Eanáir/January 1959, 10. Patsy Ó Brádaigh miscarriage: RÓB IVs; "Soldier of Destiny," *Hot Press* 15, no. 7 (April 18, 1991): 16.

95 Seán Mac Eoin: RÓB IVs; O'Farrell, *The Blacksmith of Ballinalee,* 24. As Pádraic O'Farrell notes, Mac Eoin, who was friendly with the Ó Brádaighs throughout his career, is worthy of a major biography. Ruairí Ó Brádaigh remembers attending the funeral of an IRA veteran the morning after the raid of the British base at Omagh in October 1954. Mac Eoin leaned over and asked him, "Did they capture it?"

95 RÓB released from prison; speech in Mullingar: "Sinn Féin T.D. Welcomed Home: Released After Prison Term," *The United Irishman,* Iúil/July 1960, 5, 11. The article includes his University College Dublin graduation photograph; he is wearing academic robes and holding his diploma.

97 1960 IRA convention: Frank Skuse to the author, December 19, 1997; Bell, *The Secret Army,* 329–331; RÓB IVs. This is Ó Brádaigh's interpretation of his behavior as chairman. It is worth noting that he was so even-handed that Frank Skuse thought Ó Brádaigh supported him. As Skuse describes it, "Rory was the convention chairman and as I spoke I searched his face for an affirmative response. I felt I was getting it." He was mistaken.

98 Seán Cronin's arrest, the letter from the United States, and his resignation: Bell, *The Secret Army,* 329–331.

98 RÓB replaces Cronin as chief of staff; Seán and Ruairí Ó Brádaigh edit the *United Irishman:* RÓB IVs; Seán Ó Brádaigh interview.

99 1960 local elections and beginning of broader politics: "At Issue in the Local Elections," *The United Irishman,* Aibreán/April 1960, 8–9; see also, "Vote Sinn Féin," *The United Irishman,* Meitheamh/June 1960, 14; "Sinn Féin L.G. Candidates," *The United Irishman,* Meitheamh/June 1960, 14; "Features of Election," *The United Irishman,* Lúnasa/August 1960, 12; "Sinn Féin Successes," *The United Irishman,* Lúnasa/August 1960, 12; "Sinn Féin Meeting Representatives Confer," *The United Irishman,* Meán Fómhair/September 1960, 8; "Sinn Féin Meeting," *The United Irishman,* Samhain/November 1960, 1, 12; *The United Irishman,* Nollaig/December 1959, 6, 8; Bell, *The Secret Army,* 326.

101 RÓB's 1960 arrest at Midleton: RÓB IVs; "Sinn Féin Deputy's Arrest in Cork," *Longford Leader,* December 12, 1960, 1+; "Sinn Féin T.D. Arrested in Co. Cork: Statement by Ruaidhrí Ó Brádaigh, T.D., to a Meeting of Longford-Westmeath Comhairlí Ceantair of Sinn Féin in Longford on December 11, 1960," *The United Irishman,* Eanáir/January 1960, 5.

102 IRA's conflict with the RUC: Bell, *The Secret Army,* 311, 323–332; "2 Irish Republicans Jailed," *New York Times,* October 28, 1958, 28; "Three Held in Irish Killing," *New York Times,* January 29, 1961, 30. James Crossan: *The Last Post,* 81; J. Bowyer Bell, *IRA Tactics and Targets* (Swords, County Dublin: Poolbeg Press, 1990), 73–77; RÓB IVs; "Story of 'Campaign,'" *Belfast Newsletter,* February 27, 1962. Around this time an IRA unit in Sligo informed the Army Council that Lord Mountbatten regularly vacationed in Sligo with no security precautions. Ó Brádaigh was amazed, but because there was a danger of conflict with the state's forces, he tucked the information away for future reference.

103 Ireland's application to the Common Market: In January 1963, Charles de Gaulle rebuffed the British and Irish applications. Lyons, *Ireland since the Famine,* 597–598; Lee, *Ireland, 1912–1985,* 370–371. In addition to focusing more on social and economic issues, the Republicans pushed for breaking the "link with sterling." At the time, the Central Bank in Ireland did not control credit, and interest and exchange rates moved in sympathy with sterling, which did not always suit the Irish economy. The link was formally broken in 1979.

103 1961 Leinster House election Loch Bán Aeríocht: The 1961 count in Longford-Westmeath is notable for an interesting anecdote. Paddy Cooney, nephew-in-law of Seán Mac Eoin, was a Fine Gael candidate. It was discovered during the fifth count that a "spoiled vote" had been included when first-count votes were distributed. The vote was a first-preference vote for Ó Brádaigh, and it should have been ruled invalid and removed from the count. This vote, it was ultimately determined, led to the incorrect elimination of Cooney. Cooney was later elected to Leinster House and in the 1970s was Fine Gael's minister for justice. RÓB IVs; RÓB notes; "Sinn Féin Candidates," RÓB IVs; *The United Irishman,* Meán Fómhair/September 1961, 12; "My Election Guarantee Redeemed—Mr. Brady, T.D.," *The Longford Leader,* February 4, 1961, 11; "Sinn Féin and Leinster House Attitude to 26-Co. Assembly Outlined," *The United Irishman,* Bealtaine/May 1961, 2; "Sinn Féin Candidates Joint Address to Electorate," *The United Irishman,* Meán Fómhair/September 1961, 9; "S.F. Election Manifesto," *The United Irishman,* Meán Fómhair/September 1961, 3; see also "Consider These Facts," *The United Irishman,* Meán Fómhair/September 1961, 10; "Speakers Call for Unity behind National Struggle: Republican Aeríocht at Loch Bán," *The United Irishman,* Meán Fómhair/September 1961, 5; "Fine Gael Can Lead Surely, Successfully," *The Longford Leader,* September 30, 1961, 13; "Leinster House Election First Preference Votes," *Irish Independent,* October 6, 1961, 14; "Election Count Delayed," *Longford Leader,* October 14, 1961, 1, 5. Concession speech; thanks: "Letters to the Editor: Candidate's Vote of Thanks," *Longford Leader,* October 21, 1961, 8; RÓB Notes.

105 IRA incident levels, 1957 versus 1959: Bell, *The Secret Army,* 328–329.

105 November 1961 IRA attack: see Bell, *The Secret Army,* 332–333.

106 Military tribunals: Bell, *The Secret Army,* 333; see also "The Military Tribunal Statement by Sinn Féin Publicity Committee," *The United Irishman,* Márta/March 1962, 5.

106 Decline in morale, dismissal of the Dublin volunteer, and Paddy Doyle: RÓB IVs.

106 Ending the Campaign: Joe McGarrity, who was born in County Tyrone in 1874, emigrated to Philadelphia and was a key figure in Irish-American politics until his death in 1940. "Revolt in the North, 1956–62," *SAOIRSE,* Eanáir/January 1997, 8–9. On Joe McGarrity, see Seán Cronin, *The McGarrity Papers* (Tralee: Anvil Books, 1972; New York: Clan na Gael Books, 1992); "Campaign in Six Counties Halted," *The United Irishman,* Márta/March 1962, 1; "The Roll of Honour," *The United Irishman,* Márta/March 1962, 1; "I.R.A. Statement: Editorial," *Belfast Newsletter,* February 27, 1962. See also "Surrender of I.R.A. Arms Will Convince Ulster: Welcome—and Warning," *Belfast Newsletter,* February 28, 1962.

106 Campaign summary: Bell, *The Secret Army,* 284, 306–307; Coogan, *The IRA* (1987 ed.); Seán Cronin, *Irish Nationalism: Its Roots and Ideology* (Dublin: Academy Press, 1980), 171–175, 332–335; M. L. R. Smith, *Fighting for Ireland? The Military Strategy of the Irish Republican Movement* (New York: Routledge, 1995), 71–72.

109 IRA not engaging in sectarian attacks and Cronin's "Appeal to Unionists": Denis Barritt and Charles F. Carter, *The Northern Ireland Problem* (Oxford: Oxford University Press, 1972), 131, cited in Cronin, *Irish Nationalism,* 172–173 and 284n190.

109 Ruairí Ó Brádaigh–Seán Mac Stiofáin conversation: RÓB IVs.

109 Michael Farrell quotation: Michael Farrell, *Northern Ireland: The Orange State,* 221.

Chapter 8

110 Split in Sinn Féin: Jack Holland, *The American Connection: U.S. Guns, Money & Influence in Northern Ireland* (New York: Penguin Books, 1987), 76; GHQ memo; see also Bell, *The Secret Army,* 338–339. Even after he was expelled from the movement, McLogan was not finished. At the time of his death, he was arranging arms shipments with George Harrison, a native of County Mayo living in New York. Presumably the arms were for a future IRA campaign. At the age of 65 he was found dead in the garden of his Dublin home on July 21, 1964. He had been shot in the head; found by his side was a pistol and a spent cartridge. There is speculation that McLogan was assassinated by Republicans opposed to his politics and activities. It is unlikely that McLogan, a devout Catholic who was said to be in good spirits by his friends, committed suicide. The coroner ruled that the wound was self inflicted, probably by accident.

111 Acting officers: "Sinn Féin Conference," *The United Irishman,* Lúnasa/August 1962, 5. Mac Giolla's reinstatement: *The United Irishman,* Lúnasa/August 1962, 1; RÓB IVs.

111 Influence of Tony Magan and Paddy McLogan on RÓB: RÓB IVs; Coogan, *The IRA* (1987 ed.), 324–325; Ruairí Ó Brádaigh, "Footnote on the Death of Pádraig Mac Lógán, ex-M.P.," in MacEoin, *The IRA in the Twilight Years,* 875–877; Holland, *The American Connection,* 64, 76–79; "Shot Wound Caused Death of Publican," *Irish Independent,* July 30, 1964.

112 Brian Faulkner's announcement and the Irish government's position: "North's Security Precautions to Continue, Says Faulkner," *Irish Times,* February 28, 1962; see also "I.R.A. End Ulster Campaign but Organisation to Stay Intact: No Relaxation—Mr. Faulkner," *Belfast Newsletter,* February 27, 1962; "Civic Guard to Stay on Border," *Irish Times,* February 28, 1962.

112 Release of prisoners: "I.R.A. Members Freed" and "Ireland Releases 29 in Wake of Pledge to Stop Attacks," *New York Times,* April 21, 1962, 3:6; "In Jail for Free Ireland," *The United Irishman,* Aibreán/April 1962, 10; "The Released Men," *The United Irishman,* Bealtaine/May 1962, 1; "Prisoners Reception," *The United Irishman,* Lúnasa/August 1962, 5.

112 Dáithí O'Connell–Deirdre Caffrey courtship: Deirdre Caffrey O'Connell interview.

112 Tomás Mac Giolla at Bodenstown, 1962: RÓB IVs; "Move Forward with Enthusiasm: Bodenstown Speaker on Next Phase of Struggle," *The United Irishman,* Iúil/July 9, 1962, 4.

113 RÓB reinstated: RÓB IVs; "The Power of Coercion," *The United Irishman,* Bealtaine/May 1962, 12; "R. Ó Brádaigh Applies for Post," *The United Irishman,* Lúnasa/August 1962, 3.

114 IRA "shattered"; 1962 convention: Bell, *The Secret Army,* 339; RÓB IVs.

114 Cathal Goulding: RÓB IVs. Ó Brádaigh states that Goulding was not involved in Sinn Féin until the 1960s: RÓB IVs; J. Bowyer Bell, *The Secret Army: From 1916–,* 240–241, 339; *Rebellion Handbook,* with introduction by Declan Kiberd (1916; repr., Dublin: Mourne River Press, 1988), 72.

115 Army Council after the 1962 convention: RÓB IVs; see also references in Bell, *The Secret Army.* Although Ó Brádaigh will not discuss the composition of the IRA Army Council after 1969, he confirms that Mulcahy, Costello, and McInerney were on the seven-person council at various points in the early 1960s.

115 Denis McInerney not interned: Denis McInerney interview.

115 Séamus Costello: see "Séamus Costello: One of the Greatest Leaders in 800 Years," *An Camcheachta/The Starry Plough,* October 1977, available online at http://irsm.org/irsp/costello/costellobio.html, accessed March 16, 2005.

115 Seán Garland and 1960s IRA: J. Bowyer Bell, *The IRA, 1968–2000: Analysis of a Secret Army* (London: Frank Cass Publishers, 2000), 64, 115, 301; Bell, *The Secret Army,* 343.

115 1962 Sinn Féin Ard Fheis; reorganizing Roscommon Sinn Féin: RÓB IVs; "Roscommon Reorganises," *The United Irishman,* Eanáir/January 1963, 4.

115 1962 Sinn Féin Officer Board and Ard Chomhairle: *The United Irishman,* Nollaig/December 1962, 4.

116 Tom Maguire described: see Ó Brádaigh, *Dílseacht,* 42; see also "Major Repairs to Co Roscommon IRA Memorial," *SAOIRSE,* Meán Fómhair/September 1998, 11; Robert White, *Provisional Irish Republicans: An Oral and Interpretive History* (Westport, Conn.: Greenwood Press, 1993), 175–176n1.

117 Seán Cronin quotations: Seán Cronin interview.

117 Tomás Mac Giolla presidential address: "Sinn Féin President's Address," *The United Irishman,* Nollaig/December 1962, 3, 5.

117 Wolfe Tone Society: Cronin, *Irish Nationalism,* 185, 288; Patterson, *The Politics of Illusion* (1997 ed.), 96–112.

118 Jack Bennett, Anthony Coughlan, and Roy Johnston; "because they wouldn't": quotation is from the Roy Johnston interview; Anthony Coughlan interview; Patterson, *The Politics of Illusion* (1997 ed.), 96–99; "Jack Bennett," *An Phoblacht/Republican News,* December 7, 2000, 17. Pat Walsh quotation of Roy Johnston: Pat Walsh, *Irish Republicanism and Socialism: The Politics of the Republican Movement, 1905 to 1994* (Belfast: Athol Books, 1994), 51.

118 Republican Movement rejects communism: Connolly Association: "No Link with Connolly Association, *The United Irishman,* Lúnasa/August 1960, 12; "Sinn Féin Opposes E.E.C. Tie: Ard-Chomhairle Statement of Vital Issues: Irish People to Fight Sell-Out," *The United Irishman,* Márta/March 1962, 6–7.

119 Speculation that a "radical" Republican political party would emerge: "A Radical Political Party May Emerge," *Belfast Newsletter,* February 28, 1962.

119 1964 and 1965 Ard Fheiseanna: Walsh, *Irish Republicanism and Socialism,* 51; White, *Provisional Irish Republicans,* 49; RÓB IVs.

119 1965 extraordinary IRA convention and Sinn Féin Ard Fheis: RÓB IVs; "Attempt to Take over Republican Movement," *An Phoblacht,* Feabhra/February 1970, 2–3; Patterson, *The Politics of Illusion* (1997 ed.), 93. Seán Mac Stiofáin states that there were nine proposals, but in fact there were ten: *Memoirs of a Revolutionary* (London: Gordon Cremonesi, 1975), 92–94.

120 Split in the Army Council and Tomás Mac Giolla's membership: RÓB IVs; Mac Stiofáin, *Memoirs of a Revolutionary,* 99–100; Justin O'Brien, *The Arms Trial* (Dublin: Gill & Macmillan, 2000), 27; Ed Moloney, *A Secret History of the IRA* (New York: W. W. Norton & Company, 2002), 59–60; see also Chapter 9 of this volume.

120 RÓB on 1960s political developments: RÓB IVs; Peadar O'Donnell, *There Will Be Another Day* (Dublin: Dolmen Press, 1963); Peter Hegarty, *Peadar O'Donnell* (Cork: Mercier Press, 1999).

121 Seán Mac Stiofáin versus Roy Johnston: RÓB IVs; see Mac Stiofáin, *Memoirs of a Revolutionary,* 93; Cronin, *Irish Nationalism,* 204; White, *Provisional Irish Republicans,* 34–35. In his memoir *Memoirs of a Revolutionary,* Mac Stiofáin does not identify Johnston as the "Marxist whom I knew to be Moscow-oriented." In *Irish Nationalism: A History of Its Roots and Ideology,* Seán Cronin states that Seán Mac Stiofáin "was something of an anti-Communist zealot, his memoirs suggest."

121 RÓB as "leader of the militarists": Tomás Mac Giolla interview; RÓB IVs. Mac Giolla also states that Ó Brádaigh was "very intensely anti-socialist," which is questionable. Ó Brádaigh certainly was wary of links with communists and their implications for the movement, but in his words and actions, he was committed to social change along socialist lines. In *Memoirs of a Revolutionary,* Mac Stiofáin tends to place himself as the leader of a number of initiatives, beginning in the mid-1960s through his period as chief of staff of the Provisional IRA. With respect to the 1965 extraordinary convention, Ó Brádaigh remembers himself as the leader of those opposed to ending abstentionism. Mac Stiofáin was a central figure through these years, but perhaps not quite as central as he presents. This reflects Mac Stiofáin's tendency to promote himself and the fact that *Memoirs of a Revolutionary*, published in 1975, is the only public account available by one of the founders of the Provisional IRA. He could not write on the roles of others without compromising them. He writes that he had "a certain amount of support" in confronting Johnston. This is a reference to Ruairí Ó Brádaigh and Paddy Mulcahy.

121 Editor of the *United Irishman*: "Birth of the Provos: Conspiracy Theorist," *Irish News*, January 31, 1990, 6; Bell, *The Secret Army*, 346. "Live Horse" article and reactions to it: Walsh, *Irish Republicanism and Socialism*, 56–57.

122 Joe Cahill resigns; quotations: White, *Provisional Irish Republicans*, 49–51; RÓB IVs; Díóg Ní Chonaill, "A Drink from the Lee," Republican Sinn Féin Cabhair Testimonial, 1991, 7–8; Walsh, *Irish Republicanism and Socialism*, 60–61; Deirdre Caffrey O'Connell interview; Patterson, *The Politics of Illusion* (1997 ed.), 141. Cahill became active in the National Graves Association, which is politically nonaligned and supports the preservation of the graves of people who have died in the cause of the Irish Republic. Various sources suggest that many people resigned from the IRA because they opposed the direction advocated by Goulding, Mac Giolla, and their followers. Careful examination suggests that few people resigned for this reason. In *Irish Republicanism and Socialism*, Pat Walsh states that Dáithí O'Connell emigrated from Ireland in the mid-1960s. In *The Politics of Illusion*, Henry Patterson states that O'Connell had drifted out of the movement, "disillusioned by its 'communist links.'" Each is incorrect. After his release from Crumlin Road and their marriage, Dáithí and Deirdre Caffrey O'Connell lived in Cork, where he helped establish a Wolfe Tone Club. They moved to Gorey in County Wexford, where he trained for work as a vocational school teacher. After passing his qualifying examinations, he took a job in Carrick and Ballyshannon Vocational Schools in Donegal in 1968. In Donegal, Dáithí O'Connell became involved in the cooperative activities of Father James McDyer, by whom he was much influenced. Throughout this period he was involved in the Republican Movement.

Chapter 9

124 Viscount Brookeborough; Terence O'Neill; Rev. Ian Paisley: see W. D. Flackes and Sydney Elliott, *Northern Ireland: A Political Directory, 1968–99* (Belfast: Blackstaff Press, 1999), 190, 378–379; 385–390; Farrell, *Northern Ireland: The Orange State*, 90–91.

124 Modernization of the northern economy and educational opportunities: Northern Ireland Civil Rights Association (NICRA), *We Shall Overcome: The History of the Struggle for Civil Rights in Northern Ireland, 1968–1978* (Belfast: NICRA, 1978), 3; Belinda Probert, *Beyond Orange and Green* (Dublin: The Academy Press, 1978), 77–78; Derek Birrell, "Relative Deprivation as a Factor in Conflict in Northern Ireland," *The Sociological Review* 20 (1972): 317–343.

125 Homeless Citizens League and The Campaign for Social Justice: Conn McCluskey, *Up Off Their Knees* ([Belfast, Northern Ireland]: Conn McCluskey and Associates, 1989), 10–11.

125 The Nationalist Party: Farrell, *Northern Ireland: The Orange State*, 60–62, 189, 238–239.

125 National Unity and Conn McCluskey quotation: McCluskey, *Up Off Their Knees*, 62.

125 RÓB candidate in Fermanagh–South Tyrone: "Republican Candidates Selected," *The United Irishman*, Márta/March 1966, 1; RÓB IVs; Godfrey Fitzsimons, "Today on the Election Front—My Main Worry Is Apathy, Says the Marquis," *Belfast Telegraph*, March 30, 1966; "Republican Manifesto Issued," *Irish Times*, March 26, 1966; Wesley Boyd, "Unionists' Majorities Nearly All Fall: Encouraging Election for N.I. Labour and Anti-Partitionists," *Irish Times*, April 2, 1966; "Fitt's Victory Shakes Morale of Unionists," *Irish Independent*, April 2, 1966; Flackes and Elliott, *Northern Ireland: A Political Directory*, 258–259.

128 Coalisland in 1966: "20,000 Gather at Tyrone Centre," *Irish Independent*, April 2, 1966."

129 Richard Behal meets Ruairí Ó Brádaigh: Richard Behal interview; RÓB IVs.

130 The *Brave Borderer*: The resolution, passed at the 1960 IRA convention, was one of the two resolutions Ruairí Ó Brádaigh had opposed. They were formally repealed at the 1962 convention, but they had set a precedent for such activity. No one was ever convicted for the attack on the *Brave Borderer*. The Boyes rifle recovered by the police was missing its firing pin. Behal's discussion of the incident is based on his understanding of what happened. See Bell, *The Secret Army*, 342; Richard Behal interview.

130 Richard Behal's escape: Richard Behal interview; Bell, *The Secret Army*, 343; "Manhunt Continues," *The United Irishman*, Márta/March 1966. Behal will neither confirm nor deny how he escaped.

131 Arrest of Cathal Goulding and Seán Garland; Behal's minor campaign: Bell, *The Secret Army*, 343; "Cathal Goulding Remanded," *The United Irishman*, Márta/March 1966.

131 Richard Behal at Easter 1966 arrest; Richard Behal interview; RÓB IVs.

131 Roy Johnston's conflict with Seán Mac Stiofáin: Walsh, *Irish Republicanism and Socialism*, 60–61; Mac Stiofáin; *Memoirs of a Revolutionary*, 96–97.

131 Denis McInerney on the Johnston-Mac Stiofáin disagreement: Denis McInerney interview. RÓB on the disagreement: RÓB IVs. James Monds: *The Last Post*, 134.

132 Richard Behal court-martial: RÓB IVs; Richard Behal interview; Colman W. Richards, "The Fate of Richard Behal," *Hibernia*, October 1966.

133 1966 IRA convention: In *Memoirs of a Revolutionary*, Seán Mac Stiofáin did not identify the "neutral" person, stating that he was "ambiguous" and remained so for three more years. In *A Secret History of the IRA*, Ed Moloney identifies the convention chairman as Tomás Mac Giolla. Mac Giolla was also identified as a member of the 1966 Army Council in an obituary for Cathal Goulding. Andrew Bushe, "Ex-IRA Big Goulding Dead at 76," *Irish Echo*, January 6–12, 1999. Ruairí Ó Brádaigh confirms Mac Giolla's status. He remembers him consistently voting with those opposed to change until June 1969, at which point he switched and supported Goulding. RÓB IVs; Mac Stiofáin, *Memoirs of a Revolutionary*, 99–100; O'Brien, *The Arms Trial*, 27; Moloney, *A Secret History of the IRA*, 59–60; *Irish Echo* 74, no. 40 (October 3–9, 2001).

133 Tomás Mac Giolla's 1966 presidential address: "Sinn Féin Presidential Address: The Text in Full of Tomás Mac Giolla's Speech," *The United Irishman*, Eanair/January 1967, 5; see also "Integration with Britain Suicidal: Sinn Féin President Slams Agreement," *The United Irishman*, Nollaig/December 1966.

134 Sinn Féin leadership in 1966: "Integration with Britain Suicidal: Sinn Féin President Slams Agreement," *The United Irishman*, Nollaig/December 1966; RÓB IVs; Coogan, *The IRA* (1987 ed.), 420. In 1916, Joe Clarke participated in the Battle of Mount Street Bridge in Dublin. Born in 1881, he was a year older than Éamon de Valera. For Republicans in the IRA and Sinn Féin, especially those victimized by his policies, de Valera personified the word traitor while people like Joe Clarke and Tom Maguire personified loyalty and fidelity to the Republic. As he aged, one of Clarke's ambitions was to outlive de Valera. In 1966, at 85 years of age, he ran a small bookshop in Dublin. It appears that only one senior member of Sinn Féin resigned in the mid-1960s, Seán Caughey, who was vice president of Sinn Féin in 1965. Caughey resigned because he believed the movement was not becoming political fast enough, in contrast to Joe Cahill, who left the IRA because it was becoming too political.

134 1966 Irish presidential election: see Earl of Longford and O'Neill, *Éamon de Valera*, 461–462. Thomas O'Higgins was the nephew of Kevin O'Higgins, the vice president of the Free State who had been assassinated by IRA members acting unofficially in 1927.

135 Expulsion of the North Kerry Comhairle Ceantair: RÓB IVs; Bell, *The Secret Army*, 363–364.

135 *An Phoblacht* in the mid-1960s; Saor Éire; the Saor Éire Action Group: Smith, *Fighting for Ireland?* 76, 84; Joe Dillon interview; Coogan, *The IRA* (1987 ed.), 420–421; Patterson, *The Politics of Illusion* (1989 ed.), 95–96; Liz Walsh, *The Final Beat: Gardaí Killed in the Line of Duty* (Dublin: Gill and Macmillan, 2001), 1–22; Mac Stiofáin, *Memoirs of a Revolutionary*,

95; RÓB IVs; Díóg Ní Chonaill, "A Drink from the Lee," Republican Sinn Féin Cabhair Testimonial, 1991, 7–8; Deirdre Caffrey O'Connell interview. Because Provisional Sinn Féin's newspaper was titled *An Phoblacht,* M. L. R. Smith speculates that Ruairí and Seán Ó Brádaigh and Dáithí O'Connell, and "possibly" Seán Mac Stiofáin organized the Committee for Revolutionary Action and *An Phoblacht* of the 1960s. Ruairí Ó Brádaigh, who received copies of *An Phoblacht* in the mail, states, "I know nothing of the Committee for Revolutionary Action and cannot recollect having heard of it. Dáithí O'Connell, Seán Mac Stiofáin and Seán Ó Brádaigh never mentioned it at any time." *An Phoblacht* was mailed from Cork, which had been home to O'Connell and Mac Stiofáin. By 1967, however, each had moved. Mac Stiofáin took a job transfer and left Cork in July 1966 for the small Gaeltacht in County Meath, outside of Navan. In 1967, O'Connell lived in Wexford and was training to become a vocational school teacher. Ó Brádaigh and the others were also not involved in the Saor Éire Action Group. In 1973, the group was disbanded and their members were directed to support to the Provisional Republican Movement as the upholder of the All-Ireland Republic.

135 Cathal Goulding at Bodenstown in 1967: "Oration by Cathal Goulding," *The United Irishman,* Iúil/July 1967, 10–11.

136 RÓB and cooperatives: "Republican Education: Conferences Held at Two Venues," *The United Irishman,* Eanáir/January 1967.

137 Republican Movement declares for a democratic socialist republic: see Patterson, *The Politics of Illusion* (1997 ed.), 113; "Change in the North: Sinn Féin President on Republican Tradition," *The United Irishman,* Nollaig/December 1967, 3; Cronin, *Irish Nationalism,* 189; RÓB IVs.

137 Sinn Féin political developments in the south: see "Integration with Britain Suicidal: Sinn Féin President Slams Agreement," *The United Irishman,* Nollaig/December 1966. On ownership of Ireland: "Sinn Féin's Policy on Land Deals," *The Irish Times,* January 16, 1967. On fish-ins: RÓB IVs.

137 Dublin Housing Action Committee: "Controversial Group Wants Action on Housing: Aims of D. H.A.C. Explained," *Irish Times,* June 17, 1968; "26 Arrested in Eviction Brawl: Uproar as Bailiffs Move In," *Evening Herald,* January 15, 1968; Séamus Ó Tuathail interview; Bell, *The Secret Army,* 346.

138 Northern Ireland civil rights movement: Cronin, *Irish Nationalism,* 187–189; NICRA, *We Shall Overcome;* McCluskey, *Up Off Their Knees,* 104–140; Deutsch and Magowan, *Northern Ireland, 1968–73,* 1:154.

138 Squatting in Caledon: Tomás Mac Giolla interview; Farrell, *Northern Ireland: The Orange State,* 245–246; "Sinn Féin protest meeting," *Longford Leader,* March 31, 1967. Although Austin Currie claims that "it is a distortion of history to credit local Republicans for the squatting at Caledon," Ó Brádaigh insists that the two people squatting with Currie were Sinn Féiners. Austin Currie, *All Hell Will Break Loose* (Dublin: O'Brien Press, 2004), 96–98; RÓB IVs.

138 Coalisland–Dungannon march: McCluskey, *Up Off Their Knees,* 106–108; Mac Stiofáin, *Memoirs of a Revolutionary,* 108–109; RÓB IVs; Tomás Mac Giolla interview; Bernadette Devlin, *The Price of My Soul* (New York: Alfred A. Knopf, 1969), 97–101; Michael Farrell, *Northern Ireland: The Orange State,* 246–247.

Chapter 10

140 October 5th march: Farrell, *Northern Ireland: The Orange State,* 240–241, 246–247; J. Bowyer Bell, *The Irish Troubles: A Generation of Violence, 1967–1992* (New York: St. Martin's Press, 1993), 58–86; Niall Ó Dochartaigh, *From Civil Rights to Armalites: Derry and the Birth of the Irish Troubles* (Cork: Cork University Press, 1994), 20–21. Derry's name is derived from the Irish word *doire* (oak grove). The city was taken by the English in 1600 as part of the Elizabethan conquest. The prefix "London" was added in 1613; London merchants financed some of its development. Referring to the city as "Derry" or "Londonderry" became an indicator of one's political allegiance and religion. Nationalists tend to use "Derry"; Unionists use "Londonderry." The neutral label is "Maiden City." The City Council officially changed the city's name to Derry in 1984.

140 William Craig; creation of People's Democracy: see Deutsch and Magowan, *Northern Ireland, 1968–73,* 1:10–12.

141 1968 IRA convention: see Bell, *The Secret Army,* 359; Mac Stiofáin, *Memoirs of a Revolutionary,* 110; O'Brien, *The Arms Trial,* 26–27; RÓB IVs.

141 1968 Ard Fheis: "Ard-Fheis 68," *The United Irishman,* Eanáir/January 1968, 6; RÓB IVs; Henry Patterson, *The Politics of Illusion* (1997 ed.), 115–119; "Abstention," *The United Irishman,* Eanáir/January 1969, 7; Bell, *The Secret Army,* 359. The commission's report, *Ireland Today and Some Questions on the Way Forward,* was published in March 1969. One recommendation was that the movement should develop a "broad based anti-Unionist anti-imperialist alliance" and integrate the leadership of Sinn Féin and the IRA more closely. The latter was interpreted by Goulding's opponents as a sign of marginalizing the IRA.

142 Terence O'Neill speech: Eamonn McCann, *War and an Irish Town* (London: Pluto Press, 1981), 49; Deutsch and Magowan, *Northern Ireland, 1968–73,* 1:13. Ironically, the first bombs in Northern Ireland after October 1968 were set by Loyalist paramilitaries, in March and April of 1969. However, no organization claimed them, and the incidents were attributed to the IRA and helped drive Terence O'Neill from office.

142 People's Democracy march: Ó Dochartaigh, *From Civil Rights to Armalites,* 39–41; Deutsch and Magowan, *Northern Ireland, 1968–73,* 1:13–14; Devlin, *The Price of My Soul,* 135; Bowes Egan and Vincent McCormack, *Burntollet* (London: L.R.S. Publishers, 1969); McCann, *War and an Irish Town.*

142 Stormont and Westminster elections: see relevant dates in Deutsch and Magowan, *Northern Ireland, 1968–73,* vol. 1; Bell, *The Irish Troubles,* 82–91; Devlin, *The Price of My Soul,* 185–194.

143 Continuing unrest and the deaths of Sammy Devenny and Francis McCloskey: Deutsch and Magowan, *Northern Ireland, 1968–73,* 1:24, 34–35; McKittrick, Kelters, Feeney, and Thornton, *Lost Lives,* 32–33.

143 Army Council meeting after Burntollet: Bishop and Mallie, *The Provisional IRA,* 92–93; Walsh, *Irish Republicanism and Socialism,* 86–87, 100–101. Seán Keenan's support for abstentionism: Des Long interview; Mac Stiofáin, *Memoirs of a Revolutionary,* 112–113.

143 IRA meeting in May 1969: RÓB IVs; Bishop and Mallie, *The Provisional IRA,* 92–93; Mac Stiofáin, *Memoirs of a Revolutionary,* 112–113; Ruairí Ó Brádaigh, "The I.R.A.," *Irish Press,* January 29, 1971, book review page; Walsh, *Irish Republicanism and Socialism,* 86–87, 100–101.

144 Barnes and McCormack funeral: RÓB IVs; Roy Johnston interview; Tomás Mac Giolla interview; "Barnes and McCormack," *The United Irishman,* Samhain/November 1967, 12; "Barnes and McCormack," *The United Irishman,* Feabhra/Feabhra 1969, 12; "No State Tributes as Bodies Arrive: Comrades Shoulder Coffins," *The Irish Times,* Saturday, July 5, 1969, 1; "Ex-I.R.A. Man Claims He Planted Bomb," *The Irish Times,* Monday, July 7, 1969, 1; Walsh, *Irish Republicanism and Socialism,* 100; Peter Taylor, *Behind the Mask: The IRA and Sinn Féin* (New York: TV Books, 1997), 60–62; "Remains of Two Executed I.R.A. Members Re-interred in Irish Soil," *Westmeath-Offaly Independent,* July 12, 1969, 1, 10; "Patriots' Remains Return," *The United Irishman,* Iúil/July 1969, 1; "Barnes and McCormack . . . The Last Salute," *The United Irishman,* Lúnasa/August 1969, 5.

145 August 1969: Devlin, *The Price of My Soul,* 235; Deutsch and Magowan, *Northern Ireland, 1968–73,* 1:50, 55; McKittrick, Kelters, Feeney, and Thornton, *Lost Lives,* 36; Ó Dochartaigh, *From Civil Rights to Armalites;* MacEoin, *The IRA in the Twilight Years,* 460, 875; Raymond J. Quinn, *A Rebel Voice: A History of Republicanism, 1925–1972* (Belfast: The

Belfast Cultural and Local History Group, 1999); Bishop and Mallie, *The Provisional IRA,* 103–118; McKittrick, Kelters, Feeney, and Thornton, *Lost Lives,* 33–41; *Belfast Graves* (Dublin: The National Graves Association, 1985), 64; Bell, *The Irish Troubles,* 87–128.

146 Reaction of southern Republicans to August 1969: "Sinn Féin Meetings in Connaught," *Irish Times,* August 15, 1969.

146 Lynch's speech: O'Brien, *The Arms Trial,* 42–43; Bell, *Irish Troubles,* 105. There is some controversy over whether Lynch said that his government "can no longer stand by" or that it "can no longer stand *idly* by." The text in Justin O'Brien's *The Arms Trial* omits "idly," but the speech is often quoted with "idly" included.

146 Belfast IRA seeks weapons: Coogan, *The IRA* (1987 ed.), 462; Brendan Anderson, *Joe Cahill: A Life in the IRA* (Dublin: The O'Brien Press, 2002), 176; *The Politics of Revolution: The Main Speeches and Debates from the 1986 Sinn Féin Ard-Fheis including the Presidential Address of Gerry Adams* (Dublin: Sinn Féin, 1986), 22. Seán Mac Stiofáin leads attack on Crossmaglen RUC station: Bishop and Mallie, *The Provisional IRA,* 115.

146 Charles Haughey: Flackes and Elliott, *Northern Ireland: A Political Directory,* 273–275.

147 Fianna Fáil–IRA meeting and the Belfast coup: In *The Arms Trial,* Justin O'Brien claims that Charles Haughey met with Cathal Goulding in September 1969 and that "an arms deal was arranged between the minister's brother, Pádraic (Jock) Haughey, and Goulding (page 104; see also pages 84–85). There is controversy about the nature of contact between Fianna Fáil and the IRA at this time. Some have argued that Fianna Fáil machinations led to the split of the Republican Movement. In this view, Fianna Fáil was threatened by the political development of the IRA and events in the north, so it took steps to hinder the organization. This seems far-fetched; it is hard to believe that a political party in power would be threatened by *potential* developments associated with a movement with no elected representatives at the national level. It makes more sense that some in Fianna Fáil were genuinely concerned by events but did not want to be caught associating with the IRA and Sinn Féin, whose members publicly challenged the legitimacy of the Dublin government. The split would have occurred without the involvement of Fianna Fáil, but funds and encouragement probably made it easier for some people to opt for a split. As it happened, government relief funds went to both Provisionals and Officials in Belfast, who were members of neighborhood Defence Committees and on full-time duty, therefore unable to work at their regular jobs. RÓB IVs; O'Brien, *The Arms Trial*; Peter Taylor, *States of Terror: Democracy and Political Violence* (London: BBC Books, 1993), 137–138; "Fianna Fáil and the I.R.A.," n.d., n.p. (in author's possession); Walsh, *Irish Republicanism and Socialism,* 96; Patterson, *The Politics of Illusion* (1997 ed.), 133–135; Bishop and Mallie, *The Provisional IRA,* 125–133; Leo Martin interview; Billy McKee interview; J. Bowyer Bell, *The Gun in Politics: An Analysis of the Irish Political Conflict, 1916–1986* (New Brunswick, NJ: Transaction Books, 1987), 185.

148 The Hunt Commission; rioting: McKittrick, Kelters, Feeney, and Thornton, *Lost Lives,* 42; Deutsch and Magowan, *Northern Ireland, 1968–73* 1:41, 48; Flackes and Elliott, *Northern Ireland: A Political Directory,* 289; McKittrick, Kelters, Feeney, and Thornton, *Lost Lives,* 42.

148 IRA after the Belfast coup; Goulding quotations: "Republicanism: Why It Has Failed," *This Week,* July 31, 1970. Abstentionist alternative: "Where Sinn Féin Stands," *An Phoblacht,* Márta/March 1970, 1.

148 Staying in the fold; "maximizing" position: Ó Brádaigh tried to avoid publicly challenging the leadership. In Athlone early in the fall, Caitlín Uí Mhuimhneacháin accosted him, asking, "Where do you stand? Do you stand with Belfast or Dublin?" He replied, "You'll see very clearly where I stand." He suspected that she knew his views but wanted him to confirm them publicly. Many dissidents wanted people to behave like Jimmy Steele, but Ó Brádaigh did not want to end up on the sidelines like Steele. RÓB IVs; O'Brien, *The Arms Trial,* 86.

149 Personality clashes: Bell, *The Secret Army,* 240–241; Mac Stiofáin, *Memoirs of a Revolutionary,* 130–137. "Bad marriage" quotation: "Birth of the Provos: Not an Inch," *Irish News,* January 29, 1990, 6. Some real friendships were lost in the split. John Joe McGirl and Cathal Goulding had been the best of friends, having been comrades since the 1940s. Mac Stiofáin's memoir suggests that in spite of Goulding's attitude toward him, he respected Goulding right up until the split.

149 Suspension of Dáithí O'Connell: RÓB IVs; Leo Martin interview. Ó Brádaigh agrees with Martin's assessment of O'Connell.

149 1969 IRA convention: Denis McInerney interview; RÓB IVs; Bishop and Mallie, *The Provisional IRA,* 86, 100; Ruairí Ó Brádaigh, "The I.R.A.," *Irish Press,* January 29, 1971, book review page; Mac Stiofáin, *Memoirs of a Revolutionary,* 131, 134–137. The location of the convention is given in Taylor, *States of Terror,* 142–143. See also O'Brien, *The Arms Trial,* 91–93; Bell, *The Secret Army,* 366.

151 Meeting after the convention: Mac Stiofáin, *Memoirs of a Revolutionary,* 137; RÓB IVs; Taylor, *States of Terror,* 142–143. Meeting at the Delaney home: private communication.

151 Provisional IRA convention: At the first convention, twelve delegates of those present voted against recognizing Leinster House, Stormont, and Westminster. Four others that pledged to reject the motion were not picked up, making sixteen total delegates opposed to recognizing the Parliaments. Two Cork delegates who voted "No" as instructed by their unit were personally in favor of the motion and remained with the Officials. This reduced the abstentionist delegates to fourteen. Another did not participate with the Provisionals until Official Sinn Féin formally declared for Leinster House, Stormont, and Westminster at the 1970 Ard Fheis in January. Thus, there were thirteen abstentionist delegates at the second convention. Most observers accept Bishop and Mallie on the first Army Council, *The Provisional IRA,* 137–138; see also Mac Stiofáin, *Memoirs of a Revolutionary,* 138. Joe Cahill quotation: White, *Provisional Irish Republicans,* 54. Ruairí Ó Brádaigh does not discuss the issue.

153 "inspired leaking": "'Inspired Leak' Condemned by I.R.A.," *Irish Times,* December 29, 11. One report has O'Connell suggesting "P. O'Neill" as a play on Terence O'Neill, using "P" instead of "T."

153 Tom Maguire statement: "I.R.A. Decision Criticised by Veteran," *Irish Press,* January 5, 1970.

154 Official IRA and *The United Irishman:* "The IRA Speak Out," *The United Irishman,* 1970, 1; "The IRA in the 70s," *The United Irishman,* 1970, 8.

154 Galway-Roscommon IRA meeting: RÓB IVs.

154 1970 Sinn Féin Ard Fheis: "Walk Out: A Personal View by the Editor," *The United Irishman,* Feabhra/February 1970, 4; "Birth of the Provos: Conspiracy Theorist," *Irish News,* January 31, 1990, 6; Séamus O Tuathail interview; Mac Stiofáin, *Memoirs of a Revolutionary,* 150; Ruairí Ó Brádaigh, "The I.R.A.," *The Irish Press,* January 29, 1971, book review page; Bell, *The Secret Army,* 359. Ó Brádaigh denies Goulding's allegation that the Provisionals arranged for people who were not members of Sinn Féin to vote against the leadership. Given that the Officials were in charge of the organization and everyone knew that a tough vote was on the agenda, it would be surprising to learn that nonmembers were allowed into the Ard Fheis to vote. Ó Brádaigh alleges that Séamus Costello totaled the Wicklow membership, divided it by five (the minimum for a *cumann*) and produced twenty-two delegates at the Ard Fheis, when the number should have been far less. Costello irritated a number of people in the 1968–1970 period. A member of Wicklow County Council and Bray Urban Council, he was so strident in his opposition to abstentionism that Goulding suspended him from the IRA for a period in 1968. At the Leitrim unit convention in 1969, Costello, representing general headquarters, refused to wait for ten minutes for delegates who were running late. Goulding recalled that "[t]his infuriated the Leitrim delegates."

156 Reassembling at Parnell Square: Seán Ó Brádaigh interview; Des Long interview; Frank Glynn interview; RÓB IVs; "Attempt to Take Over Republican Movement," *An Phoblacht,* Feabhra/February 1970, 4–5; "Ard-Fheis Appoints Caretaker Executive," *An Phoblacht,* Feabhra/February 1970, 1; "Where Sinn Féin Stands: Open Letter from Chairman of Caretaker Executive," *An Phoblacht,* Márta/March 1970, 1.

158 *An Phoblacht:* "On This We Stand: The Rock of the Republic," *An Phoblacht,* Feabhra/February 1970, 1; "Birth of the Provos: Not an Inch," *Irish News,* January 29, 1990, 6; Seán Ó Brádaigh interview; "20,000 Copies Sold," *An Phoblacht,* Márta/March 1970, 1; RÓB IVs; "Comhar na gComharsan," *An Phoblacht,* Feabhra/February 1970, 6–7; see also Walsh, *Irish Republicanism and Socialism,* 102–104. On January 17th a statement from the caretaker executive gave five major reasons for the walkout. They were, in order: recognizing Westminster, Stormont, and Leinster House; extreme socialism leading to totalitarian dictatorship; failure to protect people in the North in August 1969; disagreement over the issue of abolition of Stormont and direct rule from Westminster; and internal methods in operation in the movement for some time (e.g., the dismissal of the North Kerry Sinn Féin). Of these, abstentionism was the most important.

158 Provisional Sinn Féin and socialism: "New Light on the Split in Sinn Féin," *Irish Press,* January 13, 1970. The day after the split, Seán Ó Brádaigh appeared on *Féach* (*Look Here*), an Irish-language current affairs program on Radio Telefís Éireann. He noted that many of those who walked out had participated in recent political protests sponsored by the movement. He agreed with Tomás Mac Giolla's political goals but said that they could not be achieved by "going into parliamentary institutions that maintained a capitalistic system established here by England." In *This Week* in July 1970, Cathal Goulding noted that among the founders of the Provisional IRA were some "good revolutionaries and good socialists" who disagreed with parliamentary participation. It is not clear if Goulding included Ruairí or Seán Ó Brádaigh among the "good" socialists. "Belfast and Bogside and Why the IRA Failed," *This Week,* August 7, 1970.

158 Strength of the Provisionals: "The Numerous Faces of the I.R.A.," *This Week,* May 29, 1970.

159 Defense of St. Matthews; Lower Falls curfew: Bishop and Mallie, *The Provisional IRA,* 145; Quinn, *A Rebel Voice,* 164–169; Billy McKee interview; Bell, *The Secret Army,* 376–377; Bell, *The Irish Troubles,* 178; McKittrick, Kelters, Feeney, and Thornton, *Lost Lives,* 52–55; Farrell, *Northern Ireland: The Orange State,* 273–274.

159 Bodenstown 1970: "The Republican Position," *An Phoblacht,* Iúil/July 1970, 8; "5,000 People Honour Tone at Bodenstown: Republican Movement Is Intact—Future Looks Bright," *An Phoblacht,* Iúil/July 1970, 1.

160 Meeting with Conor Cruise O'Brien: O'Brien, *States of Ireland* (New York: Vintage Books, 1973), 222; Conor Cruise O'Brien interview; *Yeats's Poems,* edited and annotated by Norman Jeffares with an appendix by Warwick Gould (Dublin: Gill and Macmillan, 1989), 311; Walsh, *Irish Republicanism and Socialism,* 96–97; RÓB IVs. See also O'Brien, *The Arms Trial.*

160 Jimmy Steele funeral: RÓB IVs; "Republican News," *An Phoblacht,* Iúil/July 1970, 8; "Jimmy Steele: An Appreciation," *An Phoblacht,* Meán Fómhair/September 1970, 8; "Jimmy Steele," in *Belfast Graves,* 57–58.

160 Roddy Carlin rally: "Lynch Aids Crown," *An Phoblacht,* Meán Fómhair/October 1970, 8.

161 *This Week* interviews: "The Provisionals Answer Cathal Goulding," *This Week,* August 14, 1970; "The I.R.A. Part Four: The Attitudes of Blaney and Boland," *This Week,* August 21, 1970. Haughey's career probably suffered the most, but neither Blaney nor Haughey lost his seat in Leinster House/Dáil Éireann.

161 1970 IRA convention: "IRA Hold Convention: Provisional Period Over Says Publicity Bureau," *An Phoblacht,* Samhain/November 1970, 1; Ó Brádaigh, *Dílseacht,* 45. Membership on the Council is based on Bishop and Mallie, *The Provisional IRA,* and McGuire, *To Take Arms,* 32.

162 Ruairí Ó Brádaigh, "Address to the Ard-Fheis," *An Phoblacht,* Samhain/November 1970, 2, 7. In spite of his plea, the label "Provisional" stuck—it sounded great and was easily abbreviated as "Provos" or "Provies." The press also adopted the habit of referring to the two Sinn Féins by their addresses, Sinn Féin Gardiner Place and Sinn Féin Kevin Street.

Chapter 11

164 RÓB as chief of staff: RÓB IVs; "Ó Brádaigh: I'm Not I.R.A. Leader," *Irish News* August 30, 1971. Ó Brádaigh reviews J. Bowyer Bell's *The Secret Army*: Ruairí Ó Brádaigh, "The I.R.A.," *Irish Press*, January 29, 1971, book review page.

164 Altercation with Cathal Goulding: RÓB IVs; see also McGuire, *To Take Arms*, 30; London Sunday Times Insight Team, *Northern Ireland: A Report on the Conflict* (New York: Vintage Books, 1972), 89–90. McGirl saw them coming and "disappeared": This made the confrontation easier. If McGirl had been there, Ó Brádaigh would have felt obligated to invite them in. Others who were threatened include Leo Martin and Dáithí O'Connell. There are reports that Martin, Ó Brádaigh, and O'Connell started carrying pistols for protection. Ó Brádaigh neither confirms nor denies carrying a personal weapon.

165 Origins of Éire Nua I: Roy Johnston interview; "The Provisionals Answer Cathal Goulding," *This Week*, August 17, 1970; RÓB IVs.

165 Wolfe Tone quotation; development of Éire Nua; and Julius Nyerere: "What Is Irish Republicanism?" *Irish Independent*, December 9, 1970; Ruairí Ó Brádaigh, "Introduction," in *Aisling 1916–1976*, (Dublin: Elo Press, Ltd., 1976), 3; "We Publish Here the Introduction to the New Sinn Féin Social and Economic Programme," *An Phoblacht*, Feabhra/February 1971, 10; "Restore the Means of Production to the People," *Irish Press*, December 3, 1970, part of the series "What Social and Economic System Would Serve Ireland Best?" that was republished in Ruairí Ó Brádaigh, *Our People, Our Future* (Dublin: Sinn Féin, 1973).

165 Deaths of Robert Curtis, James Saunders, and Bernard Watt: Bell, *The Irish Troubles*, 188; McKittrick, Kelters, Feeney, and Thornton, *Lost Lives*, 62–65.

165 Ó Brádaigh-Mac Giolla war of words: "'Face the Common Enemy'—S.F. Man Mac Giolla Hits Out at Ó Brádaigh,'" *Sunday Press*, February 2, 1971; "Call for Republican Unity by Mac Giolla," *Irish Times*, February 11, 1971; "'Publicity Game' Says Ó Brádaigh: Mac Giolla 'Faces Eclipse,'" *Irish Press*, February 15, 1971.

166 Official–Provisional IRA feud: Bell, *The Irish Troubles*, 194–195. Charlie Hughes: *Belfast Graves*, 72; "Tragic Events in Ulster," *The United Irishman*, Aibreán/April 1971, 8.

166 The Scottish soldiers; Brian Faulkner succeeds James Chichester-Clark: McKittrick, Kelters, Feeney, and Thornton, *Lost Lives*, 70–72; Deutsch and Magowan, *Northern Ireland, 1968–73,* 1:96–99.

167 Brian Faulkner and the SDLP: Deutsch and Magowan, *Northern Ireland, 1968–73,* 1:111; Ian McAllister, *The Northern Ireland Social Democratic and Labour Party: Political Opposition in a Divided Society* (London: Macmillan, 1977), 67–71; Paul Routledge, *John Hume: A Biography* (London: Harper Collins, 1977), 99–100.

167 Séamus Beattie and Desmond Cusack shootings: McKittrick, Kelters, Feeney, and Thornton, *Lost Lives*, 75–77.

167 Sinn Féin rally in Derry: Deutsch and Magowan, *Northern Ireland, 1968–73*, 1:114; Michael Heney, "Sinn Féin Call to Bogside People: Speakers Allege 'Murder,'" *The Irish Times*, July 12, 1971.

168 SDLP response to the Derry rally; Máire Drumm's arrest and conviction: Deutsch and Magowan, *Northern Ireland, 1968–73*, 1:114, 116; Routledge, *John Hume*, 100–101; Pat Walsh, *From Civil Rights to National War: Northern Ireland Catholic Politics 1964–1974* (Belfast: Athol Books, 1989), 62–63. The SDLP did establish their own alternative assembly, which met twice.

168 John Rooks interview: *Belfast Telegraph*, July 28, 1971, reprinted in *An Phoblacht*, Meán Fómhair/September 1971, 8. Ó Brádaigh's comments here echo his remarks to Godfrey Fitzsimons in 1966.

169 Internment and aftermath; McKittrick, Kelters, Feeney, and Thornton, *Lost Lives*, 79–91; Bell, *The Irish Troubles*, 215–232; "Dungannon Call for Total Opposition," *Irish Times*, August 10, 1971; John McGuffin, *Internment!* (Tralee: Anvil Books, 1973).

170 British Army and Joe Cahill press conferences: Bell, *Irish Troubles,* 222–223.

170 RÓB excluded from Britain; Joe Cahill excluded from the United States: "Ó Brádaigh: I'm Not I.R.A. leader," *Irish News,* August 30, 1972; "IRA Boss Is Kicked Out of U.S.," *Daily Mirror,* September 9, 1972, 1.

170 IRA cease-fire offer: "Ceasefire Offer by IRA," *Irish Press,* September 6, 1971.

170 Leave of absence and staying in Roscommon: RÓB IVs; Patsy Ó Brádaigh interview; Díóg Ní Chonaill, "A Drink from the Lee," Republican Sinn Féin Cabhair Testimonial, 1991, 7–8. Irish law had changed and Patsy was eligible for full-time work. But with six young children, part-time work was a better option.

171 Letter bombs: McGuire, *To Take Arms,* 113–114; Mac Stiofáin, *Memoirs of a Revolutionary,* 239–240. Over time, Ó Brádaigh was sent several letter bombs. The most serious incident was probably a book bomb that was sent to his brother, Seán, in 1977. Seán was on holiday and Ruairí was staying at his home, in Dublin. A neighbor with a key accepted a package addressed to Seán and placed it in the home. Several days later, Ó Brádaigh was in the house with Fred Burns O'Brien, an Irish-American active in the Irish National Caucus and an employee of the U.S. Treasury Department (and now with the Department of Homeland Security). Burns O'Brien recognized that the package fit the description of a book bomb sent to Jimmy Drumm about 10 days earlier and told him to throw it in the garden. Ó Brádaigh tore open a corner and saw that it contained an old book. Burns O'Brien took the package, threw it in the garden, and insisted that Ó Brádaigh phone the Special Branch. Ó Brádaigh, never having called them in the past, at first refused but then recognized that the package threatened others in the neighborhood. The Irish Army bomb disposal squad carried out a controlled explosion on the package, which probably contained 4–6 pounds of explosives. They informed Ruairí that the person opening the book, and anyone in the room where the book was opened, would have been killed. RÓB IVs; Fred Burns O'Brien interview; "Blast at O'Bradaigh home," *Sunday Press,* April 9, 1977.

171 Monaghan convention: Des Fennell interview; "Dáil Uladh," *An Phoblacht,* Meán Fómhair/September 1971, 3; "Offices for Dáil Uladh," *An Phoblacht,* Meán Fómhair/September 1971, 2; "Dáil Uladh," *An Phoblacht,* Samhain/November 1971, 11; Kevin O'Kelley, *The Longest War: Northern Ireland and the I.R.A.* (London: Zed Books, 1978), 158–159.

172 Des Fennell: RÓB IVs; Des Fennell interview; Desmond Fennell, *Beyond Nationalism: The Struggle against Provinciality in the Modern World* (Swords, County Dublin: Ward River Press, 1985).

172 Comhairle Uladh meeting: "Dáil Uladh," *An Phoblacht,* Samhain/November 1971, 11.

172 Dáil Chonnacht: "Dáil Chonnacht," *An Phoblacht,* Samhain/November 1971, 11; Fennell, *Beyond Nationalism,* especially 156–166.

172 1971 Sinn Féin Ard Fheis; exclusion of the British press and treatment of Joe Cahill and Ruairí Ó Brádaigh: David Wright, "IRA Boss Is Kicked Out of U.S.," *Daily Mirror,* September 9, 1972, 1; "Gallagher Baby's Death: What Mr. Brady Told Pressmen," *Irish News,* September 8, 1971. Dorothy Maguire, Maura Meehan, Martin Forsythe, and Pat Murray: McKittrick, Kelters, Feeney, and Thornton, *Lost Lives,* 107–109; *Belfast Graves,* 77–79. Ard Fheis election: "Sinn Féin," *An Phoblacht,* Samhain/November 1971, 1. Mac Stiofáin's "Army Statement": *An Phoblacht,* Samhain/November 1971, 1–2. 1971 presidential address: "Our Duty and Our Privilege: Ard-Fheis Address by Ruairí Ó Brádaigh, Uachtaráin, Sinn Féin," *An Phoblacht,* Samhain/November 1971, 12. In Dáil Uladh and in trying to make the north ungovernable the Provisionals were trying to create a revolutionary situation, as had existed in Ireland in 1920–22. Éire Nua II, in 1972, extended this to Ireland as a whole. In a revolutionary situation, there is "the presence of more than one bloc effectively exercising control over a significant part of the state apparatus." See Charles Tilly, *From Mobilization to Revolution* (New York: Random House, 1978), 189–193.

175 Development of the Ulster Defence Association, the Ulster Freedom Fighters, and the Ulster Volunteer Force: see Flackes and Elliott, *Northern Ireland: A Political Directory;* Steve

Bruce, *The Red Hand: Protestant Paramilitaries in Northern Ireland* (Oxford: Oxford University Press, 1992).

175 North becoming ungovernable: Deutsch and Magowan, *Northern Ireland 1968–73,* 1:130; McKittrick, Kelters, Feeney, and Thornton, *Lost Lives,* 102–103, 105, 131; Bell, *The Irish Troubles,* 288–189; O'Kelley, *The Longest War,* 158.

175 Bloody Sunday: "Army Commander Describes Shooting as Defense Action," *Irish Times,* January 31, 1972, 1; Bell, *The Irish Troubles,* 249–275; Flackes and Elliott, *Northern Ireland: A Political Directory,* 184–185. The first British inquiry into the event, conducted by Lord Widgery, accepted the British Army's version of events, found that the soldiers were fired on first, and noted that no one would have been killed if the illegal march had been called off. Many people considered the report a whitewash. The causes and consequences of Bloody Sunday are still debated. The Saville Inquiry, which was established in 1998, continues to consider the event more than thirty years later.

175 Aftermath of Bloody Sunday: Deutsch and Magowan, *Northern Ireland, 1968–73,* 2:152–155; "The Provos Are the Force in Ireland To-Day," *An Phoblacht,* Márta/March 1972.

176 Abercorn Restaurant bomb in Belfast: Deutsch and Magowan, *Northern Ireland, 1968–73,* 2:160; Dáithí Ó Conaill, "Wilson-I.R.A. Talks 1972," *SAOIRSE,* Eanáir/January 1989, 5.

176 Unilateral cease-fire: Ó Conaill, "Wilson-I.R.A. Talks 1972," *SAOIRSE,* Eanáir/January 1989, 5; McGuire, *To Take Arms,* 111–112; John O'Connell, *Dr. John: Crusading Doctor and Politician* (Swords, County Dublin: Poolbeg Press, 1989), 127–135.

177 Joe Cahill's list: O'Connell, *Dr. John,* 134.

177 Fall of Stormont: Deutsch and Magowan, *Northern Ireland, 1968–73,* 2:164–165; "Events Leading to Crisis Outlined," *Irish Times,* March 25, 1972, 8; McGuire, *To Take Arms,* 11, 14, 114–115; RÓB IVs.

178 Ó Brádaigh and Mac Stiofáin statements and their relationship: Ó Brádaigh, "Suspension of Stormont," in *Our People, Our Future,* 15; McGuire, *To Take Arms,* 114–116; Deutsch and Magowan, *Northern Ireland, 1968–73,* 2:167; "Ó Brádaigh Criticises the Cardinal," *Belfast Telegraph,* April 4, 1972; "Reply to Cardinal Conway," in Ó Brádaigh, *Our People, Our Future,* 16–17; RÓB IVs.

179 Noraid: Holland, *The American Connection.* There have been charges that Noraid activists funneled money and material to the IRA. In a famous court case, members of the organization, including Michael Flannery, were found not guilty of arms smuggling.

179 Meeting William Craig: RÓB IVs; Seán MacConnell, "When Craig and S.F. Chief Met," *Sunday Press,* May 14, 1972; McGuire, *To Take Arms,* 103; "When Provo's Chief Met William Craig," *Daily Mirror,* May 19, 1972.

180 Growth of the IRA: Bell, *The Secret Army,* 372–392.

180 Resentment of the southern leadership: Brendan Hughes interview; Mac Stiofáin, *Memoirs of a Revolutionary.* The perception is important but not accurate. Although Mac Stiofáin was chief of staff, the IRA leadership throughout the early 1970s was national in scope with representation from both sides of the border that included Leo Martin, Joe Cahill, and Billy McKee from Belfast. During the early 1970s, the southern IRA leadership, including Mac Stiofáin and Dáithí O'Connell, tried to tour and meet with northern IRA units regularly.

180 Sectarian violence: Maria McGuire claims that Ó Brádaigh's questioning of the IRA prompted another phone call from Seán Mac Stiofáin, who "screamed" at him for not justifying the shooting. In the RTÉ interview, Ó Brádaigh noted the possibility of a third actor, the British security forces, who were contributing to the sectarian tension. Some explosions and shootings could not be accounted for. For example, on May 12th, Patrick McVeigh, a Nationalist civilian, was shot dead in West Belfast from a passing car. The evidence suggests that the shooting was the work of undercover British soldiers. Richard English, *Armed Struggle: A History of the IRA* (London: Macmillan, 2003), 372, 375; McGuire, *To Take Arms,* 127–129; McKittrick, Kelters, Feeney, and Thornton, *Lost Lives,* 182–183; Deutsch and Magowan,

Northern Ireland, 1968–73, 2:177; "Protestant Backlash 'the Last Thing' Desired by Republican Leadership: Ó Brádaigh Rejects Sectarianism," *Irish Times,* May 19, 1972;

181 Official IRA cease-fire: "I.R.A. Wing Orders End of Armed Ulster Action," *New York Times,* May 30, 1972, 1:3; McKittrick, Kelters, Feeney, and Thornton, *Lost Lives,* 189–190; Bell, *The Irish Troubles,* 320–322.

181 Roy Johnston resignation: Henry Patterson, *The Politics of Illusion* (1997 ed.), 153–154; Roy Johnston, "Why I Quit Sinn Féin," *Sunday Press,* January 23, 1973.

181 May 1972 arrests: RÓB IVs; Deutsch and Magowan, *Northern Ireland, 1968–73,* 2:182; Alvin Shuster, "Dublin Holds 2 Leaders of I.R.A. Militant Wing," *New York Times,* June 1, 1972, 4:4. A local officer later told Ó Brádaigh that they had been instructed to raid the house and see if they could find anything that might connect him with the IRA. The documents were the best they could do.

182 Collective decision to go on hunger strike: RÓB IVs; Mac Stiofáin, *Memoirs of a Revolutionary,* 342.

182 Visit with Patsy Ó Brádaigh: RÓB IVs; Patsy Ó Brádaigh interview.

182 Hunger strike and Ó Brádaigh in Mountjoy: RÓB interview; McGuire, *To Take Arms,* 135; "O'Brady Brothers on Hunger Strike," *Irish Times,* June 3, 1972.

183 First court appearance: "Another Remand for Ó Brádaigh: Court Statement about Activities," *Irish Times,* June 7, 1972; "Sinn Féin Chief Is Remanded," *Belfast Newsletter,* June 7, 1972.

184 Patsy Ó Brádaigh and Mary Delaney on hunger strike: Patsy Ó Brádaigh interview; RÓB IVs.

184 Second court appearance: "Sinn Féin Cleared," *The Daily Telegraph,* June 14, 1972; "Rory O'Brady Cleared of All Charges," *Belfast Telegraph,* June 13, 1972.

184 Ending the hunger strike: When a person goes on a hunger strike, the stomach shrinks. The high-protein but liquid form of the egg flip allows a person to go off hunger strike with minimal cramping. RÓB IVs; Ruairí Óg Ó Brádaigh interview; O'Donnell, *The Gates Flew Open,* 100.

186 IRA demands: The demands were: 1) release of all political internees; 2) abolition of the Special Powers Act; 3) removal of the ban on Sinn Féin in the north; 4) withdrawal of all political test oaths and their restrictions on candidates contesting elections; 5) removal of the oath of allegiance to the British Crown as a condition of employment; 6) confirmation of the proportional representation system of election. Deutsch and Magowan, *Northern Ireland, 1968–73,* 2:190.

186 Billy McKee hunger strike; bilateral truce: Bell, *The Irish Troubles,* 329–332.

186 Ulster Defence Association and the bilateral truce: McKittrick, Kelters, Feeney, and Thornton, *Lost Lives,* 205–206, 209–210; Deutsch and Magowan, *Northern Ireland, 1968–73,* 2:190–191.

186 Éire Nua II: RÓB IVs; Deutsch and Magowan, *Northern Ireland, 1968–73,* 2:191; "Interview with Ruairí Ó Brádaigh," *An Phoblacht,* Iúil/July 1972, 3; "A Federal Solution," *This Week,* July 31, 1970.

188 IRA delegation: RÓB IVs; Seán Mac Stiofáin, personal communication; Mac Stiofáin, *Memoirs of a Revolutionary,* 278–279; Bell, *The Irish Troubles,* 333; Bishop and Mallie, *The Provisional IRA,* 226–227n17; Gerry Adams, *Before the Dawn: An Autobiography* (London: Heinemann, in association with Brandon Books, 1996), 205.

188 Truce ends: After the riot but before the shooting started, Dáithí O'Connell telephoned William Whitelaw, but nothing developed from their conversation. There are rumors that the Belfast IRA, which was suspicious of the truce and perhaps the southern IRA leadership, engineered the crisis and forced the breaking of the truce. McKittrick, Kelters, Feeney, and Thornton conclude that of the ten people killed in Belfast on July 9, 1972, the Provisionals killed a member of the Ulster Defence Association, a member of the Territorial Army, two Protestant civilians, and a Catholic civilian. At Lenadoon, the British Army killed two Republicans who were engaged in non-Republican activity—they were trying to aid others who had been shot by British Army marksmen. Ciarán de Baróid, *Ballymurphy and the Irish War* (Baile Átha Cliath: Aisling Publishers, 1989), 174–175; Deutsch and Magowan, *Northern Ireland, 1968–73,* 2:194–195; Bell, *The Irish Troubles,* 336–337; "Ó Brádaigh Blames One-Sided Policy: U.D.A. Favoured by British," *Irish Times,* July 11, 1972; "Ó Brádaigh Criticises Cardinal," *Irish Times,* July 11, 1972; McKittrick, Kelters, Feeney, and Thornton, *Lost Lives,* 215–217; Adams, *Before the Dawn,* 198–208; Anthony McIntyre, "Sisyphus," *The Blanket: A Journal of Dissent,* July 25, 2002, available online at http://lark.phoblacht.net/sisyphus.html.

189 RÓB meets Merlyn Rees: RÓB IVs; Merlyn Rees, *Northern Ireland: A Personal Perspective* (London: Methuen, 1985), 26–28.

190 Harold Wilson's message: RÓB Notes.

190 Bloody Friday: Rees, *Northern Ireland: A Personal Perspective,* 26–28; Deutsch and Magowan, *Northern Ireland, 1968–73,* 2:199. "Bomb blitz": Bell, *IRA Tactics and Targets,* 85.

190 Terrorism chronologies: The Vice President's Task Force on Combating Terrorism, *Terrorist Group Profiles* (Washington: Government Printing Office, 1988), 56–58. Events perpetrated by Western governments, including Bloody Sunday, often do not appear on such lists.

190 Claudy explosions and the toll for the month: Deutsch and Magowan, *Northern Ireland, 1968–73,* 2:202; McKittrick, Kelters, Feeney, and Thornton, *Lost Lives,* 209–242.

Chapter 12

191 Growth of Sinn Féin: Éamon Mac Thomáis, "Our New Offices," *An Phoblacht,* Meán Fómhair/September 1972, 10; "We Are Going Fortnightly!" *An Phoblacht,* Meán Fómhair/September 1972, 10.

191 William Whitelaw's challenge: Deutsch and Magowan, *Northern Ireland, 1968–73,* 2:210; "Call to Sinn Féin 'Unfair,'" *Sunday Independent,* August 27, 1972; "Lift Ban: Call to Whitelaw," *Sunday Press,* August 27, 1972; "Ó Brádaigh and L.G. Elections," *Irish Independent,* August 28, 1972; Bell, *The Irish Troubles,* 347.

191 Decision not to contest elections: RÓB IVs; "No Elections," *Republican News,* 2, no. 57, October 20, 1972; "Ard-Fheis Address," in Ó Brádaigh, *Our People, Our Future,* 23–30; Adams, *Before the Dawn,* 213–215. Whitelaw postponed the election until the spring.

191 Maria McGuire exposé: "Ó Brádaigh Hits at Máire Maguire Story," *Irish News* September 5, 1972; "IRA Gun Girl Flees," (London) *Observer,* September 3, 1972, 1, and "I Accuse Seán Mac Stiofáin," (London) *Observer,* September 3, 1972, 9; RÓB IVs; McGuire, *To Take Arms,* 167–170; Mac Stiofáin, *Memoirs of a Revolutionary,* 306–307. Maguire/O'Connell quotation: "Boost for Mac Stiofáin," *Sunday Observer,* September 10, 1972.

192 Long-term consequences of Maguire's "revelations": Robert White, "The Irish Republican Army: An Assessment of Sectarianism," *Terrorism and Political Violence* 9, no. 1 (1997): 20–55; Steve Bruce, "Victim Selection in Ethnic Conflict: Motives and Attitude in Irish Republicanism," *Terrorism and Political Violence* 9, no. 1 (1997): 56–71; Robert White, "The Irish Republican Army and Sectarianism: Moving beyond the Anecdote," *Terrorism and Political Violence* 9, no. 2 (1997): 120–131.

192 RÓB job status: "Fight Now for Truth in the News," *An Phoblacht,* Deireadh Fómhair/October 29, 1972, 6; Deutsch and Magowan, *Northern Ireland, 1968–73,* 2:220; "Ó Brádaigh Job to Be Filled, Says Minister," *Irish Times,* September 21, 1972; "Committee Told: 'Sack Ó Brádaigh,'" *Irish Press,* September 21, 1972; "Ó Brádaigh Is Still on Leave of Absence," *Irish Independent,* October 20, 1972. In September 1972, the minister dismissed Dáithí O'Connell from his teaching post in Ballyshannon. By that point, O'Connell had already resigned the position and moved to Dublin.

193 Closing the Sinn Féin office: "Fight Now for Truth in the News," *An Phoblacht,* Deireadh Fómhair/October 29, 1972, 6; "Sinn Féin Hits Back," *An Phoblacht,* Deireadh Fómhair/October 15, 1972.

193 Comhairle na Mumhan and Comhairle Laighean: "200 Delegates Establish Comhairle na Mumhan," *Irish News,* October 9, 1972; "Proposed Provincial Government Seen as Revolutionary Weapon," *Irish News,* October 9, 1972; "Ó Brádaigh to Speak on Regionalism," *Irish Times,* October 21, 1972; "Dáil Laighean 4 Provincial Councils Now Established," *An Phoblacht,* Samhain/November 12, 1972, 2.

193 1972 Ard Fheis: "Sinn Féin Leaders Attacks Éire PM," *Newsletter,* October 30, 1972; "Ard-Fheis Sinn Féin," *An Phoblacht,* Samhain/November 1972, 4; Bishop and Mallie, *The Provisional IRA,* 33 and note 9; Ó Brádaigh, *Our People, Our Future,* 23–30; "The Clean Slate," *Irish Independent,* October 30, 1972, Editorial: "Unsteadily Forward," *Irish Times,* October 30, 1972.

195 Seán Mac Stiofáin's arrest and hunger strike: Mac Stiofáin, *Memoirs of a Revolutionary,* 337–364; "Mass Demonstrations," *An Phoblacht,* Samhain/November 26, 1972, 8; "Dublin I.R.A. Chief Gets Prison Term: Leader of Provisional Wing, Weakened by Fast, Vows Defiance of Court," *New York Times,* November 26, 1972, 1:5, 8:1; Deutsch and Magowan, *Northern Ireland, 1968–73,* 2:244, 245; "Violence on the Way for Éire, Says Rory Brady," *Daily Mail,* November 28, 1972. Kevin O'Kelly appealed his conviction and, according to Mac Stiofáin, served only a few days of his sentence.

197 Amendment to Offenses Against the State Act: "Sinn Féin Statement," *An Phoblacht,* Nollaig/December 10, 1972, 1; Deutsch and Magowan, *Northern Ireland, 1968–73,* 2:245–247; Bell, *The Irish Troubles,* 355.

197 Inaugural meeting of Irish Civil Rights Association: "Work to Be Done, Says S.F. President," *An Phoblacht,* Eanáir/January 7, 1973, 6; "Irish Civil Rights Association Draft Resolution at the Inaugural Meeting of the Association," *An Phoblacht,* Eanáir/January 7, 1973, 6.

197 Attempted arrest of Dáithí O'Connell: Deutsch and Magowan, *Northern Ireland, 1968–73,* 2:251; "Rory O'Brady Arrested by Special Branch," *Daily Telegraph,* December 30, 1972.

197 RÓB statement on the border bombings: "Border Bombings," in Ó Brádaigh, *Our People, Our Future.*

197 RÓB arrested in December 1972: "Sinn Féin Leader Arrested," *New York Times,* December 30, 1972, 6:5; "British Agents Succeed: Sinn Féin President Ruairí Ó Brádaigh Jailed," *An Phoblacht,* Eanáir/January 7, 1973; "Ruairí Ó Brádaigh Arrested by Special Branch in Dublin," *Irish News,* December 30, 1972; "Sinn Féin Leader Arrested," *Irish Independent,* December 30, 1972; RÓB IVs; "Provisional Sinn Féin President Rory Brady Was Arrested by Special Branch Men in Dublin Last Night," *Daily Mail,* December 30, 1972; "No Plan for Round-Up of Republican Sympathisers," *Irish Times,* December 30, 1972; "Special Court Trial for O'Brady?" *Belfast Telegraph,* December 30, 1972.

198 December 31st court appearance: "Trial Is Fixed for Jan. 11," *Sunday Independent,* December 31 1972; "Ó Brádaigh Sent for Trial on IRA Charges: State's Plea for More Time Rejected," *Irish Press,* January 1, 1972.

199 Martin McGuinness and Joe McCallion: RÓB IVs; "More Arrests . . . ," *An Phoblacht,* Eanáir/January 7, 1973; Liam Clarke and Kathryn Johnston, *Martin McGuinness: From Guns to Government* (London: Mainstream Publishing, 2002), 79–80; "McGuinness: 'I Quit IRA Nearly 30 Years Ago,'" *UTV Internet,* 5/11/2003, available online at http://www.utvlive.com/newsroom/indepth.asp?id=39065&pt=n.

199 January 11th court appearance: Deutsch and Magowan, *Northern Ireland, 1968–73,* 2:261; "Ó Brádaigh Is Given Prison Sentence," *Irish Independent,* January 12, 1973; "Ó Brádaigh Sentenced as Member of I.R.A.: Court Accepts Statement in Evidence of Chief Superintendent Fleming," *Irish Times,* January 12, 1973; Peter Doyle, "To Jail, in 12 Words. . . . Police Brand O'Brady as I.R.A. Man," *Daily Express,* Friday, January 12, 1973; "Ó Brádaigh Jailed As I.R.A. Member: Taken to Curragh Camp to Serve Six-Month Term," *Irish Times,* January 12, 1973; "Sinn Féin President Gets Jail Sentence," *Irish Press,* January 12, 1973; RÓB Notes.

201 London *Times* editorial: Denis Taylor, "The Importance of Rory O'Brady's Trial," (London) *Times,* January 15, 1973.

201 Glasshouse: The Glasshouse was a square building with a compound in the center. The cells, which had windows, were along the walls. If cell doors were closed, the compound would be in darkness. Therefore, the roof was made of glass to let light in.

201 Seán Mac Stiofáin and Martin McGuinness in the Curragh; Seán Mac Stiofáin, *Memoirs of a Revolutionary,* 363–364; RÓB IVs; Clarke and Johnston, *Martin McGuinness,* 81–82, quote on 82; "The Curragh," *An Phoblacht,* Márta/March 16, 1973, 7.

201 Protestants interned and unrest generated: Deutsch and Magowan, *Northern Ireland, 1968–73,* 2:269–270.

202 William Craig calls proposals "absurd": Deutsch and Magowan, *Northern Ireland, 1968–73,* 2:282.

202 Sinn Féin response to the white paper and decision not to contest the Assembly elections: RÓB IVs; RÓB telephone conversation, July 30, 1999; Bishop and Mallie, *The Provisional IRA,* 264–266, 472n3; Adams, *Before the Dawn,* 215–216; Ruairí Ó Brádaigh, "Sinn Féin Address," in *Our People, Our Future,* 23–30; "No Elections," *Republican News,* October 20, 1972.

202 1973 Leinster House election and coalition government: Garret FitzGerald, *All in a Life: An Autobiography* (London: Macmillan, 1991), 294; Conor Cruise O'Brien, *Memoir: My Life and Themes* (Dublin: Poolbeg, 1998), quote on 354; Bell, *The Irish Troubles,* 355–356, 373–376; Conor Cruise O'Brien interview.

203 Conditions in the Curragh: "The Curragh Statement on Conditions in Curragh Military Detention Camp," *An Phoblacht,* Márta/March 16, 1973, 7.

203 Release from the Curragh: Peter Doyle, "The Kiss That Says It's Great to Be Free," *Daily Express,* May 15, 1973; "Rory O'Brady Comes Out Fighting," *Belfast Telegraph,* May 14, 1973; "Ó Brádaigh Is Freed from the Curragh," *Irish Times,* May 15, 1975. In quoting O'Donovan Rossa, Ó Brádaigh echoed a similar comment from Seán Mac Stiofáin, who had been released a little earlier.

203 IRA leadership, 1970–1975: McGuire, *To Take Arms,* 137, 140–141, 149; Bell, *The Irish Troubles;* Bell, *IRA Tactics and Targets,* 15–17; "Éamon O'Doherty," *SAOIRSE,* Nollaig/December 1999, 15; "Provo Jail Break," *An Phoblacht,* Lúnasa/August 24, 1974. If Ruairí Ó Brádaigh was on the Army Council in May–June 1972 or in December 1972, he would have been replaced each time he was arrested. Dáithí O'Connell was never chief of staff; he was director of publicity and, for a time, adjutant general.

203 Seán Mac Stiofáin's credibility: see Bishop and Mallie, *The Provisional IRA,* 245.

204 Harassment: "Garda Watch on Ó Brádaigh," *Irish Times,* November 24, 1973; "Ó Brádaigh Complains of Harassment," *Irish Press,* November 26, 1973.

204 Dismissed from job: "Ó Brádaigh Dismissed as Teacher," *Irish Times,* January 25, 1974; "Ó Brádaigh Retains Committee's Support," *Irish Times,* February 27, 1974; "Minister Insists Ó Brádaigh Has Lost Job," *Irish Times,* April 24, 1974. As the committee searched for a way to support Ó Brádaigh, it was suggested that his position be declared vacant so that he could reapply. A member of the committee, Miss Mary O'Flanagan, who was also the niece of Father Michael O'Flanagan, who was president of Sinn Féin in the 1930s and was twice censored by his bishop, commented, "Is that another way of spitting in their eye? If so, let's spit."

204 Dáithí O'Connell appearances: Deutsch and Magowan, *Northern Ireland, 1968–73,* 2:293, 348; Deutsch and Magowan, *Northern Ireland, 1968–73,* 3:41; McKittrick, Kelters, Feeney, and Thornton, *Lost Lives,* 438–439.

205 IRA bombs in London: Deutsch and Magowan, *Northern Ireland, 1968–73,* 2:278–280.

205 Shane O'Doherty: Shane O'Doherty, *The Volunteer: A Former IRA Man's True Story* (London: Harper Collins, 1993).

205 Hunger strikes of and quotations about Marion and Dolours Price, Gerry Kelly, Hugh Feeney, Michael Gaughan, and Frank Stagg: Sister Sarah Clarke, *No Faith in the Sys-*

tem: A Search for Justice (Cork: Mercier Press, 1995), 44, 47; Gerry Kelly, *Words from a Cell* (Dublin: Sinn Féin Publicity Department, 1989), 9–11. *Daily Mirror* editorial on Michael Gaughan: "Who Are the Murderers?" *Daily Mirror,* June 5, 1974; Deutsch and Magowan, *Northern Ireland, 1968–73,* 3:89; "Why Strikers Ended Their Fast Protest," *An Phoblacht,* Meitheamh/June 14, 1974, 8; "Stagg's Love of Irish," *An Phoblacht,* Meitheamh/March 14, 1974, 8.

206 Michael Gaughan funeral: Deutsch and Magowan, *Northern Ireland, 1968–73,* 3:96–97, 99. O'Connell quotation: "New Life into Irish Hearts: O'Conaill Oration at Graveside," *An Phoblacht,* Meitheamh/June 14, 1974, 8.

207 Launch of *Our People, Our Future:* "Policy Stand of SF Clarified: Ó Brádaigh Book Launched," *Irish Press,* August 14, 1973.

207 1973 Ard Fheis and comments on Conor Cruise O'Brien: "Presidential Address to the 69th Ard-Fheis," in Ó Brádaigh, *Our People, Our Future,* 49–58; "Separate State and Church, Ó Brádaigh Tells Sinn Féin: Wants Assembly, with Provincial Rule," *Irish Times,* October 22, 1973; "Further Example of 'Dictatorial Zeal,' Says Ó Brádaigh," *Irish Times,* March 1, 1974.

208 Mary Gaffney interview: "'The Politics of the Clergy Are Not the Word of God': Ruairí Ó Brádaigh Talking Frankly to Mary Gaffney," *Sunday World,* October 28, 1973; McGuire, *To Take Arms,* 75–76.

209 July 1973 U.S. tour; deaths from plastic bullets: "Sinn Féin Appeal for Support from U.S.," *Irish Independent,* July 27, 1973; "IRA's American Branch," RÓB letter to the editor, *Irish Press,* August 27, 1973; McKittrick, Kelters, Feeney, and Thornton, *Lost Lives,* 179, 226–227, 360.

209 August 1973 trip to Washington, D.C.: "Ireland 'Denies' Human Rights," *Irish Independent,* October 13, 1973; Seán Cronin, "Letter from New York: Ó Brádaigh Barred Because of Dublin Government Pressure, Says Politician," *Irish Times,* January 21, 1974; "Ó Brádaigh in America," *An Phoblacht,* Samhain/November 2, 1973; "US Department of Justice Memo," New York, December 26, 1973; "US Department of Justice Memo," Washington, December 27, 1973 and "Department of State Telegram," October 10, 1973 (copies in author's possession); the photo appeared in the *Irish Press,* October 17, 1973. Among those attending the O'Neill-Conte reception was Senator Barry Goldwater. Secretary of State Henry Kissinger sent Goldwater a letter that included, ". . . We have received correspondence from the British Embassy who were alarmed by the event." Goldwater's reply included, "Perhaps the Department could assist in a solution that would gain for the people of Ireland the freedom we enjoy." Copies in author's possession.

210 January 1974 tour, visa revocation: "US Government Memorandum, From 'SAC' to Director, FBI, February 21, 1974"; "Memo to the United States Secretary of State, Washington, from the American Embassy, Dublin," October 25 1973; "Memo to Secretary of State, Washington, from American Embassy, Dublin," January 16, 1974; "Federal Bureau of Investigation Communications Section Memo 2217132," January 25, 1974; "FBI Communications Section Memo 121631Z, March 14, 1974"; "U.S. Shuts Door on Rory Brady," *Daily Mirror,* January 17, 1974; "United States Department of Justice Federal Bureau of Investigation Memo," May 24, 1974; "Memo from Secretary of State to American Embassy in Dublin," June 23, 1977; "Suspected Leaders of I.R.A. in Belfast Denied U.S. Visas," *New York Times,* April 28, 1975, 58:5. Ó Brádaigh denies that he would have used the trip to raise funds for the IRA. He phoned the U.S. embassy and was informed that the State Department had discovered that Peter R. Brady was Ruairí Ó Brádaigh, "the name he is known by in connection with his IRA related activities." He pointed out that his birth certificate and passport list him as Peter Roger Casement Brady and, according to an FBI memo, "stated that everyone knows who Peter Brady is." He was then informed that the embassy believed him to be a member of the Provisional IRA's Army Council. Documents obtained through the Freedom of Information Act show that the State Department spent some time confirming that Peter R.

Brady was in fact Ruairí Ó Brádaigh. Others whose visas were revoked include Joe Cahill, Séamus Loughran, Máire Drumm, and Seán Keenan. Cited memos in author's possession.

210 Patsy Ó Brádaigh trip to New York: Patsy Ó Brádaigh interview; "S.F. President Represented by Wife," *Irish Times,* January 19, 1974; Seán Cronin, "Letter from New York: Ó Brádaigh Barred Because of Dublin Government Pressure, Says Politician," *Irish Times,* January 21, 1974.

211 Trieste conference: RÓB IVs; "Provisional S.F. Men to Attend Trieste Conference," *Irish Times,* July 12, 1974; "Ó Brádaigh Put Case to Trieste Conference," *Irish Times,* July 23, 1974; "Ó Brádaigh in Trieste," *An Phoblacht,* Iúil/July 26, 1974; "'Ireland Fighting for Her Existence'—Mayor of Trieste," *An Phoblacht,* Lúnasa/August 2, 1974, 3; "Sinn Féin in Trieste," *An Phoblacht,* Lúnasa/August 2, 1974, 4; "Two-Sided Talks on North Hint," *Irish Independent,* July 17, 1974; "Secret Talks Hint," *Irish News,* July 17, 1974; "Must Be Warned," *An Phoblacht,* Iúil/July 26, 1974; "Ó Brádaigh Against 'No Warning' Bomb," *Irish News,* July 19, 1974; "European Trip by Ó Brádaigh," *Irish Independent,* July 23, 1974.

211 Constitutional politicians reject Éire Nua: Des Fennell interview; Fennell, *Beyond Nationalism,* 157–159.

212 1973 Assembly election; Sunningdale: Deutsch and Magowan, *Northern Ireland, 1968–73,* 2:317, 324, 360–361, 376–378.

213 Desmond Boal proposals and Paddy Devlin reaction: Deutsch and Magowan, *Northern Ireland, 1968–73,* 3:1–3.

213 Reaction to the Boal proposals: RÓB Notes; "Ó Brádaigh Hails Boal's Federal Plan: 'Step to Permanent Peace,'" *Irish Press,* January 9, 1974; "Ó Brádaigh Backs Boal Proposal," *Irish Times,* January 9, 1974; "Boal's Peace Plan," *An Phoblacht,* Eanáir/January 25, 1975, 2; Deutsch and Magowan, *Northern Ireland, 1968–73,* 3:2; "Des Boal's New Ireland," *Hibernia,* January 18, 1974, 3; W. D. Trimble, "Loyalists' First Aim Must Be to Preserve the Union: Independence May Be the Only Alternative to United Ireland," *Sunday News,* January 20, 1974; Henry McDonald, *Trimble* (London: Bloomsbury, 2000), 47–48.

213 1974 Westminster election: Paddy Devlin, *The Fall of the N.I. Executive* (Belfast: Paddy Devlin, 1975), 8; Bishop and Mallie, *The Provisional IRA,* 264–266; Paul Bew and Gordon Gillespie, *Northern Ireland: A Chronology of the Troubles, 1968–1999* (Dublin: Gill and Macmillan, 1999), 78, 80–81.

213 Merlyn Rees's balancing act: Rees, *Northern Ireland: A Personal Perspective.*

213 John Joe McGirl arrest: "Ó Brádaigh Raps Detention of McGirl," *Irish News,* April 18, 1974.

214 *Weekend World* appearance with Craig and Smyth: In *The Red Hand,* Sammy Smyth is described by Steve Bruce as the "sometime editor of *Ulster Militant* and a loose cannon who enjoyed an exciting and erratic relationship with the UDA." He was shot dead by the IRA in March 1976. In his conversation with Ó Brádaigh, Smyth estimated that the Unionist majority in the nine counties of Ulster would last only ten years. Ó Brádaigh replied that it was up to that community; in 2004, they are still in the majority. Smyth was also concerned that control of military forces in the provinces would rest at the federal (national) level. Ó Brádaigh replied that in a peaceful Ireland, the military would not be an instrument of repression and added that he visualized a Swiss-style volunteer army and territorial army with units in Republican and Unionist areas. "O'Brady to Meet UDA Man," *Belfast Newsletter,* April 6, 1974; "UDA Man Meets Ó Brádaigh on TV Programme," *Irish Times,* April 6, 1974; Deutsch and Magowan, *Northern Ireland, 1968–73,* 3:39; "UDA and Sinn Féin Air Views," *Belfast Newsletter,* April 8, 1974; "IRA and UDA Say Britain Must Go," *Daily Mail,* April 8, 1974; "UDA and Sinn Féin Air Views," *Belfast Newsletter,* April 8, 1974; RÓB IVs; RÓB telephone conversation, June 30, 1999; "Protestant Reaction to Éire Nua," *Éire Nua Newsletter* 2, no. 2 (June 1993); McKittrick, Kelters, Feeney, and Thornton, *Lost Lives,* 631–632. The Congo: "Patrice Lumumba and the Revolution in the Congo," *The Militant* 65, no. 28 (July 23, 2001), available online at http://www.themilitant.com/2001/6528/652850.html.

215 May 1974 Dublin and Monaghan bombs: J. Bowyer Bell, *In Dubious Battle: The Dublin and Monaghan Bombings, 1972–1874* (Dublin: Poolbeg, 1996), quote on 82; McKittrick, Kelters, Feeney, and Thornton, *Lost Lives,* 447–453. Responsibility and motive for the bombings have never been fully determined. The evidence suggests that they were the work of the Portadown Ulster Volunteer Force, but suspicion remains that British agents were also involved.

215 Ulster Workers' Council strike: Robert Fisk, *The Point of No Return: The Strike Which Broke the British in Ulster* (London: Times Books, 1975); Bew and Gillespie, *Northern Ireland: A Chronology,* 84–90.

215 Liam Cosgrave blames the Republicans and RÓB response; Deutsch and Magowan, *Northern Ireland, 1968–73,* 3:80; "Set Withdrawal Date—Ó Brádaigh," *Irish Independent,* May 30, 1974.

216 June 1974 local elections: "SF Men Not Intimidated—Ó Brádaigh," *Irish Independent,* May 30, 1974; "Provisional S.F. Seek More Seats," *Irish Times,* May 30, 1974; "Election Campaign Gathers Impetus," *An Phoblacht,* Bealtaine/May 31, 1974, 6; "Ó Brádaigh Hits Out at 'Harassment,'" *Irish Press,* May 14, 1974. Walter Lynch quotation: U. Ó Loinsigh, "A Success the Media Tried to Keep from the Voter Election Analysis," *An Phoblacht,* Iúil/July 19, 1974; "Give Our Men Your Support," *An Phoblacht,* Bealtaine/May 10, 1974, 5; "Sinn Féin Election Success," *An Phoblacht,* Meitheamh/June 28, 1974.

216 Longford election; Lynch farm raided: Seán Lynch interview. Ó Brádaigh quotation: "Sinn Féin Election Success," *An Phoblacht,* Meitheamh/June 28, 1974.

216 Seán Mac Eoin funeral; RÓB IVs; O'Farrell, *The Blacksmith of Ballinalee.*

217 Funeral of May Brady Twohig: RÓB IVs; Seán Cronin interview; "Late Mrs. May Twohig," *An Phoblacht,* Lúnasa/August 23, 1974, 8; "Graveside Oration at Republican Funeral," *Longford Leader,* August 16, 1974, 1, 8; RÓB IVs.

Chapter 13

219 Growth of *An Phoblacht*: "Éamon Mac Thomáis," *An Phoblacht/Republican News,* August 29, 2002.

219 IRA campaign in England: Martin Dillon, *The Enemy Within: The IRA's War against the British* (London: Doubleday, 1994), 132.

219 1974 data: In 1974, there were 3,206 shooting incidents, 685 bombings, 2,828 plastic or rubber bullets fired by the security forces, 74,914 homes searched, and 303 people killed in activities related to the Northern Ireland conflict. The Provisional IRA accounted for 133 of the deaths. McKittrick, Kelters, Feeney, and Thornton, *Lost Lives,* 1473–1476, Tables 1–3; Flackes and Elliott, *Northern Ireland: A Political Directory,* 681–689; Irish Information Agenda, *Agenda Information Service on Northern Ireland,* 6th ed. (London: Irish Information Partnership, 1990); Malcolm Sutton, *Bear in mind these dead . . . An Index of Deaths from the Conflict in Ireland, 1969–1993* (Belfast: Beyond the Pale Publications, 1994).

219 South Armagh: Toby Harnden, *"Bandit Country": The IRA & South Armagh* (London: Hodder & Stoughton, 1999); quotation is from Pat Holmes, "Memorial to an IRA Man: Ó Brádaigh at Ceremony," *Irish Press,* November 18, 1974; McKittrick, Kelters, Feeney, and Thornton, *Lost Lives,* 401–402; "S. Armagh Liberated Area, Says O'Brady," *Belfast Telegraph,* November 18, 1974.

220 Ó Brádaigh and 1972–1974 communication between IRA and British: RÓB IVs; Taylor, *Behind the Mask,* 153–154, 195–199; Clarke and Johnston, *Martin McGuinness,* 86.

220 1974 Ard Fheis: quotation in Liam Ryan, "Republicans Fear Another Congo—Ó Brádaigh," *Irish Independent,* September 30, 1974; "Ó Brádaigh at Ard-Fheis," *An Phoblacht,* n.d.

220 U.S. embassy summary of the Ard Fheis: In his autobiography, *All in a Life,* Garret FitzGerald states that he and John Hume were concerned about a possible British withdrawal.

Memo "From AMEMBASSY DUBLIN TO SECSTATE WASHDC," October 1, 1974 (in author's possession); FitzGerald, *All in a Life,* 255.

220 Bombs in England, fall 1974: McKittrick, Kelters, Feeney, and Thornton, *Lost Lives,* 481–483, 490–491.

220 O'Connell-Holland interview: Alan Smith, "IRA Threat to Spread Terror," *Guardian,* November 18, 1974; O'Connell quotation in "I.R.A. to Escalate Its Campaign in Britain," *Irish Times,* November 18, 1974.

221 Birmingham bombings: Chris Mullin, *Error of Judgement: The Truth about the Birmingham Bombings* (Swords, County Dublin: Poolbeg, 1986).

221 RÓB reaction to Birmingham: RÓB IVs.

221 O'Connell on Birmingham: "When Mercy Died," *Sunday World,* November 24, 1974; "Ó Conaill on Birmingham," *Sunday Press,* December 1, 1974; Mullin, *Error of Judgement,* 260–261, 266. Dáithí O'Connell's investigation of the Birmingham bombings led him to believe that IRA personnel were not involved. As evidence accumulated that those found guilty of the bombings were innocent, journalists undertook their own investigations and concluded that those who were responsible lied to O'Connell. In 1985, Joe Cahill publicly admitted that Birmingham was the work of the Provisional IRA. In 1997, in a television interview with Vincent Browne, Ó Brádaigh stated that the IRA had not sanctioned Birmingham.

221 Prevention of Terrorism Act: Bell, *The Irish Troubles,* 432; Paul Wilkinson, *Terrorism and the Liberal State,* 2nd ed. (London: Macmillan, 1986), 169–172. Wilkinson states that the Prevention of Terrorism Act was not a "panic measure," that the legislation was under way prior to Birmingham, which finally convinced the public and MPs that the legislation was necessary.

221 Birmingham Six; Guildford Four: McKittrick, Kelters, Feeney, and Thornton, *Lost Lives,* 479–482, 496–500; Mullin, *Error of Judgement*; Grant McKee and Ros Franey, *Time Bomb: Irish Bombers, English Justice and the Guildford Four* (London: Bloomsbury, 1988); Bell, *The Irish Troubles,* 803. Another victim was Judith Ward, who was wrongfully convicted in 1974 for involvement in IRA bombings. She was released, after eighteen years in prison, in 1992.

221 Feakle meeting: RÓB IVs. Arlow quotation: Bishop and Mallie, *The Provisional IRA,* 270. See also Bell, *The Irish Troubles,* 433–434; Ken Heskin, *Northern Ireland: A Psychological Analysis* (Dublin: Gill & Macmillan, 1980), 79–80. Butler and McKee quotations: Taylor, *Behind the Mask,* 206.

223 Interviews after Feakle: RÓB IVs; "Ó Brádaigh Found Talks 'Fruitful,'" *Irish Times,* December 13, 1974; "Ó Brádaigh Off the Air Again," *Irish Press,* December 13, 1974; "Always Willing to Talk—Ó Brádaigh," *Irish News,* December 3, 1974; "Brady Interview Banned," *Belfast Telegraph,* December 13, 1974; Deutsch and Magowan, *Northern Ireland, 1968–73,* 3:174.

223 Provisional IRA response to the clergymen: Rees, *Northern Ireland: A Personal Perspective,* 149–151.

223 Constitutional Convention and Rees's meeting with the clergymen: Bell, *The Irish Troubles,* 444–483; Michael J. Cunningham, *British Government Policy in Northern Ireland 1969–89: Its Nature and Execution* (Manchester: Manchester University Press, 93–94); Rees, *Northern Ireland: A Personal Perspective,* 151–153.

224 Interviews after cease-fire announcement: Deutsch and Magowan, *Northern Ireland, 1968–73,* 3:178; "Britain's Move—Ó Brádaigh," *Belfast Telegraph,* December 21, 1974; "IRA Ceasefire Could 'Become Permanent': General Welcome for Peace Move," *Irish Press,* December 21, 1974; "How Dublin Can Help—Ó Brádaigh," *Irish Press,* December 21, 1974; "Britain's Move—Ó Brádaigh," *Belfast Telegraph,* December 21, 1974.

224 Meeting of RÓB, intermediary, and Army Council; RÓB "astonished": Taylor, *Behind the Mask,* 208–210.

225 Internee releases and January 1, 1975, march: "Wilson Meeting Raises Hopes of

Churchmen: Sinn Féin Chief Demands a 'Positive Response,'" *Belfast Telegraph,* January 2, 1975; Deutsch and Magowan, *Northern Ireland, 1968–73,* 3:182; "Release of 53 Prisoners Was Not Positive Enough Says Ó Brádaigh," *Irish Times,* January 2, 1975; Jack Kenealy, "Provos in 'Get Out' Demand to Wilson," *Daily Mirror,* January 2, 1975.

225 McKee-Oatley meeting and RÓB statement: Taylor, *Behind the Mask,* 214; Gerard Kemp, "Optimism over Cease Fire," *Daily Telegraph,* January 8, 1975.

225 Rees at the House of Commons: Rees, *Northern Ireland: A Personal Perspective,* 165–166.

226 Ó Brádaigh "depressed" and Rees quotation: "Ó Brádaigh 'Saddened, Depressed,'" *Irish Press,* January 17, 1975; Bew and Gillespie, *Northern Ireland: A Chronology,* 98.

226 January 17th phone call; formal meetings between Republicans and British: "Background to Renewal of Truce and Subsequent Negotiations," RÓB Truce Notes; Taylor, *Behind the Mask,* 212–214; Nollaig Ó Gadhra, *Margáil na Saoirse* [*Bargaining for Freedom*] (Baile Átha Cliath: Cló na Buaidhe, 1988); FitzGerald, *All in a Life,* 260; see also Bishop and Mallie, *The Provisional IRA,* 273–274, 278; and Clarke and Johnston, *Martin McGuinness,* especially 87–88. RÓB notes of meetings: Although Ó Brádaigh introduced the intermediary to the Army Council and participated in the meetings, this does not necessarily indicate that he was a council member. It does indicate his importance to the movement. His notes were typed up after each meeting, save the notes for the last meeting, which were typed several years later. He also kept notes on the January 17th phone call. Several persons were given code names. Ó Brádaigh was "Michael." The notes are available through the James Hardiman Library at the National University of Ireland, Galway. Only two other times, to the author's knowledge, have they been made available to researchers. In 1988, Irish journalist Nollaig Ó Gadhra quoted from them extensively, in English, in his Irish-language book, *Margáil na Saoirse* [*Bargaining for Freedom*]. In the 1990s, British journalist Peter Taylor was allowed to use them for the television program and subsequent book with the same title, *Behind the Mask: The IRA and Sinn Féin.* Taylor accepts that the notes are a valid representation of the meetings albeit from one perspective. In his autobiography, *All in a Life,* Garret FitzGerald states that in February 1975 the British ambassador to Dublin, in secret, confirmed that the British-IRA discussions were "broadened to include 'one or two others,' including Ruairí Ó Brádaigh"; this is consistent with Ó Brádaigh's notes. Liam Clarke and Kathryn Johnston's biography, *Martin McGuinness: From Guns to Government,* suggests that the intermediary was Dennis Bradley, then a priest in Derry. It was not Bradley. Billy McKee confirmed his own involvement in the meetings to Peter Taylor. Ó Brádaigh confirms only his own involvement.

227 "freedom of movement," right to "carry concealed short arms," continued meetings "toward securing a permanent ceasefire": RÓB Truce Notes.

227 January 1975 IRA activity: McKittrick, Kelters, Feeney, and Thornton, *Lost Lives,* 511–514; Bew and Gillespie, *Northern Ireland: A Chronology,* 98.

227 "evading agreeing to practical arrangements"; January 23rd instructions: "Instructions 23.1.75," RÓB Truce Notes.

228 Truce agreement: "7th Feb. 1975," RÓB Truce Notes; "Formal Meeting, 25th August 1975," RÓB Truce Notes. In *Margáil na Saoirse,* 108–109, Nollaig Ógadhra presents the Republican and British terms. Rees quotation; "signed documents": see FitzGerald, *All in a Life,* 259–260.

229 Assurance from Frank Cooper: "7th Feb. 1975," RÓB Truce Notes.

229 Truce incident centers: RÓB IVs; "Instructions 8th Feb. '75," RÓB Truce Notes; "Provisionals Set Community Aims: Ó Brádaigh Explains Task," *Irish Times,* April 7, 1975; Bew and Gillespie, *Northern Ireland: A Chronology,* 98–99. See *An Phoblacht,* editions of Samhain/November 7 and 14, 1975.

229 Incident center in Dungannon: Tommy McKearney correspondence.

231 Jimmy Drumm, Proinsias Mac Airt, and operation of the incident centers: RÓB IVs; Bell, *The Secret Army,* 419–420; Coogan, *The IRA* (1987 ed.), 483, 499–500.

231 Martin McGuinness and the incident center in Derry: Clarke and Johnston, *Martin McGuinness,* 88–89.

231 Danny Morrison, Tom Hartley, and the Belfast incident center: Danny Morrison interview.

231 Situation as the IRA entered the truce: RÓB IVs; "The Wolf in Sheep's Clothing," *The Economist,* February 15, 1975, 14; FitzGerald, *All in a Life,* 264. Lord Gardiner directed an inquiry on the relationship between the fight against terrorism in Northern Ireland and human rights and civil liberties; see Flackes and Elliott, *Northern Ireland: A Political Directory,* 264–265.

232 Sinn Féin–IRA relations with the coalition government: "Gardaí Attack Funeral," *An Phoblacht,* Márta 28, 1975; "Port Laoise: Persistent Harassment of Prisoners," *An Phoblacht,* Meitheamh/June 20, 1975; "IRA: Dublin Gets Tough," *The Economist,* February 8, 1975, 23; Gerard Kemp, "Mallon's Capture 'Sabotaging Ceasefire,'" *Daily Telegraph,* January 9, 1975. O'Hagan's arrest: *Republican News,* January 25, 1975, 3.

232 Decision to accept the truce: There are reports that Kevin Mallon "disapproved" of the negotiations at Feakle and that two northern members of the Army Council—perhaps Mallon and J. B. O'Hagan—opposed the cease-fire at Christmas. O'Hagan and Mallon, however, had been arrested by February. According to Ó Brádaigh, these accounts are inaccurate and the council entered the truce in unanimous agreement; he states that the decision was important enough that the leadership had to proceed in full agreement. RÓB IVs; McKee and Franey, *Time Bomb,* 183; Bishop and Mallie, *The Provisional IRA,* 269–271.

232 Loyalist activity February 10 and 19, 1975: McKittrick, Kelters, Feeney, and Thornton, *Lost Lives,* 516–518.

233 Ó Brádaigh's personal life: "Ó Brádaigh: Longfordian, Republican, and Key Figure in Northern Peace," *Longford Leader,* March 7, 1975, 12.

233 Irish National Liberation Army and feud with the Officials: Jack Holland and Henry McDonald, *INLA: Deadly Divisions: The Story of One of Ireland's Most Ruthless Terrorist Organizations* (Dublin: Torc, 1994). On Billy McMillan, see McKittrick, *Lost Lives,* 538; "Formal Meeting, 25.2.75," RÓB Truce Notes.

233 Stephen Tibble and formal meetings: Bew and Gillespie, *Northern Ireland: A Chronology,* 101; McKittrick, Kelters, Feeney, and Thornton, *Lost Lives,* 521. "Truce in acute danger," "Formal Meeting, 28.2.75," RÓB Truce Notes; "Instructions 19.2.1975," RÓB Truce Notes. On the permits, see Clarke and Johnston, *Martin McGuinness,* 88. "Parallel scheme": RÓB Truce Notes.

233 "sign that H.M.G. no longer wants to dictate events in Ireland," "advocate an all-Ireland convention," and "produce ideas which would lead to agreement," "Formal Meeting, 5.3.75," RÓB Truce Notes; "four weeks of genuine and sustained suspension of hostilities," "patience in negotiation and the discipline of R.M. are acknowledged by H.M.G.," and could not "interfere in the processes of law once law-breakers are arrested": "Formal Meeting, 16.3.75," RÓB Truce Notes.

234 March 1975 IRA communiqué: "Formal Meeting, 5.3.75" and "Per Sinn Féin, 10.3.75," RÓB Truce Notes.

234 Response to IRA communiqué, repatriation of the Price sisters: Coogan, *The IRA* (1987 ed.), 515; "Formal Meeting, 13.3.75" and "Formal Meeting, 16.3.75," RÓB Truce Notes.

234 Constitutional Convention election and Sinn Féin boycott: "Convention Election Boycott Call," *Irish News,* April 7, 1975.

234 Easter 1975: "Memorial Unveiled to 29 Provisionals," *Irish Times,* March 31, 1975; "Convention Rejected by Ó Brádaigh," *Irish Press,* March 31, 1975; Rees, *Northern Ireland: A Personal Perspective,* 224; Bew and Gillespie, *Northern Ireland: A Chronology,* 102.

235 "bombing and statement . . . were not helpful"; "acceptability of R.M. as a respectable movement has greatly increased"; "circumstances out of which the structures of disengagement can naturally grow"; "then you have deceived us": April 2nd and 17th formal meetings. Feeney and Kelly repatriation: "Formal Meeting, 4.2.75," and "Formal Meeting, 17.4.75," RÓB Truce Notes; "Sé Bhur mBeatha Abhaile," *An Phoblacht,* Aibreán/April 25, 1975.

235 Convention election results: Bew and Gillespie, *Northern Ireland: A Chronology,* 103–104; "70% in North Oppose Britain: More Backed Boycott than UUUC," *An Phoblacht,* Bealtaine/May 9, 1975, 1; Bell, *The Irish Troubles,* 449; "Instructions, 6.5.75," RÓB Truce Notes.

236 Shane O'Doherty arrest; Paul Gray killed: O'Doherty, *The Volunteer,* 181–183, 190; McKittrick, Kelters, Feeney, and Thornton, *Lost Lives,* 540; "Formal Meeting, 14.5.75," RÓB Truce Notes. The charges against O'Doherty for crimes committed in Northern Ireland were dropped. He was released, arrested by the Metropolitan Police (London), charged with bombings in London, and flown to London by the Royal Air Force. He was convicted and sentenced to thirty life sentences. O'Doherty, upset that the IRA engaged in sectarian killings and about the pain and suffering caused to civilians by IRA bombs in England, later renounced violence and disassociated himself from the IRA.

237 Campaign against the EEC: RÓB Truce Notes; Bew and Gillespie, *Northern Ireland: A Chronology,* 103–104; "The Referendums of 1973 and 1974," available online at http://www.ark.ac.uk/elections/fref70s.htm.

237 Loyalist and IRA activity in May and June: McKittrick, *Lost Lives,* 540–545. It was later discovered that Francis Rice, one of the Catholic victims, had been an IRA volunteer.

238 Intermediary signals: "Meeting between S. and B.: Report and Assessment 24.5.75," RÓB Truce Notes. "Hot and cold," RÓB Notes.

238 Formal meetings in June and the "murder triangle": "Formal Meeting, 4.6.75," "Instructions 5.6.75," "Formal Meeting, 11.6.75," "Note, 19th June 1975," all in RÓB Truce Notes; "Óráid an Uachtaráin," *An Phoblacht,* Samhain/November 7, 1975, 4.

238 Release of internees: Steve Wright reports that there were more than 500 Republican internees in December 1974. It appears that over 1975, the monthly number of internees released was approximately as follows: 29 in January, 16 in February, 101 in March, 52 in April, 15 in May, 34 in June, 29 in July, 27 in August, 22 in September, 19 in October, 77 in November, and 93 in December. Steve Wright, "A Multivariate Time Series Analysis of the Northern Ireland Conflict 1969–76," in Yonah Alexander and John M. Gleason, eds., *Behavioral and Quantitative Perspectives on Terrorism* (New York: Pergamon Press, 1981), 283–328.

239 British seek additional meetings: "Notes 1.7.75" and "S. to M., Report, 3. 7. 75," both in RÓB Truce Notes.

239 IRA bombs in Derry: "'We'll Continue to Keep Low Profile'—Derry IRA," *An Phoblacht,* Iúil/July 18, 1975.

239 IRA attack in South Armagh: McKittrick, Kelters, Feeney, and Thornton, *Lost Lives,* 552–553.

239 British Parliament: Rees, *Northern Ireland: A Personal Perspective,* 198–199; "Note, 19th June 1975," RÓB Truce Notes.

239 O'Connell arrest; Ó Brádaigh quotation: "Deadly Blow at Fragile Truce," *An Phoblacht,* Iúil/July 18, 1975. Fleming and twelve-month sentence: "Special Lies: O'Connell Jailed," *An Phoblacht,* Lúnasa/August 1, 1975; Bew and Gillespie, *Northern Ireland: A Chronology,* 105–106; Bell, *The Irish Troubles,* 453–454.

239 Provisional–Irish National Liberation Army relations: Holland and McDonald, *INLA: Deadly Divisions,* 60, 75n2.

239 Tit-for-tat killings in April 1975: McKittrick, Kelters, Feeney, and Thornton, *Lost Lives;* Bell, *The Irish Troubles,* 441.

239 Miami Showband: Bell, *The Irish Troubles,* 452; McKittrick, Kelters, Feeney, and Thornton, *Lost Lives,* 555–557.

240 Bayardo Bar: McKittrick, Kelters, Feeney, and Thornton, *Lost Lives,* 560–562; O'Doherty, *The Volunteer,* 195.

240 Frank King statement: King believed that in December 1974 the British were winning the war and that releasing internees would strengthen the IRA. Paul Wilkinson agrees with King's assessment, stating that by December 1974 the British Army had "practically beaten the Provisional I.R.A." Rees, *Northern Ireland: A Personal Perspective,* 156, 225–228, 235; Flackes and Elliott, *Northern Ireland: A Political Directory,* 307; Wilkinson, *Terrorism and the Liberal State,* 160–161.

240 Unionists suspect Merlyn Rees; Twomey not arrested: Rees, *Northern Ireland: A Personal Perspective,* 235–237; "'We Stay' No Matter What—Rees: Anger as Six More Go Free," *News Letter,* August 27, 1975.

240 Garret FitzGerald's concerns: RÓB IVs; Rees, *Northern Ireland: A Personal Perspective,* 238–239; FitzGerald, *All in a Life,* 270–274, quote on 272; Bell, *The Irish Troubles,* 454.

240 Robert Fisk article: Rees, *Northern Ireland: A Personal Perspective,* 235.

240 British memo of July 16th: "16th July, 1975," RÓB Truce Notes.

241 British had to give the convention a chance: "H.M.G. is waiting for consensus of opinion in Britain," "danger of a Congo-type situation resulting," and "why continue to fight," "Formal Meeting, 31.7.75"; British army there "to separate the communities," "open war on the people," and "firing wildly from the hip," "Formal Meeting, 13.8.75," all in RÓB Truce Notes.

241 July and August formal meetings: "Formal Meeting, 22nd July 1975"; "Formal Meeting, 31.7.75"; "Formal Meeting, 13.8.75"; "Formal Meeting, 25th August 1975"; "Formal Meeting, 5th September 1975." All in RÓB Truce Notes.

241 Violence in early September 1975: Bew and Gillespie, *Northern Ireland: A Chronology,* 105–106; McKittrick, Kelters, Feeney, and Thornton, *Lost Lives,* 574–575, 577; Martin Dillon, *The Enemy Within,* 149–150.

241 John Hume, Austin Currie, William Craig, and the voluntary coalition: Bell, *The Irish Troubles,* 454–455.

241 Formal meeting September 16th: "Formal Meeting, 16th September 1975," RÓB Truce Notes.

242 Merlyn Rees denial and September 22nd bombs: Rees, *Northern Ireland: A Personal Perspective,* 238–241; Bell, *The Irish Troubles,* 457; Martin Dillon, *The Enemy Within,* 150.

242 Moment of truth press conference; "The Moment of Truth," *An Phoblacht,* Deireadh Fómhair/October 3, 1975; "Ó Brádaigh Says There Is Truce Agreement," *Irish Times,* September 26, 1975.

242 Northern tour in fall and Ard Fheis: Ruairí Óg Ó Brádaigh interview; "What Sinn Féin Have Been Doing," *An Phoblacht,* Meán Fómhair/September 12, 1975; "Ard-Fheis '75," *An Phoblacht,* Deireadh Fómhair/October 31, 1975; Bell, *The Irish Troubles,* 462–464; "Óráid an Uachtaráin," *An Phoblacht,* Samhain/November 7, 1975, 4.

243 Provisional IRA–Official IRA feud: McKittrick, Kelters, Feeney, and Thornton, *Lost Lives,* 590–595; RÓB IVs; O'Kelley, *The Longest War,* 240–241. The feud was resolved through the work of a number of parties, including Belfast priests Des Wilson and Alex Reid, with whom Ó Brádaigh met. In *Lost Lives,* McKittrick, Kelters, Feeney, and Thornton state that Fathers Wilson and Reid "negotiated a settlement." Other sources state that the death of Michael Duggan, chairman of the Falls [Road] Taxi Drivers Association, prompted a resolution. After his death, more than 300 taxi drivers refused to work, which severely affected the transportation of everyday people in West Belfast. Duggan's death helped the efforts of Wilson and Reid to negotiate.

244 Subintermediary complains about "P.I.R.A. . . . display of violence," "Mr. Rees' public denial . . . has not helped," and "purpose of the meetings to be the devising of structures of British disengagement from Ireland," "Formal Meeting, 25.9.75"; "what accommodation could be reached with the Loyalists by the Republican Movement?" "Formal Meeting, 22.10.75." All in RÓB Truce Notes.

244 Communication between IRA and British: "Message received per sub-intermediary, 6.30 p.m. Thursday, 25.9.'75"; "S. to L. [IRA Leadership] 30th September 1975"; "2nd Oct.

'75"; "Message from the Brits, 22.10.'75"; "Instructions, 28.10.'75"; "S. to M. 23.11.'75 (Explanatory Notes to be read with written communication from H.M.G. dated 10.11.'75 Paragraph 3 of 10.11.'75"; "Statement Issued from Northern Ireland Office at 10.00 a.m. 12.11.'75"; all in RÓB Truce Notes.

244 Internment ends; Derry IRA blows up the incident center: Bew and Gillespie, *Northern Ireland: A Chronology,* 108–109; Rees, *Northern Ireland: A Personal Perspective,* 246.

244 Merlyn Rees claims no additional talks: Rees, *Northern Ireland: A Personal Perspective,* 248.

245 South Armagh killings: McKittrick, Kelters, Feeney, and Thornton, *Lost Lives,* 609–614; Toby Harnden, *"Bandit Country,"* 134; RÓB IVs. In *"Bandit Country,"* Toby Harnden alleges that the attack was sanctioned by Seámus Twomey with the urging of Brian Keenan, a central IRA figure in Belfast who was director of IRA operations in England. Harnden reports that the attack was not sanctioned by the Army Council. But Twomey did not sanction the attack; Ó Brádaigh was with him when he learned of the attack after the event.

245 British response to Kingsmills: "RM–HMG Dec '75, Jan & Feb, '76 Notes," RÓB Truce Notes; Bell, *The Irish Troubles,* 467–468.

245 RÓB's response to Kingsmills and end to sectarian killings in the area: "Ó Brádaigh Initiative Successful," *An Phoblacht,* Eanáir/January 16, 1976; Harnden, *"Bandit Country,"* 134–138; Coogan, *The IRA* (1979 ed.), 550–551; "Pleas for End to Retaliation 'Even at This Late Hour,'" *Irish Times,* January 6, 1976, 4; "Feakle Churchmen Turn Down Plea by Ó Brádaigh for Intervention," *Irish Times,* January 8, 1976, 4; "Cautious Welcome from Feakle Churchmen," *Irish Times,* January 10, 1976, 5.

245 February 11, 1976, formal meeting: "Formal Meeting February 10th or 11th, 1976," RÓB Truce Notes; "RM—HMG Dec '75, Jan & Feb, '76," RÓB Truce Notes; "Notes, September 1996," RÓB Truce Notes. Ó Brádaigh typed the notes from this final meeting much later.

246 M. L. R. Smith quotations: Smith, *Fighting for Ireland?* 128–133. In an otherwise meticulously researched book, Smith, it appears, did not interview any member of the Republican leadership. This may have resulted in some key mistakes. Smith claims that the Army Council at this time was divided between hard-liners and politicos, who were allegedly led by Dáithí O'Connell. Smith characterizes O'Connell as "the one leader with sufficient stature to be able to steer the Provisionals in a more flexible direction." His arrest, which Smith dates in the spring of 1975, was a "critical" loss as Ó Brádaigh became the leader of the moderates, carried "little weight," and could not counter the hard-liners. Actually, O'Connell was arrested in July 1975, after the truce had started to fall apart. It was Ó Brádaigh, not O'Connell, who met with the British. Finally, while some were more interested in political than military matters, from 1970 to 1975, all members of the Army Council were hard-liners or they would not have been there—and it was a collective leadership.

246 Frank Stagg: "Onóir don Mhairtír," *An Phoblacht,* Feabhra/February 27, 1976, 8; "Funeral Oration," *An Phoblacht,* Feabhra/February 27, 1976, 8; McKittrick, Kelters, Feeney, and Thornton, *Lost Lives,* 626; Coogan, *The IRA* (1976 ed.), 520–521. The Stagg family split; some members of the family, who held the Provisionals responsible for Frank Stagg's death, objected to a paramilitary funeral, while other members of the family supported it.

Chapter 14

248 Leadership optimistic; Joe Clarke: "Partition States Must Be Replaced—*Easter Message,*" *An Phoblacht,* Aibreán/April 23, 1976; "Brits Are Going: The Economic Case," *An Phoblacht,* Meitheamh/June 11, 1978, 4. Joe Clarke did outlive fellow 1916 veteran Éamon de Valera, who died in 1975 at the age of 92. De Valera was given a state funeral; Clarke was given a Republican funeral.

248 Habitat conference: RÓB IVs. "World stage" quotation: "Provisional Sinn Féin Meet Foreign Rebels," *Belfast Telegraph,* June 23, 1976; "Republicans at U.N. Conference," *An*

Phoblacht, Iúil/July 2, 1976, 5; Ruairí Ó Brádaigh, "Introduction," in *Aisling 1916–1976* (Dublin: Sinn Féin, 1976), 4; On Seán MacBride, see Anthony J. Jordan, *Seán Mac Bride* (Dublin: Blackwater Press, 1993), 173–174.

249 Sinn Féin foreign policy; visits to embassies and Algeria: RÓB IVs.

250 Patrick Cannon and Christopher Ewart-Biggs: Bell, *The Irish Troubles,* 475–476; McKittrick, Kelters, Feeney, and Thornton, *Lost Lives,* 663–664; Sutton, *An Index of Deaths from the Conflict in Ireland,* 89; Lee, *Ireland, 1912–1985;* "Provisional Sinn Féin Deny Court Policy Switch," *Irish News,* October 6, 1976; Coogan, *The IRA* (1987 ed.), 522; Michael Mills, "There Is No Deal, Says Cabinet," *Irish Press,* April 23, 1977; "Hunger Strikers Give in to Dublin's Firm Stand," *Guardian,* April 23, 1977; "Port Laoise Pledges Must Be Honoured," *An Phoblacht,* Aibreán/April 26, 1977, 1, 8. An IRA statement that was issued six weeks later mentioned the death of Peter Cleary, an IRA volunteer who was shot after he had been captured by the British Army in South Armagh. The IRA regarded Ewart-Biggs's death as a reprisal and viewed the ambassador as a top British intelligence agent. An outcome of the Ewart-Biggs assassination was the resignation of Ireland's president, Cearbhall Ó Dálaigh. The Cosgrave government brought in repressive legislation. President Ó Dálaigh sent the bills to the Irish Supreme Court to test their constitutionality before signing them. The minister for defence, Patrick Donegan, denounced him. Taoiseach Liam Cosgrave refused to discipline Donegan, and Ó Dálaigh resigned in protest. From 1973 to 1977, the coalition government took a very hard line against the Republicans, especially in Port Laoise. O'Connell and O'Neill were charged with assault and IRA membership. They were found not guilty on the assault charge. O'Connell did not deny IRA membership and was found guilty. The government had raised the penalty for IRA membership from two to seven years in prison. O'Neill was charged under the old procedure and faced two years in prison. In a test case, he denied IRA membership and was found not guilty. RÓB IVs; "Provisional Sinn Féin Deny Court Policy Switch," *Irish News,* October 6, 1976.

250 RÓB and Seán Keenan arrest: "Sinn Féin Leaders Arrested North and South," *An Phoblacht,* Iúil/July 30, 1976, 1; "Rees Has Signed Detention Order Against Ó Brádaigh—Sinn Féin Claim," *Irish Times,* July 24, 1976.

250 RÓB in Castlereagh and exclusion order: RÓB IVs. The RUC presumably had access to the same press clippings on Ó Brádaigh that the Northern Ireland Office collected. These were later donated to the Political Collection of the Linenhall Library. The file included the article "Ó Brádaigh Against 'No Warning' Bombs," *Irish News,* July 19, 1974. Following his release from Castlereagh in July 1976, Ó Brádaigh received a message from the British participants in the 1975–1976 talks through the intermediary; the message was that they had read the transcript of Ó Brádaigh's interrogation while in Castlereagh and appreciated that he had not disclosed matters discussed during the talks. See "A Sop to the Loyalists," *An Phoblacht,* Lúnasa/August 13, 1976; "British Bent on Military Solution—Ó Brádaigh," *Irish Times,* August 4, 1976.

251 Danny Lennon; the Maguire family; the Peace People: McKittrick, *Lost Lives,* 669–670; Bell, *The Irish Troubles,* 482–488.

252 Majella O'Hare: "Crown Murders O.K. to Belfast Peace Women" and "Unaware," *An Phoblacht,* Lúnasa/August 27, 1976, 1, 8; McKittrick, Kelters, Feeney, and Thornton, *Lost Lives,* 671–672.

252 RÓB on the Peace People: RÓB IVs; "New Attack on Peace Women," *Irish Independent,* October 18, 1976; "Sinn Féin Makes Britain an Easy Withdrawal Offer," *Daily Telegraph,* October 12, 1976; "Honourable Peace Offered to Crown," *An Phoblacht,* Deireadh Fómhair/October 19, 1976, 1, 3; "Ard-Fheis," *An Phoblacht,* Deireadh Fómhair/October 26, 1976, 7.

252 Decline of the Peace People: McKittrick, *Lost Lives,* 669–670; Bell, *The Irish Troubles,* 489–490, 500–501, 522. A Peace People organization still exists.

252 Criminalization; Kieran Nugent: Bew and Gillespie, *Northern Ireland: A Chronology,* 107; Bishop and Mallie, *The Provisional IRA,* 350.

252 Prisoner issues; 1976 Sinn Féin Ard Fheis: "Ó Brádaigh Attacks Movement for

Peace, Urges New Talks," *Irish Times,* October 18, 1976, 8; "Ard-Fheis: A Plea for the Prisoners," *An Phoblacht,* Deireadh Fómhair/October 19, 1976, 8; see also *An Phoblacht,* edition of Nollaig/December 14, 1976.

253 RTÉ ban on Sinn Féin: "Provisional Sinn Féin Propaganda Wing of Criminal Body—Cruise O'Brien," *Irish News,* October 20, 1976. Lee, *Ireland, 1912–1985,* 476–484; O'Brien, *Memoir,* 357–359.

253 Máire Drumm assassination and funeral; "beleaguered people": "Crowds Gather to Mourn Mrs. Drumm: Provisionals Plan Elaborate Funeral," *Irish Press,* November 1, 1976; "Máire Drumm Given I.R.A. Military Rites," *New York Times,* November 2, 1976, 11:1; McKittrick, Kelters, Feeney, and Thornton, *Lost Lives,* 684–685; Bell, *The Irish Troubles,* 491–492; RÓB IVs; "Thousands in Last Salute to Mrs. Drumm," *Irish Independent,* November 2, 1976; "IRA Chief Twomey at Drumm Funeral," *Daily Telegraph,* November 2, 1976; "Máire Drumm: A Tribute by Ruairí Ó Brádaigh," *An Phoblacht,* Samhain/November 2, 1976, 3. Security net quotation: "Low-Key Funeral for Mrs. Drumm," *Irish Times,* November 2, 1976. Several stints in prison had left Mrs. Drumm in poor health.

254 Prisoner discussion groups and dissatisfaction with the truce: Kevin Bean and Mark Hayes, eds., *Republican Voices* (County Monaghan, Ireland: Seesyu Press, 2001), 21; Laurence McKeown, *Out of Time: Irish Republican Prisoners, Long Kesh, 1972–2000* (Belfast: Beyond the Pale Publications, 2001), 27–48; Brendan Hughes interview: Bishop and Mallie, *The Provisional IRA,* 284. It is reported that during the 1975 Official-Provisional feud, Gerry Adams sent a letter from Long Kesh demanding information on the situation. There are no reports that he received a reply. Joe Cahill and Mitchel McLoughlin quotations: White, *Provisional Irish Republicans,* 138–139. See also Bishop and Mallie, *The Provisional IRA,* 310–311; Smith, *Fighting for Ireland?* 143–144. Even among his Belfast critics, Billy McKee is still highly regarded, which has limited criticism of his involvement in the truce. It was much easier for the younger people, especially in Belfast, to criticize Ó Brádaigh and Dáithí O'Connell, even if McKee and Séamus Twomey also were in the IRA leadership in 1975. Ó Brádaigh agrees that the truce lasted longer than it should have, but he does not know why. *When* the IRA would end the truce depended on Séamus Twomey's decision, not on him. It was a purely military matter. It was only later, for example, that he learned from Dáithí O'Connell that commanders had been told to start mobilizing in early July 1975. In *A Secret History of the IRA,* Ed Moloney confirms that the IRA leadership was northern based throughout the truce.

255 Awareness of truce issues: Taylor, *Behind the Mask,* 233–234. Peter Taylor states that after the truce, Billy McKee seriously considered ending the campaign and discussed this with Séamus Twomey. Ó Brádaigh does not remember McKee being pessimistic, and either way he was not ready to end the campaign. Compared to 1962, when Ó Brádaigh was chief of staff, or 1950, when he joined, the movement was much stronger. Things were not going as well as in 1972, but they were still in a position of strength and opportunity compared to the 1950s.

255 Gerry Fitt quotation: "Mr. Fitt Replies to Ó Brádaigh," *Ulster Gazette,* August 14, 1975.

256 RUC and enhanced interrogations: Kevin Boyle, Tom Hadden, and P. Hillyard, *Ten Years on in Northern Ireland: The Legal Control of Political Violence* (London: Cobden Trust, 1980); Flackes and Elliott, *Northern Ireland: A Political Directory,* 177–178; Peter Taylor, *Beating the Terrorists? Interrogation in Omagh, Gough and Castlereagh* (Penguin: Middlesex, England, 1980). An Amnesty International inquiry and the Bennett Report (1979) confirmed that many of these confessions were the result of mistreatment of prisoners.

256 Northern Command; Martin McGuinness: Bishop and Mallie, *The Provisional IRA,* 311. In 2003, Martin McGuinness stated that he left the IRA in the mid-1970s.

256 Ivor Bell; reorganization of active service units: McKeown, *Out of Time,* 42.

256 Effect of the long war on the IRA: Clarke and Johnston, *Martin McGuinness,* 95–99; Robert White and Terry F. White, "Revolution in the City: On the Resources of Urban Guerrillas," *Terrorism and Political Violence* 3 (Winter 1991): 100–132; Smith, *Fighting for Ireland?* 188–189. Intelligence report quotation: Cronin, *Irish Nationalism,* 339–357, quotation on 356.

257 Gerry Adams; Danny Morrison; Billy McKee: Danny Morrison interview; Adams, *Before the Dawn,* 247; Danny Morrison, *Then the Walls Came Down: A Prison Journal* (Dublin: Mercier, 1999). Gerry Adams's self-presentation had a similar effect on many people. See Moloney, *A Secret History of the IRA,* 188.

257 Brownie column; Ó Brádaigh's politics: A Brownie article, "In Defence of Danny Lennon," echoed Ó Brádaigh's comments on Angela Gallagher in 1971. Adams wrote, "I am deeply sorry that the three young children died. . . . Children are always innocent. The Maguire family were not Danny Lennon's enemies and he was not their enemy. *They were victims of circumstances created when he was shot dead*" (emphasis added). The article was published in both *Republican News* and *An Phoblacht.* Compare Ó Brádaigh's 1972 Ard Fheis address with "Active Republicanism," by Brownie, *Republican News,* May 1, 1976, 4. RÓB quotation, "Revolutionary Ireland and the Third World," *An Phoblacht,* Deireadh Fómhair/October 12, 1976, 4. See also "Ó Brádaigh Interview with Steve Jones," *An Phoblacht,* Iúil/July 1976, 5; Gerry Adams, "In Defence of Danny Lennon," in Adams, *Cage Eleven* (Dingle, Co. Kerry: Brandon Books, 1990), 134-137.

258 Release of Gerry Adams from Long Kesh and subsequent involvement in the movement: Adams, *Before the Dawn,* 252–253; Colm Keena, *A Biography of Gerry Adams* (Cork: Mercier Press, 1990), 83–84; Bishop and Mallie, *The Provisional IRA,* 315; Bell, *The Irish Troubles,* 531. Notice of Ard Chomhairle election of 1977: *An Phoblacht,* October 29, 1977, 7; Mary Ward interview. Séamus Twomey, seeking to broaden the council, occasionally stepped off it to allow a new person on. As chief of staff, he would remain involved in discussions. That is how Adams may have joined the council in 1977. A similar situation occurred in 1960–1962, when Ó Brádaigh was chief of staff even though he had refused to join the council.

258 Jimmy Drumm at Bodenstown: "Annual Commemoration of Wolfe Tone, Bodenstown, Given by Jimmy Drumm," *An Phoblacht,* Meitheamh/June 18, 1977; Adams, *Before the Dawn,* 264; Bishop and Mallie, *The Provisional IRA,* 332–333.

259 RÓB reaction to Jimmy Drumm oration: RÓB IVs. Ó Brádaigh quotation, see Chapter 12 and "Ard Fheis Sinn Féin," *An Phoblacht,* Samhain/November 1972, 4; Ó Brádaigh quotation in *Our People, Our Future,* 23–30. "Brady Gives Backing to Drumm View," *Belfast Telegraph,* June 14, 1977; see also "M. Ó Callanáin's letter, Postmhála: Republican Manifesto Requested," *An Phoblacht,* Deireadh Fómhair/October 19, 1977.

259 Loyalist meetings, Seán MacBride and Desmond Boal talks, and meetings with Séamus Costello: RÓB IVs; Bell, *The Secret Army,* 432–433; McKittrick, *Lost Lives,* 736; Bell, *The Irish Troubles,* 518–520; Anthony J. Jordan, *Seán MacBride* (Dublin: Blackwater Press, 1993), 173–174; Adams, *Before the Dawn,* 258–260; McKittrick, Kelters, Feeney, and Thornton, *Lost Lives,* 895–896. Ó Brádaigh was struck by how well he got along with the Loyalists. Gerry Adams claims that *he* was involved in these talks. Ó Brádaigh does not remember Adams's involvement. John McKeague was shot dead by the Irish National Liberation Army in January 1982.

260 White House and U.S. Democratic Party interest in Ireland: Bell, *The Irish Troubles,* 509–510.

261 RÓB denied U.S. visa; meeting with congressmen: Memo from AMEMBASSY DUBLIN to RUEHC/SECSTATE WASH DC NIACT, June 21, 1977 and "Department of State Telegram, from AMEMBASSY DUBLIN," June 20, 1977 (both in author's possession); "Ó Brádaigh Beats Visa and Broadcast Ban," *An Phoblacht,* Iúil/July 20, 1977; Jack Holland, *Hope Against History: The Course of Conflict in Northern Ireland* (New York: Henry Holt, 1999), 101–102; Holland, *The American Connection,* 140–141; *Northern Ireland: A Role for the United States: Report by Two Members of the Committee on the Judiciary, Ninety-Fifth Congress, Second Session, Based on a Factfinding Trip to Northern Ireland, the Irish Republic, and En-*

gland, August/September 1978 (Washington, D.C.: U.S. Government Printing Office, 1979); "Ian Smith Granted Visa to U.S. While Ruairí Ó Brádaigh Is Denied Entry," *An Phoblacht,* Deireadh Fómhair/October 14, 1978, 2. In their meeting with the congressmen, Ó Brádaigh demonstrated his excellent memory. John Joe McGirl could not remember when he had been arrested in Belfast and some other dates. Ó Brádaigh helped him out with, for example, "Well, as I remember it, John Joe, you were arrested on Easter Sunday in '74 in Belfast." In *Hope Against History: The Course of Conflict in Northern Ireland,* Jack Holland places Ó Brádaigh and Martin McGuinness in New York in 1978 to purchase weapons. Ó Brádaigh denies this. U.S. State Department and FBI records, which are available under the Freedom of Information Act, do not report him in the United States at the time—legally or illegally. In *The American Connection: U.S. Guns, Money & Influence in Northern Ireland,* Holland places Ó Brádaigh, Dáithí O'Connell, and Gerry Adams as observers at a conference at Belfast's Europa Hotel in 1979. The conference, organized by U.S. congressman Mario Biaggi, brought together Loyalist and Republican paramilitary groups. Ó Brádaigh's presence is not credible. He remembers meeting Biaggi in Dublin but not in Belfast. He was willing to step out of a crowd at Milltown Cemetery at Easter 1979, but he was not foolish enough to participate in a conference at a prominent hotel in the center of Belfast. Ó Brádaigh does not discuss whether or not he entered the United States illegally.

262 Basque history; ETA and EIA: RÓB IVs; Cynthia Irvin, *Militant Nationalism: Between Movement and Party in Ireland and the Basque Country* (Minneapolis: University of Minnesota Press, 1999). In *A Secret History of the IRA,* Ed Moloney states that the contacts with the Basques, Bretons, and Corsicans that Ó Brádaigh helped establish "increased political cooperation and mutual understanding, but they also facilitated the mutual acquisition of weaponry and military expertise" (8–9). Ó Brádaigh will not comment on this.

262 RÓB, Richard Behal, and Ted Howell in the Basque country: RÓB IVs; "Message to Basques," *An Phoblacht,* Eanáir/January 4, 1978, 1; Le Eldrida, "Cúrsaí Eachtracha Foreign Affairs: Euskadi's Freedom Struggle," *An Phoblacht,* Eanáir/January 4, 1978, 6, 8; see also "Sinn Féin President Visits Basque Country," *An Phoblacht/Republican News,* March 29, 1980, 11.

262 RÓB visits Portugal, Sardinia, and the prisoners' conference in Dublin: "Portuguese Told of Irish Fight for Freedom," *An Phoblacht,* Aibreán/April 29, 1978, 3; "Ruairí O'Brádaigh's Speech in Basque Country," *An Phoblacht/Republican News,* February 24, 1979, 11; "National and Social Liberation Are Two Sides of the Same Coin," *An Phoblacht/Republican News,* March 31, 1979, 10; Paul Rooney, "European Political Prisoners Conference: Irish Prisoners Lead the Struggle," *An Phoblacht/Republican News,* April 28, 1979, 2.

263 RÓB on his trips: RÓB IVs; Seán Ó Brádaigh interview; "Ó Brádaigh Barr-ed from Frost," *An Phoblacht/Republican News,* May 19, 1979, 2.

264 Billy McKee and the Official IRA: Brendan Hughes interview.

264 Gerry Adams confronts Billy McKee: Tommy Gorman interview; Moloney, *A Secret History of the IRA,* 88–89, 166–169. Provisional IRA involvement in the feud had not been sanctioned by the Army Council. McKee was probably the commanding officer of the Belfast Provisionals. In *A Secret History of the IRA,* Ed Moloney reports that Adams and McKee had a strained relationship that dated from 1970. He also notes that Adams did not use the involvement of the Belfast IRA in sectarian attacks against McKee. He also states that Ó Brádaigh was the only person to defend Billy McKee. Sectarian attacks in Belfast, especially North Belfast, were a constant problem. In 1977, Tommy Gorman was offered the position of Belfast commanding officer. He indicated that he would take the position if sectarian attacks by the Belfast IRA were ended. He never received a reply. On sectarian attacks in North Belfast, see Robert White "The Irish Republican Army: An Assessment of Sectarianism," *Terrorism and Political Violence* 9, no. 1 (1997): 56–71.

264 La Mon House and arrest of Gerry Adams: "Screams and Shouts as Deadly Blaze Erupted," *Belfast Telegraph,* February 18, 1978; Bell, *The Irish Troubles,* 537–538. Jack Lynch quotation: "Callous Beasts Who Have No Place in Society—Lynch," *Belfast Telegraph,* February 18, 1978. Ó Brádaigh statement: "La Mon 'Totally Inexcusable'—SF," *Irish News*, February 21, 1978.

265 Martin McGuinness becomes chief of staff: Bell, *The Irish Troubles*, 537–538.

265 Long Kesh 1978: McKeown, *Out of Time*, 52–53; Adams, *Before the Dawn*, 273–274; McKittrick, Kelters, Feeney, and Thornton, *Lost Lives*, 771.

265 Statement of Archbishop Ó Fiaich: J. Bowyer Bell, *The Irish Troubles*, 552.

265 Campaign against the H-Blocks and support for the prisoners: *An Phoblacht*, Deireadh Fómhair/October 7, 1978, 8; *An Phoblacht/Republican News*, May 26, 1979, 6.

265 Trial of Gerry Adams: Colm Keena, *A Biography of Gerry Adams*, 81–84; Adams, *Before the Dawn*, 274–275.

265 Adams briefs Ó Brádaigh on Long Kesh: Adams, *Before the Dawn*, 274–275; Keena, *A Biography of Gerry Adams*, 84.

266 RÓB wary of Adams: RÓB IVs.

Chapter 15

267 *An Phoblacht/Republican News* merger: Danny Morrison interview; Moloney, *A Secret History of the IRA*, 179–180; RÓB IVs.

268 RÓB at Milltown: "'A New Generation Is Setting the Pace,'" *An Phoblacht/Republican News*, April 21, 1979, 8. Ó Brádaigh was aware for some time that a new generation with its own ideas would eventually take over the movement. Even in the early 1970s there was evidence this would happen. Once, while drinking tea with a family in Belfast, they were discussing politics when the 1950s campaign came up. Their teenage daughter dismissed that IRA campaign with, "The 1950s, it was a bunch of guys running around with gunpowder in the cuffs of their trousers." He about fell off his chair, as it was the same comment that his generation had made about the 1940s IRA. RÓB IVs.

269 Economic and Social Research Institute and Northern Ireland Attitude Survey and federalism: Edward Moxon-Browne, *Nation, Class and Creed in Northern Ireland* (Aldershot: Gower, 1983); E. E. Davis and Richard Sinnott, *Attitudes in the Republic of Ireland Relevant to the Northern Ireland Problem*, vol. 1, *Descriptive Analysis and Some Comparisons with Attitudes in Northern Ireland and Great Britain* (Dublin: The Economic and Social Research Institute, 1979). Perhaps most interesting, the Northern Ireland Attitude Survey also asked respondents to rate their "least liked solution." Overall in Northern Ireland (2.7 percent) and among Catholics in Northern Ireland (0.7 percent), the *smallest percentage of respondents* chose a federal Ireland as their "least liked" solution in the Republic. Among Protestants in Northern Ireland, the third smallest percentage (3.8 percent) of respondents chose it as their least liked solution; 3.3 percent chose "devolution-power-sharing" and 2.1 percent chose "governed directly from London" as their least-liked solution.

269 First issue of *An Phoblacht/Republican News*: "Out of the Ashes," *An Phoblacht/Republican News*, January 27, 1979; Seán Ó Brádaigh interview.

269 Conflict at Ard Chomhairle meetings: Seán Ó Brádaigh interview; David Sharrock and Mark Davenport, *Man of War, Man of Peace? The Unauthorised Biography of Gerry Adams* (London: Macmillan, 1997), 151–152; Moloney, *A Secret History of the IRA*, 493–497, Appendix I. Danny Morrison quotation: Danny Morrison interview;

270 Adams asks Ó Brádaigh for minutes: RÓB IVs; Adams, *Before the Dawn*, 261–262.

270 Billy McKee and Joe Cahill as Belfast IRA commanding officers: Bishop and Mallie, *The Provisional IRA*, 171, 178–179.

271 Westminster election and Margaret Thatcher: Margaret Thatcher, *The Downing Street Years* (London: Harper Collins, 1993), 385; "Sinn Féin Win 30 Seats," *An Phoblacht/Republican News*, June 16, 1979; "Óráid an Uachtaráin," *An Phoblacht*, Samhain/November 11, 1978, 5; "Sinn Féin Councillors," *An Phoblacht/Republican News*, June 16, 1979, 9. The election was necessary because the Labour government lost, by one, a vote of no confidence put forward by Margaret Thatcher, leader of the Conservative opposition. Frank Maguire, who could have supported the government, abstained and thereby helped force the election. In Northern Ireland, Unionists won 10 of 12 seats. Of the two nationalists, Gerry Fitt won in West Belfast and Maguire won in Fermanagh–South Tyrone.

271 Airey Neave: Paul Routledge, *Public Servant, Secret Agent: The Elusive Life and Violent Death of Airey Neave* (London: Harper, 2002).

271 Warrenpoint and Mountbatten attacks: Bell, *The Irish Troubles*, 570–574; McKittrick, Kelters, Feeney, and Thornton, *Lost Lives*, 793–799. J. Bowyer Bell states that in the early 1970s, Ó Brádaigh suggested seizing Mountbatten's Irish home and offering it to northern refugees. They would not have been able to keep it, but it would have made great news copy.

271 Pope John Paul II visit: RÓB IVs; George Weigel, *Witness to Hope: The Biography of Pope John Paul II* (New York: Cliff Street Books, 1999), 344–345; Bell, *The Irish Troubles*, 369–370.

272 Decision not to contest the 1979 European election: RÓB IVs; Moloney, *A Secret History of the IRA*, 200–201; "Why Sinn Féin Must Fight EEC Elections," *An Phoblacht/Republican News*, January 25, 1978, 5.

273 Bernadette McAliskey and 1979 European election: Séamus Boyle, "A Tragedy Not a Farce," *An Phoblacht/Republican News*, Meitheamh/June 2, 1979, 6–7; see Bell, *The Irish Troubles*, 568–569; Moloney, *A Secret History of the IRA*, 201–202. Ed Moloney states that Gerry Adams and Martin McGuinness actively opposed McAliskey's campaign while the Sinn Féin leadership in Dublin supported her. Ó Brádaigh did not support her, but he did not oppose her either. An *An Phoblacht/Republican News* article described her positively, noting that "only an anti-repression candidate of the stature of Bernadette McAliskey could have hoped to ensure a sizeable turn-out from the nationalist working-class people." John Hume and Paddy Devlin, in contrast, are described as "slavish and slobbering . . . discredited political hulks lying shipwrecked on the treacherous sands of collaboration in the 1974 'power sharing' assembly."

273 1979 Sinn Féin Ard Fheis: *Éire Nua: The Social, Economic and Political Dimensions* (Dublin: Sinn Féin, n.d.), 3–4; see also "Éire Nua—The Social Dimension," "Radical Update of Éire Nua," "Presidential Address of Ruairí Ó Brádaigh," and "The Incoming Ard-Chomhairle," all in *An Phoblacht/Republican News*, Sinn Féin Ard-Fheis Special Supplement, January 26, 1980.

274 1980 Sinn Féin Ard Fheis: "A Serious Debate—Overshadowed by H-Block Hunger-Strike," *An Phoblacht/Republican News*, November 8, 1980. Ó Brádaigh felt that in the event of immediate withdrawal, UN forces should supervise the situation. He had discussed this with Seán Mac Bride. Those pushing for "immediate" withdrawal did not mention UN intervention.

275 1980 Sinn Féin Ard Fheis; Women's Department: RÓB IVs; "A Serious Debate—Overshadowed by H-Block Hunger-Strike," *An Phoblacht/Republican News*, November 8, 1980, ii–iii; "Sinn Féin Ard-Fheis 1980: Women in the New Ireland," *An Phoblacht/Republican News*, November 8, 1980, iv.

275 Joe Clarke and Larry Grogan: see "Larry Grogan," *An Phoblacht/Republican News*, December 1, 1979, 11.

275 Walter Lynch, Cathleen Knowles, and Seán Ó Brádaigh: Seán Ó Brádaigh interview; Cathleen Knowles McGuirk interview. Knowles McGuirk, who was from a Republican family, was recruited into Sinn Féin by Dáithí O'Connell in the early 1970s.

275 Opposition to a hunger strike: Adams, *Before the Dawn*, 283–289; Moloney, *A Secret History of the IRA*, 206; RÓB IVs.

276 Formation of the National H-Block/Armagh Committee; Jim Gibney: Brian Feeney, *Sinn Féin: A Hundred Turbulent Years* (Dublin: The O'Brien Press, 2002), 284–286.

276 1980 hunger strike: Bishop and Mallie, *The Provisional IRA*, 357; McKeown, *Out of Time*, 72–77; RÓB IVs; Brendan Hughes interview. Ó Brádaigh was invited to Margaret McKearney's wedding but was traveling that day. He stopped by and wished the couple well.

See also McKee and Franey, *Time Bomb,* 196; "Victory to the Hunger-Strikers! Victory to the Irish People!" *An Phoblacht/Republican News,* November 8, 1980.

276 Hunger strike protests: "Hunger-Strike Protests: South," *An Phoblacht/Republican News,* November 15, 1980, 8; "Sinn Féin Power Moves North: Decisive Shift as Adams Is Set to Lead Party," *Irish Press,* November 12, 1983.

277 Margaret Thatcher and Charles Haughey meeting: Thatcher, *The Downing Street Years,* 388–391.

277 Gerry Adams, Martin McGuinness, and Michael Oatley negotiations: Moloney, *A Secret History of the IRA,* 207.

277 1980 hunger strike ends: "Crisis Resolved: But Vigilance Now Needed," *An Phoblacht/Republican News,* December 27, 1980, 5; McKeown, *Out of Time,* 75–76, 243n3 (of Chapter 6).

278 Brendan Hughes promises Seán McKenna he will not let him die: Bean and Hayes, eds., *Republican Voices,* 83–84.

278 Second hunger strike: RÓB IVs; Brian Campbell, Laurence McKeown, and Felim O'Hagan, eds., *Nor Meekly Serve My Time: The H-Block Struggle, 1976–81* (Belfast: Beyond the Pale Publications, 1994), 146; Adams, *Before the Dawn,* 288–289; McKeown, *Out of Time,* 77.

278 Dáithí O'Connell suggests Sands as a candidate: RÓB IVs; Moloney, *A Secret History of the IRA,* 211.

277 Sands nomination: Adams, *Before the Dawn,* 292; RÓB IVs; Brian Feeney, *Sinn Féin: A Hundred Turbulent Years* (Dublin: O'Brien Press, 2002), 288–289; Cathleen Knowles McGuirk interview; RÓB IVs. Gerry Adams and Jim Gibney claim that the Sands candidacy was Gibney's idea. On this, Ó Brádaigh comments, "Success has many fathers." The Ard Chomhairle minutes show that it was O'Connell's suggestion. As an IRA volunteer, Sands's candidacy was also subject to IRA approval, which was granted. In his memoir *Before the Dawn,* Adams claims that he and Gibney visited Noel Maguire to persuade him to not stand for the seat. In Brian Feeney's history of Sinn Féin, it is curious that while Gibney claims it was his idea to run Sands as a candidate, he also admits to being unaware of Sinn Féin's history in the constituency.

278 Dáithí O'Connell meets Noel Maguire: RÓB IVs.

278 Jim Gibney meets Bernadette McAliskey: David Beresford, *Ten Men Dead: The Story of the 1981 Irish Hunger Strike* (London: Grafton, 1987), 96.

279 Meeting in Clones: Moloney, *A Secret History of the IRA,* 211–212; Bell, *The Irish Troubles,* 610; Liam Clarke, *Broadening the Battlefield: The H-Blocks and the Rise of Sinn Féin* (Dublin: Gill and Macmillan, 1987), 141–142.

279 Sands campaign: Adams, *Before the Dawn,* 291; Colm Keena, *Gerry Adams,* 93; RÓB IVs; Ruairí Óg Ó Brádaigh interview; Bishop and Mallie, *The Provisional IRA,* 367.

279 Bobby Sands elected: David Beresford, *Ten Men Dead,* 113–114; Bell, *The Irish Troubles,* 612; RÓB IVs. Censorship was so tight in the south that RTÉ interviewed Harry West, who lost, but could not interview Owen Carron, Sands's election agent.

279 Death of Bobby Sands: Tom Collins, *The Irish Hunger Strike,* 132–134, 249; Bell, *The Irish Troubles,* 612; Richard Behal interview.

280 Deaths of Francis Hughes, Raymond McCreesh, Patsy O'Hara, Julie Livingstone, and Carol Ann Kelly: McKittrick, Kelters, Feeney, and Thornton, *Lost Lives.*

280 Raymond McCreesh funeral: RÓB IVs; Tom Collins, *The Irish Hunger Strike* (Dublin: White Island, 1986), 197–238; "The Funeral of Raymond McCreesh," *An Phoblacht/Republican News,* May 30th, 1981, 22–23.

281 1981 Leinster House election: RÓB IVs. Ard Chomhairle minutes: "General Election: Meeting in Head Office," May 29, 1981 (in author's possession); Lee, *Ireland: 1912–1985,* 506–507; Liam Clarke, *Broadening the Battlefield,* 168–169; see also "Dáil Elections since 1918," available online at http://www.ark.ac.uk/elections/gdala.htm#d22. Sinn Féin did contest a by-election in Wicklow in 1968.

281 Support for hunger strikers declines: "Only 400 Take Part in Dublin Protest over H-Block Crisis," *Irish Times,* Saturday, July 11, 1981, 7; Collins, *The Irish Hunger Strike,* 394–395; Bew and Gillespie, *Northern Ireland: A Chronology,* 151–152; "The Funeral of Joe McDonnell," *An Phoblacht/Republican News,* July 18, 1981, 16–18; "Ten-Year History of Rioting over NI," *Irish Times,* July 20, 1981, 6; "IRA Slam FitzGerald," *An Phoblacht/Republican News,* August 8, 1981, 10; "Ó Brádaigh on Kieran Doherty's Death," *An Phoblacht/Republican News,* August 8, 1981, 10.

282 Pyrrhic victory: McKeown, *Out of Time,* 87–120; Bell, *The Irish Troubles,* 620–621. After the 1981 hunger strike, the prisoners were allowed their own clothes, education was substituted for prison work, and association (separation from other prisoners under their own officers) was conceded. They made the most of the new situation; under these relaxed conditions, nineteen IRA prisoners escaped from Long Kesh, the most secure prison in Western Europe, in September 1983.

282 End of hunger strike: In *Blanketmen,* Richard O'Rawe, who was in the prison leadership, states that the prisoners accepted a proposal offered by the British after four hunger strikers had died and the fifth, Joe McDonnell, was dying. With the proposal, "it seemed that the underlying substance of our demands was being conceded to us." O'Rawe and Brendan McFarlane, who was in the prison leadership, accepted the offer only to be informed that it had been rejected by the Army Council. Years later, O'Rawe determined that the prisoners' acceptance of a settlement was not as widely known among the Republican leadership outside of the prison as it should have been. It is not clear why the Army Council rejected the settlement, but one interpretation is that someone or some persons let additional hunger strikers die in order to generate sympathy and support for the election of Owen Carron. The key person O'Rawe implicates in this decision is Gerry Adams, who may or may not have passed on to the Army Council the information that the prisoners accepted the British proposal. See Richard O'Rawe, *Blanketmen: An Untold Story of the H-Block Hunger Strike* (Dublin: New Island Press, 2005), see especially 176–182, 184–185, 219–223, and 254–259. The commanding officer of the prisoners in Long Kesh at that time, Brendan McFarlane, denies that the prisoners accepted a settlement. The citation for this is, Ireland's OWN: The Hungerstrikes. 12 March 2005. "Former comrades' war of words over hunger strike." By Steven McCaffrey, *Irish News.* http://irelandsown.net/orawe.html.

Chapter 16

283 Francie Molloy suggests that Owen Carron take his Westminster seat: RÓB IVs.

283 Division of the Ard Chomhairle into camps and quotation: Cathleen Knowles McGuirk interview.

283 1981 Ard Fheis: RÓB Notes; "Federalism Rejected, Positive Electoral Policy Adopted," *An Phoblacht/Republican News,* November 5, 1981, 6–7. Ed Maloney quotations: "Northern Notebook: SF Modernists versus the Traditionalists," *Irish Times,* November 12, 1983. See also Flackes and Elliott, *Northern Ireland: A Political Directory,* 358, 372; "An Historic Year: Presidential Address of Ruairí Ó Brádaigh," *An Phoblacht/Republican News,* November 5, 1981, 5.

283 1982 Leinster House election: RÓB IVs; RÓB Notes; Moloney, *A Secret History of the IRA,* 291; "Sinn Féin Election Candidates Announced: Fighting Stand," *An Phoblacht/Republican News,* February 4, 1982, 1–2; "Two More," *An Phoblacht/Republican News,* February 11, 1982, 2; "Sinn Féin Stand Seven," *An Phoblacht/Republican News,* February 11, 1982; "Censorship Rocked," *An Phoblacht/Republican News,* February 18, 1982, 1–2; RÓB IVs; "Dáil Elections since 1918," available online at http://www.ark.ac.uk/elections/gdala.htm#d23. Ó Brádaigh was consistently outvoted on the issue of contesting elections, both at the leadership level and at Ard Fheiseanna, and not just by "young northerners." In 1973, Máire Drumm and Séamus Twomey led the charge against participation. In 1980, five days into the first hunger strike, he lost out when the Belfast delegates to the Ard Fheis succeeded in forbidding the incoming Ard Chomhairle from contesting the upcoming (May 1981) local elections in the north. He felt that the hunger strike could change the political complexion north of the border. Bobby Sands died on May 5 and there was not enough time to summon an extraordinary Ard Fheis to reverse the decision and contest the local elections. In *Before the Dawn,* Gerry Adams, in commenting on the situation in the mid-1970s, suggests that Ó Brádaigh was the impediment to Sinn Féin's involvement in elections. "Politically, however, we encountered resistance to the direction we were pursuing, particularly when we argued for the development of an electoral strategy. Ruairí Ó Brádaigh was quite logically concerned that if we became involved in electoralism we would have to get rid of abstentionism, an important constitutional issue within the party. I didn't understand that then, but he did, and so he resisted the electoral approach" (264). Ó Brádaigh's willingness to go with the majority on these issues is an indicator of his leadership style. He did not try to impose his will on Sinn Féin and did not threaten to quit or withdraw from the leadership as a result of these decisions.

286 Falklands War: RÓB IVs; Margaret Thatcher, *The Downing Street Years,* 173–235.

286 1982 Assembly election: Bew and Gillespie, *Northern Ireland: A Chronology;* "Election Campaign Underway," *An Phoblacht/Republican News,* September 16, 1982, 2; "Leading Figures," *An Phoblacht/Republican News,* September 30, 1982, 1; Hilda McThomas, "Sinn Féin Will Contest Northern Elections," *An Phoblacht/Republican News,* April 29, 1982, 3; Bishop and Mallie, *The Provisional IRA,* 379–380.

287 Ó Brádaigh-Adams confrontation: RÓB IVs; Moloney, *A Secret History of the IRA,* 181–183.

288 1982 Ard Fheis and Ard Chomhairle changes: "Federalism Removed," *An Phoblacht/Republican News,* November 4, 1982, 6; "Sinn Féin Ard-Chomhairle," *An Phoblacht/Republican News,* November 4, 1982, 5; "Editorial Change," *An Phoblacht/Republican News,* November 4, 1982, 3; Damien O'Rourke, "Charlie McGlade Laid to Rest," *An Phoblacht/Republican News,* September 23, 1982, 6. "Left like rocks" quotation: RÓB IVs.

288 Private attacks: private communication. Ed Moloney reports that Ó Brádaigh interrupted the interrogation of Christine Elias, only to be held at gunpoint by the IRA; Moloney, *A Secret History of the IRA,* 190–194.

289 RÓB's contribution to the 26-county election report: Ruairí Ó Brádaigh, "The Effects of the Developing of Such a Strategy of Sinn Féin's Attitudes to, for Example, Armed Struggle, Abstentionism, Social Policy, Etc.," submission to the Ard Chomhairle subcommittee, Electoral Strategy in the 26 Counties (copy in author's possession). See also Frances Fox Piven and Richard Cloward, *Poor People's Movements: Why They Succeed, How They Fail* (New York: Vintage Books, 1979). Austin Currie, a prominent supporter of the rent and rates strike, became minister for housing, local government, and planning on the Executive and was therefore charged with implementing the SDLP's decision to end the strike. In doing so he referred to "the inconsistency of being in government and, at the same time, maintaining support for civil disobedience." In his autobiography, *All Hell Will Break Loose,* he commented, "That speech and the decisions it contained was the most difficult I had had to make in my ten years in politics. In so doing, I was coming to terms with the realities of political life. It was necessary, inevitable and unavoidable." He added that his speech "two-and-a-half years earlier, that rent should not be paid and should never be paid," was "to me, equally necessary and unavoidable." See Currie, *All Hell Will Break Loose,* especially 252–258.

290 RÓB in Canada: "Ó Brádaigh in Canada," *An Phoblacht/Republican News,* March 31, 1983, 7; RÓB IVs; "European Support for Sinn Féin," *An Phoblacht/Republican News,* May 19, 1983, 9.

291 1983 Westminster election: "'Election a Turning Point'—Ó Brádaigh," *An Phoblacht/Republican News,* June 16, 1983, 3; "Huge Vote for Freedom," *An Phoblacht/Republican News,* June 16, 1983, 6–7.

291 Adams at Bodenstown, 1983: "The Legacy of Tone," *An Phoblacht/Republican News,* June 23, 1983, 6–7.

292 RÓB upstaged by Danny Morrison: RÓB IVs; Seán Ó Brádaigh interview.

292 Hospitalization and plans of Ó Brádaigh, Dáithí O'Connell, and Cathleen Knowles: RÓB IVs; Cathleen Knowles McGuirk interview; Dáithí O'Connell's resignation letter (copy in author's possession); "Sinn Féin Power Moves North," *Irish Press,* November 12, 1983; "New Ard-Chomhairle," *An Phoblacht/Republican News,* November 17, 1983, 7; "Sinn Féin Face Crunch That Could Force Split," *Irish News,* October 19, 1983; "Adams to Take Over from Ó Brádaigh," *Sunday Independent,* November 6, 1983.

293 1983 Ard Fheis: "Statement by Outgoing President Ruairí Ó Brádaigh to Ard-Fheis of Sinn Féin on Sunday Afternoon, November 13th, 1983" (copy in author's possession); "Sinn Féin—the Most Progressive Political Force on This Island," *An Phoblacht/Republican News,* November 17, 11 (Ó Brádaigh's outgoing presidential address); Kevin Burke, "A Party on the Move," *An Phoblacht/Republican News,* November 17, 1983, 7; "Presidential Address," *An Phoblacht/Republican News,* November 17, 1983, 8–9; "Gerry Adams' Address to Ard Fheis 1983" (copy of typewritten speech in author's possession).

295 Ó Brádaigh family automobile accident and recovery: RÓB IVs. Gerry Adams and Margaret Thatcher also were almost killed in 1984. In March, Gerry Adams survived an assassination attempt; he was shot four times by Loyalist paramilitaries. In October, the IRA tried to assassinate Margaret Thatcher. An IRA bomb blew up the site of the annual Conservative Party conference, killing five people and injuring several others, but not Thatcher. Bell, *The Irish Troubles,* 676, 685–687.

297 Ivor Bell's reported attempt to oust Gerry Adams in the IRA leadership: Liam Clarke, *Broadening the Battlefield,* 228–229; Moloney, *A Secret History of the IRA,* 244–245. Ruairí Ó Brádaigh had no involvement in the Bell affair. If he was a member of the IRA leadership into the early 1980s, he no doubt lost this status with his automobile accident.

297 1985 north and south local elections: "Sinn Féin Strength Confirmed," *An Phoblacht/Republican News,* May 23, 1985, 8–12; Maeve Armstrong, "Belfast Council Walk-Out," *An Phoblacht/Republican News,* November 7, 1985; "Analysis of Sinn Féin's Election Performance: Definite Advance," *An Phoblacht/Republican News,* June 27, 1985, 3.

297 Anglo-Irish Agreement: Bew and Gillespie, *Northern Ireland: A Chronology,* 189–193. In the 1970s, in a series of boundary changes, Northern Ireland was given five additional seats at Westminster, bringing the total to seventeen MPs for the province. Of these, all fifteen Unionists resigned in 1985 because of the Anglo-Irish Agreement.

297 1985 Ard Fheis: "Electoral Strategy," *An Phoblacht/Republican News,* November 7, 1985, 13; RÓB letter to the author.

299 Des Long removed from the Ard Chomhairle: Des Long interview.

299 1986 IRA convention: The vote at the IRA convention was three to one in favor of ending abstentionism. Only those in attendance know for sure who attended. Séamus Twomey's presence is confirmed in "Volunteer Séamus Twomey 1919–'89: A Tribute," published by An Phoblacht/Republican News, n.d. Jimmy Drumm's vote is based on private communication. In *Martin McGuinness,* Liam Clarke and Kathryn Johnston state that McGuinness was placed in charge of the IRA campaign. McGuinness claims that he left the IRA in the mid-1970s. In *A Secret History of the IRA,* Ed Moloney places Adams and McGuinness at the convention. McGirl, O'Hagan, and Cahill's support for dropping abstention from Leinster House and for Adams and McGuinness is evident from their subsequent behavior. They need not have been present to have made their views known to the delegates. It is likely that all three were at the convention. Ó Brádaigh will neither confirm nor deny his presence. Clarke and Johnston, *Martin McGuinness,* 164–166; Moloney, *A Secret History of the IRA,* 292–293. See also, "IRA Council's Shock Move: Provos May Take Seats," *Irish News,* October 15, 1986.

299 Ó Brádaigh-Adams meeting: RÓB IVs; Brendan Hughes interview. According to Hughes, a fourth person was there. Ó Brádaigh, who was concentrating on his meeting with Adams, does not remember a fourth person. Hughes, then a long-time friend and supporter of Adams, today believes that Adams used him.

300 Runup to the 1986 Ard Fheis: RÓB letter to the author, June 27, 1997; Moloney, *A Secret History of the IRA,* 296–297; "Historic IRA Convention," *An Phoblacht/Republican News,* October 16, 1986, 1; [Jim Sullivan], "Abstention Contortions," *Irish News,* October 14, 1986; Letters to the editor, *Irish News,* October 27, 1986; "Adams Welcome for IRA Move on Abstention," *Irish Press,* October 16, 1986; "Adams Welcomes IRA Decision to End Abstentionism," *Irish Times,* October 16, 1986; "Recognising Realities of Political Life," *Irish News,* October 29, 1986, 5; "Entering Leinster House: A Veteran Speaks," Republican Sinn Féin literature, n.d.

301 University College Dublin Sinn Féin *cumann:* Ruairí Óg Ó Brádaigh interview.

302 Saturday lunchtime confrontation at the 1986 Ard Fheis: Joe O'Neill interview; RÓB IVs; Des Long interview. See also Bell, *The Irish Troubles,* 732; Moloney, *A Secret History of the IRA,* 289, 294–295.

303 1986 Ard Fheis: RÓB IVs. In 1985, when the motion on abstentionism was reached, the Ard Chomhairle rose and left the stage, except for John Joe McGirl, Tom Hartley, and Caoimhghin Ó Caoláin. Ó Brádaigh saw it as a signal that the Ard Chomhairle was unwilling to provide leadership on a fundamental principle. He watched John Joe McGirl vote against the motion and Tom Hartley and Caoimhghin Ó Caoláin vote in favor. With respect to the 1975 truce, in the three months preceding the IRA's December 1974 cease-fire (September–November 1974), the IRA killed sixteen members of the security forces. In the three months immediately following the 1975 truce (October–December 1975), the IRA killed thirteen members of the security forces. After the IRA adopted the long war strategy, its activity levels declined significantly. Gerry Adams, Martin McGuinness, Joe Cahill, and John Joe McGirl quotations are from *The Politics of Revolution: The Main Speeches and Debates from the 1986 Sinn Féin Ard-Fheis including the Presidential Address of Gerry Adams* (Dublin: Sinn Féin, 1986). Editorial on McGirl: "Letting the IRA Go to the Polls," *Longford Leader,* November 7, 1986. See also "1986 Split: The Provo Desertion. Live Debates from the 1986 Sinn Féin Ard-Fheis on the Motion to Abandon Abstentionism and Enter Leinster House," published by the National Education and Culture Committee, Sinn Féin, 223 Parnell Street, Dublin 1, April 2000; "Abstentionism: An Historic Decision," *An Phoblacht/Republican News,* Samhain/November 6, 1986, 11; RÓB Notes; Sutton, *An Index of Deaths from the Northern Ireland Conflict.* Ruairí Ó Brádaigh's contribution to the debate: "Never, I Say to You, Never," *Magill,* November 13, 1986, 12. Vote totals: Moloney, *A Secret History of the IRA,* 296.

Chapter 17

308 In Joe O'Neill's van: Joe O'Neill interview; RÓB IVs.

308 At the West County Hotel: Gerald Barry, "The Two Traditions Struggle for Spirit of 'Real' Sinn Féin," *Sunday Tribune,* November 9, 1986; see *Republican Bulletin,* Samhain/November 1986; "Revolution Not Reform: 83rd Ard-Fheis," *SAOIRSE,* Samhain/November 1987, 4 (presidential address of Ruairí Ó Brádaigh); Frank Glynn interview. Dáithí O'Connell quotations: "Night of the Golden Oldies," *Sunday News,* November 9, 1986. Cathleen Knowles McGuirk remembers O'Connell saying "Not yet!" in response to the question of whether or not Republican Sinn Féin had an army. Cathleen Knowles McGuirk interview.

308 Recount and margin of victory: Moloney, *A Secret History of the IRA,* 296–297; RÓB IVs. The vote was 429 in favor, 161 opposed, and 38 abstentions; 419 was required for a two-thirds majority. Those who walked out later learned that the counterfoils of the delegate cards, which are raised in the air to signify the delegates' vote, were destroyed the next morning. They are usually held at the head office for some time. With the counterfoils destroyed, a recount was impossible. Of the 130 or so people at the West County Hotel, about 100 were delegates and 30 were visitors.

309 The Continuity IRA: J. Bowyer Bell, "Republican IRA, an Emerging Secret Army,"

SAOIRSE, Meán Fomhair/September 1996, 2–3. Because there was no immediate Continuity IRA campaign, some people drifted away—most notably Seán Tracey, who was later killed in a workplace accident.

310 Provisional IRA founders at 1987 Republican Sinn Féin Bodenstown Commemoration: RÓB IVs; Bishop and Mallie, *The Provisional IRA,* 137.

310 Visits from Provisional IRA representatives: "Ó Brádaigh Firm on British Withdrawal," *Irish Echo,* September 14–20, 1994, 4; RÓB letter to the author, April 19, 1999; RÓB IVs.

311 Citing RÓB versus citing "Republican Spokesperson" on calendar: Republican Resistance Calendar, Provisional Sinn Féin, 1989.

312 Organization of Republican Sinn Féin; 1987 Republican Sinn Féin Ard Fheis; Ó Brádaigh quotations: "Revolution Not Reform: 83rd Ard-Fheis," *SAOIRSE,* Samhain/November 1987, 4 (presidential address of Ruairí Ó Brádaigh); Ó Brádaigh, *Dílseacht,* 44–45; "Michael Flannery Elected Patron of Republican Sinn Féin," November 16, 1993, in Dermot O'Reilly, ed., *Accepting the Challenge: The Memoirs of Michael Flannery* (Dublin: Irish Freedom Press, 2001), 197. RÓB IVs; Ruairí Óg Ó Brádaigh interview; Cathleen Knowles McGuirk interview. Others who sent messages of support for Republican Sinn Féin included Jim Monsell (Chicago), Tom Falvey and George Harrison (New York), the John Boyle O'Reilly Club (Springfield, Mass.), Dan McCormick (San Francisco), and John Morrison, Alex Murphy, and Jim Kane (Chicago). Supporters of the new organization included relatives of Republicans killed in the 1940s by de Valera's government, including Elizabeth Plant (sister of executed Protestant Republican George Plant), the Casey family (Longford), the O'Neill and Kerins families (Kerry), the sisters of Richard Goss (Dundalk), and the son of Tony D'Arcy (Galway). Others who attended Republican Sinn Féin commemorations included the Harte family (Lurgan) and the McNeelas (Dublin). Tom Maguire was Patron of Republican Sinn Féin until his death in 1993. At the 1994 Republican Sinn Féin Ard Fheis, the 200 delegates unanimously elected Michael Flannery patron of Republican Sinn Féin. Flannery held the position until his death in 1994. It is rumored, incorrectly, that Flannery willed his home to Republican Sinn Féin. Funds for the organization did pass through him, and it is suspected that he was the source, but when questioned he consistently replied that the source was a "wee woman up in Connecticut." Prominent Irish-American George Harrison, a veteran of the East Mayo Battalion of the IRA and an active supporter of international liberation struggles, was patron of Republican Sinn Féin until he passed away in 2004.

314 Enniskillen; Loughgall; the Eksund capture; and the nationwide search for weapons: McKittrick, Kelters, Feeney, and Thornton, *Lost Lives,* 1077–1080, 1094–1098; Moloney, *A Secret History of the IRA,* 3–6, 304–325; Taylor, *Behind the Mask,* 321. Among those killed at Loughgall was a civilian, Anthony Hughes, who drove onto the scene and was mistaken for an IRA member.

315 Gerry Adams quotation on the "next" election: "Presidential Address by Gerry Adams to the 82nd Annual Sinn Féin Ard-Fheis," in *The Politics of Revolution: The Main Speeches and Debates from the 1986 Sinn Féin Ard-Fheis including the Presidential Address of Gerry Adams* (Dublin: Sinn Féin, 1986), 13.

315 1987, 1989, 1992 Leinster House elections: Bishop and Mallie, *The Provisional IRA,* 451–452; RÓB quotation; Republican Sinn Féin press statement, November 27, 1992.

315 Test oath in Northern Ireland and quotation: "Where Are They Now?" and "Swallowing a British Oath," *SAOIRSE,* Feabhra/February 1989, 1.

315 1987 and 1992 Westminster elections: Flackes and Elliott, *Northern Ireland: A Political Directory;* Bew and Gillespie, *Northern Ireland: A Chronology,* 242, 258.

315 The Provisionals' behind-the-scenes contacts with Fianna Fáil, the SDLP, and the Irish Catholic Church: Moloney, *A Secret History of the IRA,* 269–280; Eamonn Mallie and David McKittrick, *The Fight for Peace: The Secret Story Behind the Irish Peace Process* (London: Heinemann, 1996), 72–91; Paul Routledge, *John Hume,* 207–229. Belfast priest Father Alex

Reid, with the support of Cardinal Ó Fiaich, played an important role in linking the Provisionals with the SDLP and Fianna Fáil.

316 Period of transition: RÓB IVs; Patsy Ó Brádaigh interview.

317 Death of Dáithí O'Connell and RÓB oration: "The Final Salute," *SAOIRSE,* Eanáir/January 1991, 1; "Death of Dáithí O Conaill," *SAOIRSE,* Eanáir/January 1991, 5.

317 Tom Maguire at 100; Maguire's death and funeral: see *SAOIRSE,* Eanáir/January 1994, 5; Ó Brádaigh, *Dílseacht,* 50, 68–75.

318 Mary Ó Brádaigh Delaney's illness; RÓB's health problems and fight to regain his job: RÓB IVs. One of Ó Brádaigh's strongest supporters in the pension struggle was Canon Graham, a Protestant minister in Roscommon. Ó Brádaigh learned that when his situation was discussed at a Roscommon Vocational Educational Committee meeting, those involved referred to him as "Mr. Ó Brádaigh." After some discussion, the minister, who never spoke at meetings, raised his hand, was recognized by the chair, and said that "Ruairí" was entitled to his pension. As he had paid in his 5 percent over the years, it was natural and just that he get his entitlement. The committee agreed. Throughout the process, Ó Brádaigh had their support.

319 Republican Sinn Féin activities, political program, and Saol Nua: "Republican Sinn Féin Backs Ó Brádaigh Programme," *Irish News,* November 16, 1992; *Saol Nua: A New Way of Life. The Social and Economic Programme of Sinn Féin Poblachtach* (Dublin: Sinn Féin, 1993); "Republican Sinn Féin Unveils Plan," *Irish Times,* November 16, 1992; Ruairí Ó Brádaigh, "Presidential Address to the 88th Ard-Fheis of Sinn Féin, in the Spa Hotel, Lucan, County Dublin, November 14–15, 1992," *SAOIRSE,* Samhain/November 1992, 9; Mary Ward interview; Ruairí Óg Ó Brádaigh interview.

321 Provisional Republican contacts with the British; Brooke talks: McKittrick and Mallie, *The Fight for Peace,* 105–108, 111, 115–117, Brooke quote on 107; see also Adams, *Before the Dawn,* 318; Bew and Gillespie, *Northern Ireland: A Chronology,* 230, 242, 247–249. Three important sources on the peace process are Moloney, *A Secret History of the IRA*; McKittrick and Mallie, *The Fight for Peace*; and Bew and Gillespie's *Northern Ireland: A Chronology.*

322 Benefits of a cease-fire: Danny Morrison was arrested in 1990 and subsequently imprisoned. A letter from Morrison to Gerry Adams in October 1991 offers insight on the perspective of the Provisional Sinn Féin leadership at the time. Morrison suggested that the Provisionals view the SDLP "more sympathetically" and noted that the Provisional IRA could "fight on forever and can't be defeated [but] . . . this isn't the same as winning or showing something for all the sacrifices." In an interview he commented that the Unionists "couldn't handle" the Provisionals becoming more friendly with the SDLP and that a cease-fire "would expose the weaknesses of the Six-County state." Danny Morrison, *Then the Walls Came Down: A Prison Journal* (Cork: Mercier Press, 1999), 240–242; Danny Morrison interview.

323 Hume-Adams report; Bew and Gillespie, *Northern Ireland: A Chronology,* 276–277. John Hume and "lasting peace": Routledge, *John Hume,* 245; McKittrick and Mallie, *The Fight for Peace,* 189–193.

323 Downing Street joint declaration: Bew and Gillespie, *Northern Ireland: A Chronology,* 277–286; McKittrick and Mallie, *The Fight for Peace,* 256–269.

323 RÓB and Republican Sinn Féin response to the joint declaration: "Opposition Grows to Major-Reynolds," *SAOIRSE,* Eanáir/January 1994, 1.

323 Continuity IRA response to the joint declaration: "Final Salute to Comdt-General Tom Maguire," *SAOIRSE,* Feabhra/February 1994, 2.

324 Martin McGuinness quotation: "'Splits' Claim Ridiculed: Unionist Veto Must Go—McGuinness," *An Phoblacht,* February 17, 1994, 2.

324 Benefits of the peace process: "Councillor's Live Interview—20 Years On," *SAOIRSE,* Feabhra/February 1994, 3; Bew and Gillespie, *Northern Ireland: A Chronology,* 287; McKittrick and Mallie, *The Fight for Peace,* 276–286.

324 Gerry Adams visits the United States in February 1994: "Cheers for Adams Raise NY Roof," *An Phoblacht/Republican News,* February 3, 1994, 3.

324 Continued meetings and British promise of peace negotiations to follow a Provisional IRA cease-fire: Adams, *Before the Dawn,* 320–323; Maloney, *A Secret History of the IRA,* 424–427; Brendan Anderson, *Joe Cahill,* 341–354. The Albert Reynolds quotation is in Bew and Gillespie, *Northern Ireland: A Chronology,* 292–293.

324 Republican Sinn Féin and RÓB reaction to the cease-fire; Bernadette McAliskey quotation: "Provos Halt Campaign but No British Withdrawal," *SAOIRSE,* Meán Fómhair/September 1994, 1.

325 Combined Loyalist Military Command cease-fire: Bew and Gillespie, *Northern Ireland: A Chronology,* 297–299.

326 Post-cease-fire situation: McDonald, *Trimble,* 140–141, 162–163; Anderson, *Joe Cahill,* 352; Adams, *Before the Dawn,* 320–321; McKittrick, Kelters, Feeney, and Thornton, *Lost Lives,* 1379; Flackes and Elliott, *Northern Ireland: A Political Directory,* 224–225; see also Dean Godson,, *Himself Alone: David Trimble and the Ordeal of Modern Unionism* (London: HarperCollins, 2004). The Provisionals did not help their cause when they shot dead a postal worker, Frank Kerr, in a raid on a Royal Mail office in November 1994. The process was also slowed by a change in Irish governments. A coalition, led by Fine Gael with John Bruton as Taoiseach, took power in Dublin in December 1994. Ironically, as peace in Northern Ireland was being forged, the new political party Democratic Left, which developed out of yet another split in The Workers' Party, was a participant in the Dublin government. Proinsias de Rossa, a former Curragh internee, became minister for social welfare.

325 Prisoner issues and release of Lee Clegg: McKittrick, Kelters, Feeney, and Thornton, *Lost Lives,* 1207–1210; "Double Standards of British 'Justice,'" *SAOIRSE,* Iúil/July, 1995, 1. Lee Clegg was also allowed to rejoin the British Army.

326 Gerry Adams in the United States; RÓB quotation: Bew and Gillespie, *Northern Ireland: A Chronology,* 296–297, 299; "Provisionals Have Not 'Delivered' All Republicans," *SAOIRSE,* Aibreán/April 1995, 3.

326 RÓB quotation, January 1995: "NIR Interview: Talking with Ruairí Ó Brádaigh," *Northern Ireland Report,* January 11, 1995, 6–8.

326 Ban on RÓB's visa: "The Message They Don't Want Heard," *SAOIRSE,* Meitheamh/June 1995, 1.

326 Recruitment to Republican Sinn Féin from Provisional Sinn Féin: private communication.

326 Indications of another IRA: "Six Sentenced by Special Court in Dublin," *SAOIRSE,* Feabhra/February 1996, 3.

326 Republican Sinn Féin's criticism of the Provisionals: private communication; "NIR Interview: Talking with Ruairi O'Bradaigh," *Northern Ireland Report,* P.O. Box 9086, Lowell, Massachusetts, 01853; RÓB IVs. Such comments were irritating enough that, privately at least, leading members of Provisional Sinn Féin accused Ó Brádaigh of trying to wreck the cease-fire. A pointed comment was "Ruairí Ó Brádaigh couldn't do the job when he had the chance." Ó Brádaigh, asked to comment, replied that he had not been consulted prior to the cease-fire and therefore was free to speak as he desired. He added, "I never led the Movement down a cul de sac."

326 Teach Dáithí Ó Conaill: "New Head Office in Dublin," *SAOIRSE,* Meitheamh/June 1995, 10; "Dublin Head Office Opened on New Year's Day," *SAOIRSE,* Eanáir/January 1996, 8.

326 Josephine Hayden and evidence of another IRA: Flackes and Elliott, *Northern Ireland: A Political Directory,* 421–422.

327 Emergence of the Continuity IRA: "Statement of Recognition by Comdt General Tom Maguire," *SAOIRSE,* Feabhra/February 1996, 9; "'Revolutionary' IRA Emerges," *SAOIRSE,* Feabhra/February 1996, 1.

327 Mitchell Commission report and reaction: George A. Mitchell, *Making Peace* (New

York: Alfred A. Knopf, 1999), 22–41, especially pages 35–37; Bew and Gillespie, *Northern Ireland: A Chronology,* 315–319.

328 Provisional IRA cease-fire ends; Bew and Gillespie, *Northern Ireland: A Chronology,* 320–324.

328 1996 Forum election: Republican Sinn Féin, because they had never accepted the "political test oath" for candidates, was not allowed to put forward nominees for the Forum election. They called for a boycott and argued that it would inevitably lead to a Unionist assembly and constitutionalism on the part of the Provisionals. Just prior to the election, Gerry Adams announced that Sinn Féin agreed to the Mitchell principles. The "Tallyman" columnist in the *Sunday Tribune* commented that this "effectively committed the Shinners to a constitutional Republican position" and added "Ó Brádaigh was right." Mitchell, *Making Peace,* 39–45; "Boycott Election Farce," *SAOIRSE,* Aibreán/April 1996, 1; "Election Plan Gives Unionists Their Assembly," *SAOIRSE,* Aibreán/April 1996, 3; "May 30 Election Leads to 'All-Party Talks' and to a New Stormont," *SAOIRSE,* Bealtaine/May 1996, 3; "Adams Commits Provisionals to Constitutional Position," *SAOIRSE,* Meitheamh/June 1996, 3.

328 Election results; Provisional Sinn Féin excluded from Forum and Manchester bomb: Bew and Gillespie, *Northern Ireland: A Chronology,* 329–330; Mitchell, *Making Peace,* 48–53.

328 Unrest in Portadown (Garvaghy Road), Derry, and the Killyhevlin Hotel: Bew and Gillespie, *Northern Ireland: A Chronology,* 331–332; "Nationalist Crushed by British APC," *SAOIRSE,* Lúnasa/August, 1996, 1; "Bombing of Hotel Diminishes Hopes for Ulster Peace," *New York Times,* July 15, 1996, A4; "1,250 1b. Bomb Wrecks Enniskillen Hotel," *SAOIRSE,* Lúnasa/August 1996, 8; "Republican IRA, an Emerging Secret Army," *SAOIRSE,* Meán Fómhair/September 1996, 2–3; Jim Cusack, "Splinter Group Thought to Be Small but Capable of Making Large Bombs," *Irish Times,* October 1, 1996, 8.

330 Suzanne Breene article: Ó Brádaigh charges that Adams rewrote history in *Before the Dawn,* beginning with his claim that he was not in the Intercontinental Hotel when Sinn Féin split in 1970. In a letter to the *Sunday Tribune,* he reminded readers of Jim Sullivan's 1986 letter to the *Irish News,* which placed Adams at the Ard Fheis and not among the walkouts. In general, Ó Brádaigh fares well in Adams's autobiography. Adams describes him as "quite liberal in his political outlook on social and economic matters" (263). Concerning the movement to electoral politics, Adams, as noted earlier, stated: "Ruairí Ó Brádaigh was quite logically concerned that if we became involved in electoralism we would have to get rid of abstentionism, an important constitutional issue within the party. I didn't understand that then, but he did, and so he resisted the electoral approach." Ó Brádaigh's reaction to this statement was amazement at Adams's naiveté. It was a point he had been trying to make for years. Ó Brádaigh's usually accurate memory failed him in the letter to the editor of the *Sunday Tribune,* where he identified Des O'Hagan as the author of the 1986 letter to the *Irish News.* Suzanne Breene, "Down through History, the Working Class Has Been Cannon-Fodder in Wars," *Belfast Telegraph,* September 30, 1996; Adams, *Before the Dawn,* 261–262; RÓB letter to the editor, *Sunday Tribune,* September 22, 1996.

330 RÓB's biography of Tom Maguire: Ó Brádaigh and Maguire were discussing the Tourmakeady ambush when Maguire, to Ó Brádaigh's surprise, asked if he would like to see the rifle, which Maguire held illegally. In the 1940s, Maguire loaned it out to the local IRA for training purposes.

331 Unionists squabble: Mitchell, *Making Peace,* 71–73, 84–87.

331 1997 Westminster and local elections in Northern Ireland: Flackes and Elliott, *Northern Ireland: A Political Directory,* 589–590; Bew and Gillespie, *Northern Ireland: A Chronology,* 341–342. Tony Blair quotation and Bertie Ahern: Mitchell, *Making Peace,* 101–106; see *An Phoblacht/Republican News,* June 12, 1997.

332 1997 Provisional IRA cease-fire: Bew and Gillespie, *Northern Ireland: A Chronology,* 343, 346–347; "New Ceasefire: Same Sell-Out: Another False Peace," *SAOIRSE,* Lúnasa/August 1997, 1.

333 Continuity IRA bombs; split in the Provisional IRA: It is reported that a group of

Provisionals in the Quartermaster Corps, led by Mickey McKevitt, reportedly a member of the Army Council, came to believe that they had been lied to; that assurances that Provisional Sinn Féin would never enter into a Northern Irish Assembly were untrue. They left the Provisional IRA and formed yet a third IRA, called the Real IRA. They also took with them a significant amount of weapons, which were returned some days later. A public organization, the 32-County Sovereignty Committee, which was reported to be affiliated with the Real IRA, was also formed. The committee's membership included McKevitt's wife, Bernadette Sands McKevitt (the sister of hunger striker Bobby Sands), and a number of Republicans in Counties Louth and Dublin, including Joe Dillon, Fra Browne, and Val Lynch. On May 1, 1998, Rónán Mac Lochlainn of the Real IRA was shot dead by Gardaí in County Wicklow. He was involved in an attempted robbery. Bew and Gillespie, *Northern Ireland: A Chronology,* 350; Moloney, *A Secret History of the IRA,* 478–479; McKittrick, Kelters, Feeney, and Thornton, *Lost Lives,* 1433–1434.

333 Good Friday Agreement and Provisional Sinn Féin Ard Fheis: Bew and Gillespie, *Northern Ireland: A Chronology,* 358–360, 370; Mitchell, *Making Peace,* 143–183; Moloney, *A Secret History of the IRA,* 480–481; "Unbowed . . . Unbroken," *An Phoblacht/Republican News,* May 14, 1998, 14–15.

334 Cathal Goulding quotation: "The Birth of the Provos: Conspiracy Theorist," *Irish News,* January 31, 1990, 6.

Epilogue

The CAIN (Conflict Archive on the Internet) Web service has been invaluable in tracking recent developments in Northern Ireland. The Web site address is http://cain.ulst.ac.uk.

336 RÓB as a socialist: One of the young northerners' criticisms against Ó Brádaigh was that he was too conservative. After the Good Friday Agreement, the commitment to socialism of these critics has been questioned. Ironically, some U.S. supporters of Republican Sinn Féin have complained about the socialist aspects of the party's policies. As evidenced by successive policies that he helped develop, Ó Brádaigh is a socialist.

337 European Union: Ó Brádaigh is not a communist, but his continued critique of the European Union and his view that it is a new form of imperialism are consistent with Marx and Engels's view of history in *The Communist Manifesto.* They write, "The bourgeoisie, by the rapid improvement of all instruments of production, by the immensely facilitated means of communication, draws all nations, even the most barbarian, into civilization. . . . Independent, or but loosely connected provinces, with separate interests, laws, governments and systems of taxation, become lumped together into one nation, with one government, one code of laws, one national class interest, one frontier, and one customs tariff." Karl Marx and Frederick Engels, *The Communist Manifesto* (1948; repr., New York: International Publishers, 1999), 13; John McCormick, *The European Union: Politics and Policies* (Cambridge, Mass.: Westview Books, 2004); John Rentoul, *Tony Blair: Prime Minister* (London: Time Warner Paperbacks, 2001), 73–74, 83–84, 584–586.

338 Pragmatism of RÓB: Ruairí Ó Brádaigh's commitment to federalism is based on his belief that the policy offers a real solution to what has been an intractable conflict. The Provisionals were not the first to propose a federal solution for Ireland. It was discussed by a number of parties in the 1960s, including Neil Blaney of Fianna Fáil, Eddie McAteer of the Nationalist Party, and Humphrey Berkeley and Quentin Hogg of the Conservative Party. A federal Ireland was Nationalist Party policy, with McAteer advocating Armagh as its capital. The wedding of a social and economic program to a multitiered federal Ireland, with specific designs for Dáil Uladh, was unique to the Provisionals. For perspectives on federalism in Ireland, see "A Federal Solution," *This Week,* July 31, 1970; Brian Caul, *Towards a Federal Ireland* (Belfast: December Publications, 1995); Brendan O'Leary and John McGarry, *The Politics of Antagonism: Understanding Northern Ireland* (London: Athlone Press, 1993), 277–311.

338 Cathal Goulding quotation; split in Workers' Party; formation of Democratic Left: Henry MacDonald, "The Birth of the Provos: Conspiracy Theorist," *Irish News*, January 31, 1990, 6; see also Flackes and Elliott, *Northern Ireland: A Political Directory, 1968–1999*, 224–225, 320, 511–512. In 1993, Tomás Mac Giolla was appointed the lord mayor of Dublin. Proinsias de Rossa served as minister for social welfare in the "rainbow coalition," and by most accounts his performance was highly commendable.

338 Ó Brádaigh on constitutional politics: In the 2001 Westminster election, four Provisional Sinn Féin candidates were elected as abstentionists: Gerry Adams (re-elected in West Belfast), Martin McGuinness (re-elected in Mid-Ulster), Pat Doherty (West Tyrone), and Michelle Gildernew (Fermanagh–South Tyrone). It was Provisional Sinn Féin's best result ever. They represented 4 of 659 MPs. In the 2002 Leinster House election, Provisional Sinn Féin took five seats, including Caoimhghin Ó Caoláin's re-election in Cavan-Monaghan. The election was perceived as a major breakthrough for the party, much like the 1957 election which saw Ó Brádaigh and three others elected. They were 5 of 166 Leinster House TDs. See also Gerard Murray and Jonathan Tonge, *Sinn Féin and the SDLP: From Alienation to Participation* (Dublin: The O'Brien Press, 2005).

339 Gerry Adams combines revolution and constitutionalism: Some of Adams's critics charge that he sold out his revolutionary principles long ago, that the compromises of the 1990s reflect conscious decisions that he made over the course of his career. With the benefit of hindsight, they find evidence of this in his past behavior—his denial that he was a member of the IRA in the 1970s, pushing Ó Brádaigh and O'Connell out in the 1980s, dropping abstention from Leinster House, and so on. From this view, personal qualities associated with Adams—perhaps a desire for office or the need to lead—led him down the path of constitutionalism. This ignores the essence of Ó Brádaigh's view—that Adams and those before him who chose constitutionalism are trapped by a political system rather than their personal failings. Adams is as astute a politician as anyone, but it is hard to believe that he foresaw the impact that the hunger strike in 1981 would have on the movement. Instead of taking the view that he sold out long ago, perhaps it is best to take the view that Adams kept his options open as he pursued "the Republic"—that if the Provisionals had been militarily successful he would have accepted the victory but when they were not successful, he turned to constitutionalism, and this choice led to compromise.

339 June 1998 Northern Assembly election: The Ulster Unionist Party, led by David Trimble, won the most seats (28). Trimble was elected first minister. The Ulster Unionist Party was followed by the SDLP (24 seats), Ian Paisley's Democratic Unionist Party (20 seats), and Provisional Sinn Féin (18 seats). The rest of the 108 seats were scattered across a number of smaller political groups. Trimble endorsed the Good Friday Agreement and had the support of a majority of party members, but some Ulster Unionist Party members who were elected to the Assembly campaigned on an anti-Assembly ticket. Ian Paisley's Democratic Unionist Party rejected the agreement and campaigned against it. Roughly a quarter (28) of the representatives elected to the Assembly were anti-agreement Unionists. Trimble, who with John Hume was awarded the Nobel Peace Prize in August 1998, has had to fight a constant rearguard action against those accusing him of selling out the Unionist cause. See the CAIN Internet archive; Bew and Gillespie, *Northern Ireland: A Chronology*, 396; "Provos' Final Surrender," *SAOIRSE*, Nollaig/December 1999, 1.

340 Decommissioning: "Stormont Saved—Arms Destroyed," *SAOIRSE*, Samhain/November 2001, 1. "'Treachery Punishable by Death,'" *SAOIRSE*, Nollaig/December 2001, 1; English, *Armed Struggle*, 330–336; CAIN archive; "IRA Clarifies Its Position," *An Phoblacht/Republican News*, Deireadh Fómhair/September 30, 2003, 1; "Irish Republican Army orders an end to armed campaign," Provisional IRA statement, July 28, 2005.

340 Attack on Michael Donnelly: "Vicious Attack on Republican Family," *SAOIRSE*, Iúil/July 1998, 3; see also "McGuinness Confronted by Martina Donnelly," *SAOIRSE*, Iúil/July 1998, 3.

340 Omagh bombing: Early speculation suggested that the Real IRA and the Continuity

IRA might merge into a more formidable organization. In *The Irish Echo,* Jack Holland went so far as to report on a discussed merger of the Real IRA, the Continuity IRA, and the Irish National Liberation Army. There has been speculation that the three organizations were in the process of trying to form a joint military strategy and that the Omagh bombing was a joint operation involving each. If this is correct, it would be similar to collaborations between different Republican military organizations that have resulted soon after splits—as in 1975, when Provisional IRA members cooperated with or left for the Irish National Liberation Army. As they work to find out who they are and what they represent, there is opportunity for collaboration. If there was cooperation between these groups, the Omagh bombing ended it. More important, even without the Omagh bombing, political differences guaranteed that the groups would not merge. There was and is a major ideological divide between these groups, centered on the splits in 1969/1970 (with respect to the INLA and the CIRA) and in 1986 (with respect to the Real IRA and the CIRA). For any kind of merger, INLA and Real IRA supporters would have to revert to an abstentionist position or Continuity IRA supporters would have to ignore the former's recognition of Leinster House. Neither is likely to happen. Some members of the Real IRA resent the fact that from 1986 to 1994, the Continuity IRA was on the sidelines while they (in the Provisional IRA) carried on the war effort. Some Continuity IRA volunteers, in turn, resent that some Real IRA members threatened and tried to intimidate them during these years. As for Ó Brádaigh, at least some supporters of the Real IRA and the 32-County Sovereignty Movement respect his sincerity but believe he lacks pragmatism, to the point of being an elitist. To paraphrase one (in a reference to the Arborfield raid in 1955), "he [Ó Brádaigh] would lead an IRA unit into a British army base, but he would not rob a bank." Ó Brádaigh, who would use the word "raid" rather than "rob," would not automatically reject raiding banks for fund-raising operations (as his predecessors had done in the 1920s and 1940s), but he would also be very concerned about the taint of gangsterism. It should be noted that the Provisionals have not confined their intimidation to political opponents; they have continued to police some nationalist areas in the north. In May and June 1999, it is alleged, they shot persons who were allegedly engaged in drug-dealing in Northern Ireland. McKittrick, Kelters, Feeney, and Thornton, *Lost Lives,* 1437–1461; "Omagh Slaughter Unjustifiable," *SAOIRSE,* Meán Fómhair/September 1998, 1; "For the Record," *SAOIRSE,* Deireadh Fómhair/October 1998, 4; "Provo Action: Denial of Freedom of Speech and Political Expression," *SAOIRSE,* Deireadh Fómhair/October 1998, 2; Bew and Gillespie, *Northern Ireland: A Chronology,* 373. Information on Provisional IRA assaults on other Republicans may be found in the CAIN archive; Richard English, *Armed Struggle,* 320–321; and Anthony McIntyre, "Provisional Republicanism: Internal Politics, Inequities and Modes of Repression," in Fearghal McGarry, ed., *Republicanism in Modern Ireland* (Dublin: University College Dublin Press, 2003), 178–198. The interested reader may want to examine the archives of the online journal *The Blanket,* available online at http://lark.phoblacht.net; McKittrick, Kelters, Feeney, and Thornton, *Lost Lives,* 1470, 1472; and Jack Holland, "Republican Extremists Talk of Merger," *The Irish Echo,* May 27–June 2, 1998.

340 Death of Joe O'Connor: The text of Marion Price's oration may be found on the Web site "Ireland's Own: Women Freedom Fighters": Marian [*sic*] Price, "Graveside Oration for Vol Joe O'Connor by Ex Hungerstriker Marian Price," available online at http://irelandsown.net/price3.html, accessed March 18, 2005.

341 Sectarian attacks: McKittrick, Kelters, Feeney, and Thornton, *Lost Lives,* 1434–1436, 1471–1472.

341 Transformation of Northern Ireland: Provisional Sinn Féin tends to reject the reforms as not going far enough. As an example, as of this writing they refuse to appoint representatives to the Police Board. Along with the reforms, there is evidence that as Catholics/Nationalists have become less marginalized in Northern Ireland, Protestants have become more marginalized. Cunningham, *British Government Policy in Northern Ireland,* 136–138; Arthur Aughey, "British Policy in Northern Ireland," in S. P. Savage and R. Atkinson, eds., *Public Policy under Blair* (Hampshire: Palgrave, 2001), 205–220; Joanne Hughes and Caitlín Donnell, "Ten Years of Social Attitudes to Community Relations in Northern Ireland," in Ann Marie Gay, Katrina Lloyd, Paula Devine, Gillian Robinson, and Deirdre Heenan, eds., *Social Attitudes in Northern Ireland: The Eighth Report* (London: Pluto Press, 2002), 39–55. "To Some in Ulster, Celebration of I.R.A. Pledge is Early," *New York Times,* July 30, 2005, A3.

341 Reform or revolution: Robert Michels, *Political Parties: A Sociological Study of the Oligarchical Tendencies of Modern Democracy* (New York: Free Press, 1966); Rosa Luxemburg, *Reform or Revolution?* (New York: Pathfinder Press, 1982), 49–50.

342 Harassment: Harassment of Ó Brádaigh is a constant possibility, depending in part on the personality of a given police officer who sights him. In recent years he has been stopped and informed that he had driven onto a highway too slowly. He assumes that his telephone is tapped. The police often monitor the comings and goings at Republican Sinn Féin offices. They always monitor the Republican Sinn Féin Ard Fheis.

342 Shankill Cross, Roscommon: RÓB IVs; "Roscommon Memorial Unveiled," *SAOIRSE-Irish Freedom,* Samhain/November 2003, 8.

343 RÓB and John Joe McGirl relationship: RÓB IVs.

343 RÓB on Seán Mac Stiofáin: Ruth Dudley Edwards claims that Ó Brádaigh ordered Mac Stiofáin off his hunger strike. This is incorrect. Ó Brádaigh, who was in the Curragh, was not in a position to order Mac Stiofáin, who was in the Curragh's military hospital, off the strike. "Seán Mac Stiofáin—A Tribute," *SAOIRSE,* Meitheamh/June 2001, 7; Ruth Dudley Edwards, "A Funeral Can't Kill off Adams's Hypocrisy," *Sunday Independent Online,* Sunday, May 27, 2001, available online at http://www.ruthdudleyedwards.co.uk/Irnews1.htm.

343 Good Friday Agreement compared to Sunningdale: In *All Hell Will Break Loose,* Austin Currie commented: "In many ways Sunningdale was a better deal for Irish nationalists and republicans. . . . The question obviously arises, following comparison between the two Agreements: What were the Troubles about? And especially, do the differences justify the loss of one life, never mind the loss of over 2,000, as occurred between the fall of Sunningdale and the Good Friday Agreement?" While he praises Adams and McGuinness and the Republican leadership that led to the Good Friday Agreement, it is worth noting that his question parallels Ó Brádaigh's September 1994 question: "What were the sacrifices of the past 25 years all about?" Austin Currie, *All Hell Will Break Loose,* 430–434. In 1972, John Hume suggested an SDLP–Provisional Sinn Féin pan-Nationalist front to Dáithí O'Connell. In Donegal, and in the presence of Joe O'Neill, Hume told O'Connell that it was "time to cash the cheque the Republican Movement has accumulated. The SDLP and the best of the Republican Movement could make an irresistible force in Irish politics." O'Connell said "No." Two years later, Hume sent a message to Ó Brádaigh through a friend in Maynooth College, asking for a meeting. Ó Brádaigh considered, consulted with colleagues, and refused. He was very aware of the approach to O'Connell.

343 Patrick Doucy story: RÓB interviews.

WORKS CITED

Adams, Gerry. *Before the Dawn: An Autobiography.* London: Heineman, in association with Brandon Books, 1997.

Alexander, Yonah, and John M. Gleason, eds. *Behavioral and Quantitative Perspectives on Terrorism.* New York: Pergamon Press, 1981.

Anderson, Brendan. *Joe Cahill: A Life in the IRA.* Dublin: The O'Brien Press, 2002.

Augusteijn, Joost. *From Public Defiance to Guerrilla Warfare: The Experience of Ordinary Volunteers in the Irish War of Independence, 1916–1921.* Dublin: Irish Academic Press, 1996.

Baróid, Ciarán de. *Ballymurphy and the Irish War.* Baile Átha Cliath: Aisling Publishers, 1989.

Barritt, Denis P., and Charles F. Carter. *The Northern Ireland Problem.* Oxford: Oxford University Press, 1972.

Bean, Kevin, and Mark Hayes, eds. *Republican Voices.* County Monaghan, Ireland: Seesyu Press, 2001.

Bell, J. Bowyer. *In Dubious Battle: The Dublin and Monaghan Bombings, 1972–1974.* Dublin: Poolbeg, 1990.

———. *The Gun in Politics: An Analysis of the Irish Political Conflict, 1916–1986.* New Brunswick, N.J.: Transaction Books, 1987.

———. *The Irish Troubles: A Generation of Violence, 1967–1992.* New York: St. Martin's Press, 1993.

———. *IRA Tactics and Targets.* Swords, County Dublin: Poolbeg Press, 1990.

———. *The IRA, 1968–2000: Analysis of a Secret Army.* London: Frank Cass Publishers, 2000.

———. *The Secret Army: The IRA from 1916–.* Revised ed. Dublin: The Academy Press, 1979.

Belfast Graves. Dublin: National Graves Association, 1971.

Beresford, David. *Ten Men Dead: The Story of the 1981 Irish Hunger Strike.* London: Grafton, 1987.

Bew, Paul, and Gordon Gillespie. *Northern Ireland: A Chronology of the Troubles, 1968–1999.* Dublin: Gill and Macmillan, 1999.

Biggs-Davison, John, and George Chowdharay-Best. *The Cross of St. Patrick: The Catholic Unionist Tradition in Ireland.* Bourne End, Buckinghamshire, England: Kensal Press, 1984.

Bishop, Patrick, and Eamonn Mallie. *The Provisional IRA.* Aylesbury Bucks, England: Corgi Edition, 1989.

Boyle, Kevin, Tom Hadden, and P. Hillyard. *Ten Years on in Northern Ireland: The Legal Control of Political Violence.* London: Cobden Trust, 1980.

Bruce, Steve. *The Red Hand: Protestant Paramilitaries in Northern Ireland.* Oxford: Oxford University Press, 1992.

Campbell, Brian, Laurence McKeown, and Felim O'Hagan, eds. *Nor Meekly Serve My Time: The H-Block Struggle, 1976–81.* Belfast: Beyond the Pale Publications, 1994.

Carroll, Denis. *They Have Fooled You Again: Michael O'Flanagan (1876–1942)— Priest, Republican, Social Critic.* Blackrock, County Dublin: Columba Press, 1996.

Caul, Brian. *Towards a Federal Ireland.* Belfast: December Publications, 1995.

Clarke, Liam. *Broadening the Battlefield: The H-Blocks and the Rise of Sinn Féin.* Dublin: Gill and Macmillan, 1987.

Clarke, Liam, and Kathryn Johnston. *Martin McGuinness: From Guns to Government.* London: Mainstream Publishing, 2002.

Clarke, Sister Sarah. *No Faith in the System: A Search for Justice.* Cork: Mercier Press, 1995.

Coleman, Marie. *County Longford and the Irish Revolution, 1910–1923.* Dublin: Irish Academic Press, 2003.

Collins, Tom. *The Irish Hunger Strike.* Dublin: White Island, 1986.

Columb, Frank. *The Shooting of More O'Ferrall.* Cambridge: Evod Academic Publishing Company, 1996.

Coogan, Tim Pat. *Michael Collins.* London: Arrow Book, Limited, 1991.

———. *The IRA.* 1979; repr., Glasgow: Fontana Collins, 1987.

Cronin, Seán. *Irish Nationalism: Its Roots and Ideology.* Dublin: Academy Press, 1980.

———. *The McGarrity Papers.* Tralee: Anvil Books, 1972; repr., New York: Clan na Gael Books, 1992.

Cunningham, Michael J. *British Government Policy in Northern Ireland 1969–89: Its Nature and Execution.* Manchester: Manchester University Press, 2001.

Currie, Austin. *All Hell Will Break Loose.* Dublin: O'Brien Press, 2004.

Deutsch, Richard, and Vivien Magowan. *Northern Ireland, 1968–73: A Chronology of Events.* Vol. 1, *1968–1971.* Belfast: Blackstaff Press, 1974.

———. *Northern Ireland 1968–73: A Chronology of Events.* Vol. 2, *1972–73.* Belfast: Blackstaff Press, 1974.

———. *Northern Ireland 1968–73: A Chronology of Events.* Vol. 3, *1974.* Belfast: Blackstaff Press, 1974.

Devlin, Bernadette. *The Price of My Soul.* New York: Alfred A. Knopf, 1969.

Devlin, Paddy. *The Fall of the N. I. Executive.* Belfast: Paddy Devlin, 1975.

Devoy, John. *Recollections of an Irish Rebel.* Shannon, Ireland: Irish University Press, 1969.

Dillon, Martin. *The Enemy Within: The IRA's War against the British.* London: Doubleday, 1994.

Duiker, William J. *Ho Chi Minh.* New York: Hyperion, 2000.

Egan, Bowes, and Vincent McCormack, *Burntollet.* London: L. R. S. Publishers, 1969.

English, Richard. *Armed Struggle: A History of the IRA.* London: Macmillan, 2003.

Farrell, Michael. *Northern Ireland: The Orange State.* Belfast: Pluto Press, 1980.

Feeney, Brian. *Sinn Féin: A Hundred Turbulent Years.* Dublin: O'Brien Press, 2002.

Fennell, Desmond. *Beyond Nationalism: The Struggle against Provinciality in the Modern World.* Swords, Co. Dublin: Ward River Press, 1985.

Fisk, Robert. *The Point of No Return: The Strike Which Broke the British in Ulster.* London: Times Books, 1975.

FitzGerald, Garret. *All in a Life: An Autobiography.* London: Macmillan, 1991.

Flackes, W. D., and Sidney Elliott. *Northern Ireland: A Political Directory, 1968–99.* Belfast: Blackstaff Press, 1999.

Gay, Ann Marie, Katrina Lloyd, Paula Devine, Gillian Robinson, and Deirdre Heenan, eds. *Social Attitudes in Northern Ireland: The Eighth Report.* London: Pluto Press, 2002.

Godson, Dean. *Himself Alone: David Trimble and the Ordeal of Modern Unionism.* London: HarperCollins, 2004.

Hall, Michael. *20 Years: A Concise Chronology of Events in Northern Ireland from 1968–1988.* Newtownabbey, Northern Ireland: Island Publications, 1988.

Handbook for Volunteers of the Irish Republican Army: Notes on Guerrilla Warfare. 1956; repr., Boulder, Colo.: Paladin Press, 1985.

Hanley, Brian. *The IRA: 1926–1936.* Dublin: Four Courts Press, 2002.

Harnden, Toby. *"Bandit Country": The IRA & South Armagh.* London: Hodder & Stoughton, 1999.

Hegarty, Peter. *Peadar O'Donnell.* Cork: Mercier Press, 1999.

Heskin, Ken. *Northern Ireland: A Psychological Analysis.* Dublin: Gill & Macmillan, 1980.

Holland, Jack. *Hope against History: The Course of Conflict in Northern Ireland.* New York: Henry Holt, 1999.

———. *The American Connection: U.S. Guns, Money, & Influence in Northern Ireland.* 1987; repr. New York: Penguin, 1998.

———, and Henry McDonald. *INLA: Deadly Divisions.* Dublin: Torc, 1994.

Irish Information Agenda. *Agenda Information Service on Northern Ireland.* 6th ed. London: Irish Information Partnership, 1990.

Irvin, Cynthia. *Militant Nationalism: Between Movement and Party in Ireland and the Basque Country.* Minneapolis: University of Minnesota Press, 1999.

Jordan, Anthony J. *Seán Mac Bride.* Dublin: Blackwater Press, 1993.

Keena, Colm. *A Biography of Gerry Adams.* Cork, Ireland: Mercier Press, 1990.

Kelly, Gerry. *Words from a Cell.* Dublin: Sinn Féin Publicity Department, 1989.

The Last Post. 3rd ed. Dublin: National Graves Association, 1985.

Lee, J. J. *Ireland, 1912–1985: Politics and Society.* Cambridge: Cambridge University Press, 1989.

London Sunday Times Insight Team. *Northern Ireland: A Report on the Conflict.* New York: Vintage Books, 1972.

Longford, Earl of (Frank Pakenham), and Thomas P. O'Neill. *Éamon de Valera.* Boston: Houghton Mifflin, 1971.

Lyons, F. S. L. *Ireland Since the Famine.* Rev. ed. London: Fontana, 1973.

Mac Eoin, Seán. *With the IRA in the Fight for Freedom: 1919 to the Truce.* Tralee: The Kerryman Ltd., n.d.

Mac Eoin, Uinseann. *The IRA in the Twilight Years, 1923–1948.* Dublin: Argenta Publications, 1997.

Mac Stiofáin, Seán. *Memoirs of a Revolutionary.* London: Gordon Cremonesi, 1975. Reprinted as *Revolutionary in Ireland.* Letchworth, Hertfordshire: Free Ireland Book Club, 1979.

Macardle, Dorothy. *The Irish Republic.* Revised ed. New York: Farrar, 1965.

Mallie, Eamonn, and David McKittrick. *The Fight for Peace: The Secret Story Behind the Irish Peace Process.* London: Heinemann, 1996.

McAllister, Ian. *The Northern Ireland Social Democratic and Labour Party: Political Opposition in a Divided Society.* London: Macmillan, 1977.

McCann, Eamonn. *War and an Irish Town.* 1974; repr., London: Pluto Press, 1981.

McCluskey, Conn. *Up Off Their Knees.* [Belfast, Northern Ireland]: Conn McCluskey and Associates, 1989.

McDonald, Henry. *Trimble.* London: Bloomsbury, 2000.

McGee, Eugene. *St. Mel's of Longford.* Longford: St. Mel's Diocesan Trust, 1996.

McGuffin, John. *Internment!* Tralee: Anvil Books, 1973.

McGuire, Maria. *To Take Arms: My Year with the IRA Provisionals.* New York: Viking, 1973.

McKee, Grant, and Ros Franey. *Time Bomb: Irish Bombers, English Justice and the Guildford Four.* London: Bloomsbury, 1988.

McKeown, Laurence. *Out of Time: Irish Republican Prisoners, Long Kesh, 1972–2000.* Belfast: Beyond the Pale Publications, 2001.

McKittrick, David, Séamus Kelters, Brian Feeney, and Chris Thornton. *Lost Lives: The Stories of the Men, Women and Children Who Died as a Result of the Northern Ireland Troubles.* London: Mainstream Publishing, 1999.

Mitchell, George A. *Making Peace.* New York: Alfred A. Knopf, 1999.

Moloney, Ed. *A Secret History of the IRA.* New York: W. W. Norton & Company, 2002.

Morrison, Danny. *Then the Walls Came Down: A Prison Journal.* Cork: Mercier Press, 1999.

Mullin, Chris. *Error of Judgement: The Truth about the Birmingham Bombings.* Swords, Co. Dublin: Poolbeg, 1986.

Murray, Gerard, and Jonathan Tonge. *Sinn Féin and the SDLP: From Alienation to Participation.* Dublin: The O'Brien Press, 2005.

Northern Ireland Civil Rights Association (NICRA). *We Shall Overcome: The History of the Struggle for Civil Rights in Northern Ireland, 1968–1978.* Belfast: NICRA, 1978.

Ó Brádaigh, Ruairí. *Dílseacht: The Story of Comdt-General Tom Maguire and the Second (All-Ireland) Dáil.* Dublin: Irish Freedom Press, 1997.

———. *Our People, Our Future.* Dublin: Sinn Féin, 1973.

Ó Dochartaigh, Niall. *From Civil Rights to Armalites: Derry and the Birth of the Irish Troubles.* Cork: Cork University Press, 1994.

Ó Gadhra, Nollaig. *Margáil na Saoirse [Bargaining for Freedom].* Baile Átha Cliath: Cló na Buaidhe, 1988.

O'Brien, Conor Cruise. *Memoir: My Life and Themes.* Dublin: Poolbeg, 1998.

———. *States of Ireland.* New York: Vintage Books, 1973.

O'Brien, Justin. *The Arms Trial.* Dublin: Gill & Macmillan, 2000.

O'Connell, John. *Dr. John: Crusading Doctor and Politician.* Swords, Co. Dublin: Poolbeg Press, 1989.

O'Doherty, Shane. *The Volunteer: A Former IRA Man's True Story.* London: Harper Collins, 1993.

O'Donnell, Peadar. *The Gates Flew Open.* Cork: The Mercier Press, 1966.

———. *There Will Be Another Day.* Dublin: The Dolmen Press, 1963.

O'Farrell, Padraic. *The Blacksmith of Ballinalee: Seán Mac Eoin.* Rev. ed. Mullingar: Uisneach Press, 1993.

———. *Who's Who in the Irish War of Independence.* Dublin: Lilliput Press, 1997.

O'Hegarty, P. S. *The Victory of Sinn Féin: How It Won It and How It Used It.* Dublin: Talbot Press, 1924.

O'Higgins, Brian. "My Songs and Myself." *Wolfe Tone Annual 1949.* Dublin: Wolfe Tone Annual, 1949.

O'Kelley, Kevin. *The Longest War: Northern Ireland and the I. R. A.* London: Zed Books, 1988.

O'Leary, Brendan, and John McGarry. *The Politics of Antagonism: Understanding Northern Ireland.* London: Athlone Press, 1993.

O'Malley, Ernie. *On Anther Man's Wound.* 1936; repr., Dublin: Anvil Books, 1994.

O'Reilly, Dermot, ed. *Accepting the Challenge: The Memoirs of Michael Flannery.* Dublin: Irish Freedom Press, 2001.

O'Farrell, Pádraic. *Who's Who in the Irish War of Independence.* Dublin: Lilliput Press, 1997.

———. *The Blacksmith of Ballinalee: Seán Mac Eoin.* Rev. ed. Mullingar: Uisneach Press, 1993.

O'Mahony, Seán. *Frongoch: University of Revolution.* Killiney, Co. Dublin: FDR Teoranta, 1987.

O'Rawe, Richard. *Blanketmen: An Untold Story of the H-Block Hunger Strike.* Dublin: New Island Press, 2005.

Patterson, Henry. *The Politics of Illusion: A Political History of the IRA.* London: Serif, 1997.

Probert, Belinda. *Beyond Orange and Green.* Dublin: The Academy Press, 1978.

Quinn, Raymond J. *A Rebel Voice: A History of Republicanism, 1925–1972.* Belfast: The Belfast Cultural and Local History Group, 1999.

Rafter, Kevin. *The Clann: The Story of Clann na Poblachta.* Dublin: Mercier Press, 1996.

Rees, Merlyn. *Northern Ireland: A Personal Perspective.* London: Methuen, 1985.

Routledge, Paul. *John Hume: A Biography.* London: Harper Collins, 1977.

———. *Public Servant, Secret Agent: The Elusive Life and Violent Death of Airey Neave.* London: Fourth Estate, 2002.

Savage, S. P., and R. Atkinson, eds. *Public Policy under Blair.* Hampshire: Palgrave, 2001.

Sharrock, David, and Mark Davenport. *Man of War, Man of Peace? The Unauthorised Biography of Gerry Adams.* London: Macmillan, 1997.

Smith, M. L. R. *Fighting for Ireland? The Military Strategy of the Irish Republican Movement.* New York: Routledge, 1995.

Sutton, Malcolm. *An Index of Deaths from the Conflict in Ireland, 1969–1993.* Belfast: Beyond the Pale Publications, 1994.

Taylor, Peter. *Beating the Terrorists? Interrogation in Omagh, Gough and Castlereagh.* Penguin: Middlesex, England, 1980.

———. *Behind the Mask: The IRA and Sinn Féin.* New York: TV Books, 1997.

———. *States of Terror: Democracy and Political Violence.* London: BBC Books, 1993.

Thatcher, Margaret. *The Downing Street Years.* London: Harper Collins, 1993.

Tilly, Charles. *From Mobilization to Revolution.* New York: Random House, 1978.

Walsh, Liz. *The Final Beat: Gardaí Killed in the Line of Duty.* Dublin: Gill and Macmillan, 2001.

Walsh, Pat. *From Civil Rights to National War: Northern Ireland Catholic Politics 1964–1974.* Belfast: Athol Books, 1989.

———. *Irish Republicanism and Socialism: The Politics of the Republican Movement, 1905 to 1994.* Belfast: Athol Books, 1994.

Weigel, George. *Witness to Hope: The Biography of Pope John Paul II.* New York: Cliff-Street Books, 1999.

White, Robert. *Provisional Irish Republicans: An Oral and Interpretive History.* Westport, Conn.: Greenwood Press, 1993.

Wilkinson, Paul. *Terrorism and the Liberal State.* 2nd ed. London: Macmillan, 1986.

INDEX

Page numbers in italics indicate photographs and illustrations.
The abbreviation RÓB denotes references to Ruairí Ó Brádaigh.

abortion, 275
abstentionism: and the Army Council,
    299, 301; and Carron, 286; and
    changing leadership, 297–304;
    and civil rights movement, 141;
    debates on, 133–34; and elections,
    104, 403n; Johnston on, 119;
    Mac Stiofáin and, 119–20, 123,
    148, 149–50, 155, 363–64n; and
    peace negotiations, 234; and the
    Provisionals, 152–53, 154–57,
    369n; and republican movement,
    137; and rifts, 142–43; and RÓB,
    95–97, 119–20, 141, 148–51,
    155, 289, 294, 299, 300–303,
    305–307, 337–38, 394–95n,
    401n, 403n; and Sinn Féin, 49–
    50, 119–20, 121–22, 300, 301–
    302; and social issues, 121–22;
    and splits, 148–49, 309, 310–11,
    337–38, 369n, 397n; votes on,
    394–95n, 396n
Adams, Gerry: and abstentionism,
    297–304, 334, 337–39, 403n;
    at Ard Fheis, *273, 305;* and the
    Army Council, 258, 264–65, 274;
    arrests, 265; assassination attempt,
    396n; attempted ouster, 297; auto-
    biography, 330; and Blair govern-
    ment, 332; and cease-fires, 399n;
    on child casualties, 389n; and
    constitutional process, 401n; and
    critics of RÓB, 333; at Easter
    Commemorations, 267–68; and

Éire Nua, 270; and elections, 272,
    278–79, 281, 287–88, 291–92,
    315, 392n; and federalism, 269,
    284–85, 345; as focus of study,
    xvii; and hunger strikes, 277–78;
    imprisonment/internment, 254;
    and J. Drumm speech, 259; and
    leadership changes, 264, 389n;
    leadership roles, 276–77; and
    M. Drumm assassination, 253–
    54; and McKee, 390n; and mili-
    tary campaigns, 257; and peace
    negotiations, 323, 324, *329,*
    388n; political style, 403n; and
    prison issues, 276, 394n; and
    recruitment, 283; release from
    prison, 186; RÓB on, 266, 326,
    336, 341; on Sands, 393n; and
    secrecy, xiii–xvii; and socialism,
    274; support for, 405n; and
    walkouts, 307, 311, 313; and
    Whitelaw meeting, 188; Wolfe
    Tone Commemoration, 291–92
Agnew, Kevin, 138
Agnew, Paddy, 281
Aiken, Frank, 14
All Hell Will Break Loose (Currie),
    395n, 405n
All in a Life (FitzGerald), 382n
Allan, James, 220, 226–27, 239
Amritsar Massacre, 80
An Phoblacht: on blanketmen, 253;
    "Brownie" column, 257; circula-
    tion, 219; on Drumm assassina-

Robert W. White is Dean of the Indiana University School
of Liberal Arts at Indiana University-Purdue
University Indianapolis and a Professor of Sociology. He is
author of *Provisional Irish Republicans: An Oral and
Interpretive History* (1993) and co-editor of *Self, Identity, and
Social Movements* (with Sheldon Stryker and Timothy J.
Owens, 2000). His scholarly articles have appeared in the
American Sociological Review, the *American Journal of
Sociology,* and *Terrorism and Political Violence.* His
examinations of the causes and consequences of small group
political violence are noteworthy because he draws on the
personal accounts of activists.